Pedagogy and Student Services for Institutional Transformation: **Implementing Universal Design in Higher Education**

Jeanne L. Higbee and Emily Goff
EDITORS

Pedagogy and Student Services for Institutional Transformation is funded by the U.S. Department of Education, Office of Postsecondary Education.
Project #333A050023ACT1

Copyright © 2008 by the Regents of the University of Minnesota, Center for Research on Developmental Education and Urban Literacy, College of Education and Human Development, University of Minnesota, Minneapolis, MN.

All rights reserved. No part of this publication may be reproduced, stored in a retrieval system, or transmitted, in any form or by any means, electronic, mechanical, photocopying, recording, or otherwise, without prior written permission of the publisher.

Printed in the United States of America.

The University of Minnesota is committed to the policy that all persons shall have equal access to its programs, facilities, and employment without regard to race, color, creed, religion, national origin, sex, age, marital status, disability, public assistance status, veteran status, or sexual orientation.

This publication/material can be made available in alternative formats for people with disabilities. Direct requests to the Center for Research on Developmental Education and Urban Literacy, General College, 340 Appleby Hall, 128 Pleasant Street SE, Minneapolis, MN, 55455, 612-625-6411.

"Making a Statement" (2003), "Universal Instructional Design in a Legal Studies Classroom" (2003), "Computer-Mediated Learning in Mathematics and Universal Instructional Design" (2003), "Universal Instructional Design in a Computer-Based Psychology Course" (2003), "Implementing Universal Design in Learning Centers" (2003), "Universal Design in Counseling Center Service Areas" (2003), "The First-Year Experience" (2003), "Residential Living for All: Fully Accessible and "Liveable" On-Campus Housing" (2003), "Disability Services as a Resource: Advancing Universal Design" (2003), "Community Colleges and Universal Instructional Design" (2003), "Charting New Courses: Learning Communities and Universal Design" (2003), originally published in J. L. Higbee (Ed.), *Curriculum Transformation and Disability: Implementing Universal Design in Higher Education.* Minneapolis: University of Minnesota, General College, Center for Research on Education and Urban Literacy. Reprinted with permission from The Center for Research on Developmental Education and Urban Literacy. Copyright © 2003, The Center for Research on Developmental Education and Urban Literacy. All rights reserved.

"Enhancing the Inclusiveness of First-Year Courses Through Universal Instructional Design" (2004), originally published in I. M. Duranczyk, J. L. Higbee, & D. B. Lundell (Eds.), *Best Practices for Access and Retention in Higher Education.* Minneapolis: University of Minnesota, General College, Center for Research on Education and Urban Literacy. Reprinted with permission from The Center for Research on Developmental Education and Urban Literacy. Copyright © 2004, The Center for Research on Developmental Education and Urban Literacy. All rights reserved.

"Universal Learning Support Design: Maximizing Learning Beyond the Classroom" (2006) originally published in *The Learning Assistance Review.* Reprinted with permission from The Learning Assistance Review. Copyright © 2006, National College Learning Center Association. All rights reserved

Designed by Heidi Sandstad, University of Minnesota Printing Services.

PASS IT PROJECT PERSONNEL

Anthony Albecker
David Arendale
Heidi Barajas
Betty Benson
Carole Broad
Tom Brothen
Heidi Cardinal
Harvey Carlson
Robert Copeland
Bobbi Cordano
Ellyn Couillard
Renee DeLong
Irene Duranczyk
Annia Fayon
David Ghere
Emily Goff
Jay Hatch
Jeanne Higbee
Pat James
Dana Lundell
Na'im Madyun
Don Opitz
Bob Poch
Peggy Mann Rinehart
Bruce Schelske
Jennifer Schultz
Brian Shapiro
Cheryl Stratton
Mary Ellen Shaw

PASS IT SUMMER INSTITUTE PARTICIPANTS

Julie Alexandrin
Karen Parrish Baker
Catalina Bartlett
Carol Beckel
Terrance Blackman
Lydia Block
Kris Bransford
Deborah Casey
Michael Chance
Axely Congress
Alex Crittenden
Debbie Cunningham
Donna Dawson
Jillian Duquaine-Watson
Colleen Evans
Robert Fox
Amy Gort
Deborah Greenwald
Danielle Hamill
Tom Hanley
Mary Hennessey
Beth Hill
Gail Himes
Bryan Johns
Amanda Jojola
Themina Kader
Amy Kampsen
Kim Kvale
Maria Lam
Theresa Leko
Karen Lemke
Miriam Luebke
Ken Marquez
Samuel Matthews
Kimberlee Moorning
Karen Moroz
Karen Myers
Kim Nakano
Vijaya Narapareddy
Linda Nelson
John Plude
Mark Pousson
Mary Susan Potts-Santone
Frank Primiani
Vicki Roth
Susan Roush
Cynthia Seltzer
Erin Sember
Nancy Sharby
Gladys Shaw
Michael Sidoti
Dereck Skeete
Alfred Souma
Charles Stinemetz
Dale Swartzentruber
Veronica Udeogalanya
Melanie Wagner
Paula White

PASS IT PROJECT ADVISORY BOARD

Heather Hackman
Saint Cloud State University

Nancy Evans
Iowa State University

Karen Kalivoda
University of Georgia

Sue Kroeger
University of Arizona

Jane Larson
Minneapolis Community and Technical College

Judy Schuck
Emerita
University of Minnesota

EDITORIAL BOARD

Betty Benson
Lydia Block
Tom Brothen
Annia Fayon
Amy Gort
Mary Hennessey
Karen Kalivoda
Sue Kroeger
Jane Larson
Dana Lundell
Don Opitz
Bob Poch
Vicki Roth
Judy Schuck
Erin Sember
Brian Shapiro
Gladys Shaw
Esther Smidt
Cheryl Stratton

Acknowledgements

We are indebted to many individuals and organizations who contributed in myriad ways to the publication of this book. First and foremost, we want to recognize that this book and its dissemination in multiple formats were made possible by a grant from the U.S. Department of Education's program of "Demonstration Projects to Ensure Students With Disabilities Receive a Quality Higher Education," grant # P333A050023. In particular, we want to express our appreciation to program officer Shedita Allston for her ongoing support.

We also want to thank all those who have been involved in the Pedagogy and Student Services for Institutional Transformation (PASS IT) project since October, 2005, and even before when we first developed the idea for the grant proposal, including Roberta Cordano, previous director of the University of Minnesota-Twin Cities' Disability Services and DS staff members Peggy Mann Reinhardt and Betty Benson.

In addition to expressing our appreciation to the authors whose manuscripts are included within this volume, it is important that we recognize the efforts of the reviewers who provided feedback to guide these authors' work. Double-masked peer review is an important part of the scholarly publication process. We value the new insights we gain by opening up our work for critique by others.

We thank Cheryl Stratton, who has served as external evaluator for the project as a whole, Heidi Cardinal, our undergraduate student worker, and AmeriCorps volunteer Ellyn Couillard, who assisted with preparation and implementation for both PASS IT summer institutes.

Finally, we thank our PASS IT external advisors, faculty, staff, and participants. Many of them have written chapters for the book, and all have contributed in critical ways to the ideas presented here.

– Jeanne & Emily

PEDAGOGY AND STUDENT SERVICES FOR INSTITUTIONAL TRANSFORMATION

Table of Contents

Professional Preparation

Student Perspectives

Administrative and Practical Considerations in Implementing Universal Instructional Design in Higher Education

Concluding Thoughts

CHAPTER 1

Introduction

Emily Goff and Jeanne L. Higbee
University of Minnesota

Abstract
This chapter provides a brief introduction to the concepts of Universal Design and Universal Instructional Design and why we believe this model holds so much promise as an inclusive approach to higher education. We then introduce the Pedagogy and Student Services for Institutional Transformation (PASS IT) project. The chapter concludes by introducing the chapters to follow.

This book builds on the work of many professionals, not only in education, but in the field of architecture as well. Universal Design (UD) began as an architectural concept, a proactive response to legislative mandates as well as societal and economic changes that called for providing access for people with disabilities (Center for Universal Design [CUD], 2007). Universal Design promotes the consideration of the needs of all potential users in the planning and development of a space, product, or program—an approach that is equally applicable to architecture or education. It also supports the notion that when providing an architectural feature—or educational service, for that matter—to enhance accessibility and inclusion for one population, we are often benefiting all occupants or participants. One of the most often cited examples is the curb cut, which is used by people on roller blades or skate boards, parents pushing strollers, travelers hauling luggage, people making deliveries with hand carts, and others, as well by people with disabilities. Similarly, many people benefit from the provision of automatic doors, elevators, door handles instead of knobs, and so on.

The Universal Design principles (CUD, 1997) have been adapted to education through a number of models that emerged in the last decade, including Universal Design for Learning (UDL; Center for Applied Special Technology, n.d.; Rose, 2001; Rose & Meyer, 2000), Universal Design for Instruction (UDI; Scott, McGuire, & Shaw, 2001, 2003), and Universal Instructional Design (UID; Silver, Bourke, & Strehorn, 1998). We do not see these models as competing, but rather as complementary—all with much to offer.

At the University of Minnesota's General College (Higbee, Lundell, & Arendale, 2005) we adopted UID in conjunction with a project funded through the U.S. Department of Education's Office of Postsecondary Education (grant # P333A990015), Curriculum Transformation and Disability (CTAD; Higbee, 2003). The "universal" in UID is not meant to imply that "one size fits all"; instead the focus of UID is universal access. One goal of UID is to reduce or eliminate the need to provide customized individual academic accommodations, and particularly those that publicly identify or segregate students with disabilities. It is important here to distinguish between academic accommodations such as providing copies of notes or PowerPoint slides in advance of lecture or extended time on tests, from structural features such as ramps or appropriate heights for signs, desks, counters, and shelves, or technological accommodations such as screen readers or captioning on videos. Although implementation of UID may not eliminate the need for sign language interpreters, books in Braille or on tape, and other accommodations that are part of daily living for people with disabilities, it can prompt educators to reconsider teaching methods that tend to exclude some students unnecessarily. Many students can benefit from electronic access to faculty PowerPoint slides or extended time to complete exams.

UID's guiding principles are based on the work of Chickering and Gamson (1987) and include: (a) creating welcoming classrooms; (b) determining the essential components of a course; (c) communicating clear expectations; (d) providing constructive feedback; (e) exploring the use of natural supports for learning, including technology, to enhance opportunities for all learners; (f) designing teaching methods that consider diverse learning styles, abilities, ways of knowing, and previous experience and background knowledge; (g) creating multiple ways for students to demonstrate their knowledge; and (h) promoting interaction among and between faculty and students (Fox, Hatfield, & Collins, 2003). We are frequently asked, "then what distinguishes UID from what is simply good teaching?" It is a fair question. But our experience is that even for those of us who have always been very intentional and reflective in our work, UID has simultaneously broadened and focused our thinking. We think more broadly about the diversity of our students and how students' social identities can shape their learning experiences, and meanwhile we are also more focused on how we can ensure that no students are excluded or marginalized.

Although UD and UID may be familiar concepts to disability service providers, we believe that it is important to share this information postsecondary professionals working throughout the academy in a way that makes the theory and use of Universal Design meaningful to them. With this in mind, a team from the University of Minnesota sought external funding for the Pedagogy and Student Services for Institutional Transformation (PASS IT) project.

The PASS IT project began as a collaboration at the University of Minnesota among faculty and staff of the former General College, the Center for Research on Developmental Education and Urban Literacy (CRDEUL), and the staff from the Disability Services Office. The goal of the PASS IT project, which is funded by the U. S. Department of Education (grant #P333A050023ACT1), has been to provide professional development for postsecondary administrators, faculty, and staff in the theory and practice of Universal Design and Universal Instructional Design. These concepts are often unfamiliar to instructors and student affairs personnel who are not directly involved in disability support services. In order to increase awareness and use of UD and UID in a variety of postsecondary venues, the PASS IT project has created a corps of trainers to facilitate professional development workshops in the implementation of UD and UID. We have sought to empower postsecondary educators to implement UID using a "train the trainer" (or "pass it on") format to teach others and disseminate materials that focus on implementing UID in specific academic disciplines, student services, and administrative areas. We have engaged in a series of different and complimentary activities in order to pursue this goal.

First, 30 participants representing both public and private, 2- and 4-year colleges and universities from across the United States were selected to participate in an intensive 3-day summer institute on UD and UID in 2006. These participants made a commitment to share what they had learned at the summer institute and disseminate through workshops on their home campuses or through presentations at local or national professional meetings. A unique aspect to the training model of PASS IT is the role that these trainees play in their own professional development and in the training of others. Built into the project are rewards for the development and dissemination of discipline- and work area-specific training materials. The response of the 2006 participants was overwhelming and the trainees who attended the first summer institute went on to share their knowledge of UD and UID with others in their disciplines and in their institutions through journal articles, conference presentations, and on-campus professional development activities.

The summer institute for 2007 invited back one participant from each disciplinary working group, who assisted as a facilitator, as well as five additional individuals from different teaching or administrative units from each of the same campuses as the returning participants. We invited teams from Adams State College (CO), Concordia College (MN), Medgar Evers College (NY), Northeastern University (MA), St. Louis University (MO), Ohio Wesleyan University (OH), and a coalition of community college professionals from Green River Community College and Seattle Central Community College (WA). Participants in the second summer institute spent time in both disciplinary working groups and institutional working groups. The goal of the 2007 summer institute was to develop measures to transform curricula and student services at the seven participating institutions and then to disseminate how these transformations are accomplished as well as to develop additional discipline- and work scope-specific professional development materials.

Along with the faculty and staff trainings that have followed both of the summer institutes on the campuses of participants across the country and the professional development offered at professional conferences, it is imperative to explore theoretical foundations and philosophical and ethical issues related to UD and UID. To that end, we are excited about the publication of *Pedagogy and Student Services for Institutional Transformation: Implementing Universal Design in Higher Education*. We hope that this book will fulfill a need in higher education for both practical and theoretical information by and for experts in a wide array of postsecondary work settings. This book features reprints of some of the most popular chapters from the successful and now out-of-print book, *Curriculum Transformation and Disability: Implementing Universal Design in Higher Education,* funded by a previous grant project. In addition to the reprinted chapters, there are over 20 new chapters from authors who participated in PASS IT professional development activities.

Pedagogy and Student Services for Institutional Transformation: Implementing Universal Design in Higher Education is organized into six sections, each dealing with a different aspect of the implementation of UD and UID in higher education. The first presents theoretical frameworks beginning with a chapter by Nancy Evans that explores the historical roots of attitudes toward disability and provides the theoretical foundations for UID and then illustrates intersections between UID and student development theory. Evans urges that awareness of inclusive pedagogy is not enough; it is also imperative that educators understand students with disabilities. Evans' chapter is followed by another powerful theoretical perspective, Heather Hackman's critique of UID as viewed through the lenses of Social Justice Education and Critical Multicultural Education theories. Hackman argues that to make learning truly inclusive for all, educators must consider what it really means to implement the guiding principles of UID within social contexts and provides examples of how this might be accomplished. Closing the theoretical section of the PASS IT book is a chapter by Na'im Madyun, "Linking Universal Instructional Design and Cultural Capital: Improving African American College Outcomes," in which Madyun contends that in order to have a positive impact on the learning outcomes for all students, there is a need to examine the universality of the access points to cultural capital in higher education.

The pedagogical section of the book opens with a reprint of "Enhancing the Inclusiveness of First-Year Courses Through Universal Instructional Design," by Jeanne Higbee, Carl Chung, and Leonardo Hsu followed by a reprint of "Making a Statement," by Mark Pedelty, in which he discusses the value of going beyond the usual syllabus statement to communicate to students that he is interested in providing equal access to his classroom and the impact that this communication has had on his teaching and on all students' learning. The first new chapter in this section is "Practicing Universal Design in Visual Art Courses," by Patricia James and Themina Kader. This chapter uses assignments from two courses—an art education course for upper-level students majoring in elementary education, taught by Kader, and a general art course for first-year students, taught by James—in order to demonstrate examples of art instruction that use principles of UID to respond to student diversity and make art available to all. Next is "Universal Instructional Design in a Legal Studies Classroom," a reprinted chapter in which Karen Miksch describes how she engages students in mock trials in her legal studies classroom. In "Writing Assignments and Universal Design for Instruction: Making the Phantom Visible," Renee DeLong discusses the guiding principles of a parallel model, Universal Design for Instruction (Scott, McGuire, & Shaw, 2003), as applied to writing across the curriculum. She urges faculty and instructional staff to provide clear expectations for student writing. Next. David Arendale and David Ghere contribute a chapter that describes a practical model for social science teachers to integrate the best practices of UID using specific examples and teaching techniques from two history courses. In "Successful Undergraduate Mathematics Through Universal Design as Essential Course Componants, Pedagogy, and Assessment," Irene Duranczyk and Annia Fayon provide a framework for understanding the importance of UID in the college mathematics classroom. This section of the book closes with three reprinted chapters. In "Computer-Mediated Learning in Mathematics and Universal Instructional Design," D. Patrick Kinney and Laura Smith Kinney describe how the use of computer-mediated learning in the mathematics classroom can eliminate the need for most individual accommodations. In "Universal Instructional Design in a Computer-Based Psychology Course," Thomas Brothen and Cathrine Wambach discuss the use of the Personalized System of Instruction (PSI), another computer-assisted model, to teach a universally-designed psychology course. Rashné Jehangir explores the role learning communities can play in implementing Universal Design and Universal Instructional Design in "Charting New Courses: Learning Communities and Universal Design."

The third segment of the book explores the implementation of UD and UID in academic support and student development programs and services. This section opens with a new chapter by Jeanne Higbee that offers a list of nine components of Universal Design for Student Development as well as providing a holistic model for understanding the application of UD to both pedagogy and student services. In "Universal Learning Support Design: Maximizing Learning Beyond the Classroom," reprinted from *The Learning Assistance Review,* Donald Opitz and Lydia Block present a model for the universal design of learning centers and learning support services. In the reprint of "Implementing Universal Design in Learning Centers," Jeanne Higbee and Shevawn Eaton discuss both physical facilities and educational programs when considering the implementation of Universal Design in college and university learning centers. In the reprinted "Universal Design in Counseling Center Service Areas," Kathleen Uzes and Daley Connelly apply the same principles to counseling centers and provide case studies that demonstrate that students with disabilities face the same developmental tasks as all students, but may have to overcome additional obstacles in approaching these tasks. In the next chapter, "Universal Design in Advising: Principles and Practices," Mary Ellen Shaw, Carole Anne Broad, Amy Kampsen, and Anthony Albecker discuss connections between student development theory and a Universal Design approach to academic advising. They provide specific recommendations for implementing UD principles with diverse student populations. In a reprinted chapter, Jeanne Higbee and Karen Kalivoda discuss the implementation of Universal Design principles in the first-year experience, from admissions and orientation to models for "best practices." This chapter leads naturally to Martha Wisbey and Karen Kalivoda's examination of residence life. In this reprinted chapter, the authors address Universal Design as a means to create welcoming living spaces and to provide inclusive social and educational programs. In the reprinted chapter, Disability Services as a Resource: Advancing Universal Design, Karen Kalivoda and Margaret Totty discuss Disability Resource Centers and discuss the ways in which these offices can be used in concert with the concepts of Universal Design. In the last chapter of this section, "Ensuring Smooth Transitions: A Collaborative Endeavor for Career Services," Jeanne Higbee, Emily Goff, Karen Kalivoda, Margaret Totty, Janice Davis Barham, and Christopher Bell present a model for collaboration between a university's Disability Resource Center and Career Center.

The next section of the book addresses the application of UD and UID to professional preparation programs in higher education. In the first chapter of this section, "Infusing Universal Instructional Design Into Student Personnel Graduate Programs," Karen Myers presents ideas for integrating disability issues and UID in student affairs graduate preparation programs and provides a sample syllabus for a course on disability. Nancy Sharby and Susan Roush explore ways in which UID has the potential to mitigate problems that students with a disability may encounter with the experiential education model in "The Application of Universal Instructional Design in Experiential Education." Deb Casey's chapter, "Universal Design Strategies in Allied Health Sciences Classroom and Clinical Settings," outlines steps that administrators working in postsecondary allied health sciences professional preparation programs can take to create policies and procedures that ensure access while also protecting students, patients and clients, clinical settings, academic programs, institutions, and themselves. She provides a comprehensive case study to illustrate key concepts of importance to administrators. In "Training Professional and Faculty Advisors in Universal Design Principles," Debbie Cunningham, Al Souma, and Kaycee Gilmore-Holman describe how two very different institutions have reflected on their own advising practices and implemented UD principles to enhance student satisfaction. This chapter also includes the findings from the 2006 PASS IT Working Group on Advising, which were that advising practices should be: (a) developmentally appropriate, (b) accessible, (c) student-centered, (d) learning centered, (e) inclusive, (f) respectful, and (g) holistic. The authors introduce two figures that demonstrate how course requirements can be presented in different formats to address students' preferred learning styles. In the last chapter of this section, Karen Myers, Jo Nell Wood, and Mark Poussan discuss the need for the inclusion of UID in pre-service and in-service training for educators working in the elementary through secondary (K-12) levels. They highlight developing professional learning communities as one means of encouraging the implementation of UID.

The section of the book dedicated to student perspectives on the use of Universal Instructional Design opens with a chapter that Jeanne Higbee coauthored with University of Minnesota undergraduate students Pa Houa Lee, James Bardill, and Heidi Cardinal, in which undergraduates share and evaluate their personal experiences with UID in a psychology course. Also included in this section is a chapter from Julie Alexandrin, Ilana Schreiber, and Elizabeth Henry on the complicated process of disclosure for students with documented disabilities. Next Jeanne Higbee, joined by coauthors Pat Bruch and Kwabena Siaka, contributes a chapter relating the results of the Multicultural Awareness Project for Institutional Transformation (MAP IT) that are specific to students with disabilities. In the reprinted "Empowering Students With Severe Disabilities: A Case Study," Jay Hatch, David Ghere, and Katrina Jerik provide a case study that demonstrates how developing accommodations for a student with multiple disabilities benefit the entire class.

The last section of the book addresses administrative and practical considerations in implementing UD in higher education. The first chapter by David Arendale and Robert Poch, "Using Universal Design for Administrative Leadership, Planning, and Evaluation," includes a planning and assessment tool that can be used by higher education administrators to evaluate the accessibility of their programs and services. In "Computing Technologies, the Digital Divide, and 'Universal' Instructional Methods," Jillian Duquaine-Watson challenges the idea that technology is a panacea for all issues of access in higher education.

In her chapter, Melanie Wagner describes the comprehensive plan of action undertaken at Lake Sumpter Community College (LSCC) to develop collaboration across academic and student affairs to enhance student success. Although focusing on the community college, LSCC's model could be implemented anywhere. Next, in their reprinted chapter Judy Schuck and Jane Larson discuss the role community colleges play in providing access to postsecondary education for all students, and particularly for students with disabilities. They explain the attributes of community colleges that facilitate the implementation of Universal Design and Universal Instructional Design, as well as the unique challenges for both faculty and students. In the last chapter in this section, "Assistive Technology," Margret Totty and Karen Kalivoda describe some of the technology tools that are available to increase student access.

In the book's conclusion, Jeanne Higbee expands on her conclusion to *Curriculum Transformation and Disability: Implementing Universal Design in Higher Education,* coauthored by Heidi Barajas and offers an expanded set of guidelines for extending UID as a model for multicultural postsecondary education.

References

Center for Applied Special Technology. (n.d.). *UDL questions and answers.* Retrieved November 29, 2007, from http://www.cast.org/research/faq/index.html

The Center for Universal Design. (2007). *About UD: Universal Design history.* Raleigh: North Carolina State University. Retrieved November 29, 2007, from http://www.design.ncsu.edu/cud/about_ud/udhistory.htm

The Center for Universal Design. (1997). *The principles of Universal Design* (Version 2.0). Raleigh, NC: North Carolina State University. Retrieved December 11, 2006, from http://www.design.ncsu.edu/cud/about_ud/udprinciplestext.htm

Chickering, A. W., & Gamson, Z. F. (1987). Seven principles for good practice in undergraduate education. *AAHE Bulletin,* 39(7), 3-7.

Fox, J. A., Hatfield, J. P., & Collins, T. C. (2003). Developing the Curriculum Transformation and Disability (CTAD) workshop model. In J. L. Higbee (Ed.), *Curriculum transformation and disability: Implementing Universal Design in higher education* (pp. 23-39). Minneapolis: University of Minnesota, General College, Center for Research on Developmental Education and Urban Literacy. Retrieved November 29, 2007, from http://cehd.umn.edu/CRDEUL/books-ctad.html

Higbee, J. L. (Ed.). (2003). *Curriculum transformation and disability: Implementing universal design in higher education.* Minneapolis: University of Minnesota, General College, Center for Research on Developmental Education and Urban Literacy. Retrieved November 29, 2007, from http://cehd.umn.edu/CRDEUL/books-ctad.html

Higbee, J. L., Lundell, D. B., & Arendale, D. R. (Eds.). (2005). *The General College vision: Integrating intellectual growth, multicultural perspectives, and student development.* Minneapolis: University of Minnesota, General College, Center for Research on Developmental Education and Urban Literacy. Retrieved November 29, 2007, from http://cehd.umn.edu/CRDEUL/books-thegcvision.html

Rose, D. H. (2001). Universal design for learning: Deriving guiding principles from networks that learn. *Journal of Special Education Technology, 16*(2), 66-67.

Rose, D. H., & Meyer, A. (2000). Universal Design for Learning. *Journal of Special Education Technology, 15*(1), 67-70.

Scott, S. S., McGuire, J. M., & Shaw, S. F. (2001). *Principles of Universal Design for Instruction.* Storrs, CT: University of Connecticut, Center on Postsecondary Education and Disability.

Scott, S. S., McGuire, J. M., & Shaw, S. F. (2003). Universal Design for Instruction: A new paradigm for adult instruction in postsecondary education. *Remedial and Special Education, 24*(6), 369-379.

Silver, P., Bourke, A., & Strehorn, K. C. (1998). Universal Instructional Design in higher education: An approach for inclusion. *Equity and Excellence in Education, 31*(2), 47-51.

Theoretical Frameworks

CHAPTER 2

Theoretical Foundations of Universal Instructional Design

Nancy J. Evans
Iowa State University

Abstract
This chapter begins with a brief introduction to historical views of disability and the various theories that have guided the ways in which disability has traditionally been understood and used to guide educational interventions. A longer discussion of social constructionist and social justice perspectives on disability that provide a foundation for Universal Instructional Design (UID) follows. I then briefly review relevant student development theories and their relationship to disability, stressing the ways in which these theories can enhance the development of learning outcomes and pedagogical design using a UID approach.

A staff member in the Disability Resources office has been invited to discuss principles of University Instructional Design (UID) at the fall faculty retreat. While some faculty seem interested in what she has to say, others appear resistant. A faculty member in chemistry challenges the idea that students with disabilities even belong in college. Another faculty member in art suggests that it is just up to the students to make the necessary adjustments to get through her class. The chairperson in sociology, who has worked with many students with disabilities, finds the ideas of UID intriguing and plans to try them out, as he wants to provide an inviting and supportive environment for all his students. How can faculty hold such different perspectives about students with disabilities? One reason is their underlying beliefs about disability. In this chapter, I review various theoretical perspectives on disability and their historical underpinnings. I also suggest ways in which these perspectives shape educational practice in working with students with disabilities, noting specifically how UID is supported by two of these theories of disability.

Knowing how to create an inclusive environment is a necessary but not sufficient condition for working effectively with students with disabilities. Educators must also understand the students themselves. In this chapter, I also introduce theories of student development that are useful to educators working with students with disabilities and, indeed, students in general. Psychosocial, cognitive-structural, and social identity theories help faculty and student affairs administrators and staff members to use UID intelligently in their work with students, taking into account the developmental tasks, cognitive processes, and self-identification issues that students experience during their years in college.

A History of Ableism

Throughout history, disability has been variously viewed as a sign of spiritual depravity, a cause for ridicule, a genetic weakness to be exterminated, something to be hidden away, a source of pity, a community health problem, and a problem to be fixed (Griffin &

McClintock, 1997). These views of disability have shaped the ways in which individuals with disabilities have been treated in society. They also influence the theoretical perspectives that guide current strategies for addressing the issues of people with disabilities in educational settings.

Griffin and McClintock's (1997) summary of the history of ableism is a helpful reminder of the various perspectives that have shaped interactions between society and people with disabilities. Griffin and McClintock noted that during the Middle Ages, physical and mental illness and disability were considered evidence of having fallen out of favor with God and many people with such impairments were prosecuted as witches. At the beginning of the 17th century, people with disabilities were evicted from hospitals and poor houses and were forced to beg on the streets, where they were often ridiculed.

As the authority of science replaced religion in the 19th century, disability came to be viewed as a genetic deficit rather than a spiritual weakness and people with mental and physical impairments became the responsibility of medical personnel (Griffith & McClintock, 1997). Institutionalization of individuals with disabilities in hospitals, asylums, or other institutions away from mainstream society was common during this time. Alternatively, individuals with disabilities were treated as "human curiosities" (p. 219), appearing in "freak shows" (p. 219). The eugenics movement, which began around 1850, favored improvement of the human gene pool by controlling reproduction to ensure that only desirable traits were passed on and strengthened negative attitudes toward individuals with disabilities of any kind. Sterilization and euthanasia were advocated as ways to eliminate the "defective" (p. 221) from society. As late as the 1950s, laws still existed in some states "prohibiting persons 'diseased, maimed, mutilated, or in any way deformed so as to be an unsightly or disgusting object' from appearing in public" (p. 222).

The mid-1950s saw the start of the deinstitutionalization movement, when many individuals with disabilities became the responsibility of their communities without appropriate support (Griffith & McClintock, 1997). Part of this movement was the mainstreaming of children with disabilities into public schools. The poor treatment of people with disabilities following deinstitutionalization led to the independent living movement, which was begun in the 1970s by people with disabilities to establish control over their lives and to gain the same rights that other citizens had. Out of this movement came the 1973 Rehabilitation Act (Section 504) that "prohibited discrimination against 'otherwise qualified handicapped' individuals in any program or activity receiving federal assistance" (Griffin & McClintock, p. 223). This bill ensured the rights of persons with disabilities to be involved in decision making regarding their treatment and also addressed architectural and transportation barriers. In 1990, the Americans with Disabilities Act extended and clarified the Rehabilitation Act to "[require] access and [prohibit] discrimination in public accommodations, state and local government, [and] employment" (p. 225). Vestiges of these historical perspectives are reflected in the various theories that guide how disability is understood and addressed currently.

Disability Theories

In this section, I review the most common theories for explaining disability and discuss how adherents of the theory might view individuals with disabilities and their participation in education.

The Medical Model

Dating back to the 18th century and still prevalent, the medical model considers disabilities as medical conditions to be treated and people with disabilities as invalids (Hughes, 2002). The focus is on what the person cannot do and individuals with disabilities are expected to accept and adjust to their conditions (Michalko, 2002). Because the individual is viewed as sick, participation in "normal" activities, such as attending college, is seen as inappropriate or impossible. In this model, disability is treated by means of medical interventions, such as medication or surgery, that are used to address symptoms of, or problems associated with, a disability. It is up to doctors and other medical professionals to determine how the individual will live his or her life, rather than individuals with disabilities themselves.

The Functional Limitations Model

In society, there are normally accepted ways of performing daily activities and each person is expected to conform to these prescribed behaviors. Disability, however, often prevents activities from being carried out in a normative manner. For instance, if one cannot walk, entering buildings with steps is impossible. Adherents of the functional limitations model assume that it is up to the individual to adapt to the situation created by his or her disability (Michalko, 2002). Like the medical model, the functional limitations approach views disability as a matter the individual must deal with and overcome (Jones, 1996). Because the "problem" of disability lies within the individual, persons with impairments must find ways to adjust to the environment (Michalko). This is accomplished through rehabilitation and adaptation. Persons with disabilities are subject to extensive evaluation and assessment to determine the full extent of their inabilities. Attempts are then made to find ways to accommodate the individual or "make up for" the deficiency.

This perspective provides the theoretical rationale upon which service providers in higher education base the identification of accommodations that will enable students with disabilities to attend college and complete classes successfully. Often such accommodations create a "separate but equal" mentality because individuals with disabilities must take tests in a different location than their classmates or use a special entrance to a building that requires ringing a bell for admission. Attitudinally, those providing accommodations may believe that they are doing the student a favor and may convey pity, condescension, or contempt for being asked to provide these services.

The Minority Group Paradigm

With the growth of the disability rights movement in the 1970s, a new perspective of disability developed that focused on the experiences of people with disabilities as members of an oppressed group (Michalko, 2002). Similar to the experiences of nondominant ethnic, racial, and sexual identity groups, people with disabilities were seen as sharing commonalities based on the discrimination and alienation they dealt with in mainstream society (Jones, 1996). Taking ownership of their lives, people with disabilities rejected society's view of disability as an impediment and took on a disability identity that was political in nature (Michalko). Some proponents of this model have suggested that the unique shared experiences of people with disabilities creates a distinct disability culture; at the least, as Scheer (1994) noted, they share an understanding of life as a person with a disability that creates a bond. Although this model does empower individuals with disabilities, disability is still assumed to be an individual trait and individuals with disabilities assume the role of victims of oppression (Jones, 1996).

In the college setting, adherents to the minority group model strive to create a group consciousness among students with disabilities, providing vehicles for students to come together to advocate for their rights. Increased visibility and awareness of the issues and injustices faced by students with disabilities would be a goal of service providers using this perspective. Although admirable goals, the onus for change is still left to individual students and the institution is not held responsible for seeing that all students are treated as equally worthy of an inclusive education.

The Social Construction Model

Unlike the minority group model, the social construction model focuses on the source of the stigmatization and oppression experienced by individuals with disabilities, finding it in the norms of society that privilege certain ways of being over others (Marks, 1999). In effect, society "creates" disability by considering some forms of being and doing as normal and correct and others as dysfunctional and not normal. In this model, the source of the "problem" of disability is a biased and excluding environment rather than an impaired individual (Marks). It is the environment that needs to be changed rather than the individual (Fine & Asch, 2000).

Proponents of this model work to ensure that environments are barrier-free and welcoming to all people. This perspective has led to the development of Universal Design (UD) principles, both in architecture and instruction. However, critics have argued that its exclusion of the person from consideration goes too far (Paterson & Hughes, 1999). Hughes (2002) argued that the lived experiences of individuals with disabilities must be considered, as they shape the ways in which the environment is experienced.

The Social Justice Perspective

The social justice perspective, which combines elements of the minority group model and the social construction model, takes both the individual and the environment into consideration. This model emphasizes the role played by privilege and oppression in determining the experiences of individuals with disabilities. Social justice theorists stress that individuals without disabilities in society have traditionally possessed the privilege and power to determine how individuals with disabilities—the oppressed group—are viewed and treated. A major goal for social justice advocates is the elimination of "ableism"—the "pervasive system of discrimination and exclusion that oppresses people [with] . . . disabilities on . . . individual, institutional, and societal/cultural levels" (Rauscher & McClintock, 1997, p. 198). Like the social constructionists, social justice theorists argue that what causes persons to be disabled are "unnecessary social, economic, and environmental barriers rather than . . . physical, psychological, or developmental conditions or impairments" (Griffin, Peters, & Smith, 2007, p. 336). An additional social justice goal is to achieve a reinterpretation of normality so that physical, mental, and sensory differences are no longer viewed as abnormal (Griffin et al.). The social justice perspective also considers the interaction of impairment with other social identities, such as gender, sexual orientation, or ethnicity, as well as the environmental contexts in which individuals find themselves and the specific nature of their impairments; in this way, individuals are viewed as multidimensional and unique (Castañeda & Peters, 2000; Griffin et al.). Because Universal Instructional Design focuses on changing the environment rather than requiring the individual to adjust to it, social justice advocates view this intervention positively. In addition, the principles of UID are based on a respect for the human dignity and self-authorship of all students, as stressed in this model (Griffin et al.).

How Theories of Disability Guide Educational Practice

Understanding the theoretical underpinnings of educational interventions for students with disabilities is important as they—intentionally or unconsciously—shape the attitudes, expectations, and motivations of educators providing instruction and advice. For example, the medical model suggests that education, at least at the college level, is not appropriate or attainable for individuals with disabilities, who are better off under the care of medical personnel. Faculty members with this belief, such as the chemistry professor in the opening scenario, may be unwilling even to consider UID as they see enrollment of students with disabilities in college as inappropriate in the first place.

According to the functional limitations model, the purpose of education is rehabilitation and the role of service providers is helping individuals to adjust to their impairments and make the best of the situation in which they find themselves. Faculty members adhering to this perspective, such as the art professor mentioned in the introduction, take the position that it is the student's job to adjust to classes as presented rather than expecting the class to be designed proactively to allow students with disabilities to participate fully. If asked, they might be willing to accommodate a request for modification.

In the minority group paradigm, individuals with disabilities are seen as members of an oppressed identity group who must fight for their rights against a dominant society; however the "problem" of disability and the responsibility to deal with it is still centered in the individual. This perspective would indicate to educators that they have no real obligation to make any changes in how they work with students with disabilities, other than to treat them with respect, which of course is a positive step forward but not a comprehensive intervention.

In contrast to these individual perspectives, the social construction view of disability shifts the focus to the environment and clearly requires that persons who control the educational environment make modifications to ensure that individuals with disabilities have access to equitable opportunities in the classroom without having to request such changes. Thus, UID would be viewed as a reasonable strategy for modifying the classroom environment. However, how the individual is viewed and treated in this process is deemphasized within this framework.

A social justice perspective, on the other hand, incorporates both environmental and individual components, with the environment being seen as the source of the disability and therefore the necessary focus of interventions that will enable students with disabilities to receive an equitable education, and individuals being viewed as multifaceted and unique, responsible for their own decisions, and worthy of respect and consideration from those around them, including instructors and service providers. While either a social constructionist or a social justice perspective can provide a foundation for Universal Instructional Design, social justice is the most inclusive model for ensuring that individuals are valued and included in implementation of specific interventions. The sociology professor introduced in the opening scenario appears to take a social justice perspective in that he is concerned both about creating a welcoming environment and respecting the students with whom he works.

Student Development Theories

While disability theory provides guidance in determining the overall nature of the educational intervention faculty and staff might find appropriate, student development theory assists them in understanding students themselves—those with disabilities and those who do not have disabilities. In this section I present an introduction to the various theories of student development and how they can guide educators in their work with students. In particular, I focus on implications of the theories for students with disabilities.

Psychosocial Theories

Psychosocial theories of development focus on the personal and interpersonal issues affecting individuals' lives (Evans, Forney, & Guido-DiBrito, 1998). Psychosocial theorists posit that development occurs when internal psychological or physical change causing an internal crisis for the individual collides with an external social demand to cause a developmental crisis. The result is a series of developmental tasks or stages in which the individual's "thinking, feeling, behaving, valuing, and relating to others and oneself" (Chickering & Reisser, 1993, p. 2) changes. Stages are generally (but not rigidly) sequential, cumulative, and culture specific (Evans et al.). The degree of success in resolution of crises affects later development. Some of the developmental issues faced by students include developing competence, managing emotions, establishing identity, and developing purpose (Chickering & Reisser). Other theories of psychosocial development focus on the role played by challenge and support (Sanford, 1966); transitions (Schlossberg, Waters, & Goodman, 1995); life events (Fiske & Chiriboga, 1990); and timing, agency, and interactions with others (Elder, 1995) on development. Some theorists included in this family also focus on specific developmental issues, such as career development (Super, 1990).

Psychosocial theories focus the attention of educators on aspects of the lives of students with disabilities. For instance, Sanford's (1966) theory of challenge and support reminds educators that students with disabilities face unique personal and societal challenges, such as exclusion from participation in mainstream activities, and need individual and institutional support to succeed. Universal Instructional Design can be an important source of support because its goal is to provide an inclusive classroom environment in which no student is singled out.

In considering Chickering and Reisser's (1993) vectors of development, educators need to be aware that students with disabilities must address the same developmental tasks as other students, but the issues involved in doing so may be more complex. For example, intellectual competence issues may be harder to resolve when students have been told all their lives that they are incapable of learning. UID provides conditions that help to dispel this belief.

Life events theories suggest to educators that the onset of a disability, such as the loss of sight, is a major life event that will affect individuals in significant ways that can affect academic performance. Students who have to learn new ways to negotiate their environment and approach academic material can be easily overwhelmed. The existence of UID, which will allow them alternative means of studying and learning, will be an important vehicle to maintain control of their lives.

Life course theories (e.g., Elder, 1995) purport that timing, agency, and interactions with significant others all affect the manner in which individuals experience and respond to a disability, important factors to keep in mind when interacting with students with disabilities. Students who experience brain injuries in accidents during college are certainly greatly affected by the life implications of this event, perhaps more so than if the event had happened later in life. Likewise, individuals' sense of agency and the support, or lack thereof, from family and friends will shape how they handle the experience. Understanding these factors can assist faculty in working with students and introducing alternatives for studying and engaging in classes.

Finally, career development theories (e.g., Super, 1990) can assist educators in working with persons with disabilities, who face unique personal and environmental challenges in identifying a career direction. Students may be very realistic about their abilities and how they might be applied in specific careers or they might have given very little thought to this aspect of their lives. Faculty and advisors who understand career development models can assist students in investigating options using various approaches suggested by UID.

Cognitive-Structural Theories

Cognitive-structural theories focus on the process of reasoning that individuals use and describe changes in this process from simple to complex (Evans et al., 1998). They illuminate changes in the way people think, but not what they think. According to cognitive-structural theorists, both heredity and environment are important in intellectual development; individuals must be ready and the environment must present challenges for development of cognitive processes to occur. Individuals move through a series of stages, or "sets of assumptions people use to adapt to and organize their environments" (Evans, 1996, p. 173), which always arise in sequential order regardless of cultural influences. When confronted with new information, individuals first try to make sense of it using their current set of assumptions; if that does not work, they develop new, more complex assumptions (Evans et al.). Development, while following an order progression, takes place at an irregular rate and not every person reaches the highest stages of cognitive functioning. Cognitive-structural theories focus on intellectual development (Perry, 1968); reflective judgment (King & Kitchener, 1994); and epistemological development (Baxter Magolda, 1992); as well as moral development (Gilligan, 1982; Kohlberg, 1976); faith development (Fowler, 1981; Parks, 2000); and self-evolution (Kegan, 1994). Each of these theories has implications for working with students with disabilities.

Theories of intellectual and epistemological development (e.g., Baxter Magolda, 1992; King & Kitchener, 1994; Perry, 1968) suggest that the complexity of cognitive reasoning used by students with disabilities will affect how they make sense of their experiences. For instance, students who think dualistically (e.g., in concrete, absolutist terms) will look for answers from authorities and expect faculty to tell them what to do and how to do it. They may have difficulty with options provided in a UID approach.

Moral development theories (e.g., Gilligan, 1982; Kohlberg, 1976) remind educators that students with disabilities, like other students, will make meaning of moral dilemmas in different ways. Some dilemmas may relate to decisions involving their impairment, diagnosis, or disability. For instance, cheating is an option that many students with learning disabilities report considering to achieve the grades they want in classes (Evans, Assadi, Herriott, & Varland, 2004). The support of UID strategies for completing assignments might deter students from using this option.

Faith development theories (Fowler, 1981; Parks, 2000) focus on the role of spirituality and faith in a person's life. How individuals view and approach disability may be related to their spiritual beliefs. For instance, some religious belief systems still equate illness and disability with sin or see it as punishment for wrong-doing. In earlier stages of faith development, such a viewpoint would be unquestioned. In a UID classroom, where various abilities are accepted, students may come to a greater sense of self-acceptance.

Kegan's (1994) theory of self-evolution suggests that a person's sense of self evolves based on relationships with others. How one handles having a disability and what one expects from other people in one's life can be partially explained by this theory. In earlier stages of Kegan's model, individuals are very dependent on others for their sense of self-worth. Faculty using UID who respect and value the contributions of students with disabilities may provide them with positive support that will assist them in developing the sense of self-authorship evident in later stages of Kegan's model.

Social Identity Theories

Social identity theories examine how individuals come to understand their social identities (race, ethnicity, gender, sexual orientation, class, etc.) and the roles played by these identities in their lives (McEwen, 2003). Social identities are contextual and fluid; they vary across time as well as national, geographic, and cultural environments. Identities are socially constructed within hierarchies of privilege and oppression, with some identities being dominant and others being subordinate. Thus, social identities exist within power relationships; they are not merely different. Social identities influence how individuals view themselves and influence their day-to-day experiences. Identities are also embedded in and influence what happens in society, communities, and social institutions—ideological, political, and economic. Each person has many social identities that influence each other and are part of every social interaction and personal experience (Jones & McEwen, 2000). Development of social identities consists of increased awareness and abandonment of internalized oppression (McEwen). More complex development is valued as a goal and is associated with increased mental health. Social identity theories include theories of minority identity (Atkinson, Morten, & Sue, 1998); racial identity (Cross & Fhagen-Smith, 2001; Ferdman & Gallegos, 2001; Helms, 1995; Kim, 2001; Renn, 2004); ethnic identity (Phinney, 2003; Sodowsky, Kwan, & Pannu, 1995; Torres, 1999); sexual identity (Cass, 1979; D'Augelli, 1994; Fassinger, 1998); gender identity (Lorber, 2000), disability identity (Olkin, 1999); and multiple identities (Jones & McEwen, 2000).

As the social justice model discussed earlier stresses, how individuals experience and view disability is influenced by their race, ethnicity, gender, class, sexual orientation, religious identity, and other aspects of the self. The various social identity theories can be very helpful in understanding identity development processes. For example, students with disabilities may also be questioning their sexual orientation. In gay male communities, physical appearance is often a factor in social acceptance (Guter & Killacky, 2004). This realization may make it especially difficult for a student to develop a positive identity as either a person with a disability or a gay man. As another example, African Americans are often inappropriately placed in special education based on the mistaken assumption that their learning abilities are inferior to those of Whites (Obiakor, 1992). As a result, Ball-Brown and Lloyd Frank (1993) have noted that many African American students avoid using services for students with disabilities or even refuse to acknowledge having a learning impairment. This may be particularly the case if students are in the immersion stage of racial identity development (Cross & Fhagen-Smith, 2001), when distrust of Whites is high. The lowered stress of a classroom designed using UID principles would be of great assistance in enabling students to address their social identity concerns while also staying on top of their studies.

Atkinson et al.'s (1998) minority identity model centers on how individuals who are members of minority groups view themselves, members of their own group, and members of the majority group. These attitudes, which develop through five stages of increasing acceptance of self and others, can be applied to how persons with disabilities view themselves, other individuals with disabilities, and those who do not currently have a disability. Olkin's (1999) minority identity model of disability uses a similar five-stage model in which individuals move from denial of having a disability to advocating for disability rights. Olkin also noted various psychosocial factors that influence this developmental process, such as degree of impairment, level of uncertainty associated with the impairment, and the likely outcome of the impairment. Understanding how a student views his or her disability and disability in general is very helpful to faculty and staff in working with the student. A student who is in denial of even having a disability likely will not want to discuss various ways in which that disability might affect his or her academic work. UID would be particularly helpful to such students because it would not require that they disclose their impairments or ask for accommodations.

Finally, Jones and McEwen's (2000) multiple identity model underscores that individuals have many social identities that may or may not be salient at various times and locations. In some classes, for example, a disability might be much more salient because of the types of learning activities involved. In another instance, being the only student of color in a class may be a more salient identity for this same student. Faculty must be careful not to assume that being a person with a disability is always the most salient identity for a student. Again, UID is helpful in that no demands are made of students to disclose should they not feel the need or desire to do so.

Conclusion

Understanding the theoretical underpinnings of disability and of student development provides faculty and staff with a foundation upon which to design interventions to assist students with disabilities to be successful in college. In particular, these theoretical approaches provide a strong rationale for the use of Universal Instruction Design principles in the classroom and in advising and working individually with students. In addition, faculty who can provide an appropriate theoretical rationale for their learning outcomes and pedagogical strategies will be more effective in convincing others to follow their lead in the implementation of UID.

References

Americans With Disabilities Act of 1990, 42 U.S.C. § 12101 *et seq.*

Atkinson, D. R., Morten, G., & Sue, D. W. (1998). *Counseling American minorities: A cross-cultural perspective* (5th ed.). Dubuque, IA: McGraw Hill.

Ball-Brown, B., & Lloyd Frank, Z. (1993). Disabled students of color. In S. Kroeger & J. Shuck (Eds.), *Responding to disability issues in student affairs.* (New Directions for Student Services, no. 64, pp. 79-88). San Francisco: Jossey-Bass.

Baxter Magolda, M. B. (1992). *Knowing and reasoning in college: Gender-related patterns in students' intellectual development.* San Francisco: Jossey-Bass.

Cass, V. C. (1979). Homosexual identity formation: A theoretical model. *Journal of Homosexuality,* 4, 219-235.

Castañeda, R., & Peters, M. L. (2000). Ableism. In M. Adams, W. J. Blumenfeld, R. Castañeda, H. W. Hackman, M. L. Peters, & X. Zúñiga (Eds.), *Readings for diversity and social justice* (pp. 319-323). New York: Routledge.

Chickering, A. W., & Reisser, L. (1993). *Education and identity* (2nd ed.). San Francisco: Jossey-Bass.

Cross, W. E., Jr., & Fhagen-Smith, P. (2001). Patterns of African American identity development: A life span perspective. In C. L. Wijeyesinghe & B. W. Jackson III (Eds.), *New perspectives on racial identity development: A theoretical and practical anthology* (pp. 243-270). New York: New York University Press.

D'Augelli, A. R. (1994). Identity development and sexual orientation: Toward a model of lesbian, gay, and bisexual identity development. In E. J. Trickett, R. J. Watts, & D. Birman (Eds.), *Human diversity: Perspectives on people in context* (pp. 312-333). San Francisco: Jossey-Bass.

Elder, G. H., Jr. (1995). The life course paradigm: Social change and individual development. In P. Moen, G. H. Elder, Jr., & K. Lüsher (Eds.), Examining lives in context: *Perspectives on the ecology of human development* (pp. 101-139). Washington, DC: American Psychological Association.

Evans, N. J. (1996). Theories of student development. In S. R. Komives, D. B. Woodard, Jr., & Associates, *Student services: A handbook for the profession* (3rd ed., pp. 164-187). San Francisco: Jossey-Bass.

Evans, N. J., Assadi, J., Herriott, T., & Varland, C. (2004, April). *Compliance is not inclusion: Social integration of students with disabilities.* Paper presented at the annual convention of the American College Personnel Association, Philadelphia, PA.

Evans, N. J., Forney, D. S., & Guido-DiBrito, F. (1998). *Student development in college: Theory, research, and practice.* San Francisco: Jossey-Bass.

Fassinger, R. E. (1998). Lesbian, gay, and bisexual identity and student development theory. In R. L. Sanlo (Ed.), *Working with lesbian, gay, bisexual, and transgender college students: A handbook for faculty and administrators* (pp. 13-22). Westport, CT: Greenwood.

Ferdman, B. M., & Gallegos, P. I. (2001). Racial identity development and Latinos in the United States. In C. L. Wijeyesinghe & B. W. Jackson, III (Eds.), *New perspectives on racial identity development: A theoretical and practical anthology* (pp.32-66). New York: New York University Press.

Fine, M., & Asch, A. (2000). Disability beyond stigma: Social interaction, discrimination, and activism. In M. Adams, W. J. Blumenfeld, R. Castañeda, H. W. Hackman, M. L. Peters, & X. Zúñiga (Eds.), *Readings for diversity and social justice* (pp. 330-339). New York: Routledge.

Fiske, M., & Chiriboga, D. A. (1990). *Change and continuity in adult life.* San Francisco: Jossey-Bass.

Fowler, J. W. (1981). *Stages of faith: The psychology of human development and the quest for meaning.* San Francisco: Harper & Row.

Gilligan, C. (1982). *In a different voice: Psychological theory and women's development.* Cambridge, MA: Harvard University Press.

Griffin, P., & McClintock, M. (1997). History of ableism in Europe and the United States--A selected timeline. In M. Adams, L. A. Bell, & P. Griffin (Eds.), *Teaching for diversity and social justice* (pp. 219-225). New York: Routledge.

Griffin, P., Peters, M. L., & Smith, R. M. (2007). Ableism curricular design. In M. Adams, L. A. Bell, & P. Griffin (Eds.), *Teaching for diversity and social justice* (2nd ed., pp. 335-358). New York: Routledge.

Guter, B., & Killacky, J. R. (Eds.). (2004). *Queer crips: Disabled men and their stories.* New York: Harrington Park Press.

Helms, J. E. (1995). An update of Helms' White and People of Color racial identity models. In J. G. Ponterotto, J. M. Casas, L. A. Suzuki, & C. M. Alexander (Eds.), *Handbook of multicultural counseling* (pp. 181-198). Thousand Oaks, CA: Sage.

Hughes, B. (2002). Disability and the body. In C. Barnes, M. Oliver, & L. Barton (Eds.), *Disability studies today* (pp. 58-76). Cambridge, UK: Polity Press.

Jones, S. R. (1996). Toward inclusive theory: Disability as a social construction. *NASPA Journal,* 33, 347-354.

Jones, S. R., & McEwen, M. K. (2000). A conceptual model of multiple dimensions of identity. *Journal of College Student Development, 41*, 405-413.

Kegan, R. (1994). *In over our heads: The mental demands of modern life.* Cambridge, MA: Harvard University Press.

Kim, J. (2001). Asian American identity development theory. In C. L. Wijeyesinghe & B. W. Jackson III, (Eds.), *New perspectives on racial identity development: A theoretical and practical anthology* (pp.67-90). New York: New York University Press.

King, P. M., & Kitchener, K. S. (1994). *Developing reflective judgment: Understanding and promoting intellectual growth and critical thinking in adolescents and adults.* San Francisco: Jossey-Bass.

Kohlberg, L. (1976). Moral stages and moralization: The cognitive-developmental approach. In T. Lickona (Ed.), *Moral development and behavior: Theory, research, and social issues* (pp. 31-53). Austin, TX: Holt, Rinehart, & Winston.

Lorber, J. (2000). "Night to his day": The social construction of gender. In M. Adams, W. J. Blumenfeld, R. Castañeda, H. W. Hackmann, M. L. Peters, & X. Zúñiga (Eds.), *Readings for diversity and social justice* (pp. 203-213). New York: Routledge.

Marks, D. (1999). *Disability: Controversial debates and psychosocial perspectives.* London: Routledge.

McEwen, M. R. (2003). New perspectives on identity development. In S. R. Komives, D. B. Woodard, Jr., & Associates, *Student services: A handbook for the profession* (4th ed., pp. 203-233). San Francisco: Jossey-Bass.

Michalko, R. (2002). *The difference that disability makes.* Philadelphia: Temple University Press.

Obiakor, F. E. (1992). Self-concept of African American students: An operational model for special education. *Exceptional Children, 59*(2), 160-167.

Olkin, R. (1999). *What psychotherapists should know about disability.* New York: Guilford.

Parks, S. D. (2000). *Big questions, worthy dreams: Mentoring young adults in their search for meaning, purpose, and faith.* San Francisco: Jossey-Bass.

Paterson, K., & Hughes, B. (1999). Disability studies and phenomenology: The carnal politics of everyday life. *Disability & Society, 14,* 597-610.

Perry, W. G., Jr. (1968). *Forms of intellectual and ethical development in the college years: A scheme.* New York: Holt, Rinehart, & Winston.

Phinney, J. S. (2003). Ethnic identity and acculturation. In K. M. Chun, P. B. Organista, & G. Marin (Eds.), *Acculturation: Advances in theory, measurement, and applied research* (pp. 63-81). Washington, DC: American Psychological Association.

Rauscher, L., & McClintock, M. (1997). Ableism curriculum design. In M. Adams, L. A. Bell, & P. Griffin (Eds.), *Teaching for diversity and social justice* (pp. 198-229). New York: Routledge.

Rehabilitation Act Amendments of 1973, 29 U.S.C. § 701 *et seq.*

Renn, K. A. (2004). *Mixed race students in college: The ecology of race, identity, and community on campus.* Albany, NY: State University of New York Press.

Sanford, N. (1966). *Self and society: Social change and individual development.* New York: Atherton.

Scheer, J. (1994). Culture and disability: An anthropological point of view. In E. J. Trickett, R. J. Watts, & D. Birman (Eds.), *Human diversity: Perspectives on people in context* (pp. 244-260). San Francisco: Jossey-Bass.

Schlossberg, N. K., Waters, E. B., & Goodman, J. (1995). *Counseling adults in transition* (2nd ed.). New York: Springer.

Sodowsky, G. R., Kwan, K. K., & Pannu, R. (1995). Ethnic identity of Asians in the United States. In J. G. Ponterotto, J. M. Casas, L. A. Suzuki, & C. M. Alexander (Eds.), *Handbook of multicultural counseling* (pp. 123-154). Thousand Oaks, CA: Sage.

Super, D. E. (1990). A life-span approach to career development. In D. Brown, L. Brooks, & Associates, *Career choice and development: Applying contemporary theories to development* (2nd ed., pp. 197-261). San Francisco: Jossey-Bass.

Torres, V. (1999). Validation of a bicultural orientation model for Hispanic college students. *Journal of College Student Development, 40,* 285-298.

CHAPTER 3

Broadening the Pathway to Academic Success: The Critical Intersections of Social Justice Education, Critical Multicultural Education, and Universal Instructional Design

Heather W. Hackman
Saint Cloud State University

Abstract
In this chapter I present a brief description of the theoretical and pedagogical foundations of Social Justice Education (SJE), Critical Multicultural Education(CME), and Universal Instructional Design (UID) in order to provide a critical analysis of UID through SJE and CME frameworks. This is followed by a discussion of how to combine SJE and CME with UID in the service of establishing the highest level of accessibility possible in our classrooms.

Picture the following scenario: A White male film studies professor at an urban community college with a highly diverse student population is facilitating a class discussion of the film *North by Northwest* (Hitchcock, 1959). He has been introduced to Universal Instructional Design (UID) and therefore has created a welcoming classroom environment, thoroughly explained the essential components of the course, given the class clear expectations and feedback about how to analyze film, used small group discussions to support learning, implemented varied instructional strategies, created a range of ways for students to demonstrate knowledge, and has been available for interactions with students in and out of class. Anyone observing this class for its structural accessibility and its openness to students with a range of learning styles would say that this professor has done an excellent job. However, as he begins to facilitate the discussion of the film, and particularly of Cary Grant's character Roger Thornhill, he states that "everyone can relate to the main character, right?" And in that moment all of the structural accessibility in the world does not compensate for the fact that he has just assumed that everyone in the room can relate to the experience of a White middle-class male. The students of color, the poor and working class students, and the women in the room are all expected to identify with the White, male, middle-class experience and, in so doing, deny their own. Some of the students of color in the class ask him about the contradiction inherent in his assumption and he, not knowing what to do about such discussions and assuming that he has done everything right in his class, tells the students to stay on point and that their questions are not really pertinent to the discussion of the film.

Although this may seem like an exaggerated or even fictitious account, it is actually a story relayed to me by a dean of students in an urban community college where this scenario took place. The impact on the diverse group of students in this class was significant—they told the dean that they felt like this was just one more class that ignored their life experience and they no longer believed the instructor was able to teach or even understand who they were. The disenfranchisement felt by these students, and millions of others like them in classrooms across the country, speaks to the undeniable need for Social Justice Education (SJE) and Critical Multicultural Education (CME) approaches to accompany that of UID. As seen in this example, structural accessibility alone does not equate to or promise accessibility in its deepest sense for all students. Unless educators have an awareness of students' social identities and the connection of power and privilege to those identities, as well as cultural competency in relating to those identities, there is a strong likelihood that even in a classroom where UID is deeply integrated, students from nondominant groups will be alienated. The cumulative impact of this marginalization of students based on race, class, gender, sexual orientation, disability, and so on, is a society completely unable to address the most powerful barriers that are currently plaguing our education system, such as increasingly high levels of racial and economic segregation (Kozol, 2005), high drop-out rates for various marginalized communities in our society, and the inability of students to engage critically with the world around them.

Given this film class and its problematic outcome, the importance of the conversation regarding the combination of Social Justice Education and Critical Multicultural Education with Universal Instructional Design, and the promise this amalgam holds for educational equity for all students, is quite clear. By discussing the incorporation of SJE and CME with UID, I am in no way questioning the fundamental efficacy of UID. While no educational approach is a panacea, UID does present educators with both a theoretical framework and a set of practical tools for helping all students achieve academic success and personal empowerment. Its focus on eliminating the structural barriers for all students and creating more accessible classrooms, if widely adopted, could significantly transform the landscape of U.S. education. However, I also contend that UID is lacking in some critical areas for which its combination with SJE and CME would compensate and give educators an even greater chance of addressing some of the core issues denying full educational access for many students in the U.S.

It should be noted that while I have been teaching about Social Justice Education and Critical Multicultural Education for 15 years, I am not an expert in the field of Universal Instructional Design and thus I invite practitioners of UID to take my analysis to deeper levels and apply it in more specific ways to their teaching or professional areas than I am able to in this chapter. Despite these limitations, however, I am clear that by combining UID's ability to create structurally accessible classrooms with SJE's analysis of systemic power and focus on equity and CME's culturally relevant and engaging educational strategies, we can significantly broaden the reach and impact of Universal Instructional Design. If UID is going to move from being seen and experienced as an approach serving primarily students with special needs to an approach that is viewed as useful for all students, it needs to make more critical and compelling connections to other educational theories.

Theoretical Foundations

In this section I present the basic theoretical and pedagogical tenets of Social Justice Education, Critical Multicultural Education, and Universal Instructional Design.

Social Justice Education Theory

Born out of the humanistic education movement in the 1970s in combination with grassroots, nonformal education practices throughout the 20th century (Freire, 1970), Social Justice Education has as its primary focus an analysis of systems of inequity and a commitment to the transformation of these systems in our society. More specifically, Lee Ann Bell (1997) suggested three important aspects of SJE theory: empowerment, social responsibility, and the transformation of systems of oppression and inequality to ones of social justice and humanity. Today many teachers hear the word "empowerment" and associate that with self-esteem building in the classroom or other cursory approaches to personal empowerment. In Social Justice Education, however, student empowerment refers to both the acquisition of knowledge *and* an understanding of what to do with that knowledge both in students' personal lives and in the greater society. This leads to Bell's second point, social responsibility, whereby students realize their interconnectedness in society and on this planet and begin to take up the charge of responsibility for their community, their society, and the world. By necessity, this process leads students to analyzing issues of power and privilege, systemic inequality, and social transformation in the service of creating a socially just school, community, and society.

Those reading this chapter may see this model as a lofty goal but too difficult to actually implement in the classroom. To the contrary, there are numerous educators across the country effectively utilizing a social justice approach in their classrooms and there is a growing body of literature that speaks to the processes of teaching from an SJE perspective. For example, Adams, Bell, and Griffin (1997) have edited a widely read text, *Teaching for Diversity and Social Justice,* which speaks very specifically to the theory and practice of Social Justice Education in our postsecondary settings. Similarly, Schniedewind and Davidson (2006), in their book *Open Minds to Equality,* have produced an excellent tool for teaching from an SJE perspective in upper elementary and middle school settings. While not as well known as multicultural education, a Social Justice Educational approach grounded in the works of authors such as Paulo Freire (1970), Marilyn Frye (1983), and bell hooks (1994) helps educators create more access for students to both the knowledge within the classroom and the world outside the classroom and thus has a great deal to offer to practitioners of Universal Instructional Design.

Social Justice Education Pedagogy

The principle goals of Social Justice Education have been described previously and thus the following is a description of what I consider five critical pedagogical components of SJE (Hackman, 2005). In considering the combination of UID with SJE, it is easy to see how these two theories can complement each other. As mentioned, Social Justice Education has a deep focus on issues of power and privilege and how they impact everything from the ability of students to learn to the ability for justice and equity to be achieved in our society. In an article I wrote for *Equity and Excellence in Education,* I offered five areas to consider when framing one's teaching from an SJE perspective: content mastery, critical thinking and tools for analysis, tools for action and social change, tools for personal reflection, and the consideration of multicultural group dynamics. Although this is not an exhaustive framework, it does give educators a place to begin in their efforts to move their teaching in the direction of an SJE approach. The first component, content mastery, is something that most schools seek in a general way but in an SJE classroom the content would be much more rigorous than the mainstream curriculum and instead represent information from a range of perspectives and experiences. To most teachers, this seems so obvious as to be naïve, and yet if one analyzes today's mainstream curriculum—history books for example—we often see a watered-down curriculum that perfectly mirrors the dominant group's understanding of the world (Loewen, 1995). SJE demands that students are given more information in order to engage critically and effectively with the world around them.

Information alone, however, is not enough to affect serious social change or even engender thoughtful student engagement, and thus students in an SJE classroom are also required to think critically about every issue presented in class. A glance at the critical pedagogy literature suggests some important aspects of critical thinking germane to an SJE classroom: (a) an analysis of content from multiple, nondominant perspectives ("Who's not at the table?" "How would 'group x' understand this content?"); (b) an analysis of systems of power and privilege in our society and the world ("Who benefits when the system runs one way versus another way?"); (c) rigorous self-reflection ("How do I *know* that what I think I know?" "Where did I get my information?"). Using critical thinking in this way allows teachers to push students well beyond simple regurgitation of classroom content and demands that they thoroughly and deeply engage with the material and find their own voice with respect to the learning taking place.

Content mastery and critical analysis, if left at that, can sometimes lead students to feel cynical and hopeless. Thus, skills and tools for social change are essential in a social justice classroom. These tools include an understanding of the history of the social change movements in this country, the underlying principles of social change processes such as nonviolent action, and the need to understand the personal motivations for engaging in social change. In line with this, the fourth dimension of an SJE classroom, tools for self-reflection, helps students constantly understand their position socially, politically, and morally in relation to the issues at hand. This focus on self-awareness is essential in helping students in a social justice classroom make the deep, personal connections to their learning that help them contextualize the content and apply it to other areas of their lives. When teaching happens in this way, students' success increases dramatically because their learning takes on greater meaning and import for their lives and their futures.

The final component in an SJE classroom is the consideration of the multicultural group dynamics and the interactions of students with one another, with the teacher, and with the school community as a whole along the lines of culture and social identity. As such, educators utilizing an SJE approach need to be aware of not only how each student's culture is impacting the class as a whole, but also to pay attention to how social identities such as class, gender, race, sexual orientation, ability, religion, and age are also impacting student learning and the dynamics of the class. More than anything, this requires a deep awareness of these issues on the part of educators themselves and an ongoing commitment to their own learning around social justice issues.

Critical Multicultural Education Theory

Arising in conjunction with the Civil Rights Movement of the 1950s and 1960s, multicultural education's initial focus was on addressing issues of increased curricular representation for people of color and creating more inclusive academic environments. The success of this work was clearly evident in the 1960s and 1970s when more inclusive classroom materials and multicultural education in general found a wide audience and its presence in U.S. classrooms increased. In these years it became clear, however, that desegregation and curricular inclusion were not enough to create safe, empowering, and academically successful educational environments for students of color. As such, the last 3 decades of multicultural education have adopted an increasingly anti-racist, anti-White privilege focus in addition to the furtherance of curricular inclusiveness through approaches like culturally responsive teaching (Gay, 2000). Writers such as James Banks (2002, 2008), Sonia Nieto (2002; Nieto & Bode 2008), Carl Grant, and Christine Sleeter (Grant & Sleeter, 2006) have aptly addressed both cultural inclusiveness and anti-racist issues over the years and put forth the idea that approaches to multicultural education exist on a continuum rather than a discreet ideological position. Sleeter and Grant advanced a model in their book, *Turning on Learning,* with four positions ranging from a "human relations" approach to one of "multicultural social justice education." Banks (2002) has also suggested a range of four approaches to multicultural education spanning from a "contributions" approach to a "decision-making and social action approach" (pp. 73-74). Nieto (2002) has proposed a five-stage model describing the range of multicultural education moving from "monocultural" to "affirmation, solidarity and critique" (pp. 8-18). While these continua use differing language and have identified slightly different characteristics for each of their "stages," one theme is strikingly consistent: the most critical forms of multicultural education not only address cultural diversity but by necessity also discuss issues of oppression, injustice, and social change. As such, the ultimate stages of all of these models, referred to as Critical Multicultural Education, are a call for transformation not only in education, but in society as a whole. In this chapter, any reference made to multicultural education will be referring to these critical, socially transformative manifestations of multicultural education and will be labeled Critical Multicultural Education.

While multicultural education is a deep and rich field with a range of essential elements, in an effort to simplify my discussion of Critical Multicultural Education I will focus on two fundamental aspects of the final stage of Nieto's model: culturally relevant teaching and rigorous student-centered engagement. In her article, "Affirmation, Solidarity and Critique," from the book *Beyond Heroes and Holidays* (Lee, Mearkart, & Okagawa-Reg, 2002), Nieto (2002), as have all critical multicultural educators, underscored the intimate connection between culture, student learning, and classroom communication. More specifically she asserted that in a CME classroom the content educators present will have a high degree of cultural relevance and the engagement of students will have a high degree of cultural competence. As a result, the life experience that the students bring into the classroom is highly valued and used as a point of entry for teaching and learning. In so doing, students find their cultural values highly regarded in a CME classroom and in general the notion of culture is central to their learning and the application of their learning to the broader society. For both teachers and students, culturally relevant teaching creates an incredibly rich and rigorous academic environment and assures that students' voices, lives, and cultural realities are not only affirmed in the classroom, but are seen as content and points of reference for all learning in the classroom. Critical Multicultural Education brings culture and identity into the classroom in powerful ways and gives students a chance to connect to the curriculum in meaningful and consistent ways. In this sense, CME is clearly about empowerment, access, and educational equity and produces engaged, participatory citizens who possess an increased awareness of others and themselves.

A second key component of a CME classroom, as stated by Nieto (2002) is that, "the most powerful learning results when students work and struggle with one another, even if it is sometimes difficult and challenging" (p. 15). As such, CME does not shy away from students deeply and rigorously engaging not only with the content but with each other. Most teachers avoid such situations as they often equate this with a loss of control in the classroom. Nieto rightly stated, however, that in fully empowering education students are strongly encouraged to think critically and through this analysis learn to voice and exchange their ideas with others. In this way, knowledge construction in a CME classroom is largely student-centered and focused on rigorous engagement instead of rote memorization.

In addition, in the book *Affirming Diversity* (Nieto & Bode, 2008), Nieto defined Critical Multicultural Education as: (a) anti-racist; (b) a basic component for all good education; (c) important for all students, not just students of color or those in culturally-diverse settings; (d) pervasive throughout the curriculum; (e) education for social justice; (f) a process, and (g) involving critical pedagogy. These educational aspects, along with cultural relevance and rigorous, student-centered engagement, can comprise a powerful addition to the fundamental aspects of Universal Instructional Design and afford students an even more empowering and accessible education.

Critical Multicultural Education Pedagogy

Of critical importance when considering the pedagogy of CME is the recognition by all educators that there is an intimate connection between culture and teaching, learning, communication styles, and academic achievement. As such, I believe practitioners of UID seeking a genuinely accessible, student-centered classroom should shift their practice of UID to include Critical Multicultural Education. To attempt to describe in detail the many processes of CME is impossible here, but I strongly encourage practitioners of UID to seek out the voluminous amount of theory and practice-based research of this field from the last 50 years. As discussed previously, I will focus here on culturally relevant teaching and rigorous, student-centered engagement.

For educators, a culturally responsive approach "can be defined as using the cultural knowledge, prior experiences, frames of reference, and performance styles of ethnically diverse students to make learning encounters more relevant to and effective for them" (Gay, 2000, p. 29). To do so, teachers need to make specific efforts to discover who is in their classroom with respect to cultural diversity and then make specific, intentional efforts to utilize that as a point of entry for learning. For example, instead of simply analyzing a passage from a text, students can be asked to analyze the text by comparing and contrasting the text to their own cultural framework. In this way, students will not be reduced to a singular analytical frame but will develop a range of analyses for the text. When this analysis is shared in small or large group discussion, it will by default add layers of complexity and critical discussion where a fairly homogenous discussion might have taken place without approaching it from a critical cultural context. This exercise can apply to any text in any classroom; therefore, CME should be incorporated into all aspects of the curriculum and not relegated to particular aspects of the curriculum such as art, music, or social studies. The importance of establishing personal contexts for knowledge construction cannot be overestimated and is one of the hallmarks of good multicultural education. If teachers are aware of the diversity of student culture in their classroom and are versed in culturally relevant instructional design, they will consistently be able to deepen student learning by making culture a standard framework of analysis in the classroom.

For students, rigorous, student-centered engagement has two dimensions. The first is an awareness of students' own cultural identities and how they shape their learning, how they make meaning of the world, and how they apply their knowledge. For example, some students may come from a culture that constructs knowledge in what is called a field-dependent manner and thus these students will need a higher degree of dialogue in the process of making meaning of the content being presented. If students are aware of this and the classroom environment is truly accessible, the students stand a better chance of being able to take ownership of their own education. Second, if students have a greater awareness of each other's culture their ability to demonstrate their learning and engage with each other is also enhanced. It is through effective cross-cultural dialogue that students can often find the complexity of content that Nieto (2002) suggested is essential to a CME classroom. Repeatedly throughout the CME literature the use of cross-cultural dialogue in conjunction with cooperative learning techniques is shown to be an incredibly effective way for students to learn, retain, and apply knowledge in meaningful ways.

In conclusion, the importance of culture in the classroom cannot be underscored and in a critical multicultural classroom it is seen as a central part of learning. As stated previously, there are myriad other aspects of CME that enhance students' learning and support the use of Universal Instructional Design and I encourage UID practitioners to investigate and make wide use of that information.

Universal Design Theory

Utilizing the notion of Universal Design (UD) in architecture and the benefits of universal accessibility for all, educational researchers have developed a range of ways that UD can be applied to the educational environment. In this section I will explore the conceptual underpinnings of the application of Universal Design to education by discussing the two most widely known approaches to doing so: Universal Design for Learning (UDL) and Universal Instructional Design. I am choosing to look at both UDL and UID in this theoretical section in order to establish a conceptual baseline for UD in education overall. The pedagogical section immediately following this, along with the rest of this chapter, will focus exclusively on UID because of its exceptional applicability to the classroom and the ease of entry for SJE and CME in its eight principles.

Universal Design for Learning (UDL), as put forth by researchers at the Center for Applied Special Technology (CAST; 2000), is an educational approach that seeks to establish classroom accessibility for all students (Meyer & Rose, 2006). Originally born out of a focus on accommodating students with disabilities in education, researchers ultimately realized that the accommodations being made and the levels of accessibility being introduced were ones that would help students from a range of learning styles and could increase the academic success of all students. While studies conducted by CAST researchers and others utilizing UDL confirm these results (Meyer & Rose), even without such data, common sense tells us that when there is increased opportunity for knowledge acquisition and application, there is increased success. Importantly, while UDL was originally focused on how to help students with disabilities be successful in the educational system, as it developed, practitioners rightly recognized that this focus was placing the locus of "the problem" on the student and instead shifted their energies to changing curricula. As a result of this awareness, and in line with the goals of the independent living movement for people with disabilities, UDL shifted its focus to helping educators—and by default the educational systems as a whole—fundamentally transform their practice. As a teaching approach, Universal Design for Learning, provides a framework that makes explicit what good teaching is. It helps teachers recognize the diversity of their classrooms—because even those that might appear to be homogenous are not. It helps them be explicit about the goals of the lessons and enables them to offer choices and alternatives for students to reach those goals." (Meo, 2006, p. 35)

The specifics of UDL and its approach are derived from neuropsychological research on the brain and the processes by which it "learns." Through the use of brain imaging technology, the developers of UDL identified three brain networks and their relation to classroom learning. As stated in Meyer and Rose's (2006) summary of these three brain networks in the preface to their book, *A Practical Reader in Universal Design for Learning,*

> Recognition networks make it possible to receive and analyze information—the "what" of learning, ... strategic networks make it possible to generate patterns and develop strategies for action and problem-solving—the "how" of learning, ... and affective networks fuel motivation and guide the ability to establish priorities, focus attention and choose action—the "why" of learning. (p. ix)

Once having identified these brain networks, the CAST group (Meyer & Rose, 2006) developed corresponding instructional frameworks (i.e., presentation, expression, and engagement) to meet the specific needs of each network. Throughout all three of these instructional responses flexibility, multiplicity, and student-centeredness are essential and put the "universal" in Universal Design for Learning. At its core, "UDL teaching is interactive and learner-centered, with an emphasis on learning concepts—rather than a traditional teacher-directed style emphasizing facts and figures" (Coyne, Ganley, Hall, Meo, Murray, & Gordon, 2006, p. 7).

Simultaneous to CAST's work, a team of researchers involved in the University of Minnesota's Curriculum Transformation and Disability (CTAD) project, "developed eight principles of 'Universal Instructional Design'—a term coined by Silver, Bourke and Strehorn (1998)—that provide a truly original synthesis" (Opitz & Block, 2006), of the fundamental tenets of Universal Design and Chickering and Gamson's (1987) generally held best practices for education. As with Universal Design for Learning, the researchers working with Universal Instructional Design stated that, "the 'universal' in Universal Instructional Design does not imply that 'one size fits all.' Instead, it refers to universal access to curricula," (Higbee, Chung, & Hsu, 2004, p.15). Although the researchers and practitioners of UID seek to address the larger issues of access for all students, it is evident that, like UDL, their work is still heavily grounded in a focus on students with disabilities. For example, though there are references to a broader student audience, Higbee, Chung, and Hsu also stated that UID is a "model for providing access to higher education for students with disabilities by rethinking teaching practices to create curricula and classrooms that are inclusive for all students" (p. 13). Unlike UDL, however, UID's principles are far more specific and more readily provide a pedagogical map for educators wishing to make their classrooms universal. The combination of Chickering and Gamson's work with the concepts of UD as applied to education, are primarily what help UID stand apart from UDL. While the UDL model does offer suggestions for educators and classroom use, UID's grounding in educational best practices affords it a much clearer application in the classroom. Adding to this, as stated in Higbee, Chung, and Hsu, "Universal Instructional Design is an outgrowth of an interactional, social constructivist approach to disability issues" (p.14) and as such I believe it lends itself more easily to the dynamism, fluidity, and evolving culture of a classroom. Taking a constructivist approach also allows for an easier connection to Social Justice Education's discussion of socially constructed dominant and subordinate identities and Critical Multicultural Education's attention to the ways society influences the constant creation and recreation of culture. As a teacher educator, I find UID to be quite user friendly and observe in my classes that pre-service and in-service teachers can more easily wrap their hands around the eight principles developed by CTAD than the three pathways and responses developed by CAST (Meyer & Rose, 2006). I believe UID's accessibility and ease of use in the classroom derives from the fact that Silver, Bourke and Strehorn's (1998) research utilized faculty focus groups in determining the most effective ways for educators to make their classrooms universal, thus heavily grounding UID in classroom practice from its inception.

Universal Instructional Design Pedagogy

The eight principles for UID are: (a) create a welcoming classroom; (b) determine the essential components of a course; (c) communicate clear expectations; (d) provide constructive feedback; (e) explore the use of natural supports for learning, including technology, to enhance opportunities for all learners; (f) design teaching methods that consider diverse learning styles, abilities, ways of knowing, and previous experience and background knowledge; (g) create multiple ways for students to demonstrate their knowledge; and (h) promote interaction among and between faculty and students (Higbee, Chung, & Hsu, 2004, p. 14). While relatively self-explanatory, the University of Minnesota's Disability Services (2007) offers the following explication of each of these points.

A first area of pedagogical issues to consider relative to these eight principles involves some preparatory work done before students even arrive in class. Determining the essential components of the course, designing teaching methods that consider diverse learning methods, and creating multiple options for students to demonstrate their knowledge are all ways faculty can work to make their classrooms universally accessible long before the first day of class. To be clear, the essential components of a course are the *outcomes* that all students need to be able to demonstrate *with or without the use of accommodations* and should be evaluated in a nondiscriminatory manner (University of Minnesota Disability Services, 2007). Understanding the difference between what is truly "essential" knowledge for a course versus what an educator would "prefer" a student to know is a vital point of clarification in helping educators effectively design diverse teaching methods and devise multiple assessment methods for a course (University of Minnesota Disability Services). Faculty who utilize PowerPoint, case studies, Web supports, and varied means of classroom discussion and group assessment, in addition to lecture and more traditional forms of assessment, not only provide varied ways for students to demonstrate their knowledge, but also give educators a much better sense of student progress and areas that may need to be further emphasized in the class. Ultimately, these three pedagogical tools in combination provide ample room for all students to be successful and to reach their fullest potential in any given class.

Moving from preparation to the initial development of a welcoming classroom, the University of Minnesota's Disability Services (2007) suggests establishing ground rules that are elicited from the class to help all students feel they have a voice in the classroom. Avoiding the process of singling out students while also valuing and recognizing the authority of students' personal experience is another way to establish a level of safety and personal value in the classroom. It is also suggested that educators share their own experiences with students not to further center themselves in the classroom but to aid in the development of trust and relationship with students. Another component in creating a welcoming classroom is to honor diversity and cultural differences. All of these steps will help educators to develop an inclusive syllabus and afford all students the same understanding of what is expected in the class. And finally, attending to the physical needs of all students is a critical step in helping them feel at home in the classroom. Once in the classroom and working with students, being able to communicate clear expectations, provide constructive feedback, and use natural supports for learning, including technology, to enhance opportunities for all learners becomes paramount. The use of study guides, practice tests, and small groups for discussion or assessment are all ways that educators can use natural supports to respond in class to the evolving needs of students (University of Minnesota Disability Services).

Taken together these eight principles provide an excellent course of action for any educator seeking to eliminate structural barriers in their classroom. Teaching in these ways clearly makes any classroom more universally accessible and creates a climate where all students can be academically successful.

Analyzing UID Through an SJE and CME Lens

As stated previously, Universal Instructional Design holds immense promise for educators seeking to transform their practice and create structurally accessible classrooms for all students. However, for all of its strengths there are some important areas where it does not fully meet its potential. An analysis of Universal Instructional Design through the lens of Social Justice Education and Critical Multicultural Education will help explicate these areas and suggest possible ways to enhance the efficacy of UID.

Analysis of Universal Instructional Design From a Social Justice Education Perspective

Two levels of analysis arise when viewing Universal Instructional Design through a Social Justice Education lens. The first includes four broad-based critiques connected to the conceptual underpinnings of UID and the second level addresses a very specific critique of the eight principles of UID.

Broadly speaking, while Universal Instructional Design does an excellent job of articulating the importance of educational accessibility for all students, it does not do a good enough job of providing a systemic critique of issues of power and privilege within which those accessibility issues arise. It is surprising to me that UID draws legitimacy for its use in all classrooms from the fact that students with disabilities have been systematically denied access to educational resources and then does not take as a central part of its approach an analysis of the very power and privilege that deny students access in the first place. If it were to do this, it would be able to ground its argument for accessibility in deeper, more systemically rooted soil and in turn be able to advocate more strongly for UID in all classrooms. The incorporation of Universal Design in general into Individual with Disabilities Education Act (IDEA, 1990) legislation is an excellent point of entry in considering the role UID can have in critiquing systems of power that serve to create barriers for students in our current education system. Without this systemic critique of power, UID cannot attend to the realities of oppression in our society and how that impacts our classrooms. For example, the role of dominance and subordinance and how they impact students' lives and realities both in and out of the classroom are completely missed in UID theory. From an SJE perspective, this lack of attention limits the accessibility of the classroom to only members of dominant groups whom the dominant norms of this society serve. Referring again to the scenario in the introduction, while students of color, women, and poor and working class students were marginalized, White, male, and middle-class students were placed at the center of the classroom and as such were given more access to academic success in that class.

A second broad critique of UID is what I perceive as its narrow focus on structural accessibility. To assume that an architectural concept addressing structural issues can be directly applied as an educational concept in a social context is inaccurate and dismisses the socially constructed nature of human communities such as schools and classrooms. Accessibility is not simply about physical access to classrooms, nor is it just about creating classroom spaces where students with various learning needs can be accommodated. In its truest sense accessibility means that *all* systematically constructed barriers to education are challenged and addressed. If Universal Instructional Design seeks to address accessibility at its roots, then it must broaden its theoretical discussion to include a more substantive critique of systemic inequality on all levels, not merely structural ones. Racism, classism, ableism, sexism, heterosexism and homophobia, religious oppression, ageism, and any other form of systemic and institutionalized oppression must become part of the "universal" in Universal Instructional Design if it is actually going to be able to meet the needs of all students. To assume that making classrooms accessible without attending to these issues is naïve at best and a reproduction of those very forms of oppression at worst.

A third broad critique has to do with the lack of connection of what UID does in the classroom to what students are doing outside of the classroom. Using the three goals of Social Justice Education mentioned previously, there is considerable room for improvement regarding UID's classroom implementation and processes. Given that UID already has a substantial understanding of individual empowerment as it relates to the academic success of students, it should be an easy step for UID practitioners to then ask students how they can apply what they are learning to larger societal issues and develop action plans for the use of this information from a social justice perspective. Because one of the central aspects of the Disability Rights Movement was independent living and self-advocacy, UID's special education roots should make it simple for practitioners and theorists alike to help expand UID's focus to include advocacy, activism, and greater participation in a diverse society. In this way SJE goals of student empowerment and social responsibility are woven into the UID curriculum and serve to deepen student learning and enhance educator options for teaching and assessment. For example, it is not enough to provide students with multiple modes of assessment and natural supports to learn about global environmental issues. An SJE approach would then push students to ask critical questions about classism, environmental racism, global consumption by the wealthy nations at the expense of other nations, the ethical concerns of multinational corporate environmental practices, why the U.S. did not sign the Kyoto Protocols, and how students can apply this analysis to their own lives. This is but a small example of what an SJE perspective would add to the depth of study and connection students have to their learning and the actions they can take with this information. All of this, as stated by UID's theoretical framework, fits well into the eight principles and is clearly an area where UID needs to give greater attention and time.

A final general critique of UID has to do with the third goal of SJE, the equitable distribution of resources. Specifically, I believe it is essential that UID address its focus on the use of technology and how that interacts with issues of systemic classism and the distribution of economic resources in our schools. Some UID and UDL authors (Coyne et al., 2006, pp.10-12) have suggested that lack of access to technology should not be seen as barrier to utilizing UID, and yet it would appear that in reality much of the UID work is technology based and there are some forms of accommodation that, without the technology, make UID next to impossible for the average teacher. Although technology does seem to make the possibilities of UID expand exponentially, there is a strong need for the authors in the field to take a more critical and social justice oriented approach when discussing this. Jonathan Kozol (2005), in his book, *The Shame of the Nation: The Restoration of Apartheid Schooling in America,* suggested that the levels of racial and economic segregation in this country are near levels before *Brown v. Board of Education* (1954). As such, it is not reasonable for UID practitioners to discuss the technology connections regarding its implementation without also addressing the socioeconomic challenges they present and how the exclusion of classism in the discussion of UID actually retrenches levels of inaccessibility with respect to education in this country.

While the previous critique holds true for UDL, UID, and perhaps to the application of UD as a whole to education, there are also some very particular aspects of UID to critique through an SJE lens. In the following paragraphs I will focus on only a few of these to illustrate the overall point of my analysis: (a) create a welcoming classroom climate; (b) determine the essential components of the course; (c) design teaching methods that consider diverse learning styles, abilities, ways of knowing, and previous experience and background knowledge; and (d) provide a variety of ways for students to demonstrate knowledge.

Throughout the literature discussing Universal Instructional Design there is next to no in-depth discussion of what it actually means to "create a welcoming classroom." More specifically, there is no discussion of student and teacher social identities or the deeper issues connected to them that alienate students from our classrooms and schools. A lack of appreciation for a students' food and holidays is not at the heart of what marginalizes and disenfranchises students of color, for example, in education in this country. Instead, a lack of access to resources and the depths of systemic inequality connected to that are what keep students of color; women; poor and working class; lesbian, bisexual, gay, and transgender (LBGT); young and old; and non-Christian students on the margins of our educational system. We can literally flood our schools with what is called a "heroes and holidays" (Lee el al., 2002) curriculum, but that will never address why a White teacher constantly calls on the Latino student in class to speak for all Latinos on a certain issue. In looking at the University of Minnesota's Disability Services (2007), Web site there are some specific suggestions listed for how to create a welcoming classroom that further demonstrate my point. For example, the notion of "honoring cultural differences" while not exploring the reasons that our society is divided along racial, cultural, and ethnic lines seems paltry at best. Genuine universal accessibility would require an educator to move beyond simply honoring differences, and instead delve into the realities of those differences in this country and what can be done about them in our classrooms to create real inclusiveness and a feeling of being welcomed. Similarly, the notion of "establishing groundrules" can be problematic without a stronger critique of how power, privilege, and social justice issues play into what one group perceives as "acceptable" or "normal" ways of being in education. Too often the "groundrules" established in U.S. classrooms are really White, male, middle-class ideals being disguised as a neutral set of beliefs. This of course is problematic because it automatically defaults to what the dominant society presumes is welcoming and safe in terms of classrooms, or society as a whole, and leaves students from subordinate social identity groups once again on the margins.

Likewise, when "determining the essential components of a course", I have yet to see the UID literature mention social responsibility and an ability to apply classroom knowledge critically and thoughtfully to the larger society as an essential component or skill. Much of the commentary about this UID principle seems instead to be about content acquisition and skill development as it pertains to the retention of knowledge and its narrow application on classroom assessments. SJE suggests that when educators determine the essential components of a course, they need to broaden the scope of this idea to include a consideration of how students' knowledge can be applied to the larger society and therefore more critically understood. To discuss the need to determine the essential components of a course without including this SJE component opens the door for the reproduction of canonical knowledge and does not create spaces where all students can find themselves in the class. This is another example where unless we mitigate for and address dominant group ideas about what is the norm or standard in education and what is not, we stand the chance of producing knowledge that has historically only represented the views, beliefs, opinions, and experiences of some of the population instead of our society as a whole. By suggesting this, SJE is not saying that UID practitioners should take a particular position on how this knowledge should be applied or in what ways students can or cannot think critically about the content as that would undermine the personal agency central to an SJE approach. It is saying, however, that some form of social responsibility and critical application of student learning to the larger society is vital for deeply integrated learning and helps make classrooms more accessible to a broad range of students.

Finally, I believe that the notion of "designing teaching methods that consider diverse learning styles" and "providing a variety of ways for students to demonstrate knowledge" again have the potential to reproduce dominant ways of knowing and learning even as they attempt to create new and innovative ways for students to engage in the class. An SJE focus here would give educators a more critical lens such that they would consider not only structural accessibility issues, but racist, classist, and sexist undercurrents in our educational system that have led to a very long history of oppressive teaching models and inaccessible assessment tools. Whether a quiz is done individually in class, as a take home, or in small groups is irrelevant if the questions on it are inherently biased to White, male, middle-class ways of knowing, thereby making it still inaccessible to a wide range of students. The lack of attention in the UID literature to the SJE issues mentioned here undermines the efficacy of its eight principles and leaves UID coming up short in terms of making classrooms accessible for all students.

Analysis of UID From a CME Perspective

Once again beginning with a broad critique of UID, the most noticeable gap in the literature is the almost complete absence of any discussion of culture. Interestingly, there is an exceptional level of conversation regarding how to implement UID in one's classroom in student-centered ways, but a dearth of conversation about how issues of culture play into this student-centered approach or the use of UID in general. Given the emphasis on student involvement in learning, a deeper understanding of the importance of culture in the classroom and how teachers can use it as a point of entry into content will undoubtedly improve educators' implementation of UID's eight principles. Thus, the essential critique of Universal Instructional Design from a Critical Multicultural Educational standpoint is the lack of attention given to students' culture, the socio-cultural location of students in the classroom in relation to each other, and how culture can enhance teaching and learning. More specifically, there is very little discussion in the literature about what "culture" actually is, what dimensions of it are being invited into the classroom, or how students would intentionally utilize that culture in their learning. Certainly, having students involved in the general practices of cooperative learning and group work, both of which are mentioned throughout the UID literature, is effective. But, if UID's commitment to academic success for all students is to be met, attending to the cultural realities of the classroom is a must.

This critical frame can be applied directly to UID in the following ways. First, when considering the processes of "creating a welcoming classroom" educators can utilize the fundamental tenets of CME by critically considering the powerful implications that culture has on classroom interactions and overall climate. The literature on UID, unfortunately, does not adequately address the importance of critically addressing cultural issues and in so doing opens the door to cultural stereotyping and the alienation of students in response to a superficial approach to their culture. To mention culture simply in passing does more harm than good by presenting culture as an insignificant aspect of student learning and the classroom environment. In fact, as CME clearly demonstrates, student culture is one of the most important aspects that informs student learning and academic success. The necessity of the attention to culture for student comprehension and application of content cannot be overstated. Authors such as Gay (2000) suggested that culturally relevant teaching often means the difference between academic success and academic marginalization for students who are not members of this society's dominant groups. Thus, while UID recognizes that not all students in the classroom are a homogenous group with respect to their learning styles and needs, culturally relevant teaching goes even deeper and recognizes that the affective, emotional, social, and cognitive experiences of students relative to their cultural identities are also not homogenous. A second point, similar in nature to the first, is that when considering "use of varied instructional methods", a deeper understanding of the importance of students' culture helps all educators broaden their repertoire with regard to the instructional methods. Educators cannot teach what they do not know, and though their intentions may be good, without a deeper and more critical understanding of how culture operates they will still be relegated to their small palate of instructional ideas.

A final point is the importance of a Critical Multicultural Education approach to the various aspects of teacher-to-student communication, whether it be in communicating clear expectations for the class, providing students with feedback, or enhancing faculty-student contact. In all cases an awareness of culture and how it informs communication styles—both verbal and nonverbal—as well as relational styles in an academic environment is extremely important for the successful communication of teachers with students and vice versa. I have had experiences early on in my own teaching where no amount of office hours would bring students to come meet with me because my cultural framework and awareness were so limited. Students from cultural backgrounds other than mine—White, middle class, and from the U.S.—recognized quite quickly that while I was trying to find creative ways for them to connect with me, I was stuck in such a small cultural frame of reference that I could not connect with them. This had a significant impact on my teaching and more importantly on their academic performance. It was and always is my responsibility to meet students where they are, and my inability to understand deeply and practice the aspects of Critical Multicultural Education mentioned previously severely limited my success in serving students.

Combining UID With SJE and CME

In this section I will utilize the previously discussed analyses to suggest both conceptual and practical ways to combine UID with SJE and CME using the eight principles of UID. In combination, these approaches ask educators to do more than just "add on" new information and instead demand a significant shift in their entire approach to teaching. Because of this many educators turn away from SJE or CME under the cover of statements such as "it is too much work", "it takes too much time", and "it is not part of the standards being tested", while others resist because they are afraid of raising contentious issues in the classroom or of looking at their own issues regarding social justice or multicultural content. In my pre-service and in-service classes this latter set of resistant responses seems to be closer to the truth and what fundamentally blocks many educators from using SJE and CME frameworks in their teaching. Unlike other pedagogical or technical teaching approaches where book knowledge of the content is sufficient for the transmission of the information, Critical Multicultural Education and Social Justice Education require high levels of self-awareness and personal understanding of the content.

For example, CME's need for a high degree of cultural competency in the classroom also suggests a level of self-awareness regarding one's own culture before the application of CME in the classroom can be most effective. Similarly, Social Justice Education authors and practitioners such as Bell, Washington, Weinstein, and Love (1997) have suggested that deep success in teaching from an SJE perspective arises out of an educator's personal awareness of and experience with empowerment, social responsibility, and oppression and liberation issues in their lives. Thus, the process of combining UID with SJE and CME is not merely about suggesting practical ways that UID can be joined with SJE and CME in the classroom. Instead, it highlights the importance for all users of UID to become ever more aware and critical of social justice and multicultural issues in their own lives and how that awareness informs what they bring into the classroom. Unfortunately, there is not enough room in this chapter to address the complexities of teacher self-awareness and teacher preparation regarding the use of CME and SJE. Resources in both of these theory bases abound, however, and I strongly encourage educators to investigate this as they seek to include CME and SJE in their work.

The Eight Principles of UID Combined With SJE and CME

In attempting to create a welcoming classroom, one issue an SJE and CME combination would lead educators to consider is the social and cultural identities of the students in their classrooms. For example, in teaching my class I consider students' racial, ethnic, gender, class, sexual orientation, religious, and disability identities with respect to educational and societal barriers they may face and use that information to understand better how I can develop responses to offset those socially constructed barriers in support of their academic success. Specifically, I may make changes in my syllabus, class readings, assignments and assessments, classroom expectations, and the like, in order to create specific points of entry for all students. At times this may mean presenting the skeleton of the syllabus on the first day and, with student input, later developing the final version to meet their needs. To quell the conservative cry against what might be perceived as "special treatment," I am not suggesting anything of the kind. I am, however, asserting quite clearly that the educational experiences of students from dominant groups versus those of subordinate groups in this nation's schools are markedly different and have tremendous influence on their performance in class; to deny this is simply reinforcing dominant norms and power structures in the classroom and denying full accessibility for everyone. Similarly, I make an effort to get to know students' cultural backgrounds and use that information as a guide in determining groundrules and class norms that would engender a greater sense of safety and comfort for all. Although these are just two examples, it should be noted that these steps go far beyond the mere honoring or celebration of differences and instead seek to help educators address the socially constructed roadblocks found in education today.

In determining the essential components of a course, an SJE approach combined with UID would have, for example, the application of classroom knowledge to community or societal issues as a must. Whether it be a high school sociology class, a third grade reading unit, or a middle school geometry problem, there are always ways that students can apply what they are learning to their community and society and use that knowledge to support social change. Understanding how the social construction of race and gender impact everything from their hallway conversations to the presidential race in 2008, students must know that we are not in the business of educating for the test and need to be able to find ways that the content matters beyond the classroom. Similarly, when combining a CME approach with UID, students will be told that cultural competency regarding the material is an essential component for the course. Questions to support this would include asking "what is the cross-cultural application of this knowledge? How would a member of 'x' group view this content? How would a member of 'y' view it? What is the cultural significance of these potentially differing viewpoints?" All of these questions push students to see that the knowledge they are learning is always embedded in a cultural context and that it is vitally important that they understand how to read each different context. CME urges educators to "teach complexity" (Nieto, 2002, p. 16) and to use in their classrooms the cultural frameworks that mirror the myriad cultural challenges in our society. In these ways, CME and SJE seek to prepare students to be active, informed, prepared, and engaged citizens with a broad repertoire of life skills. Anything less does a disservice to the true purpose of education and reduces our classrooms to mechanistic and lifeless places for our students. As such, educators combining CME with UID would have cultural competence as an essential component.

In providing clear expectations and feedback SJE affords UID a reminder that power and privilege in this society and their connection to systems of oppression have often led various social identity groups to experience "expectations" differently, and often to be given different expectations altogether. Furthermore, much of the SJE literature also suggests that educator bias regarding expectations along social identity lines is rarely conscious and therefore often goes unnoticed and unchecked. As bell hooks (1994) asserted in *Teaching to Transgress,* teachers must be critically aware of their biases and continually be willing to investigate any and all assumptions they make about students. There has been ample research on the effect of differing teacher expectations regarding gender, race, and class on student performance and I encourage all educators to incorporate that awareness into the processes by which they share expectations and feedback. A CME approach also helps educators regarding expectations and feedback by strongly encouraging student input into what those expectations are and the pathways of feedback that will be given. Using student-centered methods to co-create expectations and feedback mechanisms gives a culturally relevant base to these classroom processes and helps educators to de-center their cultural frame and allow for a more genuine multicultural experience. Adopting an SJE and CME approach when implementing this third component of UID goes a long way in making the classroom more accessible.

When exploring ways to use natural supports for learning, the benefits of a CME framework in combination with UID are clear. The more culturally relevant teachers are, the more varied their awareness of which natural supports will be effective. For example, some cultural groups do not do well in small group settings in class while others flourish. Similarly, some cultural groups like to study independently while other cultural groups are more field dependent in their learning and utilize study groups on a regular basis.

Some form of informal, anonymous assessment of who is in your classroom in terms of social identity, learning style, and cultural identity will equip any culturally aware educator with ample amounts of information regarding which supports will be most effective in their classroom. When establishing these supports, such as a small in-class discussion group, it is also very important for educators to consider power dynamics along the lines of social identity. For example, with respect to gender issues, questions to consider for these small groups would include: "Who is always the note taker in these small groups? Who talks more? Who talks the least? How are the differing communication styles with respect to gender identity affecting the productivity of the group? How might issues of race, ethnicity, age, class, or disability also be playing out with respect to these questions?" To base natural supports on cultural identity without also paying attention to power dynamics addressed in an SJE perspective would leave an educator a little short. However, the combination of all three—UID, CME, and SJE—gives educators a well balanced template from which to design the most accessible natural supports possible.

Gary Howard (1999), in his work around challenging racism and White privilege in education, suggested quite rightly that we cannot teach what we do not know through his study of White teachers in multiracial schools. Understanding this, if educators have not explored SJE or CME teaching methods, there is a good chance they will be highly limited in their teaching repertoire despite their best intentions to create varied and accessible instructional methods for all students. In their book *Teaching for Diversity and Social Justice,* Adams, Bell, and Griffin (1997) compiled a broad and deep range of teaching and training methods for educators to consider when addressing social justice issues. Their presentation of teaching methods outside of the generally known teacher education canon can, when combined with UID, assist educators in stepping even further out of traditional, limited approaches to teaching. Similarly, CME has a substantial base of research and pedagogical resources to help educators teach in a culturally relevant and academically rigorous student-centered manner. *Beyond Heroes and Holidays* (Lee, et al., 2002), curricular materials from the Rethinking Schools group, and classroom supports from Teaching Tolerance (n.d.) all provide educators with an excellent base from which to begin to utilize CME in their classrooms. The companion to the above commentary regarding instruction, of course, is the importance of providing students with a variety of ways to demonstrate their knowledge. Here again, all the resources mentioned previously provide ample examples of non-canonical, unstandardized assessment and ways to help students demonstrate their knowledge in applied, culturally relevant ways. And finally, in addressing the use of technology, Paul Gorski (2005) published a resource suggesting ways educators can utilize technology to enhance students' understanding of multicultural and social justice issues and increase their overall academic success. Obviously, outlining all the means of using SJE and CME to enhance UID methods and assessment is impossible in this section. The critical message to take from this discussion is that educators who have not exposed themselves to the SJE and CME pedagogical resources will most likely miss the chance to make their classrooms fully accessible via the widest range of teaching methods.

A final connection I will make between UID, CME, and SJE is the issue of faculty-student contact. This is where rigorous self-awareness, as suggested by Bell et al. (1997) has a vital importance for educators. My awareness of both my socially constructed identities and my cultural identities has an enormous impact on how I relate to others and the world around me. For example, my ideas about communication styles, personal space, time orientation, the role of teachers in a community, and the like, derived from my social and cultural identities, all have a tremendous impact on how I will or will not connect with students. Many educators, particularly dominant group members, do not consider that these issues are culturally and socially relative and instead view their ways of being as the "normal" way of moving through the world. This myopic view will inevitably result in ineffective communication between teachers and students and ultimately leave the students whose framework is not the same as the teacher's at a disadvantage. If educators wish to extend a genuine hand to students, it is necessary to question assumptions constantly, step out of comfort zones, and continually interrogate how power, based on socially identities, is playing out in interactions with students.

Taken together, all of these ways of combining SJE and CME with UID help to increase not only the accessibility of one's classroom, but increase the efficacy of education as a whole. Below are two curricular examples where SJE and CME are combined with UID, and while they are not exhaustive, they do indicate the direction that this overall combination can take.

Classroom Example One

My first example involves the discussion of how to place percentages into a pie chart in a fifth grade math class. A classroom utilizing Universal Instructional Design would first provide various presentation mechanisms such as models, computer examples, or games for understanding how to turn percentages into a pie chart, followed by a range of opportunities for students to demonstrate their knowledge outside what would be considered a "standard" form of assessment. To maintain student engagement an educator might offer a variety of ways to apply this to students' personal interests such as sports, music, or video games.

In a classroom utilizing Critical Multicultural Education and Social Justice Education processes the lesson would look a little different. While the range of content presentation options found in a UID approach would remain, CME might then invite students to do a cultural inventory of their family—those who are adopted or living with nonbiological caregivers can use the cultural identity about which they have the most information or with which they most closely identify—to determine the percentage of cultural representation they have. They would then place that information on a pie chart and those charts would be posted around the room. Students could then gather in three different affinity groups based on their three largest percentages. Their first groups would gather based on their largest percentage; then they would all rotate and gather in groups by their second largest percentage, and so on, to discuss where they came from, when their family arrived in North America (unless they are Native American, of course), and how their families came to be here. Critical questions about colonization, slavery, genocide, or immigration and the relevance of those issues today could easily be provided for each group to discuss in small groups and then as a whole class.

Following this activity, the teacher would then use the pie charts around the room to discuss critically, from a social justice perspective, "What makes someone an 'American'?" Students could engage in small groups around this question and others regarding nationalism, patriotism, democracy, freedom, and identity posed by both the teacher and members of the small groups. Out of these discussions, the class will identify three good questions to ask around the topic of "What makes someone an American?" and conduct interviews with people in their lives over the next 3 days. On the fourth day, the teacher will ask students to compile their interview data and create a class-wide pie chart for the responses that people gave in their interviews. The lesson will conclude with a class discussion about the current immigration debate, racism, and misinformation that may be part of that national debate, and what truly determines whether someone is an American or not.

By combining Critical Multicultural Education and Social Justice Education with the teaching tools of Universal Instructional Design, educators can deepen students' connection to the content, can create more critical ways for students to engage, and can offer them opportunities to apply this knowledge to our society in ways that are critically important for their success. Pie chart information, by itself, may or may not seem relevant to students. Creating pie charts that connect to their own lives and then to society as a whole, however, gives students a greater opportunity to integrate this learning and thus remember and apply it at a later time.

Classroom Example Two

The second example I will present is from a high school science class where they are discussing DNA. UID would allow for a wide range of methods for presenting this information such as lecture, reading, double-helix models in the classroom, computer models, and DVDs discussing DNA and its location in the nucleus of a cell. Students would then be given opportunities to research and discuss the role of DNA in their lives (e. g., looking at their genetically determined traits such as hair color, skin color, height) and express their knowledge through a range of assessment mechanisms. The process of tying this context into individual student traits also aids in supporting their engagement with the material and applying it to their lives.

A classroom utilizing Social Justice Education and Critical Multicultural Education would take this content further. In this classroom the teacher would then tie the genetic determination of skin color to issues of race, culture, and ethnicity. Students would then be asked to differentiate between race (i.e., skin color, physical features), culture (values, traditions, beliefs), and ethnicity (ancestry, carrier of culture). In this discussion students would then have the opportunity to discuss critically how our society often confuses these terms and uses them interchangeably when in fact they are distinctly different.

Critical questions such as, "How does one's melanin determine which cultural traditions one observes?" can help students understand that, in fact, socially constructed racial categories do not indicate anything about a person's culture. This would lead to a critical discussion of the social construction of race in the United States and how the *assumption* that skin color does tell us about culture and ethnicity supports the structure of racism and racial profiling. An examination of the pseudo-science of the 19th century would open the door to a critical discussion of scientific racism and ultimately help students understand that DNA's determination of skin color carries with it societal issues such as stereotypes and access—or not—to systems of power and privilege in this country, but not a scientifically proven connection to culture. Additionally, students would be able to see that culture is distinct from race and how to value diverse cultures while avoiding the traps of racial stereotyping.

In this lesson students are shown not only the scientific information about DNA and how it applies to their own genetic make up, but also how, when misunderstood and misused, genetics has had severe implications for our society as a whole, such as the eugenics movement. In this way, students can actually apply their knowledge of DNA in navigating the complexity of this society and have more informed discussions and interactions regarding the very serious issue of racism in the United States.

Conclusion

In closing I would like to repeat that my critique of Universal Instructional Design is not meant to diminish its import or viability as an empowering approach to education, but rather to open up areas for its improvement and the furtherance of its use in our classrooms. The power of a UID approach to learning is readily apparent and I hope at this point the reader can also see the power of combining both a Critical Multicultural Education and Social Justice Education approach with UID's eight principles. These two fields have long and powerful histories of their own and have a proven record of providing students with significant tools for self-actualization in the classroom. I look forward to seeing future research, writing, and application regarding the combination of Social Justice Education and Critical Multicultural Education with Universal Instructional Design and hope that the issues addressed in this chapter will support those better versed in UID to do so. In a time when the range of hope and possibilities regarding progressive education seems to be contracting rather than expanding, I believe the combination of these educational approaches can counter that trend and increase classroom accessibility, student empowerment, and ultimately the academic success of all of our students.

References

Adams, M., Bell, L. A., & Griffin, P. (1997). *Teaching for diversity and social justice.* New York: Routledge.

Banks, J. (2002). Approaches to multicultural curriculum reform. In E. Lee, D. Menkart, & M. Okazawa-Rey (Eds.), *Beyond heroes and holidays: A practical guide to K-12 anti-racist, multicultural education and staff development* (2nded.; pp. 73-74). Washington, DC: Teaching for Change.

Banks, J. (2008). *An introduction to multicultural education* (4th ed.). Boston: Pearson.

Bell, L. A. (1997). Theoretical foundations for social justice education. In M. Adams, L. A. Bell, & P. Griffin (Eds.), *Teaching for diversity and social justice* (pp. 1-15). New York: Routledge.

Bell, L. A., Washington, S., Weinstein, G., & Love, B. (1997). Knowing ourselves as instructors. In M. Adams, L. A. Bell, & P. Griffin (Eds.), *Teaching for diversity and social justice* (pp. 299-310). New York: Routledge.

Brown v. Board of Education of Topeka, 347 U.S. 483 (1954).

Center for Applied Special Technology. (2000). *CAST.* Retrieved November 15, 2007, from http://www.cast.org

Chickering, A. W., & Gamson, Z. F. (1987). Seven principles for good practice in undergraduate education. *AAHE Bulletin, 39*(7), 3-7.

Coyne, P., Ganley, P., Hall, T., Meo, G., Murray, E., & Gordon, D. (2006). Applying Universal Design for Learning in the classroom. In D. Rose & A. Meyer (Eds.), *A practical reader in Universal Design for Learning* (pp. 1-13). Cambridge, MA: Harvard Educational Press.

Freire, P. (1970). *Pedagogy of the oppressed.* New York: Continuum.

Frye, M. (1983). Oppression. In M. Frye (Ed.), *The politics of reality: Essays in feminist theory.* (pp. 1-15). Trumansberg, NY: The Crossing Press.

Gay, G. (2000). *Culturally responsive teaching: Theory, research and practice.* New York: Teachers College Press.

Gorski, P. (2005). *Multicultural education and the Internet: Intersections and integrations* (2nd ed.). Boston: McGraw Hill.

Grant, C., & Sleeter, C. (2006). *Turning on learning: Five approaches for multicultural teaching plans for race, class, gender and disability* (4th ed.). Indianapolis, IN: Wiley.

Hackman, H. (2005). Five essential components for social justice education. *Equity & Excellence in Education, 38*(2) 103-109.

Higbee, J. L., Chung, C. J., & Hsu, L. (2004). Enhancing the inclusiveness of first-year courses through Universal Design. In I. M. Duranczyk, J. L. Higbee, & D. B. Lundell (Eds.), *Best practices for access and retention in higher education* (pp. 13-26). Minneapolis: University of Minnesota, General College, Center for Research on Developmental Education and Urban Literacy.

Hitchcock, A. (Director). (1959). *North by Northwest* [Motion Picture]. United States: MGM.

hooks, b. (1994). *Teaching to transgress: Education as the practice of freedom.* New York: Routledge.

Howard, G. (1999). *We can't teach what we don't know: White teachers, multiracial schools.* New York: Teachers College Press.

Individuals with Disabilities Education Act of 1990, P.L. 101-476. (October 30, 1990). 20 U.S.C. 1400 et seq: U.S. Statutes at Large, 104, 1103 – 1151.

Kozol, J. (2005). *The shame of the nation: The restoration of apartheid schooling in America.* New York: Crown.

Lee, E., Mearkart, D., & Okagawa-Ray, M. (2002). Beyond heroes and holidays: A practical guide to K-12 anti-racist, multicultural education and staff development (2nd ed.). Washington, DC: Teaching for Change.

Loewen, J. (1995). *Lies my teacher told me: Everything your American history textbook got wrong.* New York: Touchstone.

Meo, G. (2006). Frequent questions about Universal Design for Learning. In D. Rose & A. Meyer (Eds.), *A practical reader in Universal Design for Learning* (pp. 33-38). Cambridge, MA: Harvard Educational Press.

Meyer, A., & Rose, D. (2006). Preface. In D. Rose & A. Meyer (Eds.), *A practical reader in Universal Design for Learning* (pp. vii-xi). Cambridge, MA: Harvard Educational Press.

Nieto, S. (2002). Affirmation, solidarity and critique: Moving beyond tolerance in education. In E. Lee, D. Menkart, & M. Okazawa-Rey (Eds.), *Beyond heroes and holidays: A practical guide to K-12 anti-racist, multicultural education and staff development* (2nd ed.; pp.7-18). Washington, DC: Teaching for Change.

Nieto, S., & Bode, P. (2008). *Affirming diversity: The sociopolitical context of multicultural education* (5th ed.). Boston: Pearson.

Opitz, D., & Block, L. (2006). Universal learning support design: Maximizing learning beyond the classroom. *The Learning Assistance Review, 9*(2), 33-45.

Rethinking Schools. (1998). *Beyond Heroes and Holidays.* Washington, DC: Author. Retrieved November 15, 2007, from www.rethinkingschools.org.

Rose, D., & Meyer, A. (Eds). (2006). *A practical reader in Universal Design for Learning.* Cambridge, MA: Harvard Educational Press.

Schniedewind, N., & Davidson, E. (2006). *Open minds to equality: A sourcebook of learning activities to affirm diversity and promote equity* (3rd ed.). Milwaukee, WI: Rethinking Schools.

Silver, P., Bourke, A., & Strehorn, K. C. (1998). Universal Instructional Design in higher education: An approach for inclusion. *Equity & Excellence in Education, 31*(2), 47-51.

Teaching tolerance. (n.d.). Retrieved November 15, 2007 from http://www.tolerance.org

University of Minnesota Disability Services. (2007). *Teaching students with disabilities: Universal Instructional Design.* Retrieved November 15, 2007, from http://ds.umn.edu/faculty/teaching.html

CHAPTER 4

Linking Universal Instructional Design and Cultural Capital: Improving African American College Outcomes

Na'im Madyun
University of Minnesota

Abstract

Social integration literature has identified a relationship between institutional connectedness and student outcomes. Unfortunately, there is an unhealthy disparity in the level of social integration among cultural groups. These differing levels most often result in differences in social network quality, which translates into disparities in cultural capital formation. It is not realistic to equalize the amount of cultural capital normally accumulated by different groups when coming to college. However, increasing retention and graduation rates may depend upon reducing the cultural capital gap and thus on the universality of the programs and extracurricular activities that most often lead to a healthy institutional connection.

The demographic landscape of the United States is dramatically changing. The baby boom generation will begin retiring around 2010, and by 2050 the U.S. will have a non-White majority. These concurrent changes place pressure on U.S. institutions to prepare the next generation of people of color to become productive citizens. A critical proportion of the responsibility is on our institutions of higher learning. Due to the magnitude of the cultural change, it is plausible that a seamless transition will translate into developing the next generation to continue the traditions of the previous one. On the surface, the previous statement appears quite innocuous. However, it is deeply intertwined with social and cultural capital and begs for the application of Universal Design (UD) and Universal Instructional Design (UID) in all courses, programs, and services.

Cultural Capital Theory

Bourdieu (1977) introduced the concept of cultural capital as the vehicle by which cultural traditions are transmitted to the next generation with the goal of maintaining the social patterns of the generation that preceded it. If there is a hierarchy of social class, a disparity in gender equality, or an achievement gap, cultural capital is the means by which these existing conditions and order are usually maintained. It is important to note that the maintenance of the social order that precedes a current generation is accomplished by individuals in a "tacit calculation of interest" (Swartz, 1997, p. 290). Individuals in social structures do not, for the most part, intentionally perpetuate disparities, but this perpetuation is a consequence of "habitus" or a "cultural unconscious" (Swartz, p. 101) that occurs in the field (i.e., social setting). Bourdieu characterized habitus as "an ideal type of action that is habitual, practical, tacit, dispositional, and at the same time structured" (p. 290). These tacit behaviors are programmed actions and reactions to specific contexts and are developed through social and cultural capital (Swartz). An example of a specific context in higher education that is common among many students yet varies based on a student's habitus is the selection of a seat in a challenging class. In order to reduce the anxiety that is normally generated from a challenging class, a student may subconsciously have developed an inexplicable practice—in the sense that at some level the student is aware of the behavior yet still does not fully understand its presence or cause—of identifying a place in the classroom to sit. This calculated system varies depending on the classroom demographics, time of day, and the student's perceived level of preparedness, in addition to the larger context of a challenging class. This calculation will also consider seating options that are most likely to mask this anxiety-reducing logic. This behavior is not unlike seat-choosing behavior when booking a flight. The type of passengers likely to be present (e.g., vacationers, business people, sports fans), time of day, and the type of experience one would like to have (e.g., sleeping, chatting with other passengers, leisure reading, preparing a talk) are all factored into what type of attitude one is prepared to have when boarding the plane. Depending upon an individual's social and cultural experiences, a better understanding of how to ensure a particular attitude leads to a better manipulation of the aforementioned factors. Maybe time of day is the most critical factor, or perhaps finding a seat close to the front of the plane has a higher probability of increasing productivity due to one's own idiosyncrasies. Knowing to even consider the front versus rear of the plane option or understanding the importance of time of day may have come from a sophisticated blend of conversations with other passengers and lessons learned from previous flights. For many students in the classroom, these sophisticated blends are poorly informed. The student's choice of seat location may be more to reduce anxiety than to improve performance, not realizing that improving performance is the more critical factor. As a result, the student leaves the course feeling successful with surviving, even though there was failure to achieve excellence. Better informing the sophisticated blend between social cultural resources and experiences that create the likely behaviors in a specific context or habitus is critical to the success of the African American college student.

African American Retention and Graduation

It is no secret that the retention and graduation rates of African American college students are less than ideal. The average African American high school senior graduates with the tested knowledge of the average White eighth grader (Roach, 2004). To many this is not of grave concern considering college enrollment for students of color is much higher than 20 years ago. However, only 40% of eligible African American students go to college (American Council on Education, 2001), with less than half of that population graduating within 6 years (Astin & Oseguera, 2005). These outcomes have naturally led to an investment in effective retention models for African American college students.

Carreathers, Beekmann, Coatie, and Nelson (1996), as reported in Jones (2001), reviewed several programs specific to African American student retention and found that the most effective models consistently had 11 characteristics: they (a) have the support of the administration, (b) recruit faculty for participation, (c) provide motivational lectures, (d) deliver proactive financial aid counseling, (e) get students involved with programming, (f) maintain up-to-date knowledge on retention issues, (g) assess program effectiveness regularly, (h) incorporate early assessment and intervention, (i) encourage faculty mentoring, (j) offer leadership seminars, and (k) develop a caring and competent staff. What is key about this checklist of characteristics is that the focus is not only on academic preparation, but more importantly on socially integration (Tinto, 1975). According to Tinto, motivation and persistence to graduate will be optimized the more connected and invested a student is into the social fabric of the college or university. Many researchers have argued for understanding social integration for African American students utilizing a different lens (Guiffrida, 1993; King-Saulsberry, 2002; Nettles & Johnson, 1987).

African American Habitus in College

The familiarity of the college experience and its continuity from high school for the average African American student is a critical barrier to social integration (Jones, 2001). African American students are more likely to exhibit social and academic behaviors in reaction to this unfamiliar, incongruent context that dilutes academic motivation and persistence (Moore, 2001). These behaviors again result from their habitus, which is in turn dependent upon their cultural capital (Bourdieu, 1973). To acquire the necessary cultural capital to navigate college successfully, students must first possess the capacity or cultural experience to receive and decode it (Katsillis & Rubinson, 1990). The aforementioned unfamiliarity and discontinuity suggests that many African American college students arrive on campus without having developed the necessary knowledge and skills. Even though colleges implicitly demand the existence of cultural capital or the ability to receive and decode it, they do not intentionally or explicitly assist in its development (Dumais, 2002). Researchers have found that the cultural capital gap in education is most often reduced through extracurricular participation (Dumais; Eitle, & Eitle, 2002).

The link between extracurricular activities and student achievement is not new social science research, but it has only recently been explained through Bourdieu's (1977) conceptualization of cultural capital (Eitle & Eitle, 2002). According to cultural capital theory, college-specific habitus or the informal rules of navigation are learned through study groups, student organizations, and connections with faculty and staff. My argument is not that African American students are not involved or connected to their institution, but that the effect of cultural capital varies depending on the status of its possessor (Bourdieu) and African American students are not rewarded in academia for their cultural capital in the same critical manner as White students (Roscigno & Ainsworth-Darnell, 1999). So, the issue centers on the factors that lead to the disparity in educational returns on cultural capital investments between African Americans and Whites.

Social Networks in College

Part of the variability can be explained by the habitus or the uniqueness of the manner in which African American students adapt to and navigate through the same environment encountered by other students. For instance, African American students are more likely than White students to have a less diverse social network (Antonio, 2001; D'Augelli & Hersberger, 1993; Pike & Kuh, 2006). Social networks are basically the organization of social ties or the relationships that allow and lead to the development and transmission of cultural capital. When compared to that of White students, the African American social network is more likely to include other African Americans and less likely to include other college students (Antonio; D'Augelli & Hersberer). This cultural reality, although positive in many respects, can lead to differential outcomes in higher education.

Current social theory posits that poor academic performance stems from weakened or poor quality social networks (Coleman, 1988; Sander & Putnam, 1999), which have been identified as a main cause of declining student achievement (Coleman). Literature on social and cultural capital has shown that social networks play a key role in educational outcomes (Coleman; Uekawa, Aladjem, & Zhang, 2005). Informal knowledge, expectations, mentoring, modeling, ideas, and decision making can all be delivered or influenced through social networks (Oh, Chung, & Labianca, 2004). This finding suggests that poor quality social networks can directly lead to low student achievement by reducing both cultural capital development and proper modeling of how to use this capital. Through their social networks, White students are not only able to get academic support from their college friends, but also support for adjustment and attachment (Kenny & Stryker, 1996). For African American students, adjustment and attachment support most often come from the family because of the smaller number of social ties with other college students.

One positive aspect of a less diverse social network is that norms are constructed, exchanged, and adapted with little resistance (Reagans, Zuckerman, & McEvily, 2004). However, issues arise when the need to construct multiple strategies or a more complex habitus is paramount over simply completing a task (Reagans et al.). Expanding the social network informally provides an individual or group with many more options and resources not regularly available and can function to uncover talents and skills that otherwise would lie dormant. Not only does an expansive, diverse social network provide a more thorough and affirming awareness of African Americans' own academic ability, but it can function to increase the cultural awareness and capital of all stakeholders (Antonio, 2001, 2004).

Peer Influence on Cultural Capital

Research has shown that peer influence at the collegiate level is much more significant than faculty or staff influence (Bank, Slavings, & Biddle, 1990). This knowledge is not new or surprising, but is important when considering the development of education-specific cultural capital. Bank et al. also found that normative social influence was much more significant than role modeling in predicting persistence toward graduation. This finding is consistent with previous research on identity development (Erikson, 1968) and college transitions (Chickering, 1969), as well as more resent research on social influence (Myers, 2005). As students engage in the psychosocial search for identity, they become more independent and less willing to accept the influence of the parent. In college correct decision making is still important, the student becomes even more susceptible to normative social influence (Myers). The normative referent group is comprised of college peers. This is critical knowledge for two reasons. First, the standards and goals of behavior and the scripts for achieving social and academic goals in college are most influenced by peer groups (Pike & Kuh, 2006; Antonio, 2001). Therefore, unwittingly, the student transfers the traditional model of what to do and what not to do to college peers. Secondly, self-awareness increases in importance. Sedlacek (1987) has argued that African American students are not always accurate in their appraisal of their goals or their ability to achieve them. If the scripts students adopt are not appropriate for their own ability or character, they may set the student up for isolation and failure (Moore, 2001). Therefore, participation in the types of programs and extracurricular activities that are most consistent with transmitting the informal, tacit knowledge of the institution becomes critical to social integration and ultimately success.

A multicultural campus—that is, one that is not only diverse but also embeds multiculturalism in all aspects of campus life (Higbee et al., 2004; Higbee, Siaka, & Bruch, 2007; Miksch et al., 2003)—may lead to different outcomes due to differences in access to and use of college resources. How accessible are the cultural capital mines of the campus to multiple ethnic groups? It is imperative that institutions assess (Miksch et al.) the many layers of learning and human interaction—both formal and informal—in order to expand and enhance the implementation of the guiding principles of UD and UID to serve *all* students at the institution. (Also see Chapters 3 by Hackman, 35 by Wagner, and the concluding chapter by Higbee.)

Universal Design for Multiculturalism

Cordano and Mann Rinehart (Higbee, Lundell, Barajas, Cordano, & Copeland, 2006) developed the following UD principles for multiculturalism:

1. Create spaces and programs that foster a sense of community for all students, particularly students from underrepresented communities.
2. Build barrier-free welcoming environments with attention paid to attributes that include disability, diverse content, access to artwork and graphic design, and geographic location relative to function.
3. Design accessible and appropriate physical environments that provide ease of use for people who use different modes of interacting or communicating and allow for confidential use based on the services, programs, or benefits being delivered.
4. Create inclusive and respectful policies and programs that, from the beginning, take into consideration the diverse student and employee populations at the institution and provide natural and cognitive supports to ensure full utilization of programs by students and employees.
5. Hire and develop personnel who understand, respect, and value the institution's diverse community of students and employees.
6. Ensure that non-electronic information environments are accessible and appropriate so that information is delivered in formats (e.g., Braille, captioning, different languages) understandable and easily usable by diverse users without requiring unnecessary steps or

"hoops" to jump through for completion.

7. Design and maintain Internet and other electronic environments to ensure accessibility and appropriate confidentiality or privacy for those who use various adaptive equipment, hardware (that may vary in age and capacity), and software and for those that require or need confidentiality or privacy.

These principles should be applied to a cultural capital assessment to function as a guide for improving the access of students of color to areas or contexts rich in cultural capital. These principles can also help to assess whether the cultural capital valued at the institution is advantageous to the interests and habits of one group over another and whether sources of cultural capital are equally available to all.

One aspect of UD that can be used to assess the cultural capital at an institution of higher education is that of the creation of spaces and programs that foster a sense of community. There must be rich areas of cultural capital on campus that are intended to help both the in-group and out-group foster networks and affirmation. When the areas of cultural capital are created, they must be seen as part of a larger connected community. Is there an African American student center on campus, and if so, where is it located? Does it intentionally position African American students close to other peer groups and resources? This positioning will increase the probability that African American students will be exposed to and integrated into areas on campus rich in cultural capital and expand their own social networks. What type of space is available for group interaction and hanging out? A critical component of creating barrier-free environments requires being sensitive to the many ways students want and need to congregate. It also underscores the importance of moving beyond universal access and toward universal practices that promote engagement.

Although the removal of cultural capital access barriers would be a significant accomplishment, part of the vision must include how to engage, retain, and develop students once access is gained. How well do these programs intentionally engage African American students with other successful students who are not part of their social network?

Strides toward student development, engagement, and retention are made when administrators, faculty, and student services staff members understand, respect, value, and reflect the background of the students. Creative methods for improving engagement are more likely when diverse perspectives are included. The hiring of diverse faculty increases the potential for enhancing the growth of comfortable social networks for students from historically marginalized populations. Faculty recruiters must be careful to monitor the net that the language of job descriptions can cast. Are the descriptions implicitly designed to exclude some cultural groups, whether intentionally or unintentionally? Are recruitment efforts focused on areas rich in cultural capital that are not normally accessed by candidates of color?

Barriers to Cultural Capital Transmission in "Rich" Contexts

Although larger structural and programmatic areas are critical pockets of social capital, the classroom, advising system, and organization of extracurricular activities can function as barriers to social integration into these critical pockets and should not be overlooked.

Classroom Issues

Are students of color full participants in study groups both within and outside the classroom? Are their opinions truly valued or only validated when supported by a White peer? Are African American students given opportunities to test their own biases and assumptions and to reflect on their subconscious strategies for success, or are they protected and reinforced for not expanding their cultural identity? Classroom practices must become culturally universal. The beauty of multiculturalism in the classroom is that it challenges participants from the dominant culture to test the generalizability of their assumptions. However, we must be careful not to structure the social discourse in such a way that White students are increasing their cultural capital in the African American field more than African Americans are adding to their ability to navigate the higher education field.

Advising

Even though peer influence is dominant at the college level, advisers are critical agents in shaping the habitus of students. The tacit knowledge should flow easily and often between the adviser and advisee. However, ingrained distrust and poor past relationships between the African American community and educational institutions (Lareau & Horvat, 1999), coupled with the perceived and acquired accumulation of cultural capital by members of dominant cultural groups, function as barriers (Kalmihn & Kraaykamp, 1996). The pride, ego, and past painful experiences of some African American students may lead to little faith in the adviser's knowledge and level of caring. Advisers may sometimes "detect" a resistance to educational culture rather than an underdeveloped habitus and thus be less likely to pass on their own cultural capital. This can result in overlooking opportunities to increase social networks or navigational capacity for students because those opportunities do not have the "necessary" cultural supports. Although tailoring counseling and advising is important (e.g., Stebleton, 2007; Swanson, 2004), we must encourage advisers to be more cognizant of potential barriers in order to improve the access and use of the advising system.

Extracurricular Activities

One of the more critical barriers to social integration is the segregation that exists in campus groups and organizations. Often educational disparities are perpetuated because colleges and universities are in the unique position to justify differential access and participation pockets of cultural capital under the guise of academic or interest groups. Bourdieu (1977) argued that the academic or interest label falsely put the responsibility in the possession of the student. Several questions could logically follow: What if African American students are less likely to join a traditionally White sorority or fraternity, yet the network of those groups is deeply intertwined with the transmission of cultural capital at the institution? Should inclusion efforts be a focus of special interest groups? Are support services on campus positioned in a way that leads to more or less social integration? Are faculty of color recruited to advise student organizations, including those that do not have a focus related to a specific social identity?

If we do not respond to this call and remove the perception that the classroom, the advising system, and campus groups and organizations are more welcoming to some students over others, the results will be a lack of institutional connectedness, insufficient graduation rates, and ultimately an inadequate replacement of the baby boomers in the halls of academia.

Conclusion

In recognizing these gaps, I am not suggesting intentionality nor declaring fault. I am merely recognizing the natural evolution that higher education has always undergone in response to its demographics and functions (e.g., services for war veterans). This process has been effectively smart and steady. However, we are now entering a period where steady may not be adaptive and dynamic enough to be smart.

Institutions of higher education need to examine the universality of access points to cultural capital. This is neither an argument for color blindness nor against recognizing, understanding or accommodating differences. Those factors will always be critically important. I am arguing for an efficient way to increase the probability that African American students and students from other historically marginalized groups will be able to connect with the cultural capital inherent in institutions of higher learning. If we are truly concerned about whether we will produce future generations of citizens, we must focus on how, what, and to whom college navigational skills are transmitted. By focusing on the universal design of cultural capital areas in universities, we will.

References

American Council on Education. (2001). *Minorities in higher education: Eighteenth annual status report*. Washington, DC: Author.

Antonio, A. L. (2001). Diversity and the influence of friendship groups in college. *Review of Higher Education, 25,* 63-89.

Antonio, A. L. (2004). When does race matter in college friendships? Exploring men's diverse and homogeneous friendship groups. *Review of Higher Education, 27,* 527-551.

Astin, A. W., & Oseguera, L. (2005). *Degree attainment rates at American colleges and universities* (rev. ed.). Los Angeles: University of California, Higher Education Research Institute.

Bank, B. J., Slavings, R. L., & Biddle, B. J. (1990). Effects of peer, faculty, and parental influences on students' persistence. *Sociology of Education, 63*(8), 208-225.

Bourdieu, P. (1977). Cultural reproduction and social reproduction. In J. Karabel & A. H. Halsey (Eds.), *Power and ideology in education* (pp. 487-511). New York: Oxford University Press.

Carreathers, K. R., Beekmann, L., Coatie, R. M., & Nelson, W. L. (1996). Three exemplary retention programs. In H. A. Belch, (Ed.). *Serving students with disabilities* (pp. 35-52). (New Directions for Student Services, no. 91, pp. 35-52). San Francisco: Jossey-Bass.

Chickering, A. W. (1969). *Education and identity.* San Francisco: Jossey Bass.

Coleman, J. S., (2002). Social capital in the creation of human capital. In A. H. Halsey, H. Lauder, P. Brown, & A. S. Wells. (Eds.), *Education: Culture, economy, society (*pp. 80-95). New York: Oxford University Press.

D'Augelli, A. R., & Hersberger, S. L. (1993). African American undergraduates on a predominantly White campus: Academic factors, social networks, and campus climate. *The Journal of Negro Education, 62,* 67-81.

Dumais, S. (2002). Cultural capital, gender, and school success: The role of habitus. *Sociology of Education,* 75, 44-68

Eitle, T. M., & Eitle, D. J. (2002). Race, cultural capital, and the educational effects of participation in sports. *Sociology of Education, 75*(2), 123-146.

Erikson. E. (1968). *Identity: Youth and crisis.* New York: WW Norton.

Guiffrida, D. (1993). African American student organizations as agents of social integration. *Journal of College Student Development, 44,* 304-319.

Higbee, J. L., Lundell, D. B., Barajas, H. L., Cordano, R. J., & Copeland, R. (2006, March). *Implementing Universal Instructional Design: Resources for faculty.* Presentation made at the 22nd Annual Pacific Rim Conference on Disabilities, Honolulu, HI.

Higbee, J. H., Miksch, K. L., Jehangir, R. R., Lundell. D. B., Bruch, P. L., & Jiang, F. (2004). Assessing our commitment to providing a multicultural learning experience. *Journal of College Reading and Learning, 34*(2), 61-74.

Higbee, J. L., Siaka, K., & Bruch, P. L. (2007). Assessing our commitment to multiculturalism: Student perspectives. *Journal of College Reading and Learning, 37*(2), 7-25.

Jones, L. (2001). *Retaining African Americans in higher education: Challenging paradigms for retaining students, faculty and administrators.* Sterling, VA: Stylus.

Kalmijn, M., & Kraaykamp, G. (1996). Race, cultural capital, and schooling: An analysis of trends in the United States. *Sociology of Education, 69,* 22-34.

Katsillis, J., & Rubinson, R. (1990). Cultural capital, student achievement, and educational reproduction: The case of Greece. *American Sociological Review, 55,* 270-279.

Kenny, M. E., & Stryker, S. (1996). Social network characteristics and college adjustment among racially and ethnically diverse first-year students. *Journal of College Student Development, 37,* 649-658.

King-Saulsberry, L. (2002). *Patterns of academic success for first generation, African American college students.* Unpublished doctoral dissertation, University of Minnesota, Minneapolis.

Lareau, A., & Horvat, E. M. (1999). Moments of social inclusion and exclusion: Race, class, and cultural capital in family-school relationships. *Sociology of Education, 72,* 37-53.

Miksch, K. L., Higbee, J. L., Jehangir, R. R., Lundell, D. B., Bruch, P. L., Siaka, K., & Dotson, M. V. (2003). *Multicultural Awareness Project for Institutional Transformation: MAP IT.* Minneapolis: University of Minnesota, General College, Multicultural Concerns Committee and Center for Research on Developmental Education and Urban Literacy. Retrieved December 10, 2007, from http://cehd.umn.edu/CRDEUL/pdf/map_it.pdf

Moore, J. L. (2001). Developing academic warriors: Things that parents, administrators, and faculty should know. In L. Jones (Ed.), Retaining African Americans in higher education: *Challenging paradigms for retaining students, faculty and administrators* (pp. 77-90).

Sterling, VA: Stylus.

Myers, D. (2005). *Psychology* (7th ed.). New York: Worth.

Nettles, M. T., & Johnson, J. R. (1987). Race, sex, and other factors as determinants of college students' socialization. *Journal of College Student Personnel, 28,* 513-524

Oh, H., Chung, M-H., & Labianca, G. (2004). Group social capital and group effectiveness: The role of informal social ties. *The Academy of Management Journal, 47,* 860-875.

Pike, G. R., & Kuh, G. D. (2006). Relationships among structural diversity, informal peer interactions and perceptions of the campus environment. *The Review of Higher Education, 29,* 425-450.

Reagans, R., Zuckerman, E., & McEvily, B. (2004). How to make the team: Social networks vs. demographics as criteria for designing effective teams. *Administrative Science Quarterly, 49,* 101-133.

Roach, R. (2004). The great divide. *Black Issues in Higher Education, 21,* 22-25.

Roscigno, V.J., & Ainsworth-Darnell, J.W. (1999). Race, cultural capital, and educational resources: Persistent inequalities and achievement returns. *Sociology of Education, 72,* 158-178.

Sander, T. H., & Putnam, D. R. 1999. Rebuilding the stock of social capital. *School Administrator, 56.* Retrieved October 7, 2007, from http://infotrac.galegroup.com/itw/informark/

Sedlacek, W. (1987). Black students on White campuses: 20 years of research. *Journal of College Student Personnel, 28,* 484-495.

Stebleton, M. J. (2007). Career counseling with African immigrant college students: Theoretical approaches and implications for practice. *Career Development Quarterly, 55,* 290-312.

Swanson, C. (2004). Between old country and new: Academic advising for immigrant students. In I. M. Duranczyk, J. L. Higbee, & D. B. Lundell (Eds.), *Best practices for access and retention in higher education* (pp. 73-81). Minneapolis: University of Minnesota, General College, Center for Research on Developmental Education and Urban Literacy. Retrieved September 15, 2007, from http://www.cehd.umn.edu/crdeul

Swartz, D. (1997). *Culture and power: The sociology of Pierre Bourdieu.* Chicago: University of Chicago Press.

Tinto, V. (1975). Dropout from higher education: A theoretical synthesis of recent research. *Review of Educational Research, 45,* 89-125.

Uekawa, K., Aladjem, K. D., & Zhang, Y. (2005). *The role of social capital in comprehensive school reform.* Retrieved October 7, 2007, from http://www.air.org/news/documents/AERA2005Role%20of%20Social%20Capital%20in%20CSR.pdf

Implementing Universal Design in the Classroom

CHAPTER 5

Enhancing the Inclusiveness of First-Year Courses Through Universal Instructional Design

Jeanne L. Higbee, Carl J. Chung, and Leonardo Hsu
University of Minnesota

Abstract

This chapter is reprinted verbatim from Best Practices for Access and Retention in Higher Education, *and was originally published in 2004. This chapter describes the theory behind Universal Instructional Design (UID), an educational application of the architectural concept of Universal Design. UID is a model for creating inclusive curricula that are accessible to a larger proportion of students, especially those with disabilities. Components of UID include creating welcoming classrooms, determining essential course components, using diverse teaching strategies, and enabling students to demonstrate knowledge in multiple ways. Three faculty members who teach traditional first-year core curriculum courses in physics, symbolic logic, and psychology discuss implementation and benefits of UID-inspired teaching techniques.*

Universal Instructional Design (UID; Bowe, 2000; Silver, Bourke, & Strehorn, 1998) is a relatively new pedagogical model for providing access to higher education for students with disabilities by rethinking teaching practices to create curricula and classrooms that are inclusive for all students. Although federal legislation assures access for postsecondary students with disabilities (Kalivoda & Higbee, 1989, 1994), research (Kalivoda, 2003) indicates that faculty members continue to perceive barriers to providing academic accommodations. Lack of time and resources are among the constraints listed by faculty members, who often are more likely to be rewarded for acquiring grants and producing publications than for excellence in teaching (Kalivoda; Smith, 1997). Training (Fox, Hatfield, & Collins, 2003; Hatfield, 2003; Junco & Salter, 2003) can yield more positive attitudes but will not necessarily alleviate some faculty members' skepticism about the fairness of providing accommodations for students with documented disabilities, especially when considering "hidden" disabilities such as psychological disabilities, Attention Deficit Hyperactivity Disorder (ADHD), and learning disabilities (Kalivoda; Williams & Ceci, 1999). Universal Instructional Design does not ask faculty to "make exceptions" for students with disabilities. Instead, through UID all students have the opportunity to learn more effectively and to earn grades that reflect their knowledge. Furthermore, although it takes some time "up-front" to implement UID in a course, the eventual result is a net savings of time for the faculty member because fewer accommodations will then need to be made upon request for individual students with disabilities.

The purpose of this article is to review the theory behind UID and to present examples of how three faculty members implement UID in their courses. UID is especially appropriate for core curriculum courses, and particularly first-year courses because the first year is when students in postsecondary education experience the greatest number of transition-related issues and are thus the most vulnerable to dropping out (Noel, Levitz, & Saluri, 1985; Upcraft, Gardner, & Associates, 1989). Because UID-inspired approaches have helped each of us create more welcoming learning environments and increase meaningful student-to-student and student-to-faculty interactions, we argue that UID is a useful framework for guiding curricular development and for enhancing the success of first-year students (e.g., Hatch, Ghere, & Jirik, 2003).

Components of Universal Instructional Design

An architectural concept, Universal Design (Center for Universal Design, n.d.) provides the foundation for Universal Instructional Design. When planning a space, the architect takes into consideration the needs of all potential users of that space. As a result, ramps, elevators, expanded doorways, signs, bathrooms, and other features do not have to be added or modified at additional expense after the completion of a building. Some of the same architectural features that accommodate people with disabilities also benefit many others, including senior citizens, families with young children, and delivery people. Universal Instructional Design applies this same concept, advance planning to meet the needs of all learners, to curriculum development. Steps in this process, which are based on the work of Chickering and Gamson (1987), include: (a) creating welcoming classrooms; (b) determining the essential components of a course; (c) communicating clear expectations; (d) providing constructive feedback; (e) exploring the use of natural supports for learning, including technology, to enhance opportunities for all learners; (f) designing teaching methods that consider diverse learning styles, abilities, ways of knowing, and previous experience and background knowledge; (g) creating multiple ways for students to demonstrate their knowledge; and (h) promoting interaction among and between faculty and students (Center for Universal Design, 1997; Fox, Hatfield, & Collins, 2003). For purposes of this article, we will focus specifically on four of these steps.

Creating Welcoming Classrooms

In order to encourage retention, it is imperative that faculty teaching first-year courses communicate to students that they are welcomed and valued. Many of the students who drop out during or at the end of the first year of college do so for nonacademic reasons. They are choosing to leave, as opposed to being suspended or dismissed from the institution because they have not achieved the grades required to remain. Reasons for leaving are numerous, including financial and family pressures and other issues over which neither students nor faculty may have much control. However, faculty members can control the manner in which they choose to communicate with students. In the film *Uncertain Welcome* (2002), which can be downloaded free of charge from the World Wide Web, students with disabilities discuss some of the factors that make them hesitant to disclose their need for accommodations.

For students with physical disabilities, many traditional classroom spaces are daunting. For example, the student using a wheel chair is often relegated to the end of the aisle of the first or last row of seating, rather than having the same freedom of choice afforded to any other student in the class, and may or may not be provided with an appropriate writing surface for note taking. For the student who is blind, navigating across and throughout the campus poses multiple challenges. Although faculty may have little control over some of the physical barriers that students with disabilities must overcome on a daily basis, they can pay heed to their own attitudes and the tone they set in their own courses.

In the past, students with disabilities have been stigmatized (Johnson & Fox, 2003) by a medical model approach, in which these students have been perceived as "deficient" rather than merely "different." Universal Instructional Design is an outgrowth of an interactional, social constructivist approach to disability issues. Instead of providing accommodations on a case-by-case, situation-by-situation basis, this model explores how individuals interact with the environment to construct knowledge (Aune, 2000; Groce, 1985; Johnson & Fox, 2003; Jones, 1996).

One of the first steps in integrating rather than segregating students, whether physically or metaphorically, is to create a syllabus statement (Pedelty, 2003) that clearly states that students with disabilities will have equal access and equal opportunity. However, too often the syllabus statement is treated as an administrative or legal requirement, rather than as a means of assuring students with disabilities that their requests for accommodations and modifications are reasonable and will be met. Pedelty argues the importance of "performing" this statement aloud, rather than just assuming students will read it for themselves. By publicly addressing access for students with disabilities in the classroom, teachers communicate that they welcome all students in their course and that they want all students to have equal opportunity to succeed.

Determining Essential Components

What are the essential skills and knowledge that a student should be able to demonstrate upon completion of the course? In an introductory college-level general biology course, for example, is it necessary for a student to physically perform a dissection, or can the same knowledge be gained and demonstrated in other ways (Hatch, Ghere, & Jirik, 2003)? Would the answer to this question be different in a biology course for premedicine majors? Can introductory biology laboratories be offered online through the use of computer simulations? In addition to students with mobility or vision impairments, distance learners and students whose religious or moral beliefs prevent participation in dissection can benefit from the use of other teaching and learning strategies in biology labs, as long as students are fulfilling the essential requirements of the course.

Designing Diverse Teaching Methods

All students can benefit from the opportunity to learn material in multiple ways. Many students prefer learning through visual and interactive means rather than by listening to lectures and reading a text (Higbee, Ginter, & Taylor, 1991). Faculty members who explore alternative teaching styles often find adopting new methods to be rewarding for students and teacher alike. For example, a faculty member teaching a developmental college algebra course learned that by introducing collaborative small group activities she was able to address affective barriers to learning math, enhance confidence, and engage students who had not seemed particularly attentive during her lectures. Students' grades in subsequent credit-bearing mathematics courses were higher than the grades of students who participated in more traditional developmental math classes (Higbee & Thomas, 1999; Thomas & Higbee, 1996). Furthermore, a student with a hearing impairment emerged as a leader in small group discussions.

Several years later, the same faculty member was asked to offer one section of her course on cable-access television (Thomas & Higbee, 1998). In order to face the television camera, she was forced to work from an overhead projector, rather than turning her back on students to perform math problems on the board. This change in behavior had an immediate impact on her teaching, enhancing communication with all members of the class. The televised section created access for a wide variety of students and provided a community service as well. Students enrolled in other sections of the course could watch or videotape the televised section to make up what they missed due to absences. One student with multiple severe disabilities used her videotapes of the class when working with her tutor, stopping the tape to work through the problems.

Just as some students can excel at learning math at a distance, particularly those for whom the course is serving as a review in preparation for other quantitative courses, other students need to attend class to achieve (Thomas & Higbee, 2000) and prefer having immediate access to the teacher and to one another. As demonstrated in another developmental mathematics program (Kinney & Kinney, 2003) where students can choose between computer-assisted or more traditional classrooms, allowing students to select among sections offering different formats to find a good match between preferred learning and teaching styles can be just as effective as offering a wide array of teaching strategies within a single course section. The "universal" in Universal Instructional Design does not imply that "one size fits all." Instead, it refers to universal access to curricula.

Demonstrating Knowledge in Multiple Ways

Courses that use a single format to assess content mastery discriminate against many students, not just those with disabilities. For example, first-year courses in which students' only means of demonstrating knowledge is computer-based, randomly-generated multiple choice tests can disadvantage less affluent students who come from homes and schools that did not provide access to computers on a regular basis. Similarly, first-year composition courses in which students compose in-class essays at a computer terminal can benefit many students with learning disabilities but can pose multiple barriers to achievement for students who have limited proficiency with computers. For some students, trying to master computer skills while simultaneously completing an evaluative task can cause performance-impairing anxiety, especially if the student is also surrounded by students who are competent and comfortable with computers. When designing assessments for first-year courses, it is imperative to consider issues beyond cost-effectiveness, especially in large lecture classes that can already seem impersonal to students.

In the following sections of this article, three faculty members who teach first-year core curriculum courses provide personal accounts of their efforts to implement these components of Universal Instructional Design in their classes. By planning at the outset to meet the needs of all learners, including students with disabilities, these faculty members are able to make appropriate use of available resources during course development. Although it may be argued that these examples merely illustrate good teaching practices (Chickering & Gamsom, 1987; Hodge & Preston-Sabin, 1997), Universal Instructional Design takes good teaching one step further. How many faculty members, for example, take into consideration when choosing instructional materials or designing the day-to-day activities for their courses whether those materials and activities might serve to exclude a student who is blind? Until a student with a severe vision impairment actually enrolls in one of their courses, do most faculty members think about whether their means of disseminating information would be equally accessible to a student who is blind? Do they try to imagine understanding a chart or graph that one cannot see? Do they explore the availability of raised images that make diagrams (e.g., of the human digestive tract) accessible? Are they aware descriptive services that can make films accessible to people with vision impairments? Have they explored all possible ways of integrating accommodations in their teaching rather than segregating students with disabilities?

Although some students with disabilities will still need accommodations (e.g., a sign language interpreter for a student with a hearing impairment), faculty members who practice UID are less likely to find themselves dealing with the time constraints that are inevitable when trying to accommodate a student with a disability at the last minute, often when receiving a letter from the institution's office of disability services hand-delivered by the student on the first day of class. In the following pages, three faculty members each describe how they have implemented Universal Instructional Design in their first-year courses in physical science, logic, and psychology.

The Physical Science Course Taught by Leon Hsu

"Physical Systems: Principles and Practices" is a physical science course in which students learn some fundamental concepts in physical science and the framework through which scientists view the world. The majority (85%) of the students are non-science majors taking the course to fulfill a science core curriculum requirement. The remaining students are interested in majoring in a scientific or technical field, but are looking for a refresher before taking the introductory physics course offered by the physics department.

The essential skills and knowledge that I expect my students to gain from this class are to be able to:

1. Demonstrate an understanding of basic physics concepts by: (a) applying those concepts to solve problems using a variety of representations, including equations, diagrams, and graphs; (b) using the concepts flexibly to solve problems both in familiar and unfamiliar contexts; and (c) recognizing their applicability to real-world situations.
2. Write scientific arguments and explanations using commonly accepted scientific principles as supporting evidence.

3. Obtain accurate measurements in the laboratory, identify possible sources of error, and organize data in the form of charts and graphs.

4. Work collaboratively with peers in solving problems on paper and in the laboratory.

The structure of the Physical Systems class is fairly traditional, with two 75-minute lecture periods and one 2-hour lab. The lecture periods, however, have been modified using UID principles. The 75-minute period is divided into three or four learning cycles, each involving a new concept or skill for the students to learn. During each cycle, I lecture for about 10 minutes on the new topic and students spend the next 5 to 10 minutes working on a related problem either by themselves or with their neighbors. Then I call the class back together and lead a large group discussion to go over a solution to the problem. By breaking the 75-minute lecture period into smaller chunks, students assimilate new knowledge in more manageable pieces. In addition, since students are performing a variety of activities, they are not forced to sit silently and maintain their concentration for a long period of time. Finally, integrating problem solving into the lecture gives students a chance to assess their knowledge of the material being presented, helping them to self-monitor their understanding.

I also give students copies of notes that I have written to go along with the lectures. The class notes serve several different purposes. First, they help to focus the students' attention on the most important parts of new concepts. Each set of notes is preceded by a one-page summary of the important information for that lecture period. This summary provides a handy reference that is easier to use as a reference than a 15-page chapter in a science textbook. Second, the notes free students from feeling like they must copy down everything I write on the board, enabling them to devote more attention to what is actually happening in class. To encourage students to attend class and practice using the concepts by working the in-class problems, some parts of the notes are purposely left blank, to be filled in during class. The notes are posted on the class Web site before each class so students can download them to prepare for class. Lastly, because the notes exist in electronic form, they can easily be translated into alternative formats for any students with disabilities in the class. During the semester in which I had a student who is blind, this practice eliminated the need for a note-taker for this particular student. Similarly, this approach enables students with learning disabilities and ADHD to get organized in preparation for class.

Students have additional opportunities to learn by interacting with their peers in the laboratories associated with the class. During the labs, students work in groups of three. These groups are switched only once during the semester to enable students to form social bonds with a few of their classmates, to provide a support network for students, and to help them find study partners. The labs are run by undergraduate teaching assistants who have recently taken the course themselves and thus can sometimes provide students with more effective help than the instructor.

The labs also give students a chance to work with the concepts in a concrete manner. Students perform experiments using everyday objects such as Hot Wheels cars, pennies, or their own bodies and apply the concepts learned in the course to interpret their observations. This experience allows students to practice using the concepts in both concrete (lab) and abstract (lecture) contexts, making the material accessible to students with a range of learning styles. For example, Tinkertoys were used to help students visualize the addition and subtraction of vectors, giving them something tangible to hold and move around instead of just drawing lines on a piece of paper. This activity was particularly helpful for a student who is blind.

Traditionally, students' grades in science classes are based largely on their performance on exams. To make the course more inclusive, the grade in my physical science class is distributed more evenly among homework (20%), lab (20%), the in-class problems (10%), and exams (50%). This approach allows students to demonstrate their knowledge of the concepts by solving problems in timed or untimed contexts (e.g., exams or homework) or by writing a detailed analysis of a physical situation including making tables and graphs (lab).

I write the course exams so that a typical student can complete it in about 75% of the allotted time. This eliminates much of the time pressure from the students by giving all of them some extra time. As a side benefit, students with disabilities have never needed to take the exams outside of the usual classroom situation, relieving them of having to inadvertently disclose their situations.

The Symbolic Logic Course Taught by Carl Chung

Ideally, the UID framework could be used to dramatically reinvent a particular course, rendering "special" accommodations for any student unnecessary. However, in the real world of day-to-day practice, it is also possible to use the basic ideas and tools of UID to tinker with and gradually improve even more traditional courses. Alternatively, it is possible to adopt UID as a more global framework within which to think about how existing course components might or might not contribute toward an inclusive student experience. A good example of this is my own course in introductory symbolic logic, which targets first-year students who are, for different reasons, "math phobic." By mastering basic logical concepts (e.g., argument, premise, conclusion, valid form, etc.), developing the ability to translate English sentences into symbolic notation, learning how to identify and evaluate patterns of reasoning, and becoming proficient at constructing geometry-style proofs of argument forms, students can satisfy my institution's "mathematical thinking" requirement without having to take algebra or calculus.

My course is taught fairly traditionally. I lecture, assign weekly homework problem sets, give quizzes, and administer in-class examinations. However, UID principles have helped me to improve how I teach the course and the UID framework has allowed me to step back and consider how different course components function together to promote inclusiveness. For example, UID's emphasis upon creating a welcoming classroom in which students feel valued has helped me to be mindful of establishing a supportive tone and rapport with students. On the first day of class as we are going over the mechanics of the course, I stress that doing symbolic logic will be hard for some students at first because of its unfamiliarity. I draw an analogy to how one might feel when visiting a foreign country such as Greece, Russia, or Japan, with a radically different alphabet. At first, it feels very disorienting and frustrating not being able to get around as easily as we are used to—not being able to make sense of signs, for example—but eventually as we learn the language and become more familiar with our surroundings things get easier. Approaching the topic in this manner also resonates with students who are non-native speakers of English, and particularly those who are recent immigrants, a growing population on many college campuses. At the University of Minnesota, for example, we have experienced a significant influx of Somali, Hmong, and Russian students. Addressing different symbol systems is a means of acknowledging learning differences among a wide range of students from diverse backgrounds, including students who communicate via American Sign Language or Braille.

To drive this point home, I then ask students to take out a sheet of paper and engage in a thought experiment. In this experiment I ask them to copy down a short definition of a logic concept that I write on the board. But the "trick" is that they must use their "opposite" hands to write and I ask them to imagine that their entire course grade depends upon how quickly and neatly they can copy the definition. Finally, I ask them to verbalize what they are feeling as they write by answering the following questions: How does what you are producing look? How do you feel about what you are producing? What do you think about having your entire grade determined by this assignment? Usually, of course, what they are putting down on paper resembles scribbling, and as I walk around the room reminding them that their entire grade is at stake, students laugh nervously, express their frustration, or just shake their heads.

There are two main points to this exercise. First, I draw an analogy between students' hands trying to copy the definition and students' brains trying to learn symbolic logic. At first, doing the work will feel awkward, frustrating, and difficult, I tell them. But if they stick with it, I argue, it will get easier, just as it would get easier writing with that opposite hand given enough practice. Second, the exercise acknowledges student anxiety and allows them to face it and express it publicly without singling out individuals. In this way, I believe I communicate to the students that their anxiety is understandable, that they are all "in the same boat" because everyone has some level of anxiety, but that every one of them can succeed in the course if they just stick with it and take advantage of the support structures built into the course.

A second example involves learning cycles that are very similar to those discussed by Leon Hsu in the previous section. From the students' point of view, a typical class period comprises several of these learning cycles, which look like this:

1. The instructor lectures briefly on a new concept or technique.
2. Students ask questions.

3. The instructor works examples.

4. The students have another opportunity to ask questions.

5. The students work examples individually, in pairs, or in small groups.

6. The instructor asks questions such as "How should we start this problem?" "Why won't this work?"

7. The students engage in a large group discussion of the problem(s).

8. The instructor moves on to a new concept or technique, and the cycle repeats.

In this way, there is ongoing interaction between instructor and students, and students alternate between more passive and more active modes of engaging course material.

The daily learning cycles are embedded in a larger learning cycle that centers on the exams: read text, take notes in class, ask questions, practice examples, do homework, ask questions, take quiz on homework, do a mock exam, review, take in-class exam. In this way, students can demonstrate proficiency in a series of manageable steps. Early in the cycle, students have lots of support (e.g., in-class practice and feedback with instructor and peers) that—within the classroom setting—gradually diminishes as students begin the homework set (i.e., working on problems at home away from class, possibly with peers), move on to the quiz (exam conditions but with relatively few points at stake), and, finally, work on a mock examination with solutions. This gives students time to master the material gradually and to build confidence as they work toward the in-class examinations.

For me, the transition from straight lecturing to learning cycles came about as I wondered how to help students who struggle to understand all the different concepts and rules of logic as a coherent system. Whether due to a learning disability, lack of background, lack of confidence, or a preference for learning styles that are active, concrete, and hands on, some students understand parts of what we are doing in isolation but have trouble tackling new or complicated problems. Learning cycles break complicated material into discrete components, build in repetition, practice, and immediate feedback, and require students to actively engage and apply new ideas. By proceeding in this manner, I, as the instructor, know right away whether students "get it" and are ready to move on. Although I originally conceived of learning cycles as a way to help struggling students, it is a technique that improves learning for all students in my class.

Even though the majority of my course revolves around these recurring learning cycles, around the tenth week of the semester we take a break from this routine and do something different. Instead of the usual focus on new logical concepts or techniques, students come to class, break into small groups, and work together on a structured discussion project. Students are given a philosophy article and must reconstruct and identify the author's pattern of reasoning. This requires students to work together to find the author's conclusion and main premises and to determine how the premises support the conclusion. Each group must submit a written summary of its answers to questions and main points of discussion. Then we reconvene as a large group and discuss the project and whether the students accept the author's conclusion, which provocatively argues that those of us living in affluent societies are morally obligated to donate much of our income to help people who are starving, homeless, or unable to get adequate medical care.

The educational goal of the project is to show students first-hand that what they are reading outside of class also has logical structure, and that applying what they have learned in class is useful. But the project also promotes inclusiveness since all students can read through parts of the article and participate meaningfully in their group's discussion even if they don't completely understand the logical concepts. In fact, students often end up re-teaching each other the concepts being applied. Because the project does count toward the final course grade and because it draws upon a different set of skills--discussion in a small group, working together to write a coherent summary of that discussion--than is usually emphasized in class, it is one example of an alternative way for students to demonstrate knowledge related to the course.

In the context of UID, I use learning cycles and the different activities to deliberately structure and package a variety of teaching methods (i.e., lecture, small group work, whole group discussion, active learning, problem solving, written summaries of peer discussions) to try to maximize learning opportunities for all students and to promote inclusiveness. However, what goes on outside of class can be equally important for realizing these UID-inspired goals.

One example of this is what I call the "logic lab." The logic lab is a two-hour block of time that I purposely schedule away from where I usually meet with students (e.g., the classroom or my office). The lab is informal, optional, and unstructured. Students can just come sit and work on their homework, receive supplemental instruction, work additional practice problems, or catch up if they missed class. The informality of the logic lab results in a wider range of students taking advantage of it compared to office hours. Often students will start talking to and helping each other, coming to me only when they get really stuck. In this way, I believe students develop a sense of community and ownership of the course, and it affords me the opportunity to interact individually with more of them. Clearly students who are struggling stand to benefit the most from the logic lab, but because it is open to all students and because students can come and initiate the kind of interaction they want and need, whether with me or with peers, this simple alternative to standard office hours also allows me to maximize learning opportunities and to promote inclusiveness in my class.

The Psychology Course Taught by Jeanne Higbee

"The Psychology of Personal Development" is a challenging first-year course that applies psychological theory to students' everyday lives. The following objectives describe the essential knowledge and skills required for successful completion of the course:

1. Students will become acquainted with prominent psychological theories and the theorists who espoused them.
2. Students will be able to define key psychological concepts.

3. Students will learn the relationship between psychological constructs and those of other fields of study, including history, political science, sociology, economics, and anthropology.

4. Students will become familiar with research methodologies.

5. Students will be introduced to basic statistical concepts such as central tendency and correlation.

6. Students will develop the skills and knowledge necessary to critique psychological research.

7. Students will learn about psychological assessment.

8. Students will apply psychological theory and concepts to their own development and relationships.

9. Students will learn to identify key ideas in a psychology textbook.

10. Students will further develop their writing skills.

11. Students will use higher-order thinking skills to analyze, synthesize, and evaluate course materials.

12. Students will use knowledge acquired in the course to propose creative solutions to real life problems.

13. Students will become aware of the ways in which people from diverse cultures are similar.

14. Students will work collaboratively to complete tasks.

15. Students will facilitate their own learning.

On the first day of class, I reassure students about the challenges ahead as I go over the syllabus. I also introduce myself by disclosing some personal information and sharing some of my values, meanwhile explaining that it is not my intent to impose those values on my students. I want them to think for themselves, not tell me what they think I want to hear. I try to create a classroom environment that will be welcoming to students. However, I recognize that it will still be difficult for some students with disabilities to approach me in person, so I ask all students to complete a "student information form" that seeks basic information. On that form I reiterate my commitment to providing accommodations for students with documented disabilities, and give students the opportunity to self-disclose privately and in writing rather than having to approach me in front of the class.

The course text for the Psychology of Personal Development, *Psychology Applied to Modern Life,* by Weiten and Lloyd (2003), is frequently used for upper-level psychology of adjustment courses. In order to assist students in mastering the material in the text, I have developed my own study guide for each chapter. Each study guide asks students to define key terms in their own words and then poses a series of short essay questions. Some of the essays are purely factual (e.g.,"Outline Freud's five psychosexual stages" or "Describe one intervention to assist in overcoming prejudice"), merely requiring comprehension of a theoretical framework. Other questions demand the use of higher-order thinking skills (Barbanel, 1987; Bloom, 1956), as illustrated in the following examples:

1. "Discuss how feedback from others and cultural guidelines can shape self-concept."

2. "Provide an example of each of the following common defense mechanisms:

(a) denial of reality, (b) fantasy, (c) intellectualization (isolation), (d) undoing, and (e) overcompensation."

3. "Give an example of how you have used an impression management strategy."

4. "What are steps *you* can take to enhance *your* self-esteem?"

5. "Describe a snap judgment you have made about someone in the recent past. Did it turn out to be accurate?"

These study guides differ significantly from the standard guides often published to accompany textbooks, which are more likely to be made up of objective questions. Although the study guides are time consuming for students, each is worth only 10 points, for a total of 150 out of the 1,000 possible points available in the course. The purposes of the study guides are to: (a) assist students in navigating the text and determining how to read for main ideas; (b) ensure that students have an understanding of the theories upon which class activities are based; and (c) prepare students for weekly quizzes, which usually cover one textbook chapter.

The quizzes consist of objective questions (e.g., multiple choice, true-or-false, matching) and are worth 25 points each. On quiz days, class begins with a question-and-answer period so students can review and clarify any confusing material. Students typically take 10 to 20 minutes to complete a quiz, but they are given the remainder of the 50-minute class period to do so. When students turn in their quizzes, they receive the study guide for the next chapter, which they then begin in class. Students with documented disabilities that indicate accommodations like extended time for tests are given the option to take the quizzes in another location, but seldom choose to do so because the entire class receives extended time, and they prefer not to "advertise" their disabilities by being "absent" on each quiz day. Even if their disability is one for which a less distracting testing environment might be beneficial (e.g., students with ADHD), students will often express a preference for remaining in the classroom. My response is to have the student try taking a quiz in class and see how it goes. Because students do not feel constrained by time, if they are prepared they usually do well on quizzes. Class means for each of the 13 quizzes generally fall in the 80 to 85% range. Students may drop their lowest quiz score, but there are no "make-up" quizzes.

The quizzes serve as preparation for the final exam, also objective, worth 100 points. In addition, over the course of the semester the students write four papers, with a minimum of two double-spaced pages each, worth 50 points each. These assignments enable students who are not skilled in taking objective tests to demonstrate their knowledge using a different format. Students have a choice of 12 essay topics, although only the first four will have been covered at the time the first essay is due. Each topic requires students to apply the subject matter to their own lives. Students may also choose to write a fifth essay to replace one quiz grade, but the fifth paper is then worth only 25 points. Thus, if a student is absent on two quiz days, the student can drop one zero grade, and replace the other with an essay grade. If a student has documented extenuating circumstances (e.g., hospitalization) for missing more than two quizzes, I allow the student to write additional essays in lieu of make-up quizzes. As a result, I do not have to prepare two separate quizzes for each chapter, which would require considerable additional time, yet I can still accommodate all students, including students with disabilities, who have legitimate reasons for missing class.

My favorite assignment in the course is the final project, worth 100 points. Although one option is to write a research paper, few students choose that path. Instead they can create a game, draw or paint a picture, produce a video, write a short story or poem, make a collage, or propose their own idea, and then present their project to the class. I am always impressed by the imagination and creativity displayed in these presentations.

Students earn the remaining 150 points for the course via participation in a wide range of in-class activities. I seldom lecture. Students respond to psychological assessments and then critique them. They engage in a series of activities that might be classified as "left brain" or "right brain" and then evaluate their own performance, as well as exploring the concept of hemisphere dominance. They create a research question and a series of hypotheses, develop an idea for an experiment to test their hypotheses, and then explore the limitations of research with human subjects. They watch a contemporary film and then describe how scenes from the film depict key terms from the text. In addition to the captioning for people with hearing impairments now available on all recent releases, films are also available on videocassette in formats that are accessible to students with visual impairments through DVS Home Video, 1-800-736-3099, with major funding provided by the U.S. Department of Education. For each chapter I endeavor to use a film or provide an activity that enables students to learn and demonstrate knowledge in a unique way.

The first time I taught this course, which occurred just as my introduction to Universal Instructional Design began, I was filling in at the last minute for a hospitalized colleague. I had no time to prepare. In a class of 40 students, I had one student with a severe hearing impairment, four with learning disabilities, one with a mobility impairment, one with a psychological disorder, and three recent immigrants for whom English was a second, third, or fourth language. In retrospect, I am sure that the first week was a disaster. I lectured from overheads and bored myself. The grades on the first quiz were dismal. It was my first semester in a new job and I was just imagining the impression that first set of teaching evaluations would give, and rightfully so, because the students were obviously not learning. Thanks to my involvement in faculty development in the area of UID, what began as a nightmare for students and teacher alike turned into an opportunity to rethink pedagogy and provide a learning experience that enabled students with diverse backgrounds, ways of knowing, abilities, and preferred learning styles to excel.

The Importance of Faculty Development

The concept of Universal Instructional Design in higher education has achieved broad acceptance among disability services providers, but information has not been disseminated widely to administrators and faculty members, who would have primary responsibility for its implementation. Through a grant from the U.S. Department of Education

(Curriculum Transformation and Disability [CTAD], n.d.; Higbee, 2003), a team comprised of faculty, campus disability services providers, and external consultants in specific areas of disability developed a series of training models that can be used on any campus (CTAD; Fox, Hatfield, & Collins, 2003). Components of the training include: (a) approaching disability from the perspective of the interactional model, rather than perceiving disability as a deficiency; (b) familiarizing faculty with legal issues and establishing their responsibility under the law; (c) attending to student perspectives; (d) understanding the underlying principles of UID and applying these principles to instruction; (e) learning about assistive technologies; (f) investigating local resources; (g) responding to case scenarios; and (h) creating an individual action plan. A guidebook for the training modules is available online *(Curriculum Transformation,* n.d.).

Participants in training sessions held on several campuses between 2000 and 2002 evaluated the workshops very highly, with overall means exceeding 5.0 on a 6-point Likert-type scale, except for the pilot training session, for which the overall evaluation of workshop content was 4.8 (Fox, Hatfield, & Collins, 2003). One participant wrote:

> What I left with is the most valuable and that is the wider view regarding disabilities, a more positive outlook on various approaches to use, a renewed sense of "what I should be doing," tons of useful knowledge regarding the law, access issues, and what [my campus] has to offer. (Fox, Hatfield, & Collins, p. 32)

Throughout the nation, however, campus disability services providers continue to be challenged by faculty who have been briefly introduced to the concept of Universal Instructional Design, and understand its practicality and benefits as a pedagogical tool, but still want more guidance about how to implement UID in their own courses. Typical questions posed at sessions on UID at professional conferences where the training model has been introduced begin with statements like, "OK, I can see how this might work in a composition class, but I teach chemistry." One of the purposes of this article has been to demonstrate how three faculty members teaching in different disciplinary areas have reconceptualized their teaching in order to integrate Universal Instructional Design in their work.

Conclusion

Although Universal Instructional Design may be considered "just good teaching" (Chickering & Gamson, 1987; Hodge & Preston-Sabin, 1997), it goes one step further. It involves our purposeful attention to differences among learners, and provides an excellent model for multicultural education (Barajas & Higbee, 2003) because its goal is inclusion. Through advance planning, faculty members who endeavor to implement UID find that it can be liberating, enabling them to bring more creativity to their teaching, and also rewarding, because students are responsive to more inclusive pedagogy. Although UID cannot eliminate all needs for individual accommodations for students with disabilities, it can be surprising how much less time faculty members must devote to making modifications "upon demand." Furthermore, UID benefits all students and counteracts the criticism that accommodations for students with disabilities disadvantage other students competing for grades in the same classes.

Finally, UID-inspired change can make a significant contribution toward the success of all first-year students. That is, although success in the freshman year involves more than just what transpires in the classroom, as Upcraft, Gardner, and colleagues remind us, "First and foremost, freshmen must succeed academically and intellectually" (Upcraft et al., 1989, p. 2). But how can instructors help first-year students to achieve the basic "academic and intellectual competence" (Upcraft et al., p. 2) they need in order to thrive in college? Our experience shows that UID offers both a theoretical framework and practical guidance that are worth considering. By foregrounding the importance of welcoming classrooms, essential course components, diverse teaching methods, and multiple paths for demonstrating knowledge, UID has helped each of us in different ways—to get students intellectually involved in our courses, to emphasize interaction among students to promote learning, and always to keep in mind the role of instructor contact and involvement (Upcraft et al., pp. 4-5) in the success of students in our first-year courses. We firmly believe UID can help other instructors do the same.

References

Aune, B. (2000). Career and academic advising. In H. Belch (Ed.), *Serving students with disabilities* (pp. 55-67). New Directions in Student Services, no. 91. San Francisco: Jossey-Bass.

Barajas, H. L., & Higbee, J. L. (2003). Where do we go from here? Universal Design as a model for multicultural education. In J. L. Higbee (Ed.), *Curriculum transformation and disability: Implementing Universal Design in higher education* (pp. 285-290). Minneapolis: University of Minnesota, General College, Center for Research on Developmental Education and Urban Literacy.

Barbanel, J. (1987). Critical thinking for developmental students: An integrated approach. *Research & Teaching in Developmental Education, 4*(1), 7-12.

Bloom, B. S. (Ed.). (1956). Taxonomy of educational objectives: Cognitive domain/ Affective domain. New York: David McKay.

Bowe, F. G. (2000). Universal Design in education—Teaching nontraditional students. Westport, CT: Bergin & Garvey.

Center for Universal Design. (n.d.). *What is Universal Design?* Retrieved March 6, 2002, from http://www.design.ncsu.edu:8120/cud/univ_design/udhistory.htm

Chickering, A. W., & Gamson, Z. F. (1987). Seven principles for good practice in undergraduate education. *AAHE Bulletin, 39*(7), 3-7.

Curriculum Transformation and Disability (CTAD). (n.d.). Available: www.gen.umn.edu/ research/ctad.

Fox, J. A., Hatfield, J. P., & Collins, T. C. (2003). Developing the Curriculum Transformation and Disability (CTAD) workshop model. In J. L. Higbee (Ed.), *Curriculum transformation and disability: Implementing Universal Design in higher education* (pp. 23-39). Minneapolis: University of Minnesota, General College, Center for Research on Developmental Education and Urban Literacy.

Groce, N. (1985). *Everyone here spoke sign language: Hereditary deafness on Martha's Vineyard.* Cambridge, MA: Harvard University Press.

Hatch, J. T., Ghere, D. L., & Jirik, K. N. (2003). Empowering students with severe disabilities: A case study. In J. L. Higbee (Ed.), *Curriculum transformation and disability: Implementing Universal Design in higher education* (pp. 171-183). Minneapolis: University of Minnesota, General College, Center for Research on Developmental Education and Urban Literacy.

Hatfield, J. P. (2003). Perceptions of Universal (Instructional) Design: A qualitative examination. In J. L. Higbee (Ed.), *Curriculum transformation and disability: Implementing Universal Design in higher education* (pp. 41-58). Minneapolis: University of Minnesota, General College, Center for Research on Developmental Education and Urban Literacy.

Higbee, J. L. (Ed.). (2003). *Curriculum transformation and disability: Implementing Universal Design in higher education.* Minneapolis: University of Minnesota, General College, Center for Research on Developmental Education and Urban Literacy.

Higbee, J. L., Ginter, E. J., & Taylor, W. D. (1991). Enhancing academic performance: Seven perceptual styles of learning. *Research & Teaching in Developmental Education, 7*(2), 5-10.

Higbee, J. L., & Thomas, P. V. (1999). Affective and cognitive factors related to mathematics achievement. *Journal of Developmental Education, 23*(1), 8-10, 12, 14, 16, 32.

Hodge, B. M., & Preston-Sabin, J. (1997). *Accommodations--Or just good teaching?* Westport, CT: Praeger.

Johnson, D. M., & Fox, J. A. (2003). Creating curb cuts in the classroom: Adapting Universal Design principles to education. In J. L. Higbee (Ed.), *Curriculum transformation and disability: Implementing Universal Design in higher education* (pp. 7-21). Minneapolis: University of Minnesota, General College, Center for Research on Developmental Education and Urban Literacy.

Jones, S. R. (1996). Toward inclusive theory: Disability as social construction. *NASPA Journal, 33,* 347-354.

Junco, R., & Salter, D. W. (2003, April). *Stimulating change in the attitudes of faculty and student affairs staff towards students with disabilities.* Paper presented at the annual convention of the American College Personnel Association, Minneapolis, MN.

Kalivoda, K. S. (2003). Creating access through Universal Instructional Design. In J. L. Higbee, D. B. Lundell, & I. M. Duranczyk (Eds.), *Multiculturalism in developmental education* (pp. 25-34). Minneapolis: University of Minnesota, General College, Center for Research on Developmental Education and Urban Literacy.

Kalivoda, K. S., & Higbee, J. L. (1989). Students with disabilities in higher education: Redefining access. *Journal of Educational Opportunity, 4,* 14-21.

Kalivoda, K. S., & Higbee, J. L. (1994). Implementing the Americans with Disabilities Act. *Journal of Humanistic Education and Development, 32,* 133-137.

Kinney, D. P., & Kinney, L. S. (2003). Computer-mediated learning in mathematics and Universal Instructional Design. In J. L. Higbee (Ed.), *Curriculum transformation and disability: Implementing Universal Design in higher education* (pp. 115-125). Minneapolis: University of Minnesota, General College, Center for Research on Developmental Education and Urban Literacy.

Noel, L., Levitz, R., & Saluri, D. (Eds.). (1985). *Increasing student retention: Effective programs and practices for reducing the dropout rate*. San Francisco: Jossey-Bass.

Pedelty, M. (2003). Making a statement. In J. L. Higbee (Ed.), *Curriculum transformation and disability: Implementing Universal Design in higher education* (pp. 71-78). Minneapolis: University of Minnesota, General College, Center for Research on Developmental Education and Urban Literacy.

Silver, P., Bourke, A., & Strehorn, K. C. (1998). Universal Instructional Design in higher education: An approach for inclusion. *Equity and Excellence in Education, 31*(2), 47-51.

Smith, K. L. (1997). Preparing faculty for instructional technology: From education to development to creative independence. *Cause/Effect, 20* (3), 36-44.

Thomas, P.V., & Higbee, J. L. (1996). Enhancing mathematics achievement through collaborative problem solving. *The Learning Assistance Review, 1*(1), 38-46.

Thomas, P.V., & Higbee, J. L. (1998). Teaching mathematics on television: Perks and pitfalls. *Academic Exchange Quarterly, 2*(2), 29-33.

Thomas, P.V., & Higbee, J. L. (2000). The relationship between involvement and success in developmental algebra. *Journal of College Reading and Learning, 30*(2), 222-232.

Uncertain welcome [video]. (2002). Minneapolis, MN: Curriculum Transformation and Disability, General College, University of Minnesota. Available: www.gen.umn.edu/research/ctad.

Upcraft, M. L., Gardner, J., & Associates. (1989). *The freshman year experience.* San Francisco: Jossey-Bass.

Weiten, W., & Lloyd, M. A. (2003). *Psychology applied to modern life* (7th ed.). Belmont, CA: Thomson Learning, Wadsworth.

Williams, W. M., & Ceci, S. J. (1999, August 6). Accommodating learning disabilities can bestow unfair advantages. *The Chronicle of Higher Education,* B4-B5.

CHAPTER 6

Making a Statement

Mark Pedelty
University of Minnesota

Abstract
This chapter is reprinted verbatim from Curriculum Transformation and Disability: Implementing Universal Design in Higher Education, *and was originally published in 2003. After participating in the Curriculum Transformation and Disability (CTAD) workshop, the author began presenting a concerted oral accommodation and access statement on the first day of class. The results were immediate and positive, as illustrated with three examples. The author argues that individual accommodations, like those illustrated here, are an essential part of the process of developing Universal Instructional Design (UID) courses.*

My participation in the Curriculum Transformation and Disability (CTAD) workshops yielded numerous benefits. The most significant outcome was a course remodeled with Universal Instructional Design (UID) principles in mind. With UID and access as the goal, I completed a fairly radical remake of my Introduction to Cultural Anthropology course. I turned what was a course mixing mini-lectures, multiple modes of student writing, performance, oral presentation, and independent field research projects to a lab largely based on student research projects tailored to their individual and collective needs, abilities, and interests. What could be more universal than curricula designed by and for students in collaboration with their instructor?

However, perhaps the most important course modification to come out of my participation in the workshops was also the simplest and easiest to institute. In fact, it only took a few minutes. I added an oral statement to my written syllabus statement concerning disability, accommodation, and access issues. Although I had put accommodation statements in previous syllabi, I had never thought to perform an oral accompaniment in class. Part of the reason is that I find repeating syllabi page by page to be a fairly perfunctory ritual. As a result of this general antipathy for the typical syllabus introduction, I had never before thought to orally reinforce the written accommodation statement. The CTAD workshop motivated me to do so, with positive results.

The results of the oral announcement were immediate and profound. In previous semesters I often had to wait weeks before discovering that a student needed accommodation. The written statement simply was not sufficient. However, in several of the courses I have taught since adding the announcement, students have approached me that same day to tell me about their particular needs and, in a few cases, to request accommodations. I have been reminded that the seemingly insignificant act of articulation makes all the difference. More of a text based learner myself, I often forget that for many people information is not relevant until put into oral, and perhaps even dialogic, form.

This chapter is about the oral accommodation statement I now perform in my classes. After a short description of that performance, I will describe three cases where it has made a difference. I will then discuss the ancillary benefits of making the statement. The goal is not simply to argue for the inclusion of an oral statement, but also to examine the role of accommodation, in general, as it relates to Universal Instructional Design (UID). I suggest that minor acts of accommodation, such as those described here, help us move closer to the ultimate goal of creating courses with universal access.

The Statement

My typical method for presenting the syllabus is to give students an "open syllabus" quiz on the first day of class. The quiz questions relate to the most essential elements of the syllabus and get students in the habit of using it as a working document. A quiz question concerning the accommodation statement can help emphasize the point.

However, nothing is as useful as oral performance in getting across a point, especially when the rest of the presentation is more text based. The move from text to talk signals that something important is about to be announced. With that in mind, I decided to add a short statement after we discuss the open syllabus quiz. Rather than repeat the written statement, I put down my syllabus for an impromptu lecture on the point. I said something like the following:

> I want to say a few words about access. I think that it is very important for all students to have complete access to the course. Sometimes there are aspects of a course that make it difficult for some students to fully participate. For example, students with disabilities may need accommodations so that they will have the same level of access to the course as other students. I encourage you, if you have a disability that requires such an accommodation, to approach me after class, visit office hours, or contact me immediately so that together we can make such arrangements. Also, if you have not visited Disability Services to receive a letter certifying and explaining your disability, you should do so as soon as possible. You will find them very helpful. If you have never been diagnosed with a learning disability, but have reason to believe that you have a learning disability, I encourage you to visit Disability Services to be tested and, if so, receive the help you need and deserve to have full access to your college education. Every student has a right to full educational access and I want to do whatever is necessary to make certain that you gain such access in this course. Please read the syllabus statement for further information, including the campus address for Disability Services.

As is true in much of teaching, the performative act of delivering the statement is more important than its specific content. I make a point of presenting the accommodation invitation with a level of inflection, eye contact, and projection that goes beyond that which I typically use for delivering course content.

I have been struck by the amount of attention students pay to the statement. The glossy-eyes and distant stares that normally greet introductory syllabus presentations give way to rapt interest. Either this issue is of intrinsic interest to the students or the statement works as intended, raising student awareness of and interest in access issues. It is probably a bit of both. Regardless of the reason, the statement has worked to a surprising degree. I am pleased to have discovered the importance of the oral performance, while at the same I am a bit embarrassed that I did not think of doing it earlier in my teaching career. If it were not for CTAD, I might never have bothered.

Student Impact

The statement produced immediate results. In the first case, a student with a visual impairment asked me to change the color of my PowerPoint font from blue to black. It was a subtle change, and extremely easy to execute. However, it was remarkable in the sense that rarely before had a student asked me for accommodation after the very first class meeting. Usually, students would wait to feel comfortable with me before making such an approach. In other words, the statement worked; it produced a more immediate sense among the students that I was approachable, particularly when it came to questions of access, diversity, and equity.

I might have written off that very cursory experience had I not continued to experience the same response in subsequent classes. The next semester, a student came up to me, thanked me for making the statement (a sad commentary on students' low expectations) and told me about his particular learning disability. It would be inappropriate to provide further details for reasons of anonymity, but suffice it to say that the invitation produced the intended results once again.

The student presented his Disability Services letter after the next class meeting and we discussed potential accommodations. Because I do not use timed tests and allow students to choose from a variety of methods to communicate their learning, there was not need for significant accommodations. However, my awareness of his disability and the relationship we began to establish as a result bore obvious fruit. The student did well in the course.

A third and final case took place during a course involving field study in Mexico. I made another pitch concerning the need for all students to have full access to the course, including the experiential field components. I did not want any students to encounter obstacles to the field experience. For example, we were planning on climbing a pyramid at Teotihuacan and reading a short story from the summit. In addition to trying to ascertain the accommodation needs of individual students, I designed the statement to appeal to students who might begrudge a modified course schedule. Hopefully, if they were aware that there could be students among them requiring other options, they might be less resistant to group changes.

A student approached me that day, noting that he had limited mobility and several health conditions that I should be aware of. Once again, it would be inappropriate to elaborate. However, it is fair to say that more learning was made possible thanks to the student's helpful approach. He specifically cited the oral statement as his motivation for doing so. Would he have climbed the pyramid if I had not made the statement? Would he risk health and learning for sake of participation in an activity for which there were definite collective alternatives?

We met at the base of the pyramid, in a delightful garden that was more conducive to discussion anyway. Those who desired to climb would have plenty of time to do so later. I have adopted that as my metaphor for the issue of accommodation, in general, and the importance of making the oral statement, in particular. I imagine generations of students struggling to climb over educational barriers, simply because I never bothered to invite them to talk to me about obstacle-free alternatives.

As a result, I have begun to think of it not as a statement, per se, as much as an open invitation. The oral performance provides a more personal and human invitation to the student to engage in collaborative discussion. Not one of the three students mentioned here had an obvious disability. I would have remained unaware had they not approached me. Based on comparative experience, I doubt any of them would have approached me based on the written statement alone. The resulting discussions have produced not only individual remedies, but also permanent course modifications in the spirit of UID.

Universal Design and Access

I have discovered several other benefits to the oral performance of the accommodation statement. For example, it has helped me deal with the occasional gratuitous or manipulative use of disability claims. We would like to believe that this never happens, but I have experienced it three times, each time involving Attention Deficit Disorder (ADD). On each occasion, students who were off task during class have shouted something like, "But I've got ADD!" when asked to get back to class work.

My response to such a statement would be the same, regardless of whether or not I made the oral statement. I later take the student aside and suggest that the student should visit Disability Services, if he or she has not done so already, and I discuss potential accommodations with the student. As might be expected for students who present their disability in that public and vocal fashion, they often do not follow up when encouraged to do so. Either these students are not dealing well with their ADD or ADHD (i.e., Attention Deficit Hyperactivity Disorder) and are not looking for the help they need, or, in certain cases, they may not even have been diagnosed as ADD or ADHD, but are instead making an extremely bad joke out of a very serious learning problem. This is the sort of disingenuous and manipulative act that causes other students and faculty to question the validity of some learning disabilities (LD) attention deficit diagnoses and makes the lives of those struggling with disabilities like LD, ADD, and ADHD that much more difficult (Williams & Ceci, 1999).

This is certainly not to say that ADD and ADHD claims should be dismissed. To the contrary, the general constellation of behaviors that we in the United States have defined as ADHD are also evident in other cultural contexts, albeit there is great variability in terms of how children exhibiting such "behaviors are evaluated and managed" (Brewis, Schmidt, & Meyer, 2000, p. 826). It is a serious problem for those who experience it. However, the students in question use public exclamation of their condition to excuse extremely disruptive behavior. Having established that I am open to matters of accommodation by presenting the introductory statement, I feel on much more solid ground when dealing with these potentially gratuitous uses of very serious disabilities later in the course.

On a related point, making the introductory statement helps to establish a relationship of trust with students with disabilities. Many students harbor a well-founded fear that they will be treated differently in class if they reveal their disability to the professor. There are numerous pedagogical benefits to that sort of trust. For example, I challenge students constantly, asking them to take risks and stretch in order to learn. Without trust, that is difficult to achieve. Students think that I am picking on them. They invent reasons why I would select them in particular. For example, students with disabilities might think that it has something to do with their disability. The relationship of trust first forged by the initial statement and contact with the student facilitates this later work. I do not have to be overly concerned that students will think of my challenges as something related to their particular abilities or some perceived lack thereof.

The most interesting and unanticipated benefit of the statement, however, is the effect it has upon the general student population. As mentioned above, nearly all students demonstrate inordinate attention to the statement, regardless of whether or not they have a diagnosed disability. Part of this may be the nature of my performance. As I mentioned earlier, I indicate by verbal and physical cues that the statement is of special importance. However, I believe that it goes beyond that. I teach in a developmental education program. That means that students are often stigmatized by their placement in my classes. They often see it as punishment for past academic failures and, therefore, they view me as judge and jury. In short, they are wary of me.

The statement begins to chip away at the executioner's mask students project upon me. They interpret my statement concerning accommodation as an indication that I maintain a positive orientation toward student success in general. The statement thus sets a positive tone for the course and allows me to start establishing a relationship of trust with the class as a whole.

Accommodation and UID

The meaning of the accommodation statement goes beyond the fairly limited intent denoted in the words (i.e., to find reasonable accommodations for students with disabilities). The accommodation statement performance connotes deeper meanings, particularly in a developmental education setting. It reaches all students at some level, presaging, acknowledging, and speaking toward potential feelings of discrimination and resistance, while positively signifying the instructor's intent to make the course universally accessible and adaptable to students' needs and proclivities.

The outcomes of the three examples of accommodation described above may help illustrate the point. After changing my PowerPoint fonts, I was that much more aware of the need for clearer text and redundant methods for delivering essential information. Similarly, after being approached by the field study student, I reconstructed the field assignments so that the basic core of the experience could be accomplished regardless of physical abilities. Now those particular accommodations will no longer be necessary, because they have been built into the course. Just as the curb cut evolved from a disability-based accommodation to a design used for a range of access purposes, so too, these seemingly small course accommodations can accrete to produce more robust and accessible courses benefiting all students.

The same was true of the third case. The student taught me how to better teach others with his particular disability. I learned in practice what I had read in theory: that students with that particular condition need extra time. Instead of my typical, often frenetic teaching style, I began to develop a more sedate approach, to the benefit of all students. Particularly when dealing with students with the learning disability in question, I now sit, often silently, for long periods, and generally mirror their pace of communication, so that our conversation can produce meaningful results. Instead of simply expecting students to accommodate my own, often dysfunctional means and methods of communication, I reciprocate by adapting to and accommodating their communication and learning styles as well.

The difference between being slow, in the colloquial definition of the term (i.e., "slow" as in "lacking intelligence") and deliberate was made particularly clear to me in that case. The student in question produced perhaps the best work in the class, not despite his different mode of learning, thinking, and communicating, but because of it. He made me more aware of the problem many people like me have, that of going too fast. Although there can be conundrums involved (e.g., how does one teach courses where students in the same class require both faster and slower-paced communicational modes?), simply asking these difficult questions can lead to innovative and effective solutions.

Conclusions

As these fairly basic examples demonstrate, minor accommodations can lead to greater access for all students. In other words, accommodation is not necessarily a developmental step that needs to be surpassed in order to achieve the more lofty aims of UID. Rather, accommodation is part and parcel of the process of working toward what is ultimately an impossible goal: universal access. Just as considerations of accommodation gave rise to Universal Instructional Design in the field of Disability Studies, so too, careful attention to questions of accommodation by individual instructors may aid in the development of courses that respond better to a diverse range of students' proclivities and abilities.

Accommodation is the possible process that helps us continue working toward universal curricular access. In fact, accommodation is a prerequisite for teaching any student. We constantly ask students to adapt to our universe. In other words, we ask them to accommodate our way of communicating and thinking as teachers, and adapt to our instructional needs, interests, and idiosyncrasies. We must in turn learn to adapt to students' needs, interests, and desires, accommodating them so that effective learning can take place. Teaching always involves adaptation and accommodation. That process can begin with a simple statement.

References

Brewis, A., Schmidt, K. L., & Meyers, M. (2000). ADHD-type behavior and harmful dysfunction in childhood: A cross-cultural model. *American Anthropologist, 102,* 823-828.

Williams, W. M., & Ceci, S. J. (1999, August 6). Accommodating learning disabilities can bestow unfair advantages. *The Chronicle of Higher Education,* B4-B5.

CHAPTER 7

Practicing Universal Instructional Design in Visual Art Courses

Patricia James
University of Minnesota

Themina Kader
State University of New York at New Paltz

Abstract
Visual art courses challenge students to be attentive to visual cues, to make connections among diverse kinds of information, and to take creative risks. There are likely to be cognitive, emotional, and cultural factors that both hinder and enhance learning in art. Universal Instructional Design provides a valuable framework for teaching art in ways that are accessible and meaningful for all students. We explore issues related to disability and diversity in visual art and provide examples of art instruction that respond to students' diverse abilities and use this diversity as a vital resource for teaching and learning.

The open-ended, interpretive, and creative nature of the visual arts presents college students with challenges that may be different from other academic courses. Whether students are making, looking at, or learning to teach art, there are likely to be cultural, perceptual, cognitive, physical, emotional, and social factors that both hinder and enhance learning. Although there may be times in which it is necessary to work with specific disabilities on a case-by-case basis, it is most beneficial to anticipate individual student needs by designing whole-class instruction that explicitly addresses diverse abilities (Scott, McGuire, & Shaw, 2003). Universal Instructional Design (UID) provides a valuable framework for teaching artistic concepts and processes in ways that are accessible and meaningful for all students (James, 2000b).

Some art courses require students to have specific visual or physical abilities if they are going to be able to learn essential components of the course, such as drawing realistically or welding with a torch. It may be difficult for a person who is blind to perform certain tasks related to color, or for a person who has limited mobility to use tools that may prove to be potentially dangerous. In these cases, judgments may need to be made about whether the course is appropriate. It is important, however, to ask first if there are ways to approach these processes other than by traditional methods. Many organizations provide resources that expand our understanding of what people with disabilities are able to accomplish in the arts. For example, VSA Arts (2003-2006), in which the V stands for "Vision of an inclusive community," the S for "Strength through shared resources," and the A for "Artistic expression that unites us all", and the National Arts and Disabilities

Center (1998-2007), offer articles, directories, examples of successful programs for artists with disabilities, samples of artists' work, and educational materials that increase disability awareness, communication, and self-esteem in classrooms and communities. These resources show us that disability does not need to be thought about in terms of limitations; dyslexia, for example, has been shown to enhance visual and spatial skills (Arts Dyslexia Trust, n.d.).

In addition to technical skills, there are underlying concepts and processes that cut across many kinds of studio and non-studio art courses. For example, if students are learning to make, study, or teach art, they must be open minded about unfamiliar ideas and experiences. They also must be able to find visual and conceptual relationships between the parts and the whole and make connections among disparate ideas, and use their personal and cultural knowledge as resources. It is also important for students to be able to seek insight rather than make fast judgments, to deal with complexity and ambiguity, and to explore materials and ideas. In short, students need to be both perceptive and creative. Instead of assuming that students are already artistic—or not artistic, we have to ask the question: What are the essential artistic concepts and processes that students need to understand, and how can we teach them in ways that make sense to all students? It is equally important to ask: How can we use students' knowledge and abilities as catalysts to a richer art experience for all students?

In this chapter, we provide examples of art instruction that use principles of Universal Instructional Design to respond to students' diversity, and which use that diversity as a vital resource for teaching and learning (Barajas & Higbee, 2003). We sketch some of the hidden disabilities that become evident in art classes and explore UID principles that help students understand art. We then describe assignments from two courses: an art education course for upper-level students majoring in elementary education, taught by Themina Kader, and a general education art course for first-year students, taught by Pat James. Our goal is to suggest multiple ways to make the arts accessible for many kinds of students.

Encountering Difficulties in the Arts

Perhaps the most common challenge in learning art at the college level—particularly for students who are not majoring in art—centers around creative thinking, which can be defined as a "meaningful response to any situation which calls for finding a problem and solving it in one's own way" (Wakefield, 1992, p. 13). Creative thinking in the arts includes adapting established artistic concepts and techniques to suit one's own expressive needs and engaging in open-ended interpretation of artwork. These processes, however, can be problematic for many students. Although we often think of creativity in relationship to "talent" or to childhood play, adult students can learn strategies and dispositions that promote creative thinking.

In this section, we describe some of the hidden problems, or "blocks" (Cropley, 1992; Hallman, 1987; James, 1999-2000; Jones, 1993), that often occur when college students learn to make, study, or teach art. "Block" is a useful metaphor for what happens when students are confused, conflicted, or withdrawn when doing assignments. Some blocks are "enduring personality characteristics and long term cultural influences," and others are "of a more temporary nature or related to specific current circumstances" (Jones, p. 41). These hidden barriers, which are sometimes dismissed as lack of imagination—or even stupidity—often mask students' potential for creative thinking and may manifest themselves in stubbornness and resistance. Such blocks can result in work that is clichéd, poorly designed, badly crafted, or conceptually shallow.

Creative blocks can be thought about in terms of four categories: (a) cultural, (b) conceptual and perceptual, (c) emotional and personal, and (d) social. Although the blocks described in this chapter may not constitute a disability, they can seriously affect learning. The goal here is not to analyze how the blocks developed, but to highlight some of the factors that often inhibit students' thinking and performance in art classes and to offer strategies that help students become "unblocked." We include samples of students' quotes to illustrate how these problems affected their performance. Many of the quotes were obtained from first-year students' reflective writing as part of James' (1999-2000, 2000c, 2000c); ongoing qualitative study of a general education art course; others were gathered through conversations and students' evaluative writing in Kader's art education classes.

Culture

Cultural beliefs shape students' willingness or ability to understand artistic concepts and processes and inform students' understandings of the meaning and worth of their own and others' work. Art classrooms include students from diverse cultural backgrounds who hold varying values and beliefs about learning, art, creativity, and other people. These beliefs are shaped by factors such as ethnicity, gender, religion, sexual orientation, and ability, as well as by popular culture and schooling. For example, a commonly held belief that school is supposed to be practical, factual, and certain often makes it difficult for students to think creatively. As a first-year student who was struggling with creative thinking wrote: "most of my schooling and jobs require logical thinking." Many students dismiss what they are learning in art classes because they have been taught that mathematics, logic, and linear thinking are marks of intelligence, but emotions, senses, and imagination are inadequate or inferior ways of knowing.

Students' beliefs about the origins of creativity and who can be creative also hamper their learning. Many students believe that only naturally talented people can be artists or that creativity originates from "inspiration," not hard work. The first-year student who wrote, "creativity comes up and hits you in the face" believed that something was wrong with him because nothing creative happened right away. When students understand that creativity is an evolutionary process usually based on hard work, not sheer inspiration, they become more free to experiment.

Students' beliefs about art also can affect how they learn. Many students believe that art should maintain their cultural traditions and make them feel good, and they resist thinking about art that is different from what they expected. As one first-year student wrote:

"I like it kind of simple and kind of pretty—not too bizarre. Just simple and homey." Students often experience discomfort with the ambiguous nature of art and have a difficult time understanding—or even looking at—art that unsettles them, calls into question their social values and norms, or reveals painful emotions and human conditions.

In addition, beliefs about factors such as race, ethnicity, gender, class, and religion can make it difficult for students to think about works of art that were created by people who are culturally different from them. Narrow beliefs may prevent students from learning from other people and make it difficult for others to feel safe expressing their own experiences. Students' beliefs also inhibit students from critically examining their own culture and social positions. For example, when seeing slides in an art education course, students thought that the use of henna as a medium to make patterns on the palms of a Muslim girl's hands was "gross." They were unable to think about body art within a larger context; yet in their personal lives, permanent tattoos are often considered not only acceptable but also desirable.

One strategy that helps students understand and broaden their knowledge of other peoples' experiences and dispels stereotypes is to give an assignment that asks them to appreciate and critique their own cultural backgrounds. In some cases, students from a dominant culture are offended when asked about their ancestry; "I am an American" may be their assertive response. Acknowledging that a Caucasian American can trace ancestry to a country in Europe marks a shift in the way students begin to relate to the concept of multiculturalism and diversity. A name game during the first week of the class is an effective way for all students to think about their own ancestry. In this activity, students freewrite about the origins and meaning of their first and last names. Students and teachers then talk about the origins of their names and the effects their names have on how others perceive them. This helps students to see the range of cultures in the class and to know something personal about each individual. The activity also informs students' assignments over the rest of the semester (James, Jehangir, & Bruch, 2006).

Another way to expand students' cultural beliefs is to provide artistic examples from diverse cultures as well as art that deals explicitly with multicultural issues. This practice helps students expand their repertoire of approaches to art at the same time that they confront their own beliefs. After viewing a video by a challenging contemporary Mexican performance artist, for example, a first-year student wrote, "I realized that yes, I do have prejudices—but I never thought of myself as a racist before. I guess I am, yet." Multicultural examples of artists representing African American, Asian American, Native American, and other cultures are available in hundreds of DVDs, books, and Web sites. These resources provide the historical, geographical, social, spiritual, political, and economic knowledge students need to make art germane to the students' own culture. It is also valuable to show the work of artists with disabilities. For example, Chuck Close, a painter who has dyslexia and is a quadriplegic (Marmor, 1997), and Elizabeth Layton (Lambert, 1995), who used drawing to heal depression, are excellent models of artists with disabilities who use art to express their thinking and to heal.

When working with multiculturalism in the arts, however, it is important not to duplicate superficial characteristics of style. Conflicted cultural beliefs are often evident in art education courses in which students are training to become teachers. Many students are willing to "try out diversity" by using the superficial markers of a culture, but they have difficulty working with the deeper aspects of belief and practice. They declare their love for teaching multicultural art but approach it on a superficial level. For example, an art education student planned to introduce a unit on Egyptian art by having fourth grade students make mummies in the shape of American children out of plaster and bandages. She was excited that students could take their mummies home to show their parents. This student was unwilling, however, to examine the relationship of mummies to the funerary practice of ancient Egypt or to examine funeral practices in her own culture. She thought it would upset the children if she talked about death, and parents might complain.

The goal in working with cultural diversity should not be to create a lesson "making our own African masks" out of paper and other recyclable material or "our own Navaho sand painting" using sand or powder tempera paint. Instead, assignments should help students understand and appreciate the ideals of authenticity, reverence, and celebration that are at the core of many traditional cultures. It is also important for students to understand the social and historical factors that inform multicultural art. One way to do that is to find relationships between traditional artifacts and the artifacts of contemporary culture. For example, art education students doing a mask project expressed relief when they found out they would be taking a contemporary approach to mask-making rather than making copies of African masks, which they knew about only through seeing a video. Instead, they studied masks used in make-up, sports, and various professions to understand the psychology, practice, and metaphoric meanings of masks in their own culture. By making explicit connections between the arts and other subjects such as sociology and history, students can ground their images and interpretations in facts and well-developed theories rather than myths and stereotypes.

Perception and Concepts

Many students experience "a mental set or predisposition toward seeing the situation in a certain way, no matter how closely or thoroughly we look at it" (Simberg, 1987). Although some students have physical disabilities related to vision, many with good vision experience problems discriminating colors, shapes, and formal qualities. They can see the image or object, but they have trouble identifying nuances and attending to formal relationships. In other words, they see what they want to see rather than what is actually there. This lack of perception affects how students think about their own and others' artwork. For example, a first-year student who was very frustrated with his own work wrote: "I look at something and say 'it sucks' and don't look [at] why it sucks." In many cases, students automatically judge their work before examining qualities in the work itself: "Sometimes I ... do not focus on the specific problem."

Students need to learn how to think critically about art. By designing developmental assignments that explicitly help students attend to visual information, analyze relationships within a composition, and make interpretive connections to ideas, experiences, and emotions, students are able to slow down and really see and think about artistic images and objects. There are many ways to teach art criticism; in the most basic model, students systematically learn to describe, analyze, interpret, and evaluate art (Cromer, 1990). An important aspect of interpretation is metaphor, but many students are not accustomed to interpreting visual metaphors. The book *Reading Images: Meaning and Metaphor* (Feinstein, 1996) suggests using cognitive mapping to help students make connections between form and idea. In *Metaphorical Ways of Knowing: The Imaginative Nature of Thought and Expression* (Pugh, Hicks, & Davis, 1997), the authors provide theory and various exercises that promote metaphorical thinking.

In addition to critical skills, it is important that students develop strategies, confidence, and appreciation for creativity. Creative processes are often messy, ambiguous, and unpredictable; many students, however, prefer certainty, closure, and obvious meanings. As one student wrote: "I like things to be in control." Other students, such as a student who wrote, "Why does everything have to have meaning?" retreat when they are asked to think metaphorically, conceptually, and critically rather than in literal and fixed ways. As another first-year student wrote: "I felt confusion about the abstractness of it all." Students often struggle when they try to go beyond received information and imagine alternatives. For example, a student who wrote, "I can't do it—I don't think that way!" did not know how to play with ideas or experiment with materials, so she stopped working until she was helped to see possibilities in what she had already done.

There are many strategies that can help students go beyond their own preconceived creative limits. For example, technical, formal, conceptual assignment guidelines inform students what to work toward and offer them enough flexibility to go in directions that are relevant to their own expressive needs. Exercises and assignments that use a variety of modes of representation, including verbal, aural, visual, and kinesthetic, enable students to learn in ways that make sense to them and expand their repertoire of modes of representation. A performance assignment in James' class, for example, asks students to engage in expressive movement, spoken word performances, small group creativity exercises, reflective writing, drawing, and listening to poetry and music before they begin their final project.

Readings and group discussions also provide opportunities for students to learn more about creative processes. Although written primarily for a business audience, books such as *A Whack on the Side of the Head* (von Oech, 1998) or *The Creative Spirit* (Goleman, Kaufman, & Ray, 1993) help students better understand the factors that inhibit creativity. *Art Synectics: Stimulating Creativity in Art* (Roukes, 1982) offers many suggestions for developing visual creativity. By learning a repertoire of strategies, including brainstorming, thinking metaphorically, experimenting with materials and ideas, producing thumbnail sketches, researching ideas and techniques, and thinking divergently, students can become self-directed in their creative work (Eisner, 1998). Over time, students become more willing and able to imagine new possibilities.

Taking creative risks is, perhaps, the single most frightening learning strategy a student encounters in art. In a group activity creating installation art, for example, an art education student said he had never heard of installations and expressed fear about how he would contribute to this assignment. Once he jumped into the assignment, however, the work itself provided feedback and direction, and the student became more comfortable exploring the unknown. After he had worked with other students creating the installation, this student beamed with smiles. He had not expected the assignment to be such fun, and he looked forward to adapting it to his sixth grade class during his field experience.

As they work, students transform materials, ideas, and forms to create something that has never existed before (James, 2000c). To promote creativity, teachers themselves have to be willing to model risk-taking and vulnerability and to value the diverse products that students develop. It is especially important to help students to understand the unpredictability of creativity and to recognize and interpret emerging information in their own work.

Emotions and Personal Experiences

Although art is often thought to be a means for emotional understanding and expression, many students have a difficult time identifying, understanding, and expressing emotions (Chickering & Reisser, 1993). Parker Palmer (1999) argued that the educational system of this country may work against students' ability to deal with emotions because it forces students to live out of the top inch and a half of the human self; to live exclusively through cognitive rationality and the powers of the intellect; to live out of touch with anything that lay below that top inch and a half—body, intuition, feeling, emotion, relationship (p. 17).

Emotional blocks in art often "result from desensitization to our own and to other people's feelings. The psyche, as a means of self-protection from pain or overwhelming emotion, simply blocks the mechanism of feeling; difficult feelings are 'forgotten'" (Downing, 1997, p. 22). When students are not able to recognize or understand their own emotions, they often have difficulty accepting their own ideas and trusting their artistic images and interpretations. They also have problems accessing their "aesthetic sensibility," which is "an intuitive mode of sensing, feeling, judging, organizing [that] transcends expertise" (Dudek & Côté, 1994, p. 144).

Many students experience negative emotions in relationship to art because they think that their difficulties are a reflection of their own intelligence and personality. The student who wrote, "I don't have an ounce of creativity in me" believed that she was incapable of making or understanding art. Many students anticipate failure: "I really don't like mine at all, and I have a feeling I won't like it at the end. I think mine is going to be a disaster." Other students become overwhelmed when they try to represent themselves through art:

> The process … was long and grueling. I had to come up with what I wanted to say, how I wanted to say it, envision it, and then do it. It was not always as simple as that though. I became so distraught and I even wanted to give up.

Another student wrote, "I am so lost until I want to scream. It's like I know what to say, but I have a memory block."

Poor physical or emotional health, chemical or alcohol abuse, or personal crisis also affect students' ability to think creatively. As one student wrote, "The demon of depression is trying to constantly pull me down." Other students are coping with multiple responsibilities, including children, family obligations, and jobs, as exemplified by the first-year student who wrote: "I had a lot of things going on in my life both personally and culturally and I think it was affecting everything else too much."

To help students gain confidence and a sense of purpose, and to address cultural and personal diversity, it is valuable to design assignments and classroom environments in which students use their own ways of making sense of the world. By helping students validate, articulate, and understand the structure of their own knowledge, they "have the feeling of being on familiar ground, already knowing much about how to know, how knowledge is organized and integrated" (Bateson, 1994, pp. 205-206). Reflective assignments help students understand, express, and value their own knowledge. Ongoing reflection, whether through writing or discussions, helps students to make meaningful connections between what they are learning and their own lives, to critique their learning difficulties and strengths. Reflection also promotes transfer between the arts and other educational situations (Perkins, 1994).

Full participation is more likely when students think that what they are doing is authentic, self-expressive, and relevant. Part of the challenge of creative thinking is making use of available resources. Many students find that using their own abilities and limitations as part of the content of the work helps them create work that is distinctive and meaningful. For example, two older women in James' art course were challenged by social phobia, agoraphobia, and obesity. Performing in front other people was very frightening to them, but they became more comfortable over time by engaging in informal movement exercises with the younger students. At the end of the semester, every student had to create a live multimedia performance. To cope with the assignment at the same time that they coped with their disabilities, the two women students devised a way to do a very humorous performance behind a screen that hid them from the audience. As raucous music played on a CD player, the two women threw clothing over the edge of the screen as if they were doing a strip tease. The women enjoyed themselves, and the younger students learned a valuable lesson about coping with disability.

Social Climate

Learning is not only an individual endeavor; it is also shaped by social interactions and inter-subjectivity (Bruner, 1986). Art is often thought to be a solitary individual process, in which artists work alone in their studios without the influence of other people. In reality, however, art is enriched by multiple voices. Social interactions add diverse possibilities to the study of art, but they also can hinder student involvement. Students in art classes are often asked to expose thoughts and feelings publicly through their work, but concern about other people can make it difficult for students to think effectively. Many young adults have a need to conform to social norms: "I don't like appearing stupid in front of others and I often find myself wondering 'what will others think?'" Other students worry that their peers will perceive them as strange or different: "I am often unable to create because I am scared of what others will think of my work."

Even if they are not directed at a specific person, classmates' comments can create an inhibiting environment for students who perceive themselves as different from others. During a discussion of Keith Haring's works, for example, one art education student talked forcefully about her beliefs about homosexuality. She said she would never touch on such a subject in high schools because she believed that high school students were innocent and should not be exposed to such "weird" behaviors.

In addition to judging others, students frequently judge themselves by how well they think their work stands up to that of their peers. The student who wrote, "I want to do something that makes people say 'wow!'" ended up doing mediocre work because she could not settle on an idea that would fulfill her expectations. Others become stuck when they compare themselves negatively to other students. For example, a student who did not want others to see what she was working on wrote,

> I have no idea. I was like "duh." The class wasn't productive at all. I was ashamed … 'cause I didn't know what everybody else's was like. And being since I haven't had very much work with art, I had no idea. Some of these people in here are so creative. And I'm not.

Students' interactions with instructors also can inhibit learning. As authority figures, instructors' comments have consequences that go far beyond their intended effect. Many students seek approval for each move they make; they have difficulty acting independently and want the instructor to be directive: "I was basically looking for [the instructor] to tell me if it was good or not." A student who believed that the instructor was judging him wrote, "[The teacher] said it was constructive criticism, but it still hurts." Students often become confused and resistant if they interpret the instructor's feedback as commands rather than suggestions. Even constructive suggestions can have deleterious effects, as in the case of the student who wrote: "[The instructor's] input just made me not want to put it together. Maybe if she would have said, 'oh, that looks nice,' maybe I would have proceeded more with it."

To help students work with their social fears and to use the social diversity of the class as a source of meaning in the class, it is important to construct a welcoming classroom community. A shared sense of purpose and mutual growth enables students to deepen their understanding of artistic concepts and to take artistic risks. By working together, students learn to negotiate similarities and differences among their peers and establish close bonds. An intentional community promotes students' diverse voices and helps them engage in meaningful dialogue with people who are different from themselves (Jehangir,

2003). In the process, students build a shared sense of excitement about making and exploring works of art. Cultural, personal, conceptual, and social blocks can be dealt with as a community rather than only on an individual basis.

One way to construct a supportive social climate is to alternate among individual, partnered, small group, and all-class levels of involvement. Class participation is an intimidating process for many students, so multiple levels of participation can create bridges for students to feel confident in their own ideas and to risk sharing their ideas with classmates. By working in small groups, students articulate their own points of view, hear diverse perspectives, and help each other learn difficult concepts. For example, after studying a painting with a partner, a student wrote:

It was very interesting that people could come up with two totally different things from looking at the same picture. It shows that art can be looked at in very different ways and it depends a lot on where a person grew up or what their heritage is.

A student in a pre-service art education class observed: "When we brainstormed how we would team teach a lesson on tessellations, it really helped to gel our ideas together. Like some things I wouldn't have thought of on my own." Working with others on matrices and cognitive maps helps students put order to their multiple perspectives. Students can also collaborate on projects such as public sculpture, installation art, and murals.

Classroom Examples

The best way to explain UID strategies and conditions for teaching art is to describe how they have been enacted in two very different art courses. Kader describes a systematic exercise in which elementary education students learn to go beyond their previous knowledge about color theory to think about color in new and more individualized ways. James describes an assignment in a general education art course for first-year students in a multicultural program, few of whom plan to become art majors. In this assignment, students go through a series of developmental exercises to learn to create photomontages.

Learning Color With Themina Kader

It is increasingly common for elementary education majors to be asked to practice interdisciplinarity in their teaching. ART 355: "Teaching of Art" is a required course in which future teachers learn basic artistic concepts and techniques. To succeed in the course, college students must overcome their own blocks about art and creativity at the same time that they learn how to teach art to elementary school children. Students who enroll in this course have varied levels of exposure to, ability in, motivation for, and fear of art in general. Typical comments are, "the last time I did art was in grade school," or, "I like art and I'm really looking forward to this course," or "I can't draw, but I like making crafty things." I reassure students that drawing is but one facet of a multi-layered course, and that keeping an open mind and not worrying too much about grades are ingredients in the recipe for success.

On the first day of class, I ask students three questions:

1. What is art?
2. Who is afraid of art?
3. Why are you afraid of art?

As they answer the questions, students articulate different opinions about art, and some even give definitions. The responses to the second question, however, reveal some deep-seated fears related to getting an A, which seems unattainable to students if they believe they are not talented and cannot draw. For most non-art majors, talent and drawing are synonymous, and the latter is a by-product of the former. Traumas resulting from bad teaching practices in the art room when they were children, and preconceived notions of what and how many assignments they will have to turn in all contribute to the trepidation with which Art 355 is perceived. Fortunately, the variety of activities outlined in the syllabus and the very large T-shirt that I wear alleviate some of their concerns. The class bursts into laughter when they read "FEAR NO ART" on my T-shirt (Figure 1).

To give every student an equal opportunity, I start the first activity of this course with exercises in understanding and applying the elements and principles of art. I use a still life with various fruits to teach about one element—color. My unorthodox approach seems like heresy to some students who have seen very slick laminated posters of the color wheel in schools and remember constructing color wheels themselves when they were in Grade 4. After I remind them to "fear no art," students get started. To help focus students' thinking, I arrange the tables in a semi-circle, and each student receives a palette with five colors—red, yellow, blue, black, and white; a container of water; three brushes—wide, medium, and small; and six pieces of 10 x 12 inch paper. Students are not allowed to use a pencil, an eraser, or a ruler. Around the room on the bulletin boards are posters showing several representations of still life in color and in black and white. In front of the semi-circle is a low table on which I arrange a large, tall bottle and some fruits—a pineapple, two bananas, and a cantaloupe.

By systematically walking students through the exercises, I relieve them of unnecessary but real stress. Regardless of their abilities, all students have a common starting point. Their individual predilections and abilities manifest themselves in the final product. On Paper #1, students use the large brush and one primary color to draw an outline of the object that is closest to them. Referring to an example of a still life on the bulletin board, I encourage students to fill the space on the paper. On Paper #2, students draw the same object again with the second primary color. They repeat the process on Paper #3 using the third primary color. Students wash and clean their brushes after painting with each primary color. They discover that if a brush has the residue of a color used previously, it adulterates a pure primary color. Later on in the exercise, one color mixing into another becomes a boon.

On Paper #4, students draw the same object with the mixture of any two of the three primary colors, which gives them a secondary color; the addition of black gives a shade

Figure 1. Themina Kader in her FEAR NO ART t-shirt

of the color. On Paper #5, students repeat the process, but instead of using black they use white, which introduces them to tints. On the last piece of paper, students draw the same object with a full palette. At this stage, they can experiment with any color combination they wish. They also add a background color that helps them experience the concepts of contrast and harmony of colors.

By the time they introduce the neutral black and white paint, hands are raised to ask, "Can I use textures? Is it OK to draw more than one fruit? What about the bottle? I like it. Can I put that next to the pineapple?" Hesitance, timidity, puckered brows, and groans because a blob of paint goes where it should not have are replaced by smiles and "oh, I like this, this is so much fun, kids would love to do this." The progression from primary to secondary colors and a full-palette picture as the finale convinces students that what they have drawn is not a "photo-realistic" rendition of objects, but a picture that shows a highly personal use of color that reflects their individual personalities.

This approach has a Universal Instructional Design appeal. It frees students from laboriously copying a laminated color wheel, which is a standard method for teaching color. In the age of Adobe Photoshop and the zillion colors that one can get at the click of a mouse, this physical approach to teaching about color provides immense satisfaction to all students because they can mix colors as they like, without having to agonize over whether they have the correct measure of white, black, or any other combination of colors. And everyone's picture looks different!

Traditionally, elementary education students are asked to draw a geometrically accurate color wheel that has to be divided into a specific number of shapes to accommodate the three primary colors, their secondary colors, the opposite complementary colors, and the analogous colors. To add to the stress level, students also have to grapple with the exact quantity of each color to obtain the "exact" intensity of shades and tints. In my class, however, by not being able to use a pencil and an eraser, students are forced to concentrate on the objective of the lesson—colors—and how to see and use them. Furthermore, it places those students who have a natural flair for drawing but do not like "messing with paints" at the same level as those who think they cannot draw, because the lesson is about colors, color mixing, and color combinations. I overheard one student say to his neighbor, "I would never have thought of using blue to paint a pineapple."

Students complete the exercise in the time allotted—1 hour and 15 minutes. They display their work on the bulletin board and revel in their accomplishment. Students can see each other's work and believe that they should "FEAR NO ART." This lesson is successful because it offers every student, if not completely unsighted, an equal opportunity to learn color and practice creative thinking. It also models ways to introduce Universal Instructional Design in elementary classrooms.

Learning Creative and Metaphoric Thinking With Pat James

In the first major assignment in "Creativity Art Lab: Experiences in the Media," I ask my first-year students to make two photomontages by cutting out pictures from magazines and then altering, juxtaposing, and organizing them into coherent and meaningful compositions that relate to their own lives. One should be a metaphoric self-portrait and the other a portrait of their family or ancestors. Because photomontages often undermine logical, literal, and so-called normal ways of seeing and thinking (Ades, 1976), students have to draw on their imagination, emotions, and personal and cultural knowledge in ways that may, at first, seem strange to them.

Before students begin this assignment, they do several ungraded activities that offer practice in looking carefully at art and thinking metaphorically and creatively. First, I ask students to do "I am" writing by choosing one portrait from among dozens of prints and then free-writing three paragraphs: (a) as if they are inside a work of art; (b) as if they are an object in the painting, such as a chair, an eye, or the sky; and (c) how they are similar to the person in the painting (James, 2000a).

By doing expressive writing about a work of visual art, students make immediate connections between the artwork and their own thoughts and feelings, and they spend extended time looking at qualities in the image itself. Students who are particularly verbal practice visual thinking, and visual thinkers practice translating visual information into verbal language. This expressive writing helps students understand the metaphoric nature of art, promotes open-ended empathy with the work rather than judgmental closure, and helps students concentrate on their own perceptions before sharing their ideas with other students. Introverted students make their ideas concrete before they talk with other students, and extroverted students slow down and identify their own perceptions before engaging socially.

The "I am" writing also helps students articulate emotions and cultural knowledge they may never have put into words. For example, a male African American student chose a portrait of an African American woman. He wrote:

> I am a young woman with a tired soul. With memories of the olden days lingering in my mind. All the struggles my life has endured has aged my brown skin, and exercised my soul. Able to instill fear in anyone walking, for I am wise and strong. I hear the troubles rapping at the doorstep of the next generation while they are fast asleep. I have done my part to take this family where it needs to be, but I can carry them no longer. My breath is harder to come by but sounds of golden harps come nearer. My tired soul will have happiness one day.

In the paragraph in which he wrote about how he, personally, was similar to the woman in the painting, this student wrote:

> Our souls deeper than anyone of our age, our life experiences held tightly between our soul and the heart. Not allowing anyone to see to pain, discomfort, and trials of our lives, we stand as an image of strength. Happy to have touched one life everyday with a warm thought, hug, or smile forgetting our problems to help someone with theirs. Often feeling weak or too much pressure to go on but never giving up or

> letting anyone know about us. Inside our eyes lay a story that can break the strongest man and soften the hardest heart!

After individual writing, students read their paragraphs to a partner. Working one-on-one promotes empathy with a classmate and helps students understand that their thoughts and feelings are not unique or wrong. Reflecting with a partner about what it was like to do this activity helps students better understand their own thinking processes and hear other approaches. We also reflect about the activity as a class.

Second, I show a variety of self-portrait slides by established artists so that students can learn how to analyze art and see diverse ways to express oneself artistically, including expressionism, realism, surrealism, and conceptualism. We stop for a longer time on one slide and students write and discuss a list of 10 things they observe. Hearing students describe what they see is a way for students with vision impairments to know what is in the work and for all students to pay close attention to visual information. Then students write and share individual "I am" statements about the work. Third, to help students see themselves as capable of producing images about their own experiences, I show a number of photomontages that were created in my previous classes by students with similar backgrounds. These examples exemplify the qualities that I will evaluate, including effective design, good craftsmanship, and meaningfulness. Fourth, students try out ideas in a small, ungraded practice photomontage, which takes about 40 minutes. When we pin their practice photomontages on the board and talk about them, students are able to observe multiple approaches to the assignment.

When I hand out the written photomontage assignment, students learn that it includes specific constraints as well as opportunities for individual approaches. The constraints serve as a kind of fence within which students can organize their thinking; students may "jump over" the constraints, but they have to justify their decision to do so (James, 2000c). One constraint is size: because students will be color photocopying their finished photomontages, they must work on paper that fits into photocopy machines. The second constraint is subject matter: students have to do two portraits that include some part of a person. One is to be a self-portrait, and the other should be about their ancestors, which they may interpret as their actual family or their broader cultural heritage.

Students spend two class sessions and time outside of class working on their two photomontages. As they work in class, I give individual students feedback, but I also address the whole class about problems and successes that I see emerging in their work. On the day the photomontages are due, students write "I am" paragraphs about one of their own images. They read their writing to each other and compare interpretations. After they hang their work on the bulletin board, students stand up to read their paragraph to the whole class. By this time in the semester, shy students have practiced reading out loud and now feel relatively comfortable in front of their peers.

Figure 2. Untitled self-portrait photomontage by a Hmong American student

It is always exciting to see students' photomontages hanging together on the bulletin board. Although the images fit within the size and subject constraints, students have taken many different approaches to their work. Some are social critiques, others are images of their family's journey from their home country to the U.S., and others are deeply personal images about their emotions. Students who thought they would never be able to create anything meaningful find that they have touched other students with their art work. In addition, students learn about each others' experiences and cultures. In Figure 2, for example, a Hmong student made a mysterious photomontage about spirituality. Her "I am" writing about the masked young woman in the bottom left corner reveals multiple levels of meaning:

It's dark and I am afraid. I am praying and lighting this incense to help me get rid of this bad spirit. I feel sucked through another world of bad thoughts, bad images. But I see a light glowing near by. I try to reach for it, but that figure seems to be stronger than I. I try to fight back, but I can feel it in me.

Conclusion

All students benefit when teachers use UID principles to address their diverse knowledge and abilities. By engaging in the activities in our classes, students gain confidence thinking about art in their preferred learning style, but they also practice approaches that may be uncomfortable for them and stretch their repertoire of ways to learn. Students who prefer an open-ended approach to learning are able to construct multiple ways of thinking about one thing, but they also practice making lists, mapping, and other ways to structure their thinking. In learning color theory, for example, they go beyond their habituated mode of learning to experiment with color. Students who prefer structure have opportunities to work in organized ways, but they also experience open-ended expression and interpretations. In addition, students of different cultures have contributed alternative ways of creating and thinking about works of art. By keeping the principles of Universal Instructional Design in mind as we teach, we use multiple approaches to enhance students' diverse abilities. Equally important, students' diversity adds complexity and richness to their learning about art.

References

Ades, D. (1976). *Photomontage.* New York: Pantheon Books.

Arts Dyslexia Trust. (n.d.). *Arts Dyslexia Trust Internet Service.* Retrieved March 31, 2007, from http://legacy.rmplc.co.uk/orgs/nellalex

Barajas, H. L., & Higbee, J. L. (2003). Where do we go from here? Universal Design as a model for multicultural education. In J. L. Higbee (Ed.), *Curriculum transformation and disability: Implementing Universal Design in higher education* (pp. 285-292). Minneapolis: University of Minnesota, General College, Center for Research on Developmental Education and Urban Literacy.

Bateson, M. C. (1994). *Peripheral visions: Learning along the way.* New York: Harper Collins.

Bruner, J. (1986). *Actual minds, possible worlds.* Cambridge, MA: Harvard University Press.

Chickering, A. W., & Reisser, L. (1993). *Education and identity* (rev. ed.). San Francisco:

Jossey-Bass.

Cromer, J. (1990). *History, theory and practice of art criticism in art education.* Reston, VA: National Art Education Association.

Cropley, A. (1992). *More ways than one: Fostering creativity.* Norwood, NJ: Ablex.

Downing, J. P. (1997). *Creative teaching: Ideas to boost student interest.* Englewood, CO: Teacher Ideas Press.

Dudek, S. Z., & Côté, R. (1994). *Problem finding revisited. In M. A. Runco (Ed.), Problem finding, problem solving, and creativity* (pp. 130-150). Norwood, NJ: Ablex.

Eisner, E. W. (1998). Does experience in the arts boost academic achievement? *Art Education, 51*(1), 7-15.

Feinstein, H. (1996). *Reading images: Meaning and metaphor.* Reston, VA: The National Art Education Association.

Goleman, D., Kaufman, P., & Ray, M. (1993). *The creative spirit.* New York: Plume.

Hallman, R. J. (1987). Techniques of creative thinking. In G. A. Davis & J. S. Scott (Eds.), *Training creative thinking* (pp. 220-224). New York: Holt, Rinehart & Winston.

James, P. (1999-2000). Blocks and bridges: Learning artistic creativity. *Arts and Learning Research Journal, 16*(1), 110-133.

James, P. (2000a). "I am the dark forest:" Personal analogy as a way to understand metaphor. *Art Education, 53*(5), 6-11.

James, P. (2000b). Practicing the principles of UID in an art course. In J. A. Fox & D. Johnson (Eds.), *Curriculum transformation and disability workshop facilitators' guide* (pp. 88-90). Minneapolis: University of Minnesota, Curriculum Transformation and Disability, Retrieved June 18, 2007 from http://www.gen.umn.edu/research/ctad

James, P. (2000c). Working toward meaning: The evolution of an assignment. *Studies in Art Education, 41*(2), 146-163.

James, P., Jehangir, R., & Bruch. P. (2006). Building bridges: Communities, identities, and agency in a multicultural learning community. *Journal of Developmental Education, 29*(3), 10-19.

Jehangir, R. R. (2003). Charting new courses: Learning communities and Universal Design, In J. L. Higbee (Ed.), *Curriculum transformation and disability: Implementing Universal Design in higher education* (pp. 79-92). Minneapolis: University of Minnesota, General College, Center for Research on Developmental Education and Urban Literacy.

Jones, L. (1993). Barriers to creativity and their relationship to individual, group, and organizational behavior. In S. G. Isaksen, M. C. Murdock, R. L. Firestien, & D. J. Treffinger (Eds.) *Nurturing and developing creativity: The emergence of a discipline* (pp. 133-154). Norwood, NJ: Ablex.

Lambert, D. (1995). *The life and art of Elizabeth "Grandma" Layton.* Waco, TX: WRS.

Marmor, J. (1997). *Close call.* Retrieved November 17, 2006, from http://www.washington.edu/alumni/columns/june97/close1.html

National Arts and Disability Center. (2006). *Home page.* Retrieved April 5, 2007, from http://nadc.ucla.edu

Palmer, P. (1999). The grace of great things: Reclaiming the sacred in knowing, teaching, and learning. In S. Glazer (Ed.), *The heart of learning: Spirituality in education* (p. 17). New York: Jeremy P. Tarcher.

Perkins, D. (1994). *The intelligent eye: Learning to think by looking at art.* Santa Monica. CA: The Getty Center of Education in the Arts.

Pugh, S. L., Hicks, J. W., & Davis, M. (1997). *Metaphorical ways of knowing: The imaginative nature of thought and expression.* Urbana, IL: National Council for Teachers of English.

Roukes, N. (1982). *Art synectics: Stimulating creativity in art.* Worcester, MA: Davis.

Scott, S. S., McGuire, J. M., & Shaw, S. F. (2003). Universal Design for adult instruction in postsecondary education. *Remedial and Special Education, 24,* 369-379.

Simberg, A. L. (1987). Obstacles to creative thinking. In G. A. Davis & J. K. S. Scott (Eds.), *Training creative thinking* (pp. 19-135). New York: Holt, Rinehart, & Winston.

von Oech, R. (1998). *A whack on the side of the head.* New York: Warner Business Books.

VSA Arts (2003-2006). *VSA arts' disability awareness guide.* Retrieved November 19, 2006, from http://www.vsarts.org

Wakefield, J. F. (1992). *Creative thinking: Problem-solving and the arts orientation.* Norwood, NJ: Ablex.

CHAPTER 8

Universal Instructional Design in a Legal Studies Classroom

Karen L. Miksch
University of Minnesota

Abstract
This chapter is reprinted verbatim from Curriculum Transformation and Disability: Implementing Universal Design in Higher Education, *and was originally published in 2003. This chapter was generated after the author attended the Curriculum Transformation and Disability (CTAD) workshop and implemented Universal Instructional Design (UID) principles in her Law in Society course. The chapter begins by describing an accessible Web page. The author then discusses the use of mock trials in which students can play a variety of roles that fit their individual learning styles. The chapter concludes with a discussion of how to broaden course and student service content to include disability rights.*

I had the opportunity to attend the first Curriculum Transformation and Disability (CTAD) workshop in January 2000. It helped me to reflect on how I could make my courses and services more accessible. I teach legal studies classes to first and second year undergraduate students in a developmental education program. I also act as a pre-law advisor. This chapter was generated from my experiences implementing Universal Instructional Design (UID) in my courses and advising.

Designing a course and pre-law Web page was my first step in implementing a "learning support" and will be discussed in the initial section of this chapter. I will then discuss how I redesigned my participation assessment and how I utilize mock trials so that students can play a variety of roles that fit their individual learning styles. The chapter concludes with a discussion of how to broaden course and student service content to include disability rights.

Designing and Incorporating a Web Page to Provide a UID Learning Support

After attending the CTAD training, I decided that I wanted to create a universally designed course Web page (Miksch, 2001). In order to create an accessible Web page I first went to the Bobby Web site. Bobby is a free service provided by the Center for Applied Special Technology (CAST, 2001) to help Web page authors identify and repair significant barriers to access by individuals with disabilities. Bobby will run a diagnostic program on your Web page and give you tips to make it more accessible. It will also "approve" your Web site if you incorporate UID principles.

Next, I thought about the purpose of having a course Web page. I realized that the disability accommodations that I have made for students in the past are also just good teaching practices. In the past, I have made copies of my power point lecture slides as a reasonable accommodation for a student with a disability. In universally designing my Web page, I decided to include copies of my power point lecture slides on my Web page so all students could access my notes. I post the notes weekly and many students have told me they use my lecture slides in order to check their notes for completeness, clarification, and spelling errors. Students no longer miss the big picture because they are madly trying to write down definitions and details.

I have started posting my assignments, a plagiarism and proper documentation guide, and other helpful handouts on public speaking and how to read cases on the Web page, in addition to giving students a paper copy. This assists all students, including students with learning and psychological disabilities. If students need to start an assignment early, they can do so. Tutors in the Writing Center also have access to the assignment guides and find them useful in understanding what I expect of my students. Posting a course syllabus to a Web page not only assists students currently enrolled, it also provides helpful information to advisors and prospective students about course content, goals, and the instructor's teaching style. After I realized that other staff and prospective students benefited from the increased information, I added a section for students interested in attending law school. The new section provides links to online information as a way to supplement the pre-law workshops that I conduct. As my Web page has grown, I continue to go back to the Bobby Web site for design suggestions to make sure the information is readily accessible by all prospective users.

Assessment of Participation That Respects Divergent Learning Styles

An important goal of Law in Society is for students to gain better oral communication skills and hone their ability to think critically. When I implemented UID I wanted to make sure that I was taking into account diverse learning styles when assessing participation. I have learned a lot from my students and colleagues about how to teach legal concepts in a first year developmental education course. As Higbee, Ginter, and Taylor (1991) advocated, I present the information utilizing methods that are congruent with my students' learning styles. Reading cases, hearing lectures, and reading and listening to Supreme Court oral arguments complements print and aural learning styles. Debates, mock hearings, and trials are excellent methods for interactive learners. Visual learners comprehension of material is enhanced by timelines, maps, videotapes, and power point slides. Finally, performative movement during the mock trial reaches kinesthetic learning styles.

Prior to attending the CTAD training, I assessed classroom participation mainly via debates, small group presentations to the entire class, and large group discussions. Although I want to maintain participation as a requirement for the course, I also want to recognize that there are a variety of ways for students to engage with the material and provide their unique perspective to all of us involved in the course. My syllabus now reads:

Your participation in class is highly valued. Our class will be a collective effort in which our efforts to understand law and society will depend on the exploration of a number of perspectives and viewpoints. I recognize that not all students feel comfortable speaking in front of large groups of people. Class participation therefore includes a variety of ways to contribute to the course development, including: meaningful contribution to class discussions, small group work, debates, presentations, email communication, office hour discussions, reviewing drafts of other student's work and providing useful written and/or oral comments.

I assign a mock trial in my classes and participation is a major portion of the grade. For the assignment, I write a fact pattern and witness statements based on a current U.S. Supreme Court case. Students choose whether they want to play the role of an attorney or a witness. Working together in six to eight person teams, students spend three weeks preparing the trial and then conduct a jury trial in class. In rethinking the mock trial to make sure it is universally designed, I have developed the assignment so students can play a variety of roles that fit their individual learning styles. For example, visual learners can create charts and power point slides for use as visual aids during the trial. This also enables jury members who are print and visual learners to better follow the case. Visual aids also assist students playing the role of an attorney to organize opening statements and to remember important case names. Witnesses, especially those who must remember a key dollar figure, also may use visual aids. In the past I made accommodations for students with a learning disability and allowed the use of notes. Now, all witnesses can use visual aids if they want help remembering a key fact.

Mock trial is an effective way to learn about the U.S. legal system, work on oral communication, and enhance critical thinking. The majority of students rate the mock trial as the assignment that best helped them meet course goals on end of semester evaluations. Interactive and kinesthetic learners excel in the mock trials and often gain confidence that enhances their large group participation and written work. Print learners also provide a key skill by digesting the written information in the case packet. Aural learners follow the mini-lectures that I conduct on argumentative strategies and provide constructive feedback to team members on delivery of opening and closing statements and witness testimony. In their peer assessment forms of their own and each other's participation, many students remark that each team member played a different, yet key role in preparing the case.

I continue to work on designing the mock trials so that different forms of participation are assessed and valued. Students are assessed by me and by each other on how well they work with other team members and not just on the actual trial performance. I have noticed that students who are initially nervous about the public speaking component of the course are much more successful and report a more positive experience now that I have incorporated more UID principles into both the assignment and assessment of the mock trial.

Broadening Content to Include Disability Rights

I also assessed the content of my classes to ensure they are universally designed. As James Banks (1993) and Ronald Takaki (1993) have advocated, integrating multicultural education into course content is an effective way to make courses more inclusive. I want to integrate disability rights into my courses and agree with Geneva Gay (1995) that there are multiple appropriate ways to teach in a multicultural manner. Initially I incorporated a separate section on disability rights and am now rethinking the way in which I teach to incorporate UID principles.

When students see themselves reflected in the curriculum, they are more engaged with the underlying subject matter of the course (Takaki, 1993). To this end, I have incorporated more information on people with disabilities in all of the social science classes that I teach. The legislative history, major federal laws, and seminal cases surrounding disability rights are part of Civil Rights content of the Law in Society class. However, now rather than segregating disability rights to a separate section of the course, we discuss the emergence of equal protection and evolving definitions of legal equality. Within this discussion, disability is discussed and analyzed along with race and ethnicity, gender, class, age, and sexual orientation. Disability is not relegated to a separate "ism," but seen within the context of a major Civil Rights issue.

I also decided to incorporate disability, race, class, sexual orientation, and gender issues as they relate to education law. I have found that education law and policy is an issue that all students relate to and offers a way for them to engage with course content. Students read a number of cases, including *Brown v. Board of Education* (1954), and learn about laws, such as the Americans with Disabilities Act of 1990 (ADA, 1994/1997), that govern education. For example, when we discuss education law, we read the provisions in Section 504 of the Rehabilitation Act of 1973 (1994) and Title II and III of the ADA that apply to higher education and prohibit discrimination on the basis of disability. There are a number of articles and publications that provide detailed information on Section 504 and the ADA that assisted in my curriculum development (Blanck, 1998; Council on Law in Higher Education [CLHE], 2000; Rothstein, 2000; Tucker, 1996).

Including disability rights content also reinforces my syllabus statement regarding disability accommodations. Furthermore, students who may have misinformation about psychiatric or learning disabilities learn important information and together we shatter some of the stereotypes about accommodations (e.g., students are faking it, makes course too easy, etc.). Perhaps most importantly, we discuss the Individuals with Disabilities Education Act (IDEA) of 1994 and how it differs from the ADA. Students who had IDEA accommodations when they were in high school need to know that, unlike in primary and secondary schools, when they enter higher education the onus is on them to register with the college or university disability services office and contact individual instructors to obtain reasonable accommodations. Without understanding this distinction, and that testing may no longer be free, many students may incorrectly believe they are automatically eligible for accommodations received in high school.

Discussions about disability culture and the movement for disability rights have led to a number of benefits. My perception is that students are more willing to self-disclose learning and psychiatric disabilities to me during office hours than they were when disability issues were not integrated into my courses. Hopefully this change is also due to less stigma being attached to being labeled "learning disabled" or having a psychiatric disability. In past course offerings where I focused primarily on issues of equality surrounding race, class, and gender, some students dismissed the issue as "discrimination that used to happen, but doesn't anymore." With the inclusion of disability and sexual orientation integrated into our discussion of equality, it is more difficult to dismiss inequality as just a historical problem. Students are also able to see more of a link between themselves as individuals and the legal system, a major goal of Law in Society.

Conclusion

Since incorporating UID principles in my classes, I have had several students bring me letters detailing the accommodations they require. The students notice that the most common accommodations (i.e., copies of lecture notes and additional time on assignments) have already been incorporated into the course design to benefit all students. I explain that I have attempted to incorporate more learning supports into the course with the goal of inclusive pedagogy. The mock trial, which is the best way I have found to teach students about the U.S. legal system, seems to increase course retention now that I have incorporated multiple ways to participate. Most importantly, integrating disability rights issues into the Civil Rights and education law sections of the course content has provided a valuable learning experience. In attempting to meet Sonia Nieto's (1994) challenge to move from tolerance to acceptance in multicultural education, hopefully more students are seeing themselves reflected, respected and affirmed in the curriculum.

References

The Americans with Disabilities Act of 1990, 42 U.S.C. §§ 12101 to 12132 (West 1994 & Supp. 1997).

Banks, J. (1993). Multicultural education as an academic discipline: Goals for the 21st century. *Multicultural Education, 1*(3), 8-11, 39.

Blanck, P. (1998). Civil rights, learning disability, and academic standards. *Journal of Gender, Race & Justice, 2,* 33-58.

Brown v. Board of Education, 347 U.S. 483 (1954).

Center for Applied Special Technology (CAST) (2001). Bobby home page. Retrieved November 12, 2007, from http://www.cast.org/bobby/

Council on Law in Higher Education (CLHE) (2000). *Disability law for campus administrators: Meeting the needs of students.* Retrieved November 12, 2007 from, www.clhe.org

Gay, G. (1995). Bridging multicultural theory and practice. *Multicultural Education, 3*(1), 4-9.

Higbee, J.L., Ginter, E.J., & Taylor, W.D. (1991). Enhancing academic performance: Seven perceptual styles of learning. *Research and Teaching in Developmental Education,* 7(2), 5-9.

Individuals with Disabilities Education Act, 20 U.S.C. §§ 1400-1485 (1994), as amended by 20 U.S.C.A. §§ 1400-1487 (West 1997).

Miksch, K. (n.d.) *Home page for Karen Miksch*. Retrieved November 12, 2007 from, http://www.gen.umn.edu/facultyStaff/miksch/

Nieto, S. (1994). Moving beyond tolerance in multicultural education. *Multicultural Education, 1*(4), 9-12, 35-38.

Rehabilitation Act of 1973, 29 U.S.C. § 701 (1994).

Rothstein, L. (2000). Higher education and the future of disability policy. *Alabama Law Review, 52,* 241-270.

Takaki, R. (1993). *A different mirror: A history of multicultural America.* Boston: Little, Brown.

Tucker, B. (1996). Application of the Americans with Disabilities Act (ADA) and Section 504 to colleges and universities: An overview and discussion of special issues relating to students. *Journal of College & University Law, 23,* 1-41.

CHAPTER 9

Teaching College History Using Universal Instructional Design

David Arendale and David Ghere
University of Minnesota

Abstract
This chapter provides a practical model for social science teachers to integrate the best practices of Universal Instructional Design (UID). The approach was used in a developmental education context where academic skill training has been embedded in introductory courses in American history and world history. Use of UID principles not only reduced classroom barriers for students with disabilities, but enhanced the learning of a much larger student group, those who have academic preparation issues for rigorous college courses. In some cases, the same practices had utility for both student groups as well as improving outcomes for the general student population.

Implementing Universal Instructional Design (UID) at a major research university not only supports higher learning outcomes for students with disabilities, but fosters an improved learning environment for all students within the class. The mission of the Department of Postsecondary Teaching and Learning (PsTL) in the College of Education and Human Development at the University of Minnesota requires instructors to be innovative and varied in their teaching methodology while systematically embedding best learning principles to widen access to a diverse study body. PsTL courses retain the rigorous content standards and high performance expectations of college-level courses while integrating activities and assignments that enhance the access of students and support their ability to perform college-level work. This goal requires a transformative approach to course design, including the revision of course procedures, classroom activities, written assignments, evaluation methods, and feedback to students. This chapter explores our experience in teaching history in PsTL and provides a practical model as well as specific activities for incorporating the best practices of UID into these and other social science courses.

The Challenge of Embedding UID Within Core Curriculum Courses

Historically access to postsecondary education has generally increased in the United States, even though in recent years the choice among specific institutions may have become more restricted (Barton, 2002; Bastedo & Gumport, 2003; Slaughter & Rhoades, 2004). A variety of factors have fostered this increased access: growth in the number of postsecondary institutions and satellite campuses, expanded financial aid offerings, and more aggressive marketing of public and private institutions for tuition revenue (Shaw, 1997). This increased access has been accompanied by an increased diversity of the students attending postsecondary education institutions, such as students who are the first generation in their families to attend college and students from historically-underrepresented groups

(Kipp, Price, & Wohlford, 2002). These increases in access and diversity have occurred despite the concurrent rise of admissions standards at many institutions. It is difficult to maintain both increasing academic standards and access to more students simultaneously with improvements in student outcomes like course material mastery, reenrollment rates, persistence in the academic major, scores on examinations administered upon exit from the institution, and graduation rates.

The student body of PsTL has changed recently due to the merging of the old General College (Higbee, Lundell, & Arendale, 2005) with three other academic units to form the new College of Education and Human Development at the University of Minnesota. The academic preparation level of the students admitted to PsTL has risen, with most graduating in the top quartile of their high school class. In the old General College students generally ranked in the top half of their graduating class. Best practices of developmental education and learning assistance were integrated throughout the old college's approach in academic and student affairs to meet the needs of the students who often had academic preparation issues in one or more of their college courses. Rather than providing the traditional stand-alone, developmental-level courses in reading, study skills, and writing, the instructional staff employed an enriched pedagogy that benefited all students, not merely those considered "underprepared" by the institution (Higbee, Lundell, & Arendale). The student affairs component of the old college also provided a variety of services that met the needs of the students. Because PsTL's current mission is directed toward the first year experience, many of these same strategies can be used to enhance all students' transitions from high school to college. The ethnic diversity of the students remains nearly the same with about half of those admitted to PsTL being students of color. The students continue to be predominately the first generation in their families to attend college.

It appears that the percentage of students in PsTL with invisible and visible disabilities mirrors that of the general student population at the University of Minnesota. The University's Disabilities Services, a unit of the Office of Equity and Diversity, states that more than 9% of the University's students have one or more disabilities (Disability Services, 2007). In a recent annual report, the rate of expenditures for providing individual accommodations for students has escalated nearly every year for more than a decade. The budget grew by more than 11% in the most recent reporting year (Disability Services, 2005).

These statistics from the University of Minnesota appear to mirror national statistics concerning students with disabilities. Historically the faculty from the old General College and the new PsTL Department have believed that the classroom must provide seamless integration of both teaching and learning mastery with the professor as a catalyst for both. Enhancing the learning environment within an introductory core curriculum course such as history is a viable alternative to requiring students with academic preparation issues to enroll in separate courses or students with disabilities to receive separate accommodations as needed to meet special learning needs. The transformation of the classroom learning experience to meet the needs of these two student populations often enriches the experience for all other students enrolled in the class. This decision requires a reengineering of the course and a significant change in the learning culture. Previous publications have presented models for enriching the core curriculum course (Arendale & Ghere, 2005; Ghere, 2000; 2001; 2003; Wilcox, delMas, Stewart, Johnson, & Ghere, 1997). This chapter offers practical suggestions that instructors could utilize to implement UID in a wide variety of courses.

Educational Theory Supporting UID in the Classroom

Universal Instructional Design is an approach to education in which systemic changes are made to the learning environment to accommodate the needs of students with a disability (Higbee, 2003). There has been considerable debate within education at the elementary, secondary, and postsecondary levels about the mainstreaming of these students. Advocates for UID argue that a dramatic cultural transformation is mandated in the learning environment for all students. They state that an expansion in learning modalities will result in the creation of an enriched learning environment that meets the needs of not only those with disabilities, but of all students (Silver, Bourke, & Strehorn 1998).

Through spirited dialogue and review of educational outcomes, it has been clearly demonstrated that all students within the classroom benefit from these changes, which increase the accessibility of knowledge and the environment in which learning activities occur. Burgstahler (2005) stated that, "In terms of learning, universal design means the design of instructional materials and activities that make the learning goals achievable by individuals with wide differences in their abilities to see, hear, speak, move, read, write, understand English, attend, organize, engage, and remember. Universal design for learning is achieved by means of flexible curricular materials and activities that provide alternatives for students with differing abilities."

UID provides a fresh approach to the issue of meeting the needs of an increasingly diverse student population. It is practically impossible, cost-prohibitive, and counterproductive to provide separate programs to meet the needs of each student subgroup. As educators have increasingly come to understand, placing students within categories and subcategories has had unanticipated outcomes. By implementing UID, the institutional culture creates a more inclusive and enriched learning environment (Pliner & Johnson, 2004). This pedagogical approach is based on a core set of premises that affirm high academic expectations for students while providing a transformed learning environment more conducive to learning by a broader range of students, including those with a disability. These premises include:

1. Student academic success is achieved most effectively when the classroom learning experience is enriched in rigorous, core curriculum courses, rather than providing services in isolation outside of the course.
2. The institution must adapt itself to the entering students rather than expecting them to join the student body quickly and quietly.
3. Students with a disability are best served when mainstreamed with all students within the classroom.
4. Activities and services originally designed to meet the needs of those with a disability often have high utility for all students within the class.

The educational practices contained within this chapter were selected first because of their grounding in educational theory and second for their utility within the classroom. We followed a set of guiding principles for Universal Design identified by Scott, McGuire and, Shaw (2003) with our history courses. The nine elements are (a) equitable use, (b) flexibility in use, (c) simple and intuitive, (d) perceptible information, (e) tolerance for error, (f) low physical effort, (g) size and space for approach and use, (h) a community of learners, and (i) instructional climate (pp. 375-376). A full discussion of the similarities and differences among the terms Universal Design for Learning, Universal Instructional Design, and Universal Design for Instruction are provided elsewhere in this book.

UID (Higbee, 2003) was originally conceptualized as a transformation of the classroom environment for mainstreaming of students with disabilities (Silver, Bourke, & Strehorn, 1998). The approach has now been extended for the transformation of the classroom experience to increase learning and outcomes for all students. The same practices that benefited the newly mainstreamed students with disabilities also enhanced the learning environment for all other students within the same class (Higbee, Chung, & Hsu, 2004). This paradigm requires the institution to present a transformed learning environment that capitalizes on existing student strengths and builds upon them throughout the course.

Finally, it is recognized that most students learn best as a member of a cohort of peers (Johnson, Johnson, & Holubec, 2002; Johnson, Johnson, & Smith, 1991; Vygotsky, 1978). The unique traits of students—demographic, cultural, intellectual—are important ingredients and resources for their learning experiences. In this sociocultural perspective, Vygotsky stated that the education enterprise should be viewed as a learning community dependent upon the active participation of all members. Various educational activities associated with the course encourage extensive student dialogue, various ways to express mastery of academic content and demonstration of acquired skills, and small peer-group cooperative learning activities.

Overview of the PsTL Introductory History Courses

The Department of Postsecondary Teaching and Learning has implemented this integrated and embedded approach to UID in many of its courses. To help set the context for the use of UID within the introductory history courses, some background information about the courses follows. One course is Perspectives in American History (PsTL 1231), a one-semester survey of American history, and the other history course is World Civilization Since 1500 (PsTL 1251). Both classes enroll from 35 to 45 students per section. Both courses fulfill the same liberal education requirement for graduation from the University—Historical Perspectives. In addition, PsTL 1231 fulfills the University's Cultural Diversity graduation requirement while PsTL 1251 fulfills the International Perspectives requirement.

PsTL 1231 is also a writing-intensive course as determined by the University. These courses develop students' writing ability, particularly in research papers, beyond the level provided by the required freshman-level composition courses. Students must successfully pass four writing-intensive courses in order to graduate from the University. In PsTL 1231 students need to complete three different types of writing assignments: (a) short five-to-seven-sentence essays in the form of 12 weekly writing assignments and six questions on each of three exams, (b) a long essay question on each of three major exams, and (c) a 10- to 12-page formal paper. Because the course is writing intensive, a graduate teaching assistant (GTA) is available to critique and grade the weekly writing assignments and provide a detailed critique of the first draft of the formal paper. These scores are then confirmed or adjusted by the instructor, who grades all the long essays and the final draft of the paper. A review sheet is distributed one week before each test containing study questions and announcing the long essay question.

Writing assignments also occur throughout PsTL 1251, but not at the same intensity and frequency as in the other history course. Each of the four major exams requires completing three essay questions. In advance of each exam a number of potential essay questions are placed on a study guide. A short paper of one to two pages is required concerning a "field trip" to a historically-related event or film from a list provided by the course instructor. Finally, eight short in-class writing assignments occur during class sessions to allow students to summarize major components of course material or to reflect on a learning activity that occurred during class. Because of the class size and course expectations, an undergraduate teaching assistant (UGTA) facilitates optional study review sessions outside of class 3 days per week. These sessions are called Peer Assisted Learning (PAL) Groups and follow similar procedures as other peer cooperative learning programs such as the Emerging Scholars Program (Treisman, 1985); Peer-Led Team Learning (Dreyfus, 2004); Structured Learning Assistance (Doyle & Kowalczyk, 1999); and Supplemental Instruction (Arendale, 1998).

Universal Instructional Design requires the instructor to determine the essential components of each particular course so that it can be redesigned without impacting the quality of the course. PsTL 1231 and PsTL 1251 have the same essential components. Students will become more knowledgeable about historical vocabulary, concepts, personalities, and perspectives. Students will gain a better understanding of historical cause and effect situations, of relationships between individual events and their historical context, and of how these circumstances change over time. Students will engage in student-centered learning giving voice to student concerns and choice in student actions as they actively engage in the construction of knowledge. Students will develop improved writing and critical thinking skills as well as the ability to view individuals, events, and circumstances from multiple perspectives.

Learning Experiences Before and After the Class Session

Due to the time constraints of the class session, speed of learning activities, and complexity of the varying learning situations, it is critical for many students with a disability or those with academic preparation issues to be prepared before the beginning of the class session and then to reflect carefully on what occurred during the session. Before the integration of UID within the courses, some of these activities or resources would have been provided in a confidential manner only to those students who presented an official letter from the University's Disability Services unit. Students who were academically underprepared might not have been admitted to the University and instead directed to a local community college to enroll in developmental-level courses. After retooling of the course through UID, these activities are available for all students within the course. The following activities have been used in one or both of the history courses.

Web-Based Access to Knowledge

Accessing Web-based course-related materials, whether created by the instructor or provided by the textbook publisher, provides an opportunity for the student to study and practice with the material in privacy and to decide how much time to invest in the activity. Syllabi, course calendars, assignment guidelines, review sheets, topic outlines, and discussion questions are placed on the course Web site, as well as links to documents, maps, charts, images, resource sites, and PowerPoint lecture slides. Students with visual impairments as well as some other disabilities can more easily use the material through text readers, enlarged print, and other adaptive technology. All students have an opportunity to be better prepared for class sessions and to be more confident in participating in small-group and class-wide discussions.

For teachers who seek to include Web-based resources, especially those provided by the textbook publisher, it is critical to practice extensively with accessing the materials from a computer and to explore all components of the package. Sometimes the test banks are heavily focused on knowledge-level questions of material that is obscure, even for course instructors. Encouraging students to test themselves with this type of material can be demoralizing and counterproductive. Secondly, the difficulty in accessing Web-based materials can be challenging, even for experienced computer users. It is best to demonstrate the use of such Internet resources in class. It would be a mistake to assume that today's students are equally savvy concerning use of computing resources. A cautionary note about relying upon Web resources is that not all Web sites have been modified to allow their use by students with vision or hearing disabilities. In such cases the material needs to be made available in an accessible format or it should be eliminated so as not to provide an unfair disadvantage for some students who are using screen readers and other adaptive technologies.

Preparation for Lectures and Learning

A challenge for some students is the difficulty of navigating a rich, fast-moving, and sometimes complicated college classroom learning environment. Student completion and comprehension of assigned readings could be enhanced by providing questions to be answered or key points to be identified in class discussion. Furthermore, instructors could expect students to be prepared for class discussion over those questions or key points. Providing lecture outlines ahead of time or hiring a fellow student to provide copies of notes are not uncommon practices for accommodating some students with a disability. The introduction of PowerPoint slide presentations to accompany class lectures has accentuated this problem for other students within the class as well because the amount of content information presented is often larger and the class moves at a faster pace.

PowerPoint lecture notes. In the world history course the instructor provides an incomplete copy of the upcoming PowerPoint lecture slides ahead of time. The slides are provided through the course WebVista site. The slides are provided in the Acrobat PDF format. The slides are printed in the format that places three slides on the left side of the page with the right side of the page blank for the addition of student notes. Use of the PDF format alleviates the need for students to need the PowerPoint software. Instead, a free copy of the Acrobat PDF reader software must be downloaded onto the student's computer. The course Web site has Internet links for this and other free software packages. The PowerPoint slides provided are incomplete; only the major points of the slide are visible. The secondary and tertiary material is only displayed during class to encourage more student interaction with the lecture material. Experience in the history class with providing complete sets of PowerPoint slides has revealed that some first-year students make the assumption that this is the only relevant material presented during class and therefore they attend class infrequently, much to their academic detriment.

For students with a diagnosed disability, the complete set of PowerPoint slides with all secondary and tertiary points is provided ahead of time. During a previous academic term, a student with severe sight impairment was able to use this complete set of slides on his computer in advance of the class lecture. Using the PowerPoint software program, he first converted the slides into the outline view and then used the adaptive software installed on his computer to convert the written outline into an audio narration of the complete slides. Similarly, students who are deaf must divide their attention between the text and images on the PowerPoint slides, the gestures and facial expressions of the instructor, and the sign language interpreter conveying the instructor's words. These students can benefit greatly from examining the PowerPoint slides in advance.

Wiki Web page study guide. In the world history course the students create an online study guide to prepare for the major exams. Each student in the class is assigned to write a one-page outline of an answer for one of the potential essay questions or create a narrative summary of the chapter. Because there are more students than questions or chapters, there are up to six responses for each. This practice provides a great opportunity for student voice in the class by observing how they value the course materials and express them through the writing assignment. After being assigned their task and the completion date, students work at their own pace independently outside of class on creating their section of the wiki Web page. The course instructor monitors the student contributions and edits as necessary to eliminate major factual errors. Course evaluations rate this activity very high in usefulness.

Weekly course podcasts. Students in the world history course are assigned various roles with a weekly Internet radio show that serves as a course supplement and study guide for upcoming exams. While a common approach to the use of podcasting is to record the class lectures, this use of the technology was for the students, course instructor, and others to co-create meaningful content from the students' point of view. The course instructor audio recorded student contributions for the 30-minute show. The financial investment was relatively modest with a microphone and use of a computer with GarageBand, a program within the inexpensive iLife (Apple, 2007a) software suite from Apple Computer, Inc. The episodes were made available free of charge through the iTunes Web Internet site (Apple, 2007b).

Students had choices regarding their contributions. Some students provided chapter summaries for the weekly episodes. Others selected music from different parts of the world and provided an overview of the music and how it related to contemporary culture for the country that was being studied during the class sessions. The course instructor contributed an analysis of the potential exam essay questions and suggestions on how best to respond to them. The teaching assistants for the course provided suggestions for study strategies that they had found useful in their own college studies. The student assistant who helped to edit the episodes and place them on the Internet also contributed a short piece on tips for using free software tools and programs available through the Internet. To add some more variety and student interest in the weekly episodes, one student added one or two songs from an independent music artist who provided music cleared for this purpose. This audio format could be listened to through visiting the course Web site (Arendale, 2007) or by downloading the episode to a portable MP3 device like an iPod, iRiver, or similar. Written transcripts of the shows were available by use of inexpensive speech-to-text translation computer software. End of course evaluations revealed that students found the podcasts useful as a study aid.

Out-of-class Peer Assisted Learning (PAL) groups. A frequently used support for some students with disabilities is providing private tutors to assist with processing the course material. This unfortunately can create a socially isolating environment and can be fairly expensive for supporting just one person. The same funds and efforts can be used to create an out-of-class peer cooperative learning group. In both history courses the undergraduate teaching assistants hold multiple weekly study review sessions for all students in the class. The PAL sessions provide typical activities that might be experienced in other nationally-known programs such as Supplemental Instruction and Peer-led Team Learning (Arendale, 2004). The PAL groups supported the students with academic preparation issues as well as the general students in their mastery of rigorous course material.

Modifications of the Classroom Learning Environment

Following is a sample of the activities and modifications to the classroom learning environment for either or both the American history and world history courses. The wide variety of activities is incorporated into the class sessions to provide a rich selection of ways for students to interact with the course material, with one another, and to have multiple ways to express their mastery of rigorous course material. Although the activities were initially promoted to accommodate students with disabilities, class evaluations suggest widespread support for these varied approaches by most students in the class.

Classroom Questioning Techniques

The instructor needs to recognize the effects of various questioning techniques in the classroom. Questions addressed to the whole class usually result in responses from the same small group of students. This allows other students to avoid contemplating the question because the answer will be provided by that small group of students. However, if the instructor systematically calls on other students, then all students can be actively involved in the class discussion. Students who are unprepared for class or confused about the course material, as well as those who are naturally shy, introverted, or lacking confidence can all be included in class discussion. Moreover, once students become familiar with the instructor's questioning methods, students should come to class better prepared and should consider each question as it is posed, because the instructor may call on them. The pauses between the asking of each question and the selection of the student to answer each question may become the most intellectually-stimulating moments in the class.

The previous paragraph provides an illustration of the benefits for students who have academic preparation issues or the general student population. These questioning techniques also benefit students with disabilities. Students utilizing sign language interpreters or augmentative communication devices may be left out of typical class discussions due to the delay in the communication of the questions and the communication of the student's answers. A brief pause after each question would enable those students to participate actively in the discussion and access to questions before class would further facilitate this outcome. Students with learning disabilities, for example, need time to consider each question and formulate a thoughtful answer. Past experience may have made some of these students reluctant to participate in class, but a thoughtful instructor, questioning students systematically, can create positive engagement of students with disabilities in the class activities and discussion. Other students have experienced frustration in the past, and will be excited by the opportunity to participate in class discussion offered by these questioning techniques.

Valuing the Textbook and Course Materials

Students sometimes act on the maxim that the amount of time that an instructor spends on an issue in class is related to its overall relative importance. This mismatch of expectations is especially profound regarding the use of the course syllabus, textbook, ancillary course materials, and associated Web-based resources. Instructors need to value such materials and procedures throughout the course term so that students understand that the material is important, relevant, and meets their learning needs (Martin, Blanc, & Arendale, 1994). One of the most important resources for the course is the syllabus. Instructors often spend large amounts of time carefully crafting course syllabus documents and then quickly rush through them on the first day of class so that the first lecture can be delivered. From an instructor's point of view it might seem reasonable to instruct students by telling them to read the syllabus on their own. In both the American and world history classes the instructors bring the syllabus to class daily, and frequently consult it in front of class when questions arise about assignments, due dates, grading criteria, or all the other issues that have been carefully addressed.

The same comments from the previous paragraph also apply to the textbook. In both the American and world history courses, textbooks are valued continually throughout the academic term by the course instructor in a variety of ways. First, the instructor always brings the textbook with him to class each day and finds ways to refer to material on specific pages. Examples for use of the textbook include drawing attention to specific questions listed in the chapter overview designed to guide the reading; moderating discussion concerning the meaning of maps, charts, illustrations, or brief historical primary documents in the book that are sometimes overlooked by the reader; illustrating the utility of the glossary or index in the back of the book to locate information quickly; or other activities.

In both history courses nongraded classroom assessment techniques (Angelo & Cross, 1993) are frequently used to build metacognitive awareness and motivation for academic behavior changes. Helping students to see the link between their behavior and grades is a difficult task. The goal is for students not to be surprised with results from their major examinations. Sometimes this is still a surprise, so in the world history course an activity is used in class on the day that the exams are returned to students. Students are asked to respond to a survey that lists nearly 30 activities that they might have completed before the exam; for example, studied with a friend or reread the textbook. Some of the questions ask how long they engaged in the activity. The instructor then summarizes the data and shares the results with the students during the next class period to allow them to compare themselves with others in the class regarding their study habits. In American history, an exam is critiqued on the day it is returned to the students. The discussion addresses which multiple choice questions were missed most often and why, what arguments and content were frequently or effectively used in the essays, and what arguments and content were not used that could have improved the essays.

Many first-year students report difficulty with the shift from secondary school testing procedures, methods, and vocabulary to those at the college level. Instructors can eliminate this concern by discussing the types of questions on the tests, the level of preparation needed for that type of question, and the instructor's expectations for breadth and depth and specificity for the essay questions. In the world history course, a handout details the recommended strategies for answering different question types: true or false, multiple choice, and essay. Opportunities to practice with questions that emulate the style and format of those on the exams are provided during class time with mock examinations. Instructors help students identify key language in directions, common terms used with essay questions and their specific meanings, and methods for using one part of the exam (i.e., vocabulary matching and multiple choice) to help answer the essay and short-answer questions. Other instruction regarding test-taking strategies occurs by using the frequent classroom assessment techniques as an opportunity also to analyze the strategies used for completing them.

In-Class Peer Cooperative Learning Activities

Previously in this chapter the use of out-of-class peer cooperative learning groups was described. These groups are also an integral part of the in-class activities as well. Such activities play a vital part of the class learning environment for the following reasons. Small group learning engages students in their own intellectual, personal, and professional development. Student content knowledge, depth of understanding, frequency of class participation, and level of course involvement are enhanced by the interpersonal and interactive nature of cooperative learning groups (Fry, Ketteridge, & Marshall, 2003). Group learning benefits good students who must formulate their understanding of course concepts to present them to others while students who are underprepared benefit from the reiteration of those concepts from a student perspective (Barkley, Cross, & Major, 2005). Interactive student activities increase student engagement, build learning networks, encourage students to see one another as learning resources, and increase content mastery of challenging material (Astin, 1993; Bruffee, 1993; Cooper, Prescott, Cook, Smith, & Mueck, 1990; Light, 2001).

Peer cooperative learning groups are frequently formed for short-term tasks in each of the history classes. These activities include identifying the key points in a section of the text, examining a newspaper article, analyzing a historical document, or discussing a historical documentary shown during class. Students are more likely to engage the material and have increased confidence to participate in class discussion through use of carefully assigned and monitored peer cooperative learning activities (Johnson, Johnson, & Smith, 1991). "There is a large amount of empirical evidence that small groups of peers learning together have advantages for academic achievement, motivation, and satisfaction" (Barkley et al., 2005, p. 25).

Cooperative learning methods can be especially effective for students with disabilities (Johnson & Johnson, 1986; O'Connor & Jenkins, 1995). Small-group peer learning may be especially important for students who may need a more interactive and slower pace of learning than with an instructor-led, fast-paced lecture presentation. Students with learning disabilities can remain actively engaged with the course content material in peer cooperative learning activities while students with speech, hearing, or sight impairments can have more opportunity to contribute their ideas in the context of the small group. A special application of this pedagogy is illustrated through fostering the development of critical thinking skills that maintain high intellectual engagement with the course material (Adams & Hamm, 1990; Chaffee, 1992; Higbee & Dwinell, 1998; Paul & Elder, 1999; Stone, 1990).

Fostering Critical Thinking Through Historical Decision-Making Simulations

Classroom simulations provide teachers with powerful learning opportunities by creating "a realistic experience in a controlled environment" (Fry et al., 2003, p. 137). They can help stimulate critical thinking skills as students confront the same issues and options from the perspective of historical decision makers. An additional benefit of this strategy is that it provides more engagement for the students because most report that they find it interesting and relevant, and they have the opportunity to work in small groups. These are just some of the many educational benefits from simulations for students. Research suggests that this increased involvement results in significantly greater retention of the content material, an enhanced interest in related topics, and a more positive attitude toward the general subject matter (Bennett, Leibman, & Fetter, 1997; Bredemeier & Greenblat, 1981; Druckman, 1995; Randell, Morris, Welzel, & Whitehall, 1992).

All simulations involve the students in active learning situations requiring some level of role playing. These roles can be very specific, such as a historical individual; more general as a representative of a country, region, or state; or very generic as a decision maker assessing the historical options that might have been available. Simulation handouts provide the background material necessary for each student to evaluate the various decision options in the historical situation and to play the role assigned. Sometimes a reward system is utilized to create a situation, which fosters competition between groups and cooperation within each group. In these "game" simulations, students articulate their positions, negotiate with other students, and compromise when necessary to reach a consensus decision or political bargain that achieves their goals. Other simulations employ maps to convey information to the students, to designate various territorial options, and ultimately to display student decisions. Following is an example of a simulation activity: "As a United Nations commission, what political organization and degree of autonomy would you recommend for a specific region based on the data provided concerning its ethnic and religious composition?" Students must analyze the question based on historical events in different geographic locations of the world that encompass different cultures and traditions: West Bank, Northern Ireland, Kosovo, and Bosnia. In this case, natural interests of role playing, competitive play, and intellectual curiosity are channeled into an educational activity that helps to foster students' critical thinking skills.

Diverse Methods and Means to Demonstrate Mastery of Course Material

There are a variety of learning disabilities that make it difficult for students to demonstrate mastery of the course material on standardized exams with a time limit that rewards students who can complete the examination quickly. The following strategies have been implemented in both history courses to uphold rigorous mastery of the course material and also to provide a variety of means for assessment of learning.

Assessment of knowledge. The most common accommodation request received from the University's Disability Services unit is extended time on major exams. Our purpose is to assess the students' knowledge and understanding of the course material, not the speed with which the students can compose their thoughts in written essays. While real time or limited time tests are appropriate in some academic disciplines, they are not part of the essential elements of the history courses. Tests with time limits advantage the free-flowing writer and disadvantage the thoughtful, meticulous writer while imposing unnecessary limits on the student's demonstration of course content mastery. Why should any students be penalized for taking time to think deeply about an essay question and to organize their answer logically? Why should a student who is an English language learner (ELL) utilizing a dictionary, a student with severe vision challenges using materials written in Braille, or a student experiencing test anxiety be rushed to answer multiple-choice questions due to a time limit?

In both the American and world history courses, tests are designed to require 60 to 75 minutes, but at the end of the 2-hour class session students are allowed to finish their work in the professor's office. The typical accommodation for students with learning disabilities (usually time-and-a-half on tests) is not needed because all students have the time necessary to convey fully their comprehension of the course material. As a result, the requests for this accommodation have diminished, and some students never need to disclose their disabilities. However, one or two students each term are approved by the University's Disability Services—a unit of the Office of Multicultural & Academic Affairs—to take their exams at Disability Services to provide an isolated environment for those who may become aurally or visually distracted by others in the room.

The provision of additional time benefits all students. It helps alleviate one source of test anxiety by eliminating time pressure. It helps students in being more reflective about taking the exam, more careful in reading exam questions, more practiced in writing short outlines for essay questions, and more proficient in gathering information from the vocabulary and multiple-choice sections of the exam that could be useful for supporting the essay question responses. Expectations can be raised by the instructor because students will have the time needed to create more reflective and analytical responses to essay questions. When quality work is not produced, the reason for the failure, whether lack of ability or lack of preparation or effort, is more apparent and the appropriate solutions more obvious to both instructor and student.

Alternative formal assessment measures. While the diversity of entering students has continued to rise, the use of diverse measures for assessing student mastery often has not changed significantly. Too often, for instance, students are expected to navigate multiple-choice examinations expertly. In addition to providing some multiple-choice questions on exams, the two history courses have employed a mix of short and long essay questions, matching exercises, short answer, and identity questions. Other formal assessment methods have included journals, short in-class or homework writing assignments, reaction papers, short and long research papers, written reviews of history Web sites, PowerPoint presentations, historically-related films, guest speakers, and museum exhibitions. In-class activities and student presentations can be evaluated by the instructor or assessed through peer review and self-review.

In the American history course, students are expected each week to answer one homework question by composing a paragraph of six or seven sentences. These questions are constructed so that the answer cannot simply be copied from the text and are of two basic types. The first type requires students to identify key points or summarize events from a 2- to 3-page section of the text. For example, "what local factors determined the work and living conditions of slaves in various areas of the English colonies?" Students must consider issues such as field hand versus household servant, labor difficulties for specific crops, and the percentage of slaves in the local population, among others. This ability to recognize the key points in a piece of text and condense the information into a short, concise paragraph will be invaluable to students throughout their lives. The second type of question asks students to assume a particular role given the background information from the assigned reading and reflect on what their actions or decisions would be in that situation. For example, "would you prefer to be a woman in colonial New England or colonial Virginia? Why?" Students must consider the issues of health concerns, property rights, and various social issues. These writing exercises gradually enhance the students' organization and analysis skills, as well as their critical thinking and creativity.

American history students take three major exams during the academic term, each including a question to be answered in a lengthy essay encompassing four to eight pages in a test booklet (i.e., "blue book"). Essay questions focus on broad themes that require students to consolidate and compare information and ideas over the span of a historical period. Essay questions are announced one week in advance of the exam so students can organize their thoughts and look for evidence to support their arguments. This practice not only develops the students' writing skills, but it also enables the instructor to have much higher expectations about the preparation for the essay and the quality of the arguments. Poor performance can be dealt with appropriately because the problem, whether the students' lack of understanding or lack of motivation to study, can be more easily determined. Essays are written in class without notes, and the bluebooks are marked to prevent students from bringing a previously written essay into class.

The basic philosophy of UID is that mainstreaming learning activities that are helpful for many students with disabilities, special needs, or academic preparation issues will also be beneficial for the entire group of students enrolled in a course. For a discussion of specific practices keyed to specific disabilities, refer to Ghere's (2003) previously published chapter "Best Practices and Students With Disabilities: Experience in a College History Course." We also previously published an extensive chapter that explored the practical means of meeting the needs of students considered academically-underprepared within introductory history courses (Arendale & Ghere, 2005).

Summary and Recommendations for Further Investigation

This chapter has been about transforming a college course so that all students, including those with disabilities and those with academic preparation issues, could maximize their benefit and have a learning environment with few, if any, barriers. The educational practices contained within this chapter can be used in whole or in part by classroom instructors in a variety of ways. Instructors of history or other academic content courses could select activities from this chapter that are appropriate to the academic preparation level of the students and the academic expectations for the particular institution. Another variable that comes into play is the resources made available to the instructor by the institution. Is there a campus faculty development center the faculty member can consult for embedding effective UID practices? Most of the recommended practices in this chapter do not require extensive preparation or formal coursework.

Embedding the best practices of UID within core curriculum subjects in PsTL has shown some elements of success. Some students with severe visible and invisible disabilities need more accommodations to the learning environment to increase their academic success. Not all students with academic preparation issues need to enroll in prerequisite developmental-level courses in reading, study skills, and writing. The old General College was able to meet the needs of students who were less academically prepared than others who were admitted to the University (Higbee, Lundell, & Arendale, 2005). Those patterns have continued with the new PsTL.

The practices described in this chapter expand the margins of academic success for a wider range of students, but still more powerful transformations of the course learning experience are needed. Not all students who could benefit from the PsTL experience are successful. One element that needs further investigation is why some students opt out of availing themselves of these resources and opportunities. Additional research and investigation concerning deeper issues of student motivation are needed. Research partnerships among cognitive psychologists, disability specialists, and content-area classroom instructors can illuminate the complicated nature of student motivation and guide institutions to adapt themselves to the needs of their students regarding the optimum learning environment.

Previous research and scholarship has often focused on the utility of UID for groups of students as illustrated in this article, such as students with disabilities and students with academic preparation issues, with an extension to the entire student group. So much of previous work has focused on increasing recognition, sensitivity, and meeting the needs of groups within the larger student body. The future for UID is to serve as a catalyst and guide for educators to understand that all students are different, individual, and unique. The reason for implementing UID will not be to meet the needs of a variety of groups within the class: rather, it will be to meet the unique needs posed by each individual learner within the classroom. A transformed classroom learning experience will be essential to help learners to reach their full potential.

References

Adams, D., & Hamm, M. (1990). *Cooperative learning: Critical thinking and collaboration across the curriculum*. Springfield, IL: Charles C. Thomas.

Angelo, T. A., & Cross, K. P. (1993). *Classroom assessment techniques. A handbook for college teachers* (2nd ed.). San Francisco: Jossey-Bass.

Apple Computer, Inc. (2007a). *iLife software suite.* Cupertino, CA: Author.

Apple Computer, Inc. (2007b). *iTunes podcast directory.* Retrieved August 24, 2007, from http://itunes.com

Arendale, D. (1998). Increasing the efficiency and effectiveness of learning for first year students through Supplemental Instruction. In J. L. Higbee & P. L. Dwinell (Eds.), *Developmental education: Preparing successful college students* (pp. 185-197). Columbia, SC: The National Association for Developmental Education and The National Resource Center for the First-Year Experience and Students in Transition, University of South Carolina. (ERIC Document Reproduction Service No. ED 423794).

Arendale, D. (2004). Pathways of persistence: A review of postsecondary peer cooperative learning programs. In I. M. Duranczyk, J. L. Higbee, & D. B. Lundell (Eds.), *Best practices for access and retention in higher education* (pp. 27-40). Minneapolis: University of Minnesota, General College, Center for Research on Developmental Education and Urban Literacy. Retrieved August 24, 2007, from http://www.cehd.umn.edu/crdeul/monographs.html

Arendale, D., & Ghere, D. (2005). Integrating best practices of developmental education in introductory history courses. In J. L. Higbee, D. B. Lundell, & D. R. Arendale (Eds.), *The General College vision: Integrating intellectual growth, multicultural perspectives, and student development* (pp. 223-246). Minneapolis: University of Minnesota, General College, Center for Research on Developmental Education and Urban Literacy. Retrieved August 24, 2007, from http://www.cehd.umn.edu/crdeul/books-thegcvision.html

Arendale, D. (Ed.). (2007). *Then and now Web site.* [On-line]. Retrieved August 24, 2007, from http://thenandnow.org

Astin, A. W. (1993). *What matters in college: Four critical years revisited.* San Francisco: Jossey-Bass.

Barkley, E. F., Cross, K. P., & Major, C. H. (2005). *Collaborative learning techniques: A handbook for college faculty.* San Francisco: Jossey-Bass.

Barton, P. E. (2002). *The closing of the education frontier?* Princeton, NJ: Educational Testing Service. Retrieved July 4, 2004, from: http://www.ets.org/Media/Research/pdf/PICFRONTIER.pdf

Bastedo, M. N., & Gumport, P. J. (2003). Access to what? Mission differentiation and academic stratification in U.S. public higher education. *Higher Education: The International Journal of Higher Education and Educational Planning, 46,* 341-359.

Bennett, R. B., Jr., Leibman, J. H., & Fetter, R. E. (1997). Using a jury simulation as a classroom exercise. *Journal of Legal Studies Education, 15,* 191-210.

Bredemeier, M. E., & Greenblat, C. S. (1981). The educational effectiveness of simulation games: A synthesis of findings. *Simulation & Gaming: An International Journal, 12,* 307-332.

Bruffee, K. A. (1993). *Collaborative learning: Higher education, interdependence, and the authority of knowledge.* Baltimore, MD: The Johns Hopkins University Press.

Burgstahler, S. (2005). *Universal Design in education: Principles and applications.* Seattle: University of Washington, Do-IT (Disabilities, Opportunities, Internetworking & Technology). Retrieved August 24, 2007, from http://www.washington.edu/doit/Brochures/PDF/ud_edu.pdf

Chaffee, J. (1992). Critical thinking skills: The cornerstone of developmental education. *Journal of Developmental Education, 15*(3), 2-4, 6, 8, 39.

Cooper, J., Prescott, S., Cook, L., Smith, L., & Mueck, L. (1990). *Cooperative learning and college instruction: Effective use of student learning teams.* Long Beach, CA: The California State University Foundation.

Disability Services. (2005). *Annual report.* Minneapolis: University of Minnesota, Office for Multicultural and Academic Affairs, Disability Services.

Disabilities Services. (2007). *Web homepage.* Retrieved August 24, 2007, from http://ds.umn.edu

Doyle, T., & Kowalczyk, J. (1999). The Structured Learning Assistance Program model. In M. Hay & N. Ludman (Eds.), *Selected Conference Papers of the National Association for Developmental Education, Volume 5* (pp. 4-7). Warrensburg, MO: National Association for Developmental Education. Retrieved August 24, 2007, from http://www.nade.net/documents/SCP99/SCP99.2.pdf

Dreyfus, A. E. (Ed.). (2004). *Internet homepage of the Peer-Led Team Learning Program* [On-line]. Retrieved June 22, 2004, from http://www.pltl.org

Druckman, D. (1995). The educational effectiveness of interactive games. In D. Crookall & K. Arai (Eds.), *Simulation and gaming across discipline and culture* (pp. 178-187). London: Sage.

Fry, H., Ketteridge, S., & Marshall, S. (2003). *A handbook for teaching and learning in higher education: Enhancing academic practice.* London, UK: Kogan Page Limited.

Ghere, D. L. (2000). Teaching American history in a developmental education context. In J. L. Higbee & P. L. Dwinell (Eds.), *The many faces of developmental education* (pp. 39-46). Warrensburg, MO: National Association for Developmental Education. Retrieved September 4, 2007, from http://www.nade.net/documents/Mono%2000/monograph00.pdf

Ghere, D. L. (2001). Constructivist perspectives and classroom simulations in developmental education. In D. B. Lundell & J. L. Higbee (Eds.), *Theoretical perspectives for developmental education* (pp. 101-108). Minneapolis: University of Minnesota, General College, Center for Research on Developmental Education and Urban Literacy. Retrieved September 4, 2007, from http://www.cehd.umn.edu/crdeul/monographs.html

Ghere, D. L. (2003). Best practices and students with disabilities: Experiences in a college history course. In J. L. Higbee (Ed.), *Curriculum transformation and disability: Implementing Universal Design in higher education* (pp. 149-161). Minneapolis: University of Minnesota, General College, Center for Research on Developmental Education and Urban Literacy. Retrieved August 27, 2007, from http://www.cehd.umn.edu/crdeul/books-ctad.html

Higbee, J. L. (Ed.). (2003). *Curriculum transformation and disability: Implementing Universal Design in higher education.* Minneapolis: University of Minnesota, General College, Center for Research on Developmental Education and Urban Literacy. Retrieved August 27, 2007, from http://www.cehd.umn.edu/crdeul/books-ctad.html

Higbee, J. L., Chung, C. J., & Hsu. L. (2004). Enhancing the inclusiveness of first-year courses through Universal Instructional Design. In I. M. Duranczyk, J. L. Higbee, & D. B. Lundell (Eds.), *Best practices for access and retention in higher education* (pp. 13-25. Minneapolis: University of Minnesota, General College, Center for Research on Developmental Education and Urban Literacy. Retrieved September 16, 2007, from http://www.cehd.umn.edu/crdeul/monographs.html

Higbee, J. L., & Dwinell, P. L. (1998). Thinking critically: The relationship between student development and the ability to think critically. *Research & Teaching in Developmental Education, 14*(2), 93-97.

Higbee, J. L., Lundell, D. B., & Arendale, D. R. (Eds.). (2005). *The General College vision: Integrating intellectual growth, multicultural perspectives, and student development.* Minneapolis: University of Minnesota, General College, Center for Research on Developmental Education and Urban Literacy. Retrieved August 24, 2007, from http://www.cehd.umn.edu/crdeul/books-thegcvision.html

Johnson, D. W., & Johnson, R. T. (1986). Mainstreaming and cooperative learning strategies. *Exceptional Children, 52,* 553-561.

Johnson, D.W., Johnson, R.T., & Holubec, E.J. (2002). *Circles of learning: Cooperation in the classroom* (5th ed.). Edina, MN: Interaction Book.

Johnson, D., Johnson, R., & Smith, K. (1991). *Active learning: Cooperation in the college classroom.* Edina, MN: Interaction Book.

Kipp, S. M., Price, D. D., & Wohlford, J. K. (2002). *Unequal opportunity: Disparities in college access among the 50 states.* Indianapolis, IN: Lumina Foundation for Education. Retrieved September 27, 2004, from http://www.luminafoundation.org/publications/monographs/pdfs/monograph.pdf

Light, R. J. (2001). *Making the most of college: Students speak their minds.* Cambridge, MA: Harvard University Press.

Martin, D. C., Blanc, R., & Arendale, D. (1994). Mentoring in the classroom: Making the implicit explicit. *Teaching Excellence Newsletter, 6*(1), 1-2.

O'Connor, R. E., & Jenkins, J. R. (1995, April). *Cooperative learning for students with learning disabilities: Teacher and child contributions to successful participation.* Paper presented at the Annual Conference of the American Education Research Association, San Francisco, CA. (ERIC Document Reproduction Service No. ED390189).

Paul, R., & Elder, L. (1999). Critical thinking: Teaching students to seek the logic of things. *Journal of Developmental Education, 23*(1), 34-35.

Pliner, S. M., & Johnson, J. R., (2004). Historical, theoretical, and foundational principles of Universal Instructional Design in higher education. *Equity & Excellence in Education, 37*(2), 105-113.

Randell, J. M., Morris, B. A., Welzel, C. D., & Whitehall, B.V. (1992). The effectiveness of games for educational purposes: A review of recent research. *Simulation & Gaming: An International Journal, 23,* 261-276.

Scott, S. S., McGuire, J. M., & Shaw, S. F. (2003). Universal Design for Instruction: An approach for inclusion. *Remedial and Special Education, 31,* 369-379.

Shaw, K. M. (1997). Remedial education as ideological battleground: Emerging remedial education policies in the community college. *Educational Evaluation and Policy Analysis, 19,* 284-296.

Silver, D., Bourke, A., & Strehorn, K. C. (1998). Universal Instructional Design in higher education: An approach for inclusion. *Equity and Excellence in Education, 31*(2), 47-51.

Slaughter, S., & Rhoades, G. (2004). *Academic capitalism and the new economy: Markets, state, and higher education.* Baltimore: The Johns Hopkins University Press.

Stone, N. R. (1990). Ideas in practice: Developing critical thinkers: Content and process. *Journal of Developmental Education, 13*(3), 20-26.

Treisman, U. (1985). A study of mathematics performance of Black students at the University of California, Berkeley. *Dissertation Abstracts International, 47*(05), 1641A.

Vygotsky, L. S. (1978). *Mind in society.* Cambridge, MA: Harvard University Press.

Wilcox, K. J., delMas, R. C., Stewart, B., Johnson, A. B., & Ghere, D. (1997). The "package course" experience and developmental education. *Journal of Developmental Education, 20*(3), 18-20, 22, 24, 26.

CHAPTER 10

Writing Assignments and Universal Design for Instruction: Making the Phantom Visible

Renee DeLong
University of Minnesota

Abstract
This chapter takes the principles of Universal Design for Instruction (UDI) and applies them to the conventions of writing assignments in higher education. Assignment sheets, peer editing, and creating a writing community are discussed. This chapter argues that if instructors approach UDI as a tool for both inclusiveness and professional development, we can examine assignment sheets and pedagogical values while also using UDI to examine our professional lives and the hidden values of the university.

When I made the transition from teaching high school English to teaching composition in a 4-year institution, I was given a few sample syllabi and a quick orientation on the college's approach. The instructors had all been trained in Universal Instructional Design (UID; Higbee 2003) in order to make the General College (Higbee, Lundell, & Arendale, 2005) of the University of Minnesota more accessible to students from many backgrounds, to increase active learning in the classroom, and to make student assessment clear in order to increase students' sense of competency. As colleagues explained why they wrote seven-page syllabi, held individual conferences before writing assignments were due, and constructed detailed yet flexible writing assignments, I wondered why they needed to explain it all to me. I took education classes when studying for my teaching license and taught for several years in public schools. Call it whatever you want, I thought, this is just excellent student-centered pedagogy. However, as I continued to question and analyze my own teaching strategies, I came to a more complex understanding of UID and its importance in writing assessment. We frequently and justifiably use writing in higher education to assess critical thinking skills and push students' development through the stages of Bloom's (1956) taxonomy to analysis, synthesis, and evaluation; yet we rarely scaffold our demands for compelling and analytical writing. I believe that critical thinking is imperative and achievable for all students, and students can be taught to showcase this critical thinking if instructors make their writing assignments clear and flexible.

In this chapter I will analyze five of Scott, McGuire, and Shaw's (2003) nine principles of Universal Design for Instruction—a slightly different but parallel model to UID—to examine the mostly unspoken traditional conventions of writing assignments in the university. (See Figure 1).

Figure 1. UDI principles and considerations for writing assignments

Principle	Definition Keywords	Considerations
Principle 2: Flexibility in use	accommodation, range of student abilities, flexibility	Do I give students some options for completing the assignment? Do I weigh these assignments equally or have a trump card assignment?
Principle 3: Simple and intuitive	straightforward , predictability, intuitive	Does my assignment sheet and rubric accurately reflect my grading requirements? Do I reinforce to students my values as an instructor? Do students understand the language I use on assignment sheets/rubrics? Do I use student models to demonstrate expectations?
Principle 5: Tolerance for error	anticipation of variation, different learning paces and skills	Do I build in rewriting opportunities? How much does grammar count? How do I admit errors?
Principle 8: A community of learners	interaction, communication, honesty	Do I make time for peer editing? How do I encourage student discussions outside of class? Do I teach students what academic honesty and plagiarism look like in my field? How do I know if students understand my assignment sheet? Do I use group writing assignments?
Principle 9: Instructional climate	welcoming and inclusive instruction, high expectations	Do I read excellent student writing to the class? How else do I motivate students to do exceptional work? Can students come in to my office to discuss drafts?

The first two columns are based on concepts from Scott, McGuire, and Shaw (2003)

This chapter is directed toward faculty, instructors, and teaching assistants who require and grade writing assignments across the curriculum. For a more in-depth discussion of UID in college composition courses, see McAlexander (2003). We can use UID or UDI to think through the practices and processes of writing at the college level in unique ways. This article has a larger audience than instructors, however. Advisers may decide to ask some of the pedagogical questions from this article when working with a student who is struggling through a writing-intensive class. Administrators implementing UID or UDI throughout their college or university may utilize this chapter to continue discussions about writing assessment with department leaders and administrators.

The Phantom in the Academy: Assignment Sheets and Expectations

I frequently ask students to tell me about the writing they are expected to do in college, and I am struck by how often they need to write essays or response papers to demonstrate understanding, yet how rarely they are given a rubric or assignment sheet. There is a silent agreement in college between the instructor and student: "Read my mind," implies the teacher, "and you might get the grade you want." Tracking the phantom of the college writing assignment would make a fascinating sociological—and perhaps metaphysical—study. Some students come to college with a "sixth sense" for seeing the unspoken values of an instructor, yet this ability often correlates with several intersections of privilege.

The one-sentence writing assignment that students often receive in lieu of an assignment sheet accompanied by a grading rubric can prevent students from doing excellent work, particularly students who are English Language Learners (ELL), students from urban high schools, students with emotional or behavioral disabilities, and students who represent the first-generation in their family to attend college. Many students fit into at least one of these categories, and they all deserve to have clear writing assignments. All students have this right.

As a student I agonized over this assignment: "Write a 15-20 page essay on a topic of your choice. It must be related to the material covered in our class." I wondered how I could ask enough questions to get some parameters for the assignment. Which questions could I ask? Now that I am sometimes on the other side of the lectern I marvel at how an instructor would even begin grading a stack of those papers. If instructors develop strong assignment sheets that ask for exactly what we want from students, such as, "use quotes from three scholarly sources" or "summarize two scholarly articles in your own words", we can create the outline for our own upcoming job of assessment. Within a well-crafted assignment students can explore their ideas and voices.

There are many reasons for assigning writing, and some of these justifications allow students space to experiment with their analysis, voice, and tone, while others carry with them the assumptions of professional—and perhaps detached-sounding—writing. A hidden benefit of using UDI principles is that we step back and analyze the ways knowledge is produced and valued in our discipline and then examine how we can assess students' knowledge while being fair and flexible. This examination links to the third UDI principle, simple and intuitive approach. Writing assignments may require students to: (a) demonstrate understanding of vocabulary; (b) demonstrate correct usage of writing conventions (Modern Language Association [MLA] style, American Psychological Association [APA] style, Chicago style); (c) organize and summarize principles or ideas from lecture or text; (d) quote and paraphrase primary and secondary sources; (e) use course material to set up new connections within and beyond field; and (f) create original (and perhaps critical) thinking in field.

Many undergraduate students taking lower-division classes will be unable to mimic the writing conventions in a new discipline within only 15 weeks, even though these students may have learned a great deal in my class. Whatever my aim is for assigning writing, I give students some tips on how to accomplish my assignment and show them what above-average writing looks like. During recitation or lecture sections, I present anonymous examples of both excellent and mediocre student work so that students learn the values and vocabulary for critiquing each writing assignment. Writing is situational; there is no essay that will earn an A in every class, and some students begin to understand this in their second year of college. Even though the Writing Center is staffed with excellent consultants, my writing assignments and the type of writing that I value are specific to my discipline and my class. Students can benefit from a direct discussion of these values.

To set up my file of student writing, I ask students for their permission to use their work in future classes. It is wise to create a short contract for students to sign that specifies how and why their work will be used, and then ask for a paper copy of their writing that has their name and any identifiers removed.

Creating Community and Peer Editing

It is then assumed that with an assignment sheet and some examples of excellent writing students should breeze through writing assignments, but for first-year college students in particular this may be an unrealistic expectation. Efficient instructors reinforce the importance of these tools with peer editing. If writing is situational, and writing is a process, then it only follows that students should be required to write rough drafts and talk through the parameters of the assignment with other students. The eighth principle of UDI emphasizes the importance of creating a community of learners, and peer editing supports this. Bruch (2003) described a community activity for creating meaning around and within an assignment long before the first draft is written. In this activity, students examine the new assignment sheet and write down their understanding of it. Working in small groups, students share their interpretations and think about "the different kinds of cultural work done by the different kinds of writing" that they could do to fulfill the assignment (p. 100). Bruch stressed that during this activity he tells students to stay open to various interpretations of the assignment and not to try to figure out which one might be correct. He also does not step in and point to a "correct" interpretation. Additionally, this activity makes reading an assignment sheet a personal act of interpretation and gives the instructor a voice in the discussion.

I hold peer editing sessions during class for selfish reasons: in most cases, I do not want to be the first person who reads a student's text. That desire is strong enough for me to plan for peer editing before each major assignment is due. Not every student has learned how to do peer editing before coming to my class, so I ask students to use the assignment sheet to read each others' first drafts. This also gives me a chance to teach students the vocabulary that I use when I assess their writing. A detailed peer-editing sheet can be an excellent tool to focus students' attention on the values written into the assignment sheet and rubric. Sometimes I rework our class schedule and save peer editing for assignments that permit students to do more creative or subjective work, and make peer editing on large papers worth several points or a percentage of the grade. Later in the semester, I assign peer editing as homework. In nearly every class, a few students complain about the quality of their feedback and I refocus their analysis on what they learned from reading other people's work. The process of sharing writing is valuable for many reasons.

Procrastination can be fear masquerading as laziness. When a deadline is broken into chunks (e.g., due date for first draft, due date for second draft, final due date), students can be motivated into working through the process. In addition, each benchmark draft becomes a time for students to come and talk to me about the project. Using UDI allows me to refocus my ideas about the curriculum of the class, and because I am invested in teaching students to seek and learn from additional readers, I value peer editing.

Admitting Errors: Using UDI to Talk About Teaching

At the beginning of this chapter, Figure 1 provides a list of questions to consider when instructors examine writing assignments using the tool of UDI. Some of the questions can be answered as we examine our teaching environments, post assignment sheets on blogs or Web pages, and create community through and beyond our classrooms. I wrote the consideration questions in column three to suggest alternate practices and not to prescribe changes. I can recall several cases when to myself I responded to a question in column three with a complaint about clunky technology or the limitations of my time and energy. In keeping with the spirit of UDI, I bring my most flexible and inquisitive self to the classroom with the understanding that there are physical and institutional limitations on the work that I do.

The fifth provocative UDI principle, and the one that can help us rethink many aspects of our teaching practice is: Tolerance for error—both student and teacher error. Making space for errors in our classrooms speaks to the humanity and the hope of the institution. I use my voice to remark on students' writing and not some "godlike" teacher voice. "I think I understand ..." or "I'm not sure this follows ..." are much more humane and conversational comments than "This doesn't follow" or mean-spirited question marks that leak from red pens. When I reject the stereotype of the professor who has all the answers, I can listen fully and continue to learn in the classroom. Making public mistakes reminds students of my fallibility and can increase their respect for the process of learning and increase their engagement with the class. Perhaps we can create knowledge and direct the class together. Perhaps I have more to learn about my discipline and how to teach it, and that is exciting.

Although UID's and UDI's acknowledgement of each student's unique needs and learning styles is practical, perhaps the most radical lesson we can learn through UID and UDI is that each member of the class, including the instructor, has lapses, questions, and spaces for growth. Faculty development programs could use UID and UDI to rethink all aspects of what it means to be a "professor" and how faculty members continue to develop over their careers.

A Conclusion and a Question of Haunting

As a graduate student I have begun to read my professors' articles or books before I take their classes, and this practice has given me a sense of what they value as excellent writing. Then I reconstitute their writing choices and hidden values to sketch out the assignment sheet that might later be missing from their writing assignments. Sometimes I still write the paper that I value more, but I do it knowing that I may not earn an A in the class. My examination of professors' texts is a process that involves reanimation, an examination of a hidden process, and maybe an act of ghostbusting. But undergraduate students cannot be expected to engage in this process. Instead, as instructors we must make what is hidden transparent.

The unspoken writing conventions of the university haunt our halls, and we must all work to make the phantom visible by creating specific guidelines and assessments for writing assignments. If we are not working on our pedagogy and continuing to develop our practices to create clarity in our classrooms, we run the risk of rewriting old texts of exclusion. Is elitism the most hallowed ghost of the university?

References

Bloom B. S. (Ed.) (1956) *Taxonomy of educational objectives, the classification of educational goals—Handbook I: Cognitive domain.* New York: McKay.

Bruch, P. L. (2003). Interpreting and implementing Universal Instructional Design in basic writing. In J. L. Higbee (Ed.). *Curriculum transformation and disability: Implementing Universal Design in higher education* (pp. 93-103). Minneapolis: University of Minnesota, General College, Center for Research on Developmental Education and Urban Literacy.

Higbee, J. L. (Ed.), *Curriculum transformation and disability: Implementing Universal Design in higher education.* Minneapolis: University of Minnesota, General College, Center for Research on Developmental Education and Urban Literacy.

Higbee, J. L., Lundell, D. B., & Arendale, D. (Eds.). (2005). *The General College vision: Integrating intellectual growth, multicultural perspectives, and student development.* Minneapolis: University of Minnesota, General College, Center for Research on Developmental Education and Urban Literacy.

McAlexander, P. J. (2003). Using principles of Universal Design in college composition courses. In J. Higbee (Ed.), *Curriculum transformation and disability: Implementing Universal Design in higher education* (pp. 105–114). Minneapolis: University of Minnesota, General College, Center for Research on Developmental Education and Urban Literacy.

Scott, S., McGuire, J., & Shaw, S. (2003). Universal Design for Instruction: A new paradigm for adult instruction in postsecondary education. *Remedial and Special Education, 24,* 369-379.

CHAPTER 11

Successful Undergraduate Mathematics Through Universal Design of Essential Course Components, Pedagogy, and Assessment

Irene M. Duranczyk and Annia K. Fayon
University of Minnesota

Abstract
This chapter juxtaposes the standards for successful undergraduate mathematics as defined by the professional mathematics organizations with the guiding principles of Universal Instructional Design (UID) and multiculturalism. It makes the case that you can not have one without the others. Specific examples of multiculturalism through UID with mathematical applications for determining essential components, deciding on pedagogical approaches, and using authentic assessment are given. Developmental mathematics is addressed, but in the context of undergraduate mathematics for all.

Students with disabilities (e.g., learning, visual, hearing, medical, mobility and motor control, attention deficit/hyperactivity, psychiatric) generally have been exposed throughout their formative years to many situations that necessitated the development of life skills in problem solving, perseverance, creativity, and mastering multiple or alternative approaches—characteristics that are generally enabling in the study of mathematics—yet few of these students will choose to pursue an undergraduate science, technology, engineering, or mathematics (STEM) degree. The number of people with disabilities in higher education has tripled in the past 25 years (Ebert, 2005), but not in STEM careers. While 13% of the members of the working population in the United States have disabilities, only 7% (≈ 365, 000) of the STEM workforce has disabilities (National Science Foundation [NSF], Division of Science Resources Statistics, 2002).

In 1999 the National Center for Education Statistics (NCES; Horn & Berktold, 1999) projected that more than 6% of postsecondary students have one or more disabilities; of those, over 29% report a learning disability; 23% an orthopedic disability; 21% a health-related disability (e.g., diabetes, asthma, narcolepsy); 16% a hearing disability; 16% a visual disability; and 3% a speech disability. Just 5 years later, the 2003-2004 NCES national survey of undergraduates in postsecondary education indicated that 11.3% of postsecondary students reported some type of disability (Horn, Nevill, & Griffith, 2006), well over the 6% of the postsecondary population projected to have disabilities in the 1999 study. The NCES 2003-2004 report identified that 21.9% of postsecondary students with disabilities have psychological or psychiatric disabilities (Horn et al., 2006); these are the two fastest growing segments of the postsecondary population with disabilities.

These data can only reflect reported documented disabilities. Students, given an option, may choose not to self-disclose (Uncertain welcome, 2002). Not knowing how their disability will be received unless the disability is obvious, students may prefer to adjust to the academy without disclosure unless there are clear and transparent signs that the environment will truly honor multiple ways of approaching and demonstrating academic knowledge or the essential components of the course.

Many students with disabilities are not encouraged in the study of mathematics (Feigenbaum, 2000). They are often perceived in the academy through the lens of a deficit model (also see Chapter 2 by Evans). The barriers or challenges they will face in the academy and STEM professions are emphasized, as opposed to acknowledging the life skills and attributes these students already possess and upon which they can draw while pursuing a STEM career. It is worth emphasizing that the challenges persons with disabilities face and overcome on a daily basis are the same entry-level skills and attributes needed in persons who study mathematics. Persons without disabilities are not as likely to be exposed to daily opportunities demanding creative solutions. Persons without disabilities may not have taken the time to work or think thorough situations and activities that individuals with physical, medical, psychological, or learning disabilities have analyzed and found adaptive ways to accomplish successfully.

Students with disabilities enter the college mathematics classroom with their history of accommodations, barriers, and frustrations, as well as their positive, empowering life experiences. When accommodations are individual to a student the message of "difference" is conveyed. When classroom spaces, curricula, pedagogy, and assessments are prepared with Universal Design (UD) in mind, all students can benefit. All students can utilize their life skills in meeting the challenges of the subject matter. Why universal access instead of accommodation? Universal access gives all students agency and authority in the classroom and in the academy. Students recognize that their experiences have prepared them for the educational environment rather than counting on the institution to accommodate their needs as they enter the new environment.

There is a mathematics educational gap for many students, not just students with disabilities. Although ACT has reported that more than 58% of postsecondary students are not ready for college-level mathematics and science, 54% of postsecondary students entering higher education have completed the college-preparatory curriculum and meet their state's guidelines for college readiness (ACT News, 2006). By weaving of principles of Universal Instructional Design (UID), ethnomathematics, ethnoeducation theory and pedagogy, and a sociocultural learning model into undergraduate education, more students can achieve the objectives of mathematics education for liberal arts and some will be able to realize a future in a mathematics-based career.

The literature emphasizes technological advances that have made access to education more universal for persons with vision, hearing, and other physical disabilities (Rose, Meyer, & Hitchcock, 2005). There are many instances where the use of technology can bridge content, pedagogy, and assessment gaps for students with learning, attention deficit/hyperactivity, or psychiatric disabilities as well. This chapter focuses on the nontechnological ways that faculty can create a learning and teaching environment that makes the cultural adjustments necessary for student access, engagement, persistence, and success. Even with technology these nontechnological approaches and "states of mind" are critical for faculty to address. Through faculty revisioning of effective teaching and learning, universal access can be achieved.

In order to illustrate how universal access can be achieved in the college mathematics classroom, the standards for successful undergraduate mathematics teaching and learning will be juxtaposed with the guiding principles of UID. Emphasis is on making essential course components transparent for all students, determining pedagogical processes that ensure equal access, and designing assessment strategies for fair and equitable evaluation of student progress. Through the dual lenses of multicultural theory and the experiences of a practicing ethnomathematician, specific examples of UID for undergraduate mathematics coursework are given. Developmental mathematics is addressed, but in the context of undergraduate mathematics for all.

Working Definitions

Working definitions of UID, ethnoeducation, sociocultural learning, and multiculturalism are needed before we proceed. These definitions provide a context for rethinking our academic content, pedagogical approaches, and assessment techniques. Each of these definitions provides a larger theoretical framework to reenvision our roles as teacher and learner. Each of these definitions can help practitioners in higher education reassess what it means to provide equal access for all students.

Universal Instructional Design

Universal Instructional Design is a process that maximizes learning for all students and minimizes the need for individual accommodations based on eight principles: creating a welcoming classroom climate, determining the essential components of the course, providing clear expectations and feedback, exploring ways to incorporate natural supports for learning, implementing varied instructional methods to share knowledge, providing a variety of ways for students to demonstrate knowledge, using technology to enhance learning opportunities, and encouraging faculty-student contact (Fox & Johnson, 2000). This definition invites faculty to rethink the content, pedagogical approaches, and assessment techniques used in the academy. It focuses on the end product and not the means for achieving that goal. The next few definitions provide a theoretical backdrop for this task—how to implement the eight guiding principles of Universal Instructional Design. Each of the UID principles are addressed in the context of an ethnoeducation and sociocultural theory model in first-year undergraduate mathematics (see Figure 1).

Ethnoeducation

As reported by Jackson (1995), ethnoeducation was first defined by Colombia's Constitution in 1986:

Figure 1. Guiding principles of Universal Instructional Design and multiculturalism with the professional standards for mathematics

Universal Instructional Design	Multicultural Perspectives	AMATYC and MAA Standards
Create a welcoming classroom climate	• Begin with students' lived experiences • Present mathematics as a cultural tool	Create an environment that optimizes the learning of mathematics for all students
Determine the essential components of the course	• Determine key concepts, language and symbolic techniques needed to reach course and curriculum objectives • Create connections from the concrete, discrete experience to key mathematical concepts, formal mathematical language, and symbolic mathematical representations	• Define and build consensus on goals and objectives of the mathematics curriculum and individual classes. • Create courses and programs based on desired student outcomes
Provide clear expectations and feedback	Provide clear expectations, feedback, and bridge building between informal cultural experiences and academic cultural knowledge	• Provide students with prompt feedback and be attentive, clear, and organized • Clearly define high expectations and communicate these to all students
Explore ways to incorporate natural supports for learning	• Promote active learning and independent thinking • Use cultural artifacts, tools, and expressions to support key mathematical concepts and ideas	Provide appropriate physical facilities and academic support resources to promote student success in mathematics and complement learning experiences
Provide varied instructional methods	• Use multiple experiential approaches to explore key mathematical ideas. • Use student-centered approaches to construct mathematical knowledge. • Incorporate the role that language and culture play in learning mathematics	Use a variety of teaching strategies that reflect the results of research to enhance student learning such as: collaborative/cooperative learning, discovery-based learning, interactive lectures and question-posing, writing, technology
Provide a variety of ways for students to demonstrate knowledge	Use multiple classroom assessment techniques as an integral part of instruction to assess student learning and use those results to adjust instructional methods and materials	Use multiple classroom assessment techniques as an integral part of instruction to assess student learning and use those results to adjust instructional methods and materials
Use technology to enhance learning opportunities	Integrate technology as a tool to help students discover and understand key mathematical concepts	Integrate technology as a tool to help students discover and understand key mathematical concepts
Encourage faculty-student contact	Encourage student-faculty contact embedded in the implementation of teaching strategies that capitalize on students' cultural knowledge and ways of learning	Encourage student-faculty contact embedded in the implementation of a variety of teaching strategies

Content	Pedagogy	Assessment

> a permanent social process, immersed in the culture, that consists of the acquisition of knowledge and values, and in the development of capabilities, in keeping with the needs, interests, and aspirations of the community, that will give to it the capacity to fully participate in the cultural control of the ethnic group. [Ministerio de Educacion 1986a:59] (p. 308)

D'Ambrosio (1985), considered the father of ethnomathematics, defined ethnomathematics as:

> the mathematics which is practised among identifiable cultural groups, such as national-tribal societies, labor groups, children of a certain age bracket, professional classes, and so on. Its identity depends largely on focuses of interest, on motivation, and on certain codes and jargons which do not belong to the realm of academic mathematics. (p. 45)

These two definitions assisted in broadening the concept of education to include cultural groups' ways of observing, documenting, theory testing, and explaining the world. Knowledge in the academy or university-based knowledge making would be one form of ethnoeducation—higher education as the cultural group's approach to education. The university as a cultural group has a view and approach to observing, documenting, theory testing, and explaining the world. It does not always include, acknowledge, or value divergent yet valid ways of knowing and learning that students from other cultures or with multiple cultural identities bring to the academy. Expanded definitions of multiculturalism, UID, and ethnoeducation honor the knowledge and skills developed by persons with multiple identities, including individuals with disabilities, as they interact with the world. They acknowledge, value, and incorporate cultural knowledge from outside of the academy with academic pursuits.

Sociocultural Learning Theory

Sociocultural learning theory provides a pedagogical umbrella for these multicultural, multiple identities concepts. This process is an adaptation of experiential learning (Kolb, 1984), culturally responsive mathematics and science education (Nelson-Barber & Estrin, 1995), and The Algebra Project's pedagogy (Moses & Cobb, 2001). Students enter college classrooms with a wide variety of informal mathematical knowledge, skills, and ways of thinking about and understanding their world. Often students leave this bank of information untouched and isolated from their academic experiences and required undergraduate academic knowledge base. Students able to function successfully in college—managing their time, money, and other resources—often are unable to demonstrate skills in using decimals, determining percents, or calculating decay rates, despite having entered the classroom having successfully calculated sales tax, tips, and transportation rates. When pressed, students who demonstrate their use of mathematical thinking, evaluating, and problem solving outside the academic setting can relate it to academic mathematics. Bridges between lived experiences and academic knowledge may need

Figure 2. An ethnomathematical and sociocultural learning model

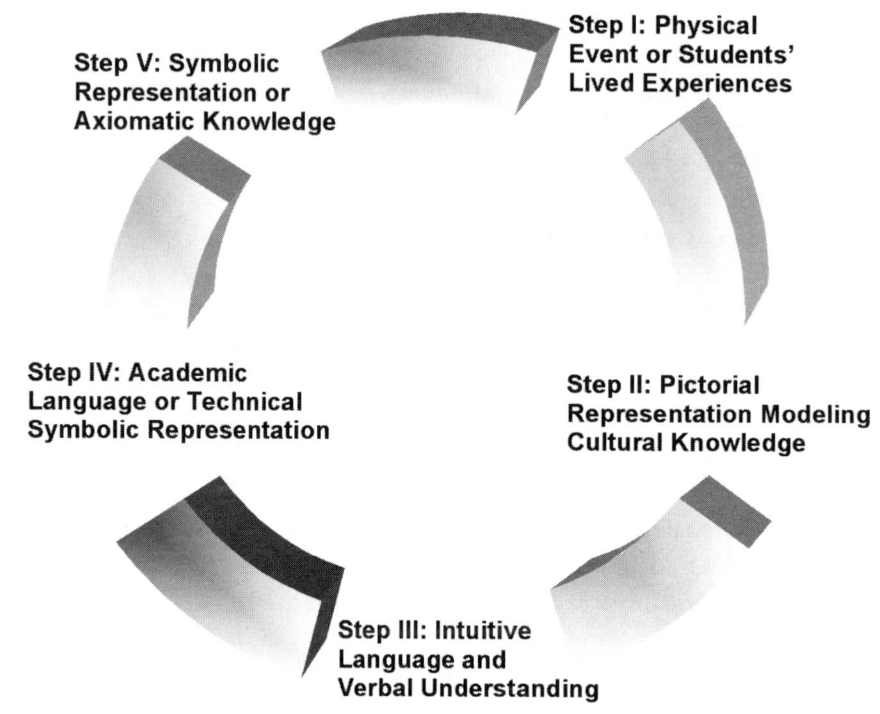

to be rebuilt or strengthened. This is the first step in the sociocultural learning model (see Figure 2).

It is not until Step IV in this learning model that a bridge is built between students' cultural representation (i.e., pictorial and verbal understanding) of the concept and the academic representation of the concept. This process acknowledges students' lived experiences and understanding and uses that information to build or restructure information for disciplinary contexts. A more complete description of this process with examples can be found in "Introductory-Level College Mathematics Explored Through a Sociocultural Lens" (Duranczyk, Staats, Moore, Hatch, Jensen, & Somdahl, 2002).

Multiculturalism

> As an idea, multicultural education seeks to create equal educational opportunities for all students, including those from different racial, ethnic, and social-class groups. Multicultural education tries to create equal educational opportunities for all students by changing the total school environment so that it will reflect the diverse cultures and groups within society and within the nation's classrooms. (Banks et al., 2001, p. 2)

Banks' (1995) five dimensions of multicultural education (i.e., content integration, knowledge construction, prejudice reduction, equity pedagogy, and empowering school culture) are all embraced in the basic components of ethnomathematics and sociocultural theory.

Ethnomathematics links students' diverse ways of knowing and learning and culturally-embedded knowledge with academic mathematics. Ethnomathematics embraces students' lived experiences, builds from that knowledge, and interfaces students' real-world knowledge with academic terms, concepts, and ways of knowing.

Integration With the Disciplinary Standards

In the new American Mathematical Association for Two Year Colleges (AMATYC) standards, Beyond Crossroads: Implementing Standards in the First Two Years of College (AMATYC, 2006), Chapter 4 is dedicated to acknowledging the diversity of our student population. As indicated in Figure 1, a review of the new standards for undergraduate education as set by AMATYC, the National Council of Teachers of Mathematics (NCTM, 2000), and the Mathematical Association of America (MAA, 2004) for undergraduate mathematics, juxtaposed with the guidelines for students with physical, psychological, or learning disabilities, reveals similar goals for course content, pedagogy, and assessment. Students who begin the postsecondary experience in a mathematics course below precalculus are primarily students who have not adjusted to traditional ways of learning posed in elementary and secondary education. They are often students who have avoided mathematics in high school and are placed in developmental education mathematics courses in postsecondary education. These are students who can benefit from UID, the sociocultural learning model, and the implementation of ethnoeducational or multicultural constructs. A multifaceted approach that integrates all three of these models embraces all students and creates natural supports for students with disabilities or developmental education needs.

The next section of this chapter will address three major areas of concern—access through the essential course components (i.e., disciplinary content and intellectual skill development); multiple teaching strategies (pedagogy); and multiple measures and formats for evaluating the attainment of essential course components (assessment). As illustrated in Figure 1, there are many natural supports and intersections when UID is viewed in context with multicultural perspectives and the disciplinary standards. Later in this chapter a section on the power of language will be addressed. The words we use in our pedagogy can be either empowering for students or send the message that students are missing key attributes needed for their academic success.

Access Through Essential Course Components

The purpose of mathematics as a mainstay in a college or university education boils down to the need for quantitative literacy in our technological world, much of which is embodied in the intellectual development skills defined by AMATYC (1995): (a) engaging in problem solving, (b) experiencing real-world modeling, (c) enhancing reasoning skills, (d) connecting mathematics with other disciplines, (e) communicating mathematical ideas, (f) developing mathematical power, (g) translating among mathematical representations, and (h) using technology to advance mathematical understanding. Along with the metaskills derived from studying mathematics, there are also standards for undergraduate mathematical content defined by AMATYC (1995). All undergraduate course work below calculus should assist students in: (a) developing enhanced number sense; (b) using symbolism and algebra for problem solving; (c) knowing when and how to apply geometry and measurement principles; (d) developing function sense, preparing the way for calculus concepts; (e) identifying and creating continuous and discrete models; (f) understanding the principles of data analysis, statistics, and probability; and (g) identifying and working through deductive proofs. There needs to be a balance between focusing on the step-by-step skills for the basic algorithms of arithmetic, algebra, geometry, trigonometry, and calculus and the intellectual "habits of the mind" (Conley, 2003) and the essential components of mathematics for the liberal arts as defined by the intellectual development and content standards (AMATYC, 1985, 2006).

Is factoring quadratic equations by grouping an essential component of an undergraduate algebra class, or is the understanding of the meaning of quadratic equation factors the essential component? Students can take a look at the many times that the "factors" of quadratic equations occur in their lives (e.g., throwing or hitting a ball; relationship between the dimensions of a quadrilateral and its area; the relationship between time, speed, and distance); be introduced to the many ways factors of quadratic equations can be found; and understand the relationships between factoring by grouping, graphing quadratic equations, using the quadratic formula or completing the square for finding factors. With this knowledge students can use nontechnological and technological approaches to finding factors of quadratic equations to solve real-world problems. This does not mean that we should not introduce students to and give them the opportunity to develop skills in the techniques used for exploring processes in mathematics. It only means that the essential components need to be clear and enable all students to achieve competency in the course goals. The emphasis needs to be on the concepts, skills, and behaviors that are core to the discipline and future studies. For some students a visual model (e.g., a graph) will be most beneficial. For other students an algebraic formula will be more informative. Yet other students will find the actual event (e.g., throwing the ball and noting the results) as the preferred method to bring the concept home. Mathematics faculty must determine how the essential components for a particular course or curriculum are defined. The faculty defines the essential components after considering the real and realistic purpose of the particular course or curriculum. What habits of mind and skills do students really need to be successful in mathematics? Are they the intellectual development skills as previously defined or are they particular algorithmic techniques?

Another example in mathematics will demonstrate this thought even further. The importance of students being able to understand algebraic concepts in words, tables, graphs, and algebraic statements or equations is well founded (AMATYC, 2006; MAA, 2004; NCTM, 2000). It is important for students to see the connections between these representations. It is also important to allow students to experiment with each of these forms yet use the form that best matches their own preferred learning styles, strengths, and thought processes. Is it imperative that a student with a vision impairment be as adept at reading and producing graphs as a student who relies on visual materials for meaning making? A student who is not a visual learner can demonstrate the interconnectedness between tables, equations, and words and be successful in understanding the relationship between variables without being adept at graph making. Will a student who is not a visual learner rely on a graphic presentation for knowledge and understanding of mathematical concepts or will the table and equation tell the greater story? The answers to these questions may vary from student to student. It is important to check for understanding of mathematical concepts. It is not essential that all students represent mathematical knowledge and understanding in exactly the same way. Students need to know mathematical conventions, but also need to express mathematical knowledge and understanding in ways that are compatible with their cultural life experiences and ways of knowing.

Access Through Multiple Teaching Strategies

Creating a welcoming environment is the first step in reducing anxiety and honoring disclosure or nondisclosure of a disability. When an instructor verbalizes a commitment to diversity, multiculturalism, universal access, and equity on the first day of class and demonstrates it in an opening activity, students' anxiety level regarding whether or not to disclose can be minimized. For instance, the faculty member can share a personal disclosure or relate a story that demonstrates a discomfort and apprehension in new situations and how that struggle shaped a new vision of teaching and learning. The faculty member might make a statement similar to the following:

> I am a proponent of discovery learning. We will use this approach. However, I would prefer not "discovering" too late that my approach to teaching and learning is not working for you. I would like an honest and clear relationship so that your time is maximized in this class and that I, too, can learn from you. We are in this together. We all learn or we all just put in time.

It is helpful if faculty acknowledge to students the belief that learning is a unique experience—rate, methods, and past experiences filter and form the base from which new knowledge can be absorbed and created. This is only the beginning. Creating a welcoming environment begins on the first day and continues to be the faculty member's habit of mind guiding or filtering the selection of all future activities, assignments, and pedagogical practices.

There is evidence that students with learning disabilities and behavioral disorders who have mediated inquiry-, activity-, or discovery-based classrooms make academic gains equivalent to those of their classroom peers and superior to most typical students in textbook-based classrooms (Dalton, Morocco, Tivnan, & Rawsom Mead, 1997; Mastropieri & Scruggs, 1994; Palincsar, Magnusson, Collins, & Cutter, 2001). There is also evidence that students who may have developmental educational needs also benefit from these same strategies. Mathematical work by students with learning disabilities may contain more numeric computation errors rather than conceptual algebraic errors (Feigenbaum, 2000). If the emphasis in the classroom is on process, numeric computation errors can be addressed in the context of reasonable answers, proof or recheck techniques, or the use of a calculator and arithmetic tools to recompute. The use of small groups in class and study groups outside of class can also give students flexibility and provide natural supports for reflecting on the results of computations.

The AMATYC (1995, 2006) standards also devote much attention to the impact of pedagogy on the teaching and learning process. The research used by the professional organization supports the key areas of pedagogy embraced by ethnomathematics, sociocultural theory, and disability studies. Instructional strategies that provide for more student-based activities, recognize student-constructed knowledge, and help students relate new information to what they already know enhance student achievement (Brophy & Good, 1986). AMATYC standards present guidelines in five areas: teaching with technology, interactive and collaborative learning, connecting with other disciplines and real-life experiences, multiple approaches, and experiencing mathematics—"projects and apprenticeships that promote independent thinking and require sustained effort" (Brophy & Good, p. 366). The research on multicultural and UID pedagogical practices verifies that there is increased achievement for all students regardless of cultural heritage or disability when these principles are incorporated into the academy (Kinney & Kinney, 2003; Staats, 2005). Although some students have and can learn through traditional lecture and drill and practice in the teacher-centered classroom, it is unlikely that anyone will be disadvantaged by a student-centered, engaged classroom.

When reviewing group activities used in the classroom, more attention needs to be given to the cultural aspects of the activity. For example, many faculty are still primarily teaching probability through the use of cards, dice, and other gambling techniques, when segments of our population have religious or cultural restrictions that disadvantage, isolate, or alienate some students when expected to engage in these activities to learn mathematics. Knowledge of the colors, number, and types of cards in a playing deck is not culturally unbiased knowledge. Presenting or having students demonstrate ways that their culture uses probability concepts in play as well as work can be more equitable, inviting, and culturally respectful. In the world of play, most cultures have other probability or counting artifacts, games, or historical representations that do not involve gambling.

Many teachers of developmental mathematics use objects and activities to demonstrate mathematical concepts. These techniques are known to increase memory and meaning making for students with disabilities (Maccini & Gagnon, 2006). Using a variety of classroom instructional activities in 10- to 15-minute segments that rely on movement; interaction; varying the size, length of time, and type of work done individually or in groups can engage all students. Again there needs to be a balance among the type and time utilized for the individual activities, the time allotted for reflection on the meaning of the activity, and the skill building focus of the essential content and intellectual develop components of the course. Tutorials that can maximize students' visual, tactile, auditory, and interactive learning preferences can become integral to in-class or out-of-class supports. Attention has to be given to strategies that tap into students' strengths and culture.

The Power of Language

Individual reflections and small group work to verbalize one's thinking and actions (e.g., what I am doing in the classroom, writing on the board, observing, or how I am lining up information) provide a powerful way to assist all students in developing meta-cognitive skills, using all their senses to take in new information, and demonstrating how thinking guides actions. Relating classroom events to real-world experiences or past activities in the classroom will also help students contextualize and build mental concept maps. Mathematics teachers can have students verbally or visually demonstrate their thinking process. This will not only help them formalize what makes sense and what does not make sense, it will help them utilize more of their physical senses and enhance memory paths. These processes help all students. Students with limited vision may benefit most from the verbalization of important aspects of problem solving, yet the demonstration will also assist a more visual learner with meaning making beyond the pictures. Talking math out loud empowers students to talk about math using both academic terminology and the words they use for less formal mathematics talk. It also helps build bridges between informal and nonmathematical language and the language of the academy. Reading mathematical punctuation and expressions can be used to clarify the similarities and differences between nonmathematical word meaning and academic mathematical terms. Verbalizing the similarities and differences between academic mathematical terminology and one's informal or other disciplinary base will help clarify mathematical concepts. In mathematics, reduce, cancel, and simplify have similar meanings but outside of the mathematical context they have very different meanings. In American Sign Language the sign for the distributive property in mathematics shares a common expression with a sign indicating a woman who has sex with more than one man. The roots of the many mathematical terms have other meanings when used by students in cultural, formal, or informal conversations. Bridging activities or exercises among conflicting concepts is an important part of meaning making and enhances one's ability to remember and recall concepts.

Access Through Alternate Measures and Formats to Demonstrate Knowledge

Advancements in the science of thinking and learning call for educational assessments that are culturally sensitive and respectful of the diversity of ways of knowing (Pellegrino, Chudowsky, & Glaser, 2001). Using a variety of culturally sensitive approaches for measuring increased knowledge and skills related to the essential components of undergraduate mathematics courses can add to this body of research. The 2006 edition of the AMATYC standards includes a chapter devoted to completing the circle—evaluating the impact of the course content and pedagogy on students' progress. These new guidelines are consistent with what has been offered in multicultural and disability studies. Assessment must take place at multiple levels: classroom, course, and program. Only when assessment is aligned at all three levels is there a feedback loop for program improvement and evaluation of *if* and *how well* the program is serving students. This chapter focuses only on meeting the diverse needs of all students at the classroom level. It is not intended to minimize the impact of the course, program, and institutional levels of assessment. For each of these levels faculty and administrators need to address sociocultural and disability issues to ensure that there is equal access and equity within the program and institution. The two key components recommended by AMATYC (2006) are multiple classroom assessment techniques integrated into the teaching and learning process and clear and transparent feedback loops between students' assessment results and adjustments in instructional methods and materials.

Operationally, untimed testing, retesting, and alternative ways to represent knowledge and skills (e.g., presentations, projects, in-class activities) may be starting points for reflecting on classroom assessment. One example drawn from rhetoric faculty is using the midterm exam as a first draft (Duranczyk & Lee, 2007). This practice reduces anxiety. Students can relax, and are thus able to recall as much information as possible, knowing that the draft can be revisited and revised to demonstrate the essential course components (i.e., skills and concepts). The emphasis is on being able to demonstrate competence, not on being able to demonstrate it *right now.* Between drafts, as in composition, students can meet with tutors or faculty to talk through concepts, skills, and presentation. Peer review is another technique used in composition that can assist mathematics faculty in revisioning class assessment activities (Duranczyk & Lee). Students can review other students' work to evaluate whether or not a problem and its solution are clearly and completely presented. Student-to-student feedback can move the assessment from a teacher-centered activity and the teacher's need for clarity in the presentation of mathematical work to a student-centered activity and the need to communicate mathematical meaning clearly with peers using conventional mathematical language and symbols. Skipping steps, not defining variables, not clearly indicating a final solution and its meaning, or leaving out connecting mathematical verbs or symbols will make peer review difficult. Students' clear presentation of mathematical ideas can only follow when there is a clear understanding of mathematical methods and concepts.

The use of rubrics to assess project-based activities, classroom and homework assignments, exams, or students' class presentations based on the essential course components, intellectual development skills, and mathematical standards can also create a venue for presenting clear expectations, feedback, and assessment. Figures 3 and 4, adapted from a model initially presented by Exemplars (2001), provide two examples of how a rubric can be designed to provide clear expectations and involve students in reflection, and be used for assessment purposes. The columns in both rubrics represent the methods (i.e., intellectual development skills) and assessment forms promoted by the mathematics professional organizations based on research on teaching and learning in mathematics (AMATYC, 2006; MAA, 2004; NCTM, 2000).

Summary and Implications for Mathematics Faculty and Administrators

The mathematical professional associations' standards, best practices in multiculturalism, and UID principles support, enhance, and advance undergraduate teaching and learning. This chapter draws clear demarcations between content, pedagogy, and assessment for presentation purposes only. The integration of a purposeful theoretical framework that values the contributions of all students, embracing their diversity in cultural heritage, abilities, race, religion, age, language, gender, income, sexual orientation, and so on, coupled with a purposeful institutional approach in determining essential course components and multiple pedagogical and assessment approaches to explore and assess how well students achieve those essential components will make UID and equity possible. It is also important to note that the mathematical practitioner's commitment to move toward a more

Figure 3. Project activities grading rubric

Levels	Problem Solving	Reasoning and Proof	Communication	Connections
Novice 2 points	No plan is identified or a plan is started but not complete. Little or no evidence of drawing on some relevant previous knowledge is present. Lacks evidence of some relevant engagement in the task.	Positions are made without support. No reasoning or justification for reasoning is present.	No clear presentation of ideas. Little or no communication of an approach is evident. Everyday, familiar language is used to communicate ideas but not related to formal mathematical language.	No connections are made linking this activity with life experiences and academic mathematics.
Apprentice 3 points	A partially correct strategy is chosen, or a correct strategy for solving only part of the task is chosen. Evidence of drawing on some relevant previous knowledge is present, showing some relevant engagement in the task.	Some arguments are made and are supported. Some correct reasoning or justification for reasoning is present but not a clear, complete, systematic presentation.	Some communication of an approach is evident through verbal or written accounts and explanations, use of diagrams or objects, writing, and using mathematical symbols. Some connections between informal and formal math language is used, and examples are provided to communicate ideas.	Some attempt to relate the task to other subjects or to own interests and experiences is made.
Practitioner 4 points	A correct strategy is chosen based on the mathematical situation in the task. Planning or monitoring of strategy is evident. Evidence of solidifying prior knowledge and applying it to the problem-solving situation is present.	Arguments are constructed with adequate mathematical reasoning. A systematic approach or justification of correct reasoning is present including: (a) clarification of the task, (b) Exploration of mathematical phenomena, and (c) Noting patterns, structures and regularities.	Communication of an approach is evident through a methodical, organized, coherent, sequenced, and labeled response. Informal and formal math language is used throughout the solution to share and clarify ideas.	Mathematical connections or observations are recognized.
Expert 5 points	An efficient strategy is chosen and evidence of evaluating progress toward a solution is present. Adjustments in strategy, if necessary, are made along the way or alternative strategies are considered. Evidence of analyzing the situation in informal and formal mathematical terms and extending prior knowledge is present.	Deductive arguments are used to justify decisions and may result in more formal proofs. Evidence is used to justify and support decisions made and conclusions reached. This may include: (a) testing and accepting or rejecting of a hypothesis or conjecture, (b) explanation of phenomena, and (c) generalizing and extending the solution to other cases.	Communication beyond the practitioner level is achieved. Communication of arguments is supported by mathematical properties used. Precise math language and symbolic notation are used to consolidate math thinking and to communicate ideas.	Mathematical connections or observations are used to extend the solution.
My rating of this portfolio:				
Professor's Rating:				

Note. Modified from the original version of NCTM Standard Rubric by Exemplars, 2001. Available from http://exemplars.com/ resources/ rubrics/nctm.html. Copyright 2004 by Exemplars. Adapted with permission.

Figure 4. Grading rubric for portfolios

Levels	Assigned activities/ reflections/ documents charting progress toward course objectives	Revisions to first drafts as appropriate to show progress toward course objectives	Additional representations of learnings or progress toward course objectives	Daily notes used for capturing in-class and out-of-class progress toward course objectives
Not Serious 1 point	No completed assignments	No revisions made on assignments	No additional work present	No class or study notes present
Novice 2 points	Less than 50% of the assignments completed	Less than 50% of the revisions completed on assignments	Some additional work present but not labeled or organized to show progress toward course objectives	Some class and study notes present but not labeled or organized to show progress toward course objectives
Apprentice 3 points	At least 50% of the assignments completed but less than 75%	At least 50% but less than 75% of the revisions completed on assignments	Some additional work present but not addressing weaknesses as identified in assignments; some labeling and organization is present showing progress toward course objectives	Some additional class and study notes present but 50% or fewer of the course objectives have notes that are labeled and organized
Practitioner 4 points	At least 75% of the assignments complete	At least 75% of the revisions on assignments complete	Additional work present addressing some of the areas of weaknesses as identified in the assignments;. the work is labeled and organized	More than 50% of the course objectives have class and study notes clearly labeled and organized
Expert 5 points	More than 90% of course assignments completed and turned in on time	More than 90% of the course assignments have completed revisions and were turned in on time	Additional work present addressing all of the areas of weakness identified in the assignments; all work is labeled and organized	There are class and study notes for each of the course objectives that are clearly labeled and organized
My rating of this portfolio:				
Instructors rating				

equitable classroom must be supported by a department and institution that also value and support equity and access in words and actions.

More research is necessary at the institutional, departmental, and classroom levels. More qualitative and quantitative classroom-based research is needed to demonstrate the advances for all students when studying in a universally-designed classroom. Armed with this knowledge, further advances can be made in access and equity. Our world is being flattened because of our global economies and interconnectedness beyond national boundaries—a flattened world in the sense that the competitive playing fields between industrial and emerging market countries have been leveled. Our classrooms need to be flattened to prepare all students for an uncertain, challenging future with many undefined, unknown needs. The essential components of mathematics are essential components for the advancement of all cultures in our technological world. With attention to our delivery system, students can be prepared for the undefined needs and careers ahead. Through a theoretical framework embracing UID and multiculturalism, mathematical success can be realizable for all students.

References

ACT News. (2006). *2006 ACT national score report news release.* Retrieved Feb 6, 2007, from http://www.act.org/news/releases/2006/ndr.html

American Mathematical Association of Two-Year Colleges. (1995). *Crossroads in mathematics: Standards for introductory college mathematics before calculus.* Memphis, TN: Author.

American Mathematical Association of Two-Year Colleges. (2006). *Beyond crossroads: Implementing mathematics standards in the first two years of college.* Memphis, TN: Author.

Banks, J. A. (1995). Multicultural education: Historical development, dimensions, and practice. In J. A. Banks & C. A. M. Banks (Eds.), *Handbook of research on multicultural education* (pp. 3-24). New York: Macmillan.

Banks, J. A., Cookson, P., Gay, G., Hawley, W. D., Jordan Irvine, J., Nieto, S., Ward Schofield, J., & Stephan, W. G. (2001). *Diversity within unity: Essential principles for teaching and learning in a multicultural society.* Seattle: University of Washington, School of Education, Center for Multicultural Education. Retrieved August 17, 2007, from http://depts.washington.edu/centerme/dwu.htm

Brophy, J. E., & Good, T. L. (1986). Teacher behavior and student achievement. In M. C. Wittrock (Ed.), *Handbook of research on teaching* (3rd ed., pp. 328-375). New York: Macmillan.

Conley, D.T. (Ed.). (2003). *Understanding university success: A report from Standards for Success, A project of the American Association of American Universities and The Pew Charitable Trusts.* Eugene, OR: Center for Educational Policy Research, University of Oregon.

Dalton, B., Morocco, C. C., Tivnan, T., & Rawson Mead, P. L. (1997). Supported inquiry science: Teaching for conceptual change in urban and suburban science classrooms. *Journal of Learning Disabilities, 30,* 670-784.

D'Ambrosio, U. (1985). Ethnomathematics and its place in the history and pedagogy of mathematics. *For the Learning of Mathematics, 5*(1), 41-48.

Duranczyk, I. M., & Lee, A. (2007). Process pedagogy, engaging mathematics. *Academic*

Exchange Quarterly, 11, 31-35.

Duranczyk, I. M., Staats, S., Moore, R., Hatch, J., Jensen, M., & Somdahl, C. (2004). Developmental mathematics explored through a sociocultural lens. In I. M. Duranczyk, J. L. Higbee, & D. B. Lundell (Eds.), *Best practices for access and retention in higher education* (pp. 43-53). Minneapolis: University of Minnesota, General College, Center for Research on Developmental Education and Urban Literacy.

Ebert, J. (2005). Scientists with disabilities: Assess all areas. *Nature, 435,* 552-554.

Exemplars. (2001). *NCTM standard rubric.* Retrieved August 24, 2007 from http://exemplars.com/resources/rubrics/assessment.html

Fox, J. A., & Johnson, D. (Eds.). (2000). *Curriculum transformation and disability (CTAD): Workshop facilitator's guide.* Minneapolis: University of Minnesota, General College & Disability Services. Retrieved September 12, 2007, from http://www.gen.umn.edu/research/CTAD/publications.htm

Horn, L., & Berktold, J. (1999). *Students with disabilities in postsecondary education: A profile of preparation, participation, and outcomes* (NCES 1999-187). Washington, DC: U.S. Department of Education, National Center for Education Statistics. Retrieved December 10, 2007, from http://nces.ed.gov/pubs99/1999187.pdf

Horn, L., Nevill, S., & Griffin, J. (2006). *Profile of undergraduates in U.S. postsecondary education institutions: 2003-04 with a special analysis of community college students.* Washington, DC: U.S. Department of Education, National Center for Education Statistics, Institute of Education Sciences. Retrieved September 14, 2007, from http://nces.ed.gov/pubs2006/2006184.pdf

Jackson, J. (1995). Preserving Indian culture: Shaman schools and ethno-education in the Vaupes, Colombia. *Cultural Anthropology, 10,* 302-329.

Kinney, D. P., & Kinney, L. S. (2003). Computer-mediated learning in mathematics and Universal Instructional Design. In J. L. Higbee (Ed.), *Curriculum transformation and disability: Implementing Universal Design in higher education* (pp. 115-125). Minneapolis: University of Minnesota, General College, Center for Research on Developmental Education and Urban Literacy.

Kolb, D. A. (1984). *Experiential learning: Experience as the source of learning and development.* Upper Saddle River, NJ: Prentice Hall.

Maccini, P., & Gagnon, J. C. (2006). Mathematics instructional practices and assessment accommodations by secondary special and general educators. *Exceptional Children, 72,* 217-234

Mastropieri, M. A., & Scruggs, T. E. (1994). Text-based vs. activities-orientated science curriculum: Implications for students with disabilities. *Remedial and Special Education, 15,* 72-85

Mathematical Association of America. (2004). *Undergraduate programs and courses in the mathematical sciences: CUPM curriculum guide 2004.* Retreived August 24, 2007, from http://www.maa.org/cupm/cupm2004.pdf

Moses, R. P., & Cobb, C. E. (2001). *Radical equations: Math literacy and civil rights.* Boston: Beacon Press.

National Council of Teachers of Mathematics. (2000). *Principles and standards for school mathematics.* Reston, VA: Author.

National Science Foundation (NSF), Division of Science Resources Statistics. (2002). *Women, minorities, and persons with disabilities in science and engineering.* (NSF 03-312). Arlington, VA: Author.

Nelson-Barber, S., & Estrin, E. T. (1995). Culturally responsive mathematics and science education for Native students. San Francisco: WestEd.

Palincsar, A. S., Magnusson, S. J., Collins, K. M., & Cutter, J. (2001). Making science accessible to all: Results of a design experiment in inclusive classrooms. *Learning Disabilities Quarterly, 24,* 15-32

Pellegrino, J., Chudowsky, N., & Glaser, R. (Eds.). (2001). *Knowing what students know: The science and design of educational assessment.* Washington, DC: National Academy Press.

Rose, D. H., Meyer, A., & Hitchcock, C. (Eds.). (2005). *The universally designed classroom: Accessible curriculum and digital technology.* Cambridge, MA: Harvard Education Press.

Staats, S. K. (2005). Multicultural mathematics: A social issues perspective in lesson planning. In J. L. Higbee, D. B. Lundell, & D. R. Arendale (Eds.), *The General College vision: Integrating intellectual growth, multicultural perspectives, and student development* (pp. 185-199). Minneapolis: University of Minnesota, General College, Center for Research on Developmental Education and Urban Literacy. Retrieved December 10, 2007, from http://cehd.umn.edu/CRDEUL/pdf/TheGCVision/section2.pdf

Uncertain welcome [video]. (2002). Minneapolis: University of Minnesota, General College and Disability Services. Retrieved December 10, 2007, from http://www.gen.umn.edu/research/ctad/publications.htm

CHAPTER 12

Computer-Mediated Learning in Mathematics and Universal Instructional Design

D. Patrick Kinney
Wisconsin Indianhead Technical College

Laura Smith Kinney
Northland College

Abstract
This chapter is reprinted verbatim from Curriculum Transformation and Disability: Implementing Universal Design in Higher Education, *and was originally published in 2003. Interactive multimedia software is creating new opportunities for mathematics educators to implement Universal Instructional Design to meet the needs of all students. The software delivers the course content, provides immediate feedback, and allows students to work at their own pace and from remote locations. The instructor is freed up from lecturing and is available to work with students individually or in small groups as needed. Instruction of this type, referred to as computer-mediated learning, allows students of varying ability levels to meet the course standards in a way that provides flexibility in terms of pace, modes of learning, and location. This work was supported in part by the National Science Foundation (DUE 9972445).*

Students in introductory college mathematics courses are increasingly becoming a diverse group of learners. Historically, most introductory postsecondary mathematics courses have been taught using the lecture format, in which the instructor provides direct instruction. Rosenshine and Meister (1987) noted that direct instruction usually includes (a) presenting new material in small steps, (b) modeling of the procedure by the teacher, (c) thinking aloud by the teacher, (d) guiding initial student practice, (e) providing systematic corrections and feedback, and (f) providing expert models of the completed task. Instructors may also engage students in discussions and use some form of collaborative or group work.

For many students, however, lecture classes do not adequately meet their needs for a variety of reasons. For example, listening to lecture may not be the preferred learning style for a particular student. There is evidence that instruction that allows students to learn using their preferred learning styles can lead to improved student outcomes (Higbee, Ginter, & Taylor, 1991; Lemire, 1998). Also, traditional lecture classes often fail to fully meet the needs of students with disabilities, even when instructors do their best to provide appropriate accommodations.

Computer-Mediated Learning

In recent years, computer-mediated mathematics courses incorporating interactive multimedia software have increasingly been used to offer students an alternative to lecture courses. Gifford (1996) defines computer-mediated learning as a learner-centered model of technology-mediated instruction. The computer-mediated courses discussed in this chapter incorporated software from Academic Systems (AcademicOnline 2000, 2000) and reflect the implementation model used at the General College at the University of Minnesota. The software: (a) presents the concepts and skills using interactive multimedia; (b) embeds items requiring student interaction within the instruction; (c) includes provisions for the development of skills; (d) provides immediate feedback, including detailed solutions after the second attempt on an item; (e) offers online quizzes; and (f) includes a course management system that tracks students' progress and time on task.

In a computer-mediated classroom the instructor, who does not lecture, is able to move about the room during the entire class period to provide individual or small group assistance to all students as needed. Because the instructor does not lecture, the instructor can work with individual students for longer periods of time than is usually possible in lecture classes. When interacting with students, the instructor may clarify an explanation of a concept provided by the software, aid in troubleshooting errors in the development of procedural skills, and discuss with students their progress so that they remain on track. The course management system provides detailed information about each student's progress. This enables instructors to quickly identify the students most in need of assistance.

The reviews of research on technology-mediated instruction have consistently found that instruction of this type can have positive effects on student learning (Becker, 1992; Khalili & Shashaani, 1994; Kulik & Kulik, 1991; Niemiec, Samson, Weinstein, & Walberg, 1987). In mathematics courses from prealgebra through college algebra, the technology of choice is interactive multimedia software. Software that is interactive allows students to control both the pace of their learning and the navigation path. Najjar (1996) reviewed the research related to interactivity by Bosco (1986), Fletcher (1989, 1990), and Verano (1987) and concluded, "Interactivity appears to have a strong positive effect on learning" (p. 131). Multimedia is the use of text, graphics, animation, pictures, video, and sound to present information (Najjar).

In computer-mediated classes, students control the pace that they move through the software, although they are expected to complete lessons according to a schedule. The ability to control the pace benefits students who only need a brief review or who acquire the material quickly because it allows them to proceed through the instruction and assignments more rapidly than in a lecture class. For other students, considerably more time may be needed to process the material than is usually provided in a lecture course. The computer-mediated student can spend as much time as desired to study the mathematics on each screen, to navigate backwards to review previous material, and to take notes. Characteristics of mediated learning such as these are particularly important to students with learning disabilities.

Immediate feedback is another important component of interactive multimedia software. The research related to feedback indicates that feedback is important to the development of student self-regulation and self-efficacy (Hattie, Biggs, & Purdie, 1996; Kluger & DeNisi, 1996). Kluger and DeNisi found that feedback should be specific to the task, corrective, and done in a familiar context that shapes learning. In the mediated learning model, students receive feedback that is specific to each task that they attempt when using the software. If a student answers incorrectly on the first attempt, the software provides feedback that points the student in the right direction. This allows students to review their work and reattempt the item. If a second incorrect response is entered, the software provides a detailed explanation. In addition to the feedback provided by the software, students often receive feedback from classmates when they work together informally, as well as from the instructional staff.

Student's Selection of Computer-Mediated or Lecture Instruction

Students' responses to surveys, questionnaires, and focus groups (Kinney, 2000) indicate that they enroll in computer-mediated and lecture courses for a variety of reasons such as (a) they prefer to learn through multimedia rather than watching and listening to an instructor; (b) they find multimedia more visual than what instructors can typically write on the board; (c) they prefer to learn independently, rather than having another person show them everything; (d) they can control the pace of the instruction and receive individual assistance as requested (Kinney, 2000); and (e) they find that multimedia, with its interactivity and immediate feedback, holds their attention better than a lecturer. Many of these students discussed negative experiences in high school with lecture instructors, citing poor explanations of the material, ineffective classroom management skills, and not treating students in a respectful manner. For some students, computer-mediated instruction is attractive simply because it allows them to avoid the possibility of another negative experience in a lecture mathematics class.

Students who enroll in lecture classes consistently expressed several reasons for preferring lecture (Kinney, 2000). They prefer to learn by watching an instructor present the material and being able to ask questions during the presentation of the material; they valued the human interaction. They also pointed out that they frequently benefit when another student asks the instructor a question and they are able to listen to the instructor's response. Students in lecture courses prefer these types of interactions over the opportunity for more individual attention in a computer-mediated course.

It is clear from offering both computer-mediated and lecture mathematics courses that both instructional formats contribute to meeting the needs of mathematics students. In a recent semester, student's performance in the computer-mediated and lecture courses showed no significant difference on common final exams (Kinney, 2001a). What is important, especially in traditionally "high risk" courses like mathematics, is to provides students with a variety of options.

Universal Instructional Design

The concept of Universal Instructional Design (UID) suggests that as instructional design decisions are made to meet the needs of any particular student, it is worth looking for a solution that may benefit all students. The mathematics program at the University of Minnesota-General College offers both computer-mediated and lecture mathematics courses in Introductory Algebra and Intermediate Algebra. Students are allowed to self-select into the instructional format that they believe will best meet their learning preferences. To assist them in their decision, students take an inventory containing items related to computer-mediated and lecture instruction and discuss their options with their advisor.

In an attempt to provide students with the widest range of instructional materials and access to those materials, all students are provided with the textbook and software from Academic Systems (*AcademicOnline 2000,* 2000) and a study guide. The study guide, developed by faculty and staff, contains (a) the objectives for each section, (b) the location of the instruction related to each objective in the textbook, (c) instructional supplements to add to or clarify those in the textbook, (d) exercises in the homework set related to each objective, and (e) the answers to each problem. All students, whether enrolled in computer-mediated or lecture classes, are able to use the software in the mathematics learning center and where they live if they have a personal computer (PC) and Internet access.

The use of these instructional materials benefits students in several ways. First, if students miss a class for any reason, they can study the material for that class using the software in the mathematics learning center or possibly at home. This may be important to students who are ill for extended periods of time, have work or family conflicts, or have a disability that at times makes it difficult to physically get to class or interferes with their ability to learn, perhaps due to the effects of medication while in class. Second, students enrolled in lecture courses may be able to access the software for an additional presentation of the material, which may be useful if they did not fully understand the presentation provided by the lecturer or if they would like to work some additional problems where they receive immediate detailed feedback. This opportunity can be particularly helpful to students with acquired brain injuries (ABI) and other disabilities that impede retention of knowledge. Third, the study guide allows students to concentrate on learning the content, rather than spending time trying to figure out what they are expected to learn and identifying where to find the relevant instruction. The time saved can be particularly important to students with learning disabilities because they often require more time to process the material than other students.

This approach also benefits students with Attention Deficit Disorder (ADD) and Attention Deficit Hyperactivity Disorder (ADHD) who may easily be distracted and have difficulty making complex connections. Using this method, these students can focus their attention on the mathematics.

The Principles of UID as an Assessment Tool

On instructor evaluations in a recent pilot study, students were asked to evaluate their learning experiences by answering eight items based on the principles of UID (Kinney, 2001b). Traditional instructor evaluation items do not always apply to computer-mediated instruction and they may not address topics that contribute to successful and positive learning experiences for students. The goal of the General College mathematics program is to provide students with an opportunity to study mathematics that is consistent with the principles of UID, whether in computer-mediated or lecture courses. Overall, student responses in the pilot study were favorable and provided useful suggestions for identifying areas in the mathematics program that can be improved. Next, the eight items administered to students are provided along with a short discussion of how we are attempting to incorporate each principle into the mathematics program.

1. "The instructional staff created a classroom climate that fostered trust and respect." Establishing good communication with students contributes to students feeling respected, and establishes trust between students and faculty. Communication includes verbal interactions between instructors and students and written information such as the course syllabus. Instructors communicate more than mathematics when presenting lessons or working with students individually. They often implicitly communicate their own attitudes towards mathematics, what it means to learn mathematics, and their expectations about the pace and level of mastery that their students should achieve. Thus, it is important that what is communicated to students encourages them to continue attending class and working to be successful, even when they may dislike mathematics or are struggling. A classroom that fosters trust and respect may encourage students with disabilities to let the instructor know what facilitates their learning. The classroom should also encourage students to ask questions, share potential solutions, seek assistance as needed, including using office hours, and contribute to students viewing attending class as a positive experience.

2. "The instructor clearly identified the knowledge and skills students must attain to complete the course successfully." The study guide was written in part to identify the knowledge and skills that students must attain. In many textbooks, the author includes a heading called objective and then simply lists the topics to be covered in that section rather than actual objectives. Few students actually read these so-called objectives, let alone know how to use them to guide their studying. The objectives in the study guide, and links to the relevant instruction and related problems, are intended to make the instructor's expectations clear to the students. Instructors are expected to provide instruction that assists students in achieving these objectives and students are informed that the quizzes and exams are linked directly to these objectives. This approach can be particularly helpful to students with learning disabilities, ADD, ADHD, and ABI, who often need more time than other students to process the material, because it allows them to focus on learning the material rather than determining the instructor's expectations and where to access useful materials.

3. "The instructor provided clear expectations and feedback." The expectations for the course are contained in the study guide, which includes a detailed course syllabus, assignment schedule, and due dates for all assignments, quizzes, and exams. Another mechanism

for providing clear expectations is daily reminders written on the board at the beginning of class. Instructors may also communicate their expectations when working with students individually in class, during office hours, and by email.

Feedback is provided to students on all assignments, which includes homework, checkpoint questions, quizzes, and exams. Daily checkpoint questions are a single item on a recently covered concept or skill and are given in class for group work. Students are encouraged to communicate with classmates about their strategies and solutions when completing checkpoint questions, which enable them to receive peer feedback. The instructor is also available to provide feedback to students as they complete checkpoint questions. Students also receive feedback on two mid-semester reports. These reports are sent to the student and advisor and provide information about the student's progress in the course. An instructor may request that the advisor intervene if the student is not performing up to expectations academically, needs assistance in developing better study skills, or is aware of other issues that may be adversely affecting the student. For students who are reluctant to ask questions in a lecture class, such as students who have missed classes due to their disabilities and do not want to feel like they are "holding up the class" by asking questions, the computer-mediated courses offer the opportunity for extended periods of individual assistance and feedback from the instructor.

4. "The course materials (software, book, study guide, handouts, etc.), the instructional staff, and the course design were effective in supporting your learning." Students are able to select the primary mode, computer-mediated or lecture, in which they prefer to learn mathematics. For students in the lecture courses, the software acts as an ancillary resource that supports their learning in the event they missed class, were not clear about the content covered that day, or simply find that an interactive multimedia presentation of the material aids their learning. The software can be used by all students in the mathematics learning center and where they live by students with a personal computer (PC) and Internet access. The study guide supports student learning by providing all of the course objectives, references to the instruction in the textbook and corresponding problems in the exercise set for each objective, and includes answers to all problems. This supports students' learning by making clear what they are expected to learn and enabling them to quickly and easily access the desired material. All students may receive one-on-one tutoring in the mathematics learning center during regular business hours.

5. "The course materials and design provided opportunities to learn in a way(s) that fit your learning style." Students may enroll in either a computer-based or lecture course and take an inventory to assist them in making their decision. All students are provided with an interactive multimedia software package, a textbook, and a study guide. Lecture instructors make frequent use of various representations--words, algebraic, tables, graphs, and pictures--to assist students in understanding the concepts and skills. In the computer-mediated courses, students receive a multimedia presentation of the concepts and skills in various modes of representation. The animation and graphics, along with students' ability to control the pace and navigation path, provide students with a learning experience that is very different than lecture.

6. "There were enough different ways to demonstrate your knowledge of the subject and earn that grade that you deserved." Traditionally, students have been asked to demon-

strate their knowledge through homework exercises, quizzes, and exams. The resources and time available to students varies for each of these categories. Homework assignments, for example, encourage students to use any available resource, including working with classmates and tutorial assistance, and usually have no time limits other than that they are to be completed by a set date. Exams have time limits, unless a student with a disability has appropriate documentation, and often the only resource that students may use is a calculator. A mastery approach on exams, which we currently do not use but are considering if the current software is modified, would allow students more than one opportunity to demonstrate their knowledge. Furthermore, when using computer-mediated instruction, the teacher can opt to give extended time on tests to all students.

Students may also demonstrate their knowledge through innovative approaches such as checkpoint questions and learning logs. Checkpoint questions, as discussed earlier, are currently incorporated into the program. An additional approach under consideration involves learning logs, which give students further opportunities to express their ideas and demonstrate their understanding through writing. General guiding questions are given to students to help them organize their work for a particular problem in the format "introduction -- main body -- reflection." Learning logs encourage students to explore, question, and clarify their own mathematical thinking and reasoning and facilitate writing across the curriculum. A rubric focusing on the mathematical process can be designed for evaluating learning logs.

7. "The technology used in this class helped me learn the subject matter." By making interactive multimedia software available to all students, students no longer are reliant on the instructor for a presentation of the content. For some students, the most important aspect of the software is the multimedia presentation, interactivity, and control of pace. For other students, it is simply that they have control over their learning rather than the instructor. Students also have greater flexibility in terms of time and location of their learning because the software can be used in computer-mediated classrooms, the mathematics learning center, and at home.

The mathematics faculty and staff are in the process of incorporating the web platform WebCT into the regular day classes and distance education classes as a means to facilitate communication. Chatrooms, for example, allow students to ask classmates questions about the mathematics covered in each lesson and the homework assignments. For students with disabilities, a variety of technology products are available, including a software program called Zoomtext that aids visually impaired students when using the course software.

8. "The course design and instructional staff encouraged student-instructional staff contact." In the computer-based courses the instructor provides individual or small group assistance to students throughout the class, thus providing more individual faculty-student contact than generally is possible in lecture courses. E-mail and office hours, along with a classroom that fosters trust and respect, also encourage faculty-student contact.

Summary

The availability of interactive multimedia software, for use in computer-mediated courses and as additional resource for students in lecture courses, is providing new opportunities for redesigning introductory mathematics courses and programs. The principles of UID are worth reflecting on as programs change to meet the needs of all learners to the greatest extent possible. For many students, including students with disabilities, computer-mediated learning provides students with greater control over the pace and navigation of their learning, a more visual and interactive approach to learning, and more flexible times and locations for learning than lecture. The principles of UID, however, do not suggest that programs eliminate lecture classes because many students still prefer to learn mathematics through lecture. UID does suggest that solutions for some students, such as providing opportunities to learn through interactive multimedia software, be incorporated into a program so that it may support all students.

References

AcademicOnline 2000 [computer software]. (2000). Mountain View, CA.: Academic Systems.

Becker, H. J. (1992). Computer-based integrated learning systems in the elementary and middle schools: A critical review and synthesis of evaluation reports. *Journal of Educational Computing Research, 8,* 1-41.

Bosco, J. (1986). An analysis of evaluations of interactive video. *Educational Technology, 25,* 7-16.

Developmental Interactive Multimedia Mathematics (DIMM). Funded by the National Science Foundation (DUE 9972445).

Fletcher, D. (1989). The effectiveness and cost of interactive videodisc instruction. *Machine-mediated Learning, 3,* 361-385.

Fletcher, D. (1990). *The effectiveness and cost of interactive videodisc instruction in defense training and education* (IDA Paper P-2372). Alexandria, VA: Institute for Defense Analyses.

Gifford, B. R. (1996). *Mediated learning: A new model of technology-mediated instruction and learning.* Mountain View, CA: Academic Systems.

Hattie, J., Biggs, J., & Purdie, N. (1996). Effects of learning skills interventions on student learning: A meta-analysis. *Review of Educational Research, 66,* 99-136.

Higbee, J. L., Ginter E. J., & Taylor W. D. (1991). Enhancing academic performance: Seven perceptual styles of learning. *Research and Teaching in Developmental Education,* 7(2), 5-10.

Khalili, A., & Shashaani, L. (1994). The effectiveness of computer applications: A meta-analysis. *Journal of Research on Computing in Education, 27,* 48-61.

Kinney, D.P. (2000). [Student responses to survey, questionnaire, and focus group questions identifying reasons for students' enrollment in computer-mediated and lecture courses]. Unpublished raw data. Minneapolis: University of Minnesota.

Kinney, D.P. (2001a). A comparison of computer-mediated and lecture classes in developmental mathematics. *Research & Teaching in Developmental Education, 18* (1), 32-40.

Kinney, D.P. (2001b). [Instructor evaluations based on the principles of Universal Instructional Design]. Unpublished raw data. Minneapolis: University of Minnesota.

Kluger, A., & DeNisis, A. (1996). The effects of feedback interventions on performance: A historical review, a meta-analysis, and a preliminary feedback intervention theory. *Psychological Bulletin, 119,* 254-284.

Kulik, C., & Kulik, J. (1991). Effectiveness of computer-based instruction: An updated analysis. *Computers in Human Behavior, 7,* 75-94.

Lemire, D. S. (1998). Three learning styles models: Research and recommendations for developmental education. *The Learning Assistance Review, 3*(2), 26-40.

Najjar, L. J. (1996). Multimedia information and learning. Journal of Educational Multimedia and Hypermedia 5(2), 129-150.

Niemiec, R., Samson, G., Weinstein, T., Walberg, H. (1987). The effects of computer-based instruction in elementary schools: A qualitative synthesis. *Journal of Research on Computing in Education, 20,* 85-103.

Rosenshine, B., & Meister, C. (1987). Direct instruction. In M. J. Dunkin (Ed.), *The International Encyclopedia of Teaching and Teacher Education.* Oxford, UK: Pergamon.

Verano, M. (1987). *Achievement and retention of Spanish presented via videodisc in linear, segmented and interactive modes.* Unpublished doctoral dissertation, University of Texas, Austin, TX.

Zoomtext [computer software]. (2001). Manchester Center, VT: Ai Squared.

CHAPTER 13

Universal Instructional Design in a Computer-Based Psychology Course

Thomas Brothen and Cathrine Wambach
University of Minnesota

Abstract
This chapter is reprinted verbatim from Curriculum Transformation and Disability: Implementing Universal Design in Higher Education, *and was originally published in 2003. In this chapter we describe a general psychology course that is consistent with Universal Instructional Design principles and illustrate it with several case studies of students with disabilities. We show how all students' needs are met with the normal interventions of our personalized system of instruction (PSI) model. We conclude that PSI courses can effectively accommodate the needs of students with disabilities and make "accommodation" simply part of what occurs in class on a regular basis.*

In a series of articles, Twigg (1994a, 1994b, 1994c) suggested that the traditional lecture classroom is a learning technology that is simply out of date. Twigg advocated a new national learning infrastructure in which students learn more independently, test and enhance their learning with each other in cooperative learning communities, and work without the rigid time constraints of the traditional academic term. Twigg's description of higher education today as a "teaching infrastructure" rather than a "learning infrastructure" applies most clearly to the traditional classroom. The viability of a teacher centered educational system is even more problematic since passage of the Americans with Disabilities Act of 1990 (1991). That act requires educational institutions to develop policies for accommodating students with disabilities. Accommodations typically are expected to be consistent with a definition of disability that encourages individuals with disabilities to "seek adaptations to their needs and aspirations rather than simply adjusting themselves to the demands of a predominantly nondisabled society" (Hahn, 1985, p. 101). This expectation complicates matters for educational institutions, which have adapted to it in various ways (c.f., Fairweather & Shaver, 1990; Hodge & Preston-Sabin, 1997).

Most commonly, larger institutions have a disability services office that mediates relationships between faculty and students with disabilities. That office works with students to certify that their need for accommodation is legitimate and helps students decide what instructional features are necessary to facilitate their academic performance. Then the office sends official requests to faculty to provide the suggested accommodations. A study of 485 faculty members' actions to provide accommodations (Bourke, Strehorn, & Silver, 1997) showed that the more difficult the accommodation was for faculty to implement, the less likely it was to be delivered. There are also indications that requests for accommodations, especially difficult ones, cause skepticism and concerns about fairness among instructors (Williams & Ceci, 1999), especially when it comes to disabilities less "obvious" than vision, hearing, or mobility impairments (McAlexander, 1997).

Part of the problem is that instructors do not know how to respond to requests for accommodations. Writers offering guidance (e.g., Chang, Richards, & Jackson, 1996; Knox, Higbee, Kalivoda, & Totty, 2000; Lissner, 1997) are working to fill this gap with practical suggestions about working with students, applying technology to traditional classes, and dealing with the legal issues that sometimes arise. But for instructors, the letter they are likely to get from the disability services office might simply say "Extended time on tests (time and one half is recommended)" and little else. This might be an easy accommodation to make but may not adequately address the student's problem and may evoke concerns about fairness to other students. If the goal is to facilitate student learning, often much more needs to be done and it is not readily clear just what that might be.

Silver, Bourke, and Strehorn (1998) address accommodation in a new way with the concept of Universal Instructional Design (UID). They advocate placing "accessibility issues as an integral component of all instructional planning" (p. 47) and suggest that faculty adopt instructional practices such as those described in Chickering and Gamson (1987) and McKeachie (1999) as a way to provide accommodations. To us, this implies making some basic changes in the enterprise of higher education. But first college instructors need new models of instruction that meet the needs of students with disabilities and also benefit other students.

In this chapter we describe our UID model and present case studies of students with disabilities in a general psychology course we designed to meet the needs of developmental students (Brothen & Wambach, 2000a). Our purpose here is to show how a course specifically designed to improve students' academic performance may be consistent with Universal Instructional Design principles to accommodate the needs of students with disabilities effectively. We teach our class in the General College, the "open-access," developmental education unit of the University of Minnesota, and currently deliver the course via the Internet with WebCT courseware (see Landon, Bruce, & Harby, 2001 for a description and comparison of WebCT with other courseware packages).

The Personalized System of Instruction

Bloom's (1976) formulation of the mastery learning model requires students to achieve mastery over subject matter before progressing to a new unit. A highly developed and researched version of the mastery learning teaching method from the field of learning psychology is Keller's (1968) Personalized System of Instruction (PSI). Several reviews and meta-analyses over the years (Keller, 1974; Kulik, Kulik, & Bangert-Drowns, 1990; Kulik, Kulik, & Cohen, 1979; Robin, 1976; Ryan, 1974) have found superior student learning in PSI compared to traditional forms of instruction. Our UID model is based on PSI.

Written Materials

PSI emphasizes written materials rather than lecture as the major teaching activity. Instead of presenting information to students orally, instructors select and create appropriate reading materials, create behavioral objectives and study questions, and prepare multiple forms of tests that measure student progress and provide feedback. Lectures are sometimes used in PSI but the conclusion of numerous research studies is that they add little to student learning (Brothen & Wambach, 1999; Semb, 1995).

We base all assignments in our course on the structure of the 18 chapter textbook. Before they read each chapter, students complete an "electronic flashcard" psychology vocabulary development computer exercise. This exercise requires exact typing of terms or key words missing from 20 randomly selected definitions taken from those printed in the study guide. Students get two points for all 20 correct, and can repeat the exercise unlimited times, getting a new set of items each time they repeat any exercise or quiz. Then they read their text, guided by study questions that they write answers to and turn in for two points. Next they do a 10 item computerized completion exercise that requires them to fill in a key word for a "main point" phrase randomly selected from the textbook chapter. Students are to use their books and can do this exercise unlimited times. They receive three points for getting all 10 correct, two for nine correct and one for eight correct. They must get a mastery score of at least eight correct to be able to take quizzes. Their last task for each chapter is to take a 10 item proctored multiple choice chapter quiz. The items are randomly selected from a pool of over 100 that vary from easy to very difficult. Their best score of five tries counts toward their grade. To help them determine if they are ready for the quiz they can take practice quizzes also selected randomly from a large pool of items. They get two bonus points for getting all 10 correct and one for nine correct. Immediately after they finish all exercises and quizzes, WebCT presents students with information about what material they need to study further before they try again. Our research shows that over the term, students improve their ability to be successful on quizzes (Brothen & Wambach, 2000b).

Small Unit Mastery

PSI courses are broken down into manageable units that students are to master before they move on. Mastery is determined by successful completion of short unit tests that provide feedback to unsuccessful students so they may review the appropriate material before trying again. We measure learning by students' final performance on a number of small, repeatable exercises on small (i.e., one chapter) units. We encourage mastery in two ways. First, students must get 8 of 10 correct on the challenging completion exercise before continuing the chapter. Students cannot successfully complete this exercise in a reasonable time without having studied the chapter. Second, to make mastery more likely, students receive feedback on their performance and have the option to repeat exercises and quizzes.

Our exercises and quizzes deliver feedback consistent with Kluger and DeNisi's (1996) Feedback Intervention Theory (FIT). FIT describes how feedback should be structured and defines feedback interventions as "actions taken by (an) external agent(s) to provide information regarding some aspect(s) of one's task performance" (p. 255). The FIT approach demands that feedback must be (a) specific to the task, (b) corrective, and (c) done in a familiar context that shapes learning. First, general, nonspecific feedback (e.g., "You got 70% correct.") is much less performance enhancing than task information feedback (e.g., "You got an item incorrect on the differences between classical and operant conditioning, see page 312"). Second, corrective feedback should be tailored to help the individual student improve. This implies that the feedback must be delivered by a responsive person who knows the student or by "intelligent" computers that can judge and track the student's responses. Third, the task feedback should be embedded in course activities. That is, as students do coursework they should be receiving feedback on it. Our students receive feedback on all their exercises and quizzes as soon as they finish them.

Self-Pacing

In PSI courses, students pace themselves through the material, finishing assignments as they are able. Flexibility is a cornerstone of the method and is based on the realization that students have many other obligations and learn at different rates. This is especially true for adult students with careers and families and the increasing number of traditional undergraduates with heavy outside work schedules as well as for students with disabilities.

Personalized but not Individualized Instruction

Finally, undergraduate tutors have typically scored tests and helped students understand what their deficiencies are and what they need to do to deal with them. Tutors help to personalize PSI. This is different from individualized instruction in which each student pursues a different learning plan (Semb, 1995). In typical PSI courses all students have the same body of content to learn; tutors are available to help them learn it. Our teaching assistants work with students individually and our research (Brothen & Wambach, in press) shows that our computer assisted model can fulfill most of tutoring's many dimensions. Our staff is central to the operation of our instructional model. It consists of two professors assigned part time to the course, a full time course coordinator, and several undergraduate teaching assistants who completed the course in a previous semester with A grades.

Elsewhere (Brothen & Wambach, 2000a) we describe the research program we have carried out with our computer assisted PSI model. We describe below two studies over two semesters in which we have explored how students with disabilities respond to our model. In this chapter our report of these investigations is descriptive rather than experimental; we believe it illustrates the advantages of PSI in meeting the goals of UID.

Study I

We conducted the first case studies in an earlier version of the course model (Brothen, Hansen, & Wambach, 2001). Participants consisted of students enrolled in six sections of the course that met three days each week with two other days reserved for open lab during a 15 week spring semester. Students did all their computer work in a computer classroom containing 35 workstations and six quiz computers located at the back of the room (Brothen, 1992). Out of 210 initially enrolled students, a total of 187 finished the course by taking the final examination.

Methodology

We told students the first day of class that we would be studying their course progress. All read and signed an informed consent form giving us permission for the confidential use of their course data and academic progress data on file at the university. On the first day of class students completed a Big 5 personality questionnaire (John, Donahue, & Kantle, 1991) as part of a course assignment. We recorded students' scores on the Big 5 traits of agreeableness, conscientiousness, extraversion, openness to new experience, and neuroticism along with each student's cumulative completed credits and cumulative grade point average (GPA) for this study.

For each chapter students did three computer exercises (i.e., vocabulary exercise, completion exercise, progress quiz) that were self-paced with no time limits. They accessed them with a course delivery system (Brothen, 1995) that randomly selected items from chapter databases, recorded scores, and recorded time spent on each exercise in log files for subsequent analysis. We used this information to monitor student progress during the semester. Because completing exercises and amassing points is most strongly related to course success, time spent working is crucial. We selected for intervention both students spending too little time working and those spending a great deal of time but not accomplishing much.

In this study we present student progress data and other observations to detail the progress of the three students we will call Ralph, Terry, and Rene, who were identified by the university's Office of Disabilities Services as requiring accommodations during the academic term of this study. These students brought letters to us during the first week of classes requesting specific accommodations. We describe how they negotiated the course and how they illustrate our UID model.

The Students

Students registering for the course had completed from zero to 106 semester credits (M = 20.24, SD = 17.19) with cumulative GPAs ranging from zero to 4.0 (M = 2.81, SD = .72). There were 57 computer exercises to complete in the course, 3 for each of 19 textbook chapters. The 187 students who took the final exam completed from 6 to 57 exercises (M = 50.76, SD = 10.82) and they spent from 176 to 3,209 total minutes completing these exercises (M = 1,326, SD = 501). Our three students with disabilities completed all 57 exercises in from 787 to 2,319 min. The corresponding completion times for the other 77 students who completed all 57 exercises ranged from 669 to 2,277 minutes (M = 1,433, SD = 400). Students completing the final examination received scores ranging from 37 to 96 (M = 66.59, SD = 11.32). We present comparison data and case descriptions for our three students subsequently.

Student #1. Ralph was a large, friendly, and vocal student whom everyone on the staff came to know in a short time. His scores on the Big 5 all fell within one standard deviation of the class means. The letter from his Disabilities Services counselor said very little about him specifically. The first, third, and fourth paragraphs simply identified him and provided general information about whom to contact for further information. The second paragraph read:

> Accommodations for students with disabilities are individually determined with input from the student, instructor, and the Disability specialist. Your input in this process is important, as the accommodations should in no way compromise the essential elements or objectives of your curriculum. [Ralph] and I are anticipating that the following accommodations would be reasonable: Extended time on tests (time and one half is recommended).

The lack of specific information in this letter is not unusual given that students have input into how much they are willing to disclose about their disability. Perhaps Ralph's experience in previous courses showed that extra time was all that he required. Perhaps it was the only accommodation possible in his previous courses. Or, perhaps it was the only thing he would "admit" to needing. Our approach to Ralph was no different than for any other of our students; we monitored how he handled the work and responded accordingly.

Of our three students with disabilities, Ralph spent the longest time working on computer exercises—2,319 min for the semester. Although this was a high total, it was far from the highest of all our students. The staff did notice very early in the term that Ralph was spending a lot of time on and having difficulty with his computer exercises (see Table 1). However, at this point early in the term Ralph was apparently preparing adequately outside of class because even though he struggled on his first quiz attempts, his final quiz scores for both Chapter 1 and the Appendix were 9 out of 10. He did spend more time than the average student on quizzes. The Chapter 1 quiz on which he received a 9 took him 12 min. The Appendix quiz on which he received a 9 took him 20 min. Most students finish quizzes in 8 min or less. From this data it appeared that our built-in extra time accommodation was working well for Ralph.

But even though he was attending class regularly and ultimately doing well on quizzes, Ralph began falling behind early in the semester, often because he was spending so much time completing exercises, particularly completion exercises, which require students to fill in key words. We noticed this and assigned one of our undergraduate teaching assistants to work with him. While working with Ralph, our assistant soon noticed that he seemed to know the material, but had difficulty reading computer exercise items and finding answers for items in the text. He often struggled with individual words and mumbled them when reading a phrase out loud to the assistant. This led us to suspect that his disability was related to reading and affected his out of class work as well as his computer exercises. We called his Disabilities Services counselor to report that the extra time was only part of what Ralph needed and that help with reading items was crucial.

The counselor revealed that Ralph had what she described as one of the most severe cases of dyslexia her office had ever encountered.

For the first 6 weeks of the course, Ralph basically did the exercises the way we recommended, completing vocabulary and completion exercises and quizzes before moving on to the next chapter in the text. However, about the 6th week, Ralph took a quiz for Chapter 4, and then did not take a quiz again for over a month, concentrating on doing the other chapter exercises. The opinion of the assistant working with Ralph was that he was no longer reading and preparing outside of class, and was trying to do the pre-quiz exercises without carefully reading the book. For this reason, he was spending even more time on completion exercises than he was previously.

With about a month left in the course, Ralph realized that he only had a few weeks to finish quizzes for 14 chapters. Because he had completed nearly all of the vocabulary and completion exercises, most of his day in the classroom was spent reviewing for quizzes with one of our assistants, taking quizzes, studying feedback, and retaking quizzes. In general, his goal was to receive a minimum score of 7, which is a C. To finish this many quizzes in a month would be a very difficult for any student, much less for a student with a reading disability.

After discovering that Ralph's request for additional time was due to a reading disability, we regularly provided a reader for his quizzes. He would often become "stuck" on a word in a question, or he would just skip words that he could not read, and try to fill in the blank using the context of the question, a survival skill that had probably served him well in the past. However, for our multiple choice quizzes that ask students to make some very fine discriminations, that strategy does not work. We discovered that simply providing Ralph with more time to complete quizzes would not help. If he did not recognize a word, it did not matter how long he looked at the question. Providing him with a reader was by far the more effective strategy.

In addition, we wanted to induce Ralph to practice the exercises to develop fluency (cf., Johnson & Layng, 1992). Because it took him so much longer to complete vocabulary exercises where he had to search for a word and type it correctly, we told him that if he received two 19s on a vocabulary exercise, we would give him full points, just as if he had received a 20. As we expected, Ralph became faster at doing them. He completed his last nine chapter vocabulary exercises in an average of 13.1 min compared to an average of 28.8 min over the first 10 chapters. Ralph received a B- final grade for the course.

Student #2. Terry was an older returning student who appeared anxious enough on the first day of classes for us to notice. His scores on the Big 5 fell within one standard deviation of the class means on agreeableness, conscientiousness, and extraversion. But he scored nearly two standard deviations above the mean on openness and more than two on neuroticism. His letter from Disabilities Services was much the same as Ralph's except that it mentioned the nature of his disability as well as requesting an accommodation. The letter stated, "He is being treated for a chronic illness that limits his ability to manage anxiety and maintain concentration." It requested that he "be allowed to take a break during class if necessary to manage his anxiety."

Because students can enter and leave our classroom at any time, Terry did not require an accommodation to take breaks. Terry's letter also indicated that he needed a nondistracting test taking environment. We discovered that although Terry may have been anxious, he was actually not easily distracted, but incredibly focused in the environment we created for our students. Terry spent the least time completing computer exercises of our three students with disabilities and received the most points. He followed our recommended study technique to the letter, doing the exercises in the sequence noted above, restudying before repeating an exercise, and repeating earlier chapter exercises if he was having trouble on later ones. When asked at the end of the semester about following our recommendations, he said that he did not set out to follow them but simply did them in a manner he thought was logical.

From the beginning, Terry used the completion exercises to build fluency. On the difficult neuropsychology chapter he did six of them before taking a quiz, and received 10s on five of the quizzes, in as little as two min each. He took three quizzes, restudying his text after the first two, and the highest score he received was a nine. After the third try he did another completion exercise for Chapter 2, and then took another quiz and received a 10. This became a pattern for Terry. If he did not get a 10 on his first quiz attempt, he would do more completion exercises and then retake the quiz. Even though Terry took several completion exercises for each chapter, he did not spend a great deal of time on them. By the last chapters he took only one or two before achieving the maximum quiz score.

Our strategy for Terry was to stay out of his way because it appeared that the PSI structure was working fine for him without any special intervention. We tried to be encouraging and asked if he had any questions; he rarely did. We noticed fairly early that he had a strategy that was working well for him, and we let him work on his own. It became a game for Terry to see if he could get a 10 on his first try on each quiz, and we joined in by asking him if it was his first try when we would see that he received a 10. Out of 19 chapters, Terry scored 10 on his first try on 11. The only points Terry missed all semester were four points on his final exam and he received an A final grade for the course.

Student #3. Rene was a small, fragile, shy individual who could easily go unnoticed in a large class. Her scores on the Big 5 fell within one standard deviation of the class means on agreeableness, conscientiousness, extraversion and openness. But she scored two standard deviations above the mean on neuroticism. The reason for her appearance and demeanor was only hinted at in her letter from Disabilities Services. It contained basically the same "boilerplate" as the other two and described her disability as one "which impacts concentration and speed of thought." The letter requested "1.5 test time and a non-distracting test environment."

Rene spent 2200 min working on the computer exercises in the classroom, missing 4½ weeks of class time due to serious illness. Throughout the semester she was in and out of the hospital for what was apparently highly invasive medical treatment. She was very test anxious and for the first few chapters did an enormous number of completion exercises before taking quizzes. After doing fairly well on the first quiz she took for Chapter 1, a score of seven, she did nine more completion exercises before taking another quiz. She had very high expectations and when she was unhappy with a quiz score, she continued to practice to the point of using her time inefficiently.

After Rene missed 3 consecutive weeks of class early in the semester due to her illness, she contacted us via e-mail and asked for help. This gave us an opportunity to work with her on more efficient strategies, which was necessary due to the amount of time she missed. We recommended that she resume her work on Chapter 8 because the reading and study guide assignments were current for that chapter. She did only two completion exercises, both with scores of 10, in 42 min. She then took all five of her quizzes, studying feedback and asking questions between each time she took one. Her final score on this chapter was an eight (the equivalent of a B letter grade).

Rene continued this pattern for the rest of the semester, doing a few completion exercises for each chapter, taking quizzes, studying feedback, and taking quizzes again. She worked on chapters as they were assigned and on earlier chapters as she had time. She was not afraid to ask for help, and if she struggled on a chapter she would ask one of the staff to ask her questions about the material between her quiz attempts. She finished with only two quizzes below a score of eight—those chapters she took after her last episode in the hospital when she was still on heavy medication. She told us that she was having trouble organizing her thoughts the same way as she could when she was not medicated, but she also was behind and knew that she needed to catch up.

We provided a lot of support to Rene and tried not to add to the severe stress she appeared to be undergoing. We encouraged her when she was in the classroom, were available to answer her questions, and when she received a low score we offered to work with her. She used open lab times frequently when we could spend more time with her one-on-one. We allowed her to turn in her study questions late for no penalty during the time she was in the hospital and simply tried to maintain an environment in which she could be as relaxed as possible and perform her best. Rene received an A final grade for the course.

Discussion

The three students described above all performed well in the course. The PSI format allowed the instructors and staff considerable flexibility in meeting their learning needs. In a traditionally taught psychology course, one that was based on lectures, two midterms, and a final examination, it would have been more difficult to discover and respond appropriately to their needs. For example, Ralph would have been given more time to take tests, but that would not have addressed his underlying reading issue. Recording the examinations on audiotape might have worked for Ralph, but this was not requested by him or his disabilities counselor and would have been very difficult to implement. Because we had the opportunity to watch Ralph work, we could design accommodations that were more effective than those requested. Many sympathetic instructors would have recognized Rene's health problems and given her opportunities to make up missed examinations. In fact, university policy requires faculty to make alternative arrangements for students who have legitimate reasons for missing class. Our class did not have scheduled dates for tests so Rene did not require a special accommodation to complete her work. Terry's problem with anxiety would have been more perplexing to many instructors. Although psychology teachers would likely view an anxiety disorder as a legitimate disability, many instructors would be skeptical, and resist the notion that a separate exam should be scheduled for this reason. The need to accommodate psychological disabilities is the most controversial part of the American's with Disabilities Act (Higbee, Kalivoda, & Hunt, 1993). And, in our PSI course, Terry did not require anything from us. The issue of accommodating vaguely defined disabilities is further illustrated in the next study.

Study II

In this study we focus on the performance of a student we will refer to by the pseudonym of Jerry. To highlight issues we encountered with Jerry, we will also describe a student who approached our sense of the ideal, whom we will call Ben. The students were enrolled during the spring of 2001. The course was offered using the WebCT course delivery system. WebCT allowed students to complete many of the course exercises outside the classroom, which was not possible with the previous courseware. WebCT also allowed us to place time limits on some exercises. Time limits encourage students to be better prepared before they attempt exercises. When students spend less time on each exercise they are likely to attempt more exercises, consistent with our goal of encouraging more practice and opportunities for feedback.

The Students

Jerry is a student athlete. The Office of Athletic Academic Counseling carefully monitors the performance of student athletes. That office also provides a variety of learning assistance services, and supervises mandatory study sessions for student athletes. The learning specialists in the office have long term contact with individual athletes and develop a deep understanding of them as students and persons. The Athletic Department counselors and learning specialists seek feedback from instructors about student progress that they use to create interventions for these students. Many students now have learning disabilities identified at earlier stages of schooling, so more student athletes arrive on campus with disability diagnoses. Also, as more schools have developed sophisticated athlete support services, more learning disability issues among student athletes are being identified at the college level. It was through Jerry's Athletic Department learning specialist that we learned that Jerry has a learning disability and we should expect to receive a letter requesting an accommodation. That was as much information as the Learning Specialist could tell us without breaching confidentiality.

It took Jerry several weeks into the semester to bring us his letter from the Office of Disabilities Services. In the meantime we noticed that he was not making good use of his time in class. Instead of focusing on computer exercises, he would sit next to fellow athletes and whisper. When approached he would giggle and pretend to get back to work. He was accomplishing little, and quickly falling behind.

In contrast to Jerry, Ben, our ideal student, stayed focused in class. He worked quietly at the exercises and steadily completed work with close to 100% accuracy. He appeared each day at the beginning of his scheduled class period and left at the end having accomplished all he needed to do while in class. He did no computer exercises outside of class, but came to class obviously having done his reading and studying. We spoke with Ben occasionally about his accomplishments and about information from the class he found interesting, but at no point did we need to give him advice on how to become more successful. He knew what to do.

Several weeks into the semester, Jerry gave the staff a letter from disability services. The letter requested that Jerry take tests in a nondistracting environment and be given extra time to complete them. Our first hypothesis was that Jerry has a reading disability. To pursue this hypothesis, one of our staff members began talking with Jerry as he completed exercises. She observed that Jerry mispronounced many words and did not know the meaning of common words. We came to suspect that Jerry had a very weak general vocabulary and poor prior knowledge, which made it difficult for him to comprehend what he read, much less retain it. Unlike Ralph, who had trouble decoding words, Jerry could decode words, but did not understand them.

In contrast, Ben appeared to have an excellent vocabulary and good prior knowledge. We discovered that he had an ACT Composite score of 26, suggesting he had a good mastery of the high school curriculum and good general intelligence. His ability and prior knowledge allowed him to complete the work of the course efficiently.

As we worked with Jerry it became more apparent that he was an intelligent young man who was capable of learning when he expended the effort. As he mastered more vocabulary he was able to use it appropriately and generate original examples of course concepts. We discovered that he was faced with several serious decisions in his life, and was demonstrating effective problem solving as he made these decisions. We began to wonder if Jerry's learning disability was actually a deficit in prior educational background combined with lack of effort in the past. As Jerry began to experience more success in the course he responded by spending more time both in the classroom and outside of class working on computer activities.

Students' Performance

First, Jerry did more completion exercises (83) and spent more time on them (M = 27.2 min) than Ben (43, M = 13.0 min). The difference in number was primarily because Jerry was getting lower scores (M = 6.25 out of 10 possible) than Ben (M = 9.72) and had to repeat them to reach the mastery level of 8 correct. It would be reasonable to argue that Jerry's need for more time caused his low scores because many times he reached the 30 minute time limit before answering all 10 questions. However, in our experience, students typically take longer if they do not prepare well and we see the same pattern in many of our students without disabilities. Jerry eventually did what most of those students do; he put in more time and did the exercises more times, completing all 19 chapters successfully. His distractibility could also have played a role in that we often observed him talking to other students when he should have been working to finish within the time limit. He solved this problem on his own by doing more than half of his completion exercises during nonclass hours, many of them late at night.

Second, Jerry took fewer progress quizzes (46), scored lower on them (M = 5.65), and spent more time on them (M = 23.4 min) than Ben (65, Ms = 8.62; 4.5 min). The difference is primarily that Ben repeated quizzes until he got the highest score he could, getting 17 high scores of 10 and 2 of 9 on the 19 chapters. Jerry often quit when he got what seemed to him a decent grade. He got 13 high scores of 7, 5 of 8, 1 of 9, and no 10s even though he had attempts left on most of the chapters. Ben was generally better prepared for progress quizzes, getting no scores below 6 (i.e., passing) while one third of Jerry's scores were below 6.

Third, Ben's and Jerry's completion and quiz scores differed in another way. Jerry's scores were higher when he spent more time, while Ben's were lower. We correlated time spent with score on each exercise and quiz. The correlations for Jerry's completion and quiz scores were +.414 and +.356 respectively while Ben's were -.422 and -.369 (all were significant beyond the .05 level). Apparently, Ben spent more time when he was trying unsuccessfully to find or remember some material. Jerry began to spend more time on quizzes when we persuaded him that it would be helpful for an assistant to read quiz items to him. We did this to keep him focused. For example, we did not allow him to bring his cell phone to the quiz computers. It also allowed us to deal with vocabulary as we did for Ralph in our earlier study and define words that were critical to his understanding of the question but not key psychological terms on which his mastery was being tested.

Finally, Ben and Jerry differed in the way they approached the course. Ben was almost "machine like" in his approach. He proceeded exactly as we suggested and worked steadily on task. Jerry delayed getting started and fell behind early. He stayed behind for most of the semester but caught up to Ben after Spring break. Figures 1 (Completion Exercises) and 2 (Progress Quizzes) show both student's progress graphically. The size of the "bubbles" correspond to students' scores squared to show differentiation better. Dots represent quizzes below the threshold for points. The bubbles are arrayed on a matrix of chapters and days of the semester.

Ben's progress is basically linear with one gap early in the semester and one at Spring Break. Smaller bubbles precede larger ones on the chapter axis showing that his scores generally improved on subsequent attempts. His progress is consistent with that of the highest performers in our classes over the years such as Terry's in Study 1. Jerry's progress is more erratic. His chapter scores sometimes decreased on subsequent attempts due probably to inadequate restudy. He sometimes completed completion exercises for more than one chapter on the same day before taking a progress quiz, thereby losing focus on the earlier chapter. And he attempted numerous chapter exercises and quizzes on the last few days of classes in an attempt to improve earlier low scores as shown on the bottom right of the figures.

In a traditional psychology class, Ben would have earned good grades on his examinations. Jerry would have been given the extra time requested to complete the examinations, but time and a half is probably an underestimate of the time he required. It often took Jerry 20 min to complete 10 items. At this rate it would have taken him 100 min to complete 50 items, a common number of items for a mid-semester test. Typically an instructor would allow 50 min for a test of this length, and most students would be done in 30 min or less. Time and a half would be 75 min, far short of what Jerry would need.

Taking a test in a less distracting environment, the second accommodation requested for Jerry, might have allowed him to complete the exams more quickly. However, it would not have addressed Jerry's more serious problem of being distracted during class and while studying. Because our teaching method allows the instructor to observe students' work habits, we could intervene during class to help Jerry stay focused and learn to use his time more effectively.

Figure 1 says volumes about the differences between Ben and Jerry. Ben had the attitudes and skills he needed to perform well immediately, Jerry had to acquire those attitudes and

Figure 1. Completion quiz comparison student 1 and student 2.

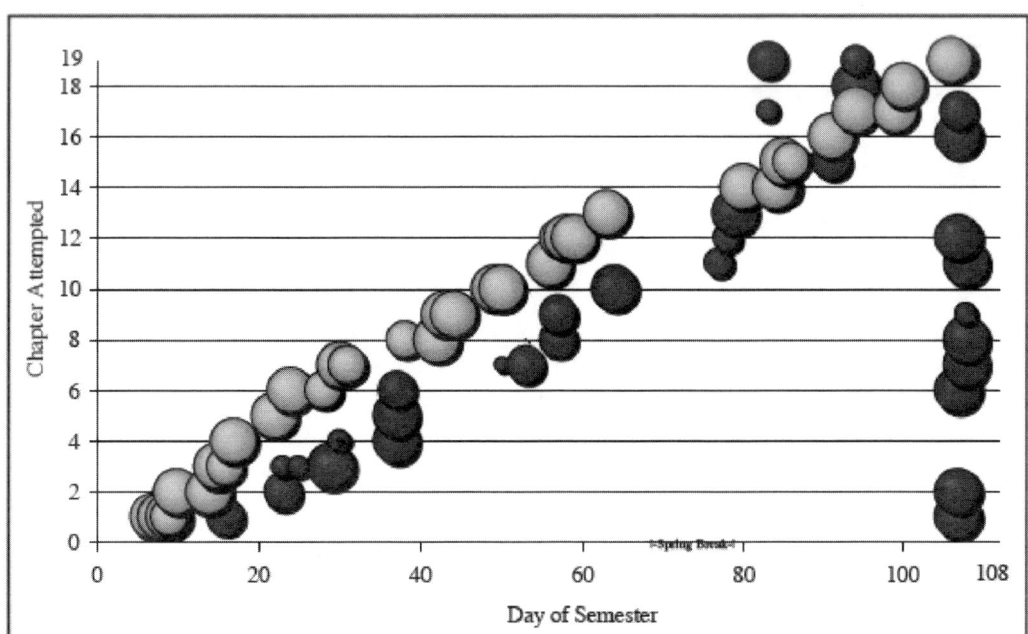

skills as he gained experience with the course. Multiple attempts at exercises allowed Ben to achieve a high level of mastery of the course material. Multiple attempts at exercises and attention from the staff gave Jerry the motivation to put in the long hours he needed to spend to pass. By the end of the term, Jerry knew what was needed to succeed and he earned a grade of B in the course.

Conclusions

PSI is a mastery learning model that fosters superior student learning compared to traditional forms of instruction. We believe that one of the reasons it is effective is that it is responsive to student needs, providing important progress feedback to them and their instructor (cf., Wambach, Brothen, & Dikel, 2000). Our computer-assisted model (Brothen & Wambach, 2000a) allows us to monitor students quickly and efficiently so that we can make appropriate interventions.

Figure 2. Progress quiz comparison student 1 and student 2

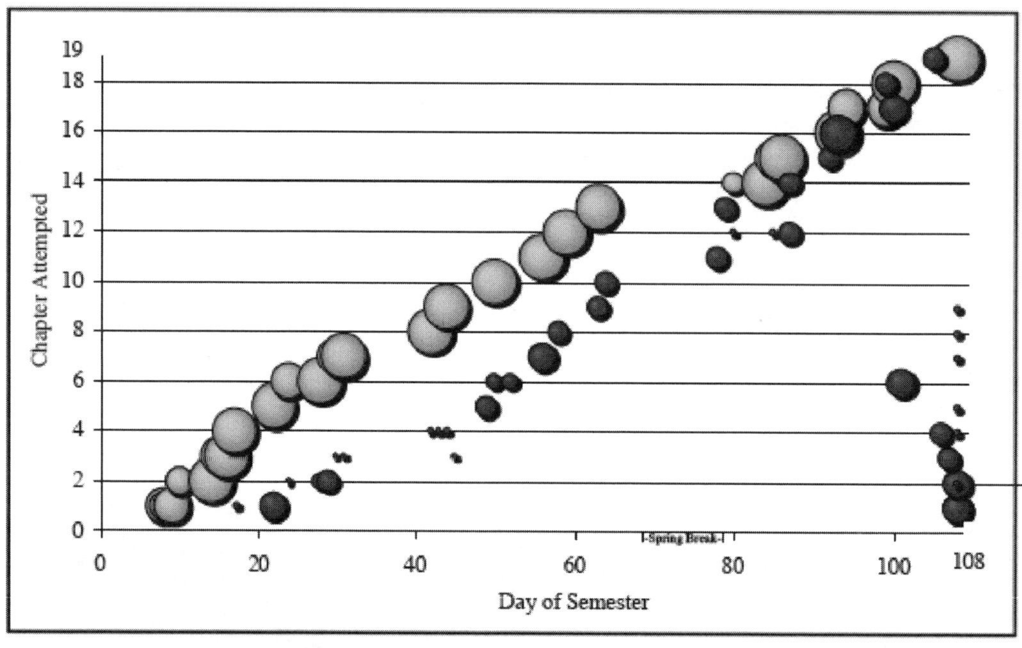

The flexibility of our method allows most students with disabilities to complete the course without special treatment. Students with disabilities can receive assistance within the classroom setting in the same environment in which other students receive assistance. For example, any student could request help reviewing a chapter, or discuss quiz-taking strategies. Although our students with disabilities received more consistent and intense assistance, the type of help was available to all. For example, a teaching assistant reading test items to Ralph or Jerry was not at all unusual. Nearly every class day saw a staff member sitting with students taking quizzes who had been having trouble with quizzes. We did this for second language students as well as for those underperforming on quizzes because they made the typical strategic errors students make on exams (e.g., rushing, "second-guessing" themselves, or picking the first alternative that seems reasonable without reading further). Staff sitting and working with students was a common sight as was our talking to them about their progress and how they were approaching their work.

Nothing in our classroom activities themselves distinguishes students with disabilities from any other student. Although two of the students in Study 1 scored high on the Big 5 neuroticism scale, which was consistent with the accommodations they requested, other students were unlikely to notice anything different about them. They did not take their exams in a different place, they did not require a student volunteer to take notes for them, or require any of the special technological interventions described by Knox, et al. (2000). Of course, new circumstances might require something more. We have, for example, had individuals provided in the past by Disability Services to read screens for students who are blind and we have had to make room for wheelchairs and Seeing Eye dogs. But our experience over the past several years has been exactly the same as the one described here. Students with disabilities have worked along with other students, albeit taking longer and so on, with similar results. We conclude from this that most students with disabilities can adapt to course requirements and that our PSI model for universal instructional design gives them the opportunity to do that quickly and effectively.

Instructors utilizing PSI will find, as we have, that this form of universal instructional design makes "accommodation" simply part of what they do on a regular basis. We believe PSI has been good for us and for all of our students.

References

Americans With Disabilities Act of 1990, Pub. L. No. 101-336, § 2, 104 Stat. 328 (1991).

Bloom, B. (1976). *Human characteristics and school learning.* New York: McGraw-Hill.

Bourke, A., Strehorn, K.C., & Silver, P. (1997, March). *Tracing the links in the chain of accommodation: A study of university of Massachusetts' faculty members' provision of accommodations to students with learning disabilities.* Paper presented at the annual conference of the American Educational Research Association, Chicago, IL. (ERIC Reproduction Service No. ED408764)

Brothen, T. (1992). A developmental education approach to computer assisted content instruction. *Journal of Developmental Education, 15*(3), 32-35.

Brothen, T. (1995). Using a new text-based authoring system to create a computer-assisted introductory psychology course. In T. Sechrest, M. Thomas, & N. Estes (Eds.), *Leadership for creating educational change: Integrating the power of technology, Vol. 1* (pp. 308-310). Austin: University of Texas.

Brothen, T., Hansen, G., & Wambach, C. (2001). *Accommodating students with disabilities: Three case studies that illustrate Universal Instructional Design.* Unpublished manuscript, University of Minnesota.

Brothen, T., & Wambach, C. (1999). An evaluation of lectures in a computer-based, PSI introductory psychology course. *Journal of Educational Technology Systems, 27,* 147-155.

Brothen, T., & Wambach, C. (2000a). A research based approach to developing a computer-assisted course for developmental students. In J. L. Higbee & P. L. Dwinell (Eds.), *The many faces of developmental education* (pp. 59-72). Warrensburg, MO: National Association for Developmental Education.

Brothen, T., & Wambach, C. (2000b), The effectiveness of computer-based quizzes in a PSI introductory psychology course. *Journal of Educational Technology Systems, 28,* 253-261.

Chang, M. K., Richards, S. J., & Jackson, A. (1996). Accommodating students with disabilities: A practical guide for faculty. (ERIC Document Reproduction Service No. ED 404827).

Chickering, A. W., & Gamson, Z. F. (1987, March). Seven principles for good practice in undergraduate education. *AAHE Bulletin,* 3-7.

Fairweather, J. S., & Shaver, D. M. (1990). A troubled future? Participation in education by youths with disabilities. *Journal of Higher Education, 61,* 332-348.

Hahn, H. (1985). Toward a politics of disability: Definitions, disciplines, and policies. *The Social Science Journal,* 22, 87-105.

Higbee, J. L., Kalivoda, K. S., & Hunt, P. (1993). Serving students with psychological disabilities. In P. Malinowski (Ed.), *Perspectives in practice in developmental education* (pp. 90-92). Canandaigua, NY: New York College Learning Skills Association.

Hodge, B. M., & Preston-Sabin, J. (Eds.). (1997). *Accommodations—Or just good teaching?* Westport, CT: Praeger.

John, O. P., Donahue, E. M., & Kantle, R. (1991). The "Big Five" Inventory—Versions 4a and 54. (University of California Technical Report). Berkeley, CA: Institute of Personality and Social Psychology.

Johnson, K., & Layng, J. (1992). Breaking the structuralist barrier: Literacy and numeracy with fluency. *American Psychologist, 47,* 1475-1490.

Keller, F. (1968). "Goodbye teacher. . ." *Journal of Applied Behavior Analysis, 1,* 79-89.

Keller, F. (1974). Ten years of personalized instruction. *Teaching of Psychology, 1,* 4-9.

Kluger, A., & DeNisi, A. (1996). The effects of feedback interventions on performance: A historical review, a meta-analysis, and a preliminary feedback intervention theory. *Psychological Bulletin, 119,* 254-284.

Knox, D. K., Higbee, J. L., Kalivoda, K. S., & Totty, M. C. (2000). Serving the diverse needs of students with disabilities through technology. *Journal of College Reading and Learning, 30,* 144-157.

Kulik, C., Kulik, J., & Bangert-Drowns, R. (1990). Effectiveness of mastery learning programs: A meta-analysis. *Review of Educational Research, 60,* 265-299.

Kulik, C., Kulik, J., & Cohen, P. (1979). A meta-analysis of outcome studies on Keller's personalized system of instruction. *American Psychologist, 34,* 307-318.

Landon, B., Bruce, R., & Harby, A. (2001). Online educational delivery applications: A Web tool for comparative analysis. Retrieved July 2, 2001, from http://www.ctt.bc.ca/landonline/

Lissner, L.S. (1997). Legal issues concerning all faculty in higher education. In B. M. Hodge & J. Preston-Sabin (Eds.), *Accommodations—Or just good teaching?* (pp. 5-22). Westport, CT: Praeger.

McAlexander, P. J. (1997). Learning disabilities and faculty skepticism. *Research & Teaching in Developmental Education, 13*(2), 123-129

McKeachie, W. (1999). *McKeachie's teaching tips: Strategies, research, and theory for college and university teachers* (10th ed.). Boston: Houghton Mifflin.

Robin, A. (1976). Behavioral instruction in the college classroom. *Review of Educational Research, 46,* 313-354.

Ryan, B. (1974). *PSI, Keller's personalized system of instruction.* Washington, DC: American Psychological Association.

Semb, G. (1995). The personalized system of instruction (PSI): A quarter century report. *Revista Mexicana De Psicologia, 12,* 145-160.

Silver, P., Bourke, A., & Strehorn, K. C. (1998). Universal Instructional Design in higher education: An approach for inclusion. *Equity & Excellence in Education, 31,* 47-51.

Twigg, C. (1994a). The changing definition of learning. *Educom Review, 29*(1), 2-25.

Twigg, C. (1994b). The need for a national learning structure. *Educom Review, 29*(2), 16-20.

Twigg, C. (1994c). Navigating the transition. *Educom Review, 29*(3), 20-24.

Wambach, C., Brothen, T., & Dikel, T. N. (2000). Toward a developmental theory for developmental educators. *Journal of Developmental Education, 24*(1), 2-4, 6, 8, 10, 29.

Williams, W. M., & Ceci, S. J. (1999, August 6). Accommodating learning disabilities can bestow unfair advantages. *The Chronicle of Higher Education,* B4-B5.

CHAPTER 14

Charting a New Course: Learning Communities and Universal Design

Rashné R. Jehangir
University of Minnesota

Abstract
This chapter is reprinted verbatim from Curriculum Transformation and Disability: Implementing Universal Design in Higher Education, *and was originally published in 2003. This chapter will examine the manner in which learning communities can serve as an effective vehicle for incorporating Universal Design into courses that are already thematically tied together. Clearly Universal Design can be incorporated successfully into individually taught courses. Learning communities, however, present the additional dimensions of affective connections, peer support, cooperative learning outcomes, and faculty collaboration that naturally lend themselves to the tenets of Universal Instructional Design (UID).*

Any college or university catalog or literature includes images and language suggesting that students who attend this institution are special. They may be especially bright, in the top 10% of their high school classes, especially talented in a broad range of extracurricular activities, or simply special because each one will be treated not as a number but as a unique individual. Interestingly enough, when these students arrive on campus and in our classrooms, the term "special" takes on a wholly different meaning. "Special populations" is the common catch phrase for adult students, students of color, student athletes, multilingual students, developmental students, and, of course, students with disabilities.

Because language shapes thought and nomenclature, it is important to consider how terminology can perpetuate the labeling that we are seeking to remove from our classrooms and communities. Terms like special populations serve only to add to the "othering process" (Anzaldua, 2001) with which students are already struggling. I am not suggesting that we assume that everyone is the same, but rather that the students bring with them a wealth of knowledge that allows us to celebrate differences rather than view them as deficient, lacking, or incomplete. In this vein, Universal Instructional Design (UID) suggests that imbedding accommodations into curricular structure benefits not only students with disabilities, but all students (Silver, Bourke, & Strehorn, 1998).

Like the implementation of Universal Instructional Design, participation in learning communities can facilitate achievement among all students. Goodsell Love (1999) argues that the growth in learning communities is the result of two recent shifts in higher education. The first is a shift from teaching to learning (Barr & Tagg, 1995) and the second a "shift from viewing knowledge as an acquisition of information to the social construction of knowledge" (Goodsell Love, 1999, p. 6). Similarly, UID complements flexible and innovative approaches to postsecondary education such as cooperative learning and computer-assisted instruction (Silver et al., 1998). Both approaches expand the student learning experience; they equally challenge teachers to reexamine their own biases and return to the role of learner themselves. Consequently, these teaching approaches necessitate a type of interdependence between instructors and students and a focus on "student learning rather than subject-matter teaching" (Evenbeck, Jackson, & McGrew, 1999, p. 55).

Finally, the intent of these approaches is to create access to learning. There is a tendency to equate accessibility with simplicity in the same way as it is often assumed that access and excellence are mutually exclusive. Accessible education acknowledges the diversity of today's learners and uses the strengths of this diversity to create environments that make learning attainable and excellent. Universal Instructional Design presents a means of ridding ourselves of a divided curriculum and replacing it with a learning space that capitalizes on the learning styles of all students. The collaborative environment of learning communities can be a good fit for implementing an inclusive curriculum.

What Is a Learning Community?

There is a large body of literature on learning communities and their outcomes. Increased student involvement, interdisciplinary learning, retention, improved quality of thinking and communicating, a superior ability to bridge the gap between academic and social worlds, and an avenue for faculty development have been attributed to successful well-developed learning communities (Elliot & Decker, 1999; Goodsell Love, 1999; Lenning & Ebbers, 1999, Tinto, 1998). Lenning and Ebbers' review of the literature identified three specific ways that the term learning community is used:

> Most commonly, learning community refers to a curricular approach that links and clusters classes around an interdisciplinary theme and enrolls a common cohort of students. Second, in technology circles, learning community refers to a way to link students and faculty through the Internet. Third, in international circles, learning community describes linking people from different countries. (p. ix)

Other definitions reflect criteria for learning and teaching:

> A learning community centers on a vision of faculty and students-and sometimes administrators, staff and the larger community- working collaboratively towards shared, significant academic goals in environments in which competition, if not absent, is at least de-emphasized. In a learning community, both faculty and students have the opportunity and responsibility to learn and help teach each other. (University of Miami, 1998, as cited in Goodsell Love, 1999, p.1)

The intent of learning communities is to create a space for dialogue and connections between disciplines and ideas, but also to extend the intellectual into the socio-cultural experience of students. Tinto argues that most learning communities have "two things in common, shared knowledge and shared knowing" (1998, p.171). It is this relationship of collaborative, experiential, and active learning that blurs the line between the classroom and the outside world, thus setting the stage for inclusiveness and democratic thinking.

Thus, learning communities present a safe space to incorporate Universal Instructional Design. There are many different components and approaches to developing a successful learning community. For the purposes of this chapter I will focus on two aspects: cooperative learning and faculty collaboration. The three critical components for curricular development using UID include providing a flexible means of representation, a flexible means of expression and a flexible means of engagement (Orkwis,1998). The following paragraphs will explore how learning communities can be particularly effective at imbedding these components into the classroom.

To provide a context for the examples I use, it will be helpful to understand the framework for the multicultural learning community in which I teach. This learning community contains three classes: a social science course titled Multicultural Relations, a first year composition course, and Creativity Art Lab. Students registering for this community were required to register for all three classes concurrently. This learning community has been designed to help students examine issues of diversity from different lenses. Using the materials from the disciplines of writing, art, history, sociology, and psychology, the learning community as a whole will focus on an interdisciplinary examination of different ways of knowing and examining the diverse world we inhabit. While each class in the community has its own focus, the three courses relate to each other and the faculty teaching them encourage students to examine issues of diversity and critical thinking and to explore connections and distinctions between some of these ways of knowing.

Cooperative Learning

Cooperative learning has long been associated with group or team-based learning and is a natural fit for the learning community environment. The most critical components of this approach involve positive interdependence among students, shared leadership, individual accountability, development of social skills, and group processing (Johnson, Johnson, & Smith, 1991a). Placing students in situations that encourage face to face (i.e., promotive) interaction and shared resources not only enhances critical thinking skills, but also heightens affective connections between students (Johnson, Johnson & Smith; Stage, Muller, Kinzie, & Simmons, 1998). This blending of social and cognitive components sets the stage for the incorporation of UID.

Flexible means of representation requires presenting materials in multimodal ways. This challenges instructors to present information in accessible formats while acknowledging that access for one student's learning style may pose barriers for another student (Orkwis, 1998). In cooperative learning communities, presenting materials in multi-modal formats is required not only of the instructor, but also of the students. In the social science course I teach within the multicultural learning community, one of the course requirements is student presentations. Students are required to work in smaller cooperative groups and present or lead classroom discussion on a variety of topics ranging from race, class, and gender to homophobia and ableism. Most students are not practiced at preparing presentations and can be quite nervous. If being a student teacher is intrinsic to participating in a learning community, then it behooves instructors to both model and train students to learn how to present information in flexible ways.

One semester a group of students used overhead transparencies or flip charts to present an overview of their arguments and then each took turns explaining the concepts to the class. Given the comfort level that had been established, the remaining student audience was quick to point out their concerns. "The writing on the overhead is too small," or, "You are going too fast and I can't find the page you are referring to, please tell me the page number before you begin reading." Other students asked for more background on specific readings rather than jumping straight into definitions or terms. The advantage of the learning community format is that the students' time together both in and out of their linked classes creates a camaraderie, and hence a trust for honest dialogue and critique. In this particular scenario the students learned to become adept at asking for means of representation that reduced perceptual and cognitive barriers.

Instructors within a learning community have the advantage of captured time. Their students see each other and engage with each intellectually and socially more often than non-learning community students simply on the basis of time spent in linked courses. This time plays a critical role in allowing students to gain ownership of their learning experience and view themselves a "members of a distinctive learning community" (Lenning & Ebbers, 1999, p. 29). Pascarella and Terenzini's (1991) extensive research on the collegiate experience suggests that although a single college course can become a true learning community, it is not likely to happen, primarily because of lack of sufficient time together as a class and because lecturing tends to be the dominant mode of instruction.

Flexible means of expression can come about within the design of the learning community itself. In learning communities that cluster courses around a theme or metaphor, the nature of the disciplines themselves demand flexible means of expression. Because the learning community in which I teach is comprised of my social science course, a first year composition course, and a performance-based arts course, expression through student presentation, written word, and performance create opportunities for students to communicate their ideas in multiple ways. However, this is only the first layer. As one examines the limitations of any one means of expression, one can see that creating flexible means of expression within each course is also critical to student success.

Earlier I mentioned the use of student presentations in my classroom. Of course, there are challenges with that particular mode of presentation. Clearly, verbal expression is not accessible for students for "whom speech is not a viable presentation method" (Orkwis, 1998 p.3). Yet, demonstrating an understanding of central concepts in the social sciences and learning to dialogue and debate about how these concepts relate to the lived experience are essential components in my course. As a result, I have tried two strategies to incorporate UID without compromising the essential components of the course. First, students in cooperative groups can break up the responsibility of the presentation. A student who is more comfortable with visuals such as images or graphics might take the lead on that aspect of the presentation, while one who is more comfortable with organizing text may focus on creating a written outline, and a third member may serve as the reporter or present the information to the larger class. This approach allows students to draw on individual strengths for collective gain. As students familiarize themselves with the different tasks, they can be encouraged to take on roles they may have been less comfortable with at the start of the semester. Another method that encourages dialogue is via email or web-based chat rooms that are limited to students enrolled in the learning community. Both methods suggest means of reducing motor barriers to expression.

Cognitive barriers to expression also need to be considered. Explicit strategies are referred to as providing students "with a series of steps to prepare and execute" (Orkwis, 1998, p.2) an assignment. Scaffolding is "a temporary support for learning that is gradually reduced as the student develops confidence with the new content or skills" (Orkwis, p.2). These cognitive strategies are especially relevant in a learning community where students are being encouraged to learn via sharing and cooperation rather than an individualistic competitive model that is often more familiar to them.

As a community, faculty and students need to come together to create a set of ground rules for classroom behavior, debate, and healthy disagreement. This set of rules may be something to which we continue to refer until the students can incorporate these ideas into regular communication. The same can be said of small learning groups; throwing students into groups without explicit instructions on sharing workload, individual accountability, and participation can be detrimental to the success of the community. With specific assignments, different instructors within the community may create a variety of ways to provide scaffolding. In my course, students get a detailed outline on how to write their first paper. For the second paper they create an outline together in the classroom. In the composition course, students write drafts for each paper and may also engage in peer editing. Consequently, students are simultaneously engaging in flexible means of presentation, expression, and engagement in each of the three courses while examining issues of diversity and oppression from different lenses. Given that this multimodality exists both within and across the three courses, it can often serve as a road map for students who are trying to discern what types of learning are most beneficial to them.

Providing flexible means of engagement challenges us to create an environment that allows all students the opportunity to be connected to their learning. We seek to find balance between support and challenge, between novelty and familiarity, and aim to appeal to students who are at different places in their academic journey (Orkwis, 1998). It seems like an impossible undertaking. Yet, consider that in this type of learning community the same cohort of students is interacting with each other in three or more common classes. If the shared curriculum has provided space for cooperative dialogue, reflection, and process, the stage is set for engagement. Trust is also critical to flexible means of engagement.

In the multicultural learning community that I have described, sharing of oneself via writing, discussion, or performance is inherent to the experience. To share one's writing with peers is often as anxiety provoking as doing a presentation or performance. "To disclose one's reasoning and information, one must trust the other individuals involved in the situation to listen with respect. Trust is a central dynamic of promotive interaction" (Johnson, Johnson, & Smith, 1991b, p. 36). In the learning community environment, trust plays a role in the encouragement of both flexible means of expression and engagement. Without feeling supported by peers and instructors alike, students are unlikely to take risks that encourage new learning and construction of knowledge. Thus, to arrive at a place where flexible means of engagement can be successful, we as instructors need to model the very behavior we seek from our students. In presenting material, we need to consider the extent to which we might apply novel approaches to our own teaching.

In the multicultural learning community, the students were expected to write a creative, imaginative, historical short story about multicultural America. The assignment asked students to imagine what it might have been like to come to the United States, or to be here interacting with new immigrants. In the spirit of cooperation, students were invited to bring in copies of their story drafts to share with each other. This exercise required students to not only reveal their writing ability, but also to share a very personal perspective on the immigrant experience in America. I felt that it was important to model how challenging it can be to both share of oneself and also to take in constructive criticism. One way to provide a template for this activity was to do the assignment myself and allow students to critique my work. This was an attempt to normalize constructive criticism and provide an environment that was both supportive and challenging. Students also received feedback on this assignment through process and sharing, via individual meetings with peers and instructors, and in writing. Many students used some aspect of the short story as a theme in their performances for the arts course, thus linking their learning and finding new avenues to gain and express knowledge.

All of the strategies addressed above can be applied to the individual classroom. However, the collaboration and planning that is critical to learning community design is well suited to the process students and instructors would naturally engage in when creating UID based classrooms.

Faculty Collaboration

Boyer argues that the "new American college" needs to reexamine its priorities, the most germane of which include clarifying the curriculum, creating a sense of community on campus, and connecting students to the real world beyond the walls of the academy (Coye, 1997). If classrooms are to provide extensions into the real world and shape citizenship and community collaboration among instructors may be a sensible place to start. If it is fair to say that our students have been educated within an individualistic, competitive model of learning, the same can be said of those who teach. Both learning communities and Universal Instructional Design push us to think outside the parameters of our disciplines and the pedagogical structures inherent to them.

The process of being a participant in training for UID and collaborating with faculty within my learning community highlighted the connection between the two approaches.

1. Planning ahead: Teaching and learning in collaboration with others necessitates time for planning and process. Teaching cohorts must share their curriculum and also have time to discuss shared goals and vision for the learning community. This means that choosing textbooks and sharing syllabi and classroom activities can include attention to flexible means of representation, expression, and engagement. This type of preplanning allows for several instructional perspectives such that preparation for multiple means of testing or other forms of demonstrating knowledge, for presenting syllabi and text in alternate forms (e.g., books on tape) can be made available for prospective students early on.

2. Articulation of objectives and fit: UID encourages faculty to examine the essential components of their curriculum. The intent is to challenge us to pinpoint the critical objectives of the course and to examine the purpose behind the teaching activities we use. Do the teaching activities fully reflect the course objectives and do they serve the purpose they were intended for? Teaching in a learning community demands that faculty examine these very questions, but also provides a forum for shared learning and discussion with colleagues. This process involves specifying instructional objectives and examining the fit between the represented disciplines allowing for the incorporation of strategies and approaches to teaching that most benefit students. Instructors can then customize a curriculum that reflects both "academic and social skills objectives" (Johnson, Johnson, & Smith, 1991b, p. 60) with attention to the range of student abilities.

3. Examining student needs: Faculty who teach within learning communities report: A much greater appreciation of the first year experience. Since each teacher has a personal and unique approach to students, each interacts with the students differently and experiences different aspects of a student's personality. Sharing these experiences provides each faculty member with valuable insights into the possible reasons for a student's behavior and academic performance. (Strommer, 1999)

Thus, faculty collaboration not only allows for multiple ways of evaluating student performance, but can also incorporate scaffolds like time-management activities that help students acclimate to a college workload. Learning community faculty may coordinate their assignment due dates to prevent excessive overlap. In addition, they may "reinforce the topics and expectations of each other's courses" (Goodsell Love & Tokuno, 1999, p. 10). It can be helpful to have regular meetings to discuss student progress and brainstorm means of incorporating UID depending on student needs. Having a sense of students' learning styles can play a role when assigning students to small base groups for classroom activities. Faculty awareness of peer group dynamics can augment modeling social skills and supportive learning.

4. Practicing what we preach: Learning community collaboration creates collegial learning groups for faculty in the same way as their classes create communities of learning and being for their students. It is a place where cooperation builds trust and this allows for "coplanning, codesigning, copreparing, and coevaluating curricular material" (Johnson, Johnson, & Smith, 1991b, p.117). Shared learning and teaching makes us more aware of our own learning preferences and how this may bias or shape our teaching pedagogy. The nature of collaboration and collective accountability may encourage faculty

to try new UID approaches and examine the accessibility of each other's curriculum. "The commitment of physical and psychological energy to achieve the goals of improving one's instructional expertise is heavily influenced by the degree to which colleagues are supportive and encouraging" (Johnson, Johnson, & Smith, p.116). A shared space for discussing problems and sharing successes can heighten our experiences as teachers and benefit all the students we serve.

5. New directions: As with all new approaches having a forum to discuss curriculum access is important. Although faculty collaboration within a learning community can provide space for ongoing incorporation of UID, it can also present opportunities to contribute and construct new knowledge on the subject— we some times call this research.

Case Study

I will conclude with a brief case study describing the experience of a student with a disability participating in a learning community. The case study does not address all types of disabilities, nor is the intent to segregate the experience of students with disabilities from that of other learners. Rather, I hope this example illuminates the benefits of a learning community as a vehicle for implementing UID principles.

When asked, David said that he felt that he was part of the deaf culture, but being in a hearing classroom he was also part of a hearing culture. Students who are non-native English speakers may be more tentative about their class participation. David's primary language is American Sign Language and he was less likely to participate in larger discussions. However, within his small collaborative group he was far more involved and even took on the role of lead presenter. In a reflective learning log, David had an opportunity to express his thoughts without an interpreter. Describing a discussion about race and identity issues, he wrote " I felt really good about the classes discussing why we go through this within our life. It did teach that I wasn't the only one who went through it, even though other students had different colors than me." Another multiracial student wrote of the same discussion "We were able to just express our own views and experiences regarding race. It surprised me that their [sic] were not limits put on how much we can get into detail. Traditionally, I don't think that this is common."

I chose this example to illustrate the extent to which a collaborative learning environment can create trust that is necessary for students to express themselves. Providing an opportunity to reflect on racial identity issues both in class and in a reflective writing assignment was beneficial to David, but also to other students who may or may not have been comfortable speaking up in class. In addition, the cohesive environment of three classes allowed students to feel a sense of belonging to the community and a willingness to take risks in their learning. This is true for students of multiple learning styles.

The last decade has seen a shift in approaches to social diversity on our campuses (Levine, 1991). Curriculum has begun to reflect the various manifestations of power differentials and worldviews that affect our students and our teaching. As we make efforts to acknowledge, value, and celebrate the multiple means of knowing that are shaped by the race, culture, age, gender, and ethnicity of our students, we need to also take note of the extent to which a culture of ableism excludes not only students with disabilities, but also students from the aforementioned groups. Bowe (2000) urges us to become aware of our own "culture's teachings and how those affect you as an educator" (p.5). The same can be said of the teachings of your discipline. How have these models affected your approach to learning and teaching? Universal Design and the learning community design offer us models through which to examine these questions and also to view the classroom experience from the lens of others.

References

Anzaldúa, G. (2001). En rapport, In opposition: Cobrando cuentas a las nuetras. In P. Rothenberg (Ed.), Race, class, and gender in the United States: An integrated study (5th ed.) (pp. 595-601). New York: Worth.

Barr, R.B., & Tagg, J. (1995). From teaching to learning--A new paradigm for undergraduate education. Change, 27(6), 12-25.

Bowe, F. (2000). Universal Design in education. Teaching nontraditional students. Westport, CT: Bergin and Garvey.

Coye, D. (1997). Ernest Boyer and the new American college: Connecting the disconnects. Change, 29(3), 20-30.

Elliot, J.L., & Decker, E. (1999). Garnering the fundamental resources for learning communities. In J. Levine (Ed.), Learning communities: New structures, new partnerships for learning (pp.19-28). Columbia, SC: National Resource Center for The First-Year Experience and Students in Transition, University of South Carolina

Evenbeck, S.E., Jackson, B., & McGrew, J. (1999). Faculty development in learning communities: The role of reflection and reframing. In J. Levine (Ed.), Learning communities: New structures, new partnerships for learning (pp.51 -58). Columbia, SC: National Resource Center for The First-Year Experience and Students in Transition, University of South Carolina.

Goodsell Love, A. (1999). What are learning communities? In Levine, J. (Ed.). Learning communities: New structures, new partnerships for learning. (pp.1-8). Columbia, SC: National Resource Center for The First-Year Experience and Students in Transition. University of South Carolina.

Goodsell Love, A., & Tokuno, K.A. (1999). Learning community models. In J. Levine, (Ed.), Learning communities: New structures, new partnerships for learning (pp. 9-17). Columbia, SC: National Resource Center for The First-Year Experience and Students in Transition, University of South Carolina.

Johnson, D.W., Johnson, R.T., & Smith, K.A. (1991a). Active learning: Cooperation in the college classroom. Edina, MN: Interaction.

Johnson, D.W., Johnson, R.T., & Smith, K.A. (1991b). Cooperative learning: Increasing college faculty instructional productivity. ASHE-ERIC Higher Education Report, 4. Washington D.C.: The George Washington School of Education and Human Development.

Lenning, O. T., & Ebbers, L.H. (1999). The powerful potential of learning communities: Improving education for the future. ASHE-ERIC Higher Education Report, 26 (6). Washington D.C.: The George Washington School of Education and Human Development.

Levine, A. (1991). Editorial: The meaning of diversity. Change, 23(5), 4-5.

Orkwis, R. (1998). A curriculum every student can use: Design principles for student access. ERIC/OSEP Topical Brief. ERIC Clearinghouse on disabilities and gifted education. (ERIC/OSEP # E586).

Pascarella, E.T., & Terenzini, P.T. (1991). How college affects students: Findings and insights from twenty years of research. San Francisco: Jossey Bass.

Silver, P., Bourke, A., Strehorn, K.C. (1998). Universal Instructional Design in higher education: An approach for inclusion. Equity and Excellence in Education, 31(2), 47-51.

Stage, F.K., Muller, P.A., Kinzie, J., & Simmons, A. (1998). Creating learning centered classrooms: What does learning theory have to say? ASHE-ERIC Higher Education Report 26 (4). Washington D.C.: The George Washington School of Education and Human Development.

Strommer, D.W. (1999). Teaching and learning in a learning community. In J. Levine (Ed.), Learning communities: New structures, new partnerships for learning (pp. 39-49). Columbia, SC: National Resource Center for The First-Year Experience and Students in Transition, University of South Carolina.

Tinto, V. (1998). Colleges as communities: Taking research on student persistence seriously. Review of Higher Education, 21(2), 167-177.

Implementing Universal Design in Academic Support and Student Development Programs and Services

CHAPTER 15

Universal Design Principles for Student Development Programs and Services

Jeanne L. Higbee
University of Minnesota

Abstract
A number of models provide guiding principles for the implementation of Universal Design (UD) in the classroom. The purpose of this chapter is to provide a framework for implementing UD in student affairs units and other programs and services that focus on student development outside the classroom.

As noted by Opitz and Block (2006; reprinted in this volume—see Chapter 16), most of the emphasis on adapting Universal Design (UD) principles to higher education has focused on the classroom. When we developed the Pedagogy and Student Services for Institutional Transformation (PASS IT) grant proposal, one of the areas in which we believed that we needed to expand upon the work of our previous grant, Curriculum Transformation and Disability (CTAD; Higbee, 2003) was to give equal attention to student development outside the classroom. Thus, for the 2006 PASS IT Summer Institute we selected a group of participants who work in a wide array of student development programs and services and established separate working groups for those whose primary responsibility is (a) counseling or advising, (b) academic support services and developmental education, and (c) administration. At times the three working groups met independently, while at other times they met together. During one of the larger group sessions we asked participants to meet in small groups and then respond to the group as a whole to a draft of a set of Universal Design principles for student development programs and services. The small groups were set up to include participants from each of the three working groups. This chapter is a direct result of that conversation, and these principles reflect that group effort.

Background

One of the pre-readings for the PASS IT Summer Institute was *Learning Reconsidered: A Campus-Wide Focus on the Student Experience* (Keeling, 2004). We concur that there is an artificial divide between student affairs and academic affairs in U.S. higher education (also see Chapter 35). The learning that occurs outside the classroom can be equally—and at times even more—influential in the development of the student, and factors external to the classroom can have a critical impact on student retention (Astin, 1985, 1993; Chickering, 1969; Chickering & Reisser, 1993). Thus, we think that it is imperative that when discussing the implementation of UD in higher education, the entire postsecondary experience be considered. For purposes of this chapter, the term "student development programs and services" is defined broadly to include admissions, orientation, financial aid, advising, counseling, first-year experience programs, activities related to career exploration and placement, learning centers, tutorial services, academic assistance programs, residence life, Greek life, student activities and student union programs, judicial affairs, and any other services and programs that complement students' experiences in the classroom.

We also believe that Universal Design can provide a valuable framework for multicultural education in higher education settings (Barajas & Higbee, 2003; Higbee & Barajas, 2007). Although originally envisioned as a mechanism for inclusion for students with disabilities, by considering the individual learning of all students, and the backgrounds and experiences represented by their diverse social identities, Universal Design and Universal Instructional Design (UID) can contribute to inclusion for all students. Thus, we incorporated features of the *Multicultural Awareness Project for Institutional Transformation* (MAP IT; Miksch et al., 2003) guiding principles when developing UD principles for student development programs and services. The MAP IT guiding principles are listed in Chapter 32.

Guiding Principles

We propose the following "Universal Design Principles for Student Development Programs and Services":

1. Create welcoming spaces: PASS IT participants brainstormed a wide variety of suggestions for ensuring that students feel welcomed and valued. Reception areas should be cheerful, with friendly staff readily accessible, and spaces for students to congregate informally or to wait comfortably. Staff should get to know students as individuals ans seek to understand the cultural contexts that will shape their learning and development. Illustrations and photographs on all print publications and decorative artwork and posters as well as Web sites should reflect the diversity of the students, faculty, and staff at the institution. Offices should have extended hours or flexible schedules of operation so that students with diverse time commitments including to work and family have equal access to all services. Although we understand the role that making and keeping appointments can play in teaching responsibility and preparing students for life after college, we also recommend the availability of walk-in appointments not only for students in crisis, but also for when students experience an unanticipated change in their own schedules. Online calendars for making appointments can make this process equally available to anyone at any time of day. Offices should be designed to be accessible to all learners and staff members, with desks, counter tops, storage spaces, and signage at appropriate heights and easy entry and navigation within the space. Alternative formats of all materials, such as publications and handouts in Braille and large print, should be readily available at any time, rather than requiring advance notification. Web sites should be tested for accessibility and ease of navigation.

2. Develop, implement, and evaluate pathways for communication among students, staff, and faculty: Communication should be encouraged through methods that are appropriate, comfortable, and accessible to all, with appropriate accommodations (e.g., telecommunication devices for people who are deaf) readily available. When possible, information

should be shared using multiple and varied methods and technologies, and when appropriate or necessary mechanisms should be in place to ensure that messages are received, preferably through some form of return receipt. As noted by Jillian Duquaine-Watson in Chapter 34, when considering electronic forms of communication, it must be recognized that all students do not have equal access to campus computer labs because of other time commitments, and may not have a computer or access to the Internet at home. For some students these are unaffordable luxuries rather than standard household equipment and services. Every effort should be made to create pathways to make electronic communication accessible to all students.

3. Promote interaction among students and between staff and students: Once channels for communication have been established, the next step is to encourage their use. Numerous research studies support that interactions with faculty and staff outside the classroom contribute to student satisfaction and retention (Astin, 1985, 1993; Chickering, 1969; Chickering & Reisser, 1993). Why? These interactions lead to students feeling a sense of connection to the institution and foster the belief that someone cares about them. But these relationships are easier to develop for some students than others. According to Jones (2005), for many White students, "discussions with students of color are viewed as mine fields where it is safer not to tread" (p. 145). Other authors (Alimo & Kelly, 2002; Antonio, 2001; Bruch, Higbee, & Siaka, 2007; Frederick, 1995; Holt-Shannon, 2001; Levine & Cureton, 1990; Tregoning, in press a; Zuñiga, 2003) have also addressed the discomfort or inability of both students and faculty and staff to engage in multicultural conversations and the need to provide more opportunities for intergroup interaction in order to facilitate mutual understanding and respect. Similarly, some individuals lack confidence when trying to communicate in another language or are not comfortable when needing to engage in alternative forms of communication in order to converse with someone with a disability. The concept of interaction strain between those with and without disabilities has been well documented (Fichten, Robillard, & Sabourin, 1994). Tregoning (in press b) has noted that educators' attitudes toward people with disabilities may be to want to "help", but that this approach can "set up a pattern of behavior and belief in both parties that can be detrimental." Instead, we should seek mutually beneficial relationships.

4. Ensure that each student and staff member has an equal opportunity to learn and grow: Barriers to learning should be assessed, examined, and removed wherever possible. Barriers may be physical, intellectual, or attitudinal. They may be created by the individual or imposed by external sources. A wide variety of institutional assessments (e.g., MAP IT) can be used to measure campus climate. Meanwhile, individual assessments can measure factors related to student success. From a Universal Design perspective, these assessments should not be limited to those related to disability. For example, any student can have debilitating test or mathematics anxiety and a wide array of measures—both formal (e.g., test attitude inventories) and informal (e.g., the mathematics autobiography)—is available to ascertain whether this is a problem for the individual. Lack of motivation can also be an issue for anyone, but the source of the problem may be anything from unclear career goals to lack of autonomy to the perception of dissonance between individual and institutional goals. One step that is key to ensuring equal opportunity for all is to take the time to get to know the individual and to refrain from making snap judgments or

engaging in stereotypes.

5. Communicate clear expectations to students, supervisees, and other professional colleagues utilizing multiple formats and taking into consideration diverse learning and communication styles: Expectations related to performance—whether from the standpoint of employment or academic requirements and standards—must be clearly defined. No one can be held to expectations that have not been made explicit. Stating requirements orally is not adequate. Many individuals—both with and without disabilities—do not retain information well when it is communicated only by word of mouth. But not everyone learns most effectively from reading text, either. In their chapter on "Training Professional and Faculty Advisors in Universal Design Principles" (see Chapter 27), Cunningham, Souma, and Gilmore Holman illustrate how providing a "mind map" of graduation requirements can be a useful alternative to standard checklists. They do not recommend using one or the other, but instead note that the two formats can complement one another.

6. Use methods and strategies that consider diverse learning styles, abilities, ways of knowing, and previous experience and background knowledge, while recognizing each student's and staff member's unique identity and contributions: Individuals should have the right to determine how they identify and define themselves, rather than being labeled by others. Each of us has something different to offer, and it is important that our contributions are valued. Whether developing a tutor training program, a career exploration workshop, social programs for the residence halls, or a lecture series for the campus community, it is imperative to consider all possible participants and to think creatively about how everyone might be included. In our chapter on "The First-Year Experience" (see Chapter 20), first published in 2003, Karen Kalivoda and I discuss ideas for more inclusive approaches to the campus tour, a common experience during the admissions and orientation processes. But at the time that we wrote that chapter, we were still not thinking inclusively enough from a Universal Design perspective. For example, how do we include parents with limited proficiency in spoken English? How do we enable alumni to share their experiences and knowledge of the campus without dominating the activity? And what do we do when the weather is so unbearable that no one wants to go outdoors? Anyone who works on the banks of the Mississippi River in Minneapolis in the winter can relate to this dilemma! Climatic and environmental factors such as inclement weather and pollution can challenge everyone, not only those with mobility impairments or asthma, for example.

7. Provide natural supports for learning and working to enhance opportunities for all students and staff: Natural supports can come in many different forms. For example, for committees—whether of administrators and staff or student groups—meeting agendas and minutes are natural supports that can assist everyone in knowing what to expect and how to prepare in advance of a meeting and in following the progression from one subject to another and staying on task during the meeting. Additional handouts such as those to accompany PowerPoint slides can supplement the discussion and aid participants in retaining the content of the meeting. Documenting key points via notes on flip charts or overhead transparencies or by typing them and simultaneously projecting them on a screen can also enable participants to correct any misunderstandings in the content of

Figure 1. Template for evaluating student development programs and services

EVALUATION TEMPLATE
(For purposes of having students evaluate programs and services)

On a 1 to 10 scale, where 1 = "not at all" and 10 = "outstanding," please evaluate the extent to which this program or service accomplished each of the following goals:

	Not at all									Outstanding
1. Created a respectful and welcoming environment	1	2	3	4	5	6	7	8	9	10
2. Provided effective pathways for communication with staff and administrators	1	2	3	4	5	6	7	8	9	10
3. Promoted interaction among students and between staff and students	1	2	3	4	5	6	7	8	9	10
4. Ensured that I and all students have an equal opportunity to learn	1	2	3	4	5	6	7	8	9	10
5. Communicated clear expectations utilizing multiple formats and taking into consideration diverse learning and communication styles	1	2	3	4	5	6	7	8	9	10
6. Used methods and strategies that consider diverse learning styles, abilities, ways of knowing, and previous experience and background knowledge, while recognizing each student's unique identity and contributions	1	2	3	4	5	6	7	8	9	10
7. Provided natural supports such as [provide specific examples implemented in the program here]	1	2	3	4	5	6	7	8	9	10
8. Ensured confidentiality	1	2	3	4	5	6	7	8	9	10

Note: Additional specifics such as mechanisms for creating a welcoming environment or particular modes of communication can be added to each item for further clarification and to adapt the template to the goals of the program or service being evaluated.

what has been said or add further clarification. These notes can serve as the foundation for the minutes of the meeting, which can then be made available to those unable to attend. Similar practices can support tutoring sessions and other services offered to students. Another example of a natural support that might be used in a learning center or counseling, placement, or advising office is automatically-generated electronic appointment reminders for both the student and the staff member, assuming that provisions have been made for equal access to technology.

8. Ensure confidentiality: This is important to everyone, but for individuals with disabilities, even when confidentiality is supposedly assured, when programs and services are not universally designed the public provision of separate accommodations reveals that the

individual is somehow "different." In the film *Uncertain Welcome* (2002) students with disabilities discuss some of the reasons why they choose not to disclose their disability, including that they cannot always assume that their confidentiality will be protected. Disability is but one aspect of a student's identity that he or she might be hesitant to share. Students may feel awkward or embarrassed to discuss their financial status or may have experiences less than supportive responses to disclosure of other facets of identity.

9. Define service quality, establish benchmarks for best practices, and collaborate to evaluate services regularly: These Universal Design Principles for Student Development Programs and Services can guide the implementation of best practices and can be used as the basis for establishing institutional, programmatic, and individual goals and objectives. The next step is to establish a mechanism and timeline for regular evaluation, both by students and by colleagues. Figure 1 provides a template for providing an opportunity for students to evaluate student development programs and services according to these principles.

Conclusion

These principles are neither exhaustive nor mutually exclusive. The overlap in ideas and concepts is not unintentional. But woven together these principles create a framework for inclusion for student development programs and services and can serve as a "safety net" to ensure that no student is lost in the shuffle. Furthermore, these guiding principles considered side-by-side with those created for instruction and learning support (see Figure 2) provide a multifaceted institution-wide approach to inclusion.

Our goal in presenting these Universal Design Principles for Student Development Programs and Services is not to imply that we are introducing anything that is new or unique or revolutionary, and yet implementing these guidelines in a very intentional way can be transformative. Individually and collectively we can make a difference if we really take the time whenever we engage in the planning process to consider the following questions:

> "How can we ensure that everyone who wants to participate will have the opportunity to do so?"
> "What steps can we take to ensure that everyone will feel included?"
> "What do we need to do to ensure that everyone will benefit to the greatest extent possible?"

And we can document the impact of UD in student development programs and services by engaging in evaluative research to determine the extent to which students, staff, and faculty believe that the implementation of these Universal Design principles accomplishes the goal of inclusion.

Just as Universal Instructional Design is "just good teaching" (Chickering & Gamson, 1987; Hodge & Preston-Sabin, 1997), the Universal Design Principles for Student Development Programs and Services are merely guidelines for good practice. What may distinguish them from other similar standards is that they were created with inclusion at their core as the one unifying goal that binds them together.

Figure 2. Guiding principles across contexts

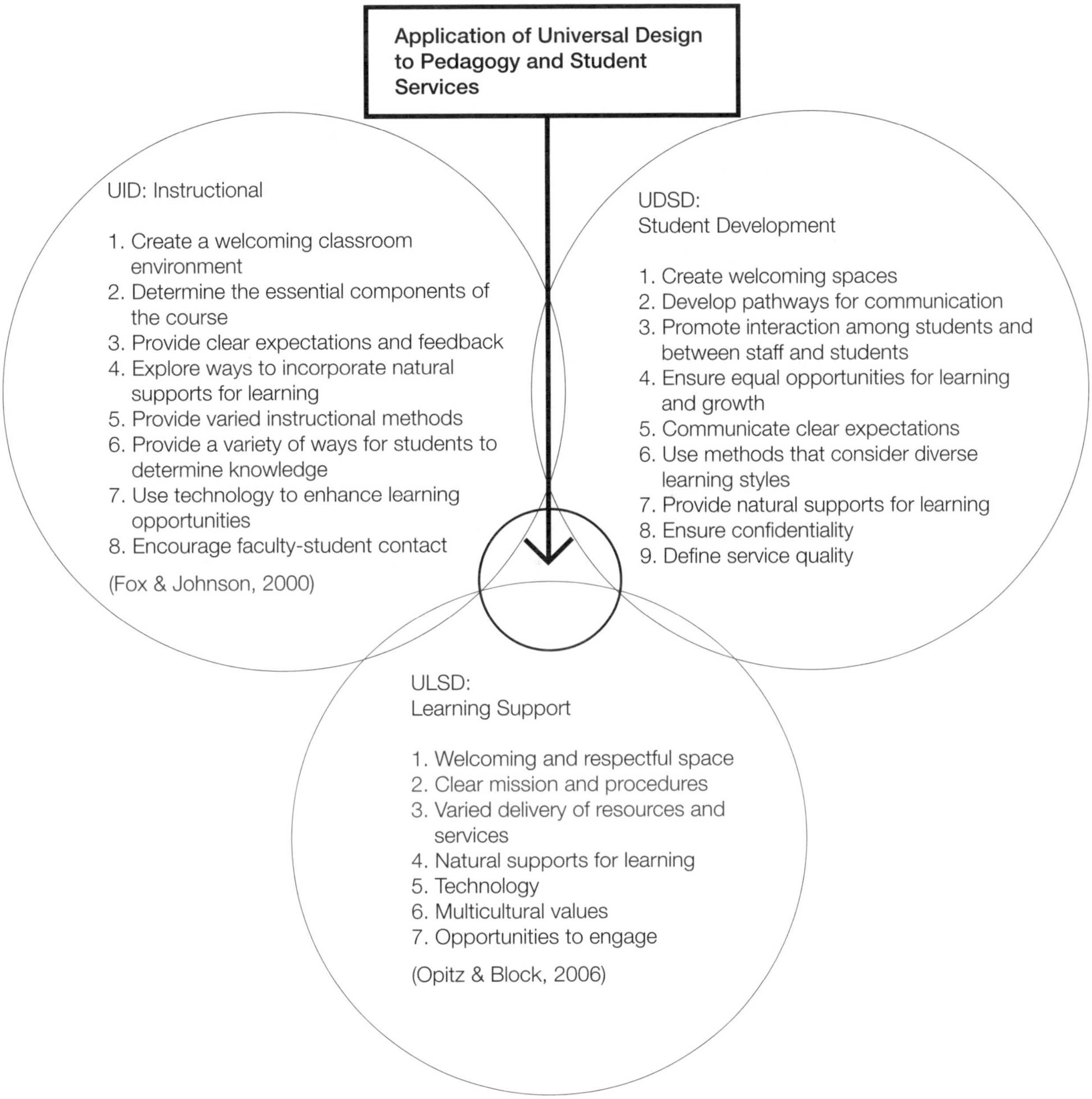

Application of Universal Design to Pedagogy and Student Services

UID: Instructional

1. Create a welcoming classroom environment
2. Determine the essential components of the course
3. Provide clear expectations and feedback
4. Explore ways to incorporate natural supports for learning
5. Provide varied instructional methods
6. Provide a variety of ways for students to determine knowledge
7. Use technology to enhance learning opportunities
8. Encourage faculty-student contact

(Fox & Johnson, 2000)

UDSD: Student Development

1. Create welcoming spaces
2. Develop pathways for communication
3. Promote interaction among students and between staff and students
4. Ensure equal opportunities for learning and growth
5. Communicate clear expectations
6. Use methods that consider diverse learning styles
7. Provide natural supports for learning
8. Ensure confidentiality
9. Define service quality

ULSD: Learning Support

1. Welcoming and respectful space
2. Clear mission and procedures
3. Varied delivery of resources and services
4. Natural supports for learning
5. Technology
6. Multicultural values
7. Opportunities to engage

(Opitz & Block, 2006)

References

Alimo, C., & Kelly, R. (2002). Diversity initiatives in higher education: Intergroup dialogue program student outcomes and implications for campus radical climate (A case study). *Multicultural Education, 10*(1), 49-53.

Antonio, A. L. (2001). The role of interracial interaction in the development of leadership skills and cultural knowledge and understanding. *Research in Higher Education, 42,* 593-617.

Astin, A. W. (1985). *Achieving educational excellence.* San Francisco: Jossey-Bass.

Astin, A. W. (1993). *What matters in college: Four critical years revisited.* San Francisco: Jossey-Bass.

Barajas, H. L., & Higbee, J. L. (2003). Where do we go from here? Universal Design as a model for multicultural education. In J. L. Higbee (Ed.), *Curriculum transformation and disability: Implementing Universal Design in higher education* (pp. 285-290). Minneapolis: University of Minnesota, General College, Center for Research on Developmental Education and Urban Literacy. Retrieved October 11, 2007, from http://www.cehd.umn.edu/crdeul

Bruch, P. L., Higbee, J. L., & Siaka, K. (2007). Multiculturalism, Incorporated: Student perspectives. *Innovative Higher Education, 32,* 139-152.

Chickering, A. W. (1969). *Education and identity.* San Francisco: Jossey-Bass.

Chickering, A. W., & Gamson, Z. F. (1987). Seven principles for good practice in undergraduate education. *AAHE Bulletin, 39*(7), 3-7.

Chickering, A. W., & Reisser, L. (1993). *Education and identity* (2nd ed.). San Francisco: Jossey-Bass.

Fichten, C. S., Robillard, K., & Sabourin, S. (1994). The attentional mechanisms model of interaction strain. *Journal of Developmental and Physical Disabilities, 6*(3), 239-254.

Frederick, P. (1995). Walking on eggs: Mastering the dreaded diversity discussion. *College Teaching, 43*(3), 83-92.

Higbee, J. L. (Ed.). (2003). *Curriculum transformation and disability: Implementing Universal Design in higher education.* Minneapolis: University of Minnesota, General College, Center for Research on Developmental Education and Urban Literacy. Retrieved October 10, 2007, from http://www.cehd.umn.edu/crdeul

Higbee, J. L., & Barajas, H. L. (2007). Building effective places for multicultural learning. *About Campus, 12*(3), 16-22.

Hodge, B. M., & Preston-Sabin, J. (1997). Accommodations—Or just good teaching? Strategies for teaching college students with disabilities. Westport, CT: Praeger.

Holt-Shannon, M. (2001). White hesitation: A message from a well meaning White person like herself. *About Campus, 6*(3), 31-32.

Jones, W. T. (2005). The realities of diversity and the campus climate for first-year students. In M. L. Upcraft, J. N. Gardner, B. O. Barefoot, & Associates, *Challenging and supporting the first year-student: A handbook for improving the first year of college* (pp. 141-154). San Francisco: Jossey-Bass.

Keeling, R. P. (Ed.). (2004). *Learning reconsidered: A campus-wide focus on the student experience.* Washington: DC: American College Personnel Association & National Association of Student Personnel Administrators. Retrieved January 16, 2007, from http://www.

naspa.org/membership/leader_ex_pdf/lr_long.pdf

Levine, A., & Cureton, J. S. (1998). *When hope and fear collide: A portrait of today's college student.* San Francisco: Jossey-Bass.

Miksch, K. L., Higbee, J. L., Jehangir, R. R., Lundell, D. B., Bruch, P. L., Siaka, K., & Dotson, M.V. (2003). *Multicultural Awareness Project for Institutional Transformation: MAP IT.* Minneapolis: University of Minnesota, General College, Multicultural Concerns Committee and Center for Research on Developmental Education and Urban Literacy. Retrieved October 10, 2007, from http://www.cehd.umn.edu/crdeul

Opitz, D. L., & Block, L. S. (2006). Universal learning support design: Maximizing learning beyond the classroom. *The Learning Assistance Review, 11*(2), 33-45.

Tregoning, M. E. (in press a). Being an ally in language use. In J. L. Higbee & A.A. Mitchell (Eds.), *Making good on the promise: Student affairs professionals with disabilities.* Washington, DC: ACPA-College Student Educators International and University Press of America.

Tregoning, M. E. (in press b). "Getting it" as an ally: Interpersonal relationships between colleagues with and without disabilities. In J. L. Higbee & A. A. Mitchell (Eds.), *Making good on the promise: Student affairs professionals with disabilities.* Washington, DC: ACPA-College Student Educators International and University Press of America.

Uncertain welcome [video]. (2002). Minneapolis: University of Minnesota, General College and Disability Services. Retrieved December 11, 2006, from http://www.gen.umn.edu/research/ctad

Zuñiga, X. (2003). Bridging differences through dialogue. *About Campus,* 7(6), 8-16.

CHAPTER 16

Universal Learning Support Design: Maximizing Learning Beyond the Classroom

Donald L. Opitz
DePaul University

Lydia S. Block
Ohio Wesleyan University

Abstract
This chapter was originally published in The Learning Assistance Review *in 2006 and is reprinted verbatim with permission. The movement for adapting Universal Design (UD), a concept from architecture, to higher education has yielded guiding principles for implementing UD in classroom and online instruction. In order to address all of the environments on college campuses, members of the Pedagogy and Student Services for Institutional Transformation (PASS IT) Institute, which met recently in Minneapolis, identified the need to adapt UD principles to the administration of learning support services. In response to this need, we propose 7 principles of Universal Learning Support Design (ULSD) that are distinct from—and yet complement—principles of Universal Instructional Design (UID). In addition, we provide a definition of learning support, a rationale for ULSD, a strategy for implementation, and future directions for dissemination.*

Originally developed for use in architectural design, the principles of Universal Design (UD) have positively impacted postsecondary settings through the collaborative work of dedicated advocates. Adapting the seven principles articulated by the Center for Universal Design (CUD) at North Carolina State University under architect Ron Mace's leadership (Center for Universal Design, 1997), postsecondary educators now have useful sets of guidelines for implementing UD in instruction (Bowe, 2000; Burgstahler, 2002; Fox & Johnson, 2000; Scott, McGuire & Shaw, 2003; Silver, Bourke & Strehorn, 1998). The need now exists to adapt UD principles to the myriad campus services that support students' classroom and online learning. Scholars in Disability Services and related areas have already called attention to the leading role that student services can play in supporting the retention and academic achievement of students with disabilities (Block, 1993; English, 1993; Hall & Belch, 2000; Hart, Zafft & Zimbrich, 2001; Kroeger & Schuck, 1993; Weir, 2004). But, as Burgstahler (2005) has noted, "Few published articles have focused on accessible or universal design of student services" (p. 23). Despite this dearth in scholarship, student services often demonstrate UD "because they provide multiple means of facilitating the acquisition of knowledge" (Higbee & Eaton, 2003, p. 233). Training and dissemination projects such as the University of Washington's Disabilities, Opportunities, Internetworking, and Technology (DO-IT), University of Minnesota's Pedagogy and Student Services for Institutional Transformation (PASS IT), and DePaul University's Productive Learning Strategies (PLuS) have led recent efforts to translate UD in areas of learning support (DePaul University, 2006b; University of Minnesota, 2006; University of Washington, 2006; U.S. Department of Education, 2006). Yet practitioners and administrators still lack a clear statement of principles that parallel what is already available for instruction. To address this situation, in this article we offer seven principles of Universal Learning Support Design (ULSD) inspired by our discussions with participants of the first summer institute of PASS IT held at the University of Minnesota August 2-4, 2006.

We begin by offering a rationale for the need and then proceed to outline seven guiding principles inspired by the principles of Universal Instructional Design (UID). We will also define "learning support" and illustrate the range of programs, resources and services that fall within its domain. We conclude with strategies for successful implementation in one key area of learning support, the campus learning center, and suggest further directions for this critical work.

Rationale

Mace (1988) and the Center for Universal Design (1997) at North Carolina State University have inspired three distinct adaptations of UD principles to instruction that are often cited in the higher education literature. Because the instructional principles provide clues for how UD may be adapted to learning support, it will first be useful to review the instructional adaptations of UD.

Concerned with assistive technologies, the Center for Applied Special Technology (CAST), a Massachusetts-based nonprofit organization, adopted three principles of Universal Design for Learning (UDL) that attend to three essential facets of learning (i.e., recognition, strategy, and affect) that are mapped to distinct brain networks (Rose, 2001; Rose & Meyer, 2000). These principles may be summarized as "multiple means of representation," "multiple means of support," and "multiple means of engagement" (Center for Applied Special Technology, 2006). Nearly simultaneously with CAST's development, two faculty teams, funded by grants from the U.S. Department of Education's Office of Postsecondary Education, developed new sets of principles by considering the relationship of UD to Chickering and Gamson's (1987) "seven principles for good practice in undergraduate education" (Fox & Johnson, 2000, p. 43; Fox, Hatfield & Collins, 2003, p. 26; Scott, McGuire & Shaw, 2003, pp. 374-376). One team, at the University of Connecticut's Center for Postsecondary Education and Disability, developed "Universal Design for Instruction" (UDI; Scott, McGuire & Shaw, 2001). UDI consists of nine principles—seven of which are the principles stated by CUD—with supplementary definitions and examples that clarify the relevance for instruction. Ultimately, a second team at University of Minnesota's Curriculum Transformation and Disability (CTAD) collaborative, developed eight principles of "Universal Instructional Design" (UID)—a term coined by Silver, Bourke, and Strehorn (1998)—that provide a truly original synthesis of CUD's principles and Chickering and Gamson's principles. In proposing UID principles, the CTAD members attempted to make the relevance of UD to instruction easily applicable (see Figure 1). Among these three versions of principles, a fundamental theme persists: universally-designed instructional environments foster equitable and multimodal means by which students possessing the broadest range of characteristics can engage with instructors and curricular materials, and thus minimize barriers to students' learning. It is important to remember this fundamental commonality because the growing number of instructional adaptations of the principles of UD can seem confusing.

Although postsecondary educators have made significant headway in disseminating and implementing adaptations of UD principles in instruction, their focus on the classroom does not account for the entire range of students' college learning experiences and environments (Chism & Bickford, 2002; Keeling, 2004; Terenzini, Pascarella, & Blimling, 1996). Clearly, if we intend to minimize barriers and maximize students' access to learning more holistically, we must ensure that the wide range of learning support offices, programs and services also support UD principles. As in the case of instruction, practitioners can benefit from a set of guiding principles and strategies for implementation. Some have already used UD, UDI, and UID to guide their efforts, but we wonder whether lock-stock-and-barrel applications of architectural or instructional principles are sufficient or even appropriate for all areas of learning support. To take an example, instruction-specific language, like CTAD's second UID principle—"determine the essential components of the course" (Fox & Johnson, 2000, p. 43)—may not always translate to services like a learning commons dedicated to supporting students' self-directed study as opposed to achieving a course-specific learning outcome. Other UID principles bring similar challenges for their application to areas of learning support. Here we need to reconsider, then, the relevant principles that apply to the design of learning supports.

Seven Principles of Universal Learning Support Design (ULSD)

We must bear in mind that CUD's seven principles undergird all design considerations. Particularly where the resource is physical space, administrators and staff must, in our opinion, first attend to architectural design before other aspects. To return to our earlier example, the dominant feature of the learning commons—an innovative design integrating many traditionally distinct services—is its highly multipurpose space. Although staff members may be present to offer a variety of support and consultation, access to key learning resources is integrated into the commons' physical design: the layout of study carrels, tables, and computer workstations intended for various kinds of study activity and often self-service access to online resources and assistive technology. However, attention must then be given to nonphysical and ephemeral features of the commons like social interactions between students and staff, printed and online information, and administrative functions that take place behind the commons' public space.

In our discussion with colleagues at the PASS IT summer institute, we arrived at a set of principles that, for us, enhances the application of architectural and pedagogical concepts to learning support functions and environments. We developed these principles further by taking into consideration Blimling, Whitt, and Associates' (1999) principles of good practice in student affairs. We view these principles as "works in progress" to be adapted in ways appropriate for the distinctiveness of individual programs and services (see Figure 1):

Figure 1. Diagram showing three sets of complementary principles of Universal Design, Universal Instructional Design, and Universal Learning Support Design

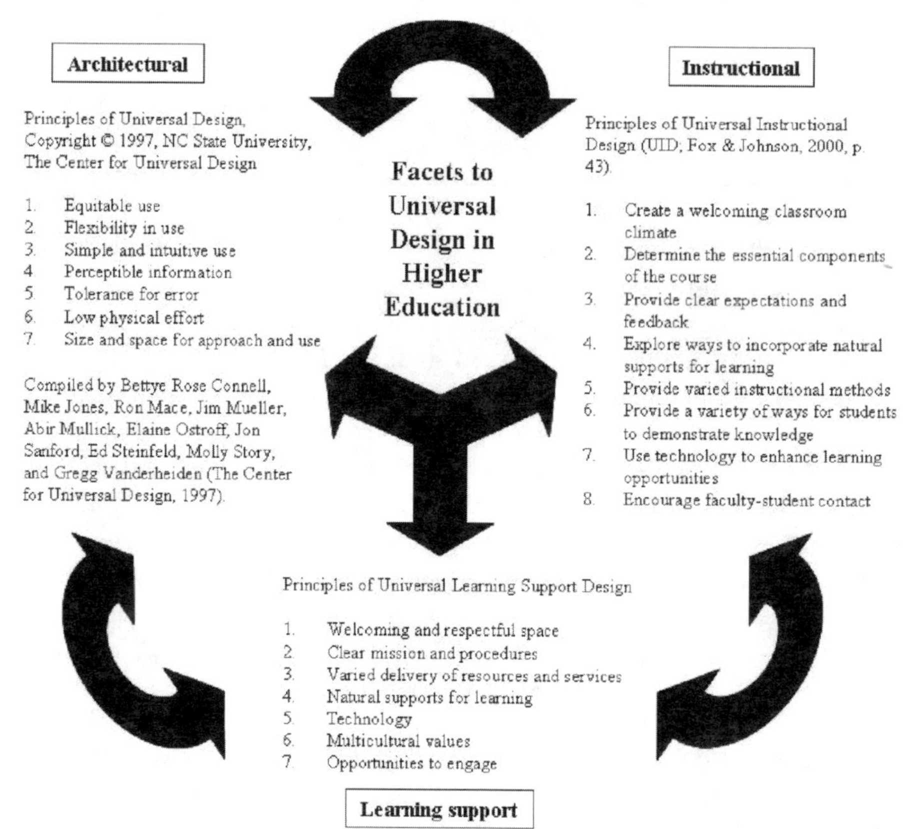

Note: The application of the Principles of Universal Design, which were conceived and developed by the Center for Universal Design at North Carolina State University, to instruction and learning support does not constitute or imply acceptance or endorsement by the Center for Universal Design.

1. Welcoming and respectful space: Features of the spaces, resources, and services are welcoming, respectful, and comfortable to students having the widest range of characteristics and abilities. All representations of the spaces are welcoming and respectful.

2. Clear mission and procedures: The purpose of resources is clear and the procedures for their use are easy to follow regardless of the students' experience, knowledge, language skills, and abilities.

3. Varied delivery of resources and services: Varied, nonstigmatizing means of delivering resources and services foster equitable and flexible use by students. Varied delivery meets the needs and interests of students having the widest range of experiences, characteristics, and abilities.

4. Natural supports for learning: Resources and services foster students' holistic learning and engagement in a developmental manner. Staff members are trained to accommodate

the diverse learning styles of students. Services empower the students using them.

5. Technology: Technology resources enhance opportunities for all students to be engaged and learn. Technology assists in implementing other ULSD principles.

6. Multicultural values: All aspects of learning support embrace the broadest characteristics, backgrounds, and interests of students. Students' knowledge and experience are incorporated into design elements and improvements.

7. Opportunities to engage: Space, resources, and services promote students, regardless of their characteristics, to be engaged in learning. Positive interactions among students and staff are fostered by resources, services, and programming.

What Is "Learning Support"?

Now that we have proposed a set of guiding principles, to which spaces, programs, and activities do they apply? We intentionally designate the target of these principles as learning support. We believe that doing so avoids the artificial dichotomization of *academic learning* and *student development* and embraces the spirit of Keeling's (2004) holistic definition of transformative learning. We also escape pinning learning support services to a particular institutional division like student affairs or academic affairs, an important strategy amid the diversity of organizational homes that maintain the range of activities we have in mind. In essence, these activities include the many ways and many places in which instruction and student services can be coupled within and beyond classrooms. It is important to adopt a fluid definition as institutions increasingly embrace innovative, integrated, and holistic approaches to student learning, as learning communities demonstrate. Where instruction is concerned, UID should be considered in addition to ULSD.

We outline here nine broad areas of learning support and provide examples of the types of services that may be included within each area. This list is a beginning. In providing it we hope that student service professionals and administrators will recognize their particular programs and services and work to adopt ULSD at *both* the programmatic *and* institution-wide levels.

1. Core Administrative Services: Learning support can include the widest range of campus services that deal with the very logistics of being a student on campus: admissions, student records, financial aid, accounts receivable, registration, transcripts, and degree conferral. Indeed, if these core administrative services maximize students' sense of welcome, access, and engagement, they can only promote students' satisfaction, sense of belonging on campus, and, ultimately, their academic achievement. Campus administrators are increasingly recognizing how simplifying their delivery of services positively impacts the quality of students' learning experience. Let's take two examples. The University of Minnesota, a large public institution, brought together registration, transcript, financial aid, and related services within a comprehensive "OneStop" identity having both online and on-site presences that reduces the bureaucracy in administering these services (University of Minnesota, 2005). Similarly, DePaul University, a large private institution, recently opened "DePaul Central" to carry out the mission: "Here, at DePaul Central, we promise to help you take care of the core administrative details (student records, financial aid, student accounts) so you can get on with your core business—learning at DePaul!"

(DePaul University, 2006a).

2. Transition Programs and Services: Another growing trend in learning support often straddles the division between student affairs and academic affairs in efforts to promote students' successful transition to college life and expectations. First-year experience programming, for example, may include a variety of welcoming activities, summer bridge programs, orientation, convocation ceremonies, Web-based communities and portals, and freshman seminars. A growing recognition of transfer and adult students' unique needs has led to tailored services for these distinct cohorts. Institutions are also increasingly attending to student transitions within and beyond their degree programs. Sophomore seminars, upper-division seminars, weekly departmental colloquia, and learning communities all embody this trend.

3. Academic Skills Development: A panoply of programs and resources that focuses on developing students' academic skills constitutes another core area of learning support: subject-based tutoring, writing consultation, Supplemental Instruction, skills workshops, library workshops, testing and assessment, learning centers, printed and Web-based resources, professional clubs, leadership programs, and student research opportunities. Increasingly, institutions are approaching academic skills development in more integrated and holistic ways through across-the-curriculum approaches to writing and mathematics instruction, learning communities, and curricula that purposefully integrate skills development and content (Higbee, Lundell & Arendale, 2005).

4. Career and Community Learning: Increasingly important for post-graduation survival, career and community learning programs provide students with opportunities and resources to connect their classroom learning to the "real world." These opportunities take on a wide variety of formats: career counseling and workshops; career centers; community and service learning centers; internship, cooperative, and "externship" programs; volunteer placement; teaching and research apprenticeships; and graduate school preparation workshops. In the context of adult, neighborhood-based and online degree programs, career and community learning may also occur through satellite campus programs and resources located within students' own workplaces and communities.

5. Engagement, Social Community and Living: Regardless of whether students live on campus, commute, or learn online, and regardless of students' abilities, research has demonstrated that a sense of connection to campus on both academic and social levels is critical to student retention (Astin, 1993; English, 1993; National Survey of Student Engagement, 2006; Tinto, 1993). In response to national recognition of this fact, universities have instituted offices and centers devoted to student engagement. Other significant providers and partners in this work are residential life offices and the wide array of student communities, cultural centers, and organizations often supported by student affairs personnel.

6. Health and Recreation: By promoting students' physical, emotional, and spiritual health, campus health services, crisis centers, counseling services, and ministry offices constitute a further closely-related set of learning supports. In addition, intercollegiate and intramural sports, recreation centers, and recreational clubs all foster students' physical health and engagement.

7. Advising: Academic advising and a variety of other advising activities are critical

supports to students' learning and development. Three predominant models for academic advising are (a) advising performed by a professionally-trained staff within distinct units; (b) advising performed by tenured and tenure-track faculty members; and (c) a blend of both—for example, advising that begins with a professional staff advisor and concludes with a faculty advisor or mentor. Other types of advising may include roles for peer mentors, student affairs personnel, research supervisors, and alumni.

8. Disability Services: Traditionally, campuses have had at least one staff member designated as the campus consultant for students with disabilities. Large universities may have a department of staff. Disability services can be housed in any number of campus divisions or offices. One place that disability expertise can be found with greater frequency is within a learning center, learning commons, or academic skills center. Emerging models of service provision situate disability services personnel as consultants to the entire campus and partners in efforts to implement UD strategies in settings for instruction and learning support (Block, 2006).

9. Holistic Learning Communities: A variety of offices and programs do not fall neatly into one or another category because of the comprehensiveness of their programming and resources and close partnerships with curriculum. Examples include some campus women's centers, multicultural centers, honors colleges, and living and learning communities.

Practitioners and administrators have the benefit of several excellent books that address the wide range of learning support services and programs highlighted here. They offer further guidance for the administration and development of these services and give some perspective on the importance of learning support work in the broader context of higher education. See especially Barr, Desler, and Associates (2000); Blimling, Whitt, and Associates (1999); Kuh, Schuh, and Whitt (1991); and Sandeen and Barr (2006).

Strategies for Implementation

To illustrate how ULSD may be implemented within particular learning support services, we will focus on one common type of learning support: the learning center. We offer the following scenario as an impressionistic window for viewing how a universally-designed learning center might appear from a student's perspective. The scenario, although idealized, is inspired by a student's real experience at the University of Minnesota's Academic Resource Center, currently affiliated with the Department of Postsecondary Teaching and Learning (Opitz & Hartley, 2005).

A Model of ULSD-Based Practice

Katrina, a 28-year old transfer student who is blind, enrolled in a college algebra course needed as a prerequisite for upper-division courses in her major, international business. Although she liked math in elementary school, negative experiences in her high school algebra class dissuaded her from continuing her math study. Given her prior negative experiences, her 15-year break from math, and the disability accommodations she will need, she is worried about falling behind in the class and failing. Dan, her disability specialist, assures Katrina that all arrangements for her accommodations have been made, including advance electronic copies of lecture notes that are in a format compatible with her laptop's screen reader. But Dan also encourages Katrina to take advantage of peer math tutoring available at her college's learning center. Fortunately, her math instructor took the class on a mini-field trip to the learning center, creating a natural opportunity for her to become acclimated to the space and services of the center. During this visit, Katrina learned that the center offered scheduled appointments with tutors and other helpful resources like wireless access to the Internet. She found the center's space easy to navigate and the student staff welcoming. The following week she returned to sign up for a weekly appointment with a tutor who was also a business major. A receptionist made the appointment and explained further resources available to her, including after-hours online tutoring and software on the center's computers that provided supplementary instruction and practice problems in an audio format. For the remainder of the semester, Katrina worked regularly with her assigned tutor, Cindy, with whom Katrina developed a good friendship. Sometimes she came with a student scribe, assigned by her disability specialist, but other times she simply dropped into the center to access the Internet, among other things, to download her class notes, or simply study. She especially liked the convenience and accessibility of the online tutoring, which she often used from home. She sometimes joined classmates at the center's study tables to review for exams. At the end of the semester, after her final, Katrina dropped by the center to share the news of her success—she got a B. She asked the tutors on-duty for their perspective on the instructor teaching her next math class, business calculus.

We chose the perspective of a student with a physical disability, but many of the center's design features implied here would benefit all students regardless of their abilities. Particularly where math learning assistance is concerned, the learning center must be welcoming and respectful so that students who already possess negative predispositions or "math anxiety" will feel comfortable. As in this scenario, centers can accommodate class visits to ensure that all students are introduced to the learning resources, a strategy that circumvents the intimidation students often feel when faced with making their initial visits alone. Design considerations for the physical space reinforce a sense of welcome and foster equitable access: bright lighting, sound absorbers like carpeting and acoustic ceiling tiles, wide aisles between tables to enable ease of movement, table heights and chairs that are suitable for the widest range of users, seating options that meet students' needs for individual or group study, a perceptible layout of resources, and a reception area. The center's mission, procedures and policies are posted and made available in a variety of formats. Staff members explain procedures to newcomers and regularly monitor whether students are getting what they need during their visits. Specific resources and services are offered through a variety means. Here, tutoring is available online, on a drop-in basis, and by appointment. Individualized and group-study options exist. Ideally, the hours and places of service also vary by students' needs. Technology enhances this flexibility and students' opportunities to learn by offering interactive service online, ancillary learning software, and assistive technology. The space and staff promote group study and other opportunities for students to interact and be engaged in their learning. In on-going training and staff development opportunities, peer tutors learn about self-directed learning, developmental education, varied instructional approaches and learning styles, multicultural and disability issues, active listening, positive reinforcement, welcoming and respectful behavior—i.e., strategies that provide natural supports for student learning. Multicultural values infuse all dimensions of the center: tutoring pedagogy, diversity of staff, interior design features, media and communications, and student-staff interactions. Based on student feedback and periodic program assessment, the design and administration of the center is further developed to ensure that all students' needs are being met and that their holistic learning is supported most effectively.

Many of these features may indeed already characterize much of learning center practice (Higbee & Eaton, 2003). ULSD provides a framework within which to name and assess such characteristics and to guide further program development. Checklists can help in the planning and assessment process (University of Washington, 2006).

Conclusion: Future Directions

We intend our conceptualization of ULSD, as presented in this article, to begin a conversation around issues of postsecondary learning that are intertwined with curriculum and extend beyond the classroom. A starting point is simply to identify a set of UD principles as they apply to learning support (i.e., ULSD), what constitutes learning support, and what a demonstration of ULSD may look like. We have offered the seven principles of Universal Learning Support Design as fluid guidelines that we hope others will interpret and develop in ways relevant to their own programs and institutions.

Moving forward, the need exists to further illustrate the applicability of these principles, share best practices, and assess the impact on student learning. To a certain degree, ULSD may very well be "just good practice" and therefore intrinsically rewarding to both practitioners and students who are engaged in holistic learning on campus.

References

Astin, A. W. (1993). What matters in college? *Liberal Education, 79*(4), 4-15.

Barr, M. J., Desler, M. K., & Associates. (2000). *The handbook of student affairs administration* (2nd ed.). San Francisco: Jossey-Bass.

Blimling, G. S., Whitt, E. J., & Associates. (1999). *Good practice in student affairs: Principles to foster student learning.* San Francisco: Jossey-Bass.

Block, L. S. (1993). Students with learning disabilities. *Responding to disability issues in student affairs* (pp. 69-78). (New Directions for Student Services, No. 64.). San Francisco: Jossey-Bass.

Block, L. S. (2006, February). *The disabilities service provider as a consultant on campus.* Paper presented at the Transition and Communication Consortium on Learning Disabilities, Columbus, OH.

Bowe, F. G. (2000). *Universal Design in education: Teaching nontraditional students.* Westport, CT: Bergin & Garvey.

Burgstahler, S. (2002). Distance learning: Universal design, universal access. *AACE Journal: International Forum on Information Technology in Education, 10*(1), 32-61. Retrieved August 26, 2006, from http://www.aace.org/pubs/aacej/

Burgstahler, S. (2005). *Students with disabilities and campus services: Building the team*. Seattle: University of Washington, Disabilities, Opportunities, Internetworking, and Technology. Retrieved August 26, 2006, from http://www.washington.edu/doit/AdminN/

Center for Applied Special Technology. (2006). *CAST: Universal Design for Learning.* Retrieved October 16, 2006, from http://www.cast.org

The Center for Universal Design. (1997). *The principles of Universal Design* (Version 2.0). Raleigh, NC: Author, NC State University. Retrieved October 16, 2006, from http://www.design.ncsu.edu/cud/

Chickering, A. W., & Gamson, Z. F. (1987, March). Seven principles for good practice in undergraduate education. *AAHE Bulletin,* 3-7.

Chism, N. V. N., & Bickford, D. J. (2002). Improving the environment for learning: An expanded agenda. In D. V. N. Chism & D. J. Bickford (Eds.), *The importance of physical space in creating supportive learning environments* (pp. 91–97). (New Directions for Teaching and Learning, No. 92). San Francisco: Jossey-Bass.

DePaul University. (2006a). *DePaul Central.* Retrieved August 27, 2006, from http://arc.depaul.edu/central/dpc.shtml

DePaul University. (2006b). *Productive Learning u Strategies.* Retrieved October 16, 2006, from http://studentaffairs.depaul.edu/plus/

English, K. M. (1993). The role of support services in the integration and retention of college students who are hearing-impaired. (Doctoral dissertation, The Claremont Graduate University & San Diego State University, 1993). *Dissertation Abstracts International, 54* (06), 2114.

Fox, J. A., Hatfield, J. P., & Collins, T. C. (2003). Developing the Curriculum Transformation and Disability workshop model. In J. L. Higbee (Ed.), *Curriculum transformation and disability: Implementing Universal Design in higher education* (pp. 23-39). Minneapolis: University of Minnesota, General College, Center for Research on Developmental Education and Urban Literacy.

Fox, J. A., & Johnson, D. (Eds.). (2000). *Curriculum transformation and disability (CTAD): Workshop facilitator's guide.* Minneapolis: University of Minnesota, General College & Disability Services. Retrieved October 16, 2006, from http://www.gen.umn.edu/research/CTAD/publications.htm

Hall, L. M., & Belch, H. A. (2000). Setting the context: Reconsidering the principles of full participation and meaningful access for students with disabilities. *Serving students with disabilities* (pp. 5-17). (New Directions for Student Services, No. 91.). San Francisco: Jossey-Bass.

Hart, D., Zafft, C., & Zimbrich, K (2001). Creating access to college for all students. *Journal for Vocational Special Needs Education, 23*(2), 19-31.

Higbee, J. L., & Eaton, S. B. (2003). Implementing Universal Design in learning centers. In J. L. Higbee (Ed.), *Curriculum transformation and disability: Implementing Universal Design in higher education* (pp. 231–239). Minneapolis: University of Minnesota, General College, Center for Research on Developmental Education and Urban Literacy. .

Higbee, J. L., Lundell, D. B., & Arendale, D. R. (Eds.). (2005). *The General College vision: Integrating intellectual growth, multicultural perspectives, and student development.* Minneapolis: University of Minnesota, General College, Center for Research on Developmental

Education and Urban Literacy. .

Keeling, R. P. (Ed.). (2004). *Learning reconsidered: A campus-wide focus on the student experience.* Washington, DC: The National Association of Student Personnel Administrators & the American College Personnel Association.

Kroeger, S., & Schuck, J. (1993). Essential elements in effective service delivery. *Responding to disability issues in student affairs* (pp. 59-68). (New Directions for Student Services, No. 64.). San Francisco: Jossey-Bass.

Kuh, G. D., Schuh, J. H., Whitt, E. J., & Associates. (1991). *Involving colleges: Successful approaches to fostering student learning and development outside the classroom.* San Francisco: Jossey-Bass.

Mace, R. (1988). *Universal Design: Housing for the lifespan of all people.* Rockville, MD: U.S. Department of Housing and Urban Development.

National Survey of Student Engagement. (2006). *NSSE 2006 institutional report.* Bloomington, IN: Author. Retrieved August 27, 2006, from http://nsse.iub.edu/html/2006_inst_report.cfm

Opitz, D. L., & Hartley, D. A. (2005). Collaborative learning beyond the classroom: The Academic Resource Center. In J. L. Higbee, D. B. Lundell, & D. R. Arendale (Eds.). *The General College vision: Integrating intellectual growth, multicultural perspectives, and student development* (pp. 395-413). Minneapolis: University of Minnesota, General College, Center for Research on Developmental Education and Urban Literacy. .

Rose, D. H. (2001). Universal Design for Learning: Deriving guiding principles from networks that learn. *Journal of Special Education Technology, 16*(2), 66-67.

Rose, D. H., & Meyer, A. (2000). Universal design for learning. *Journal of Special Education Technology, 15*(1), 67-70.

Sandeen, A., & Barr, M. J. (2006). *Critical issues for student affairs: Challenges and opportunities.* San Francisco: Jossey-Bass.

Scott, S. S., McGuire, J. M., & Shaw, S. F. (2001). *Principles of Universal Design for instruction.* Storr: University of Connecticut, Center on Postsecondary Education and Disability.

Scott, S. S., McGuire, J. M., & Shaw, S. F. (2003). Universal Design for Instruction: A new paradigm for adult instruction in postsecondary education. *Remedial and Special Education, 24*(6), 369-379.

Silver, P., Bourke, A. B., & Strehorn, K. C. (1998). Universal Instructional Design in higher education: An approach for inclusion. *Equity & Excellence in Education, 31*(2), 47-51.

Terenzini, P. T., Pascarella, E. T., & Blimling, G. S. (1996). Students' out-of-class experiences and their influence on learning and cognitive development: A literature review. *Journal of College Student Development, 37*(2), 149-162.

Tinto, V. (1993). *Leaving college: Rethinking the causes and cures of student attrition* (2nd ed.). Chicago: University of Chicago Press.

University of Minnesota. (2005). *OneStop student services.* Retrieved August 27, 2006, from http://www.onestop.umn.edu/

University of Minnesota. (2006). *Pedagogy and Student Services for Institutional Transformation.* Retrieved October 16, 2006, from http://www.gen.umn.edu/research/passit/

University of Washington. (2006). DO-IT: *Disabilities, Opportunities, Internetworking, and Technology.* Retrieved October 16, 2006, from http://www.washington.edu/doit/

U.S. Department of Education. (2006). *Demonstration projects to ensure students with disabilities receive a quality higher education.* Retrieved August 27, 2006, from http://www.ed.gov/programs/disabilities

Weir, C. (2004). Person-centered and collaborative supports for college success. *Education and Training in Developmental Disabilities, 39*(1), 67-73.

CHAPTER 17

Implementing Universal Design in Learning Centers

Jeanne L. Higbee
University of Minnesota

Shevawn B. Eaton
Northern Illinois University

Abstract
This chapter is reprinted verbatim from Curriculum Transformation and Disability: Implementing Universal Design in Higher Education, *and was originally published in 2003. This chapter defines the mission, functions, and goals of college and university learning centers and then describes how the implementation of Universal Design facilitates the achievement of these goals for all students. The authors also address testing services commonly provided by learning centers for students with disabilities. The chapter concludes with a discussion of physical accessibility issues.*

The primary mission of every postsecondary institution is to educate students effectively. Early in the history of American higher education, it became clear that effective learning also meant developing support services to meet the academic needs of students (Enright, 1994). College and university learning centers have become home to a wide variety of services that enhance learning among all students at the institution. In addition, learning centers often play a role in the delivery of services for students who require developmental support, including underprepared students and students with disabilities.

Mission, Functions, and Goals

The development of the learning center on any given campus is grounded in the history and mission of that institution. When a college or university provides access for students who have developmental needs, retention of those students often requires programmatic support beyond the curriculum. However, whether open admissions or highly selective, institutions have an obligation to engage in activities that promote the intellectual development of all students. Levels of student preparedness are always relative; at any given institution there will be students who are more talented in some disciplines than in others, and students who have developed skills and habits that are more conducive to learning than others. The nature of the support needed, the funding available, and the political position of the institution all contribute to decision-making regarding learning center functions.

Changing demographics have also influenced the nature of academic supports provided in postsecondary education. After World War II, for example, the GI Bill enabled many veterans to go to college. A large number of these students were not adequately prepared for the rigors of college work. As a result, learning assistance programs and learning centers became institutionalized to support veterans in their academic pursuits (Johnson & Carpenter, 2000; Martha Maxwell, 2000). Similarly, in the 1960s the initiation of many access-oriented programs, such as financial aid, brought another wave of diverse students to college for the first time. Meanwhile, the changing face of the work place required more adults to return to school following gaps in their education. The resulting diversity in skills and experiences created an explosion of learning centers and support services designed to meet the broad range of academic needs of students. Based on that historical change in higher education, a majority of learning centers evolved during the 1970s (Devirian et al., 1975; Enright, 1994). The emergence of learning centers has been reflective of the changes in diversity and access on a campus.

Often the origin of a center defines its function, at least initially. Prager (1991) cites three models that guide most centers: (a) those that emerged from the disciplines, such as math labs and writing centers; (b) those that grew as extensions of the library; and (c) those that were created as "stand-alone" programs, with no or limited connections to other institutional functions. Centers can provide a wide range of activities that include assessment; counseling-based services; academic assistance in mathematics, writing, reading, and the development of learning skills and strategies; and technological support. In addition to traditional models such as peer and professional tutoring, service delivery systems can include programs like Supplemental Instruction (SI) and Video-based Supplemental Instruction (Arendale, 1998; Peled & Kim, 1995) and paired, linked, or adjunct courses (Blinn & Sisco, 1996; Bullock, Madden, & Harter, 1987; Dimon, 1981; Resnick, 1993) that attach instruction in strategies such as note taking and preparing for exams to courses considered "high risk" (i.e., with low retention rates or high failure rates). Many learning centers provide services such as workshops on topics like time management and test anxiety, computer tutorials in subjects like mathematics and foreign languages, or the opportunity to participate in learning communities or collaborative study groups. Finally, centers may be the home to developmental or basic skills curricula.

Services may be provided in person, online (Johnson & Carpenter, 2000), or via videotape or cable-access television (Thomas & Higbee, 1998). Learning centers were initially born to meet the needs of students who have the capacity to succeed academically, but for a variety of reasons may require additional resources or different approaches to learning. For this reason, centers often have become the place on campus to experiment and utilize nontraditional or cutting edge delivery systems to assist students, looking to technology and instructional innovations to provide complementary ways to enhance learning (Foelsche, 1999).

Goals for learning centers may include promoting academic success, enhancing student learning, improving retention and graduation rates, and providing services for students with disabilities (Kay & Sullivan, 1978; Prager, 1991). Some learning centers are designed to support all students, and some are targeted to meet the specific needs of particular populations. Students with disabilities have long been considered one of the primary target groups for learning centers (Casazza & Silverman, 1996). Some centers evolved initially to provide exclusive services to this population (Enright, 1994). It is imperative for all learning center administrators to maintain sensitivity and openness to universal support for students. Students with hidden disabilities may come to the center to seek help, sometimes without sharing information about their particular disability or needs (Eaton & Wyland, 1996). Planning for such situations will help maintain the confidentiality of the student and create a center that is truly accessible to all students. Universal Design (UD) provides a means by which the curriculum and educational tasks can be adapted and mastered more effectively by all students, particularly those with undisclosed invisible disabilities, whose learning needs might otherwise not be met.

The philosophy of Universal Instructional Design (UID) is to design curricula in such a way so that accommodation is built into the program. In the learning center, materials and delivery systems can also include Universal Design guidelines and assumptions. The myriad programs and services that may be made available by learning centers demonstrate Universal Design because they provide multiple means of facilitating the acquisition of knowledge. However, they also represent numerous challenges for planning and implementation in a manner that is accessible to all students.

Services for All Students

It is not difficult to adapt some of the individualized services provided by learning centers for students with virtually any disability. One-to-one tutoring, for example, may require arranging for a sign language interpreter or real time captioning for a student with a hearing impairment, but if tutoring appointments are scheduled in advance for all students, making these arrangements should not pose overwhelming obstacles. Similarly, computer-assisted tutorials may require the provision of assistive technology, but it is necessary to equip some computer stations in every learning center with the technology to make all programs and services accessible to any student. If students are able to sign up for computer time in advance, students with disabilities will not have to wait for a computer terminal. On the other hand, it is important to note that providing assistive technology does not guarantee accessibility. For example, a screen reader will read across lines of columns in a table, rather than down the column. The final section of this book provides further information on creating accessible tables. When possible, computer tutorials and other programs can be placed on the server, providing accessibility to all students, whether working within the learning center or from a distance.

As indicated in the next section of this book, the implementation of Universal Instructional Design, whether within the classroom curriculum or in learning center programs like workshops, Supplemental Instruction, and paired, linked, or adjunct courses, will also require advance planning. Workshop facilitators, SI leaders, and instructors must consider how to include all learners by presenting information in a variety of ways. For example, material provided on overhead transparencies or via power point slides should also be presented orally, provided on handouts in both regular size and enlarged print, and made available on disks or to download from a web site. Workshops, SI sessions, and courses can be videotaped so that students can view the tapes in the learning center, check them out to view at home, or if possible, watch on public cable access television. Videotapes should include closed captioning.

Video services can be beneficial for all students who work, have family responsibilities that make it difficult to attend at the times that programs and services are made available, or are not able to attend due to illness. In addition, providing courses, SI lessons, or tutorial sessions on tape and TV through the learning center can make it possible for students who have disabilities like asthma or cystic fibrosis, or require surgery during the academic term, to maintain their academic responsibilities (Thomas & Higbee, 1998). Many students also benefit from being able to pause or stop videotaped lectures in order to take more accurate notes or to ensure that they really understand the material.

Online services can also benefit all students. However, for some students with disabilities, synchronous discussions can become exclusive rather than inclusive. Just as in collaborative study sessions occurring in the learning center it may be necessary to allow time for "translation" so that students with auditory impairments can participate fully when assisted by a sign language interpreter or real time captioning interpreter, synchronous online chats can disadvantage some students with visual impairments, mobility impairments, and reading-oriented learning disabilities, to name a few. These factors must be taken into consideration when creating online programs and services. Thinking inclusively in the planning stages makes all services more accessible to all students.

All web information for students, including learning center information sites as well as other online programmatic functions, must be given careful consideration for accessibility. Often, visually attractive or high tech websites can be problematic for students with disabilities. Therefore, it is important that websites be made with minimal graphic additions, or offer a "text only" version of the site that can be downloaded or modified for students with visual impairments. *Bobby Worldwide,* for example, provides guidelines and evaluative tools for the accessibility of websites (Center for Applied Special Technology, 1999). Text versions of sites also provide an excellent way of developing simple handouts for all students to use.

Finally, learning center administrators, expecting that students with disabilities will come to the center, need to offer training and increase sensitivity of staff through professional development activities. When learning center administrators anticipate needs early, staff can be prepared to change delivery systems or to direct students to different resources for assistance.

Disability Services Housed Within Learning Centers

Some learning centers provide services specifically for students with disabilities, while others physically house the institution's disability services for students. Under the latter model, especially on smaller campuses, the learning center may be the only location that provides computers with assistive technology. In this situation, students with disabilities may be less segregated than on campuses with separate facilities for disability services. However, especially at larger institutions, if assistive technology is not made available in computer labs throughout the campus, it is imperative that the learning center be centrally located and make the same hardware and software provided around campus accessible to all students. It is not appropriate, for example, for a student with a disability to be required to complete statistics assignments in the learning center when all other students are doing the assignment in the statistics lab.

Testing Services

On some campuses the learning center is the site designated for proctoring tests when extended time or other modifications are indicated as part of a student's individualized plan for accommodation. Students with Attention Deficit Hyperactivity Disorder, learning disabilities, acquired brain injuries, or some psychological disabilities may require a private testing room in order to reduce distractions. Students with anxiety disorders may require a testing environment that eliminates sources of stress, such as other students leaving when they finish early.

It would be wonderful to be able to provide extended time and a more conducive testing environment for all students who could benefit, including students who do not have a documented disability but do suffer from test anxiety. In many classrooms, time limits are placed on quizzes and tests because of the length of standard class periods, not because the time factor is an essential component of performance of the task. The ability of learning centers to provide testing with extended time for all students depends on the availability of space and staff.

Learning centers may also provide other types of testing services for students with disabilities, such as reading a test aloud for a student with a vision impairment, or transcribing audio taped oral responses for a student with a mobility impairment. Or the learning center might provide assistive technology such as a screen reader or voice recognition software to enable students with disabilities to "read" or to respond orally to exams. At the present time the cost of this software makes it prohibitive to expect learning centers to provide these technologies for all students. But as further technological advances occur, and costs diminish, it is not unreasonable to anticipate that learning centers will be able to make more choices for demonstrating knowledge available to all students if faculty members are willing to be flexible in their approaches. New forms of technology may make it easier for faculty to test the use of higher order thinking skills among students.

Physical Accessibility

Innovations in computer technology, as discussed in the final section of this book, address many issues of accessibility for students with disabilities who want to make full use of learning centers. Other considerations include how spaces are designed, flexibility in furniture arrangements, and adjustable workstations.

Welcoming Reception Areas

Reception areas should be easily accessible and welcoming. Reception counters should be 28 to 34 inches tall, so that students seated in wheelchairs have ready access to staff and to printed materials provided on the counter. Signage should be provided in contrasting colors in raised text and Braille at appropriate heights. Trained personnel should be ready to provide information about programs, make referrals, schedule appointments, and direct students to appropriate services and staff. Descriptions of services, staff directories, and handouts should be available in multiple formats, including large type, Braille, and on audiotape and computer disk.

Use of Space

Learning centers should include both individual and group rooms for tutoring and study skills counseling, if provided, as well as for testing. Entrances, corridors, rooms, pathways, and computer stations must be sufficiently large to accommodate wheel chairs and scooters. Adjustable height workstations are more comfortable for people of various sizes as well as for students with mobility impairments. Study carrels provide a level of privacy that can be appreciated by any student. Circular tables for study groups facilitate communication while also allowing flexible seating arrangements.

Lighting

Windows that allow for natural lighting can make learning spaces more welcoming if other factors are taken into consideration. Installation of windows that filter ultraviolet light will benefit all students, but are particularly important to students with disabilities like lupus and students who suffer from migraine headaches. In addition to providing window blinds to reduce glare on computer screens at different times of day, computer monitors should be equipped with glare guard. It is preferable that overhead lighting not be fluorescent, but when there is no choice, it is important to properly maintain fixtures and replace bulbs regularly. Flickering bulbs can trigger seizures. Adjustable individual work station lighting can also be beneficial for all students. Task lamps should be equipped with "soft" or "low light" bulbs.

Regulating Noise

Policies enacted to regulate noise levels (e.g., policies related to use of cell phones and pagers) benefit all students, not just those with hearing impairments. In addition, wall, ceiling, and flooring materials should be selected to minimize noise. Study carrels and partitions should be sound-absorbent. Separate spaces should be created for group activities so that the natural flow of conversation does not disrupt the concentration of individuals working on computer tutorials or studying alone. Implementing these practices to promote Universal Design creates a more welcoming and efficient learning environment for all students.

Conclusion

With forethought, learning centers are an ideal place to implement the principles of Universal Design and Universal Instructional Design. On many campuses learning centers play a vital role in enhancing student retention. It is imperative that learning centers be universally accessible.

References

Arendale, D. (1998). Increasing efficiency and effectiveness of learning for freshman college students through Supplemental Instruction. In J. L. Higbee & P. L. Dwinell (Eds.), *Developmental education: Preparing successful college students* (pp. 185-197). Columbia: University of South Carolina, National Resource Center for The First-Year Experience and Students in Transition.

Blinn, J., & Sisco, O. (1996). "Linking" developmental reading and biology. *National Association for Developmental Education Selected Conference Papers, 2,* 8-9.

Center for Applied Special Technology (1999). Bobby worldwide. Retrieved April 25, 2002, from http://www.cast.org/Bobby/

Bullock, T., Madden, D., & Harter, J. (1987). Paired developmental reading and psychology courses. *Research & Teaching in Developmental Education, 3*(2), 22-29.

Casazza, M., & Silverman, S. (1996). *Learning assistance and developmental education: A guide for effective practice.* San Francisco: Jossey-Bass.

Devirian, M. C., et al. (1975). *A survey of learning program centers in U.S. institutions of higher education.* (ERIC Document Reproduction Service No. ED112349)

Dimon, M. (1981). Why adjunct courses work. *Journal of College Reading and Learning, 21,* 33-40. Reprinted in M. Maxwell (Ed.). (1994), From access to success. Clearwater, FL: H&H.

Eaton, S., & Wyland, S. (1996). College students with Attention Deficit Disorder (ADD): Implications for learning assistance professionals. *The Learning Assistance Review, 1*(2), 5-22.

Enright, G. (1994). College learning skills: Frontierland origins of the learning assistance center. In M. Maxwell (Ed.), *From access to success: A book of readings on college developmental education and learning assistance programs* (pp. 31-40). Clearwater, FL: H&H.

Foelsche, O.K. (1999). *Implementation and implications of digital services in learning centers.* (ERIC Document Reproduction Service No. ED450707)

Johnson, L., & Carpenter, K. (2000). College reading programs. In R. F. Flippo & D. C. Caverly (Eds.), *Handbook of college reading and learning* (pp. 321-363). Mahwah, NJ: Lawrence Erlbaum Associates.

Kay, R.S., & Sullivan, L. (1978). *Learning centers: Alternatives to bridging the gap between secondary and postsecondary education.* (ERIC Document Reproduction Service No. ED155574)

Martha Maxwell: An oral history. (2000). In J. L. Higbee & P. L. Dwinell (Eds.), *The many faces of developmental education* (pp. 9-13). Warrensburg, MO: National Association for Developmental Education.

Peled, O. N., & Kim, A. C. (1995). Supplemental Instruction in biology at the college level. *National Association for Developmental Education Selected Conference Papers, 1,* 23-24.

Prager, C. (1991). *Learning centers for the 1990s.* ERIC Digest. (ERIC Document Reproduction Service No. ED338295)

Resnick, J. (1993). A paired reading and sociology course. In P. Malinowski (Ed.), *Perspectives in practice in developmental education* (pp. 62-64). Canandaigua, NY: New York College

Learning Association.
Stewart, T. C., & Hartman, K. A. (2001). Finding out what the campus needs: The process of redefining a learning center. *The Learning Assistance Review, 6* (1), 39-49.
Thomas, P.V., & Higbee, J. L. (1998). Teaching mathematics on television: Perks and pitfalls. *Academic Exchange Quarterly, 2*(2), 29-33.

CHAPTER 18

Universal Design in Counseling Center Service Areas

Kathleen B. Uzes and Daley O. Connelly
The University of Georgia

Abstract
This chapter is reprinted verbatim from Curriculum Transformation and Disability: Implementing Universal Design in Higher Education, *and was originally published in 2003. The implementation of the concept of Universal Design in counseling center service areas for students with disabilities can increase the number and diversity of students served. This in turn supports the mission statement of the counseling center and the institution's mission. By knowing and understanding the needs of students with disabilities and incorporating the concept of Universal Design, counseling centers can provide services and accommodations befitting the ever-increasing diverse populations on college campuses. This chapter will address incorporating Universal Design into service areas such as outreach programming, consultation, groups, and individual counseling. Case studies will be provided to demonstrate how students with disabilities can benefit from counseling provided by most counseling centers.*

Counseling centers on university and college campuses have mission statements that endeavor to support the personal and professional growth of students. It is the role of counseling centers to support the mission statement of the university or college (Kiracofe et al., 1994) by facilitating the mental health of as many students as possible with the resources available to them. Many counseling centers are multifaceted, offering students direct services, personal, career, and group counseling, and broader outreach programming and consultation. According to Archer and Cooper (1998), there is a

> continuing need to provide counseling for traditional-age students with "normal" career and developmental needs and crises (identity development, value clarification, sexuality and intimacy, death, relationship endings, parental divorce) as well as the need to attend to the special concerns of returning adult students (career and life changes, family and relationship issues, stress, time management). (p. 13)

Many problems and concerns are widely shared by college students whether they have disabilities or not (Cormin & Hackney, 1993; Nutter & Ringgenberg, 1993), so the types of services already provided by counseling services on many campuses will enhance the undergraduate experience of all students. For example, students with disabilities seek time-limited individual counseling services such as therapy, support, or personal development for many of the same reasons that other students seek counseling.

Counseling centers are also utilized in providing consultation and support to the college or university community when a student is in distress and for other campus emergencies.

It is no surprise that, given the great need for mental health services on campus and the ever-shrinking resources available to counseling centers, most centers adhere to different versions of what is called a "short term model" of counseling. This model allows services to the most students, while students needing years of care are referred to community resources. It is, therefore, possible that a student who is being seen by a therapist in the community can also be seen at the counseling center for short-term career counseling. Likewise, referrals can be made from agencies on campus to the counseling center for the same issues outlined by Archer and Cooper (1998). It would be important to have a consultative relationship with the referring agency. For example, if the disability services office were the referral source it would be important in some cases to obtain a release of information so that the counselor and disability specialist could work together in providing the best services for the student. It would also assist both agencies in keeping abreast of the current issues, gaining feedback on programs that are being offered, and looking for productive means of working together. In addition the counseling center can be very valuable as a resource to help refer students with disabilities who need longer term counseling that is not provided by the counseling center.

Accessibility of Counseling Services

Physical accessibility is one of the most fundamental components of Universal Design. If the counseling center were located in an architecturally inaccessible facility, then alternative access would need to be provided (Kalivoda & Higbee, 1994). For example, if the counseling center were located on the second floor of a building with no elevator and the student seeking counseling used a wheelchair or was unable to ascend or descend stairs due to a mobility impairment, then an alternative accessible place to meet the student would be needed. It should be borne in mind that there are individuals with mobility impairments that are not obvious. These individuals might have a prosthetic, be on medications, or have a chronic illness that leaves them physically weak. Any alternative meeting place used to accommodate students with mobility impairments would need to provide the same fundamental environment that would be provided for other students. If clients were normally met in a quiet one-on-one setting, then a comparable site that would ensure the same degree of confidentiality would need to be provided. On the other hand, a universally designed counseling service would be located where all students have equal access to individual and group counseling spaces.

Along with one-on-one counseling, many counseling centers also provide groups, outreach programs, and consultation with faculty and student groups. There are specific issues when presenting programs or groups that can potentially arise when the accessibility needs of the audience are not known. For example, for workshops held in residence halls, Greek organizations, or for a drop-in "lunch and learn," the number attending the programs or the needs of those attending would not necessarily be known in advance. If the program were planned for a targeted group of students, it would be important for the presenter to inquire in advance if anyone in the targeted audience needs accommodations. If the concept of Universal Design were already implemented, then not knowing the audience needs would not be an issue. All the possible needed accommodations would already be in place.

In addition to meeting in an accessible location, in a Universal Design setting counseling staff would have developed alternative forms of all handouts, thus prepared should an individual who is blind or has a visual impairment decide to attend the outreach program. Having the handouts prepared in advance and available in Braille, large print formats, on tape, and on disk would not only meet the Americans with Disabilities Act (ADA 1990) requirements, but would also provide an open and accepting environment. This allows students to feel valued (Schlossberg, Lynch, & Chickering, 1989). Also, small changes in presentation style will aid people with visual impairments. For example, when using visual aids like overhead transparencies or power point slides, it would be helpful to replace the nonspecific "this" and "that" with more specific descriptions of what is being discussed, and not to assume that everyone in the audience is able to read the text on the screen. This approach will benefit not only those with a visual impairment, but also those who are not visual learners, as well as participants who do not have a clear view of the screen. In addition, for each program a sign language interpreter would be provided in the event that a student with a hearing impairment would be attending. If the presenter is utilizing a videotape, then the videotape would be captioned and the television would have captioning capability.

Of course, some of these accommodations may be impractical or simply too costly, such as providing a sign language interpreter for all programs, whether needed or not. One alternative would be to require all participants to register in advance, and indicate if any accommodations are needed, thus allowing the program to be accessible for all those who attend. Another suggestion, particularly for counseling workshops or programs to be held in residence halls or Greek houses, is to have a contact person who knows the needs of the audience relay any accommodation needs to the presenter in advance.

The concept of accessible handouts would also apply to brochures or any other print materials that are provided or used by the counseling facility. In order to promote program access and the option of alternative formats, all advertisements of services in the form of publications and announcements would state that these accommodations can be provided. A contact person and contact information should also be provided (Kalivoda & Higbee, 1994) for all programs and services.

Counseling Concerns of Students with Disabilities

The following section presents case studies of students who were referred to the counseling center by campus agencies (e.g., disability services, housing), friends, and faculty. These case studies are examples of students with disabilities who accessed counseling services to address mental health issues in the same manner as other students. They illustrate some of the developmental concerns of students with disabilities. It is our hope that the case studies will give the reader examples of how the counseling center can be of service to help students with disabilities deal with psychological concerns.

Case Study One: Loss and Acceptance

A 24-year-old female diagnosed with a disease that caused her to become legally blind during early adolescence was referred to the counseling center to cope with the reentry to school. She was experiencing a great deal of anxiety about approaching her professors to discuss her needs for accommodations in the classroom. Much of her anxiety in these situations had to do with the anger and grief she was feeling about losing her sight, which was something she had never been able to verbalize. By working on these issues, she was able to gain more confidence in approaching others and expressing what she needed in the classroom situation. Although this issue was related to the individual's visual impairment, the counselor did not have to be an expert in the field of blindness. The counselor was not there to cure or to "fix it all." Rather, the role of the counselor was to identify the source of the difficulty and help the student develop effective coping skills to function more productively.

Case Study Two: Personal and Career Adjustment

A young man who started college as a typical freshman was involved in an accident his second semester in school that left him paralyzed from the waist down. After a year in recovery, he returned to the university using a wheelchair for mobility. He was still involved in physical therapy in the hopes that he would one day no longer need to use a wheelchair. Upon returning to school many unforeseen issues arose for him. His relationship with his friends was now very different. Going out with friends to restaurants, bars, and sporting events was no longer the casual event it once was for him. He now had to deal with transportation and accessibility concerns. He became depressed as he compared the reality of his new situation to how he once functioned, as well as the lack of understanding from his friends. In working with this student, it was important to help him through the grieving process over the feeling of overwhelming loss. The counselor also helped the student become more assertive in identifying and addressing his needs with his friends and family. There were also some career issues involved in working with this client. Before the accident he was majoring in forestry and was planning to be a forest ranger. Other opportunities in the forestry field were investigated to find a good match for him, taking into consideration his interest and his mobility issues.

Case Study Three: Interpersonal Relationships

A thirty-two year old female was referred to the counseling center to work on marital problems. She had been diagnosed with severe carpal tunnel syndrome, which resulted in surgery that left her with nerve damage to her dominant arm. Due to her limited manual dexterity, she experienced difficulty in many areas of her life, such as caring for her young child, writing, or typing for any length of time. She was also limited in her ability to drive her car. These limitations resulted in her having to rely on her husband for assistance. The client reported that her husband expressed a great deal of resentment concerning her requests for help. This ongoing situation left her feeling frustrated with his lack of assistance in her day-to-day life, as well as the lack of support for her career aspirations. Her husband was not willing to take part in couple's counseling; therefore, she was seen individually. During the therapeutic process the client became aware the absence of support had been an issue for her and her husband even before she experienced difficulties with her arm. The client made a decision to divorce and terminated counseling shortly after her divorce was final.

Case Study Four: Behavior Modification and Values Clarification

A twenty-year-old junior majoring in psychology was referred to the counseling center to explore career issues. The client reported that he wanted to continue his education in a field of study that would enable him to work with people; however, he did not have a specific career objective in mind. He disclosed that he was diagnosed with Attention Deficit Hyperactivity Disorder at the age of nine and was placed on medication at that time. He had been on and off medication since then and wanted to explore non-medical options to address the difficulties with initiative that he experienced with the Attention Deficit Hyperactivity Disorder. In working with this client, certain considerations had to be taken into account, based on his inability to sustain focus for extended periods of time. He was also able to identify areas that caused him difficulty, such as his limited attention span and his impulsive behavior. To accomplish the behavior modification, the client was instructed in self-relaxation, as well as how to anticipate instances that would exacerbate his hyperactivity. Career batteries were administered with specific emphasis on skills, abilities, and values to determine the client's strengths as well as to clarify his values. As a result, a field of study was chosen that would enable him to work with people as well as tap into the strength of his high energy level. In the end, he chose to pursue a career in working with juvenile delinquents.

Conclusion

In conclusion, it should be kept in mind that the principle of Universal Design is based on obtaining the most ideal situation in implementing services to as many students as possible. With the ever-increasing number of students with disabilities on campus, the implementation of the concepts encompassing Universal Design into the counseling center service area would help support the counseling center in its goals and mission statement.

References

Americans with Disabilities Act of 1990, 42 U.S.C A. Section 12101 et seq. (West 1993).

Archer, J., & Cooper, S. (1998). *Counseling and mental health services on campus: A handbook of contemporary practices and challenges.* San Francisco: Jossey-Bass.

Cormier, S. L., & Hackney, H. (1993). *The professional counselor. A process guide to helping* (2nd ed.). Needham Heights, MA: Allyn & Bacon.

Henderson, C. (1999). *College freshmen with disabilities.* Washington, DC: American Council on Education.

Kalivoda, K. S., & Higbee, J. L. (1994). Implementing the Americans with Disabilities Act. *The Journal of Humanistic Education and Development, 32*(3), 133-137.

Kiracofe, N. M., Donn, P. A., Grant, C. O., Podolnick, E. E., Bingham, R. P., Bolland, H. R., et al. (1994). Accreditation standards for university and college centers. *Journal of Counseling and Development, 73,* 38-43.

Nutter, K. J., & Ringgenberg, L. J. (1993). Creating positive outcomes for students with disabilities. In S. Kroeger & J. Schuck (Eds.), *Responding to disability issues in student affairs* (pp. 45-58). San Francisco: Jossey-Bass.

Schlossberg, N. K., Lynch, A. Q., & Chickering, A.W. (1989). *Improving higher education environments for adults.* San Francisco: Jossey-Bass.

CHAPTER 19

Universal Design in Advising: Principles and Practices

Mary Ellen Shaw, Amy Kampsen, Carole Anne Broad, and Anthony Albecker
University of Minnesota

Abstract
Using Universal Design (UD) in advising practices has the potential to enhance student success, retention, and graduation rates by providing developmentally appropriate, student-centered, inclusive, respectful, and holistic advising. This chapter will focus on the use of UD in advising practices for a diverse population of students, discussing principles and practices related to creating a successful advising program to serve all students.

In the summer of 2006, a group of educators with responsibility for advising programs or direct responsibility for academic advising from around the United States joined together to discuss ways that the principles of Universal Instructional Design (UID) would play out in academic advising settings. This chapter takes the framework of the rich conversation that took place in that summer and expands the discussion, especially focusing on how principles of Universal Design (UD) in advising connect to student development theory.

Current literature on the concept of UID has predominantly revolved around the use of UID in a classroom setting. In our review of available literature, little has been written about the use of Universal Design in academic advising centers on university and college campuses. What we will demonstrate in this chapter is that UD has an important place in academic advising centers and it fits well with the mission of advising services and the theoretical model commonly used in advising.

Student Development Theory

Though each campus advising program may be different, the main purpose of advising is to "assist college students in making and executing educational and life plans" (Creamer, 2000, p. 18). Creamer also asserted that in order for academic advisors to be effective in helping students achieve their educational and life goals, they must have an understanding of the theory underlying student development and learning. Perhaps the most documented theory of student development is that proposed by Arthur Chickering (1969) and updated by Chickering and Reisser (1993). Chickering and Reisser described seven developmental tasks or "vectors" that students need to resolve in order to transition smoothly through their educational experience and into adulthood. The seven developmental tasks are as follows: (a) developing competence, (b) managing emotions, (c) becoming autonomous, (d) developing mature interpersonal relationships, (e) establishing identity, (f) developing purpose, and (g) developing integrity. Students focus on each of these tasks at certain times and try to resolve the task. If the task is not successfully resolved, it may cause difficulty in resolving other tasks at later times. Although not intended as a "stage theory," each vector or task may be a building block or foundation for another task. This does not assume that students go through these tasks in the same amount of time or in the same order or manner but they will eventually touch on each of the vectors. Chickering and Reisser described this more colorfully by depicting the vectors as "major highways for journeying toward individuation" and proposed that "while each person will drive differently, with varying vehicles and self-chosen detours, eventually all will move down these major routes" (p. 35). The challenge for advisors, then, is to determine which vectors the individual student is currently navigating in order to better assist the student in moving forward on the developmental tasks. Students just entering college may need to focus on "managing emotions"; they may experience a range of emotions such as anxiety, fear, depression, or loneliness. One of the developmental tasks of this vector is to become aware of these emotions or feelings. Once aware, a student can learn how to balance or manage these emotions before they become overwhelming and affect progress. An advisor's role in this process is first to understand the theory behind the vector, and then to assist students in acknowledging significant emotions and devising strategies for managing these emotions in a way that guides the student forward in development. The advisor's understanding that there is not a "one size fits all" approach to guiding and supporting students through these developmental tasks is paramount to effectiveness and is in line with UD principles. The next section of this chapter will depict an advising model that supports this claim.

Developmental Advising Model

Chickering's (1969) theory of student development seems to promote a holistic approach to advising and supports the claim that students need more individualized attention to their unique needs around career, academic, and personal goals. The advising model that seems most closely aligned with this approach and with the concepts of UD is the developmental advising model. Ender, Winston, and Miller (1984) defined developmental advising as "a systematic process based on a close student-advisor relationship intended to aid students in achieving educational, career, and personal goals through the utilization of the full range of institutional and community resources" (p. 19). Within this model, advisors develop a caring relationship with the student by paying attention to the individual educational experience and skill levels of each student and using this as a guide to assist the student in enhancing educational success. Ender and Wilkie (2000) stated the following in regard to the developmental advising relationship:

> The very nature of a developmental advising relationship—focusing on the three major themes of *academic competence, personal involvement, and developing or validating life purpose* (italics in original) – requires that the relationship between advisor and student be (1) ongoing and purposeful; (2) challenging for the student, but also supportive; (3) goal oriented; and (4) intentional as it maximizes the use of university resources. Effective advisors therefore provide both an advising curriculum and an advising process for the student to experience. (p. 119)

King (2005) also described developmental advising as a process that focuses on the "whole" person, taking into consideration each student's individual stage of development. This approach to academic advising is consistent with UD practices in that it takes into consideration the needs of each and every individual student, thus providing a service that is intended to enhance the educational experience of all students. Therefore, any student entering an advisor's office should expect to receive the same respect for individual needs regardless of ability or disability status, race and ethnicity, sexual orientation, class, age, gender, previous educational experience, or academic preparedness.

UD as Best Practice in Meeting Diverse Student Needs

The idea of UD in academic advising is to provide equal access to effective advising and advising services for all students using an approach that considers each student's unique and individual needs regardless of demographics. To achieve this goal, advisors need to have training related to student development theory, multiculturalism, and disabilities. The student services administrative structure needs to provide for this training and also recognize that advising that encompasses the principles of Universal Design requires adequate staffing to allow for individual relationships to be built between students and advisors. The benefit for implementing UD principles will be enhanced success not only for students with disabilities but for many other groups of students, including first-generation college students, students from underrepresented populations, students with different learning preferences, and students for whom traditional program-focused advising is not effective. What follows in this chapter is a discussion of some of the principles and applications of Universal Design in advising developed by the Pedagogy and Student Services for Institutional Transformation (PASS IT) advising working group in summer 2006, beginning with a discussion of what we meant by the broad diversity of students who will benefit from this approach and a discussion of the sorts of benefits we expect Universal Design principles to provide.

Inclusive Definition of Diversity

A definition of diversity that truly reflects the populations of students we serve in higher education needs to include the following: race, ethnicity, socioeconomic class, home language, disability, gender, religion, age, and sexual orientation. In addition, no single characteristic captures any individual's identity or needs; we need to recognize the multiple and intersecting social identities claimed by an individual at any time, and also to recognize that these social identities may shift or change. This is why a Universal Design approach will benefit students by focusing on serving the student as an individual, recognizing multiple and changing identities, and not seeing the student as a static member of a category with fixed needs related to that characteristic.

Traditional Models of Serving Students With Disabilities or "Special" Student Needs

In traditional models of service for students with disabilities, the advising and the disability support have been separated. Students with disabilities have received academic advising from their university, college, or departmental advising services, and have received disability-related services from a separate office, which they have needed to seek out, sometimes feeling unwilling to do so because of the stigma attached. The interaction between postsecondary disability service offices and advising offices has not always been entirely collaborative. Disability services counselors sometimes advocate for and support student exceptions to institutional policies, or for allowing students to enroll for reduced credit loads. There is often no communication between the disability services counselor and the student's primary academic advisor, as these exceptions may be requested through a more central office. In the case of hidden disabilities such as psychiatric or learning disabilities, the student's advisor may not even be made aware of them, unless the student chooses to self-disclose.

It is understandable that the privacy of students with disabilities needs to be protected and that disclosure to an advisor is at the discretion of the student. If the student chooses not to disclose a disability, the advisor is at a disadvantage when guiding the student in course selection, appropriate time management strategies, and referral to resources. It is also beneficial for the student to disclose a disability so that advisors can support the student in developing self-advocacy skills needed when approaching faculty about accommodations. At times, advisors may rely on "early warning systems" as an opportunity to discuss possible learning disabilities with students. These systems may take the form of a report of academic progress submitted to the advisor by faculty. If a student is having difficulties in the course, advisors can use this report as a dialogue tool when initiating a conversation with the student, perhaps facilitating the likelihood of disclosure of a disability. The advisor could then work collaboratively with disability services and assist the student in communicating needs.

One way to improve collaboration between advising and disability services is for the disability services staff to train students in self-advocacy skills and encourage self-disclosure to their assigned advisor, explaining the benefits of doing so but also protecting the rights of the student. Some institutions may find that having disability services located near to other student services offices could facilitate student ease in utilizing both disability services and advising services to the fullest, and also making collaboration easier between staff members. Disability services staff and advising staff can meet to discuss best ways of collaborating or supporting each others' services, and can sponsor projects together. Advising staff members should become very familiar with disability services and normalize these services in conversation or presentations to all students, as any student may have a hidden disability. Other collaborations might also be sought with the institution's career and placement services, learning center, and other academic support programs and counseling services.

Benefits of Universal Design in Advising

We believe that applying Universal Design in advising will have many benefits; most obvious among them will be the "bottom line" benefits of enhanced student success, retention, and graduation. Because students will be able to get more of their needs met in a holistic way through their central advising resources, rather than having separate services for different needs such as for their disability needs, or for their needs related to other cultural identies, students will experience less "run-around" and frustration, and there will be fewer occasions of students "falling between the cracks" and being lost as they are referred from one site to another. Universal Design in advising is a proactive rather than reactive approach, which does not put the burden of seeking help on the student, and normalizes the sorts of assistance that might otherwise make students who had to seek out this help from special services areas feel stigmatized for needing it. This normalization of services tied to individual needs and developmental readiness enhances all students' engagement in the tasks of college learning and in negotiating developmental tasks. If services and also policies are retooled using UD principles, there will be less need for last-minute modifications of services for "special" students, less redundancy of parallel services for special student groups, and less need for appeals and requests for exceptions for all students.

Administrative and Staffing Considerations

An institution determining to apply UD principles to improve advising services and to prepare those services to serve effectively a diversity of students and student needs will need to provide the planning time, staffing, and resources that will be necessary. These changes will take advanced planning, long-term administrative commitment, and the allocation of adequate space and staffing. Policies that govern students will need to be assessed from the perspective of whether they create undue barriers for any groups of students and revised to minimize these limitations. Examples of policies that might involve needless student run-around are requirements for multiple signatures for petitions that are routinely approved, or the requirement that duplicate documentation be provided by the student to different offices in the process of requesting course drops and tuition refunds. Staff will need training and access to appropriate technologies to provide services in multiple formats for students. A key requirement will be training staff to become familiar with a broad range of resources and information, including understanding of the multiple and changing needs of diverse students and their development.

Applying UD Principles in Advising Practice

The PASS IT working group on advising agreed that there should be a cluster of high-level characteristics that should guide the creation of advising services. These services should be developmentally appropriate for all students, physically accessible and inviting, student-centered, learning-centered, inclusive, respectful, and holistic. The following discussion expands on ways to make advising services accessible and inviting.

Creating Universally-Designed Space for Advising

The following section addresses ways to create universally designed "space" for advising and student services. The purpose of UD in advising is to make advising services available and accessible for people with a broad range of abilities, disabilities, and other characteristics—to include accommodating people of different ages, learning styles, languages, cultures, and so on. Three areas are particularly important when considering how UD principles can be implemented to help make advising services accessible to everybody: (a) physical space, (b) Web space, and (c) utilization of alternative and flexible technologies.

Attending to the actual physical space of the building and office in which advising and student services take place is a good start in making sure potential barriers are eliminated and that a welcoming environment is created. The primary considerations of physical space include these: Is the building welcoming, accessible, comfortable, and organized? Is the building itself easy to get into? Are parking areas, pathways, and entrances to the building wheelchair-accessible and clearly marked? Once inside, is there enough room to maneuver a scooter or wheelchair? Are wheelchair-accessible restrooms available and near central student services offices? Are building directories and signage in large print and Braille at appropriate heights for all learners?

Advisors and student services professionals have a significant influence in creating a welcoming environment to complement or enhance the actual physical space of a building. Examples of climate setting include posting welcoming materials near an advisor's office, such as a personal welcome statement, a photograph, a statement of advising philosophy that speaks to the principles of UD and inclusiveness, or a rainbow sticker. Advisors and student services professionals can also create a welcoming climate by creating "community boards" that announce important college or university resources and events, information board topics like enhancing study skills or time management skills, or art work and academic materials that celebrate diversity.

In regard to specific advising space, it is important to follow the same physical guidelines for individual office or work spaces. A key component is that face-to-face advising interactions need to take place in a private space, where student confidentiality can be assured. Individual advisors need to have offices with doors that can close so that they do not have to make special accommodations for privacy. It is important, too, that these offices are large enough and open enough to be wheelchair accessible. This spaciousness also allows all students to choose their level of comfort with physical proximity, which accommodates students with cultural or religious needs as well as students with disabilities.

One author, Anthony Albecker, has become sensitized through awareness of UD and disability issues to how important it is to meet with students in a way that enables students to make eye contact easily. As a tall male (over six feet), he has noticed a difference when he lowers the seat on his office chair to a level that brings him to eye level with a less tall student advisee. As an example, when he first started advising, he had trouble connecting with a first-year female student who was having significant academic difficulties, noticing during their weekly meetings that she rarely made eye contact and kept her head down. This continued until about the fourth time they met, when the control adjusting the height of his office chair broke and was stuck in the lowest setting. To his surprise, this meeting with the student was completely different from previous meetings, as the student was engaged and they had really good eye contact. When Anthony asked the student what was so different from their previous sessions in terms of her engagement, she pointed out that she had been uncomfortable having to look up at him during the previous sessions. Also of note here is that Anthony took the time to explore this issue with the student, and that the student was both astute enough and assertive enough to respond once a new comfort level had been achieved.

Another UD practice that Anthony implements to create a sense of welcoming is that when students enter his office, as part of the exchange of greetings, he informs students that they have control over their environment: they have the choice whether they want the office door slightly opened or closed, and they have control over the lighting, choosing either the overhead fluorescent lighting or a calmer incandescent lamp. They also have control over the floor heater or fan. Anthony has noticed this goes a long way in breaking down boundaries and creating a welcoming environment.

Another example of creating a more welcoming, comfortable, and safe environment is illustrated by author Amy Kampsen. Amy has created a space that is free from obstructions and allows students options of where they would like to sit. There is a larger couch closest to the door, a chair by a table closer to the middle of the office, and a chair near Amy's desk. These options are intended to account for different student comfort zones regardless of cultural representations, size or mobility of the student, or mental health challenges such as anxiety. Some may prefer to sit closer to the advisor, others may want to be closer to the door, and others may want the security of a table between them and the advisor. Upon entering Amy's office, students are encouraged to sit wherever they feel comfortable.

Technology and "Virtual" Space in Advising

The use of the Web is another way to enhance the advising experience, to welcome diversity, and provide accessibility to everybody. A few key guidelines to consider when developing advising Web sites include these: (a) the advising Web page needs to be easy to navigate and organized according to standards of adaptive technologies; (b) its content should be complete, clear, current, and easy to access; (c) the Web site should include images of people of diverse backgrounds, including race, gender, age, and disability; and (d) on the Web site, the advising unit should explicitly address inclusion and accessibility issues.

Finally, advising can be augmented through the use of newly emerging technologies, to include portal systems, course management systems, and new interactive technologies such as Breeze and other video or Voice Over Internet Protocol (VOIP). These technologies will allow advising to go beyond the current options of "office-based" or "one-dimensional asynchronous" (e-mail) modes. Instead, the near future holds promise for advisors to be able to meet the needs of all students in any number of ways that transcend the traditional face-to-face, e-mail, or phone contact—in both synchronous and asynchronous ways. One example is Microsoft Breeze, where advising sessions can be facilitated via video conferencing to reach groups of students to provide more routine sorts of information without the necessity of the students physically traveling to campus. The Breeze sessions can then be recorded for student access at times convenient to the student. However, as noted by Duquaine-Watson in Chapter 34, it is also imperative to recognize that not all students have access to these technological advances.

Applying UD Principles for Specific Student Populations

UD principles in advising benefit students with disabilities, and also other student populations experiencing unique educational challenges. One such population with unique needs is the immigrant students served in the University of Minnesota's Commanding English program. Advising practices that benefit these students and can benefit other students as well include thoughtful attention to the advisor's communication with students. Author Amy Kampsen, working with this population of students, suggests the following approaches:

1. Speak clearly and without using slang or idioms.
2. Give instructions both verbally and in a different format for the student to take with them, or have students take notes and then summarize the notes with the advisor to make sure students have understood what was said. If available, use self-duplicating forms when writing down planned courses for upcoming semesters as well as referrals, expectations for the next appointment, or other advisement tasks for the student such as meeting with faculty or accessing a campus resource. This will allow the advisor to follow up on these referrals with the student.
3. Provide visual and verbal illustrations when appropriate.
4. Engage in discussion about cultural implications to better understand the students' needs or expectations.
5. Follow up shortly thereafter with an e-mail message that thanks the student for coming, summarizes advising session content, and confirms future appointments and other obligations on the part of both the student and the advisor.

Another student population that has unique needs is student-athletes. The most pressing consideration for student-athletes, which is shared by students with family responsibilities or unavoidable work obligations, is finding the time to be successful academically. Athletes also have unique pressures related to expectations placed by team members or coaches, travel responsibilities, and registration requirements related to national standards. Some approaches to use in working with this student population include considering time management strategies and a good balance of all responsibilities. It is important to work with the student on creating a schedule that is realistic and flexible to change as needed. It is also imperative to provide a safe place for the student to discuss pressures and expectations related to athletic involvement, ensuring confidentiality.

A third group with unique challenges is students who are low-income and the first generation in their families to attend college. These students have challenges with paying for their education, but also challenges learning how to navigate the university and understand typical college policies and procedures, including the terminology and acronyms used by the institution to describe degree requirements. Like students with disabilities, it is important for these students to develop self-advocacy skills. Some approaches in working with this group of students include these:

1. Take time to assist students in interpreting financial aid packages, or locate other financial resources such as scholarships. Advisors can provide recommendations for students who apply for scholarships and coaching in the monitoring of deadlines, writing

of personal statements, and filling out forms.

2. Discuss the pros and cons of working more hours and taking fewer credits versus incurring debt but graduating sooner. Assist students in determining what is a reasonable workload to balance academics and employment. Make students aware of the part-time job opportunities on campus.

3. Assume nothing about the student's knowledge about the institution or about how things work in higher education.

4. Discuss housing and transportation needs or issues. There may be students who do not understand that housing and transportation support is available to them.

5. At the student's request, Be open to communicating with parents or others in the student's extended community about university life, finances, and the like.

Practicing these approaches of exploring what students know and do not know about university life and institutional expectations, and assisting them in learning to negotiate the institution and manage their time and resources will benefit many students beyond the groups identified above, as many "mainstream" students can also benefit from discussion about finances, housing, transportation, and college policies and procedures.

Finally, UD principles in advising benefit students with disabilities, whether or not the students have sought out disability support services in the institution. Some approaches recommended in advising students with disabilities include these:

1. Be purposeful when planning courses or creating educational and career goals to consider the type of disability the student has.

2. Explain confidentiality expectations and norms at the institution, as well as federal laws protecting privacy.

3. Help the student develop and practice self-advocacy skills.

4. Facilitate the process of the student teaching the advisor about the specific disability.

Similarly, applying these approaches universally to all students, advisors should be purposeful in educational and goal planning with all students, focusing on particular strengths of the student, rather than disability. All students need to be aware of confidentiality rules, should be coached in advocating for their own educational needs, and should be facilitated in teaching advisors and faculty about their strengths.

Advisor and Student Responsibilities in Universal Design

Advisors should receive ongoing training, mentoring, and professional development in areas of multicultural and diversity theory, disability awareness, campus resources, colleague connections, student development theory, and counseling skills. Professional development opportunities need to include both academic and experiential forms to support the holistic integration of the material. This said, it is important that advisors are given the time and support to pursue this professional development, including reasonable student caseloads and adequate allocation of financial resources. Priority may be given in the hiring process as well to those candidates who can demonstrate knowledge or expertise in these areas. Creating advisor position descriptions and interview questions directly related to advising program outcomes and concepts of Universal Design is recommended.

Advisors trained in Universal Design and student development theory support and guide students in academic, personal, and career domains and take into account cognitive, affective, and behavioral development, addressing students at their level of readiness consistent with their learning style. Having advisees complete a simple, one page learning styles assessment early on in the advising relationship, perhaps during orientation, can be a useful tool for advisors to promote discussion about how the advisee learns best, and for the advisor to tailor future meetings to the student's favored learning style. It is recommended that advisors also know and share their own preferred learning styles with the student.

Knowing students' learning styles guides advisors in shaping conversations about the students' academic and personal goals. These tools help advisors see the complexity of the whole student, instead of just the intellectual piece traditionally connected to academic success, and allows for conversations about student strengths and challenges that normalize recognition of challenges and difference across the student population. Understanding student learning styles also allows the advisor to provide an appropriate balance of challenge and support to the student (Sanford, 1966).

Another advising tool that is congruent with UD principles is the Clifton StrengthsFinder (2000), a 30-minute online assessment from the Gallup Organization that reveals a person's top five strengths. Conversations with students about their strengths can help them make academic choices that are more likely to lead to success and satisfaction. At the level of the advising team, recognizing each others' strengths can lead to more effective team building and collaboration.

Another advising tool congruent with UD principles used by one author, Carole Broad, is the Responsibility Model flow chart created by Skip Downing (2007) as a way to guide students through problems. By asking students to start with the assumption that they have a fair degree of control over their educational outcomes and guiding them through imagining what they could have done differently in difficult situations, the tool helps students become "creators" rather than "victims" of the various situations they encounter in college. With advisor encouragement and support, over time students can use this approach to break self-defeating patterns.

To be effective in serving students with diverse needs and challenges, advisors need to make connections around campus to facilitate cross-training, mutual support, and collaboration on behalf of student needs. Examples of effective collaboration include a college advisor working closely with the athletic advisor or Disability Services counselor who is also connected with an advisee. An advisor should engage in institutional advocacy on behalf of student needs when appropriate, and minimize student run-around by facilitating communication between offices or sharing documentation provided by the student rather than forcing the student to visit several offices bringing duplicate documentation.

It is important that advisors communicate clear expectations for both advisor and student roles and that these expectations be communicated early on during new student orientation. A resource such as an advising syllabus, available in both printed and online forms, can contain this information as well as key contact information and calendars (Albecker, Kampsen, & Wartchow, 2007). An advisee's responsibilities outlined on such an advising syllabus might include the following:

1. Schedule regular appointments with your advisor; be prepared with questions or materials for discussion.
2. Check your e-mail every day and follow up on anything of importance.
3. Learn about college programs, degree requirements, policies and procedures.
4. Ask for assistance when needed, whether from an advisor, administrative staff, professor, or peer.
5. Begin to clarify personal values and goals in conversations with family, advisors, professors, and peers.
6. Create an action plan to meet all requirement for graduation.

A document such as an advising syllabus is only useful if is it used. Therefore, it is recommended that such a tool be designed to be interactive, requiring the student and advisor to "check off" sections as they are addressed in advising appointments. "Assignments" for the student to complete by the next appointment can easily be created from such a document. It can also be used in advisor training sessions and should be reviewed often for accuracy and relevance. Feedback from both advisors and students is a valuable source for needed changes and improvements. During advising appointments, informal feedback can be asked of the student and noted by the advisor to be reported to the staff responsible for the syllabus. Specific online or paper student survey questions about the advising syllabus should also be a tool used in the evaluation process.

Outcomes and Assessment Considerations for in Advising

We recommend that any institution of higher education have a set of measurable outcomes related to Universal Design for students, individual advisors, and advising programs as a whole. Outcomes here might be defined as overarching specific, observable characteristics developed by the advising administration that allows them to determine or demonstrate evidence that learning has occurred as a result of a specific activity (adapted from Siemion, 2007). Each of these outcome categories should be driven by the institution's mission, vision, and values as further articulated through the mission and values of the college, unit, department, program, service, and so on. For example, the mission of the College of Education and Human Development at the University of Minnesota (n. d.) states,

> The College of Education and Human Development is a world leader in discovering, creating, sharing, and applying principles and practices of multiculturalism and multidisciplinary scholarship to advance teaching and learning and to enhance the psychological, physical, and social development of children, youth, and adults across the lifespan in families, organizations, and communities.

References to "multiculturalism," "multidisciplinary," "learning," and "development" all support the concepts and practices of Universal Design in advising. There is ample literature related to the writing of mission statements and outcomes related to advising. The National Academic Advising Association (n. d.) and its related publications, conferences, and institutes are well-recognized sources for such information. For any institution wanting to integrate UD concepts into an advising program, a simple way to begin is to compare the current advising practices with the principles of UD in advising to create a "scorecard" or baseline of where the advising program is currently. Having these foundational pieces in place is essential before implementing any strategies related to Universal Design in advising. It is desirable that all parts of the institution, from the administration to the faculty, be supportive, open, and informed about the concepts of UD in general.

Having clearly written and measurable outcomes in place first, before implementation of UD strategies, allows for all planning and development for students, advisors, and the advising program to meet these outcomes. The following are examples of suggested measurable outcome statements for each of the previously mentioned categories:

Student Outcomes in a Universally-Designed Advising Program

Students participating in a universally-designed advising program will do the following: (a) schedule and participate in advisor meetings at least two times per year; (b) know and make connections with the assigned advisor and several faculty and staff; (c) take initiative to access information in various forms as needed; (d) use campus resources supportive of their transportation, housing, personal support, and mobility needs; (e) seek out and utilize academic assistance on campus when needed; (f) seek out and utilize career resources when needed; (g) identify and use Web-based resources; (h) take appropriate courses to complete their degree in a timely fashion; (i) demonstrate self-advocacy by independently pursuing help to achieve goals; and (j) appreciate differences, working effectively with others. These outcomes can be measured by a variety of means such as a review of advising notes, assessment of the advising syllabus, student surveys, or focus groups.

Advisor Outcomes in a Universally-Designed Advising Program

Advisors trained in the principles of Universal Design and student development theory will be able to do the following: (a) explain and apply student development theory in their advising practices; (b) assist students in understanding and utilizing services and policies of myriad supportive services, including disability services, at their institution; (c) design office space to be welcoming and accessible; and (d) demonstrate knowledge of differing needs and experiences students may have related to differences in race, ethnicity, socioeconomic class, home language, disability, gender, religion, age, sexual orientation, or multiple and intersecting social identities. These advisor outcomes can be measured by assessing attendance at various related professional development opportunities, specific coursework taken, advisor self-evaluation, evaluations by supervisors or peers, and student surveys and focus groups. Advisors' yearly work plans should include professional development and performance goals in each category related to the concepts of

Universal Design. The advising program mission should also be included in such a work plan to remind advisors of the relationship of their work to the mission of the institution. Ultimately, it is presumed that the overarching outcome of a program in Universal Design in advising would be an increase in the retention and graduation rates for any institution. Though advisors may not think that they have a direct influence on retention and graduation rates, the holistic nature of Universal Design in advising, encompassing so many facets of the learning process for students, is sure to affect many of the choices and decisions students make and their success in completing degrees. It will be important for programs implementing UD principles in advising to implement assessment and tracking to document improvements in student success.

Future Research and Development

One area for future research may be examining the degree to which Universal Design in advising addresses social justice issues, and ways that scholarship grounded in social justice models can inform UD practices in advising. These models broaden the scope of impact of educational practices beyond the private good of student success to the public good of inclusion and full participation of members of diverse communities. Recognizing the communities that our students come from and return to lead may shape advising practices supportive of student engagement and community service in support of both social justice and student growth and development.

Future research can also include evaluations of features in advising services representing UD principles and how these features correlate with improvements in student retention and success, especially the success of student populations currently faring less well than others. Although UD in advising cannot remove all barriers, as some students face significant financial challenges, family responsibilities, or physical limitations, a robust and thoughtful UD advising model will provide appropriate support, guidance, and response to diverse student needs to help students succeed in spite of these challenges, bringing their unique gifts to the wider community.

References

Albecker, A., Kampsen, A., & Wartchow, D., (2007). *Academic advising syllabus.* Minneapolis: University of Minnesota, College of Education and Human Development.

Chickering, A. W. (1969). *Education and identity.* San Francisco: Jossey-Bass.

Chickering, A. W. & Reisser, L. (1993). *Education and identity* (2nd ed.). San Franscisco: Jossey-Bass.

College of Education and Human Development. *Homepage.* Retrieved November 20, 2007, from http://cehd.umn.edu/college/

Creamer, D. G. (2000). *Use of theory in academic advising.* In V. N. Gordon, W. R. Habley, & Associates: Academic advising, A comprehensive handbook. San Francisco: Jossey-Bass.

Downing, S. (2007). *On course: Strategies for creating success in college and in life* (5th ed.). New York: Houghton Mifflin.

Ender, S. C. & Wilkie, C. J. (2000). *Advising students with special needs.* In V. N. Gordon, W. R. Habley, and Associates, Academic advising: A comprehensive handbook. (pp. 118-143).

San Francisco: Jossey-Bass.

Ender, S.C., Winston, R.B., & Miller T.K. (1984). *Academic advising reconsidered.* In R.B. Winston, T.K. Miller, S.C. Ender, T.J. Grites, & Associates: Developmental academic advising (pp. 9-24). San Francisco: Jossey-Bass.

King, M. C. (2005). *Developmental academic advising.* Retrieved August 10, 2007, from http://www.nacada.ksu.edu/Clearinghouse/AdvisingIssues/dev_adv.htm

The National Academic Advising Association (n. d.). *Homepage.* Retrieved November 20, 2007, from www.nacada.ksu.edu

Sanford, N. 1966. *Self and society: Social change and individual development.* New York: Atherton Press.

Siemion, G. (2007). *On Course national conference presentation* (2007), Dallas, TX, Student Learning Outcomes.

The Gallup Organization. (2000). *StrengthsFinder.* Princeton, N.J: Author. Retrieved November 20, 2007, from https://www.strengthsfinder.com/

CHAPTER 20

The First-Year Experience

Jeanne L. Higbee
University of Minnesota

Karen S. Kalivoda
The University of Georgia

Abstract
This chapter is reprinted verbatim from Curriculum Transformation and Disability: Implementing Universal Design in Higher Education, *and was originally published in 2003. This chapter discusses the implementation of Universal Design in a number of programs and services for prospective and new students, including admissions, orientation, registration, and first-year experience courses.*

The importance of Universal Design of programs and services begins even before students are enrolled. This chapter will address admissions, orientation, and first-year experience courses and programs.

Admissions

The admissions process can play a significant role in students' choice of institution. A seemingly disinterested staff member can dissuade a student from pursuing admission. An admissions web site that is difficult for anyone to navigate can frustrate applicants and create critical barriers for students with some types of disabilities.

Students are not required to disclose a disability when applying. Some students wait to share information regarding their disability until after they have been accepted at an institution because they fear discrimination. Even then, some students with disabilities are hesitant to make their disabilities known; they do not want to be labeled on the basis of disability. Some have been segregated into "special" classes or tracked in high school and are concerned about college course placements. Students have the right to withhold this information, and when they choose to exercise this right it can make planning difficult. Universal Design, planning for all potential situations, can prevent stumbling blocks from arising later, when there may not be adequate time to address them appropriately.

On the other hand, it is helpful for students to contact the institution's disability services office as soon as they have been admitted, or even before, so that they can be informed about what services are available, procedures for arranging for accommodations, testing policies, and so on. Disability services providers and students can then work together to ensure that necessary documentation of the disability is on file and develop a plan of action. Sometimes students will need to undergo another evaluation to update their documentation. For example, some institutions require that testing for a learning disability be recent, occurring within a specific time period. Students who wait to contact disability services until they experience academic difficulty may find that it is several months, perhaps even an entire term, before they can receive services or modifications or accommodations, because they need to seek further documentation. Thus, it can be beneficial for both the institution and the student to disclose a disability early in the process. It is up to the admissions office to establish rapport, create an environment that welcomes diversity, and communicate that the decision to self-disclose will not have negative ramifications. It is also imperative that the admissions office provides information regarding how to contact the disabilities services office to all new students. Some institutions include a separate postage-paid response form in all letters of admission to encourage students with disabilities to provide information to the institution, or even better, directly to the campus office for disability services.

Orientation

Once admitted, the next contact students have with the institution is often new student orientation. Implementing Universal Design in orientation programs becomes a complex process because orientation often includes testing, advising, registration, campus tours, meals, and an overnight stay in a residence hall, as well as educational and social programs. Arranging these activities is likely to involve people representing a variety of functions and offices in both academic and student affairs. It is critical for the planning process to begin with consideration of the needs of all students. If the tenets of Universal Design are central to the development of the orientation program, it will be much easier to create an experience that is welcoming to all students. Accommodations added later are likely to be perceived as afterthoughts, which indeed they are.

Testing

If placement testing occurs during orientation, testing schedules must be flexible in order to provide extended time and private testing rooms for students whose disabilities warrant these accommodations. Faculty and administrators need to reconsider the role of timed tests in the placement process. Is there any legitimate reason why students should not be allowed to complete a set of math problems or write an essay, rather than being assessed according to how much they can accomplish in a given amount of time? Would many students be likely to perform better on placement tests if given the opportunity for more time if they need it? Even if students do not need additional time, knowing that it is available can reduce stress. Would higher scores on placement tests be a negative occurrence? Have institutions conducted research to determine whether timed placement tests are more accurate predictors of academic achievement than untimed tests? At colleges and universities that require standardized tests for admission, how much additional testing is really necessary for placement? These questions are posed to encourage the reexamination of placement testing policies, not just in terms of accommodating students with disabilities, but to better serve all new students.

Advising

Aune (2000) suggests that application of student development theory, including Astin's (1993) theory of involvement and Tinto's (1993) theory of integration, can assist advisors in using what they already know about all students to better serve students with disabilities. Similarly, consideration of Chickering's (1969; Chickering & Reisser, 1993) seven vectors of college student development can remind advisors that college students are faced with multiple intersecting developmental tasks, and that although some of these tasks may pose greater challenges for students with disabilities, just as they may for students who do not have a disability, facilitating the development of "the student as a whole" (American Council on Education, 1937; reprinted in National Association of Student Personnel Administrators, 1989, p. 39) is the primary goal. Aune suggests that advisors take the following steps to implement Universal Design in providing services for all students:

> Recognize their assumptions about disability and how those assumptions affect their behavior toward students with disabilities... Create an atmosphere of mutual respect and trust... Understand how disability and the environment interact to create barriers... Use flexibility and creativity to solve problems... Address disclosure issues... Achieve a balance in focus between disability issues and issues all students face... Balance support with fostering independence... (p. 58)

Unfortunately, the duration of advising appointments during orientation is generally brief, and students often go directly from advisement to registration. Advisors may barely have time to point out options within the core curriculum, with no opportunity to become acquainted with the individual interests and needs of the student. Thus, for the most critical first term of college, students may be least prepared to make knowledgeable choices when registering for courses. There may be no time to address issues like whether to enroll in a lecture-based section or a computer-assisted section of the same course; how a student's interests, skills, past educational experiences, or disability might affect the decision to take art, music, or drama appreciation to meet a fine arts requirement; where to look up class locations to determine whether it is feasible to sign up for classes during consecutive class periods; and how to decide what time of day to schedule classes. For students with disabilities, not unlike student athletes, students who work, students who are parents, and many others, some of these decisions may have a significant impact on success during the first term of college. If questions like these are addressed in educational sessions about core curriculum choices during orientation or in advisors' groups or learning communities, advisors can then focus more of their attention on individualizing the advising process.

Registration

Online options at many institutions have enhanced opportunities to apply Universal Design to registration policies and procedures. However, registering online can also be frustrating when it is unclear why some pathways become blocked. Similarly, if registration is Web-based, it is imperative that the registration Website be accessible. (Further information on Web accessibility and assistive technology is provided in the final section of this book.) In addition to providing computer stations with assistive technology to make online registration accessible to all students, it is imperative for support staff to be available to answer questions during orientation. If registration is completed from a distance, rather than at a centralized site during orientation, individualized assistance should be available, at least during regular work hours, online and via telephone, and also via telecommunication devices such as TTY for students with hearing impairments.

Campus Tours

Walking or bus tours are common components of new student orientation. Tours must be designed so that they do not discriminate or segregate students and parents with disabilities, including mobility, vision, and hearing impairments. A common solution for accommodating students with mobility impairments, for example, is to provide separate vans for the families of wheelchair users. Thus, these students and their parents do not have the same opportunities for interaction as other families. If some participants must ride a bus with a lift, all students and parents in that group should ride the same bus. Creative approaches, such as the use of golf carts and audiotaped narratives supplemented by written text, can make the traditional campus walking tour more enjoyable for all, especially in inclement weather. Campuses can also provide universally accessible virtual tours on their Websites. Virtual tours would also be beneficial to all students when planning course schedules that allow adequate time to get from building to building, and when making housing decisions.

Housing and Meals

The residence halls used for orientation should be chosen with the most flexible room arrangements and modern facilities (e.g., elevators, air conditioning) in order to accommodate all participating students. A separate chapter of this book provides further information regarding the implementation of Universal Design in residence life facilities and programs. Meals and snacks should be planned to allow choices that accommodate diverse student needs, which can be related to food allergies, religious beliefs, and health issues. Dining facilities must be accessible to students with mobility, hearing, and vision impairments. These students must not be placed in a position in which they need to ask other students to "wait on" them.

Educational and Social Programming

In addition to "ice breakers" and other social activities, it is not unusual for orientation programs to include educational programs on topics like alcohol and drug awareness and communication in roommate relationships. Orientation is also an ideal time to provide programs that focus on multiculturalism. Workshops that include discussions of contemporary films or small group consideration of case studies are just a couple of ideas for educational programs that can be implemented in a way that is entertaining and fun. It is important that in programs like this diversity be broadly defined to include race, religion, ethnicity, home language, social class, gender, sexual orientation, and disability.

Freshman Seminars and Other First-Year Experience Courses

There are myriad models for freshman seminars and orientation-type courses. On some campuses freshman seminars are taught by faculty from departments across campus and are content-based. Many campuses also have a diversity requirement for graduation, meaning that all students are required to complete at least one course that addresses diversity issues. Content-based freshman seminars with small enrollments taught by full-time faculty members provide another ideal opportunity to engage students in discussions of multiculturalism in an environment that establishes ground rules and facilitates trust (Higbee, 2001, 2002; Jehangir, 2001).

First-year experience courses (e.g., Gardner & Jewler, 2002) often focus on skill development and adjusting to college life. Many topics that are traditionally included in these courses, such as time management and relieving stress, can be of particular importance to students with disabilities. In discussions of communication skills, an emphasis on self-advocacy assists all students in asserting themselves in a manner that commands respect and does not infringe on the rights of others. Elementary and secondary school policies and procedures, especially for students with disabilities, often place the parent in the role of advocate. Students are not in charge of requesting services for themselves; generally a team that includes parents, teachers, a counselor, and perhaps a member of the administration, decide what is best for the student. This poses a considerable challenge for new freshmen, who are suddenly responsible for communicating their own needs. For some students with disabilities, who may have very specific and immediate concerns, and may also fear being stereotyped or not being taken seriously, or who may be reticent about discussing their disability for myriad other reasons, the inability, inexperience, or unwillingness to communicate with faculty and staff may be the greatest barrier to achievement. Developing self-advocacy skills is crucial to college success.

Diverse Program Models

Hartman (1993) discusses the importance of summer transition programs for students with disabilities and describes some of the early model programs. She explains the impact of major legislation on increasing access for people with disabilities at institutions of higher education. Once the doors of educational opportunity were opened for people with disabilities, colleges and universities saw the need for the development of transition programs. In the 1980s, institutions such as Wright State University, St. Paul Technical College, the University of North Carolina at Charlotte and Central Piedmont Community College all offered programs to students with disabilities to help prepare them for college or to help them select the best college program for their needs. Although programs such as these were instrumental in enhancing access and retention for students with disabilities, many still accommodated students with disabilities by segregating them.

Samberg, Barr, Hartman, & Murray (1994) describe three model summer transition to college programs designed specifically for students with learning disabilities. These programs ranged from three days to seven weeks and were intended to supplement the general orientation program offered at the institutions. Samberg et al. identify common successful strategies used by the projects, including "training in self-advocacy skills, instruction in study skills, instruction in time management, learning strategies training, orientation to disability support services . . ." (p. 75). In addition to introducing students to academic skills for college success, these programs offered an opportunity for social interaction with peers with similar disabilities.

HORIZONS

Dale (1995) describes a federally-funded TRIO program, HORIZONS, at Purdue University, designed to facilitate transition and to increase retention of students who are first generation, low-income, and have physical disabilities. This program utilized a freshman orientation course titled "Strategies for Effective Academic Performance." The class included instruction in effective study methods and instruction on personal development. The success of the program is evident by the higher retention rate reported for students who participated in HORIZONS. Also of interest are the results of the participant evaluation of the program. Although services such as tutoring, study skills training, and computer training were valued, participants rated "just knowing that help was available" on the evaluation form as the most important service. This highlights the importance of making personal contacts with students and introducing them to a variety of available services.

Project Excel

The University of Arkansas developed Project Excel, a summer transition program for students with disabilities. The purpose of the program was to facilitate transition and to promote academic excellence (Serebreni, Rumrill, Mullins, & Gordon, 1993). A small group of 12 high-achieving students with varying types of disabilities were chosen to participate in the program. The six-week program included activities to address psychosocial adjustment, academic development, and orientation to the campus and community. The participants evaluated Project Excel as "good" to "excellent." Similar to other model programs, most participants reported that the most beneficial facet of the program was the opportunity to make contact with new people.

Student Transition and Retention Program

The Student Transition and Retention (STAR) Program at the University of Georgia (UGA) was created to assist new students with disabilities in making connections at the university and in learning how to utilize campus resources. The theoretical foundation for the program is Astin's (1984, 1985) theory of involvement. When students become involved in campus life, they are more likely to be retained at the institution and to be satisfied with their educational experience. Astin (1985) noted that one of the most critical factors is contact with faculty, becoming acquainted with members of the faculty outside the traditional classroom environment. It is not unusual for students with disabilities to feel isolated and reluctant to seek help. (Willis, Hoben, & Myette, 1995). A primary goal of the STAR program is to introduce students to one another and to some of the faculty and staff members who hold key support positions.

During the 1997-1998 academic year, the UGA Office of Disability Services (ODS) surveyed current students with disabilities regarding their adjustment to college life.

Students were asked to make recommendations for facilitating the transition for new freshmen and transfer students. The STAR program was designed to address those ideas and suggestions. In order to inconvenience families as little as possible, five one-day sessions of STAR were piloted during summer 1998 in conjunction with the university-wide orientation program; families attended STAR for an additional day following participation in orientation. Separate schedules of activities were established for students and parents. The maximum enrollment per session was 10 students, so that the program could be tailored to meet individual student needs and so that each student would have several opportunities for one-to-one and small group interaction with disability service providers and a faculty member from the Division of Academic Assistance (ACA). ACA provides learning support in the form of elective courses, workshops, tutoring, a learning center, and academic counseling in such areas as setting goals and objectives, time and stress management, motivation, learning styles, career exploration, and adjusting to college life.

The schedule of activities included (a) introductions and a tour of the Office of Disability Services, including private testing rooms and a computer laboratory that is equipped with virtually every form of technology available to accommodate students with disabilities; (b) a visit to the ACA Learning Center (LC), including the opportunity to complete two instruments on computers in the center, one to assess preferred learning styles and one to explore choice of major and career opportunities, and group interpretation of the results; (c) a videotape that relates personal style to career choice, followed by exploration of how students use their five senses to learn, and how to use their perceptual strengths to their advantage, applying this information to specific study strategies such as the Cornell format of note taking (Longman, 1999; Pauk, 1974); (d) a box lunch, which also provided an opportunity to interact informally with faculty, staff, and current students; (e) a discussion of university policies, procedures, curricula, and graduation requirements; (f) individual meetings between students and the ODS staff member who would serve as their disability specialist in the fall; and (g) role plays of self-advocacy skills.

Students and parents responded to separate evaluation forms that asked them to rate each activity on the schedule on a scale of one (i.e., not at all helpful) to five (extremely helpful). Parents' mean overall rating of the STAR program was 4.80 on a scale of one (i.e., not at all helpful) to five (extremely helpful); students' was 4.47. Parents and students were unanimous in indicating that they would recommend the STAR program to other new students with disabilities and their parents. All of the students also responded "yes" when asked, "Do you think participation in this program will help you feel more comfortable in the fall (a) seeking services at the Office of Disability Services, (b) seeking services or attending programs in the Division of Academic Assistance, and (c) making the transition to university life?" A representative parent comment was "I am feeling more confident that [student] has made the correct choice of [institution] after attending the STAR program." Several students expressed the importance of having the opportunity to meet other students with disabilities. This program, which can be easily replicated at other institutions, is considered by participants and faculty and staff alike to be a very worthwhile addition to new student orientation for students with disabilities.

Conclusion

Institutions are still grappling with how to design orientation and first-year experience programs for students with disabilities that serve specific student needs without segregating students. Althogh programs like STAR can be instrumental in allaying student fears and responding to individual concerns that cannot be addressed during regular orientation sessions, they still require an additional time commitment not asked of other students. On the other hand, they do not restrict students with disabilities from participating fully in the institution's regular orientation program. Similar issues arise when considering the possibility of offering separate sections of first-year courses for students with disabilities, or for student athletes, or for returning adult students, "underprepared" students, or any other group for that matter. Administrators must weigh the potential advantages against the barriers erected when students are segregated on the basis of any group membership. On the other hand, when student development professionals creating first-year programs consider the principles of Universal Design early in the planning process, they can embed information targeted to specific groups in the contents of integrated courses and activities, enhancing the first-year experience for all students.

References

American Council on Education. (1937). *The student personnel point of view.* Washington, DC: Author.

Astin, A. W. (1984). Student involvement: A developmental theory for higher education. *Journal of College Student Personnel, 25,* 297-308.

Astin, A. W. (1985). *Achieving educational excellence.* San Francisco: Jossey-Bass.

Astin, A. W. (1993). *What matters in college? Four critical years revisited.* San Francisco: Jossey-Bass.

Aune, B. (2000). Career and academic advising. In H.A. Belch (Ed.), *Serving students with disabilities.* (New Directions for Student Services, no. 91, pp. 55-67). San Francisco: Jossey-Bass.

Chickering, A. W. (1969). *Education and identity.* San Francisco: Jossey-Bass.

Chickering, A. W., & Reisser, L. (1993). *Education and identity* (2nd ed.). San Francisco: Jossey-Bass.

Dale, P. M. (1995). A successful college retention program. *College Student Journal, 30*(3), 354-361.

Ellis, D. B. (1985). *Becoming a master student* (5th ed.). Rapid City, SD: College Survival.

Gardner, J. N., & Jewler, A. J. (2002). *Your college experience: Strategies for success* (5th ed.). Belmont, CA: Wadsworth.

Hartman, R. (1993). Transition to higher education. In S. Kroeger & J. Schuck (Eds.), *Responding to disability issues in student affairs.* (New Directions for Student Services, no. 64, pp. 31-43). San Francisco: Jossey-Bass.

Higbee, J. L. (2001). Promoting multiculturalism in developmental education. *Research & Teaching in Developmental Education, 18*(1), 51-57.

Higbee, J. L. (2002). Addressing current events in classroom discussions. *Research and Teaching in Developmental Education, 18*(2), 85-90.

Jehangir, R. R. (2001). Cooperative learning in the multicultural classroom. In D. B.

Lundell & J. L. Higbee (Eds.), *Theoretical Perspectives for Developmental Education* (pp. 91-99). Minneapolis: University of Minnesota, General College, Center for Research on Developmental Education and Urban Literacy.

Longman, D. G. (1999). *College learning and study skills* (5th ed.). Belmont, CA: Wadsworth.

National Association of Student Personnel Administrators. (1989). *Points of view.* Washington, DC: Author.

Pauk, W. (1974). *How to study in college* (2nd ed.). Boston: Houghton Mifflin.

Samberg, L., Barr, V., Hartman, R., & Murray, T. (1994). *Educating students with disabilities on campus: Strategies of successful projects.* Washington, DC: HEATH Resource Center, National Clearinghouse on Postsecondary Education for Individuals with Disabilities, American Council on Education. (ERIC Document Reproduction Service No. ED393254)

Serebreni, R., Rumrill, P. D., Mullins, J. A., & Gordon, S. E. (1993). Project Excel: A demonstration of the higher education transition model for high-achieving students with disabilities. *Journal of Postsecondary Education and Disability, 10*(3), 15-23.

Tinto, V. (1993). *Leaving college: Rethinking the causes and cures of student retention* (2nd ed.). Chicago: University of Chicago Press.

Willis, C., Hoben, S., & Myette, P. (1995). Devising a supportive climate based on clinical vignettes of college students with attention deficit disorder. *Journal of Postsecondary Education and Disability, 11,* 31-43.

CHAPTER 21

Residential Living For All: Fully Accessible and "Liveable" On-Campus Housing

Martha E. Wisbey and Karen S. Kalivoda
The University of Georgia

Abstract
This chapter is reprinted verbatim from Curriculum Transformation and Disability: Implementing Universal Design in Higher Education, *and was originally published in 2003. On-campus housing for college students is a critical part of postsecondary educational life. Residence hall facilities and programs are typically located within the overall academic surroundings, thus making the location of where students sleep, study, eat and live in close proximity to their classrooms and to campus resources and services. Ideally, students with disabilities, like their peers, will be able to access their living spaces without any interruption or specific additional need for accommodation. The concepts of Universal Design features are those that are comfortably useable by all people, not just people with disabilities. Universal Design expands the scope of accessibility by suggesting that all spaces and environments in the community be useable by people with disabilities. This chapter addresses various aspects of residential life from a Universal Design perspective. The authors provide student affairs professionals suggestions on how to create an environment that is optimal for all students, staff, and faculty working and living in residence halls on campus.*

"I know this is a big campus but my daughter uses a wheelchair for her disability, what are the residence hall buildings like? Does she have to live in a special place in a specific dorm or are all your buildings equipped to handle wheelchair access? How close is she to classes?" Just getting off the phone after fielding several questions from a mother of an incoming student at my university, I had to take a minute to grasp the number of specific questions she had regarding her daughter's room assignment. I did not know how to respond, which was rather disturbing because I have been in the student services field for over 15 years. I promised I would get back in touch with her after I talked with several other colleagues. I was unaware of what our office could offer her daughter and had honestly never thought about some of the issues she raised. During the conversation, it became apparent that I needed to gain some knowledge about how we accommodate students with disabilities in our residence halls.

With over five different theme housing programs, 20 different buildings ranging in size from 100 to 1000 students, and housing facilities dating back to the early 1900s, I knew we had isolated spaces that would offer students with mobility impairments a place to live on campus. These spaces were designed and planned with only the intent of being able to get a wheelchair into a residence hall room and a bathroom. No other access issues were addressed in these adaptations.

As a parent, this student's mother wanted assurance that her daughter was not just in an accessible room, but also part of the mainstream of the co-curricular life that typically takes place in a residence hall. According to Ratzka (1994), when designing structures for residences, do we look at the structures for "visitability" or do we look at it from a "liveability" criterion? This mother wanted to be sure her incoming freshmen daughter would have liveability with other new students. She sought information not only about the actual room where her daughter would live, but where she would eat, how she would get around on campus, and other aspects of campus life.

As the Assistant Director for Residence Life, I knew some of our new buildings had "handicapped accessible" rooms, but they were located across campus in buildings designed for upperclass students, not in buildings where first-year students primarily lived. I could tell from the mother's tone that she hoped her daughter was able to enter college just as any student would, without any extra obstacles. Her phone call was intended to smooth the way and I knew this was new territory for me, and maybe it was new for most persons within our department. Student assignments follow a standard format for the institution; the sign up process involves the following: get the name, roommate request, if applicable, and desired building preference, then assignments are made on a first come, first serve basis. It is hard to state if the building she would be placed in would be able to provide the "seamless" entry into the University that her family was seeking.

This chapter and my subsequent journey into gathering facts about accommodating students with disabilities in residential life offers student affairs practitioners some insight into planning residential communities that apply universal design concepts. These universal concepts and principles allow students with different abilities to live side-by-side and can offer designers of residence halls "an opportunity to engage them [students] within worthwhile learning activities alongside their peers" (Blamires, 1999, p. 161).

Living Facilities for Students: Historical Overview

Residence hall facilities in the United States were established as student housing early in the history of higher education. The idea of residential colleges was brought from universities in England and was seen as places for educating the "whole" student. Faculty would spend hours after class sharing time with students in their residential living spaces (Winston & Anchors, 1993). During the period after the civil war until the early 1900s, German university influences were brought to many campuses. Professors were returning from Germany with the belief that housing students was not the intended mission of the university. During this period residence halls became less educationally defined and more distinctive facilities for "out of class" activities to take place, and typically focused on conduct issues unrelated to the overall learning atmosphere. The term dormitory signified a living space for a bed, a desk, and a few other items for living as a student on campus. The primary place for learning was designated as the classroom. The dormitory-type barrack became a standard on many college campuses (Winston & Anchors).

Over the last half of the twentieth century, dormitories transformed from just rooms with beds into living communities where students are encouraged to continue their learning process in their living spaces. Today, many residence hall buildings provide common areas where kitchens, laundry rooms, study halls, and living spaces for students provide a greater level of comfort and services. In addition, student affairs professionals are hired as residence hall staff and offer intentional programmatic opportunities for students. Programs offered range from social interaction activities to educational seminars for students to gain knowledge outside the classroom. Professors conduct lectures and informal chats with students in common areas of their residences mirroring residential living in the early days of higher education.

College Environment Issues

On large university campuses, residence halls offer smaller communities for students to meet and get to know each other. The effort is made to create smaller communities within the large campus setting to stimulate interaction among students, especially new students, and create support systems that will offer students the chance to make connections with their peers. Peer interactions, involvement on campus, and faculty contact are all important parts of student retention (Tinto, 1987). For students with disabilities, as for all students, these are a critical components of their success as students. Happiness and satisfaction in their surroundings can lead students to get involved and feel as though they matter and belong. "Students have feelings of marginality when they do not think they matter; they feel out of place, alienated, not central, lack connections, or feel as if they do not belong." (Winston & Anchors, 1993, p. 464). Students with disabilities may automatically feel like they are different because of their need for a special accommodation, or because they have a visible disability that makes them look different than their peers, such as using a wheelchair, a cane, or a guide dog.

On smaller campuses, residence halls are usually seen and utilized as extensions of the campus experience; many colleges use residential facilities to house other services for students or to create areas around residence hall buildings where recreational and other activities take place. Housing can become an important part of a student's daily life and can offer a place for creating friendships, learning new things, and developing their "home" away from home. Students with disabilities are looking for the same opportunities as their peers. They may need to articulate their specific need for accommodations, as evidenced in the initial story in this chapter, but they are not seeking spaces that are separate or even "special," they are seeking residence hall designs that are universally useable (McGuinness, 1997).

Residence Hall Universal Design Features

What would universally designed residence halls feature? In essence, any aspect of the residential hall building can be used by anyone regardless of his or her level of ability or disability. Universal features are intended to enhance building components to provide flexibility for the user. Specific components are placed in different places, or carefully selected for a variety of uses within the living setting. For example, electrical outlets can be placed higher than usual above floors for access, standard but wider doors can be selected for installation, and steps into buildings can be eliminated (Ratzka, 1994).

The intent of Universal Design is to make life simpler for everyone and make housing usable for more people at the least amount of cost to the institution. Lusher and Mace (1989) define Universal Design as an approach to design that accommodates people of all ages, sizes, and abilities. Housing professionals are faced with buildings that reflect post-World War II educational standards (McGuinness, 1997). Two different perspectives have occurred in response to making modifications based on the Americans with Disabilities Act (ADA; 1990): (a) An institution makes permanent changes by renovating a building space or room to accommodate a student, or (b) an institution makes temporary adaptations to an existing space without expensive renovation. Regardless of the response to creating an environment that meets the letter or spirit of the law to allow a student to utilize a facility, a residence hall need not look like it is designed for specific types of users. When applying Universal Design principles, planners are encouraged to start small and simple, and consider what issues are related to the look, cost, safety, gender and cultural appropriateness. Typically, it is much easier to accommodate the unique needs of a student with a disability in a newly constructed residence hall than in an existing building; however, both facilities need some time and attention and should be "developed in a sensitive and sensible manner" (Rydeen, 1999, p. 56). The idea of renovating space for an individual specific student presents unique challenges for housing professionals. For many practitioners, the daily demands of their role can serve to limit their proactive response in making specific accommodation changes in their buildings. Housing professionals may only react to the requests that they receive and only respond based on the need.

When considering the universal design of a space for all people with different abilities, housing personnel should address several different levels of design. Although it isn't always possible to think of everything when considering these issues, it is important to keep some basic ideas in mind. In addition, consulting current students with disabilities to assist in creating this environment would be an asset and a way to truly conceptualize some of the needs that might not occur to an able-bodied person. It is easy to make assumptions based on typical life experiences and to overlook some obvious and easy ways to make changes in the overall residence hall building. "Today's architects address the life cycle of buildings. It is time that they began to address the life cycle of people as well. Universal design is considerate of the human lifespan and the continuum of abilities of all individuals" (Mace, 1990, p.2).

Architectural Suggestions for Universal Design

There are a number of common issues related to moving through open spaces, including hallways, entrance ways, and open space areas. The following suggestions are offered to address possible obstacles related to moving through open spaces in hope of enhancing Universal Design in residence halls.

Moving Through Open Spaces

1. Avoid creating areas that are so small that persons cannot move back and forth with ease.
2. Provide a full-length side light at entry door.
3. Ensure space utilization is orderly and defined.
4. Install appropriate directional signs for use of space or services.
5. Assist students with visual impairments by using specific color schemes and providing Braille information.
6. Eliminate any sharp projecting objects from wall space.
7. Place any decorative benches, plants, or furniture in areas other than the main circulation routes.
8. Be sure doors have adequate width for connecting hallways to common areas and to ensure easy traffic patterns (consult architectural guidelines for required dimensions).
9. Provide open access in and out of the building via curb cuts, inclines, and ramps that are easily maneuvered.
10. Place accessible water fountains, telephones, and other service machines (e.g., vending, automated teller machine [ATM]) at heights that enable easy access.

Residence Hall Doors

Entry into student space and any other common area space must have lever handles and lighting above doorways. Automatic doors and delayed action door closer devices ease access for all students.

Bathrooms

There should be at least one, and preferably two accessible bathrooms for students on each floor. If renovations are needed, utilizing a closet or utility space can usually offer additional square footage for a universal shower stall and bathroom space. Guidelines for accessible bathrooms include: (a) slightly more square footage than a conventional bathroom, allowing for full mobility of a wheelchair; (b) fixtures provided at appropriate heights; (c) grab bars on shower or tub walls; (d) faucets for showers and tubs located at appropriate heights and close to the outside rim, making them easy for anyone to reach; (e) shower stall large enough for wheelchairs, (f) full length mirror, and (g) adjustable height showerheads.

Bedroom areas

Residence hall bedroom areas are the actual rooms where students sleep, study, socialize and spend a large portion of their time. Ideally, the space provides students with many options for creating a comfortable and easy to use environment for their clothes, books, computer, bed, any permissible appliances, and other items such as personal hygiene items, cleaning items, laundry, and trash. Beyond comfort and ease, these spaces must also provide safety features.

Suggestions for bedroom areas include: (a) notched mounting blocks to allow for closet rods to be lowered or raised accommodating students of all heights, (b) light switches and electrical receptacles located at a height that is reachable for persons at different heights,

(c) wider passageways from hallways leading into bedrooms, (d) moveable furniture that can be removed or changed to accommodate any specific furniture need, (e) desks and chairs that can be raised or lowered, (f) sinks in rooms that are lowered to accommodate students in wheelchairs but also accessible to students of all heights, (g) audio-visual fire alarm boxes, and (h) flexible lighting options for desk areas and overhead room lights.

Kitchen Areas

Accessibility considerations are critical for students who want to use the residence hall kitchen. Suggestions to improve access to kitchen areas for all residents include: (a) single-lever controls on kitchen faucets to facilitate easy operation and adjustments of water temperatures and volume, (b) light switches and electrical receptacles located at a height that is reachable for persons of different heights (c) side-by-side refrigerator in close proximity to the oven and stove, (d) front mounted controls on stove and oven, (e) adjustable height counters and cabinets, and (f) knee space under the sink and cook top.

Some of the items listed for Universal Design architectural changes can be helpful for students with both temporary and permanent disabilities. Universal Design principles in housing are also critical for residence hall entrances, bathrooms, and other common areas like the lounges, academic spaces, recreational areas, and kitchens. This overall approach to making changes throughout the building will allow all residents to remain in the community rather than being confined to a specific area in the building.

Universal Programming

Lehmann, Davies, and Laurin (2000) reported that barriers encountered by students with disabilities in their study included: (a) lack of understanding of disabilities in general on the part of fellow students, staff, and faculty; (b) lack of adequate resources or services to tackle college challenges; (c) lack of financial support; and (d) lack of self-advocacy skills. Specific programs can be offered in the residence halls to help educate peers and increase student understanding about disability related biases and stereotypes. Students with disabilities can be asked to help create programs to educate their peers also. The support of students with disabilities in offering programs can serve to help empower them. Students with disabilities must be provided with equal opportunities to serve in leadership roles, such as officer and staff positions. Inclusion and involvement can offer students a voice for sharing with their peers as well as staff and faculty. Also associated with this type of invitation is the chance for students with disabilities living in a residence hall to be able to learn new skills in advocating for themselves and taking a leadership role within the campus community. By starting at the level of their residential community, students can gain confidence in themselves and their ability to confront attitudes or actions that occur throughout their college career on campus or in society as a whole.

Residence hall staff are required to offer diversity training programs on most campuses and their efforts should expand beyond issues of race, ethnicity, and sexual orientation to include educational programs on both visible and invisible disabilities. Vander Putten (1993) found that paraprofessionals in residence halls can effectively model favorable attitudes toward college students with learning disabilities and can facilitate development of these attitudes among students on their floors and in their buildings.

Another aspect of Universal Design programming involves the inclusion of all persons in programs that are offered in the residence halls. For example, if a program on a floor is announced through a poster or written flyer advertising the date, time, and place for the activity, how can a person who is visually impaired know about the event? Ideally, staff would leave an auditory message on the student's answering machine, talk to the student personally, or if appropriate prepare the flyer in Braille and put it in the student's mailbox. However, a more universal approach might be to announce the program to all students via e-mail, especially on campuses that have designated e-mail as their official means of communication with students. Students with visual impairments can easily access e-mail with the use of assistive technology.

Careful program planning also involves identifying a location for events where students of all abilities can feel included. If the residence hall common space is a room that has only steps leading to it, and no ramp or elevator for access, it would be wise for a staff member to avoid using this location so that all students can attend the event. The ADA requires programs to move beyond the obvious needs of the mobility impaired and begin to address the highly individualized needs of the entire population of students with disabilities. Advertising the residence hall's intent to provide access allows housing staff to plan specific programs that will allow all students to participate in a program. Suggestions that may assist in making a program accessible are:

1. Include a general access statement in all publications and announcements. This lets students with disabilities know they are welcome and that they can contact a person planning the event to make specific requests.
2. Offer printed material in alternate forms. Taped versions, large print, Braille copies, and electronic media make visually oriented material available to people with vision impairments.
3. Communicate the availability of assistive listening devices for people attending programs.
4. Advertise that a sign language interpreter is available upon request.
5. Relocate programs that are architecturally inaccessible.
6. Secure accessible transportation for programs that require off-campus activities or programs in other areas beyond the residence hall.

Even if staff do not see themselves as having social barriers or discriminatory attitudes towards students with disabilities, social distance, avoidance, and lack of foresight in planning can lead students with disabilities to perceive barriers from them (Denny & Carson, 1994). Subtle symbols such as providing alternative forms of a newsletter or including sign language interpreters for an event to be sure students with hearing loss can attend will reveal to students that the office of residence life truly regards and recognizes each individual. It may take more effort and more time to be inclusive, but the messages sent to students with disabilities will factor into their overall satisfaction with the campus environment.

Staff Development Issues

In creating residence halls that have Universal Design principles, the development and training of student paraprofessional staff living with students on the halls, as well as professional staff, is crucial to the success of this concept. The philosophical aspect as well as the physical signs of change in the environment will determine how the atmosphere will impact all students in the development of community.

To fully understand and actualize the Universal Design concept in the residential living environment, staff should become knowledgeable about Universal Design. Staff, especially student staff working directly with students on the floor, need to be educated about Universal Design principles and implementation. Ideally, after they gain this knowledge, they will develop positive attitudes that promote sensitive and proactive responses to a built environment that meets all students' needs. The seven established Universal Design principles that the Center for Universal Design at North Carolina State University established can guide the design process and help in the evaluation of design work (Story, 1998). The principles are (a) equitable use, (b) flexibility of use, (c) simple and intuitive use, (d) perceptible information, (e) tolerance of error, (f) low physical error and (g) size and space for approach and use. By using these principles to train and teach staff, residence life personnel can begin to support the goals for offering this type of environment.

Students with disabilities, like other subpopulations on college campuses, may experience prejudice, discrimination, and even neglect in some cases when attempting to obtain an education in a postsecondary setting. Staff may get questions from students on a floor about a student's disability. The more that is offered to help staff recognize and embrace students as individuals, the more staff can offer in responding to fellow students. "Reduction of attitudinal barriers becomes more possible when physical barriers in the environment are removed" (Chang, Tremblay, & Dunbar, 2000, p. 154). If the residence hall has the physical indications of change to suit individual students on a floor, discussions may occur with staff and other students on why this change and this design has become a component of their living environment. The teachable moments or passive learning that staff as well as students experience may help them recognize the value and positive aspect of these changes. This type of intervention is critical to the overall success of this design approach.

Helping student staff develop a personal awareness of the environmental needs of students with disabilities can add to their overall understanding of design changes. Simulated programs that have students experience the use of a wheelchair, crutches, canes, darkened glasses, or other temporary disability can add significance to the understanding of accessibility needs for students with disabilities. Caution should be taken to advise students that because they are "pretending" to have a disability for an experience during training; they should not take on any superior knowledge in respect to another student's experience. Even though you might be in a wheelchair and gain some insight about the challenges that a student may face, the fact that you as an able-bodied student can get up and walk away from the chair separates you from the real day-to-day life of a person who utilizes a wheelchair. This factor requires discussion and may even be strengthened by inviting students with disabilities to assist with the actual student staff training.

The ultimate goal in involving staff with knowledge and attitudes that mirror the overall Universal Design concepts would be to have them engage in recognizing new and creative ways to improve the actual environment in which they work as resident assistants, graduate residents, or hall or complex coordinators. Staff members set examples for others students in the living environment and typically serve as role models. Ideally, students will gain a perspective in their residence that would extend to the rest of the campus, thus making the overall attitude towards the creation of a universal environment a common and expected part of life. "There will be direct benefits of increased convenience, accessibility, and sociability for [all] people… " (Stone, 1998, p. 12). The prevailing attitude the Universal Design philosophy would provide is that functional challenges are simply part of the norm on a college campus.

Housing and the Law

Discrimination has been a major barrier to access for persons with disabilities and others seeking to obtain adequate housing in society. In an effort to eliminate discrimination and to support the right of people with disabilities to live in the community of their choice, Congress enacted the Fair Housing Amendments Act of 1988. Congress added some special provisions to the Fair Housing Act to protect persons with disabilities and families with children (U.S. Commission on Civil Rights, 1994). It was intended to strengthen and enforce Fair Housing requirements and to extend civil rights protections for persons with disabilities. This Act covers most housing, but in some circumstances housing operated by private clubs, organizations, or institutions that limit occupancy to members can be exempt. Institutions of higher education should be responsive to the standards set by the Act.

The Act provides that modifications to a residential hall space for a student with a disability cannot be at the expense of the student. In addition, no institution can refuse to make reasonable accommodations in rules, policies, practices, or services if necessary for a student with a disability. For example, "no pets" policies must allow students with a visual impairments to keep a guide dog in their residence hall space. There are specific legal guidelines for accessibility features for new buildings after 1991 that have an elevator and four or more units. Following the architectural suggestions for Universal Design listed previously in this chapter will assist university personnel in complying with federal regulations.

Two other legislative statues that impact housing professionals in relation to students with disabilities are the ADA and Section 504 of the Rehabilitation Act of 1973. Federal and state statues constitute the relationship defining the rights and responsibilities of students and their institutions. Section 504 contains housing-specific requirements. Housing "shall be available in sufficient quantity and variety so that scope of handicapped students' choice of living accommodations is, as a whole, comparable to that of non-handicapped students" (84.45[a]). The ADA expands the rights granted under Section 504 and applies to both public and private institutions (Kalivoda & Higbee, 1989). Discrimination in public accommodations includes a failure to remove architectural or communication barriers unless the removable is not readily achievable. The criteria for evaluating whether the removal is readily achievable include the cost, the financial resources available to the facility, resources available to the entity and the type of operation. Primarily, the law provides for the goods, services, and accommodations to be provided in the most inclusive way to fit the needs of the individual (Winston & Anchors, 1993).

The Ideal Residence Hall

What would the type of hall described in this chapter look like? How would students with visual impairments feel when entering their assigned building, or how would students in wheelchairs make their way around their building? Let's look at an ideal day in the life of any new student entering University XYZ. Many of the features discussed go above the legal requirement for a postsecondaey educational institution; however, for residential living professionals who embrace Universal Design policies, the suggestions made are intended to provide some thought-provoking design ideas.

If all things were possible within a specific residence hall, a resident assistant (RA) would greet students on opening day at the side curb, complete with curb cuts appropriate for access and for allowing items to be unloaded onto hand cranks and carts for moving items to their rooms. A few volunteer student helpers would be available for the unloading process also. Students would have received a time in their assignment letter when they were asked to arrive so that traffic jams and chaos could be minimized. Upon getting things removed from their cars, they would go to the parking areas adjacent to the buildings and park, or to the parking decks where accessible buses would be driving back and forth to the specific residential halls. Refreshments, including water, would be available in the lobbics of all buildings.

The entry way to each building would be flat, with no steps leading up to the building, and the doors would be wide and electronically operated to open when a person approached. On opening day, the doors would be propped open for easy entry and the hallways and lobby would be clear of debris. Student staff would be available to answer questions, serve cold drinks, and walk parents and students around to specific service areas within the buildings.

All bathrooms would have wide entryways for access and at least one sink lower and one restroom stall large enough for a wheelchair or scooter, with grab bars installed at functional heights. At least one shower stall would be equipped with accessible shower controls, a shower chair or bench, and grab bars, and have plenty of space for maneuverability. All signage would also be in Braille and posted at accessible height. The alarm system would include both strobe and sound alarm. The water fountains, vending machines, and telephones throughout the building would be at different levels for access, at least two of each side by side to offer varying heights.

A student entering the building would be able to hear instructions on locations of specific services or see instructions through appropriate signage. The actual residence hall rooms would have outlets and light switches at varied heights. Closet rods in clothes areas would be adjustable and desks, chairs, and beds would be moveable and able to be raised, lowered, or removed if necessary. Lighting would be offered on a dimmer switch for students' specific needs in providing overhead light if beyond what is available via desk lamps. All doorknobs throughout the building would be lever handles facilitating use by people with mobility and dexterity impairments. Elevators would be available in all buildings of more than one story.

Materials that would improve acoustic considerations such as carpeting, furniture, and upholstery type, and curtains would be added to assist in absorbing noise throughout the facility. In addition, hallways would be wide and well lit for safety and ease of moving through the facility. All common areas would have open knee spaces under counters, sinks, and desks. RAs and other staff throughout the building would be representative of the overall population of students at the institution and barriers of exclusion would be removed to offer all students of all abilities the chance to get fully involved in residence hall life.

During the evening of the first day, students would be invited to participate in a welcome activity at which all staff would be present and access to the event would be available for all students, regardless of abilities. Interpreters would be present; assistive listening devices and enlarged print and Braille copies of any material handed out would be provided. The program would be planned for the different abilities of all students living in the hall.

Conclusion

Returning to the story of the mother who called regarding her daughter's accommodations, the overall barrier-free design of Universal Design would offer the residence life program buildings that normalize living space for all students. "Instead of creating 'special places' accommodating 'special' individuals" (Stone, 1998, p. 16), residence halls would be built or renovated for students with varying needs. This concept makes common sense and helps provide residential communities that are conducive to inclusion. The simple and practical mode of building spaces that are light, spacious, minimally cluttered, and attractive for students does not need to result in extra cost or create "separateness" for a student with a disability who is entering the institution. Utilizing Universal Design principles also eliminates the possible embarrassment of the professional who is unprepared to respond in a personal and regarding way to a parent or student asking about the facilities. Universal Design promises to remove the "stigmatizing burden none of us need to carry" (Stone, 1998, p. 14).

References

Americans with Disabilities Act of 1990, 42 U.S.C.A. § 12101 et seq. (West 1993).

Blamires, M. (1999). Universal Design for Learning: Re-establishing differentiation as part of the inclusion agenda? *Support for Learning, 14*(4), 158-163.

Chang, B.V., Tremblay, K. R., & Dunbar, B. H. (2000). An experiential approach to teaching Universal Design. *Education, 121*(1), 153-158.

Denny, G. S., & Carson, E. K. (1994). *Perceptions of campus climate for students with disabilities.* Fayetteville: Arkansas University (ERIC Document Reproduction Service No. ED380929)

Fair Housing Act Amendments of 1998, 42 U.S.C. § 3601 *et seq.*

Fair Housing and Equal Opportunity. (2001, July 6) *U.S. Department of Housing and Urban Development* [Online]. Available: http://www.hud.gov/fhe/fheact.html.

Kalivoda, K. S., & Higbee, J. L. (1989). Students with disabilities in higher education: Redefining access. *Journal of Educational Opportunity, 4* (1) 14-21.

Lehmann, J. P., Davies, T. G., & Laurin, K. M. (2000). Listening to student voices about postsecondary education. *Teaching Exceptional Children, 32* (5), 60-65.

Lusher, R. H., & Mace, R. I. (1989). Design for physical and mental disabilities. In J. A. Wilkes & R. T. Packard (Eds.), *Encyclopedia of architecture* (pp. 748-763). New York: John Wiley & Sons.

Mace, R. (1990). *Definitions: Accessible, adaptable, and Universal Design.* Raleigh: North Carolina State University, Center for Universal Design. Retrieved June 30, 2002, from http://www.design.ncsu.edu/cud/pubs/center/fact_sheets/housdef.htm

McGuinness, K. (1997). Beyond the basics. *American School & University, 69*(11), 39-41.

Ratzka, A. (1994, June). *Cost-benefits of universal building design.* Paper presented at the International Congress on Accessibility, Rio de Janeiro, Brazil.

Rydeen, J. E. (1999). Universal Design. *American School & University, 71*(9), 56-59.

Section 504, Rehabilitation Act of 1973, 29 U.S.C. § 794 as amended (1973).

Stone, K. (1998). Practical, beautiful, humane. *Inside MS, 16*(3), 12-17.

Story, M. F. (1998). Maximizing usability: The principles of Universal Design. *Assistive Technology, 10* (1), 4-12.

Tinto, V. (1987). *Leaving college: Rethinking the causes and cures of student attrition.* Chicago: University of Chicago Press.

U.S. Commission on Civil Rights. (1994). *The Fair Housing Amendments Act of 1988: The enforcement report.* Washington, DC: Author.

Vander Patton, J. J. (1993). Residence hall students' attitudes toward resident assistants with learning disabilities. *Journal of Postsecondary Education and Disability, 10*(2), 21-2.

Winston, R. B., Anchors, S., & Associates. (1993). *Student housing and residential life.* San Francisco: Jossey-Bass.

CHAPTER 22

Disability Services as a Resource: Advancing Universal Design

Karen S. Kalivoda and Margaret C. Totty
The University of Georgia

Abstract
This chapter is reprinted verbatim from Curriculum Transformation and Disability: Implementing Universal Design in Higher Education, and was originally published in 2003. Many institutions of higher education have established disability services offices to assist in implementing the basic regulations of the Americans with Disabilities Act (ADA; 1990). This chapter offers a brief overview of the mission of these offices and describes some common ways disability services offices can assist both students with disabilities and the campus community. Suggestions are proposed on how to utilize the support available from these standard service delivery systems and at the same time advance the concept of Universal Design.

The Americans with Disabilities Act (ADA; 1990) mandates that institutions of higher education provide equal educational opportunity to students with disabilities. Higher education administrators and student development professionals are faced with difficult decisions regarding how to provide the most efficient and cost-effective access throughout the institution. The law requires a particular person to be assigned to coordinate ADA compliance for the institution, but does not require a specific office to serve students with disabilities. However, most colleges and universities have chosen to establish offices to address specific disability concerns of students (Schuck & Kroeger, 1993).

The purpose of this chapter is to offer practical information for institutions, both public and private, small and large, to assist in implementing the ADA's basic regulations. The authors will offer a brief overview of the mission of disability services offices, describe common assistance available from disability services offices to both students with disabilities and the college or university community, and suggest how to implement Universal Design within the campus community.

Establishment of Disability Service Offices

As early as 30 years ago, institutions were challenged to set up offices through which "all assistance and activities [for students with disabilities] would be channeled" (Pinder, 1979, p. 8). Many institutions established new positions to coordinate equal access needs for students with disabilities and others assigned these extra responsibilities to an existing position such as the dean of students. Program design for disability services programs, whether comprehensive or specific, varies widely just as size and characteristics of institutions vary. With the establishment in 1977 of the Association on Handicapped Student

Service Programs in Postsecondary Education, now named the Association on Higher Education and Disability (AHEAD), disability services providers gained support on how to provide services to individuals with disabilities pursuing postsecondary education. AHEAD is an international organization of professionals with a mission to increase full participation of persons with disabilities in higher education. The growth in the AHEAD membership, from 36 charter members in 1977 to 2,200 in 2001, reflects the growth in disability services offices throughout the nation (J. Jarrow, personal communication, August 24, 2001).

These offices share a common goal of assisting institutions in fulfilling their responsibility to provide equal access to qualified students with disabilities (Kalivoda & Higbee, 1989). The term equal access means equal availability of all programs and freedom of participation for all students with disabilities. Equal access does not guarantee equal outcomes nor does it promote favoritism of one group over another or result in the lowering of academic standards.

Documentation of Disability

Federal statutes require that institutions of higher education provide appropriate accommodations and modifications for students with disabilities. Institutions are not required to provide evaluative testing to establish the presence of a disability (U.S. Department of Education, 1998). However, some institutions do have on-site evaluators that diagnose learning disabilities (LD), attention deficit hyperactivity disorders (ADHD), and psychological disorders. It is a student's responsibility to present current and adequate documentation of a disability. This procedure can be confusing to students who enter college from public secondary special education programs. Public school systems may conduct evaluations as part of students' individual plans for disability-related educational services (Silver, 1992). Should the most recent documentation from a health professional be outdated, students may be required to seek, at their own expense, more current documentation. Many institutions require diagnostic evaluations no more than three years old. Others are more flexible as long as the documentation specifically states the diagnosis and adequately addresses current level of functioning and necessary accommodations. As long as it is current, disability documentation certified by a qualified health professional should not be questioned by an institution. The institution does have the authority, however, to determine the appropriate accommodations that they should provide (Jarrow, 1997).

Health related conditions, such as lupus, cystic fibrosis, Crohn's disease, and multiple sclerosis may simply require verification from the student's health care provider. Should the condition wax and wane, the disability service representative may require frequent updates to verify flare ups that functionally limit the student. Students with cognitive deficits due to an acquired brain injury are usually asked to provide the results of neuropsychological testing. A thorough neuropsychological evaluation will provide ample information to determine necessary and appropriate accommodations for the student.

There is considerable controversy over the documentation requirements for ADHD and LD (Zirkel, 2000). AHEAD suggests guidelines to assist institutions in establishing the appropriate criteria and to encourage a general sense of uniformity in documentation requirements across the nation. Most institutions of higher education will require students to provide a recent evaluation conducted by a qualified health professional experienced in the diagnosis and treatment of ADHD and LD. Offering the student a list of qualified evaluators may facilitate prompt implementation of support services. The evaluation should address the specific academic and support service needs of the student. This information is rarely included in an evaluation report unless specifically requested from the referral source. It is recommended that a set of questions regarding the academic needs of the student be sent to the evaluator with each referral.

Program Standards

Dukes (2001) conducted research with 1000 postsecondary professionals at disability services offices in North America to determine which service components they deemed essential to ensure equal educational access for students with disabilities. Nine general categories of service delivery with 27 standards were identified as essential regardless of type of institution, funding source, location, or admissions policy. The AHEAD membership recently approved the program standards for disability services offices in higher education and they are briefly described below (Shaw & Dukes, 2001).

The first category consists of consultation, collaboration, and awareness. It includes advocating for students with disabilities and ensuring their adequate representation on campus committees. Disability personnel may find that they provide the only voices that speak to the needs of this population on campus. This makes the development of good working relationships with key departments around campus critical to the enhancement of equal opportunity. Providing academic departments with disability awareness training and information about disabilities and resources available to assist them can decrease attitudinal barriers that result in stereotyping and discrimination toward people with disabilities.

The second category, information dissemination, promotes equal access by informing the campus community about the availability of services for students with disabilities. To promote equal access to the campus community, it is important that disability services offices coordinate and provide auxiliary aids such as alternative print, interpreter services, and adaptive technology. Auxiliary aids, not limited to the college classroom, should be provided at all institution-sponsored activities and programs (Kalivoda & Higbee, 1994).

Faculty and staff awareness, the third category, involves consultation with faculty, staff, and administrators regarding appropriate academic accommodations for students with disabilities. Faculty are chiefly responsible for providing academic adjustments for students with disabilities in their classes. Instructors are not asked to lower academic standards or to provide adjustments that are excessive, but they are expected to make reasonable accommodations. If academic adjustments are not provided by faculty, students with disabilities will be at an academic disadvantage.

Academic adjustments, the fourth standard, establishes the responsibility of determining the appropriate academic adjustments with the disability services office. This is based on student interviews, analysis of appropriate documentation, consultation with health professionals, and legal guidelines.

Disability services offices are also encouraged to be actively involved in instructional interventions, the fifth category. Shaw and Dukes (2001) state that this involves encouraging institutions to provide "instruction in learning strategies (e.g., attention and memory strategies, planning, self-monitoring, time management, organization, problem-solving)" (p.85). Most institutions have an academic assistance program or learning center where students can either take classes or attend workshops on learning strategies or work one-on-one with a counselor for coaching. Hand-in-hand with this category, the sixth is counseling and advocacy, through which disability specialists help their students to learn how to advocate for themselves.

The seventh category addresses the importance of developing policies and procedures. Written policies and procedures may cover issues such as student rights and responsibilities, institutional rights and responsibilities, confidentiality, formal complaint guidelines, and the determination of reasonable accommodations (Shaw & Dukes, 2000). Jarrow (1997) states that the development of written policies and procedures is critical to "demonstrating a good faith effort on the part of the institution to meet its responsibilities to persons with disabilities in an equitable and consistent manner" (p. 7).

Following up on the importance of having an effective program, the eighth category involves program development and evaluation. Frequent evaluations to obtain student feedback on satisfaction with services will help in identifying ways to improve the program. Schuck and Kroeger (1993) emphasize the importance of a comprehensive evaluation plan that includes data on students served to justify the need for fiscal resources. The final category of standards involves the training and professional development of disability services personnel.

Support Services

To guarantee students with disabilities equal access to higher education, many institutions have or are establishing support services that uphold the nine categories of AHEAD program standards. Marion & Iovacchini (1983) assert that basic services to assure program accessibility were provided by most colleges and universities in the early 1980s. Necessary accommodations and services will vary from student to student and across institutions. The following, however, are common services available to students through disability support offices: (a) weekly meetings with a counselor or disability specialist to maintain support, monitor academic progress, and provide an early warning system so that the student receives additional services as needed; (b) time extensions on tests and assignments when appropriate; (c) adjustment and restructuring of class assignments as individually warranted; (d) test taking in a separate and quiet location to reduce distractions commonly associated with the classroom environment; (e) note takers in the classroom to supplement the student's notes; (f) the provision of assistive listening systems; (g) document conversion (e.g., from print to Braille) services; (h) sign language interpreters; (i) real-time captioning; and (j) assistive technology, which will be discussed in the final section of this book.

Additional services provided are often above and beyond legal requirements and are made available as resource allocations permit. Programs that have acquired ample financial support from the institution, federal grants, or private development activities, may develop exemplary programs and services for students with disabilities. These services constitute "best practices" in disability services offices and are offered in efforts to enrich the lives of students with disabilities who seek the goal of higher education (Shaw & Dukes, 2001). Services may include the following: (a) student support groups; (b) priority registration to ease initial frustration and tension and to enable the student to select classes at times of optimal concentration or to allow for scheduling of regular medical appointments; (c) curriculum counseling regarding course selection and scheduling; (d) written contracts to assist the student in achieving academic or personal goals; (e) academic support groups for review and discussion of barriers encountered on a college campus; (f) orientation to classrooms, buildings, and the campus, and (g) coaching to help students stay focused on specific goals, and overcome disability-related challenges (e.g., organization, prioritization, follow-through).

Universal Design

In an ideal world, Universal Design would provide access to all people in advance rather than after the fact. Aune (2000) states, "In universal design, environments and activities are designed in such a way that they are accessible to anyone, regardless of the person's functional limitations" (p.57). The following case study is offered to describe the application of Universal Design to a college setting.

Ideal Case Scenario

Caroline is a sociology major at a large public university. She is blind and obtains most of her texts and other reading assignments electronically. All her texts are available on e-text and her instructors use accessible Web designed course materials. Caroline scans last minute reading assignments handed out in class at various computer labs on campus. She has a computer and scanner in her residence hall room but she often prefers to use the computer lab with her peers. Once the material is scanned and saved onto disk, Caroline uses a computer workstation at the sociology computer lab that is equipped with speech output software. This allows her to listen to the printed material independently at her preferred time and pace.

Caroline independently navigates around campus. All crosswalks have audible signals, drivers announce each bus stop, and all facilities have signs in raised characters and Braille. Campus lectures and programming sponsored by campus activities have handouts prepared in Braille to provide Caroline the opportunity to fully participate along with her peers. The university offers audible display for all visually oriented communication (e.g., maps, computer terminals, posters, newspapers, fliers, overheads), which makes Caroline feel welcome and included in university-sponsored events.

Shared Responsibility for Equal Access

In this scenario, there is little need for disability services offices. Unfortunately, Universal Design is still an aspiration and disability services offices are continually relied upon to coordinate and provide routine equal access requests. Establishing separate administrative units to assist students with disabilities helps meet legal requirements of equal access, but may also enable others to abdicate responsibility for interacting with students who have disabilities and providing equal access. Pinder (1979) cautions institutions about relying excessively on disability support offices:

> Special, separate offices such as these also tend to reaffirm the old standards of segregation on the campus because faculty, students, and administrators are simply not used to routinely dealing with disabled students--and it is much easier to delegate this responsibility to a special office ... However, it is natural for people to be reluctant in dealing with new and different things. The separate, special bureaucratic units provide anyone looking for such avoidance with the perfect method of dealing with disabled students while not having to deal personally with them. (p. 9)

Hall and Belch (2000) concur that these special offices can serve a well-needed role of easing students into the college or university and helping them feel that they matter, but they also have to consider the unintended consequences, "... special programs and centers also relieve staff who are not located in those centers from acting on their responsibility to understand and address the diverse needs of under represented groups" (p. 13).

This dilemma demands that disability service professionals increase education about the responsibility of each faculty and administrative unit in providing equal access. There are several steps that administrators, faculty, and staff members can take to reduce or eliminate potential blocks to equal access. The top administration should publish and disseminate a policy statement regarding the legal mandate to provide accommodations. The policy statement should clearly state that the administration encourages and supports accommodations for students with disabilities and that the responsibility for providing access to all programs and activities resides with each department. For example, the administration could mail out a brochure to all faculty and staff, accompanied by a letter from the president's office. In addition, the institution might sponsor professional development workshops to educate faculty and staff regarding how to best meet the needs of students who have disabilities. Prior to scheduling such workshops, it would be helpful to survey potential attendees regarding their knowledge of legal and educational issues. This will enable workshop facilitators to prepare to address pertinent questions or dilemmas from workshop participants. Staff and faculty may also provide scenarios for role plays or small group discussion that would offer practical solutions to common problems.

Obstacles to Universal Design

The true concept of Universal Design is to create at the onset an educational environment to meet all learners' needs. In reality, however, many institutions are firmly established and have facilities and programs that do not meet this ideal. Practical suggestions for architectural and program access needs of students who have disabilities are addressed below.

Architectural Inaccessibility

Many older institutions have facilities that were constructed before the implementation of federal and state requirements for architectural accessibility. The ADA does not require the installation of elevators in all existing facilities; therefore, access to older structures may be limited to the main floor via a lift or ramp. Programs or departments located on inaccessible floors must find alternative methods of providing accessibility. The law requires what is termed "programmatic access" (Office of the Attorney General, 1991). This means that the program may be moved or the information requested (e.g., financial aid forms, admissions applications) may be brought downstairs or sent directly to the student. Equitable service needs to be provided for students with disabilities; this may require extra time and patience from program staff. Suggestions that may assist in providing programmatic access for programs and services located in facilities that are architecturally inaccessible are listed below (Kalivoda & Higbee, 1994):

1. Advertise in all publications and announcements (e.g., campus newspaper, newsletters) that programmatic access is guaranteed for people with limited mobility. Provide the name of a contact person and telephone number for obtaining information about access. A general access statement communicates to people with disabilities that they are welcome to participate in the program. The statement may read "Alternative access will be arranged for people with limited mobility. Call (person or office) by (date) for specific requests."

2. Equip the accessible floor with a campus phone for students to use to call offices located on inaccessible floors. Assure that existing and newly installed phones are at the appropriate height (48" forward approach, 54" side approach). Include the location of the phone on the building directory. Post phone numbers of offices located on inaccessible floors both on the building directory and next to the telephone.

3. Provide accessible locations for offices and services that meet important student needs and require personal rather than mail or telephone contact. Examples include counseling, career planning and placement, academic advising, multicultural affairs, language laboratories, tutorial services and disability services.

4. Provide internal and external signs to direct people where to go to obtain services or get the information they need. Buildings where there is access to at least one floor must provide accessibility information about the program on existing building directories. Buildings without a directory should request that one be installed in order to comply with the ADA. Buildings with no access should provide outside signs directing people either to an outside phone line or to an accessible building where they can obtain the information they need. The phone line should automatically ring in a designated office in the inaccessible building. A representative from that building would then meet the person

at an accessible location.

5. Request a multi-use conference room to be made available on the first floor of any building that is otherwise inaccessible. If this is not possible, network with offices on the first floor of the building and with offices in accessible buildings in the vicinity to arrange for an accessible and private meeting room.

6. Forward requests for modest renovation projects (e.g., signs, curb cuts, door handles, grab bars) to the institution's disability resource office or physical plant.

7. Relocate programs and events that are scheduled in buildings that are architecturally inaccessible.

8. Provide access to all departmental information and resources, e.g., books, bulletin board notices and information on the internet or Web sites. This may entail sending a catalogue of resources to patrons.

9. Communicate to faculty and staff in each department their responsibility to provide equal access to all people, even if it poses an inconvenience. (pp. 135-136)

Providing Program Access

Removing architectural barriers is of great importance, but it is only one of the commonly recognized barriers to access for students with disabilities. The removal of concrete and obvious physical barriers only affects a small subgroup of the disability population. Commonly overlooked obstacles that impact students with a wide variety of disabilities are programmatic access barriers. Although these are critical to ensuring equal access, they are often overlooked because they are not the easiest to implement (Jarrow, 1993). The ADA requires us to move beyond the obvious needs of students with mobility impairments and to address the highly individualized needs of the entire population of students with disabilities (Office of the Attorney General, 1991).

Kalivoda and Higbee (1994) provide suggestions that may help in making programs accessible:

1. Include a general access statement in all publications and announcements. This communicates to people with disabilities that they are welcome. The statement may read "Access provided for people with disabilities. Call *(person or office)* by *(date)* for specific requests."

2. Offer printed material in alternate forms. Taped versions, large print and Braille copies make visually oriented material available to people with limited vision. Be aware of resources for Braille printers in the community or geographic area.

3. Communicate the availability of Assistive Listening Devices (ALD) for people attending programs. One common ALD, the FM System, is a small transmitter that amplifies the speech of the speaker while eliminating background noise. An FM system can be purchased for under $1000. Several can be made available for check out through a centralized campus audiovisual service.

4. Advertise that a sign language interpreter is available upon request. This offers people who are deaf equal access to programs. Major campus-wide events should recognize the need for an interpreter and arrangements should be made well in advance. The presence of an interpreter also enhances awareness and acceptance of students with disabilities.

Interpreters can be scheduled through the institution's resource office if one exists, or assistance in locating a qualified free lance interpreter is available through each state's Interpreter Referral Service.

5. Relocate programs that are architecturally inaccessible. Develop a close working relationship with the office on campus that assists in space allocation. Identify one of the most modern and convenient buildings on campus for a possible meeting site. Assure that accessible parking spaces are readily available.

6. Secure accessible transportation for programs that are reserving university vehicles. Contact the campus department responsible for transportation or the off-campus contractor to request a lift equipped van or bus. (pp.134-135)

These suggestions are not limited to academics. Noninstructional activities are a vital aspect of college life and critical to the development of the student as a well-rounded individual; therefore, students with disabilities should be incorporated into programming available for the rest of the student body. Nutter and Ringgenberg (1993) emphasize the importance of the above activities for student affairs units to successfully invite, involve, and retain students with disabilities.

Suggestions to Enhance Learning

Functioning successfully at an educational institution can be difficult for students who have disabilities that impact learning, organization, and social interaction. Students with head injuries, for instance, may have problems with communication, memory, comprehension (especially learning new information), organization, decision making, and flexibility. This can affect registration, study skills, meeting class and administrative deadlines, and establishing relationships with faculty, staff, and other students. The following strategies are offered to assist faculty, counselors, advisors and student development professionals:

1. Try to learn more about the needs of students who have disabilities. In-service workshops conducted by campus and community disability professionals can enlighten both you and your staff.

2. Communicate your willingness to work with students' different learning and organizational needs. Express your support both in writing (e.g., on a course syllabus or in a brochure) and orally. Allow students to identify themselves as having a disability in writing rather than having to say it in the presence of their peers.

3. Attend to a student's concerns carefully and repeat back your understanding of the student's situation. When approached with a student problem, choose a quiet place to meet. Try to work through some alternatives and consequences in a systematic way. Use your expertise to make suggestions for solutions.

4. Meet with students you are instructing, counseling, or advising within the first two weeks of the academic term to determine necessary accommodations.

5. Give students step-by-step written information about your program or policy and allow an opportunity for questions or clarification of procedures.

6. Learn what your campus offers for students with disabilities. Acquaint yourself with other campus resources and key people to contact so that you can offer clear and specific referrals. It is helpful to supply the name of a contact person and location of the office or

department and phone number, so that the student can schedule an appointment.

7. Post notices announcing deadlines for advisement, registration, or various student activities in strategic places well before the deadline, but also communicate these deadlines to all students via e-mail if possible.

8. Be flexible with students who might need alternative avenues for meeting class requirements. For example, students with disabilities such as visual impairments, attention deficit hyperactivity disorders, learning disabilities, acquired brain injuries, or psychological disorders might need to have their tests provided on disk so that the printed material can be converted into an accessible form such as large print, Braille, digital format, or audiotape.

8. Put together a mediation program using someone who understands disability access issues and is interested in working out amicable solutions. Students who have disabilities that affect communication, flexibility, and organization sometimes encounter difficulties with other students in group activities due to their disorganization and poor communication skills.

9. Keep in mind that although students with disabilities are subject to the same standards as any other college student, they may need to take an alternative route to achieve those standards.

Conclusion

This chapter provides a brief overview of the mission of disability services offices, describes typical ways these offices assist students with disabilities and the campus community, and proposes suggestions on how to advance the concept of Universal Design. Universal Design considers the needs of all learners prior to the beginning of classes rather than trying to accommodate the needs of students on a case-by-case basis when requested. Regrettably, Universal Design is still an ideal. Until it becomes reality, institutions must assure that students with disabilities are provided equal educational opportunity. That is why colleges and universities have established separate administrative units to ensure that legal requirements of equal access are met.

This chapter identifies and describes common standards for disability services offices and offers practical information for faculty and administrators in the hope that they will step up and meet the challenge to enhance learning for students with disabilities. The information this chapter provides can help alleviate common concerns and questions about how to provide equal access to all programs and activities. In the meantime, both students with disabilities and their nondisabled peers will benefit from an ongoing discussion about Universal Design at institutions of higher education. Perhaps in the not too distant future, college and university representatives will assume the responsibility for meeting the needs of each individual learner rather than relying on disability services offices to accommodate students with disabilities.

References

Americans with Disabilities Act of 1990, 42 U.S.C.A. § 12101 *et seq.* (West 1993).

Aune, B. (2000). Career and academic advising. In H. A. Belch (Ed.), *Serving students with disabilities* (New Directions for Student Services, no. 91, pp. 55-67). San Francisco:

Jossey-Bass.

Dukes, L. M. (2001). The process: Development of AHEAD program standards. *Journal of Postsecondary Education and Disability, 14*(2), 62-80.

Hall, L. M., & Belch, H. A. (2000). Setting the context: Reconsidering the principals of full participation and meaningful access for students with disabilities. In H. A. Belch (Ed.), *Serving students with disabilities.* (New Directions for Student Services, no. 91, pp. 5-17). San Francisco: Jossey-Bass.

Henderson, C. (1999). *College freshmen with disabilities.* Washington, DC: American Council on Education.

Jarrow, J. E. (1993). Beyond ramps: New ways of viewing access. In S. Kroeger & J. Schuck (Eds.), *Responding to disability issues in student affairs.* (New Directions for Student Services, no. 64, pp. 5-16). San Francisco: Jossey-Bass.

Jarrow, J. E. (1997). *Higher education and the ADA: Issues and perspectives.* Columbus, OH: Disability Access Information & Support.

Jaschik, S. (1993, February). Backed by 1990 law, people with disabilities press demands on colleges. *The Chronicle of Higher Education, 39*(22), A 26.

Kalivoda, K. S., & Higbee, J. L. (1989). Students with disabilities in higher education: Redefining access. *Journal of Educational Opportunity, 4*(1), 14-21.

Kalivoda, K. S., & Higbee, J. L. (1994). Implementing the Americans with Disabilities Act. *Journal of Humanistic Education and Development, 32*(3), 133-137.

Marion, P. B., & Iovacchini , E.V. (1983) Services for handicapped students in higher education: An analysis of national trends. *Journal of College Student Personnel, 24*(2), 131-138.

Nutter, K. J., & Riggenberg, L. J. (1993). Creating positive outcomes for students with disabilities. In S. Kroeger & J. Schuck (Eds.), *Responding to disability issues in student affairs.* (New Directions for Student Services, no. 64, pp. 45-58). San Francisco: Jossey-Bass.

Office of the Attorney General, Department of Justice (1991, July). Non-discrimination on the basis of disability in state and local government services; Final rule. *Federal Register,* 28 CFR Part 35.

Pinder, P. (1979). Obligation of the disabled student: Reasonable self-help. In M. R. Redden (Ed.), *Assuring access for the handicapped.* (New Directions for Higher Education, no. 25, pp. 1-10). San Francisco: Jossey-Bass.

Section 504, Rehabilitation Act of 1973, 29 U.S.C. § 794 as amended (1973).

Schuck, J., & Kroeger S. (1993). Essential elements in effective service delivery. In S. Kroeger & J. Schuck (Eds.), *Responding to disability issues in student affairs.* (New Directions for Student Services, no. 64, pp. 45-58). San Francisco: Jossey-Bass.

Shaw, S. F., & Dukes, L. L. (2001). Program standards for disability services in higher education. *Journal of Postsecondary Education and Disability, 14*(2), 81-90.

Silver, L. B. (1992). *Attention deficit hyperactivity disorder: A clinical guide to diagnosis and treatment.* Washington, DC: American Psychiatric Press.

U.S. Department of Education, Office for Civil Rights. (1998). *Auxiliary aids and services for postsecondary students with disabilities: Higher education's obligations under section 504 and Title II of the ADA.* Retrieved June 22, 2002, from www.ed.gov/offices/OCR/docs/auxaids.html

Zirkel P. A. (2000) Sorting out which students have learning disabilities. *The Chronicle of HigherEducation, 47*(15), B15.

CHAPTER 23

Ensuring Smooth Transitions: A Collaborative Endeavor for Career Services

Jeanne L. Higbee and Emily Goff
University of Minnesota

Karen S. Kalivoda, Margaret C. Totty, Janice Davis Barham, and Christopher D. Bell
The University of Georgia

Abstract

Based on theoretical work by Aune (2000) and others, this chapter presents a model for collaboration between a university's Disability Resource Center and Career Center to ensure that appropriate career services are provided for students with disabilities. Results of a brief online interview with students approaching degree completion indicate that services provided by the Career Center were used and considered helpful.

Clearly it should be the goal of any student affairs unit to provide services that are accessible to and promote the inclusion and development of *all* students at the institution. Unfortunately, some of the attitudes portrayed by a counselor in the film *The Music Within* (Donowho, Sawalich, & Vitolo, 2007) persist in higher education and the world of work today. The counselor believed that the use of GI Bill funding to pay the postsecondary education expenses of veteran Richard Pimentel, who experienced a hearing loss as the direct result of his service in Vietnam, was a waste of money because he assumed that Pimentel would never join the work force anyway. In *Making Good on the Promise: Student Affairs Professionals With Disabilities* (Higbee & Mitchell, in press), the first-person accounts of student affairs professionals with disabilities document the extent to which assumptions and stereotypes regarding both students and colleagues continue to limit options for people with disabilities. For example, when a student affairs unit questions whether it is appropriate to hire a professional colleague with a hearing impairment due to stereotyped assumptions about the candidate's ability to communicate with students, what attitudes might administrators and staff members also be conveying to students or to employment recruiters coming to campus? Thus, although from a Universal Design (UD) perspective the preferred approach is to ensure that all programs and services are created and implemented to include all students, until that goal becomes a reality it may still be helpful to provide targeted programs and resources for students with disabilities. Meanwhile, professional development activities in student affairs must include a focus on Universal Design so that eventually the need for additional services for students with disabilities becomes obsolete.

This chapter reports feedback from online interviews conducted with 15 students who were close to completing their degree programs at The University of Georgia (UGA), where two student affairs units, the Disability Resource Center (DRC; Mann, 2007) and Career Center, have chosen to collaborate to supplement traditional services with specific programs for students with disabilities. These programs include workshops, career fairs, and joint meetings regarding choosing a major, career options, resumé review, and mock interviews. The DRC provides career counseling as it pertains to students' abilities and has a state-of-the-art assistive technology lab that assists students in preparing resumés and other job-related correspondence. The DRC also works with students' vocational rehabilitation counselors, and arranges interviews with employers such as the Federal Employment of People with Disabilities. The offices of the DRC and the Career Center are located in the same building, allowing for easier collaboration between staff members.

Responding to Diversity: A Paradigm Shift in Career Development

The face of postsecondary education is changing to include students with a wider variety of backgrounds than ever before (Horn, Nevill, & Griffin, 2006; Horn, Peter, Rooney, & Malizio, 2002; KewalRamani, Gilbertson, Fox, & Provasnik, 2007; Kipp, Price, & Wohlford, 2002; Snyder, Dillow, & Hoffman, 2007; Zhang & Chan, 2007). As discussed elsewhere in this book, students with disabilities are one of the groups enrolling in postsecondary education in ever-increasing numbers (Henderson, 1988, 1999; Hitchings, Horvath, Luzzo, Ristow, & Retish, 1998; Horn, Nevill, & Griffin). However, they—along with their peers from other underrepresented cultural groups—tend to underutilize student support services such as those offered at career centers or by career counselors (Flores & Heppner, 2002; Friehe, Aune, & Leuenberger, 1996). Additionally, a study by Hitchings et. al. found that students with disabilities are not only underutilizing career services at their institutions, but also have basic career education needs that are not being met when compared to their peers without disabilities.

Why do students with disabilities underutilize career service offerings? Friehe, Aune, and Leuenberger (1996) found that a lack of knowledge of the services offered by career centers and a perception that they did not need or would not benefit from these services were two factors that kept students with disabilities away. A a study done by Aune and Kroeger (1997) found that students experiencing negative attitudes or behaviors at one campus office were likely to assume that similar attitudes and behaviors would also be encountered at the career center, and this assumption caused some students to avoid seeking services. Flores and Heppner (2002) and Aune (2000) asserted that in addition to these barriers, negative attitudes toward diversity held by faculty and staff are also damaging. They noted that one possible reason that students from diverse backgrounds do not seek career services on their campuses is that some career counselors continue to use an approach "which disregards cultural variability and the unique strengths various cultural backgrounds bring to the career planning process" (Flores & Heppner, 182). As proposed by Stebleton (2007), theory and research as applied to practice in career development must be "inclusive, holistic, and multicultural" (p. 297) and must consider contextual factors. Stebleton and others (Blustein, 2001; Savickas, 1993) have encouraged "a paradigm shift from an emphasis on scores to stories" (Stebleton & Peterson, 2007, p. 9) through the use of narrative and other contextually-based approaches to career development. This type of paradigm shift is needed in order for career centers to better serve all students and to offer inclusive services that could be more approachable for students with disabilities. As indicated in Chapter 30, students with disabilities are often hesitant to self-disclose. Collaboration with campus disability services personnel can assist career counselors in understanding disability-related contexts and encouraging students to share their stories.

Career Services Delivery Models and Universal Design

There are a variety models for providing career services to postsecondary students with disabilities; the model that an institution implements can have a profound impact on the accessibility of those services to students. Aune (2000) described four possible models of career service delivery. The first—and the most common model—is one in which career services and disability services offices operate completely independently without any formal collaboration between the offices. In this model, the onus is placed squarely on the student to gain access to services and the career counselors may or may not have any awareness of the unique issues faced by students with disabilities. The second model is one in which the disability services office provides all academic and career advising and planning for students with disabilities. In this model, the counselors would certainly have a greater understanding of disability issues. However, the student would be effectively segregated from other students at the institution who are receiving the same services at an institution-wide career center. Additionally, as Rabby and Croft (1991) noted, this model could disadvantage these students because few disability service centers would have as many resources for placement and career counseling as a campus office dedicated exclusively to career issues.

A third option explained by Aune (2000) is for counseling and career services to work in close collaboration with the disability services office. In this model, both offices are able to advise in their areas of expertise and collaborate to provide interoffice staff training and support. Additionally, "this approach has the advantage of further integrating students with disabilities into the life of the campus community at the same time that they benefit from the expertise offered by both disability services and career advising" (p. 57).

Aune (2000) described a fourth model as an ideal situation in which collaboration between offices would be so integrated and well adapted that students with disabilities would not require additional services. This is described as the application of Universal Design to career services. In this model, the needs of all students are taken into account so that "environments and activities are designed in such a way that they are accessible to everyone, regardless of the person's functional limitations" (p. 57). This approach reflects the importance of respecting the individuality of all students, which has also been identified as an important factor in providing effective career services and counseling to students from other traditionally-underrepresented populations (Flores & Heppner, 2002). It is important to note that the practice of considering the needs of all students creates a more welcoming environment for everyone and benefits all students (Higbee, Chung, & Hsu, 2004). In this model, all students would feel comfortable and welcome in the career center and have access to high quality career counseling that would be individualized for their specific needs.

Findings

In order to gauge the reactions of students who received services from a Disability Resource Center that has forged a close collaboration with the institution's Career Center, anonymous interviews were conducted in April and May, 2007. Students were not asked demographic questions, including regarding the nature of their disability, nor were they asked to specify whether they were completing a baccalaureate or advanced degree.

Plans for the Future

Of the 15 students with disabilities who participated in the open-ended online interviews, 5 planned to graduate in May 2007; 1 in August, 2007; 5 in December, 2007; 3 in May 2008; and 4 in December, 2009, so the students were in varying stages of their preparation for "life after graduation." Three were "unsure" about their plans for after graduation; but of those three, one was "thinking about doing Teach for America or attending law school" and another "would like to travel Europe for a year and this is a real possibility." Eight of the respondents indicated that they were seeking employment, providing responses like "move to Atlanta and get a job" or "get an American dream job—with health insurance—having earned my Ed. S." or "probably move to Brazil and get a job with whatever company wants to hire me." Of these eight, four were specific about their career paths, intending to "interview for faculty positions" or "find work as a database administrator or network analyst" or "teach high school biology" or "seek social work employment in Iowa." Four of the 15 participants indicated that they would pursue further education in graduate or professional school (e.g., law, pharmacy).

Most of the responses to "How has your university experience shaped your future plans?" were very positive:

> "Leadership and community service through Kappa Alpha Order Fraternity, Inter-Fraternity Council (IFC), UGA Visitors Center, etc."

> "I got an education."

> "It has been a blast as an alternative dyslexic middle aged woman. I love the culture, sports, and intellectual stimulation in the university community."

> "The University has focused my efforts and made me want to ask for more and look for something better than just a 9 to 5 job."

> "The university has made my plans possible."

"My plans have been shaped in so many ways. Here are just a few: (a) career path, (b) son's education, (c) service to my community, (d) Esperanto language acquisition."

"I received an excellent MSW education."

"It has provided me with a quality education that has influenced my career plans and gotten me into graduate school."

"Enabled me to prepare for the future"

"It has given me the opportunity to find out more about what I am interested in."

One student simply stated "indispensable," while another wrote,

> It has opened my eyes to new fields. I came into college wanting to be a pre-med major and my experiences at UGA made me realize that I was only interested in the social side of medicine. So I began to focus on social justice issues and helping others, which led me to my current sociology and women's studies majors.

For two of the students participating in the online interview the experience was not completely positive. One wrote, "Somewhat negatively—UGA is a large school and I believe that has hindered my learning process." Another student shared, "My university experience my freshman year was awful. I was planning to go to medical school when I first entered the university, but the university did not change my plans to go to medical school."

Preparation for the Future

When asked, "What steps have you taken to prepare for the next stage of your life?" the responses were varied, but all but one student indicated taking significant positive action toward preparing for the future. Responses included: (a) preparing for and taking the Law School Admissions Test (LSAT) and Graduate Record Exam (GRE); (b) researching graduate and professional schools; (c) meeting with a pre-law advisor; (d) participating in internship programs and gaining relevant part-time work experience; (e) student teaching; (f) earning teacher certification; (g) doing online research to learn more about potential employers; (h) consulting with faculty members; (i) participating in extracurricular activities; (j) establishing a network of contacts; (k) meeting with a career counselor; (l) seeking help with revising a resumé; (m) signing up for job interviews on campus; and (n) submitting applications.

Use of Career Center Programs and DRC Transition Services

Of the 15 students who completed the online interviews, 9 had made use of the programs and services available to all students at the University's Career Center, including workshops, courses, and one-on-one counseling related to choosing a major, investigating career options, and finding a job. Of the nine responding students with disabilities who used these services, five specifically wrote about the helpfulness of resumé critiques, while others mentioned job searching tools, personality profiles, and mock interviews. When asked, "How have the Career Center offerings assisted you in developing your future plans?" one student wrote, "It has shown another world of exploring jobs and possibilities that I did not think I had access to." Another student answered, "The career center helped me choose a major when I was unhappy with my previous one." Responses like these, and that of the student who wrote, "made my resumé better and enabled me to expand my job search," indicate that the counselors in the Career Center were effective in providing the same services for students with disabilities that are made available for all students. The student who received "advice and counseling as to what would fit my interests and abilities" was clearly focused on ability, not disability, as were the students who wrote that the Career Center "helped to point me in the right direction with careers that best suit my abilities," and "it verified my beliefs that I no longer wanted to be a pre-med major and that I should focus on social work." In none of the responses was there any mention of being dissuaded from a career path because of a disability, a common thread in *Making Good on the Promise* (Higbee & Mitchell, in press). The only negative comment came from a student who had returned to school after an extensive career, and that comment did not pertain to disability: "Career counselors in their 20s do not have a clue about the real world of work."

Students were asked, "Have you made use of any of the career transition services provided by the Disability Resource Center?" Only 1 of the 15 students interviewed responded affirmatively, and focused the response on the use of assistive technologies and staff support available through the DRC's adaptive laboratory and one outstanding staff member in particular.

The next item on the interview schedule asked, "Is there any one program or service that you believe has been particularly helpful as you prepare for your post-graduation transition?" Of the five students who answered, "yes," two focused on DRC programs and services. One wrote,

> Personal tutors or student advocates. I as a mature woman was the age of my professors or older. I knew most of the hoops to jump and how but sometimes the fact that I had backup was very helpful in getting accommodation on exam taking. Also books on tape or CD or our Web-CT was great!

Meanwhile, two of the five addressed services provided by the Career Center, and specifically the mock interview and resumé review: "resumé checking and advice on what I should and shouldn't include on it—I never learned any of those skills in my core classes." The fifth student identified the academic department from which the student was receiving a graduate degree.

Student Recommendations

Finally, students were asked, "What recommendations would you make in regard to additional programs and services that would facilitate a smoother transition to your life after graduation?" Of the 15 students interviewed, 10 responded to this item, and 3 of the 10 did not make recommendations. One was unaware of the DRC's career transition services, suggesting that they should be better publicized. Another wrote, "A guidebook to the available programs and services; something that would list the programs available to me, so that I don't have to wonder what they are." Other ideas included (a) better networking opportunities, (b) classes or workshops on 401(k) investments, (c) preparation for relocating to other geographic areas, and (d) assistance creating a file of references. One student indicated that the University should establish a graduate program in Disability Studies to educate others about "this often overlooked minority." And one student used this last question as an opportunity to praise the work of the DRC: "Keep up the great work!!!! UGA's disAbility Resource Laboratory and staff is tops in only a field of 14 in the U.S."

Discussion

The students interviewed for the research study reported in this chapter represent too small a sample for drawing inferences to a larger population. However, despite not making use of the career transition services offered by the Disability Resource Center for students with disabilities, these students believed that they had been well served and received the support they needed for making the transition to graduate or professional school or the world of work. Nine of the students did take advantage of the services and resources provided by the Career Center—those services made available to all students at the University—and found them to be helpful. None of the students interviewed expressed any negative comments about these services, and one student described the experience as discovering "another world of exploring jobs and possibilities that I did not think I had access to." So rather than feeling limited, students were empowered by their experiences with the Career Center. This reflects the ideal application of Universal Design to a career center as described by Aune (2000) and from a Universal Design perspective, it would appear that the administrators and staff members Career Services at The University of Georgia have "got it right." They have been successful in assessing the needs of *all* students and providing the programs to meet these needs. The recommendations the students suggested for improving these services were not related directly to disability, and could as easily have been made by students without disabilities. One question that this research cannot answer is the extent to which the collaboration between the DRC and the Career Center, which are housed in the same building, might have influenced the development of the Career Center's programs and services in a way that is consistent with Universal Design, or enhanced the awareness of Career Center employees about equity for students with disabilities. In either case, it is a model that seems to be working for the students at The University of Georgia.

Conclusion

The University of Georgia's DRC and Career Center have created the kind of collaboration that Aune (2000) saw as being beneficial to students with disabilities. Aune described the possibility of delivering universally-designed career services as being a natural outgrowth of this type of collaboration. Based on the positive responses from students who used the services of the DRC and those of the Career Center, it appears that The University of Georgia collaboration model is taking steps in that direction. Through the reactions of students with disabilities to the services received through a Career Center that has worked closely with disability experts, it is clear that universally-designed programs and environments can have a positive impact on the quality of their postsecondary experience and beyond. Further research is needed to investigate this model and the impact that it might have on the life of students when they leave the postsecondary environment in order to enable other campuses to forge similar collaborations.

References

Aune, B. (2000). Career and academic advising. In H. Belch (Ed.), *Serving students with disabilities* (pp. 55-67). (New Directions in Student Services, no. 91). San Francisco: Jossey-Bass.

Aune, B. & Kroeger, S. (1997). Career development of college students with disabilities: An interactional approach to defining the issues. *Journal of College Student Development, 13*(1), 23-34.

Blustein, D. L. (2001). The interface of work and relationships: Critical knowledge for 21st century psychology. *The Consulting Psychologist, 29,* 179-192.

Donowho, B., Sawalich, S., & Vitolo, F. X. (Producers), & Sawalich, S. (Director). (2007). *The music within* [Motion picture]. United States: MGM.

Flores, L.Y., & Heppner, M. J. (2002). Multicultural career counseling: Ten essentials for training. *Journal of Career Development, 28,* 181-202.

Friehe, M., Aune, B., & Leuenberger, J. (1996). Career service needs of college students with disabilities. *Career Development Quarterly, 44,* 289-300.

Henderson, C. (1988). *College freshmen with disabilities.* Washington, DC: American Council on Education.

Henderson, C. (1999). *College freshmen with disabilities.* Washington, DC: American Council on Education.

Higbee, J. L., Chung, C. J., & Hsu. L. (2004). Enhancing the inclusiveness of first-year courses through Universal Instructional Design. In I. M. Duranczyk, J. L. Higbee, & D. B. Lundell (Eds.), *Best practices for access and retention in higher education* (pp. 13-25). Minneapolis: University of Minnesota, General College, Center for Research on Developmental Education and Urban Literacy. Retrieved December 7, 2007, from http://www.cehd.umn.edu/crdeul/monographs.html

Higbee, J. L., & Mitchell, A. A. (in press). *Making good on the promise: Student affairs professionals with disabilities.* Washington, DC: American College Personnel Association (ACPA)—College Student Educators International and University Press of America.

Hitchings, W. E., Horvath, M., Luzzo, D. D., Ristow, R. S., & Retish, P. (1998). Identifying the career development needs of college students with disabilities. *Journal of College Student Development, 39,* 23-32.

Horn, L., Nevill, S., & Griffin, J. (2006). *Profile of undergraduates in U.S. postsecondary education institutions: 2003-04 with a special analysis of community college students.* Washington, DC: U.S. Department of Education, National Center for Education Statistics, Institute of Education Sciences. Retrieved September 14, 2007, from http://nces.ed.gov/

pubs2006/2006184.pdf

Horn, L., Peter, K., Rooney, K., & Malizio, A. G. (2002). *Profile of undergraduates in U.S. postsecondary institutions: 1999-2000. Statistical analysis report.* Washington, DC: U.S. Department of Education, Office of Educational Research and Improvement, National Center for Education Statistics. Retrieved January 16, 2007, from http://nces.ed.gov/pubs2002/2002168.PDF

Kewal Ramani, A., Gilbertson, L., Fox, M. A., & Provasnik, S. (2007). *Status and trends in the education of racial and ethnic minorities.* Washington, DC: U.S. Department of Education, National Center for Education Statistics, Institute of Education Sciences. Retrieved September 14, 2007, from http://nces.ed.gov/pubs2007/2007039.pdf

Kipp, S. M., Price, D. D., & Wohlford, J. K. (2002). *Unequal opportunity: Disparities in college access among the 50 states.* Indianapolis, IN: Lumina Foundation for Education. Retrieved September 7, 2007, from http://www.luminafoundation.org/publications/monographs/pdfs/monograph.pdf

Mann, A. (2007). Leveling the playing field. *The University of Georgia Magazine, 87*(1), 24-29.

Rabby, R., & Croft, D. (1991). Working with disabled students: Some guidelines. *Journal of Career Planning and Employment, 5*(2), 49-54.

Savickas, M. L. (1993). Career counseling in the postmodern era. *Journal of Cognitive Psychotherapy: An International Quarterly, 7,* 205-215.

Snyder, T. D., Dillow, S. A., & Hoffman, C. M. (2007). *Digest of education statistics 2006.* Washington, DC: U.S. Department of Education, National Center for Education Statistics, Institute of Education Sciences. Retrieved September 14, 2007, from http://nces.ed.gov/pubs2007/2007017.pdf

Stebleton, M. J. (2007). Career counseling with African immigrant college students: Theoretical approaches and implications for practice. *Career Development Quarterly, 55,* 290-312.

Stebleton, M. J., & Peterson, M. (2007). Unfolding stories: Integrating positive psychology into a career narrative approach. *Career Planning and Adult Development Journal, 23*(1), 9-24.

Zhang, Y., & Chan, T. (2007). *An interim report on the Student Support Services program: 2002-03 and 2003-04, with select data from 1998-2002.* Washington, DC: U.S. Department of Education, Office of Postsecondary Education, Federal TRIO Programs. Retrieved September 15, 2007, from http://www.ed.gov/programs/triostudsupp/sss-interim2002-04.pdf

Professional Preparation

CHAPTER 24

Infusing Universal Instructional Design Into Student Personnel Graduate Programs

Karen A. Myers
Saint Louis University

Abstract
In support of the profession's core values, student affairs professionals foster inclusive, diverse, and affirming learning environments that promote human dignity and equality. Infusion of disability education and Universal Instructional Design (UID) in professional preparation programs provides students with the tools they need to ensure equal access for all members of the academic community. This chapter addresses graduate student interests and needs relative to disability education. It offers recommendations and an example for successful faculty buy-in, a plan for infusing UID into the curriculum, and a sample syllabus.

It is 7:45 p.m. Lynn, in her first year as Director of Student Activities at Midwest Metro University (a pseudonym), is anxiously gripping her clipboard as she waits in the wings of the magnificent old theater, rehearsing the introduction that she has rehearsed at least 100 times before. She has spent the last 8 months planning every detail of tonight's event. It should be perfect. Every i is dotted; every t is crossed. All is right with the world. As she peeks around the curtain, she can see audience members drifting in and filling seats. There is magic in the air and nothing, but nothing, can ruin this night. Just then she gets a text message from Sean, her assistant director: "President's wife broke leg. Is in wheelchair. Can't get into theatre." With her heart pounding in her throat, Lynn pictures the 17-stair barrier, and whispers through tears, "And I was so sure that I thought of everything."

Lynn's story is all too common for new—and not-so-new—professionals in the field of student affairs. Equal access and inclusion are often superseded by the minute details of program planning. When do thoughts of inclusion become second nature? When does equitable access become a natural part of the planning process, another box on the "to do" list, easily accomplished and quickly checked off?

Education on disability issues, learning styles, equal access, Universal Design (Center for Universal Design, 1997), and Universal Instructional Design (UID; Higbee, 2003; Silver Bourke, & Streehorn, 1998) needs to begin in student personnel graduate preparation courses, if not before. By virtue of its espoused values, the student affairs profession leads the way in creating inclusive, diverse, and affirming learning environments that promote human dignity and equality (Hall & Belch, 2000). Through pedagogical practices, awareness strategies, sensitivity training, case studies, and experiential learning, student affairs professionals can support their core values and learn to apply principles of Universal Design to their programs and services. Very little information about disability and Universal Design is incorporated into the college curriculum, including student personnel preparation programs (Evans, Herriott, & Myers, in press; Linton, 1998; Thompson, 2000). In fact, according to Dukes and Shaw (1999), little disability-specific academic preparation is provided for disability services providers, a vital student service on college campuses. Given this campus curricular void, faculty, practitioners, administrators, and graduate students should take immediate action toward infusion of these topics at all levels of the academy. This proactive approach allows professionals like Lynn to have the knowledge and expertise to confidently ensure inclusion.

This chapter addresses the importance of infusing UD and UID into student personnel and higher education graduate programs; a premise that is supported by results of an interest, needs, and awareness assessment conducted in a national graduate student study. Results from this study are presented along with suggestions for application and infusion. Recommendations for encouraging faculty involvement in the teaching and modeling of UID are also offered, and the chapter concludes with strategies for introducing and implementing the infusion plan.

Why UID in Student Affairs?

Colleges and universities are microcosms of society where students, faculty, and staff with diverse backgrounds and characteristics learn, work, and often live together with one common goal—education. While diversity highlights differences, multiculturalism embraces and celebrates those differences. Disability is an important aspect of diversity, yet it is often omitted from diversity and multicultural inquiry (Linton, 1998). Unfortunately, as Jones (1996) has noted, people see disability as a deficiency within the individual (i.e., the medical model) rather than a difference resulting from societal interaction (i.e., the social constructivist model). Celebrating disability as an integral part of the human fabric is indeed a multicultural phenomenon—one that should be examined through its social, political, and cultural properties (Linton, 2005) and recognized and embraced on college campuses.

The number of college students with disabilities has tripled over the past 20 years (Wolanin & Steele, 2004). Currently over 9% of college students have self-disclosed documented disabilities (U.S. Census Bureau, 2000), and this number continues to grow. Increases in this student population are seen across campus—in classes and student services, as well as in undergraduate, graduate, and professional degree programs. This includes student services practitioners, service users, and programmatic event attendees. "This increase is due, in large part, to the passage of legislation that opened the doors to higher education for these students" (Bryan & Myers, 2006, p. 19). Given this growing population, university personnel must be cognizant of these students and knowledgeable of student rights, needs, and expectations. The issues of students with disabilities should be given the same priority as other multicultural issues (Wolanin & Steele, 2004). Legally, institutions of higher education must provide reasonable accommodations to students with disabilities (Simon, 2000); however, utilizing the principles of UID decreases the number of individual accommodations required (Silver, Bourke, & Strehorn, 1998). Universal Instructional Design is based on the architectural concept of Universal Design, which is defined as "the design of products and environments to be usable by all people, to the greatest extent possible, without the need for adaptable or specialized design" (Center for Universal Design, 1997, p. 1). Higbee (2003) defined Universal Instructional Design as the application of Universal Design principles to the academic setting, creating inclusive and customizable curricula and programs that are accessible to all students. Through flexible multimodal teaching and learning approaches, UID provides welcoming environments and equal access to everyone (Strange, 2000).

"The development of student affairs professionals who are sensitive, aware, and knowledgeable about disability issues starts in the classroom" (Evans et al., in press). Recognizing that one size does not fit all, postsecondary institutions must prepare future faculty, administrators, and student affairs personnel to meet the challenges of providing accessible education and services to a diverse student body that has various learning styles, backgrounds, languages, and abilities. Unfortunately, few college courses address the topic of disability, which leaves graduates with little knowledge of disability issues in higher education settings (Thompson, 2000). Disciplines such as rehabilitation counseling, special education, teacher preparation, physical and occupational therapy, and other applied sciences usually provide some disability education; however, these tend to view disability through a medical lens (i.e., a deficiency to be fixed) rather than seeing disability as a socially-constructed phenomenon (Linton, 1998). As Linton (2006) pointed out, "The curriculum not only mimics but contributes to the marginalization of [people with disabilities] in society" (p. 231).

According to Pederson (1988), multicultural awareness refers to attitudes, values, and assumptions needed to work with diverse groups successfully and effectively. In living their core values of inclusion and human dignity, student affairs professionals must learn how to create learning environments that foster success for students with disabilities and for all students (Strange, 2000). These environments include, among others, admissions (Palombi, 2000); academic and career advising (Aune, 2000); student activities including recreation, sports, leadership programs, and study abroad (Johnson, 2000); and disability support services (Rund & Scharf, 2000). According to the Council for the Advancement of Standards in Higher Education (CAS; 2003), student personnel preparation programs (i.e., programs preparing student affairs professionals) should include curricula that address college culture, diversity, and student characteristics as well as their effects on college students. Courses or course modules relating to disability issues support this CAS standard. Courses or course modules relating to Universal Instructional Design go one step further by offering pedagogical solutions for inclusion for all students.

The Graduate Student Survey

Are graduate students knowledgeable about disability and inclusion issues? Do graduate students see a need for disability education in their student personnel preparation programs? Asking the graduate students themselves these questions may assist faculty and administrators in making decisions regarding the infusion of disability studies into the curriculum.

Purpose and Methodology

In response to the paucity of disability education in graduate programs, a study was conducted in 2006 to determine (a) the degree to which graduate students are knowledgeable about disability inclusion in postsecondary education, (b) whether or not graduate students see a need for disability education in their degree programs, and (c) whether or not graduate students are interested in enrolling in a course specifically designed to address disability issues relative to higher education. Using a mixed methods approach, an online survey was developed comprised of multiple choice and open-ended questions. Only two demographic questions were included; they requested type of degree program and area of study. Lists of professional degree programs in college student personnel and from related areas were obtained from the ACPA—College Student Educators International Web site and the Saint Louis University (SLU) Web site. An e-mail message was sent to the program directors at 120 institutions requesting them to forward the online survey to their students. Interested students completed and submitted an anonymous online survey.

The length of the survey was intentional, anticipating that students were more apt to respond to a short survey that would take less than 5 minutes to complete. The online survey consisted of the following seven questions:

1. I am interested in enrolling in the course, "Disability in Higher Education" as a classroom course, an online course, either one, or neither one. (multiple choice)
2. The course, "Disability in Higher Education" should be a required course, an elective course, a module within another course, or not offered. (multiple choice)
3. I see a need for this type of course in my degree program. (yes, no)
4. I believe that students with disabilities fully participate in higher education. (yes, no)
5. I know what steps to take to ensure that students with disabilities can fully participate in higher education. (yes, no)
6. My program level: Masters or Doctorate
7. My degree program (select from list of possible programs)

Results

A total of 784 respondents from 61 graduate programs in the United States voluntarily participated in the study. The majority of respondents (67%) reported they were in masters-level programs. Of masters-level respondents, 33% reported that they were in the area of higher education administration, 28% were in student personnel administration, 10% were in educational administration, and 6% were in nursing, with the remaining 23% in other disciplines. Of all respondents, 33% reported that they were in doctoral programs. Of doctoral level respondents, 44% were in higher education administration, 31% were in educational administration, and 8% were in educational studies, with the remaining 17% divided among other disciplines. Of the 784 total respondents, 71% saw a need for a disability course or module in their degree program and only 29 % saw no need for such a course or module. While 62% reported that they did not know what steps to take to ensure that students with disabilities can fully participate in higher education, that left only 38% reporting that they did know what steps to take to ensure inclusion. In response to the question regarding participation of students with disabilities in higher education, 53% reported that they do not believe that students with disabilities participate fully in higher education, while 47% believe that students with disabilities do participate fully in higher education.

Regarding the issue of disability in the curriculum, survey results indicated that 57% of the graduate students surveyed are interested in taking a disability course. Of these students, 32% preferred a face-to-face classroom course, 24% preferred an online course, and 44% did not have a preference between either a classroom or online course. When asked how the disability course or topic should be incorporated into their program, the majority of the respondents (57%) said it should be offered as an elective course, 27% would like to see disability as a module within another course, and 13% believed it should be a required course. The remaining 3% had no opinion.

At the end of the survey students were provided an opportunity to write comments. The theme that emerged from their comments was that it is time to move beyond generic cultural diversity courses. As one student stated, "Empowering student voices in the classroom [is essential]. Accessibility and voice are important enough issues to be embedded in every course." Another respondent put it this way: "Disability awareness in general should be fused into all courses, just as we expect educators to address diversity. It's all applicable."

Infusing Disability Into the Curriculum

Based on the results of this study, it is clear that graduate students in programs like higher education do see a need to understand and learn about students with disabilities. It has been over 30 years since the passage of the Rehabilitation Act of 1973 (i.e., Public Law 93-112) and 17 years since the passage of the Americans with Disabilities Act of 1990 (i.e., Public Law 101-336). Although these laws protect students with disabilities from discriminatory actions, knowledge of disability issues and appropriate communication is still limited on college campuses. It is time to address issues of disability and equal access not only through voluntary programming outside the classroom but also through academic curricula—this recommendation is clearly supported by this respondent's statement: "Included within a disabilities course should be a component on Universal Design . . . that is one of the major issues we are facing." Making access and inclusion a part of the curricular fabric and weaving it into daily pedagogical practices of faculty and student personnel administrators will only enhance the respect and equal treatment fostered on college campuses, which then is carried into the community and beyond.

The Connection Between Disability and UID

Jones (1996) described three theoretical frameworks for understanding disability: (a) functional limitations model, (b) minority group model, and (c) social constructivism model.

When disability is viewed as a functional limitation, the person is seen as "broken,"—needing to be fixed. Focus is placed upon the individual's limitations and what he or she cannot do. From the functional limitations perspective, accommodations may be needed to level the playing field.

The minority group paradigm suggests commonalities among people with disabilities and focuses on their marginalization and oppression. It requires a group identity, which in turn may perpetuate stereotypic thinking, such as that students with disabilities need help and support. Although the minority group paradigm acknowledges psychological and social consequences in the lives of persons with disabilities, it does not address students' lived experience. Schlossberg's (1989) theory of marginality and mattering fits within the minority group framework of disability. Faculty, staff, and administers can play major roles in determining a student's perceived self-worth. Through myths and stereotypes, university personnel can intentionally or unintentionally push students with disabilities to the margins, fueling feelings of inadequacy and insignificance. On the other hand, by recognizing student membership in the disability minority group, college personnel may empathize with students, sending them clear signals that they indeed matter to them, to the institution, and to society as a whole.

Jones' (1996) social constructivist model also provides a framework through which marginality can be viewed and mattering can be fostered. As a socially-constructed phenomenon, disability is defined and shaped by society. Thus, according to the social constructivist paradigm, society develops the barriers and determines how persons with disabilities are perceived and treated. Viewing disability through a social constructivist lens clearly illustrates how college students with disabilities are marginalized. On the flip side, putting the social construction framework into practice via UID principles clearly exemplifies how students with disabilities matter in the higher education community.

Teaching and Modeling UID

UID principles can be taught in depth in a specifically designed and designated disability course, they can be infused into other courses as modules, or they can be sprinkled throughout the curriculum in other creative and innovative ways. Most importantly, these "pedagogical curbcuts"—a vivid illustration of UID coined by Ben-Moshe, Cory, Feldbaum, and Sagendorf (2005)—are included in the curriculum. At Saint Louis University, UID is taught and modeled in every higher education and student personnel administration graduate course I teach. A sample UID teaching module is illustrated in Figure 1.

A course titled "Disability in Higher Education and Society" has also been developed at SLU. "Such a course should be taught by professional staff or faculty members, preferably with disabilities, who are well versed in disability theory, disability law, and disability rights issues" (Evans et al., in press). The course at SLU was created as a result of the needs and interests reported in the graduate student survey described previously in this chapter. Based on the Competency Assessment in Distributed Education (CADE) principles devel-

Figure 1. Universal Instructional design module

1. Defining of UD and UID
2. Viewing online video
3. Working in groups to address case studies
4. Developing UD/UID plan for office/workplace/classroom (individual or in groups). The purpose of this plan is to develop short-term actions that can be implemented immediately and long-term actions that are doable and will be accomplished over time.
5. Requiring students to incorporate UID into their assignments. For example, in a College Teaching course, require students to include UID in their syllabus assignment. In the Higher Education Curriculum course, require students to incorporate the use of UID principles in their new course design. In the Student Personnel Administration course, require students to incorporate UD and UID into their program development project.

oped by the Jesuit Distance Education Network (Vigilante, 2005), course competencies (i.e., learning outcomes) are divided into strategic, procedural, and factual competencies (see Figure 2.). Using a reverse design approach, the development of the course focuses first on the learner and the learner's competencies, followed by instructional processes, then resources. The course is comprised of four modules that can be used as classroom, online, or hybrid instruction, separately in other courses or together for one course. The modules are: (a) Disability as a Social Construct—Perceptions, Attitudes, and Feelings; (b) Empowerment; (c) Advocacy and Support in the Educational Experience; and (d) Fostering an Inclusive Environment. Module One addresses appropriate language, pros and cons of simulations as teaching tools, the Disability Movement, disability legislation in the U.S., and disability frameworks with emphasis on social constructivism. Module Two discusses student development theories, disability identity models, the disability experience, and disability myths and stereotypes. Module Three deals with disability accommodations, communication techniques, and working with students with disabilities in higher education settings. And Module Four addresses Universal Design and Universal Instructional Design, equal access to facilities, programs, and services, and disability in the community.

Disability in Higher Education and Society has been offered as a face-to-face course, a hybrid course, and an online course. Based on results from the national survey previously described, students see a need for disability education in their degree program, and they do not know what steps to take to ensure that students with disabilities can fully participate in higher education. These results alone indicate a desire among graduate students to learn about this increasing population of students and issues of access and inclusion. The results also reveal a void in the curriculum. It is imperative for colleges and universities to hear the call and fill the void.

According to Rauscher and McClintock (1997), disability courses should include both cognitive and affective learning by intentionally addressing students' biases, fears, and levels of discomfort regarding persons with disabilities. Through first-person accounts and personal interactions with people with disabilities, students may gain a deeper understanding of what it is like to live with a disability and how society plays a major role in the lived experience of people with disabilities. Examples for experiential learning activities and resources include student panels, guest speakers, interviews, teleconferences, site visits, group discussions, autobiographies, videos, vodcasts, podcasts, movies, and Web sites—all of which should involve persons with disabilities themselves rather than actors or persons without disabilities attempting to explain life with a disability.

An integral part of a student affairs professional preparation program is student development theory (CAS, 2003). With regard to diversity and multiculturalism, most programs address student identity theories related to race, ethnicity, culture, gender, and sexual orientation. Few disability identity theories are available and even fewer are used in graduate curricula. The following disability identity theories should be incorporated into courses on student development, disability, diversity, campus culture, and others relating to the lives of college students: (a) Gibson's (2006) disability identity model, (b) Olkin's (2003) women with disabilities theory, (c) Olkin's (2001) minority model of disability, and (d) Troiano's (2003) learning disability model.

In addition to teaching UID, or even in lieu of teaching UID, faculty members can model UID in their classes (Higbee, 2003). Modeling consists of behaviors such as providing syllabi and other materials online; providing syllabi and reading lists early, preferably prior to the first class session; offering students an opportunity to self-select assignments (e.g., papers, presentations, group work, written and oral journals, online work); allowing students to weight their assignments; using only open-captioned videos or DVDs; providing opportunities for online discussions as well as in-class discussions; utilizing multiple teaching methods to accommodate multiple learning styles; using audio podcasts, video podcasts, and other forms of technology as appropriate; and including statements on course syllabi related to disability and to UID (Pedelty, 2003). The following are examples of such statements:

One quick and easy method for determining student learning styles is to incorporate the VARK (Fleming, 2006) guide to learning styles into the course. Students may complete the 16-item VARK assessment tool online and receive immediate online results indicating the student's learning style: Visual, Auditory, Reading/Writing, and Kinesthetic. Students can e-mail results to the professor or bring a hard copy to class. A useful technique is to have students share with the class the results of their learning style assessment, possibly followed by a discussion regarding types of teaching and learning methods that are most compatible with their particular learning styles. This practice not only allows instructors

Figure 2. Sample Syllabus Statements

Students With Disabilities (a syllabus statement)

If you have a documented disability that will affect your ability to participate fully in the course or if you require disability-related accommodations, please contact the Disability Services Office at (phone number) so that appropriate accommodations may be arranged. After contacting the office, I encourage you to discuss your accommodations with me so that I may assist you in their provision.

Universal Instructional Design (a syllabus statement)

This course is designed to eliminate barriers and provide equal access for all students. All forms of diversity (e.g., learning styles, cultures, disabilities, etc.) —those unique characteristics that add richness, breadth and depth to our class— will be acknowledged and accommodated in a universal manner.

to become aware of students' learning styles so that they can enhance pedagogical practices via UID principles, but also allows the students in the class to do the same through their presentations, discussions, and other assignments involving their peers. Teachers and students alike will be modeling UID in the classroom.

Getting Faculty On Board

"Feed them and they will come. Promise them tenure and they will come in droves." Unfortunately, the second statement only occurs in higher education fairytales. The first statement, however, does work for faculty just like it does for students. As a wise mentor once said, "When recruiting faculty for anything, it is important to walk softly and carry a big cookie." Levity aside, in addition to the promise of food, faculty need to know upfront how and why this topic will benefit them and their students. As previously stated, UID is a flexible way to ensure equal access to all students. As a result, everyone benefits, including the professor. When recruiting faculty to utilize UID, there must be a mechanism to ensure their success and that they will leave training sessions with a solid plan for immediate implementation.

The concept of shared responsibility is one that must be emphasized as well. Disability and equal access issues are not the sole responsibility of the disability services office but rather of all members of the academic community (Bryan & Myers, 2006; Kalivoda & Totty, 2003). Faculty, staff, student affairs personnel, administrators, and students with and without disabilities must take personal responsibility to provide a welcoming learning environment for all students, ensuring access and inclusion.

Making Connections

In order to connect with faculty, it helps to collaborate with the department that connects with faculty the most. At SLU, the Reinert Center for Teaching Excellence (CTE) is that department. The purpose of the Center is to provide faculty with tools to enhance their pedagogy (Reinert CTE, n.d.). In collaboration with the CTE, a UID Community of Practice was formed. The Community of Practice is comprised of 11 faculty members from various departments across the University. The members were self-selected by their interest in learning about UID and willingness to teach, model, and spread the word about UID principles. In fall 2006 during a 90-minute lunch hosted by the CTE at the faculty club, the group received an overview of UID including materials, assessment tools, and resources. By the end of the meeting, the following slogan to be used in future UID training and promotion was developed: "Is your curriculum UID-friendly?" Within 6 months members of the UID Community of Practice presented sessions on UID in classes, at university meetings, and at state and national conferences. They wrote and submitted articles and chapters on UID for publication, and they were awarded an internal mini-grant to promote retention via UID programs. Forming a Community of Practice is an excellent way to tap into the expertise of bright, innovative, and enthusiastic faculty. It is also an ideal networking and innovative support opportunity.

An example of a successful faculty event is the "UID Coffee Break" implemented by the UID Community of Practice at SLU. Funded through the mini-retention grant program, two 1-hour coffee breaks were offered on both ends of the campus, providing easy access to most faculty. After refreshments and a brief presentation of UID principles and techniques by UID Community of Practice members, faculty participants applied what they learned to their own syllabi, leaving the session with an implementation plan in hand. Standing room only and positive evaluations prompted the facilitators to incorporate more UID Coffee Breaks into the faculty training program.

Spreading the Word

Once faculty, staff, and students are educated about the principles of UID, they should be encouraged to spread the UID word. Although the Saint Louis University UID Community of Practice was a faculty committee, staff from student affairs, enrollment management, alumni, development, technology services, and so on, were recruited to "board the UID bandwagon." Once recruited and trained, they also spread the principles in myriad ways, both intentionally and subliminally. Examples of intentional methods include publications in journals, books, newsletters, newspapers, and e-announcements; presentations in departmental meetings, division retreats, classes, and campus organizations; workshops and seminars at the local, state, regional, national, and international levels through colleges and universities, local schools, and professional organizations; and participating in interviews, panels, and formal group discussions. Subliminal methods of spreading the UID word include comments in meetings and classes; informal conversations with faculty, staff, administrators, and students; verbal statements during dissertation oral exams and defense; written comments on assignments and online discussion boards; participation in informal group discussions; and including the slogan "Is your curriculum

UID friendly?"

The Right Tools

Providing faculty, staff, and students with the tools needed to teach, model, and assess the principles of UID is an essential part of recruitment and training. Materials and resources in the form of books, binders, folders, Web sites, PowerPoint presentations, CDs, DVDs, videos, flash presentations, and so an are welcomed and appreciated by those who are willing to spread the word. Excellent UID materials can be found on the following Web sites: (a) the "Faculty Room" Web site and materials created by the DO-IT project at the University of Washington, (b) the Curriculum Transformation and Disability project at the University of Minnesota, and (d) the Accommodating Students with Disabilities project at Utah State University. One particularly useful tool is an assessment sheet developed by members of the Pedagogy and Student Services for Institutional Transformation (PASS IT) project summer institute at the University of Minnesota. It is a universal tool to be used by academic and student services personnel to assess their classes, departments, programs, and services to determine if they are "UID friendly." Distributing this easy-to-use tool at every UID presentation provides participants with the means to take immediate action.

The Infusion Plan

To begin the infusion plan process, it is helpful to divide the process into four steps: (a) developing the plan, (b) introducing the plan, (c) implementing the plan, and (d) assessing the plan. The following paragraphs provide some suggestions for carrying out and completing each step.

Developing the Plan

Using informal networking strategies, talk to colleagues (locally or at other institutions) who are interested in UID and/or who already have incorporated UID into their curricula.

Through formal networking, develop a UID Community of Practice comprised of faculty, staff, and students. Discuss ideas with both networks and create a proposal using CAS standards, ACPA Professional Preparation Commission standards, and appropriate institutional, departmental, and program standards. Discuss infusion ideas and the proposal with the department chairperson, dean, or appropriate person to ensure that all policies are being followed and to keep them "in the loop."

Introducing the Plan

To introduce the plan, begin by developing a marketing plan. Develop promotional materials to promote UID infusion programs, modules, course, and so on. using multimedia methods. Utilizing the suggestions mentioned earlier in this chapter, use intentional and subliminal methods for spreading the word.

Implementing the Plan

If a new course has been developed or a permanent course revised, offer the course through appropriate channels. This may include a time-consuming course approval process, so plan accordingly. Assist other faculty in infusing UID modules into their courses. Present information sessions, workshops, seminars, and so on, both on and off campus. And continue to promote UID infusion through marketing plan techniques previously developed.

Assessing the Plan

When a course has been developed or revised, keep a "finger on the pulse" of the class by informally evaluating the course and the instructor throughout the term and adjust the course as needed. Conduct a formal midterm and final evaluation and make adjustments accordingly. Incorporate a peer assessment component into classes that require group work. And include an evaluation component to each workshop, seminar, or presentation, and so on.

Conclusion

Through the infusion plan process, faculty can provide students in professional preparation programs with the tools needed to foster inclusive learning environments. Disability and UID education prepare students to be knowledgeable about disability issues and sensitive toward the diverse nature of the student and community populations. As a result, student affairs professionals, like Lynn in the opening scenario, will be proactive in their program planning and ready to provide equal access to all.

References

Aune, B. (2000). Career and academic advising. In H. K. Belch (Ed.), *Serving students with disabilities.* (New Directions for Student Services, no. 91, pp. 55-67). San Francisco: Jossey-Bass.

Ben-Moshe, L., Cory, R., Feldbaum, M., & Sagendorf, K. (2005). *Building pedagogical curb cuts: Incorporating disability in the university classroom and curriculum.* Syracuse, NY: Syracuse University, Graduate School.

Bryan, A., & Myers, K. (2006). Students with disabilities: Doing what's right. *About Campus, 2*(4), 18-22.

Center for Universal Design. (1997). *The principles of Universal Design.* (Version 2.0). Raleigh: North Carolina State University.

Council for the Advancement of Standards in Higher Education. (2003). *Masters-level graduate program for student affairs professionals.* Washington, DC: Author.

Curriculum Transformation and Disability. (n.d.) *Homepage.* Retrieved September 23, 2007, from http://www.gen.umn.edu/research.ctad

DO-IT (2007). *The faculty room.* Retrieved March 25, 2007, from www.washington.edu/doit/

Dukes, L. L., III, & Shaw, S. F. (1999). Postsecondary disability personnel: Professional standards and staff development. *Journal of Developmental Education, 23*(1), 26-31.

Evans, N., Herriot, T., & Myers, K. (in press). Integrating disability into the diversity framework of our professional preparation and practice. In A. A. Mitchell and J. L. Higbee (Eds.), *Making good on the promise: Student affairs professionals with disabilities.*

Washington, DC: ACPA—College Student Educators International and University Press of America.

Fleming, N.D. (2006). VARK: A guide to student learning. Retrieved March 26, 2007, from http://www.vark-learn.com/english/index.asp

Gibson, J. (2006). Disability and clinical competency: An introduction. *The California Psychologist, 39,* 6-10.

Hall, L. M., & Belch, H. K. (2000). Setting the context: Reconsidering the principles of full participation and meaningful access for students with disabilities. In H. K. Belch (Ed.), *Serving students with disabilities* (New Directions for Student Services, no. 91, pp. 5-17). San Francisco: Jossey-Bass.

Higbee, J. L. (Ed.). (2003). *Curriculum transformation and disability: Implementing Universal Design in higher education*. Minneapolis: University of Minnesota, General College, Center for Research on Developmental Education and Urban Literacy. Retrieved December 16, 2006, from: http://www.education.umn.edu/crdeul.

Johnson, D. (2000). Enhancing out-of-class opportunities for students with disabilities. In H. K. Belch (Ed.), *Serving students with disabilities* (New Directions for Student Services, no. 91, pp. 41-53). San Francisco: Jossey-Bass.

Jones, S. R. (1996). Toward inclusive theory: Disability as a social construction. *NASPA Journal, 33,* 347-354.

Kalivoda, K. S., & Totty, M. C. (2003). Disability services as a resource: Advancing Universal Design. In J. L. Higbee (Ed.), *Curriculum transformation and disability: Implementing Universal Design in higher education* (pp. 187-202). Minneapolis: University of Minnesota, General Colleg,e Center for Research on Developmental Education and Urban Literacy. Retrieved February 21, 2007, from http://www.education.umn.edu/crdeul.

Linton, S. (1998). *Claiming disability: Knowledge and identity.* New York: New York University Press.

Linton, S. (2006). *My body politic.* Ann Arbor: University of Michigan Press.

Olkin, R. (2001). *What psychotherapists should know about disability.* New York: Guilford Press.

Olkin, R. (2003). Women with disabilities. In J. C. Chrisler, C. Golden, & P. D. Rozee (Eds.), *Lectures on the psychology of women* (3rd ed.). New York: McGraw-Hill.

Palombi, B. J. (2000). Recruitment and admission of students with disabilities. In H. A. Belch (Ed.), *Serving students with disabilities* (New Directions for Student Services, no. 91, pp. 31-39). San Francisco: Jossey-Bass.

Pedelty, M. (2003). Making a statement. In J. L. Higbee (Ed.), *Curriculum transformation and disability: Implementing Universal Design in higher education* (pp. 71-78). Minneapolis: University of Minnesota, General Colleg,e Center for Research on Developmental Education and Urban Literacy. Retrieved February 21, 2007, from http://www.education.umn.edu/crdeul.

Pedersen, P. (1988). *Handbook for developing multicultural awareness.* Alexandria, VA: American Association for Counseling and Development.

Rauscher, L., & McClintock, M. (1997). Ableism curriculum design. In M. Adams, L. A. Bell, & P. Griffin (Eds.), *Teaching for diversity and social justice* (pp. 198-229). New York: Routledge.

Reinert Center for Teaching Excellence (n.d.). *Reinert CTE mission statement.* Retrieved July 6, 2007, from http://www.slu.edu/centers/cte/

Rund, J., & Scharf, T. (2000). Funding programs and services for students with disabilities. In H. A. Belch (Ed.), *Serving students with disabilities* (New Directions for Student Services, no. 91, pp. 83-92). San Francisco: Jossey-Bass.

Schlossberg, N. K. (1989). Marginality and mattering: Key issues in building community. In D. C. Roberts (Ed.), *Designing campus activities to foster a sense of community* (New Directions for Student Services, no.48, pp. 5-15) San Francisco: Jossey-Bass.

Silver, P., Bourke, A., & Strehorn, K. C. (1998) Universal Instructional Design in higher education: An approach for inclusion. *Equity and Excellence in Education, 31*(2), 47-51.

Simon, J. (2000). Legal issues in serving students with disabilities in postsecondary education. In H. A. Belch (Ed.), *Serving students with disabilities* (New Directions for Student Services, no. 91, pp. 69-81). San Francisco: Jossey-Bass.

Strange, C. (2000). Creating environments of ability. In H. A. Belch (Ed.), *Serving students with disabilities* (New Directions for Student Services, no. 91, pp. 19-30). San Francisco: Jossey-Bass.

Thompson, R. G. (2000). The new disability studies: Inclusion or tolerance? *ADE Bulletin, 124,* 18-22.

Troiano, P. F. (2003). College students and learning disability: Elements of self-style. *Journal of College Student Development, 44,* 404-419.

Vigilante, R. (2005). *Competency assessment in distributed education.* Washington, DC: Association of Jesuit Colleges and Universities.

Wolanin, T. R., & Steele, P. E. (2004). *Higher education opportunities for students with disabilities: A primer for policymakers.* Washington, DC: Institute for Higher Education Policy.

CHAPTER 25

The Application of Universal Instructional Design in Experiential Education

Nancy Sharby
Northeastern University

Susan E. Roush
University of Rhode Island

Abstract

Experiential education (EE) describes a formal activity that links academic and work settings. The school is responsible for preparing trainees for the demands of the EE environment; the trainee is responsible to function as a learner and a worker; and the preceptor is responsible to teach, protect, and fulfill the student's role as an employee. Some trainees may have difficulties with EE because of a disability or other difference. Universal Instructional Design (UID) has the potential to mitigate these difficulties. This chapter summarizes the practice of EE and the application of UID to EE and provides specific UID implementation suggestions through case examples.

Experiential education (EE) is a concept that has been associated with an array of learning activities that, although linked to academic objectives, take place outside of the classroom (Schambrach & Dirks, 2002), It is a term that has been associated with experiences as diverse as wilderness adventure programs (Estes, 2004), travel abroad, and service learning (Keen & Howard, 2002). EE differs from community service or other volunteer participation in that it is a more formal activity with direct links to an academic course where students learn through experiencing the connections among the community, academic knowledge, and citizenship (Reynolds, 2006). Although EE can be structured in diverse ways, in all settings learning is intentional, not incidental, and is embedded into a curriculum to support specific academic learning goals. In other words, "experiential education represents a distinctive form of education, guided by carefully selected, structured, intentional, relevant and humanistic learning experiences" (Osborn, Daninhirsch, & Page, 2003, p. 15)

This chapter will briefly describe EE in postsecondary settings and will highlight the perspectives of the academic institutions that implement these programs, the students who participate in them, and the work sites. Next we will consider how Universal Instructional Design (UID) can serve as a resource in bringing the advantages of EE to students with diverse needs. Finally, three cases will be presented to illustrate the application of UID to EE for students who have atypical learning needs.

There is no universal agreement on the terms used to label various aspects and roles of practice within EE. For the purposes of this chapter the term "preceptor" will be used to designate the person who supervises an EE student at the work site, "trainee" will be used for the learner, and "traineeship" will be used for the work experience. In the medical and health professions, preceptors are also known as clinical instructors and fieldwork supervisors, and the academic staff who coordinate EE are know as academic coordinators or directors of clinical education (ACCE) or academic fieldwork coordinators. In the literature surveyed, the vast majority of experiential placements occurred in a work site where the trainee functioned in the role of employee-in-training and was supervised by staff employed by the site. At these placements some trainees are paid a salary and expected to perform in a professional capacity along side their peers who have permanent positions. Only nursing and pharmacy reported sending faculty into the work site to supervise trainees (Jacobson, Grinel, & Lewis, 2006; Littlefield et al., 2004).

EE at the postsecondary level provides trainees a way to explore career paths and opportunities, apply classroom knowledge to the work setting, learn directly from role models how to comport themselves in the work place, and become proficient in problem solving and critical thinking (Keen & Howard, 2002; Osborn, et al., 2003; Ryan & Krapels, 1997; Zettergren & Beckett, 2004). Interdisciplinary collaboration is highly valued in health care settings and there is evidence that experiences in the clinic foster respect for other disciplines and increased willingness to share roles (Plake & Wolfgang, 1996). Many skills, especially social skills and affective behaviors that are difficult to teach or assess in the classroom, are central to these learning opportunities in real-world settings. Postsecondary education is increasingly valuing these outcomes and consequently it is increasingly common to see institutions grant academic credit for these experiences or mandate them for graduation. (Keen & Howard; Osborn, et al.; Ryan & Krapels).

Kraft and Sakofs (1988) stressed the importance of experiential learning that engages students in real-life situations with real consequences. The outcomes of the trainee's actions are not reflected in a grade, but in tangible accomplishment or failure to meet a work-related goal. The goal of the experience is to apply theories, concepts, and skills directly to the performance of real, not simulated, work functions. Because the learning takes place in a work setting, trainees are expected to perform in a manner that is safe, efficient, and effective. The trainee must adhere to technical and ethical standards, meet productivity demands, have appropriate social skills, and adapt to the culture of the work site. Experiential learning differs from employment, however, in two fundamental ways: (a) the roles and tasks are directly related to classroom activities, and (b) structured analysis of the experience facilitates reflective thinking about that learning. Embedding reflection on actions in the learning experience leads to the development of new skills, attitudes, and approaches to learning (Williams-Peres & Keig, 2002). As previously noted, some EE opportunities are embedded in paid employment while others are voluntary or have an associated tuition fee.

Allied health, teacher preparation, social work, counseling, and medical education have long considered EE vital to their educational missions, as evidenced by mandatory inclusion of EE in these curricula. Whether called clinical practica, clinical affiliations, internships, clerkships, student teaching, or cooperative education, these experiences connect learning through work with learning in the classroom. In these fields, EE may be particularly important for students as a mechanism for early exposure to the expected professional roles and responsibilities. These fields place high value on affective skills such as empathy, interpersonal skills, conflict management, attitudes, and ethics. EE is a necessary component to promote the development of these skills (Dornan & Bundy, 2004; Littlefield et al., 2004; Plake & Wolfgang, 1996; Williams-Perez & Keig, 2002; Welch, 2006). Medical education, for example, articulates the value of early EE by recognizing that "authentic (as opposed to simulated) human contact in a social or clinical context ... enhances learning of health, illness and disease, and the role of the health professional" (Dornan & Bundy, p. 840). Additionally, Dornan and Bundy proposed that EE in medical education could broaden learning and contextualize it, strengthen cognitive processes, link theory to roles and responsibilities, and promote the development of affective and interpersonal skills.

Cooperative (co-op) education is another variant of EE. This is an "educational model in which students alternate periods of study with periods of academic-related employment" (Hoffart, Diani, Connors, & Moynihan, 2006, p. 136). These employment opportunities involve working for pay in a setting where trainees are able to practice skills directly related to their major field of study. Co-op education requires coordinated teamwork among the school staff, staff at the work site, and the trainees, and each party has clearly defined roles (Keen & Howard, 2002). While on a co-op job, the trainee's first responsibility is to the employer to perform the job of being a good employee. For co-op education experiences, the educational institution typically has a co-op education coordinator who will visit sites to ensure educational quality, support student needs, and evaluate student performance.

Northeastern University (Boston, MA) and Antioch College (Yellow Springs, OH) have well-developed co-op education programs. Co-op education has been in place at Northeastern University since its founding in the early 1900s. Most academic programs structure co-op to occur as two 6-month placements as an employee at a job, with 6 or more months of classroom time between jobs. Co-op jobs are integral components of the academic curriculum and are required for most majors. Co-op coordinators, employed by Northeastern, develop work opportunities, assist students in securing jobs, and supervise their progress. The faculty depends on co-op experiences to integrate theory and practice that can be built upon when trainees return to campus. Learning becomes concrete—not abstract—when a student is able to apply classroom knowledge to problem solving or delivery of a service. Another example of co-op education occurs at Antioch College, which in 1921 became the first liberal arts school to incorporate working in full time co-op education jobs (Keen & Howard, 2002). "Every Antioch student in every major. ... [participates in] multiple, required terms of work" during their enrollment. (Antioch College, 2005).

The Academic Perspective

Effectively implementing EE requires a unique set of skills and knowledge. The school has the responsibility to prepare trainees comprehensively for the multifaceted demands of the EE environment; trainees have the responsibility to function as both a learner and a contributor in that environment; and the preceptor has the responsibility to guide, teach, mentor, and protect.

Because of these unique demands, many schools have staff specifically designated to develop work experiences and to provide on-campus support and supervision. The educational institution and the experiential work site must collaborate to form an alliance that supports trainee learning. Ideally there will be direct communication between the school coordinator and the site preceptor to agree upon expectations. There must be agreement on the types of teaching that will occur, job descriptions, performance expectations, ways of measuring performance, and how to handle problems that arise. Indeed, in majors such as health care and education where EE is mandatory, the academic liaison has an obligation to work with the training site and preceptors to ensure a quality placement and to foster the preceptors' teaching skills (Littlefield et al., 2004). In some fields this is formalized via the development of legal contracts, where in other situations the guidelines are less formal. However, the bottom line must always be effective and safe work outcomes commensurate with the trainee's level of education.

Whatever the model, schools often encounter a shortage of clinical sites for the number of trainees who need placements (Talley, 2006). Placement availability is not the only challenge facing academic coordinators. In addition, they frequently must track and maintain records on criminal background checks, cardiopulmonary resuscitation (CPR) certifications, health clearances (e.g., current immunizations), universal precautions training, and appropriate licensures (Traynor, 2004). Given the high productivity demands of the workplace and need for preceptors, some disciplines such as nursing and pharmacy find it difficult to provide meaningful real-life experiences for trainees (Jacobson, et al., 2006; Littlefield et al., 2006), unfortunately limiting the EE opportunities in these fields.

The Work Site Perspective

While academic coordinators face placement and supervisory challenges, working with students is their primary responsibility. On-site preceptors, in contrast, have dual loyalties; they are employees with their own work requirements and at the same time are the teachers. In their role as employees, they must ensure that the trainee produces a quality "product." This may be an innovative software tool, a marketing campaign, a creative teaching module, or high-quality patient care. The preceptor must always balance fiduciary responsibility to the organization with the obligation to educate and mentor. Osborn et al. (2003) summarized the generic (i.e., noncontent) responsibilities of preceptors, which include designing appropriate learning opportunities, facilitating students' engagement in problem solving, establishing boundaries, protecting physical and emotional safety, and supporting and facilitating learning.

Frequently, time is diverted from direct service delivery to attend to these teaching tasks. Often the workplace demands of the preceptor do not diminish to accommodate for the time that is spent teaching or supervising. In addition, they often have little or no formal training in pedagogy or how to facilitate a novice's learning, and as a result, treat trainees in the same way they were instructed when they were trainees. In some settings there is significant incentive to provide direct teaching, while in others supervisors treat the trainee as they would a new hire. In physical therapy there is a structured training program to teach preceptors how to be good instructors (American Physical Therapy Association, 2007). In other fields, such as business, the expectations are more ambiguous. One source reported that in one large corporation the preceptors receive training in supervision because they are already supervising novice employees. This company assesses trainees exactly as they would a novice full-time employee (Ryan & Krapels, 1997).

The Trainee Perspective

While on-site preceptors have several roles that may conflict, trainees are caught in a similar conundrum of balancing their need to learn with the need to be productive. In a co-op education experience, the trainee is working as an employee and is directed to perform delegated tasks for monetary compensation. In other types of traineeships, the goal may be skewed more toward learning and demonstrating mastery of objectives the school or credentialing agency has mandated. Some of these objectives include the ability to be productive as well as knowledgeable and skilled. Patient safety and client satisfaction must not be compromised because the work is performed by a trainee. Many business sites that participate in EE use traineeships as extended job interviews and opportunities to recruit talented trainees who will be a good "fit" for the organization (Schambach & Dirks, 2002). In these situations success at a traineeship has significant consequences that can directly impact the trainee's career. In situations where passing the traineeship is mandatory for graduation, trainees may be in a situation where they are afraid to ask for help as they feel they may be judged to be incompetent, even if they do not have the necessary skill or knowledge to perform the required task. Some trainees may have difficulties because of a hidden disability or cultural differences, but are afraid to ask for assistance because they believe that this will create stigma or affect the preceptor's attitude toward them. In some cases they are correct about these assumptions.

The stigma associated with disability can be particularly limiting. Unfortunately, ableism, or discrimination against people on the basis of a disability, is part of our culture. There are many negative attitudes about persons with disabilities, including that they need to be taken care of or that they cannot perform to the same standards as their peers who do not have a disability. Rarely is a disability thought of as merely a difference, one that might also be associated with advantages or strengths.

> From an ableist perspective, the devaluation of disability results in societal attitudes that uncritically assert that it is better for a child to walk than roll, speak than sign, read print than read Braille, spell independently rather than use a spell checker, and hang out with non-disabled kids as opposed to other disabled kids, etc. (Hehir, 2002, p. 3)

The social view of disability emphasizes the negative consequences of disability and fails to acknowledge and appreciate the positive aspects of this diverse population. It is not an easy notion for people to accept that they are influenced by this negative bias, but research suggests it is common, even among educators and helping professionals (Hehir).

One study found that negative attitudes of faculty were the most frequent obstacles to success reported by students, in contrast to faculty perceptions that physical access and lack of technology were the most significant barriers (Marks, 2000). The salience of attitudinal factors is reinforced when you consider that accommodating psychiatric disabilities is associated with more resistance than accommodating physical disabilities (Thomas, 2000). Attitudes and beliefs about persons with disabilities may be at least or perhaps even more important than legal statutes when the effectiveness of inclusion efforts is considered (Brostrand, 2006). Unfortunately, even faculty with accepting attitudes have limited knowledge about students with disabilities and their specialized learning needs (Kalivoda, 2003). They typically lack training in effective strategies for facilitating the learning environment for these students (Hehir, 2002). Given the bias against disability and lack of knowledge on how to accommodate disabilities, the reluctance of some trainees with disabilities to disclose is understandable.

EE and the Trainee With Diverse Needs: UID As A Resource

In the work environment the trainee takes on many of the roles of an employee. When the traniee is skilled, well prepared, and competent, this process goes smoothly and productivity may increase. Trainees who lack necessary skills, however, must receive assistance to support their learning and maintain patient safety, ensure client satisfaction, or meet productivity standards. Under the best circumstances, EE can be challenging for all involved, but it may be particularly complicated when the trainee has diverse needs. Trainees with special learning or cultural needs may be seen as a burden on an already overloaded system because of the additional time and effort needed to make accommodations or adjustments in the work environment. The preceptor may also anticipate spending considerably longer supervising and supporting these trainees. In these situations, trainees who struggle may be viewed as deficient and may cast a poor image on their school; consequently the site may be less likely to take trainees in the future. Applying the concepts of UID to EE, however, can increase the probability that trainees will successfully meet educational and work expectations, while minimizing the amount of remediation or additional supervision that is required of the preceptor.

UID is a powerful tool that has the potential to bring the promise of EE to a wide range of learners in higher education. UID is the application, in learning environments, of the architectural principle of Universal Design (UD), which is defined as "the design of products and environments to be usable by all people, to the greatest extent possible, without the need for adaptation or specialized design" (Center for Universal Design, 1997, p.1). UID takes these ideas and applies them to education, although authors differ in the details and language of this application (Center for Applied Special Technology, 2006; Fox, Hatfield & Collins, 2003; Scott, McGuire, & Shaw, 2001; Silver, Bourke, &

Strehorn, 1998). Opitz and Block (2006) captured the essence of all of these approaches in the following statement:

> universally-designed instructional environments foster equitable and multimodal means by which students possessing the broadest range of characteristics can engage with instructors and curricular materials, and thus minimize barriers to students' learning. (p. 35)

UID has become a robust resource for educators concerned with a wide array of "atypical" learners. UID is probably most readily associated with meeting the needs of students with disabilities. Examples include the inclusion of syllabus statements inviting those needing accommodations to contact the instructor and providing multiple modes (e.g. written, oral, visual, tactile) to present classroom information. The incorporation of UID principles in this arena has been influenced by recognition of the inherent value of the principles and the access they facilitate, and by practical concerns. Without UID, access to higher education for persons with disabilities is fundamentally linked to legal statutes such as the Rehabilitation Act of 1973 (United States Department of Health and Human Services, 2006) and the Americans with Disabilities Act (ADA) of 1990 (United States Department of Justice, 2007). Both require institutions of higher education to provide "reasonable accommodations" to otherwise qualified students with disabilities. The law requires case-by-case handling that includes verification of the disability and identification of an accommodation that reasonably balances access and academic integrity and rigor. This individual process is time consuming and labor intensive; additionally, accommodations tend to be made after a course or learning experience has been designed, requiring supplementary and often unexpected faculty effort. Examples include providing written material in large print or developing alternative test formats. Frequently, a trainee's understandable reluctance to disclose a disability and needed accommodation in a timely manner can further complicate this legally-mandated paradigm within an EE setting.

The growing numbers of higher education students with disabilities requesting these legally-protected individualized accommodations, along with the unresolved disclosure issues, have raised serious concerns. How can the administrative task of providing case-by-case accommodations be lessened? How can faculty efficiently and effectively provide accommodations in the context of typical time and resource constraints? How can the impact of society's stigmatizing of disability be lessened for students in educational environments? Although not a complete solution, UID is a powerful tool for addressing these concerns.

UID aims to reduce barriers for all learners, decreasing the need for individual, after-the-fact accommodations. Consequently, administrative involvement is reduced, students are less likely to need to disclose a potentially stigmatizing condition, and faculty can plan for the needs of students as they design their courses, not after the learning experience is underway. All of these positive outcomes associated with implementing UID in classroom settings can be realized in EE settings. Indeed, applying UID in EE holds great promise to expand the already valuable learning opportunities associated with this approach to education.

Case Studies

The setting for EE is the work environment where "real" work is the expectation. Mentoring trainees can take time and effort, but the employer is usually rewarded with the satisfaction of watching the trainee grow and contribute to workplace outcomes. Many institutions are motivated to take trainees because it is an excellent strategy to recruit new staff. However, it can also be disruptive and costly in terms of time, productivity, and safety if the student presents challenges. While the primary goal of the academic institution is teaching, the primary goal of the workplace is meeting performance expectations. Challenging trainees can place hardships on the work site, preceptor, and the relationship between the academic institution and the work site. The cost of a negative outcome can also have significant negative impact on the learner. In some situations the trainee may be unable to graduate or sit for a licensure exam until internship or other EE requirements are met. If it is serious enough, the trainee may even fail out of school altogether. Let us consider some trainee situations that may present particular challenges and how UID can prevent problems and costly mistakes.

"Lisa" (a pseudonym) is a very bright physical therapy student who has worked extremely hard to do well in her college classes. She has extensive experience working with the elderly and would like to dedicate her career to this group. In elementary school Lisa was diagnosed with a learning disability that affects language processes such as reading, spelling and organizing papers. Over the years she has found many compensatory strategies that enable her to achieve academic success, but it takes her longer than the typical student to complete her work. She relies heavily on assistance from technological equipment such as her computer and other technologies. She worries that when she gets into the hospital environment she will be unable to meet time demands and that she will have difficulty with documentation.

"Carlos" (pseudonym) is a business student who immigrated to the United States from Mexico when he was in middle school. He is fluent in Spanish, and his English is good but not always perfect. When he speaks or writes he occasionally makes errors in grammar or spelling, and sometimes cannot find the best words to express his ideas in English. These errors occur more frequently when he is rushed for time or under stress. The Latino practice of "personalismo" is still an integral part of Carlos's social interactions. He finds it important to get to know each of his colleagues well, and to spend considerable time engaging them in social conversation before he gets down to business and addresses the problem at hand. He is aware that in the world of high technology, business people are very task oriented and structured in their interactions. Carlos may not make the "right" impression with his less-than-perfect English and his penchant for spending time talking with clients about their personal interests.

"Andrea" (pseudonym) is very excited about becoming a teacher. It is something that she has wanted to do since she was in elementary school when a teacher made learning exciting for her. She has studied hard and worked summer jobs in children's camps, where she has been consistently praised for her creativity and ability to relate to "hard to reach" children. She is well prepared to begin student teaching, however, she is scared, actually she is very scared, to enter the classroom as the teacher. Every time she thinks about it, her heart races, her hands get sweaty, and she forgets all her carefully planned lessons. Her doctor has told her that she has an anxiety disorder and she is working with a therapist to learn how to manage this.

The Role of UID in Addressing Challenges

Each of the students presented in these case studies has many positive attributes that will be assets when they begin their first jobs. However, they each appear to have very different needs that would require different accommodations in their traineeships and on the job. Due to fear, embarrassment, or stigma, it is also likely that they may not choose to disclose their challenges or to make requests for accommodations. In each case, their needs would probably not become apparent until they were failing. These situations require the preceptor to be vigilant to prevent inefficiency or costly mistakes. Indeed, without intervention, each of these trainees may have a less than optimal outcome that could impact the quality of the work that is done in the traineeship, endangering the bottom line and the safety and well being of clients. By embedding the principles of UID into the structure of the internships, all trainees can be supported and the preceptor's need for competent trainees is more likely to be met without creating a burdensome amount of work. Furthermore, UID will enhance the learning environment for all trainees, supporting everyone's success without imposing undue hardship.

Many trainees, including those without atypical needs, arrive at traineeships unprepared to succeed at all aspects of their jobs. Implementing UID assists all trainees to be more successful and lessens the burden on supervisors. Let us consider how these principles can be applied in the work setting in a way that supports trainee learning while maintaining high standards and expectations. For purposes of this section, the following UID principles that are the most applicable to EE will be considered: (a) create a welcoming environment and a positive instructional climate; (b) define essential components; (c) communicate clear expectations; (d) provide constructive feedback; (e) incorporate natural supports for learning, including a community of learners; (f) use a variety of instructional methods; and (g) use multiple ways to test learning outcomes.

Creating a Welcoming Environment

Creating a welcoming environment sets the tone for all future actions. New trainee orientation is an essential part of any student program and allows new trainees to begin to understand their role in the organization and what is expected of them. The key feature in establishing a climate that facilitates trainee success is the development of a positive relationship between the trainee and the preceptor (Myrick & Yonge, 2005). All trainees will feel some degree of stress and be uncertain how to proceed. A preceptor should begin by informing the trainee that he or she is someone who is at ease with students and welcomes the opportunity to teach. Treating each trainee with respect lays the foundation for establishing a trusting relationship. This attitude allows the trainee to voice concerns and uncertainties and to feel comfortable asking questions without shame or embarrassment (Myrick & Yonge). The preceptor also sends a message about the climate of the work site and how flexible or accommodating the work site is willing to be.

Under the ADA all persons who declare a documented disability are entitled to reasonable accommodations. As previously noted, many students do not disclose that they have a disability if it is a hidden condition such as a learning disability. Rather than waiting for the trainee to make a request, or to fail because of not requesting an accommodation, a policy that encourages all trainees to discuss learning needs with their preceptor invites disclosure. This can be done by making a statement in the orientation materials about the preceptor's willingness to address differences and to offer the opportunity to discuss learning needs. The preceptor can directly inquire, "What things are important for you to be able to learn? How can I help you with that?" This practice also provides preceptors with the opportunity to explore their own teaching style and to learn new teaching strategies. The preceptor can also ask trainees directly if they will need any ADA accommodations, although this is best done in a private area that assures confidentiality is maintained.

Another important strategy for welcoming new trainees is to develop an attitude of openness and authenticity in communication. Many trainees are anxious about making the right impression, fitting in, and meeting expectations. A preceptor may be a source of both expertise and intimidation. Preceptors can be seen as more accessible if they share some of their own experiences as a learner and allow the trainee to see that they have been vulnerable at times (Welch, 2006). This may also provide a comfortable opportunity to ask trainees to discuss cultural background and how they see their beliefs or practices fitting in with the culture of the organization. Many cultural differences can be assets once they are identified and put into context.

Finally, creating a welcoming climate means taking the trainee's physical comfort into account. Pointing out the coat room, the availability of the rest rooms, where to get coffee or water, and how to find the cafeteria are important in alleviating anxiety (Myrick & Yonge, 2005). One of the authors still recalls the first day of her first traineeship when noon arrived and all the staff left for lunch. No one told her where to go, and she was alone in the staff room! It certainly did not create a sense of a welcoming environment

For a student like Andrea with anxiety, these will probably be the most important steps that a preceptor can take. Anxiety is increased with uncertainty and fear of the unknown; anxiety can be lessened by letting the student know that mistakes are an expected part of the learning process and that we all make them. As we will see in the steps that come later, this relationship of trust can be built upon by making the expectations clear, offering timely and accurate feedback, and providing natural supports.

Defining Essential Components

The second principle of UID is defining essential components of the work experience. The preceptor must determine what job responsibilities are critical and which are customary, but not essential. This can be difficult, especially in fields with rich and valued traditions. If the justification for declaring a task "essential" is that "it has always been done this way," it is probably not essential. One helpful strategy in differentiating essential from customary is to focus on outcomes. Indeed, it is the outcome that is important, even though the means of achieving that outcome may be novel or individualized. For example, in a hospital setting the nurse or therapist would be responsible for accurately documenting patient outcomes. It might take a trainee like Lisa longer to accomplish this, or she might struggle with the correct spelling of words or use of abbreviations. The product, documentation with correct spelling, is an essential function that must always be performed in an accurate and timely manner. However, there may be alternate ways this outcome can be achieved. She could carry a spell checker or write notes on a computer rather than by hand. To accommodate the increased time Lisa needs to perform these tasks she could come in early or stay later without being criticized or penalized. For Andrea, standing in front of a class and talking is likely to be uncomfortable, but it will be an essential component of the student teaching experience. She may be creative and effective at developing small group activities where the students are able to learn via active engagement with the materials instead of by listening to her talk. These are accommodations that can be available to all students and staff without considering them special exceptions to standard procedures.

For Carlos to be successful it would be important to consider what jobs within the organization best match his talents. He might be extremely successful in sales or public relations while accounting or technology support may not be the best fit for him. Given the importance of multiculturalism in today's diverse work force, his language skills and knowledge of Latino culture could be extremely important assets. He would still be expected to perform all the important functions in his job description, but would not need to perform all the jobs available at the firm.

Providing Clear Expectations

Providing clear expectations is the third UID principle to be considered. Trainees cannot succeed unless they know specifically what they will be expected to do. Many preceptors will consider this to be intuitive, but in fact, in our experience it is one of the most common reasons trainees fail. Every work site should have an orientation manual with clearly stated policies and regulations. Rules, safety procedures, and reporting protocols should be included (Welch, 2006). The preceptor should discuss relevant sections of the manual with trainees to make sure they do not overlook important components. Work sites should also consider including examples of completed forms, documentation, or reports that the trainee can use as a model. This practice can save considerable time and frustration as the trainee learns the details of each site's expectations. This is particularly important as some forms are legal documents and errors can put the trainee, preceptor, work site, client, or consumer at risk. Lists of frequently used terms, abbreviations, and resources can also be included in the student manual.

Another important topic to discuss is the trainee's schedule. It is essential to differentiate between what must be performed at a fixed time and what can be done in a flexible time frame. This knowledge allows the trainee to make appropriate modifications as needed without having to ask permission or neglect an important deadline. Lisa may need to know that before she leaves work each day all of her documentation must be complete, although she can take as long as she needs to accomplish this. Carlos, on the other hand, may be informed that he needs to see a certain number of clients each week, but he is free to make his own schedule and determine how much time he spends with each client. Lisa will need to include all essential curriculum components in her classes, but can be flexible with how much time she spends on each unit.

Learning about the culture of the training site may seem intuitive, but is often one of the most challenging aspects of meeting expectations. The preceptor should provide the trainee with information on the structure and rules of the organization, the hierarchy of the organization (who reports to whom), the formality of social interactions (how people address each other and interact), boundaries, and how roles are defined (who can do what). UID would advocate for sharing this information in both written and oral forms. Preceptors are most likely to focus on the cognitive or psychomotor skills trainees will be learning or doing. They may not attend to orienting trainees to the culture of the organization, thus setting trainees up for uncertainty. This may disrupt the smooth flow of the work process and contribute to trainee failure, co-worker dissatisfaction, and lost productivity or safety (Welch, 2006).

Providing Feedback

Once the value of sharing clear expectations is realized, implementation is usually straightforward. This is in contrast to the implementation of the UID principle of providing feedback. Even those who value the role of feedback may find it challenging to provide. Providing constructive feedback is the fourth aspect of UID that has great importance in facilitating the success of EE. Unfortunately, providing feedback is all too often perceived as confrontational, by both those giving and receiving. Informing trainees who are genuinely doing their best that their work is unsatisfactory is an important role of the preceptor. Trainees' success often depends on knowing what they have done well, what needs to be improved, and what good performance looks like. Feedback is most appropriate when it is given immediately after the incident, is given in a nonjudgmental fashion, and addresses the behavior, not the individual.

Feedback, of course, should not focus solely on deficiencies. When constructive criticism is balanced by praise and specific comments on what has been done well, feedback is less likely to seem confrontational. For example,

> Carlos, you included excellent information in your presentation and it was very well organized. I liked how you connected last week's scheduling problem with the dip in sales. However, when you were speaking it seemed that some of the group didn't understand how the computer glitch in accounting affected the scheduling. This was probably a time when giving too much information detracted from the main message

> you were trying to send. Next time, let's work together to think through what are the essential points to include that will help the staff understand what is going on, and what is probably going to overload them. We can do it together.

The more specific and concrete the feedback, the clearer it will be to the trainee what needs to change.

Creating Natural Supports for Learning

The work environment provides a wealth of natural supports for learning and finding ways to incorporate these supports into EE is valuable. Trainees can be formally placed in groups or teams with other students or staff to accomplish tasks. Some hospitals place trainees in groups of two or three so that they can learn from each other and complement each other's strengths. Alternately, trainees may be encouraged to find other trainees or staff who are willing to mentor them on an informal basis. Study groups, meetings with administrative assistants, and sharing coffee or lunch all provide natural opportunities to network and acquire information or practice skills. Interactions with "real" clients also provide natural opportunities for learning.

Consider our three students. Lisa may find that she can collaborate with other physical therapy trainees and trainees in other health fields as well. They may share ways they have learned to accomplish patient care skills and provide her with tips they have found to make documentation more efficient. The department administrative assistant may be willing to spend time with her to help her practice the computer documentation system. Carlos may find another staff person who is willing to help him to find leads for clients or projects that best suit his personality or that would benefit from his fluency in Spanish. He can also collaborate with other trainees or staff to solve potential problems with his work before he presents it to his preceptor. Andrea might find that other student teachers share many of her struggles with lack of confidence and provide her with moral support or compensatory strategies. Many work sites have technologies that can support learning at every level such as e-mail, voicemail, portable communication devices, and text messaging.

Using Varied Instructional Methods

The next principle of UID, use of varied instructional methods, is the hallmark of EE. Multiple learning activities are a fundamental characteristic of the work place, and many diverse learners actually do better with hands-on learning. In academic settings, most learning tends to be via reading, writing, or listening. However, many students are tactile, kinesthetic, or multisensory learners who require multiple opportunities to interact with the material in order to master it (Dornan & Bundy, 2004; Williams-Perez & Keig, 2002). What better place to learn anatomy than with a patient with an illness or a disability? The principles of computer science can be applied in a work situation where the trainee actually has to produce a program that solves a problem and has to test it out with multiple users. Interpersonal and affective skills can be addressed by providing opportunities to interact with other staff, clients, administrative assistants, executives, and the crew that cleans the office.

Allowing Students to Demonstrate Learning in Multiple Ways

Closely connected to the concept of using a variety of instructional methods is employing a variety of ways for students to demonstrate their learning. In the work setting some preceptors will "grill" trainees on their rote knowledge of facts. This can be intimidating—even terrifying—to trainees and would not be a good technique for finding out how much our three students know. Again, the work setting is where trainees get to apply their knowledge across multiple paradigms. Learning should be tested in all the ways that trainees will be using it when they graduate and begin their careers. The preceptor will learn far more about how well trainees can write a progress note, project summary, or student evaluation by reading one they have actually written than by having them take a test on the principles of how it should be done.

Summary

In summary, EE is an exciting alternative to traditional, classroom-based education. It extends the learning environment to real world settings, bringing with it multiple benefits to trainees, preceptors and their organizations, and the home academic institutions. In contrast to traditional classroom teaching techniques that rely heavily on learning through listening and reading, EE emphasizes hands-on learning and the practical application of knowledge. Because of these differences, EE may be particularly well suited to students with atypical learning needs, such as those with a disability or with cultural differences. The opportunity to participate in EE, however, may be lessened because of those atypical learning needs. The complex nature of EE, including the multiple demands that need to be balanced by each stakeholder and the potential stigma associated with being an atypical learner, may hinder opportunities for individuals who are perhaps ideally suited for EE. While preceptors might feel burdened by the extra time and effort it takes to establish learning experiences that use UID, it should soon become apparent that this saves time overall, and enhances the learning experience for all involved. UID is a valuable resource that can increase access to EE for those with atypical learning needs, while at the same time improving the experience for everyone. Applying UID to EE takes an already good situation and improves it for everyone!

References

American Physical Therapy Association. (2007). *APTA clinical instructor education and credentialing program.* Retrieved July 28, 2007, from www.apta.org/AM/Template.cfm?Section=Home&Template=/CM/HTMLDisplay.cfm&ContentID=21012

Antioch College. (2005). Experience counts and our employers know it best! *An overview of cooperative education.* Retrieved July 29, 2007, from www.antioch-college.edu/co-op/employer/index.html

Brostrand, H. L. (2006). Tilting at windmills: Changing attitudes toward people with disabilities. *Journal of Rehabilitation, 72*(1), 4-9.

Center for Applied Special Technology. (2006). *CAST: Universal Design for Learning.* Retrieved March 22, 2007, from http://www.cast.org

Center for Universal Design. (1997). *The principles of Universal Design.* (Verson 2.0). Raleigh: North Carolina State University.

Dornan, T., & Bundy, C. (2004). What can experience add to early medical education? Consensus survey. *British Medical Journal, 329*(7470), 834.

Estes, C. (2004). Promoting student-centered learning in experiential education. *Journal of Experiential Education, 27*(2), 141-160.

Fox, J. A., Hatfield, J. P., & Collins, T. (2003). Developing the Curriculum Transformation and Disability workshop model. In J. L. Higbee (Ed.), *Curriculum transformation and disability: Implementing Universal Design in higher education* (pp. 23-39). Minneapolis: University of Minnesota, General College, Center for Research on Developmental Education and Urban Literacy.

Hehir, T. (2002). Eliminating ableism in education. *Harvard Educational Review, 72*(1), 1-31.

Hoffart, N., Diani, J., Connors, M., & Moynihan, P. (2006). Outcomes of cooperative education in a baccalaureate program in nursing. *Nursing Education Perspectives, 27*(3), 136-143.

Jacobson, L., Grinel, C., & Lewis, B. (2006). What is happening in pre-licensure RN clinical nursing education? Findings from the faculty and administrator survey in clinical nursing education. *Nursing Education Perspectives, 27*(2), 108-109.

Kalivoda, K. S. (2003). Creating access through Universal Instructional Design.

In J. L. Higbee, D. B. Lundell, & I. M. Duranczyk (Eds.), *Multiculturalism in developmental education* (pp. 25-34). Minneapolis: University of Minnesota, General College, Center for Research on Developmental Education and Urban Literacy. Retrieved August 21, 2007, from http://education.umn.edu/CRDEUL/pdf/monograph/4-a.pdf

Keen, C., & Howard, A. (2002). Experiential learning in Antioch College's work-based learning program as a vehicle for social and emotional development for gifted college students. *The Journal of Secondary Gifted Education, XIII*(5), 130-140.

Kraft, D., & Sakofs, M. (Eds). (1988). *The theory of experiential education.* Boulder, CO: Association for Experiential Education.

Littlefield, L., Haines, S., Harralson, A., Schwartz, A., Shaeffer, S., Zeolla, M., & Flynn, A. (2004). Academic pharmacy's role in advancing practice and assuring quality in experiential education: Report of the 2003-2004 professional affairs committee. *American Journal of Pharmaceutical Education, 68*(3), S8, 1-12.

Marks B. (2000). Jumping through hoops and walking on egg shells or discrimination, hazing and abuse of students with disabilities. *Nursing Educator, 39*(5), 205-210.

Myrick, F., & Yonge, O. (2005). *Nursing preceptorship: Connecting practice to education.* Philadelphia: Lippincott, Williams and Wilkins.

Opitz, D. L., & Block, L. S. (2006). Universal learning support design: Maximizing learning beyond the classroom. *The Learning Assistance Review, 11*(2), 33-45.

Osborn, C., Daninhirsch, C., & Page, B. (2003). Experiential training in group counseling: Humanistic processes in practice. *Journal of Humanistic Counseling, Education and Development, 42*(1), 14-22.

Plake, K., & Wolfgang, A. (1996). Impact of experiential education on pharmacy students' perceptions of health roles. *American Journal of Pharmaceutical Education, 60,* 13-19.

Reynolds, P. (2006). Commentary and introduction: Service learning and community-based scholarship. *Journal of Physical Therapy Education, 20*(3), 3-7.

Ryan, C., & Krapels, R. (1997). Organizations and internships. *Business Communication Quarterly, 60*(4), 126-130.

Schambach, T., & Dirks, J. (2002). Student perceptions of internship experiences. *Proceedings of the 17th Annual Conference of the International Academy for Information Management.* Retrieved July 29, 2007, from www.eric.ed.gov:80/ERICWebPortal/custom/portlets/recordDetails/detailmini.jsp?_nfpb=true&_&ERICExtSearch_SearchValue_0=ED481733&ERICExtSearch_SearchType_0=eric_accno&accno=ED481733

Scott, S. S., McGuire, J. M., & Shaw, S. F. (2001). *Principles of Universal Design for Instruction.* Storrs: University of Connecticut, Center on Postsecondary Education and Disability.

Scott, S. S., McGuire, J. M., & Shaw, S. F. (2003). Universal Design for Instruction: A new paradigm of adult instruction in postsecondary education. *Remedial and Special Education, 24,* 369-379.

Silver, P., Bourke, A. B., & Strehorn, K. C. (1998). Universal Instructional Design in higher education: An approach for inclusion. *Equity and Excellence in Education, 31*(2), 47-51.

Talley, C. R. (2006). Experiential education for pharmacy students. *American Society of Health-System Pharmacists, 63*(11), 1029.

Thomas, S. (2000). College students and disability law. *Journal of Special Education, 33*(4), 248-258.

Traynor, K. (2004). Experiential education requirements squeeze schools, rotation sites. *American Journal of Health Care Pharmacy. 61,* 1537-1538.

United States Department of Health and Human Services. (2006). *Your rights under section 504 of the Rehabilitation Act.* Retrieved July 29, 2007, from www.hhs.gov/ocr/504.pdf

United States Department of Justice (2007). *Americans With Disabilities Act of 1990.* Retrieved July 29, 2007, from www.usdoj.gov/crt/ada/pubs/ada.htm

Welch, S. A. (2006). Understanding clinical culture: Organizational communication in the clinical practicum. *The Internet Journal of Allied Health Sciences and Practice, 4*(4).

Williams-Perez, K., & Keig, L. (2002). Experiential learning: A strategy to teach conflict management. *Nurse Educator, 27*(4), 165-167.

Zettergren, K., & Beckett, R. (2004). Changes in critical thinking scores: An examination of one group of physical therapy students. *Journal of Physical Therapy Education, 18*(2), 73-79.

CHAPTER 26

An Administrative Approach to Universal Design in Allied Health Sciences

Deborah A. Casey
Green River Community College

Abstract
Administrators working with allied health sciences programs have the opportunity to create environments in which all students can be nurtured to achieve academic success. Postsecondary administrators are conduits to promote new initiatives to enhance instructional teaching methods, develop inclusive policies, and advocate for diverse teaching across the curriculum. Administrators can take an active role in supporting these initiatives by endorsing the principles of Universal Design (UD) across the academic curriculum and co-curriculum. This chapter offers an overview and practical recommendations for developing inclusive UD practices for administrators to increase access and provide support for students and faculty.

Administrators in higher education continue to discuss aggressive recruitment, marketing, and retention strategies necessary to increase enrollment, persistence, and graduation rates of students. Declining student enrollments compounded by decreasing federal and state funding support accelerate the urgency to determine new approaches to working with diverse student populations. Postsecondary administrators are conduits to promote new initiatives to enhance instructional methods, develop inclusive policies, and advocate for diverse teaching across the curriculum and within student support services (e.g., tutoring, advising, financial aid, student programs). One example of how administrators can take an active role in supporting these initiatives is by endorsing the principles of Universal Design (UD) across the academic curriculum and co-curriculum.

The conceptual framework of Universal Design emerged from the architectural field and over the past 10 years has been studied within the field of education (Rose & Meyer, 2000). Researchers have documented content and materials developed in alternative formats that in conjunction with diverse teaching strategies offer a host of benefits to students. These initiatives allow the learner to customize and engage in instructional content specific to diverse learning styles (Abell, Bauder, & Simmons, 2004; Brown & Augustine, 2000). The principles of UD offer faculty, support services professionals, and students innovative learning possibilities. UD also promotes inclusive academic support provisions for students with and without disabilities. This chapter focuses on UD concepts and strategies for administrators working with allied health sciences faculty to compliment the Universal Instructional Design (UID) strategies addressed in other chapters of this book.

Allied Health Sciences Programs

The term "allied health" has been utilized for over 30 years to identify a cluster of health professions aligned in a higher education setting as an academic unit or department of a school, college, or university. Allied health sciences programs in the 21st century continue to be prestigious and competitive programs in higher education. Examples of allied health sciences programs include dentistry, dental hygiene, medical technology, physical therapy, occupational therapy, nursing, surgical technology, and other programs offering a medical focus with both didactic and practical academic requirements (Casey, 2007). Many of these professions require licensure or certification to practice in the specific allied health specialty. These programs evolved steadfastly over the centuries and additional professional programs such as colleges of nursing, colleges of medicine, and colleges of pharmacy now offer diverse programs for professional careers. The continued emergence of allied health sciences programs poses new challenges for administrators and institutions of higher education in regard to equal access for students with disabilities who are admitted to these programs.

Allied health sciences programs require both didactic and practical curriculum components. Students learn in both the classroom and the clinical environment how to apply the theoretical and practical applications required for their selected allied health sciences program. Students completing the necessary classroom curriculum programs in allied health sciences expect to transition into clinical experiences seamlessly. Many institutions have implemented initiatives to address seamless transitions for students (Cohen & Brawer, 2003; Echevarria Rafuls, Howard-Hamilton, & Jennie, 1999; Sausner, 2004; Townsend, 2001). The seamless transition for students from the classroom to the clinical experience provides a stable and consistent process. For example, students entering the clinical setting expect to have already acquired lab skills to help them in the clinical experience. These skills provide a smooth transition because the skills were performed first in a teaching and learning environment rather than on-site. Unfortunately, this sometimes is not the case for students with disabilities because in specific instances the clinical environment poses additional barriers such as rigorous hours, physical demands, and negative attitudes (Sowers & Smith, 2003) not encountered in the lab setting. These barriers may have intentional or unintentional effects on "weeding out" students participating in allied health sciences programs.

Legal Obligations, Accommodations, and Technical Standards

The foundation of equal access for individuals with disabilities in higher education evolved from the passage of Section 504 of the Rehabilitation Act of 1973 and the Americans with Disabilities Act (ADA) of 1990. Both laws obligate institutions of higher education to provide academic adjustments to students as long as the adjustments are not unduly burdensome and do not compromise proven essential requirements of the educational programs. Section 504 and the ADA were landmark federal laws intended to increase access for individuals with disabilities. Federal legislation provided a legal framework to bring about greater public access and equal treatment than previously offered. The case law outcomes of each act started a process of expanding the rights of people with disabilities and afforded individuals the opportunity to participate in postsecondary allied health programs.

College and university disability support services (DSS) offices offer students with disabilities assurances that federal law will be followed for access to educational programs. In postsecondary education it is the student's responsibility to initiate the process of self-identification and requests for academic accommodations. A collaborative process between DSS, the student, and faculty is a central aspect of providing academic adjustments to students with disabilities. Harris, Horn, and McCarthy (1994) stated, "Ideally an accommodation results from collaborative effort among the student, faculty, and student affairs professional designated to assist in this individualized process" (p. 40). A balance between meeting the needs of the student and maintaining academic standards is a fundamental aspect of the intent of the federal laws (Hart, Zimbrich, & Whelley, 2002).

Reasonable accommodations are any modification or adjustment to an environment that enables a qualified student with a disability to participate in the course requirements and perform essential technical standards in the clinical setting. Accommodations refer to the removal of barriers for specific disabilities allowing an individual access to the educational process. Examples of reasonable accommodations include (a) making existing facilities used by other students readily accessible to and usable by an individual with a disability, (b) restructuring a clinical timeline, (c) modifying work schedules, and (d) acquiring or modifying examinations. Universal Design refers to the creation of curriculum and services automatically built into the educational process to minimize or eliminate the need for accommodations. Faculty and student services professionals utilizing UD shift the need to accommodate a specific individual to inclusive strategies to support all student's learning outcomes.

Allied health sciences students traditionally prefer a more active, experiential learning mode in which preferred topics allow students to engage immediately (i.e., within a social context such as a lab setting or with concrete content demonstrating a specific technical procedure), allowing the student to comprehend how the material relates to professional goals and experiences. UD principles offer diverse learners a variety of alternative learning and assessment possibilities that meet the experiential learning of allied health sciences students.

In allied health sciences programs essential functions are referred to as technical standards. However, Maheady (1999) stated in her research on students with disabilities enrolled in nursing programs that technical standards were not readily available or utilized on most campuses. She acknowledged in her study that a taskforce to the Board of Directors of the Southern Council on Collegiate Education for Nursing (SCCEN) assisted in the development of guidelines for nursing education programs in the Southeast. The guidelines were developed to respond to students covered under the ADA and address safety and welfare concerns related to performance outcomes. A few examples of the technical requirements include: (a) critical thinking, (b) interpersonal, (c) communication, (d) mobility, (e) motor skills, (f) hearing, (g) visual, and (h) tactile (p. 3). Today, technical standards are applied to all students who enter a program.

Technical standards are current practices used in many allied health sciences programs. The standards also serve as guides to assist the faculty and administrators in complying with accreditation expectations. These technical standards allow students the opportunity to reflect on whether they can meet the technical functions of the program to which they are applying. Typically, each technical standard will have an example of an activity that a student must perform while enrolled in the program. Technical standards are performance indicators essential to a professional clinical practitioner.

Administrators and faculty working with allied health sciences programs consistently assert that safety is the most important aspect when dealing with patients in programs serving the community. Medical mistakes are the fifth leading cause of death in the United States (Commonwealth of Massachusetts Group Insurance Division, 2006). Human mistakes cause more deaths than car accidents, breast cancer, and AIDS. Mistakes that are not fatal can still lead to injury, disability, longer hospital stays, or longer recovery time. Allied health sciences departments and faculty are held accountable when students are placed in clinical settings.

The accountability expectations are so high that faculty and administrators use technical standards to ensure satisfactory performance in all academic and clinical coursework. Faculty and clinical coordinators spend extensive time and effort building partnerships with local clinical affiliates. A single questionable situation surrounding patient safety (Sowers & Smith, 2003) can potentially jeopardize the institutional partnerships and future clinical sites for students. A loss of one clinical affiliation can destroy an entire program if the program is located in a geographical area with few clinical site possibilities. When students are working one-on-one with patients, faculty or clinical supervisors must have confidence in the basic technical competencies of the students representing the institution and working with community members. Administrators are held accountable for protecting the institution from legal situations involving factors like patient safety that can have a direct impact on the college or university. There is always a fine line balancing priorities between student success and the institutions' reputation, credibility in the community, and accreditation.

In my research study (Casey, 2006), patient safety was the most prominent finding between and among faculty, students, and staff related to indicators of student success in allied health programs. The most revealing aspect of the safety finding was faculty and staff concerns regarding the ability of students with psychological disabilities to provide safe patient care in the clinical setting. The finding also demonstrated concerns regarding student use of medication in the clinical setting and students' emotional stability, which directly affected the safety of patients. However, it was interesting that none of the allied health sciences programs participating in my study had policies or procedures in place related to students' medication usage during clinical affiliations or mechanisms such as seminars on how to deal with workplace stressors. I also interviewed and surveyed students without disabilities who shared experiences directly related to workplace stress in the clinical environment (Casey, 2007). The students without disabilities articulated similar concerns related to emotional stability and patient safety. Faculty were also concerned about the competencies of all students when providing for the safety and welfare of patients. The need for safety procedures and the concerns of faculty regarding patient safety were enumerated in Marks' (2000) research with nursing faculty. The most important and consistent concern generated in Marks' study regarding students with disabilities was the ability of these students to provide safe patient care in clinical training settings.

Applying a UD Framework to Budgets, Policies and Procedures, Technology, and Facilities

What is the role of leadership in supporting Universal Design? Administrators and leaders in the field of allied health sciences must be able to step back and see the bigger picture, the context within which they wish to initiate change. If an administrator's role is to create systemic changes on campus, then Universal Design is one model that has long-lasting outcomes (Rohland, Erickson, Mathews, Roush, Quinlan, & DaSilva Smith, 2003). One way to create systemic change is for administrators to have an understanding of the differences between accommodations for students with disabilities and UD strategies. Systemic change also includes understanding how the use of multiple strategies and perspectives—whether it be assessments or evaluations of students' knowledge in the classroom or providing ramps for all campus users—provides a much richer institutional analysis than the use of only one view or method of accomplishing student learning or services.

Boleman and Deal (1997) viewed culture as both a product and a process: "As a product, it embodies accumulated wisdom from those who came before us. As a process, it is continually renewed and recreated as newcomers learn the old ways and eventually become teachers themselves" (p. 217). As administrators, some of us have created the product while others are in a dynamic process to continue to gain more knowledge. The conceptual framework of UD demands that administrators evaluate the process and determine ways to make policies and procedures more inclusive. Institutions are obligated under the law to provide accommodations to individuals with disabilities, but providing Universal Design truly meets an institutional mission of equal access. If the mission of the institution is to assist all students in being successful in achieving their full potential, then creating inclusive policies for admission, retention, and graduation in allied health sciences programs must be considered. UD can guide the conversations about how administrators create inclusive environments. Partnerships between allied health sciences departments and disability support services are critical to implementing UD strategies. Fostering these partnerships can enhance collaboration and identify ways to enhance teaching and learning for all students.

Allied health sciences faculty and administrators may want to consider viewing students from a social justice model rather than a medical model. A medical model focuses on individuals' inability to do things and their need to be taken care of by others (Michalko, 2002). The social justice model shifts attention from the individual to the environmental factors associated with discrimination and exclusion. As noted by Evans, Assadi, and Herriott (2005), the shift from a medical model to a social justice model eliminates ableism. Allied health sciences faculty and administrators may want to consider evaluating ableism attitudes within their departments by breaking down the cultural norms associated with what is perceived to be the ideal allied health sciences student.

Budget and Fiscal Decision Making

The fiscal environment continues to challenge leaders of higher education. Budgets are continually shrinking due to federal and state micromanagement, economic recessions, and changing student demographics. The strategic planning process allows an organization "to identify and maintain an optimal alignment with the most important key elements of the environment" (Rowley, Lujan, & Dolence, 1997, p. 15). It is obvious that linking strategic planning to the budget process is one way to ensure long-term success. Budgeting is a process through which proactive planning can support programs, services, and learning opportunities. Funding for UD professional development endeavors, marketing strategies, and technology initiatives is beneficial for administrators to consider when planning for and allocating fiscal resources. Faculty and staff in allied health sciences should be involved in the budgeting process from the planning to the allocation phases. Incorporating UD into the day-to-day operations may require budget allocations initially, but over time may decrease the need for individual accommodation requests. One example of initial budgeting costs may be the inclusion of a statement for access requests on all campus publications. At first it may be costly to edit publications, but once the initial costs are allocated the publications may serve a variety of diverse learners. Another fiscal example may be the up-front costs for Section 508 recommendations to update the college or university Web site. The benefit of having a user-friendly Web site enhances the number of individuals viewing the Web site for recruitment and retention initiatives.

Policies and Procedures

This section outlines various policies and procedures related to student rights and due process as well as notification of progress and dismissal. Each of these areas highlights ways in which administrators can transform UD strategies into practice. Policies and procedures can be created to be inclusive in practice or they have the potential to exclude individuals unintentionally, creating an unwelcoming environment. Implementing continuous evaluation of polices and procedures and combining the evaluation process with the UD framework offers administrators a template for inclusive practices.

Consistent policies and procedures within allied health sciences programs protect both the student and the institution. An administrator within a division often has the responsibility for creating and updating policies and procedures. Standards and policies are usually the result of extended discussions with faculty and administrative groups and ultimately decided by the division. Faculty and administrators must be involved collaboratively in the policy formation and implementation process. For example, one important consideration administrators can address with faculty is well thought-out policies and procedures that respond in a timely manner to student concerns, appeals, and potential grievances. The appeals process typically is initiated because of a failing grade, a dismissal from a clinical, or a code of conduct sanction. It provides direction and a road map for the student and the institution to follow when a potential complaint is made against a faculty member or the institution. Administrators have the responsibility to create open communication between themselves and the faculty involved in the complaint. This open communication creates a dialogue in which problematic issues can be discussed and addressed in a joint problem-solving manner. A consistent and fluid communication process provides a UD approach by promoting interactions among students and between faculty and administrators.

Another important aspect of the appeals process is determining if information resources prepared ahead of time outline the appeals process and are distributed to all students. For example, do student handbooks outline expected student codes of conduct, grievance procedures, appeals processes, clinical requirements, course substitution policies, and so on? This is helpful and universally designed because it communicates clear expectations to students. The materials should outline the appeals process and be offered in multiple formats taking into account diverse learning and communication styles.

UD principles can be applied to a number of other policies and procedures within allied health sciences programs including: (a) providing information and curriculum requirements in alternative formats such as print and online; (b) allowing faculty flexibility in scheduling hours of clinical rotations so a student can choose two 4-hour shifts in place of a one 8-hour shift; (c) providing students the option to read class materials such as books before the course begins; (d) allowing for adequate time to arrange for alternative formats such as books on tape; (e) requiring a mandatory and uniform institutional course syllabus statement for accessibility requests; and (f) encouraging faculty to look at the above issues and support these concepts in practice. In addition it is important to require that all publications have a statement such as, "Our goal is to make all materials and services accessible. Please inform the faculty of accessibility barriers you encounter and request accommodations that will make activities and information resources accessible to you" (Burgstahler, 2006),

Student rights and due process. Students are entitled to due process at both public and private institutions. However, public institutions are held to codes determined by state entities while private institutions are held mainly to federal mandates such as Civil Rights laws (Hollander, Young, & Gehring, 1995). Institutions must consider constitutional issues such as due process when decisions are made regarding removal or dismissal of a student from an allied health sciences program. Students at public institutions have two rights to due process, the constitutional right under the Fourteenth Amendment and a contractual right between the student and the institution.

The Fourteenth Amendment allows a student due process before an institutional body such as a departmental committee or an academic board, which is typically made up of faculty, students, and staff. A student's reputation is considered a "liberty" and enrollment at an institution is considered "a property right" (Hollander, Young, & Gehring, 1995, p. 48). A student, therefore, cannot be dismissed from a program without due process procedures. There are two types of due process: substantive and procedural. Substantive due process requires that policies and procedures must be related to institutional purpose and basic fairness must be employed. An example of a substantive due process is when a student in the medical program who is under a learning contract has contractual expectations that are related to the program and these expectations must be applied fairly by the institution. Procedural due process refers to the requirement for notice to a hearing before being deprived of a right. For instance, before being dismissed from a clinical program for misconduct or a safety violation in the clinical environment, the student should be notified of what he or she has done wrong and given a chance to express his or her side of the story. Both procedural and substantive due process provide a UD approach by applying consistent and equal access to all students.

Typically, academic due process involves substantive due process in which the student's academic competency is evaluated by academic criteria such as technical standards in the case of allied health sciences programs. In specific academic matters, there is no absolute right to procedural due process. For example, a student who jeopardizes the safety of a patient can be suspended or dismissed for academic failure. The student has the right to appeal the decision if the student believes the failing grade given was arbitrarily and capriciously assigned. Providing an appeals process incorporates UD by creating a welcoming environment and clear expectations for a student to address his or her side of the story. It also provides opportunity for open dialogue to occur between the student, the faculty, and the administration.

Notification of progress and dismissal. A student in an allied health science program should be notified of his or her academic progress. The student is made aware of the technical standards and course expectations in the admissions process, student handbook, and course syllabus. The syllabus acts as a contractual agreement between the student and the instructor or clinical site. A student who does not meet the technical standards of the course curriculum must be notified of the deficiency and allowed ample time to correct deficits in didactic or practical skills. Typically the deficiencies are noted in a learning contract. This contract is an agreement between the student and the faculty member outlining the academic deficits and the recommendations to meet the technical standards successfully. The student should be notified in writing of the deficiencies within a reasonable amount of time. The student and the instructor should both sign the learning contract agreement. A learning contract provides a UD approach by ensuring that each student has the opportunity to learn and grow in the educational process. The learning contract provides clear and consistent communication about what is expected from the student. In addition, a learning contract may be the perfect opportunity for a faculty member and the student to brainstorm alternative strategies to learn the material.

For example, if the faculty member expects students to function independently when they begin the clinical rotation or by the third clinical rotation, the expected timeline should be clearly documented. Obviously, we recognize that students need more supervision during the initial clinical experience. Allowing students time to learn, reviewing and correcting poor performance prior to making a mistake, and allowing students to repeat and practice the task until they become proficient are all UD strategies for the learning process.

Documentation of a student's progress should be maintained in a confidential file. When a student-instructor meeting is held, all information regarding the meeting should be documented with facts such as date, time, and individuals involved in the process. All documentation should be placed in the student file. Regardless of the decision to suspend or dismiss a student from an academic program, a student must be afforded certain measures of procedural fairness. A student should be notified of the rationale for removal or dismissal from a clinical site or institutional program. The student has a right to have dismissal reviewed by the department and in some cases the right to appeal to an impartial academic board. The academic board should notify the student of the results of the hearing findings and a final review of the appeal should be reviewed by an institutional designee such as the vice president, provost, or president, depending on the institution. The Family Educational Rights and Privacy Act (FERPA, 1974; U.S. Department of Education, n.d.) regulations apply when sharing information with other institutional resources or academic boards. Only those individuals directly involved in the due process and grievance procedures should have access to a student's records. Defining the process and access issues provides quality service and establishes best practices for all students.

A student must prove in the process of the dismissal appeal whether the dismissal was "arbitrary or capricious." For example, a nursing student fails a clinical course for safety reasons and is dismissed from the program. The student chooses to appeal and is then expected to show how the failing grade was given arbitrarily or capriciously. It is important in any academic dismissal proceeding that written procedures be followed and communicated with the student in a timely manner. These written procedures should be provided online, in paper format, and explained to the student verbally. Courts consistently view an institution's failure to follow its own rules and articulate those rules clearly as a violation of due process Binder & Hauser, 1995). This example illustrates UD by demonstrating how institutions and allied health sciences faculty and administrators must communicate clear expectations and procedures in alternative formats. These communications must be offered in multiple ways and take into consideration diverse learning and communication styles.

Partnerships and affiliations with clinical sites such as hospitals, laboratory settings, and out-patient clinics are critical to the success of a college or university allied health sciences program. Programs that offer a clinical affiliation have spent many hours developing rapport and partnerships with these outside affiliates, building trust and credibility for the student experience. Expecting an affiliate to become involved in the institutional due process proceedings for a student may in fact jeopardize the credibility of the faculty and the institution. In addition, it may damage the credibility of how other students from the institution are viewed. Only under extreme circumstances should a clinical site representative be called into an institutional due process proceeding. Witnesses for both the student and the department can be asked to provide statements or to attend the academic hearing in support of the institution or student.

Computer Software and Assistive Technology

Administrators can promote equal access through the provision of assistive technology for individuals with a wide range of abilities. When faculty acquire and utilize classroom technology, it opens up additional avenues of learning for students and fosters equal access. Some of the assistive technology approaches that promote UD include adjustable-height tables for wheelchair users and individuals of different physical sizes, software that enlarges screen images for students with low vision, a trackball in place of a mouse to allow those with fine motor skills limitations to maneuver easily, and wrist and forearm rests. In addition, there are interactive software teaching tools available to allied health faculty to create images providing the students a rich supplement to lectures. One example of this type of software allows the user to point, click, and identify more than 20,000 anatomical structures within fully dissectible male and female bodies in anterior, lateral, medial, and posterior views. This software allows students to view and manipulate anatomical structures, allowing the student to use technology to enhance classroom lecture material. Faculty and department Web sites can also be developed with UD principles allowing the site to be accessible for most users.

Facilities

Administrators have responsibilities that include providing a safe and accessible environment for faculty and students. Some facility considerations that employ UD approaches include: high-contrast, large-print directional signs throughout the department; elevators that have both auditory and visual signals for floors; controls that are accessible from a seated position; wheelchair-accessible restrooms; glare-free computer screens; adjustable lighting for students in the classroom; a minimization of noise and distractions in the classroom; printed materials within arm's reach; adequate work space for both left- and right-handed users; and door levers for easy operating. Careful consideration of the classroom and clinical environments for barrier-free access can benefit individuals with and without disabilities. All students want a clinical setting that embraces student learning and encourages individual growth. Providing welcoming facilities with barrier-free access demonstrates an inclusive environment for all individuals to use.

Strategic Planning for Universal Design Strategies

Administrators overseeing allied health sciences programs and departments are in a strategic position to create environments supportive of UD principles. These principles promote equal access for students and minimize the need for singling out individuals. A proactive strategic plan to infuse UD concepts into the allied health sciences department will in the end serve the greatest number of students in a more diverse manner. It should be noted that employing UD principles does not eliminate the need for some specific accommodations such as interpreters for the deaf. However, UD allows for greater participation and minimizes the need for additional accommodations.

Supporting Universal Design Professional Development

Administrators can impact student learning by arranging for faculty and staff professional development workshops focused on issues and concerns related to UD strategies. Arranging in-service training on how faculty and staff can effectively communicate and address needs of students can be accomplished in tandem with UD concepts (Getzel, Briel, & McManus, 2003). The disability support services office on campus may be well versed in UD strategies and offer expertise in working with students with and without disabilities. Strategies for assisting faculty in developing alternative methods for assessment and evaluation of student learning offer a wide range of professional development discussions. Ways to advise faculty as to how the classroom climate and physical environment may cause barriers to teaching and learning can also be addressed. Other topics for faculty and staff workshops include: alternative teaching strategies for students with diverse learning styles, creating welcoming and inclusive classroom and clinical environments, and addressing ways in which faculty can provide prompt and continuous feedback.

Case Study

The purpose of examining the following case study is to look at the course of events unfolding in a nursing program to determine what indicators or actions could be instituted to prevent a formal student grievance. The application of a UD framework and attention to universally-designed policies and procedures early on in the student's academic performance may indicate to faculty and administrators ways to resolve student problems proactively rather than reactively, as in this case. At the end of the case study sample questions are provided to facilitate a discussion.

Individuals Involved in the Case Study

1. Tashika was an above-average student in high school and volunteered at a hospital once a week. Her supervisor encouraged her to consider a career in nursing because of her excellent interactions with the hospital staff and patients. She applied and was accepted as a nursing student at a mid-size public postsecondary institution in the Pacific Northwest. As a student in the nursing program, Tashika completed all of her academic coursework and three clinical rotations with a 3.5 grade point average (GPA) and entered her last two clinical rotations of her senior year with clear hopes of graduating. Prior to her clinical rotations, all of the classroom laboratory courses she took in her academic career were interactive and cohort based. It was at the end of the first of two final clinical rotations in her senior year that Tashika was dismissed for safety errors while working with a patient.

2. Donnie Montega was an academic advisor new to the college and was assigned to advise new allied health sciences students.

3. Talibah Mahamed was the nursing clinical instructor for the course that included the clinical experience at the local hospital.

4. Genesee Brooke was the dean directly responsible for the allied health sciences programs that included nursing.

Facts of the Case

Tashika enrolled in her senior year of clinical courses fully expecting to complete her nursing degree. The previous clinical was a rigorous placement comprised of all the technical standards she had learned during her tenure as a nursing student. She enjoyed the hospital setting and had gained proficiency from her previous clinical rotations. Unfortunately, she encountered difficulties in her senior year rotation when she provided water to a patient on water restrictions, miscalculated the same patient's medication, and did not log what time she administered medication to another patient. Her clinical coordinator, Talibah Mahamed, documented the mistakes but did not share her concerns at that time.

Donnie Montega, her advisor, told Tashika at the end of clinical that she did not pass the clinical rotation. He explained that she did not meet the technical standards due to poor performance and would not go on to complete her last rotation. She was shocked by the decision and surprised to hear that she was being dismissed from the nursing program for poor performance. Tashika became depressed and angry at her advisor and clinical instructor for making this decision with one clinical rotation left to complete. She scheduled an appointment with Genesee Brooke, the dean, seeking a resolution and requesting to be allowed to finish her last rotation to graduate with her nursing cohort. The dean was unwilling to meet with Tashika and referred her to the academic appeals process. Tashika was required to show the appeals committee that the failing grade was arbitrarily and capriciously assigned.

In the past 3 years, the nursing program administered six student academic dismissals in the last quarter of clinical rotation. Each of these students initiated formal complaints against the nursing program to challenge their failing grades. In response, administrators implemented a series of workshops on UD. As a result of Tashika's recent case, legal council for the institution recommended a complete review of due process procedures and faculty professional development training.

Discussion Questions to Consider

The following questions guide the discussion on ways to incorporate UD into administrative decision-making:

1. What are the issues and problems associated with this case study?

2. Was the decision to dismiss the student for failing her clinical rotation appropriate? If so, why? How was the student assessed to determine clinical learning outcomes? How would the appeals committee view the dismissal when the student passed all of her other course work and clinical rotations?

3. Is the clinical rotation an opportunity to learn how to perform the technical standards? Are mistakes allowed during the learning process? What obligations do key personnel have to provide timely feedback? What interventions or support strategies were instituted before the dismissal?

4. What UD strategies could have been instituted to assist in the student's success in the clinical rotation?

5. Were the technical skills to evaluate the student's progress and academic success published and communicated to students?

6. How could the dean have provided a UD approach to explain to the student how she must show the appeals committee that her grade was arbitrarily and capriciously assigned?

7. What due process procedures should be followed to make sure the student is treated fairly and the institution's legal obligations are followed?

8. What typical barriers do all students face in the clinical rotations? How could these barriers be minimized or eliminated utilizing UD strategies? When answering these questions, be sure to consider pedagogy (e.g., alternative assignments, teaching strategies, flexible work locations or schedules) and professional development opportunities (e.g., learning about students with diverse learning abilities, accommodations versus universal design principles).

By introducing a case study exercise like the one provided in this chapter, individuals can reflect on ways in which faculty and administrators can become more inclusive toward others with diverse learning abilities. Although institutions have policies and procedures in place to safeguard the student and the institution, it is also important to remember how UD benefits student outcomes. Throughout this case study various universally-designed strategies could have been utilized to produce a successful outcome for the student and the institution. A few applied UD strategies include: utilizing a learning contract, introducing the technical standards expected to complete the clinical rotations, scheduling weekly individual and cohort meetings between students and faculty, evaluating and assessing student performance consistently until the student becomes proficient in performance, notifying the student in writing of poor performance, and following consistent procedures to address the student complaint.

Summary

Administrators play a significant role in supporting and integrating UD into the allied health sciences curriculum and co-curriculum. One of the most important roles administrators have is modeling a commitment to UD through policies, budget allocations, and academic professional development. Administrators can facilitate conversations and collaborative partnerships to support equity and social justice initiatives for diverse student learners. Faculty and staff professional development opportunities focused on innovative teaching and learning strategies are supportive approaches administrators can implement to create collaborative dialogue between faculty and student services regarding UD.

Universal Design benefits administrators by promoting understanding of what and how institutional decision-making structures and policies affect learning outcomes for students. Supporting fiscal and policy-driven methods to train faculty and staff to provide multimodal teaching strategies, flexible assessment methods, and physical access to services (e.g., a ramp providing access for strollers, wheelchairs, and technology carts) can minimize the need for special accommodations. Overall, UD provides inclusion for students from underserved populations and a learning environment that values individual differences. UD does not make excuses or exceptions to clear violations of policies and procedures or technical competencies. However, UD does offer a framework to incorporate strategies for providing natural supports to the learning process and enhances the opportunity to engage more students.

Administrators have the ability to make institutional systemic change. This means including UD as a systemic change initiative and institutional priority. Allied health sciences programs must recognize the diverse student demographics and ways to support student success. The combined efforts of both administration and allied health sciences faculty and staff can transform the learning experience for students. As with all innovative practices, UD takes financial resources and supportive allies to frame the conceptual principles as an investment in the mission of the institution.

References

Abell, M., Bauder, D., & Simmons, T. (2004). Universally designed online assessments. Implications for the future. *Information Technology and Disability, 10*(1). Retrieved August 26, 2004, from http://www.rit.edu/%7Eeasi/itd/itdv10nl/abell.htm.

Americans with Disabilities Act of 1990, P.L. 101-336, 42 US CA. 12, 1001-12, 213, (West Supp. 1991).

Boleman, L. G., & Deal, T. E. (1997). *Reframing organizations: Artistry, choice, and leadership.* San Francisco: Jossey-Bass.

Binder, R., & Hauser, G. (1995). Due process in fraternity and sorority hearings: A response to the Middle Tennessee State case. *Perspectives, 16*(4), 38-50.

Brown, P. J., & Augustine, A. (2000). *Findings of the 1999-2000 Screen Reading Field Test. Inclusive Comprehensive Assessment System.* Newark: University of Delaware, Educational Research and Development Center. Retrieved February 1, 2006 from www.rdc.udel.edu/Stazesky/vita.htm

Burgstahler, S. (2006). *Equal access: Universal Design of student services: A checklist for the Universal Design of campus resources* [brochure]. Seattle: University of Washington, Disability, Opportunity, Internetworking, and Technology (DO-IT).

Casey, D. A. (2006). *Indicators linked to the success for students with psychological disabilities in urban community college allied health sciences programs.* Unpublished doctoral dissertation, Florida Atlantic University.

Casey, D. A. (2007). Students with psychological disabilities in allied health sciences programs: Enhancing access and retention success. In J. L. Higbee, D. B. Lundell, & I. M. Duranczyk (Eds.), *Diversity and the postsecondary experience* (pp. 87-98). Minneapolis: University of Minnesota, General College, Center for Research on Developmental Education and Urban Literacy.

Cohen, A., & Brawer, F. B. (2003). *The American community college* (4th ed.). San Francisco: Jossey Bass.

Commonwealth of Massachusetts Group Insurance Division. (2006). Reduce your risk for medication errors. *Benefit Newsletter.* Retrieved February 1, 2006, from http://www.

mass.gov/gic/safety.htm

Echevarria Rafuls, S., Howard-Hamilton, M., & Jennie, J. (1999). Multicultural models and campus ecology theory: Application to diversity in apartment communities. In D. Casey-Powell (Ed.), *College and university apartment housing* (pp. 93-118). Columbus, OH: Association of College and University Housing Officers-International.

Evans, N. J., Assadi, J. L., & Herriott, T. K. (2005). Encouraging the development of disability allies. In R. Reason, E. Broido, T. Davis, & N. Evans (Eds.), *Developing social justice allies* (pp. 67-80). San Francisco: Jossey-Bass.

Family Educational Rights and Privacy Act. (1974). 20 U.S.C.S. §1232

Getzel, E. E., Briel, L., & McManus, S. (2003). Strategies for implementing professional development activities on college campuses: Findings from the OPE-funded projects sites (1999-2002). *Journal of Postsecondary Education and Disability, 17*(1), 59-76.

Harris, R., Horn, C., & McCarthy, M. (1994). Physical and technological access. In D. Ryan & M. McCarthy (Eds.), *A student affairs guide to the ADA and disability issues* (pp. 33-50). Washington, DC: National Association of Student Personnel Administrators.

Hart, D., Zimbrich, K., & Whelley, T. (2002). *Challenges in coordinating and managing services and supports in secondary and postsecondary options.* Retrieved February 27, 2006, from http://www.ncset.org/publications/viewdesc.asp?id=719.

Hatfield, J. P. (2003). Perceptions of Universal (Instructional) Design: A qualitative examination. In J. L. Higbee (Ed.), *Curriculum transformation and disability: Implementing Universal Design in higher education* (pp. 41-59). Minneapolis: University of Minnesota, General College, Center for Research and Development Education and Urban Literacy.

Hollander, P. A., Young, D. P., & Gehring, D. D. (1995). *A practical guide to legal issues affecting college teachers.* Asheville, NC: College Administration Publications.

The Kellogg Commission, (1998). *Returning to our roots: Student access.* Retrieved March 9, 2005, from http://www.nasulgc.org/Washington_Watch/Affirmative_Action.htm

Keyes, J. (1993, November). *Medical students with disabilities: Implications for health science programs.* Paper presented at the National Association of College and University Attorneys, Health Sciences Section meeting, Washington, DC.

Maheady, D. C. (1999). Jumping through hoops, walking on egg shells: The experiences of nursing students with disabilities. *Journal of Nursing Education, 38*(4), 162-170.

Marks, B. A. (2000). Jumping through hoops and walking on eggshells or discrimination, hazing, and abuse of students with disabilities? *Journal of Nursing Education, 39*(5), 205-210.

Michalko, R. (2002). *The difference that disability makes.* Philadelphia: Temple University Press.

National Center for Education Statistics. (1999). *Students with disabilities in postsecondary education: A profile of preparation, participation, and outcomes.* Washington, DC: Author.

National Council on Disability. (2003). *People with disabilities in postsecondary education.* Washington, D.C: Lex Frieden. Retrieved February 24, 2006, from http://www.ncd.gov/newsroom/publications/2003/education.htm

Rehabilitation Act of 1973, 29 U.S.C.794, Section 504, P.L. 93-112.

Rohland, P., Erickson, B., Mathews, D., Roush, S., Quinlan, K., & DaSilva Smith, A. (2003). Changing the culture (CTC): A collaborative training model to create systematic change. *Journal of Postsecondary Education and Disability, 17*(1), 59-76.

Rose, D. H., & Meyer, A. (2000). Universal Design for Learning. *Journal of Special Education Technology 15*(1): 67-70.

Rowley, D. J., Lujan, H. D., & Dolence, M. G. (1997). *Strategic change in colleges and universities: Planning to survive and foster.* San Francisco: Jossey-Bass.

Sausner, R. (May, 2004). *Are we shutting her out?* Retrieved February 7, 2006, from http://www.universitybusiness.com.

Sowers, J., & Smith, M. (2003). A field test of the impact of an inservice training program on health sciences education faculty. *Journal of Postsecondary Education and Disability, 17*(1), 33-48.

Townsend, B. K. (2001). *The community college transfer function in the 21st century: Where hopes and dreams collide.* Office of Community College Research and Leadership. Retrieved February 7, 2006, from http://occrl.ed.uiuc.edu/Newsletter/2001/spring2001_1.asp.

U.S. Department of Education. (2007). Family Educational Rights and Privacy Act (FERPA). Retrieved April 10, 2007 from http://www.ed.gov/policy/gen/guid/fpco/ferpa/index.html.

CHAPTER 27

Training Professional and Faculty Advisors in Universal Design Principles

Debbie Cunningham
Thomas College

Alfred Souma
Seattle Central Community College

Kaycee Gilmore Holman
Adams State College

Abstract

When academic advisors are trained to understand advising in a holistic manner, they are better prepared to serve students. Advisors can be trained to see advising in relationship to creating welcoming environments, identifying essential components, communicating clear expectations, providing constructive feedback, exploring learning supports, designing service methods that consider diversity, creating multiple ways for students to demonstrate understanding, and promoting interaction among faculty, staff, and students. This chapter describes how 2 campuses began to make application of these Universal Instruction Design principles, one as part of an advising-specific initiative and one as part of a campus-wide initiative.

Universal Instructional Design (UID) principles can easily be applied to support services such as academic advising without requiring significant financial commitment from the department or institution. Although these changes in services require little budget support, they do necessitate ongoing attention and review to maintain consistent implementation. In 2006, two campuses, Seattle Central Community College in Seattle, Washington, and Adams State College in Alamosa, Colorado, began implementing UID principles in academic advising. This chapter describes how each campus approached implementation.

Seattle Central Community College is an urban commuter campus in the heart of Seattle serving approximately 10,000 students. The college is one of the most diverse educational institutions on the west coast; 32 languages are spoken on campus. Advising is conducted by four full-time and three part-time professional advisors. Students initially see an admissions counselor, who may provide direction for undecided students. This individual session is then followed by the student orientation conference, which explains the services and programs offered at the college. Students are then referred to advising for assistance in determining specific classes to pursue.

Adams State College is a small state campus in rural south central Colorado that offers associate's, bachelor's and master's degrees. It serves a disproportionate number of first-generation, low-income college students and is designated as a Hispanic Serving Institution (HSI). Advising is divided between faculty advisors and a small staff of professional advisors. Students who are conditionally admitted to the institution or who have not yet declared their majors are advised by the advising staff. All other students are advised by faculty members.

Although Seattle Central Community College and Adams State College employ different advising approaches, serve different student populations, and approach implementing UID differently, each campus applies UID to serve the needs of both students and advisors. Neither campus has increased its budget for advising as a result of applying UID principles.

UID Principles and Desired Outcomes in Advising

Universal Design (UD) is a widely recognized architectural approach to creating accessible buildings and facilities. Examples of applications of UD principles include access features such as elevators, symbol-based signs, and curb cuts. From this school of thought—that facilities should be accessible to a wide variety of individuals without specially-arranged accommodations—has emerged a more recent innovation: Universal Instructional Design (Johnson & Fox, 2003).

UID approaches education from the perspective that instruction and services should be designed for access for a wide variety of individuals without specially-arranged accommodations (Johnson & Fox, 2003). It moves education from an accommodation model to an inclusion model. Rather than making unique and sometimes cumbersome arrangements for designated students, application of UID principles to instruction and services allows instructors and service providers to prepare for students with disabilities before difficult or uncomfortable situations arise. Of course, individual accommodations may still be necessary, because each learner's unique strengths will always need to be taken into account. However, applying UID principles will allow more students with a wider variety of abilities to be served without instruction and services being altered in unsystematic ways (Johnson & Fox).

Based on the work of Chickering and Gamson (1987) Johnson and Fox (2003) articulated UID as a distinct set of principles: (a) creating welcoming environments, (b) identifying essential components, (c) communicating clear expectations, (d) providing constructive feedback, (e) exploring learning supports, (f) designing service methods that consider diversity, (g) creating multiple ways for students to demonstrate understanding, and (h) promoting interaction among faculty, staff, and students.

Before the principles are applied, educators should first determine the purpose of the service or instruction, so the integrity of the service or instruction can be maintained. In such an effort, participants in the Pedagogy and Student Services for Institutional

Transformation (PASS IT) summer 2006 Working Group on Advising defined academic advising as:

> an interactive, transformational process through which a representative of the institution assists a student in clarifying and achieving personal, academic and career goals—the process should be based on the student's developmental level.

The Working Group subsequently determined that application of these principles to academic advising should result in advising practices that are (a) developmentally appropriate, (b) accessible, (c) student-centered, (d) learning-centered, (e) inclusive, (f) respectful, and (g) holistic.

Representatives from both Seattle Central Community College and Adams State College agree that understanding these principles and the type of advising practices that should result is important both to the advisors and to the students they serve. However, each campus took a different approach to communicating and implementing these principles.

Application of UID Principles in Advising at Seattle Central Community College

Academic advising at Seattle Central Community College is a shared responsibility utilizing the entire college community as a resource. The effectiveness of advisors is proportionate to the degree to which each advisor is informed of the functions of the student service areas available to meet the needs of students. Advisors on campus are first and foremost focused on providing accurate information as to transfer degree requirements, vocational program classes, and prerequisite requirements for classes and programs.

Advisors have an array of resources that they can access and to which they can refer students when specific needs arise. During an advising session, advisors may feel it is appropriate to refer a student to one of the following areas for further assistance: workforce training, college transfer center, career center, counseling, women's program, TRIO program, or the high school running start counselor. The key to our success is the on-going training advisors receive as to the function of each of the aforementioned referral units. To this degree we have an appropriate fit between our advising model and our institutional culture that offers optimal advising services.

Because Seattle Central advisors and other service providers are encouraged to refer students to other services throughout the campus, Seattle Central adopted a campus-wide initiative to introduce UID principles into the larger institutional culture. All principles were introduced at a college-wide in-service workshops facilitated by the disability support service coordinator and sponsored by the college retention committee. UID principles are not unique to advising but have critical application in all areas of student services.

Adams State College

Because advising practices at Adams State had not received a great deal of attention apart from self-motivated, student-oriented individual advisors, we first attempted to implement UID principles among advisors before attempting to disseminate the principles throughout the institution. In this manner, the application of UID principles offered the opportunity to take a serious look at advising practices within the academic advising unit. To make the project manageable for the small staff, Adams State initially focused on only five UID principles. The advisors worked as a team to determine how to implement the principles.

Creating Welcoming Environments

Exploring advising practices through the lens of this UID principle confirmed good practice in the area. At Adams State the professional advising staff is centrally located in the One Stop Student Services Center in the Student Union Building. This environment is welcoming to students because they do not need to traverse the campus to tend to various student issues. In this way, academic advisors have brought their services to the students. The academic advisors are located in offices that provide privacy and comfort. This privacy for what are sometimes difficult conversations for students to initiate with a campus representative, especially if the student has not been as successful as had been anticipated, is critical for creating a welcoming environment.

While office location can assist in creating a welcoming environment, the academic advisor must also create this feeling. When students come in for advising appointments, even as drop-ins, advisors greet the students and welcome them warmly. Asking the students how they did in classes they were worried about or if they have thought any more about a particular major increases the feeling of connection to the advisor. Calling students by name and recalling specifics about their situations demonstrates to the students that they are regarded as individuals.

Communicating Clear Expectations

Although the academic advisors at Adams State were clear about their responsibilities, the students did not always appear to be as clear as they needed to be to participate and benefit fully from the services. We needed to implement a new practice: providing students with a written document clarifying the academic advisor's role and responsibilities, as well as the student's role and responsibilities. The basis for such documents in advising practices is well established; examples include the National Academic Advising Association's (NACADA, 2005) Statement of Core Values and the Council for the Advancement of Standards' (CAS, 2005) Standards and Guidelines. Multiple campuses have also posted their statements online for students and others to view. We have not yet implemented a written statement of expectations, but this task has moved to a higher position on the priority list.

Providing Constructive Feedback

Academic advisors at Adams State thought that they were not focusing on providing feedback based on student goals partly because of heavy advising loads. Based on the definition of advising from PASS IT and this UID principle, we focused on providing feedback on the ways in which students might achieve their goals at Adams State primarily through the use of open-ended prompts. Intentionally asking open-ended questions sounds remarkably simple—and it is, but simply reviewing the UID principles provided a consciousness-raising exercise. Modifying a current practice has led to better advising practices and increased the likelihood that students will find the services satisfying.

Exploring Use of Learning Supports

This principle prompted us to consider the ways in which we shared information with students. While we were providing written copies of essential information, such as the General Education Requirements, and were discussing them with the students, we determined that the current written format was not necessarily a productive learning support: it was in an outline format and small font (see Figure 1). Because the General Education Requirements is an official Adams State document, we could not simply do away with the current version, but we could supplement it. Figure 2 is an example of our more visually-accessible version of the General Education Requirements. It was created by Professor Margaret Doell, Assistant Provost and Chair of the Art Department. Her participation served as an early indicator of the willingness of faculty and staff outside of the Academic Advising unit to engage in efforts to implement UID at Adams State. It also serves as an example of how very important garnering support of key administrators can be to the successful implementation of UID, as well to development of plans for campus-wide initiative.

Designing Service Methods That Consider Diverse Learners

This principle confirmed an effective practice in the area. Advisors determined that meeting with students only in face-to-face advising sessions was unrealistic, and that students would be better served by being offered phone appointments as well. As a result, several populations of students have benefited from phone appointments. Our initial target group was students who were out of the area during the summer. However, now students whose physical or emotional disabilities make getting to campus difficult are served more effectively. In addition, taking into account Adams State's large population of students of nontraditional age, phone appointments aid those students who are working full-time or at home caring for children or other family members.

Training Advisors in UID Principles

To ensure effective advising, it is important to provide appropriate training and other professional development opportunities for advisors.

Seattle Central's Approach

Advisor training at Seattle Central has been handled on an on-going basis, rather than as a workshop. The approach is not time intensive, which is important for the advisors, who have heavy, cyclical, and often unpredictable advising loads. A three-category approach (Gordon, Habley, & Associates, 2000) is used as the basis for the training:

1. Concept components: These are topics that encompass what the advisor needs to understand about the student and the institution's advising environment. They include

Figure 1. General education requirements

ADAMS STATE COLLEGE
General Education Curriculum Fall 2006

Rev 09/01/06

NAME ______________________________ ID _________________________

DATE __________________________

Technology Proficiency: All students must demonstrate baseline technological proficiency by the end of the sophomore year. The requirement may be met by scoring 70% or higher on the ASC Technology Proficiency examination or by passing an approved course with a grade of C or better. Courses meeting
this proficiency are BUS 120 (Business Computer Applications) and CSci 100 (Essentials of Info Technology). FULFILLED:_________________________

Writing Assessment: All students pursuing bachelors degrees are required to undergo an assessment of their writing during the semester in which they will have completed 60 hours of credit. Students are strongly advised to confer with the head of their department or program about the unit's writing assessment policy as soon as they have chosen a major. FULFILLED: _________________________

HOURS____ TRANS/SUB____ SEMESTER____ TAKEN____ GRADE_____

Area I. Communications - 6 credit hours required

AP SCORE OF 3+ ON ENGLISH LANGUAGE/COMP OR ACT SCORE OF 27+ SAT SCORE OF 500+ (BEFORE 4/95) 580+ (AFTER 4/95) - CREDIT
(P) IS GIVEN FOR ENG 101.

3 ENG 101 Communication Arts I [GT-CO1]

3 ENG 102 Communication Arts II [GT-CO2]

Area II. Arts & Humanities/Social and Behavioral Sciences - 15 credit hours required

Students are required to complete a minimum of 6 credits in AH courses, 3 credits in HI courses and 3 credits in SS courses. If necessary to reach a minimum of 15 credits, select 1 additional course (minimum 3 credits) in Arts and Humanities, History, or Social and Behavioral Sciences.

3 AR 103 Art Appreciation [GT-AH1]

3 MUS 100 Introduction to Music Literature [GT-AH1]

3 THTR 180 Introduction to Theatre [GT-AH1]

3 ENG 203 Major Themes in Literature [GT-AH2]

3 HGP 110 Development of Civilization [GT-HI1]

3 HGP 111 Development of Civilization[GT-HI1]

3 HIST 202 American History to 1865 [GT-HI1]

3 HIST 203 American History 1865 to Present [GT-HI1]

3 ECON 201 Economics & Today's Society [GT-SS1]

3 PSYC 101 Introduction to Psychology [GT-SS3]

3 SOC 201 The Sociological Imagination [GT-SS3]

Figure 1. continued

Area III. Mathematics – 3 credit hours required

3 MATH 104 Finite Mathematics [GT-MA1]

3 MATH 106 College Algebra [GT-MA1]

3 MATH 107 Trig & Analytical Geometry [GT-MA1]

3 MATH 120 Single Variable Calculus I [GT-MA1]

3 MATH 121 Single Variable Calculus II [GT-MA1]

3 MATH 150 Liberal Arts Math [GT-MA1]

6 MATH 155/156 Integrated Math I/II [GT-MA1] [both sections must be taken]

Area IV. Physical and Natural Sciences – 7 credit hours required

4 BIOL 101 Introductory Biology [GT-SC1]

5 BIOL 203 General Biology with Lab [GT-SC1]

5 CHEM 111 Introductory Chemistry with Lab [GT-SC1]

5 CHEM 131 General Chemistry with Lab [GT-SC1]

5 CHEM 132 General Chemistry with Lab [GT-SC1]

4 ENV 101 Introduction to Environmental Science [GT-SC1]

4 GEOL 111 Physical Geology with Lab [GT-SC1]

4 PHYS 201 Introduction to Astronomy [GT-SC1]

5 PHYS 225 College Physics with Lab [GT-SC1]

5 PHYS 230-231 General Physics (Calculus) with Lab [GT-SC1]

4 SCI 155 Integrated Science I – Physical Science [GT-SC1]

4 SCI 156 Integrated Science II – Natural Science [GT-SC1]

Area V. Required Course – 3 credit hours

3 SPCH 100 Speech Fundamentals [GT-AH1]

Figure 2. Visually accessible General Education Requirements

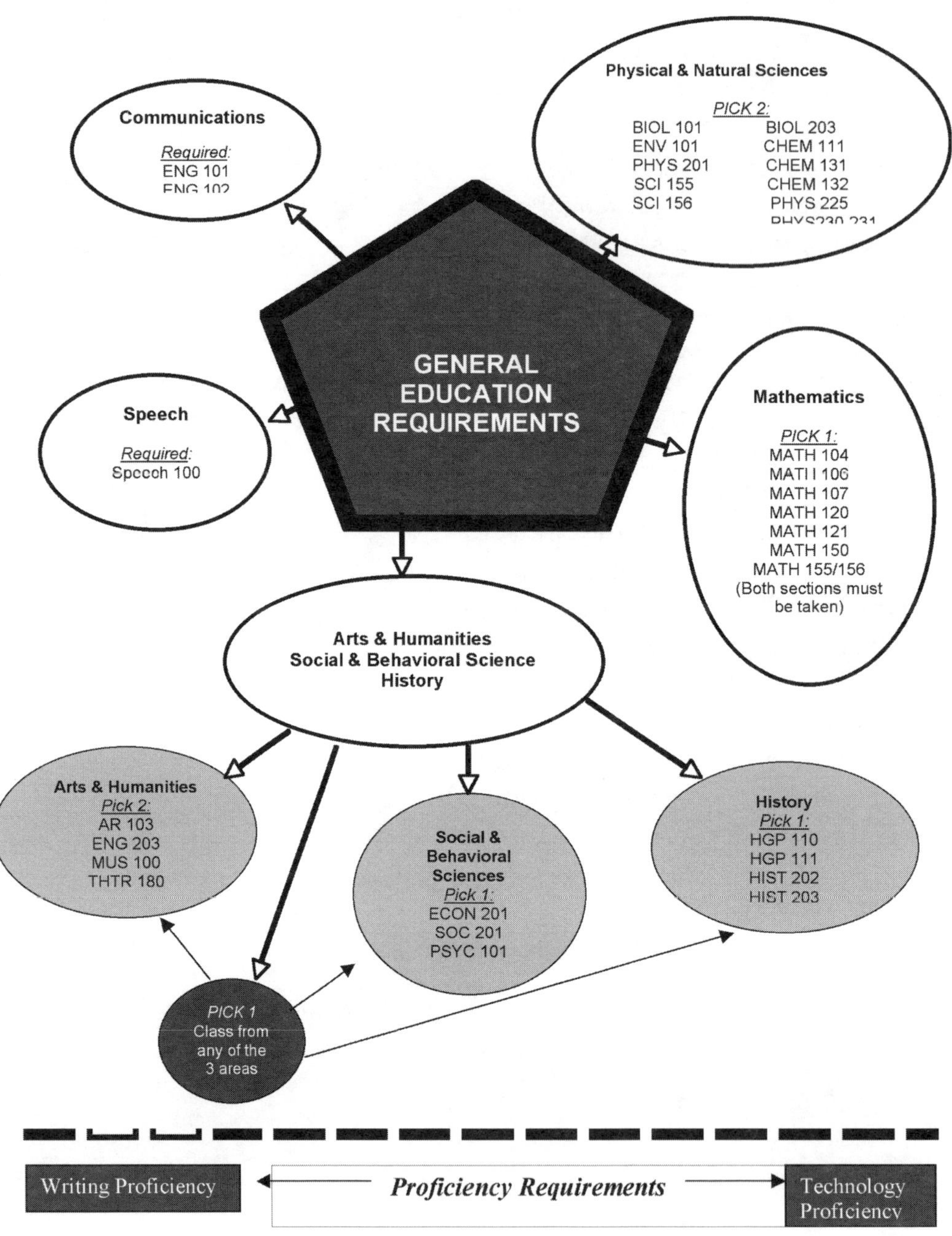

such subjects as the definition of advising, students' expectations of advising, and the rights and responsibilities of advisors and advisees.

2. Information components: These are topics about which the advisor needs to be knowledgeable, including familiar items such as institutional rules and regulations, program and course offerings, and referral sources and services.

3. Relationship components: These are behaviors that the advisor needs to demonstrate in order to be effective in advising students, including demonstrating an attitude of warmth and welcome, asking questions that invite students' involvement in discussion, and helping students use effective decision-making strategies.

To supplement their training, advisors were invited to a campus-wide workshop on UID principles. They were also encouraged to participate as part of the campus-wide speaker's series on UID. However, low participation rates among advisors demonstrated that workshops were not effective in reaching advisors due to their heavy advising loads.

Instead, we adopted a more individualized approach to working with the advisors. Advisors were provided handouts and reading material on UID principles as part of a best practices approach. The written materials allow the advisors to review the material on an "as needed" basis or as time permits. Two handouts concerning UID and advising were provided: "Equal Access: Universal Design of Advising" (Burgstahler, 2006a), and "Equal Access: Universal Design of Student Services" (Burgstahler, 2006b). These checklists allowed immediate application of UID principles.

Discussions of UID principles are handled one-on-one in relaxed sessions because the advisors are typically young professionals who are more comfortable in these types of meetings. This approach reflects the UID principles because advisors' unique learning styles are also considered during the individual sessions, which are ongoing.

Adams State's Approach

Before implementing UID principles, academic advisor training was handled in a non-uniform manner and on a one-on-one basis within the Academic Advising unit, rather than through a focused, uniform, cross-unit basis. Since implementing UID principles, we have developed and engaged staff and faculty from across campus in a uniform advising training to prepare them for their advising responsibilities and to disseminate UID principles.

The training sessions begin by reviewing the definition of advising developed by the summer 2006 PASS IT Advising Work Group. Discussion of this definition allows prospective advisors to explore their understandings and assumptions about advising—that is, to clarify their expectations of themselves and of the students they serve—as does identifying the desired outcomes of UID-enhanced advising. The remainder of the training session is spent discussing advising processes specific to Adams State, including the contents of a typical advising file, General Education Requirements, placement testing policies, and the online registration system.

Because the training involves presenting so much information in a relatively short time (about 1.5 hours), we conclude by presenting the group with several advising scenarios to role play. The scenarios cover situations that advisors typically face, as well as issues covered in the training. The role playing gives participants a chance to apply the newly acquired knowledge to a practical situation. The following scenarios are presented:

1. Gabriel is a new student on the campus. He is unsure about how to get registered for classes and has several questions about the campus in general.

2. Monique has been in college for a couple semesters. She wants to prepare to register for the upcoming semester, but is evasive about current grades. After checking her transcript, you discover that she has failed a prerequisite for a course she planned to take in the upcoming semester.

3. Rafael is a new advisee on your list. He has been reasonably successful in high school and is excited about registering for college classes. However, he complains that the PIN number you just gave him is not very useful, because he does not know how to register online.

4. Veronica is a strong student who took a year off to work and take care of an ill family member. She is returning after missing two consecutive long semesters. The campus General Education Curriculum has changed.

5. Eric has been undecided about his major, but took your advice and attended the campus Major Decisions Week events. After a workshop, he has decided to declare Pre-Engineering as his major. He is currently registered for MATH097, a developmental mathematics course.

Future Directions

At Seattle Central, the individual attention that each advisor receives concerning UID has proven to be less difficult than attempting to align all the advisors' schedules and finding other staff members to fill in for the advisors in order to schedule group trainings. Through continued individual discussions and involvement in the campus-wide initiative, we hope that advisors can contribute to making UID part of the culture of the larger institution. In approaching implementation from a multifaceted perspective, the principles can become built into the system. Both the campus-wide presentations and the individual conferences will continue as part of the retention committee's work.

At Adams State College, the evaluations of the training sessions by both professional and faculty advisors were essentially positive. Based on the evaluations, participants reported that they desire to use the UID principles in their positions. However, no follow-up plan is in place to allow the participants to articulate how or to what extent they would adopt the principles. A simple worksheet and one-on-one sessions would likely result in more effective implementation by each participant. Additionally, posting the principles in a highly visible part of the advising area and providing faculty with small, but attractive posters listing the principles might also increase campus-wide exposure to them, as well as increase recognition of their value. Having successfully begun to implement the principles in the advising unit, Adams State is ready to begin pursuing a more comprehensive implementation along the lines of Seattle Central. The plans to move forward with the campus-wide initiative including bringing a speaker to campus to rally the faculty and staff who have not yet been exposed to UID, establishing discipline-specific and student services working groups, and developing an online forum for exchange of information for faculty and staff working to implement UID.

Conclusion

Both Seattle Central Community College and Adams State College, despite differences in location, student populations, and approaches to implementing UID, have successfully applied UID principles to academic advising. In both cases, little budget was required for advising-specific application of the principles.

The campuses do not intend to represent themselves as having made ideal or complete applications of the principles. Instead, their approaches were to make progress where possible, given constrained resources, and to develop ongoing plans for further application. Seattle Central's campus-wide initiative led to approaching advisors in a way that is appropriate to its unique campus culture. At Adams State, the advisors, who are now comfortable with and committed to UID, are ready to begin to work toward campus-wide dissemination.

References

Burgstahler, S. (2006a). *Equal access: Universal Design of advising* (2nd ed.). [Brochure]. Seattle: University of Washington, DO-IT. Retrieved March 22, 2007, from http://www.washington.edu/doit/Brochures/PDF/equal_access_adv.pdf

Burgstahler, S. (2006b). *Equal access: Universal Design of student services* (4th ed.). [Brochure]. Seattle: University of Washington, DO-IT. Retrieved March 22, 2007, from http://www.galvin-group.com/assets/equal_access_ss.pdf

Council for the Advancement of Standards in Higher Education. (2006). CAS professional standards for higher education (6th ed.).Washington, DC: Author.

Chickering, A. W., & Gamson, Z. (1987). Seven principles for good practice in undergraduate education. *AAHE Bulletin, 40*(7), 3-7.

Gordon,V. N., Habley, W. R., & Associates. (2000). *Academic advising: A comprehensive handbook.* San Fransisco: Jossey-Bass.

Higbee, J. L., Chung, C. J., & Hsu, L. (2004). Enhancing the inclusiveness of first-year courses through Universal Instructional Design. In I. M. Duranczyk, J. L. Higbee, & D. L. Lundell (Eds.), *Best Practices for Access and Retention in Higher Education* (pp. 13-26). Minneapolis: University of Minnesota, General College, Center for Research on Developmental Education and Urban Literacy. Retrieved March 22, 2007, from http://www.cehd.umn.edu/crdeul

Johnson, J. M. & Fox, J. A. (2003). *Creating curb cuts in the classroom.* In J. L. Higbee, (Ed.), Curriculum transformation and disability: Implementing Universal Design in higher education (pp. 7-17). Minneapolis: University of Minnesota, Center for Research on Developmental Education and Urban Literacy.

National Academic Advising Association. *Homepage.* Retrieved August 2, 2007, from http://www.nacada.ksu.edu/

PASS IT Working Group on Advising. (2006, August). *Universal Design and student-centered advising: Reflections on Universal Design for advising.* Presentation at the PASS IT Summer Institute, Minneapolis, MN.

CHAPTER 28

Universal Instructional Design and Professional Development for Public School Teachers

Karen A. Myers, Jo Nell Wood, and Mark Pousson
Saint Louis University

Abstract
Engaging students in their own learning regardless of abilities, learning styles, developmental levels, and cultural backgrounds is a teacher's responsibility. Universal Instructional Design (UID) assists teachers in engaging students and providing access to all curricula. This chapter addresses the benefits of using UID in elementary and secondary school classrooms. Based on the results of a study of public school teachers in Missouri indicating a need for UID education, a UID professional development plan for elementary through secondary teachers is provided.

It was week 3 of the new school year. A new teacher, Nancy, had begun individually to teach a 7-year-old boy to read at his request because he admitted that he was not able to read like his friends. She began to sit with him during reading time and quickly assessed that he could tell a story from the pictures in the book. With her help he began to put words to the images on the page. He surprised himself with how quickly he caught on to reading. With growing confidence, he would pick up books on his own. He also taught Nancy that there could be more than one way to teach a child new academic skills.

Nancy decided to try to teach all the lessons in the curriculum in a variety of ways. She remembered that not all of the children were on the same reading level nor did they have the same learning styles, backgrounds, and abilities. She recalled reading an article about Universal Instructional Design (UID), a flexible, adaptable method that provides all students equal access to the curriculum and allows them to learn in their own ways. So, she chose to teach her next science lesson on the digestive system as a play rather than utilizing traditional worksheets to reinforce new information from the textbook. The children were excited and quickly took to the task of assuming roles, writing out scripts, reading and memorizing their lines, and acting out their roles in the digestive system. They had an enjoyable learning experience while accomplishing the intended learning outcomes. Nancy's universal teaching method was a success.

Nancy enthusiastically shared her success stories with her colleagues and encouraged them to use this UID approach. Although they congratulated her for trying something new that actually worked, her fellow teachers were skeptical about jumping on board. Nancy knew that all of the teachers—including her—needed to learn more about this unique theory. "Could Universal Instructional Design be one of our professional development topics this year?" Nancy asked. Her colleagues agreed that it was definitely one to consider.

Universal Instructional Design in Kindergarten Through High School

Change used as an object seems to spark resistance in people. Change connotes transition—movement involving tension from a known state into an unknown one. It requires the skill of adaptation to ever-evolving circumstances. The world is changing, society is changing, and technology is changing. With these natural changes evolving in humans and societies, the needs of students also change. How can teachers adapt their teaching methods to fit the needs of all students? UID is one response that capitalizes on adaptation to change.

UID, as an approach to instruction, is a "set of design, delivery and evaluation techniques that can enhance student achievement and teacher satisfaction . . . using flexibility and planning to provide accessible education" (Bryson, 2003, p. 110). Capitalizing on student differences in their abilities to engage their learning environments, UID promotes academic achievement through integrating the use of flexible instructional materials and activities into the curriculum (Bowe, 2000; Bryson; Higbee, 2003; Silver, Bourke, & Strehorn, 1998).

Though UID may involve additional work for educators, it does not need to overwhelm the classroom teacher, principal, school, or school district. Consider the case example. Accommodating all students' learning styles, abilities, developmental levels, and cultural backgrounds can be as complicated, overwhelming, and uncomfortable as one allows it to be. Nancy's curiosity about creating different learning environments can be a challenge for all educators teaching in heterogeneous classrooms. What flexible approaches can be built into the instructional design of educational materials used in kindergarten through high school (K-12) to ensure equal access to curricula?

Universal Instructional Design incorporates principles of Universal Design (UD) that facilitate the achievement of learning goals of individuals by acknowledging their abilities to hear, see, move, speak, read, write, understand English, attend, organize, engage, and remember (Burgstahler, 2007). When utilizing UID, student learning is achieved through a variety of methods and learning activities that allow for students with a range of abilities.

Some instructional methods consistent with UID (Argondizza, 2003) and suggestions for their use are:

1. Equitable use: Instruction is useful and marketable to all people, allowing a variety of options for students to demonstrate their mastery of required objectives. Examples include presentations, computer-assisted instruction, handouts, role playing—instructional methods that will support a diverse student population's learning needs. Bryson (2003) offered several suggestions: (a) create study guides for students needing to preview material to ensure success in evaluative processes, (b) provide alternative forms of test-

ing and examinations so that students will have an opportunity to use their strengths and preferred learning styles to demonstrate their knowledge base, and (c) provide alternative types of assignments so students can choose a format that challenges them and yet best demonstrates achievement of learning outcomes.

2. Flexibility in use: Instruction accommodates a diverse range of student preferences and abilities. Teacher presentations can take many forms including PowerPoint, handouts, and discussion groups. These alternatives benefit not only those who learn better visually and through hearing, but those who learn better kinesthetically and through oral instruction. Bryson (2003) offered several suggestions: (a) teach learning strategies as a part of the course; (b) create instructional activities that meet different physical, emotional, and social needs of the students; and (c) alternate class activities on a regular basis to maximize student attention and address varied learning styles.

3. Simple and intuitive use: Instructional devices are easy to understand regardless of students' knowledge base, language, and skills. Labeling all materials and providing simple instruction for devices used for learning can accomplish this goal.

4. Perceptible information: Instruction communicates the necessary knowledge effectively to the student, regardless of the student's sensory abilities. Open captioned videos can be used in class to assist students who learn better by reading and for students who speak English as a second language. Providing course materials in audio format will be helpful to some students. Technology can be beneficial if integrated appropriately in the curriculum from lecture to group work. Bryson (2003) suggested that technology needs to be integrated so that it serves the students' needs rather than dictating them. In addition, he suggested the following: (a) develop and implement a course-based Web site where announcements, course information, and assignments can be found; (b) begin each class with the course components that will be covered and their relationship to the learning outcomes; (c) design resource materials and handouts with various learning styles in mind; (d) end each class with a summary of the main points related to the learning outcomes.

5. Tolerance for error: Instruction maximizes learning by capitalizing on the benefits of failure. Feedback can assist in the discovery of correct performance as well as errors. Bryson (2003) suggested the following: (a) design instructional activities that encourage and critique student participation, (b) provide effective feedback during class activities, (c) conduct regular evaluations to ensure that student learning needs are being met, and (d) create opportunities to help students recall what they already know and how it relates to course content and instructional activities.

6. Low physical effort: Instruction is affected by the context in which learning occurs. Creating a comfortable environment that minimizes clutter allows for accessibility to individuals who use mobility aids. Providing alternatives to projects involving manual dexterity, eyesight, speech, and hearing allows students to participate with minimum physical effort.

7. Size and space for approach and use: Creating an environment in which size and space are realistic for the students' body size, posture, or mobility can maximize instruction. Are the chairs and workstations adaptable to the physical needs of the students? Bryson (2003) suggested creating a clear line of sight for significant course elements to

be presented and incorporating group learning so students can learn from each other and from the interactive experience.

Instructional methods and strategies such as those listed in the previous paragraphs can be applied to the elementary, secondary, or postsecondary classroom to ensure equal access for all students.

Benefits of Universal Instructional Design in K-12

Engaging students in their own learning regardless of abilities, learning styles, developmental levels, and cultural backgrounds is a teacher's responsibility. Applying UID principles to the K-12 environment assists teachers in engaging students and providing access to all curricula. Bryson (2003) outlined the following benefits for utilizing UID—benefits that easily can be applied to the elementary and secondary education setting.

First, UID is a set of principles that provides an adaptive, flexible, and user-friendly paradigm for which a variety of instructional methods can be created for use in the classroom. UID is a highly adaptive and applicable educational theory that can be built upon and developed based on the needs of the students. Second, UID is designed to accommodate the needs of all students regardless of the presence of a disability. Third, UID acknowledges that all students have a preferred learning style. Teachers benefit from helping students determine their primary means of learning by fashioning methods to ensure success in achieving the learning outcomes of the course. Thus, the course design, delivery of course content, and methods of evaluation need to be sensitive to and driven by the students' learning styles. Another benefit is that UID increases motivation for students to attend and participate in an environment that stimulates their learning on a variety of sensory levels. A dynamic, fluid environment enhances not only the students' learning experience, but the teacher's experience as well. Finally, technology is a critical component to UID in building learning environments. Technology is only as effective as the teacher allows it to be. Use of technology challenges the teacher to be creative in integrating it in the classroom and into the curriculum so that it serves to enhance, not curtail, the students' learning experience.

Both students and teachers benefit from UID. Through the use of UID principles, K-12 teachers will experience a cost effective, time efficient method for enhancing student engagement in their own learning, while reducing the need for spur-of-the-moment modifications and accommodations for students with varying needs, learning styles, abilities, and disabilities (Higbee, 2003). In order to experience these benefits, however, teachers must be knowledgeable of UID and its application.

The UID Teacher Survey

Universal Instruction Design is a fairly new concept in education. Up to this point, most of its promotion and inquiry have been in postsecondary education settings. Very little information and training has been presented to elementary and secondary school teachers and administrators. In an effort to determine the level of knowledge, use, and training of K-12 public school teachers in Missouri regarding UID, we conducted the following study.

Purpose and Methodology

Although it is possible for UID to be applied to the K-12 environment, it is important to know if elementary and secondary school teachers are aware of UID. Are K-12 teachers familiar with UID principles and have they been trained to use them in their classrooms?

In an attempt to answer these questions, a study was conducted with 50 school districts in the state of Missouri. E-mail messages were sent to the superintendents of these school districts with an explanation of the purpose of the study and a request to send the online survey link to the teachers in their districts. The survey consists of 10 questions. The first five questions are demographic, including years of teaching; grade level of teaching; type of teaching (i.e., regular or special education); type of school (rural, urban, suburban); and school size. The next four questions relate to Universal Instructional Design, prefaced with the following explanation of UID: "Universal Instructional Design (UID) is based on the concept of Universal Design, in which environments and products are designed to allow everyone to use them to the greatest extent possible. 'The basic premise of Universal Instructional Design is that curriculum should include alternatives to make it accessible and applicable to students with different backgrounds, learning styles, abilities and disabilities' (Center for Applied Special Technology, 2001)."

Question 10 is open-ended and asks for examples of how UID is used in the respondent's teaching practices.

Results

Completed surveys were submitted by 188 teachers. A snapshot profile of the respondents reveals that the 31% respondents had taught 16 or more years, 88% were teaching in suburban schools, 67% taught in schools with enrollments above 1,000 students, and 79% were teaching in special education. The grades taught by respondents were relatively equally distributed (i.e., between 11 and 18 teachers for each grade taught) except grade 12, for which there were no respondents and kindergarten, which had the largest proportion of respondents (21%).

Responses to the questions regarding UID revealed that 65% had never heard the term "Universal Instructional Design," 82% had no UID training, and 75% had never used UID in teaching. Of the 25% who reported using UID in teaching, 9% reported always using it and 20% reported using it sometimes. Of those who used UID in their teaching practices, 80% found the experience to be somewhat successful and 18% found it to be extremely successful.

The tenth question on the survey was an open-ended question asking for additional comments. Frequently-used terms in this section of the survey included "differentiated learning" and "equal access." Several teachers reported that they use differentiated learning methods, which are individualized for their students to meet each student's specific needs. Some respondents provided examples of how they use differentiated instruction for specific subject matter. Most respondents were not familiar with the term "Universal Instructional Design" but saw it as similar to the methods they were currently using. The following statements provide some examples of how the responding K-12 teachers use differenced teaching and learning: "I have groups [of] students so that there are kids from various ability levels in order to have them help each other. In addition, I try to incorporate tactile, audial [sic], and visual learning in my weekly lessons."

Another teacher responded,

> I do have in every classroom students of varying ability because I teach at a very small, rural high school where all members of a class take their subjects together. This forces me to develop units and lessons that apply to every ability level in a classroom. So often I have to modify my lessons to adapt to every ability level.

And another,

> [I] present lessons in a variety of ways for different learners, use different teaching styles & learning styles (group work, individual). We work on the floor, at desks, in small groups. Use hands on approaches as well as teacher directed methods.

Another respondent said,

> I have used adapting lesson to grade level of understanding of the student, I took a course on learning styles and received training in working with students with disabilities, some professional development in student background. I try to let the student work where it is comfortable, consider all information of their background that I can get, adapt lessons to meet their abilities to a reasonable level of understanding.

Some teachers addressed how they use differentiated teaching methods in specific classes. The following statements illustrate this use in different academic disciplines.

Language arts. "When teaching language arts, the following practices are used: choices in reading selections, choices in literature response projects, modifications in spelling expectations, assessment in writing that is based upon student individual growth, use of sign language in theatre/speech presentations and projects, collaborative group work, self-assessment by students which involves an emphasis upon metacognition, student portfolios, emphasis upon autobiographical writing which assists students in reflecting upon unique abilities or weaknesses, choice of literature that examines the influence of background on the lives of the writers as well as the readers."

Science and social studies. [I use] "differentiated instruction for Science and S.S.—lessons designed on the ability level of [students with disabilities]. hands-on lab vs. written responses performance vs. written responses."

Reading and writing and spelling. [I utilize] "teaching practices that adjust to variations in learning styles and abilities of the students' skills in reading and writing." Discussing UID in spelling curriculum, a teacher said,

> When practicing spelling we: write the words, use manipulative letters to spell them, compose sentences using them, close our eyes and 'see' them, sometimes act them out, trace their shape, make up songs to help us remember the spelling... I have not had a student that does not speak English.

Gifted. "I use UID in my teaching practices with my multi aged gifted students, via the projects we do and the way the students are grouped."

The term "UID". The following statements reflect teachers' responses:

> Since I have not heard of the term 'UID,' I can only base my knowledge of it on the small explanation provided in this survey. I don't use a program to meet my students' needs. I do whatever I can do or find to help ALL of my students to find success..."

Another teacher said, "UID contains logical concepts that effective, experienced teachers use instinctually. Providing a positive, flexible, focus on student's needs can make a teacher an successful educator." One teacher wrote,

> Even though I have never heard of the term UID it is the goal of every teacher, ... that curriculum should include alternatives to make it accessible and applicable to students with different backgrounds, learning styles, abilities and disabilities. If you asked me questions about how much training I have had on diversity, multiculturalism, learning styles, at risk, teaching students with IEPs, etc. it would be endless. We do this everyday!

Several respondents provided specific examples of how they use what they consider to be UID in their classes. From these responses, the following three themes emerged: (a) modifying and adapting lessons, (b) meeting students' needs, and (c) accommodating multiple learning styles. Whether or not the teacher indicated familiarity with the term Universal Instructional Design, many of the comments revealed that the teachers were using some type of system to ensure access to all students. Some mentioned using flexible teaching styles and learning methods. For several teachers who submitted comments to Question 10, their concern for equal access and leaving no child behind was paramount. One teacher passionately stated, "I have NEVER left any of my students out of any experience regardless of socioeconomic factors, cognitive abilities, disabilities, ethnic background, English proficiency, etc. I modify the curriculum to meet the needs of the students who need modification."

Observations Based on the Results

The results of this survey raise the following questions:

1. Why were the majority of respondents (79%) special education teachers? Did other teachers not consider the survey relevant to the populations they teach?

2. Do teachers see UID as synonymous with "differentiated learning, academic accommodations, and modifying the curriculum to meet students' needs?

3. Will knowledge of UID enhance the way school teachers teach?

4. Will years of teaching experience affect the teacher's level of interest in learning and using UID?

5. Will location of school (rural, urban, suburban) or size of the school impact interest in UID and resources to obtain UID training?

In order to answer these questions, more questions are raised. For example, did special education teachers respond to this survey because they were familiar with the term or concept of Universal Instructional Design? Was the "access for all" issue of particular interest to them? Several respondents related UID to modifying the curriculum to meet students' needs. Are these teachers using the term or concept UID in the same way they would use the term "reasonable accommodation"? Are UID and accommodation synonymous to these teachers? Will professional development efforts in UID affect the teaching practices of elementary and secondary school teachers? Based on some of the respondents' comments, their responsibilities are many, their students are many, and they are concerned with what UID means to them personally.

One teacher's confusion about the term and concern for change is evident in her statement:

> I think all teachers modify to the class of students. I am not sure if I am using UID. All students within my class do the same activities, take the same assessment, etc. Most teachers would find it difficult to modify the curriculum to EACH student.

This statement indicates that confusion exists about the definition of UID and how UID principles are applied. Modifying the curriculum for each student refers more to specific individual accommodations than it does to universal design of the curriculum, which provides access to all students. Focusing on individual deficiencies and needs falls within what Jones (1996) referred to as the "functional limitations" framework of disability. It supports a medical model that exemplifies the "broken" person who needs to be mended or healed. Universal Instructional Design views disability through a social construction lens, indicating that society has created the barriers and it is society's responsibility to remove them (Jones). Applied to education, this means developing and implementing curricula that are accessible to all students—for example, using multiple methods of teaching so that all students learn (Higbee, 2003). As Burgstahler (2003) pointed out to K-12 teachers, "Although you may receive direction regarding academic adjustments and accommodations through IEP plans and Section 504 plans for specific students, it is good to be thinking about the broad range of abilities, disabilities, and other characteristics of potential students as you design your own curriculum. This approach is called universal design of instruction" (Section 2, para. 1). UID is not an accommodation to meet an individual need, nor is it a change in the curriculum content. It does not require or endorse lowering academic standards or "watering down" assignments. Rather it encourages creative, inclusive, customizable curricula that enhance student success (Higbee).

Providing equal access is a shared responsibility (Bryan & Myers, 2006); it is not the responsibility of one office or one person. Ideally, every teacher, student, administrator, and staff member should be knowledgeable about UID principles and ready to apply them to programs, activities, services, events, and curricula both inside and outside of the classroom.

Why UID Should Be Included in the Professional Development of K-12 Teachers

Currently the K-12 classroom is focused on ensuring that all students achieve. No Child Left Behind (Public Law 107-110, 2001) has created an environment in which teachers find themselves more and more accountable for student achievement. However, in many instances teachers are at a loss as to why some students are not achieving. "The quality of teaching is the foundation that supports student success in schools. Promoting high academic standards for students must be accompanied by equal emphasis on high standards for teaching practice" (Mitchell, 1998. p. 48). Teaching practices are often the answer to the question of why some students are not achieving. In response to Garmston's (1998) article title, "Expert Teachers Carry a Satchel of Skills," the question is what skills are in this satchel and how do teachers make use of them?

Historically, K-12 teachers have moved through various trends looking for the "silver bullet" to ensure student success. Two common approaches relating to learner needs include the learning styles method that focuses on the setting in which students are placed, and the learning through different modalities tactic that attempts to provide pathways for all students to be successful. Neither of these approaches, however, has been triumphant. While both methodologies do consider the learner's needs, they have not gone in depth to determine what students need to access the curricular information for content learning most effectively.

As educators strive to help students understand curricular information, it is imperative that they consider how well they as educators understand and utilize UID. UID is a new innovation on the educational scene for most K-12 teachers. UID provides guidelines to help teachers know how to prepare lessons so that they are accessible for all students without needing to know the learning style or the academic abilities of each individual student. It considers what might be the exceptions within the classroom, not merely the norm, yet most students will benefit from the incorporation of UID into all lessons. Using UID means that teachers will take the balcony view of the lesson and ask what else they might do to make the learning even more accessible. By making learning more accessible to the needs and learning styles of all students, K-12 teachers are essentially creating "curb cuts" (Fox & Johnson, 2000) in the classroom for all students, not just for those with disabilities. Based on the results of the study described in this chapter, this information appears to be missing from the K-12 teacher's satchel of skills. Perhaps because UID is not a current part of the traditional teacher's satchel, many students are not learning as well as possible. If the U.S. school system is to provide equity for all students entering its doors, then all teachers need the information that will assist them in providing unhindered access to curricular information.

Knowing that student success will depend on teacher knowledge and skills, it is becoming more and more apparent that UID must become a part of both the pre-service learning as well as the in-service learning of teachers across this country.

UID Professional Development Plan for Teachers

In the past, there seemed to be complacency about content knowledge in both teacher training and K-12 schools.

There was an assumption that teachers get all that they need in their college major and once they begin teaching in the classroom, staff development efforts need to focus on fine-tuning instructional strategies, dealing with social and behavior problems, integrating new technology, and generally keeping abreast with our changing communities and culture. (Schenkat & Tyser, 1997, p. 33).

Lampert and Ball (1999) echoed these same concerns by reaffirming that most reform movements in education have taken aim at the common assumptions about knowing and worthwhile knowledge that have dominated public schools for decades. However, as times and mandates have changed, it has become more and more apparent that all teachers need on-going, job-embedded, high-quality professional development that puts educators into learning communities that allow them to investigate new methods of improving their craft. As with any good initiative, it is imperative that teachers be provided a pathway through which to learn new information such as UID. Within the K-12 community of schools, this is normally associated with professional development. Darling-Hammond (1997) articulated this well when she stated, "teachers who know a lot about teaching and learning and who work in environments that allow them to know students well are the critical elements of successful learning" (p. 8).

Members of a Community of Learning

To achieve buy-in for a new initiative such as UID, however, the school leaders must create a compelling vision for learning. They must be willing to allow teachers to envision what is possible and put together a plan for learning that will provide them with the knowledge and skills to implement this new format. Leaders who are willing to share leadership are those who know that they must engage teachers in leading the way in order for an initiative to continue well beyond their leadership. A vision that engages teachers in their own learning can be shared through opportunities to collaborate, dialogue, and study their work in order to enhance their craft and improve student success. This type of learning and buy-in have been evident in the incorporation of learning communities of teachers within schools across our nation. "The professional learning community calls for clarifying purpose, monitoring results, and celebrating progress so that a sense of achievement will be restored" (DuFour, 1998, p. 57). As Costa, Lipton, and Wellman (1997) stated, "Efforts to restructure schools will prove futile unless staff developers work to create an environment which signals to the staff, the students, and the community that the development of the intellect, cooperative decision making, and continual learning are central to successful change" (p. 93).

These learning communities for teachers must provide opportunities for teacher leadership around meaningful improvements that can result in student achievement. As the community of teachers begins to create its learning community, it must be clear about the knowledge that resides within the members; however, teachers must also be able to outline what is left to learn. As is true for UID, many members of the learning community may need more information prior to beginning any type of implementation process. This learning can be delivered through readings of various books or articles on the subject and then through sharing sessions with each member of the learning community taking the role of facilitator of knowledge. Additionally, there may be one member of a learning community who has studied this approach to improving lessons and can help other members of the community gain a deeper understanding of the topic. While working as a learning community, skills will need to be developed that allow members to converse and dialogue about a topic without creating any barriers. While the learning community works together, it is important for all members to hold certain concepts in high regard. Suggested concepts include the following:

1. All work will be done centered on the goal of improving student access to curricular content.
2. All members of the community will be involved in the UID implementation effort.
3. All members of the community will study theory and will attempt to put this theory into practice within their respective classrooms and lessons.
4. The members will engage in lesson study of the implementation of UID with other members of the community.

While these concepts may be central, there are also central assumptions that should be included in the work of the professional learning community. Adapting the work of Costa, et al. (1997) these assumptions might include: (a) What each learner brings to the learning process matters, (b) how we know is as important as what we know, (c) learners have a commitment to entire schemes of understanding, (d) knowledge is socially constructed, (e) exploration and dialogue with other professionals is vital.

Learning communities can use a modified lesson study approach. While working together in triads, members can begin to design a lesson that incorporates the UID approach. The triad can ensure that each lesson not only includes the vocabulary necessary for learning, but also has direct alignment to required learning standards as outlined by the state and school district. These lessons can then be brought to a sharing time within the learning community during which the lessons will be presented to the entire group one at a time. This process can be completed utilizing a "tuning protocol," a way in which "a teacher presents actual work before a group of thoughtful 'critical friends' in a structured, reflective discourse aimed at 'tuning' the work to higher standards" (Allen, Blythe, & Powel, 1996, p. 2). The tuning protocol is used so that each lesson can be presented and discussed, and dialogue can occur around the lesson and its components.

Upon the completion of the discussions and dialogues within the learning community, one member of the triad can then teach the lesson while the other members of the triad will observe both the teaching methods as well as the students' seeming grasp of the content information contained within the lesson. The observers need to pay especially close attention to and look for specific components of UID within the lesson to see if these components have provided more students better access to the curricular concepts.

Following the teaching and observation, the members of the triad should again gather to discuss what changes might still need to be made to improve the lesson prior to another member of the triad teaching the lesson with improvements. As Costa et al. (1997) stated,

> Reflection is a specialized form of thinking, arising from perplexity about a direct experience and leading to purposeful inquiry and problem-resolution . . . to support continual development of thinking and decision making time and attention must be devoted to individual meaning making of new information, different perspectives, and current theory." (p.102)

Once the lesson has been revisited, it should once again be taken to the larger learning community and presented again with its improvements for a wider discussion.

At this point, the lesson then needs to be shared outside the small learning community of teachers with a wider audience of professionals. It is through this continuous growth of feedback spirals that "a collaborative culture, based on mutual support from colleagues, can serve to foster norms of experimentation and continuous improvement and reduce discomfort with risk-taking" (Costa et al. 1997, p. 102). This pattern of teacher community study and self-reflection may allow more teachers to improve their own practice as well as allow more students better access to curricular information. "Staff development can offer opportunities for individuals to talk aloud about their internal maps, causing examination, refinement, and the development of new theories and practices" (Costa et al., p. 105). This type of learning community does not exist for one semester or 1 year only. It is ongoing over a period of years and once it is set into motion it should continue to create its own inertia such that it continues regardless of the changes in leadership or membership. It is only through the work of such learning communities reflecting on their own pedagogy and looking deeply at their students' work that continued improvement in teaching practice will result in student achievement gains.

Sparks (2002) quoted Roland Barth, "My view is that schools are there to promote the learning of all their inhabitants, whether they are called students, teachers, parents, or principals. A school must offer a culture that replenishes . . . adults" (p. 48). His statement implies that one of the most powerful forms of learning comes not from listening to the words of others, but from sharing what one knows with others and reflecting on what one does, giving it coherence, and sharing and articulating knowledge to make meaning.

Next Steps

In order for professional learning communities to be effective, they must first analyze their disaggregated data to determine possible student needs. This type of information can be gained, for example, by looking at the results from learning styles inventories for all students in the class as well as referring to the IEPs and state-provided disaggregated data for students with disabilities. Using this information along with a brief audit of student needs, learning communities can reflect on the various components of UID that need to be incorporated into lessons as they are developed.

For learning communities to be successful, the school context must provide the resources necessary for learning communities to exist. There must be time for teachers to meet together during the work day so that this learning takes place on the job and becomes job-embedded. Further, schools will need to provide training in collaboration skills and in conducting protocols so that teachers can engage in meaningful discussions and dialogues while working within their learning communities. And, finally, schools must establish a culture of expectations so that learning communities become an integral part of each teacher's environment and working conditions.

The UID professional development plan connects students' needs with teachers' needs. Only through the implementation of self-sustaining structures like established learning communities that focus on student learning, student access to curriculum, and student academic success will schools see improvement that prepares students for their futures.

Conclusion

UID is fairly new to education. Initially applied to higher education, it is just beginning to be addressed in K-12 educational settings. The Council for Exceptional Children (1999) defined universal design in education as follows:

> In terms of learning, universal design means the design of instructional materials and activities that makes the learning goals achievable by individuals with wide differences in their abilities to see, hear, speak, move, read, write, understand English, attend, organize, engage, and remember. Universal design for learning is achieved by means of flexible curricular materials and activities that provide alternatives for students with differing abilities. These alternatives are built into the instructional design and operating systems of educational materials-they are not added on after-the-fact. (p. 2).

Providing equal access is a shared responsibility (Bryan & Myers, 2006). Faculty, staff, administrators, and students can play active roles in providing and maintaining inclusive environments through the use of Universal Instructional Design. Understanding and utilizing UID requires a change in the way of thinking—a paradigm shift. Pedagogy changes from a focus on teaching all students in the same manner except for those who require accommodations (i.e.. students with disabilities may be taught differently) to utilizing various teaching methods to provide access to all students with various backgrounds, learning styles, cultures, languages, abilities, and disabilities. Curriculum content remains the same. It is how the curriculum is delivered that changes.

Professional development for K-12 teachers on the topic of Universal Instructional Design will benefit them and their students. The UID professional development plan as described in this chapter connects students' needs and teachers' needs through established, effective professional learning communities. Armed with UID principles and techniques in the satchels of skills, teachers will have the knowledge and confidence not only to utilize UID but to welcome UID initiatives from their colleagues, administrators, and enthusiastic teachers like Nancy.

References

Allen, D., Blythe, T., & Powell, B. S. (1996). *A guide to looking collaboratively at student work.* Cambridge, MA: Harvard Project Zero.

Argondizza, T. (2003). Tools for universal instruction. In L. Ben-Moshe, R., Cory, M. Feldbaum, & K. Sagendorf (Eds.)., *Building pedagogical curb cuts: Incorporating disability in the university classroom and curriculum* (pp. 101-107).Syracuse, NY: Syracuse University.

Bowe, F. (2000). *Universal Design in education: Teaching non-traditional students.* Westport, CN: Bergin and Garvey.

Bryan, A., & Myers, K. (2006). Students with disabilities: Doing what's right. *About Campus, 11*(4), 18-22.

Bryson. J. (2003). *Universal Instructional Design in postsecondary settings: An implementation guide.* Province of Ontario, Canada: Learning Opportunities Task Force.

Burgstahler, S. (2003). *Working together: K-12 teachers and students with disabilities.* Seattle: University of Washington, DO-IT. Retrieved March 26, 2007, from http://www.washington.edu/doit/Brochures/Academics/working.k12.html.

Burgstahler, S. (2007). *Universal Design of Instruction.* University of Washington, DO-IT. Retrieved March 22, 2007 from http://www.washington.edu/doit

Costa, A., Lipton, L., & Wellman, B. (1997). Shifting rules, shifting roles: Transforming the work environment to support learning. In S. Caldwell (Ed.), *Professional development in learner-centered schools* (pp. 92-114). Oxford, OH: National Staff Development Council.

Council for Exceptional Children. (1999). *Research Connections, 5*(2), 2-3.

Darling-Hammond, L. (1997). *Doing what matters most: Investing in quality teaching.* New York: National Commission on Teaching & America's Future.

DuFour, R. (1998). You won't find this on any checklist. *Journal of Staff Development, 9*(2), 57-64.

Fox, J. A., & Johnson, D. (Eds.). (2000). *Curriculum transformation and disability (CTAD): Workshop facilitator's guide.* Minneapolis: University of Minnesota, General College & Disability Services. Retrieved September 12, 2007, from http://www.gen.umn.edu/research/CTAD/publications.htm

Garmston, R. (1998). Expert teachers carry a satchel of skills. *Journal of Staff Development, 9*(2), 54-57.

Higbee, J. L. (Ed.). (2003). *Curriculum transformation and disability: Implementing Universal Design in higher education.* Minneapolis: University of Minnesota, General College, Center for Research on Developmental Education and Urban Literacy. Retrieved December 16, 2006, from http://www.education.umn.edu/crdeul/pubs/ctad.

Jones, S. R. (1996). Toward inclusive theory: Disability as a social construction. *NASPA*

Journal, 33, 347-354.

Lampert, M., & Ball, D. (1999). Teaching as the learning profession: *Handbook of policy and practice.* San Francisco: Jossey-Bass.

Public Law 107-110 (2001). *No child left behind.* Retrieved March 28, 2007, from http://www.ed.gov/nclb/landing.jhtml

Schenkat, R., & Tyser, K. (1997). Teacher content knowledge: Impact on teaching and learning. In S. Caldwell (Ed.), *Professional development in learner-centered schools* (pp. 116-130). Oxford, Ohio: National Staff Development Council.

Silver, P., Bourke, A., & Strehorn, K. C. (1998). Universal Instructional Design in higher education: An approach for inclusion. *Equity and Excellence in Education, 31*(2), 47-51.

Sparks, D. (2002). In search of heroes: Give educators a place on the pedestal: Interview with Roland Barth. *Journal of Staff Development, 23*(1), 46-50.

Student Perspectives

CHAPTER 29

Student Evaluations of the Effectiveness of Implementing Universal Instructional Design

Jeanne L. Higbee, Pa Houa Lee, James R. Bardill, and Heidi D. Cardinal
University of Minnesota

Abstract
This chapter uses multiple methods to explore student perspectives on participating in a course that was created from the bottom up with Universal Instructional Design in mind. It is coauthored by 3 undergraduate students, 1 who compiled the course evaluation statistics presented and 2 who wrote about their experiences in a universally-designed psychology course taught by the lead author. Results of course evaluations are provided.

Previous sections of this book have focused on various aspects of administrator, faculty, and staff perspectives on implementing Universal Design (UD) in higher education. This chapter instead explores how students have evaluated a psychology course taught in the Department of Postsecondary Teaching and Learning (PsTL) at the University of Minnesota that was designed from the bottom up with Universal Instructional Design (UID) in mind. The course in question, PsTL 1280: "Psychology and Personal Development," is discussed in depth in Chapter 5. The instructor has considerable autonomy and freedom to experiment with alternative pedagogies and multicultural content because PsTL 1280 is not a prerequisite for other courses in sequence. In fact, students often enroll because they must meet a social science requirement and want to do it in the least painless fashion possible. Because the course is taught during a 3-week May term, students' initial attitude toward the course often seems to be something like "I guess I can stand anything for 3 weeks." The course, which is offered for 3 credits, meets for 3 hours and 40 minutes per day—a time period that could tax the attention and persistence of students and instructor alike. But through implementation of the guiding principles of UID, the course is engaging and typically earns high (i.e., means for overall teaching ability of 6.6 to 6.9 on a 7-point scale) teacher evaluations for the instructor. However, standardized teaching evaluations cannot tell the whole story. Initially the faculty member developed a separate course evaluation form to determine whether the course met its objectives. Then she created a template for evaluating the effectiveness of implementing UID principles in any course (Pedagogy and Student Services for Institutional Transformation [PASS IT], n.d.). Finally, she collapsed the two into one evaluation instrument. This chapter presents the evaluation results from sections of PsTL 1280 offered in May 2006 and 2007.

Method

On the second-to-last day of class, students enrolled in PsTL 1280 and its earlier iteration, GC 1280, were asked to complete an anonymous paper-and-pencil version of the course evaluation form. In 2006 the form consisted only of an adaptation of the template of items based on UID guidelines. In 2007 the evaluation form also included the opportunity to rate the success of PsTL 1280 in meeting each of the course's objectives, also considered by the instructor to be the essential components of the course, as follow:

1. Students will become acquainted with prominent psychological theories and the theorists who espoused them.
2. Students will be able to define key psychological concepts.
3. Students will learn the relationship between psychological constructs and those of other fields of study, including history, political science, sociology, economics, and anthropology.
4. Students will explore psychological aspects of current and historical events both within the U.S. and throughout the world.
5. Students will become familiar with research methodologies.
6. Students will be introduced to basic statistical concepts such as central tendency and correlation.
7. Students will develop the skills and knowledge necessary to critique psychological research.
8. Students will learn about psychological assessment.
9. Students will apply psychological theory and concepts to their own development and relationships.
10. Students will learn to identify key ideas in a psychology textbook.
11. Students will further develop their writing skills.
12. Students will use higher-order thinking skills to analyze, synthesize, and evaluate course materials.
13. Students will use knowledge acquired in the course to propose creative solutions to real-life problems, both personal and global.
14. Students will explore psychological concepts within the framework of diverse cultures.
15. Students will work collaboratively to complete tasks.
16. Students will facilitate their own learning.
17. Students will demonstrate their knowledge in a variety of ways, including through assigned study guides, quizzes, exams, essays, small-group activities and other in-class exercises, and group discussions.

While the students completed the evaluations the instructor left the room. A class member volunteered to collect the forms and place them in an envelope and seal it. Students were informed that the instructor would not open the envelope until after course grades had been posted, and that the evaluations would in no way impact students' grades in the course. An undergraduate student assistant employed by the PASS IT project compiled the results into an Xcel spreadsheet and ran the statistics—mean, mode, median, and standard deviation—for each item.

Results

Of 16 students enrolled in GC 1280 in May 2006, 14 voluntarily completed the course evaluation; 17 of 18 enrolled students in PsTL 1280 completed the evaluation in May

2007. Figure 1 provides the mean, mode, median, standard deviation, and range of scores for the eight items related to the implementation of UID administered in both 2006 and 2007. Rated on a scale of 1 to 10, the means for these items ranged from 9.6 to 9.9, and the median and mode for each of the items was 10 (n = 31).

For the 17 items administered in 2007 related to the course objectives—or, in terms of the guiding principles of UID, the essential components—the mean responses on the 10-point scale ranged from a high of 9.7 for item 17 regarding demonstrating knowledge in a variety of ways, down to 8.6 for two of the items, as depicted in Table 1. Across 17 students' responses for 17 items, there were 3 ratings of 6 and a total of 12 ratings of 7; all other ratings (274 out of a total of 289 responses) were 8 or higher. The 6s and 7s came from different students for different items; there were no student "outliers." Thus,

Figure 1. PASS IT course evaluation template adapted for PsTL 1280.

Guiding Principle	*M*	Mode	*Mdn*	*SD*	Range
Dr. Higbee created a respectful learning environment.	9.9	10	10	0.30	9-10
The required course content was appropriate.	9.6	10	10	0.62	8-10
The expectations for the course and how the assignments and tests would be graded were clearly communicated via the syllabus, summary of assignments, and separate assignment sheets for each major assignment (e.g., essays, final project).	9.8	10	10	0.37	9-10
Dr. Higbee provided clear and accurate feedback.	9.9	10	10	0.30	9-10
Natural supports for learning were provided (e.g., instructor-created study guides, reviews for all quizzes and the final exam, class exercises to illustrate textbook content).	9.8	10	10	0.45	8-10
Dr. Higbee used multiple teaching strategies (e.g., short lecture, discussion, films, small group exercises).	9.9	10	10	0.30	9-10
In PsTL 1280 students were able to demonstrate their knowledge of the material in multiple ways (e.g., study guides, quizzes, essays, final project, final exam).	9.9	10	10	0.34	9-10
Dr. Higbee encouraged contact between students and the faculty member (i.e., inside and outside of class, as well by phone or e-mail).	9.8	10	10	0.37	9-10

Note: *N*=31

in general, students were very positive about the effectiveness of PsTL 1280 in achieving its objectives.

Other Indicators of Success

Another measure of the success of implementing UID can be reducing or eliminating the need to provide individual academic accommodations for students with disabilities. In PsTL 1280 all students receive as much time as they need to complete daily quizzes and the final examination, as described in Chapter 5. As a result, the three students who disclosed documented disabilities chose to take tests with the rest of the class, assuring that their disabilities remained confidential. Each of these students earned a B or higher in the course.

In fact, no student with or without a disability has failed GC or PsTL 1280 in sections taught by the author. "Noncompleters" (i.e., those who enrolled but withdrew from the course after attending at least 1 day of class) have left for time management or nonacademic reasons, including two postsecondary educational option (PSEO) students who were completing their last weeks of high school at the same time that the course was offered, several students who had initially attempted to take two courses during the

Table 1. Mean, mode, median, standard deviation, and range of student responses to course objectives evaluation items from May 2007

Course Objective	*M*	Mode	*Mdn*	*SD*	Range
1. Theories and theorists	9.1	9	9	0.93	8-10
2. Key concepts	9.2	10	9	0.81	8-10
3. Relationship to other fields	8.6	9	9	0.93	7-10
4. Current and historical events	8.6	8	9	1.12	6-10
5. Research methodologies	8.7	9	9	0.99	8-10
6. Basic statistical concepts	8.9	8	9	0.83	8-10
7. Skills and knowledge to critique	9.0	10	9	0.93	7-10
8. Assessment	8.7	8	9	0.92	7-10
9. Application to self	9.2	10	9	0.75	8-10
10. Key ideas in text	9.4	10	9	0.70	6-10
11. Writing skills	8.9	10	9	1.09	6-10
12. Thinking skills	8.8	9	9	1.01	7-10
13. Problem solving skills	9.2	10	10	0.90	8-10
14. Diverse cultures	8.8	10	9	1.19	6-10
15. Collaboration	9.1	10	8	0.99	7-10
16. Facilitation of own learning	9.1	10	9	1.14	7-10
17. Demonstration of knowledge	9.7	10	10	0.59	8-10

n =17

3-week session, and a single mother whose child became ill during the first week of class. Any student who has withdrawn has done so during the first week, and has had a passing grade at the point of withdrawal. No student who has disclosed a disability has withdrawn from the class.

In 2007 when students were assigned 2 essays from a possible list of 12, two students, James and Pa, chose to write about their experiences taking a course for the first time to their knowledge that had been designed using UID principles. They responded to the following prompt:

> Universal Instructional Design (UID) is a relatively new model for creating college and university learning experiences that engage all students. One of the purposes of UID is to ensure that students with disabilities are not segregated from all other students. However, the point of UID is that all students should benefit. Key components of UID include: (a) creating welcoming classrooms; (b) determining the essential components of a course; (c) communicating clear expectations; (d) providing constructive and timely feedback; (e) exploring the use of natural supports for learning, including technology, to enhance opportunities for all learners; (f) designing teaching methods that consider diverse learning styles, abilities, ways of knowing, and previous experience and background knowledge; (g) creating multiple ways for students to demonstrate their knowledge; and (h) promoting interaction among and between faculty and students …
>
> Have you found this approach to be helpful? What in particular worked for you? What other suggestions would you make? Would you recommend that other teachers use UID principles to design their classes?

Neither James nor Pa have a disability. Their essays, which follow, support the assertion that all students can benefit from the implementation of UID.

James' Assessment of UID in PsTL 1280

Although it is a fairly new teaching approach, Universal Instructional Design has been shown to be an effective model that allows students from many different cultural backgrounds to be able to engage in class activities and discussions with the instructor and classmates. The key purpose of UID is to allow any student an equal opportunity to learn the key concepts and themes of the course while also having the opportunity to express ideas to others.

I enrolled in a course at the University of Minnesota, PsTL 1280: "Psychology and Personal Development", which has implemented many of the key components of UID to fit the diversity of the types of educational backgrounds in the class. My instructor, Dr. Jeanne Higbee, has applied the principles of modern psychological development to the UID teaching style and it has been successful for applying the key concepts to practical situations and for individual participation in class discussions.

Some main strategies of UID that Dr. Higbee used were (a) clearly stated learning objectives, which she hoped we would remember later on in life; (b) interactive activities with other students in the class to be able to apply and understand the principles of psychological development, and finally (c) rather than basing students' entire performance evaluation (i.e., grade) on a couple quizzes and a final exam, Dr. Higbee used in-class conversations, films, and study guides in addition to exams to explore what students have really learned and to determine course grades.

For me, the best way to apply the lessons and key terms from the textbook was to think of my own experience that could be applied to the main theme of the reading, which was exactly what the study guides Dr. Higbee created for the course ask students to do. This type of processing made it much easier to understand the key concepts and also made further reading more interesting and easier to comprehend. I also think this method worked well for other members of the class because the discussions were always vocal. I remember sitting in literature classes trying to analyze themes in a book and the awkward dead silence that would fall on the class when nobody could come up with an answer; this class had the complete opposite outcome. I also thought applying concepts and key terms to videos was an effective method. The more we were able to remember a specific scene, the easier it was to remember a concept.

Because UID was an effective approach, as implemented in PsTL 1280, it is difficult to think of suggestions to make improvements. One suggestion I would make is to have the instructor come up with his or her own examples for the class to hear when dealing with tough topics to grasp. I think any class that holds discussions will be more vocal and interactive if the instructor interacts more with the students, rather than just have students answer a specific question they are asked. PsTL 1280 was good at dealing with this issue, but many others are not and the result would sometimes be instructors who would lose their tempers when the students clearly did not understand what the instructor was asking. One of my friends who attends another institution also shared recently that he has a teacher who is constantly relating the topics to his own personal experience, and my friend says that this type of interaction makes remembering the topics much easier for him as well.

Overall, I think UID is a common-sense style to approach teaching, but its practice is rare because many professors believe that the way they learned is the way others will learn, too, which is not the case. I think many of the classes I have taken here at the University would have been easier to understand if professors had applied a more one-on-one interaction with the class, rather than just a pure lecture from PowerPoint slides or straight off a chalkboard. Even if students do not encounter professors who use this type of teaching style, they can apply it themselves while reading from a text because as long as they can apply the material to previous experiences they have had in their lives, the easier it will be to remember it for a test.

Pa's Thoughts About the Benefits of Universal Instructional Design

I believe if more college courses took the Universal Instructional Design approach, more students would be inclined to participate and ultimately succeed. I wish I had taken a course with this approach in my beginning years of college because I felt so lost in all of my classes my freshman year. Also, I can honestly say that I have learned a lot more information in PsTL 1280 than in any of my other college courses due to the set-up of the course curriculum. I understand that in college students should begin to exercise their responsibilities of becoming an adult (e.g., meet deadlines without being told to), but I think the UID approach will help develop the skills needed more than hinder the skills needed to become a responsible adult.

UID is a very helpful approach to learning. In PsTL 1280 I liked the fact that I was tested and quizzed along the way instead of having to stress over studying for a midterm that includes three to five chapters of information. By getting tested or quizzed everyday, I felt like I could handle the pressure of the quizzes and I did not feel as overwhelmed when compared to taking midterms in a regular semester. The particular thing that worked very well for me in this approach was the fact that I was held accountable to show up for class if I wanted to pass the course. Not only did I have to take a quiz everyday, but participation in class activities and discussion counted in the calculation of the final grade. While taking a regular lecture course, I tend to "skip out" on lecture because I think that the professor could care less and there really is "no use" to attendance because there is no immediate result. I believe that in college, students succeed best when they receive immediate results and rewards. For example, if they know that attendance counts towards the final grade in a course, students are more prone to come to lecture; if not, students may find other things to occupy themselves during lecture.

Another reason why I really like this approach to learning is the fact that I am a really bad test taker. English is my second language and so I have a really hard time with the traditional test set up of true-false and multiple choices. I have always been slower than I want to be at interpreting the statements or questions and I am always nervous and stressed while taking an exam; somehow I am never really able to make myself relax during an exam. Whenever an exam (i.e., midterm or final) is timed and I know that it is worth a big chunk of my final grade, I get very stressed out before (while studying), during, and after taking the test. Again, I loved how I was quizzed daily on the information I learned the day before and I loved how there was no time limit on any of the quizzes in PsTL 1280. That made the atmosphere for taking the quizzes and the final exam less stressful for me.

I think it is really reasonable that the study guides we did as daily homework were incorporated into the final grade. For a student who does not do so well on tests, I believe that exams should not be the only means of measuring knowledge in the classroom. I have taken some courses where I have learned much fascinating information but ended up with a grade that did not come close to reflecting the amount of knowledge I had gained. It is always discouraging when I know I have done my best and do not receive the grade

Figure 2. PsTL 1280 summary of assignments form

Summary Of Assignments
PsTL 1280
Dr. Jeanne L. Higbee
May-June, 2007

Date Due	Assignment	Point Value	Earned
5/21	In-class activities	10	_____
5/22	In-class activities	10	_____
5/22	Study Guide (SG) 1 for Chapter (CH) 1	20	_____
5/22	Quiz (Q) 1	50	_____
5/23	In-class activities	10	_____
5/23	SG 2 for CH 2	20	_____
5/23	Q 2	50	_____
5/24	In-class activities	10	_____
5/24	SG 3 for CH 3 & 4	20	_____
5/24	Q 3	50	_____
5/29	In-class activities	10	_____
5/29	Essay 1	60	_____
5/29	SG 4 for CH 5 & 6	20	_____
5/29	Q 4	50	_____
5/30	In-class activities	10	_____
5/30	SG 5 for CH 7	20	_____
5/30	Q 5	50	_____
5/31	In-class activities	10	_____
5/31	SG 6 for CH 8 & 9	20	_____
5/31	Q 6	50	_____
5/31	Road map for final project	10	_____
6/4	In-class activities	10	_____
6/4	Essay 2	60	_____
6/4	SG 7 for CH 10 & 11	20	_____
6/4	Q 7	50	_____
6/5	In-class activities	10	_____
6/5	SG 8 for CH 12	20	_____
6/5	Q 8	50	_____
6/6	SG 9 for CH 13 & 14	20	_____
6/6	Q 9	50	_____
6/6	Final Project	100	_____
6/7	Final Exam	100	_____

Drop lowest quiz score: _____
Attendance Record: _____ *Absences (not to exceed 2)*

POINT TOTAL: (before subtracting 1 quiz)	1050	_____
POINT TOTAL: (after subtracting lowest quiz)	1000	_____

FINAL LETTER GRADE: _____

I deserve. When I come across a situation like that, I tell myself that it is not entirely my fault as long as I studied effectively for the exam. Instead the problem could have been that the questions were not well constructed or the professor did not do a good enough job of explaining the material or narrowing down which information will be important for the exam. I appreciated that in PsTL 280 Dr. Higbee conducted a review session in class prior to each quiz and the final examination.

I suggest and recommend that other teachers use the UID approach to teaching. There are many professors with whom I have taken a course who are very knowledgeable in what they are teaching, but cannot teach effectively and have unfair grading systems or do not communicate "up front" what the grading criteria are. Dr. Higbee provided a concise summary of all assignments and the maximum points available for each (see Figure 2). By the last day of class we knew exactly where we stood before we took the final exam.

Conclusion

Clearly this chapter merely provides preliminary data from a very limited sample to support the effectiveness of UID. For 2 years PASS IT has been collecting data from summer institute participants from throughout the U.S. who represent a wide variety of institutions and academic disciplines (Goff & Higbee, 2007). These data, which track course completion and pass rates, indicate that students with disabilities participating in courses taught by faculty who implement UID achieve success at a rate that is proportionally comparable to that of students without disabilities. We believe that is an important finding, but just the beginning. We are also concerned about student perceptions—do students think that UID can make a difference? As explained by Pa, many students who are not native speakers of English can certainly benefit from the implementation of UID principles in the classroom. Are there other historically underserved populations of students for whom the implementation of UID might be particularly beneficial? Overall, does implementation of UID student have an impact on student engagement and satisfaction? Does it enhance learning? More sophisticated research is needed to explore these questions further.

References

PASS IT course evaluation template. (n.d.). Minneapolis: University of Minnesota, Center for Research on Developmental Education and Urban Literacy, Pedagogy and Student Services for Institutional Transformation. Retrieved October 18, 2007, from http://cehd.umn.edu/passit/resources.html

Goff, E., & Higbee, J. L. (2007). *PASS IT annual report.* Minneapolis: University of Minnesota, Center for Research on Developmental Education and Urban Literacy, Pedagogy and Student Services for Institutional Transformation.

CHAPTER 30

Why Not Disclose?

Julie R. Alexandrin
University of Southern Maine

Ilana Lyn Schreiber
VOICES For Change

Elizabeth Henry
Saint Joseph College

Abstract

For people with hidden disabilities, the prospect of self-disclosure can be a double-edged sword. True, they sometimes benefit from disclosure, but they also can be penalized in how other people interact with them. This chapter will look at personal stories of why people disclose their hidden disabilities and why they do not. It will also discuss what supports are needed in an environment to make disclosure easier for a student with a hidden disability.

Many professionals have asked us, "Why don't students just disclose that they have a disability?" Our response is, "Is it safe for them to disclose?" Many people do not understand the risk that students take when they disclose. Why is it a risk? It is a risk because students cannot predict how others will react and subsequently treat them when they do disclose. Will others believe they have a disability, will others treat them differently once they know, or will life be easier for someone who has disclosed? Having a hidden disability (e. g., learning disability, mental illness, Attention Deficit Hyperactivity Disorder [ADHD], acquired brain injury, medical condition such as asthma or diabetes) is far from easy. In fact, when most people are asked what a disability is, they will say that a person with a physical disability will come to their mind first (Kennemer, 1997). When one asks about specific disabilities, again a person who visibly fits that disability will come to mind; for example, a student who is lazy or seeking unfair advantages is often the description of a student with a learning disability (Kravets, 1996). Hence, when asking students with a hidden disability to disclose, one is not only asking them to disclose something they have tried to hide or work against their whole life, but in addition to go against and, in effect, alter what a person with a disability looks like to others in terms of stereotypes and biases. This is not an easy task for most, and is especially difficult for someone with low self-esteem, which is characteristic of many people with a disability (Lynch & Gussel, 1996).

Many people with hidden disabilities will often state that they wish their disabilities were visible rather than unseen, a desire that represents the difficulty of disclosure. Though they will acknowledge that there are advantages to people being unaware of their disability, like not having low expectations inflicted upon them or not being stared at, the risk and fear people with hidden disabilities face over needing to disclose often outweigh the comfort of their invisibility. The questions of if, when, and how to disclose, and what the potential consequences of disclosure are, weigh heavily on their mind whenever they meet new people or are in new situations. In addition, the risk increases with the likelihood of opposing what people traditionally consider to be disabilities—something visible, a physical impairment—when stating that one has a disability that people cannot see. As a result, many people will doubt the individual with a hidden disability and even accuse the person of lying. Consider what it is like for people finally to gather up the courage to disclose and in turn have someone not only doubt them, but also think that they are lying about an essential part of who they are.

Why discuss disclosure in a book about Universal Design, which aims to create an environment where people with disabilities do not need to disclose? Even beyond Universal Design, an environment must be fostered in a manner that allows anyone to feel comfortable to disclose a disability. Without such an environment, people cannot fully be who they are, as they often feel that they need to keep their disability a secret. When an accepting and understanding environment is created, people are empowered to be fully who they are and therefore are more likely to reach their full potential. Individuals who must hide aspects of their identity are often unable to work to their full potential because so much effort is expended on keeping the disability hidden. Hence, creating a campus where students feel safe and are safe to disclose allows students with hidden disabilities to work to their full potential.

This chapter begins by examining what the literature states about students disclosing their disabilities on college campuses. The chapter then shares personal experiences of people with hidden disabilities. These experiences present how both disclosure and the choice not to disclose have been beneficial to people at times and disadvantageous or even harmful at other times. The last part of this chapter will explore how colleges and universities can better create environments where students feel safe and are safe to disclose a hidden disability. The goal in feeling safe is for students to feel supported enough so that they do not fear or encounter negative repercussions as a result of their disclosure. The ultimate goal in providing an environment where students are safe to disclose a hidden disability is to provide adequate supports and not create barriers and challenges for students after they do disclose.

Literature Review

The majority of the literature on disclosure and disabilities relates to how and when to disclose a disability. Further, much of this literature is focused on the employment sector, and most often written from the point of view of the legal rights of disclosure (Career Center-Cal Transitions, n.d.; Career Services at the University of Delaware, n.d.; Career Services at Rutgers, n.d.; Cooper, 1995; Dalgin, 2005, Disability Services - University of Wisconsin - Stout, n.d.- Frieche & Aune, 1996; Huvelle, Budoff, & Arnholz, 1984; Leahly, 1994; National Center for Learning Disabilities, n.d.; National Collaborative on

Workforce and Disability for Youth, 2005; Pearson, Ip, Hui, Yip, Ho, & Lo, 2003; Roberts & Macan, 2006; SFSU - DPRC, n.d.; Training and Technical Assistance Providers, 2005; Witt, 1992; Your Florida, n.d.). Very little literature exists addressing the need to create environments that are safe for disclosure, or discussing the impact that the lack of these safe environments can have on those with hidden disabilities. Because much of the research tends to focus primarily on finding effective ways in which to disclose (e.g., what language to use when disclosing, how much information to provide, optimal times to disclose), there is limited discussion about the personal risks a person with hidden disabilities faces upon deciding to and actually disclosing (KOKUA Program - University of Hawaii-Manoa, n.d.; Learning Plus University of Hartford, n.d.; Office of Disability Services, n.d.; University of Vermont, n.d.).

Research indicates that postsecondary institutions have been reporting a steady rise in the matriculation of students with hidden disabilities since 1978 (Lynch & Gussel, 1996). However, this rise is based on students who disclose their disabilities, and research findings suggest that the rate of students' disclosure to postsecondary institutions is low (Glover-Graf, Janikowski, & Hadley, 2003). Most colleges and universities have disclosure documentation that potential students can fill out when applying for admission. The research in this area again focuses on the legal rights a student has in disclosing, but not why it is important to disclose, or how the disclosure of a disability during the admissions process can really benefit the student, such as with special admission reviews or the provision of academic support early on the student's collegiate career.

There is a dearth of research that discusses how to create safe postsecondary environments for students to disclose. In addition, the extant research does not address the risks students take when disclosing and the double-edge sword that disclosing creates. Finally, publications related to disclosure are often either written from the point of view of someone with an apparent disability (Barga, 1996; Rocco, 2001) or someone who is an ally but does not have a disability. Many advantages do result from the support of allies by students who are disclosing. However, allies often lack the experiential knowledge of the real risks and challenges involved in disclosing. Those who have experienced the complexities of disclosure and nondisclosure can support students not only with expertise, but also with first-hand knowledge of what it is like to have a hidden disability.

Personal Experiences With Disclosure and Nondisclosure

To provide a more thorough awareness of the issues students with hidden disabilities face on college campuses, we share our own undergraduate and graduate student experiences as students with hidden disabilities.

Julie

Getting to college was a challenge. Even though I was in honors classes and had a high grade point average (GPA) in high school, I was not thought of as "college material" as I have a severe learning disability. I was not permitted to take the PSATs and my guidance counselor in high school would not support me in doing college applications or talking about to which colleges I should apply. It was, therefore, important to me to find a college that supported me as a student with a learning disability. Fortunately, I did. It was a university that provided special evaluations for students who disclosed their disabilities in the application process, which I needed as demonstrated by my verbal score in the low 400s on the SAT; had an early orientation for students with disabilities; created a peer support network for students with disabilities; and provided supports to students with disabilities on campus.

At this university I benefited by disclosing my disability. I obtained the books on tape I needed, received syllabi early in order to secure my books on tape before the semester started, utilized a tutor at the Writing Center who proofread all of my papers, and through the peer support network I found other students with disabilities with whom I could productively study. For example, one of my study partners was a student who was wonderful at reading aloud, but had little comprehension of what he read. So he read to me and I helped him understand what he had read. This demonstrates the importance of why peers with disabilities need a way to network and support each other. Beyond schoolwork, we also supported each other in the knowledge that we had an understanding of what it was like to have a hidden disability. We shared the same difficulties regarding not knowing whether to disclose, and understood how frustrating it often can be to have a disability. Through my peer network, I was able to celebrate my success of achieving a good grade on a multiple-choice test, one of my weaknesses, because my peers fully understood what an accomplishment this was for me. Most of the college professors also worked with me to meet the accommodations I needed, such as untimed tests and handing in drafts of papers so that I could make sure I was meeting all of the requirements of the papers assigned.

The one time that my disability was used against me occurred during the early part of my program for teacher certification. My advisor called me in and questioned me on whether I could really be a teacher, as my spelling is not strong and she doubted my ability to write on the board for students. Honestly, I was floored. How could one aspect of me, my ability to spell correctly, be holding me back from my goal of being a teacher? I explained to my advisor ways that I would support myself in spelling correctly on the board. In all of my field placements, I made sure I used these supports and created others, as I knew that how well I spelled on the board was being held to a higher standard than my teaching style and how I interacted with the students.

When I went to graduate school, I decided not to self-disclose. One reason was that I was at a different university, and I did not feel as comfortable or safe in disclosing. In addition, my accommodations were different. I no longer needed to rely on books on tape as much, as I am a strong sight word and context reader, as long as I am in my discipline of psychology and education. In addition, I had my own proofreader for my papers. I did disclose to my advisors, however, which was beneficial, and my disclosure helped them to understand better my writing style throughout my work on my dissertation.

I chose to self-disclose to one other professor during my graduate studies, and the resulting experience was not positive. She initially challenged the reality of my disability, as my lack of phonics awareness went against her theory that no one could possibly sight read and succeed at my level. Because the professor believed that I did not actually have a disability and therefore did not warrant appropriate accomodations, she was not helpful in providing the readings early so that I could have them put on tape. The readings were mostly medical and out of my discipline, and I had a great deal of difficulty reading them without the support of the tapes. I was unable to go to the Disabilities Support Center for assistance in convincing her to provide the accommodations I needed, as I was told at the beginning of my graduate work that these services were mostly for undergraduate students. The impact of the lack of support I received in this course is quite clear as this turned out to be the lowest grade I received during all of my graduate work.

Ilana

I was not officially diagnosed with a disability until my junior year in college, though I certainly struggled through high school due to the effects of my symptoms. Despite the lack of an official diagnosis, by my first year of high school I was distinctly aware that my learning was seriously impacted by forces beyond my control. I clearly remember the anxiety I felt when beginning the application process for college, knowing that my high school GPA and transcript did not accurately represent my abilities. Having a mental illness often disrupted my ability to concentrate, and as a result I often turned assignments in late or incomplete. When I was feeling well, I achieved high grades. Hence, my grades were all over the map. I knew that the colleges reviewing my transcripts were going to question the extreme fluctuation in my grades throughout the four marking periods of each year, as well as throughout my high school years as a whole, and I believed I had no answer. I distinctly remember at that time wishing I had an "actual" disability to disclose, so that I could not only help the college admission officers understand the variance in my grades, but also so that I would be able to ask for some support from the college that I would be attending.

Applying to college as a psychology major did provide the opportunity to disclose my difficult experiences in a way, in effect, to describe and explain how these experiences had affected my high school education, as I chose to center my entrance essays around this topic. Of course my description was neat and tidy, and quite representative of my optimism that my struggles were behind me, and conveyed how they would serve as a great learning tool as I studied to help others overcome their own difficulties. This was my belief, but I decidedly omitted from my disclosure my often overwhelming fear that my struggles were, in fact, not behind me, and would continue to affect my education as I moved on to college. Several months after deliberating over, and finally sending those essays, I was accepted to six of the seven schools to which I had applied. I chose one with a psychology program that interested me, and began my college career there the next fall.

There are many reasons why I did not formally disclose my disability in college; including my fear of the consequent perceptions of my abilities, my lack of awareness of what steps to take and to whom I would disclose, and my insecurity about whether the problems affecting my learning could and would even be classified as a disability. I attribute these and the countless other reasons that I bounced around in my mind over time to the very real stigma surrounding mental illness, and hidden disabilities in general, in our country. Had more thought been given to the need for services for students with hidden disabilities on our campus, a safe space or person would have been present to help me navigate through the process of disclosure, and hence I may have been more likely to consider seeking out the assistance that I needed. Further, I would not have questioned myself so much as to whether or not I even deserved services if mental illnesses were widely recognized as a disability and not "conditions" to "get over" or "pull yourself out of."

In reflecting back through my college years, I can clearly see how I would have benefited from both academic and peer support. This was not so clear at the time, however, and as a consequence my coursework suffered and the aspects of my disability actually became stronger and more overwhelming. As a result of the stress and frustration of often perceiving myself to be a "failure", my symptoms evolved into extreme anxiety and a gradual downslide into a deep depression. It was at this point, midway through my junior year, that I realized I had no choice but to reach out for help. I had been researching under a psychology professor for several years as part of my curriculum, and had come to know and trust her quite well. I met with her in her office one afternoon, and fell apart. Once we began talking and I felt reassured that she was a safe person to disclose to, I needed for her to "see" my struggles because hiding had simply become too difficult. Though we never discussed the possibility of academic support, this faculty member was fully able to help me navigate through the process of finding a professional to provide the emotional support that I so desperately needed at that point. With her support and guidance, I found a therapist with whom I would work until the summer after I earned my degree. However, there was one large piece missing from my encounter with the faculty member that consequently affected me for years to come. She inadvertently confirmed my hesitancy towards disclosing officially, as she never recommended that I receive academic support services or even discuss my eligibility. Thus, she did not confirm for me that my mental illness was indeed a disability at all. She did, though, remain a great source of emotional support, and she also became my academic advisor in order to help me balance my course load more appropriately than I had previously. Despite my difficulties, and several dropped courses, I was able to earn my degree the summer after my scheduled graduation date, and I was able to walk at graduation with my class. I have a photograph from my graduation day of my professor and me, and I feel very fortunate to have had her support and academic advice that helped me to achieve what so often felt impossible.

When I went to graduate school to pursue a master's degree in social work (MSW), I again was unaware that I could qualify for services for my hidden disability, which had by then been diagnosed as a mental illness. I did debate disclosing my illness early on. However, I was not sure that having my hidden disability officially documented would actually provide an avenue for support or recourse if my symptoms were to interfere with my ability to complete my coursework or field placements. I did not, however, think of disclosing as a proactive approach in receiving support to prevent such issues. Apparently neither did the college, as it did not offer any support once I did make the official disclosure. Disability Services simply sent me a form to document my illness and a copy of the portion of my social work handbook that detailed steps to take if problems occurred due to a disability. Because the support available was not clear, and due to the lack of reinforcement that a mental illness would qualify me for support just as if I had a "more accepted" disability, I never accessed any services during my graduate studies. As a result of this lack of support, and several encounters with unsupportive professors who were unwilling to accommodate my needs, I was unable to finish my degree and left school on a leave of absence. I did decide to withdraw from this college, and hope to finish my degree at a different institution sometime in the near future. When I am seeking out a new graduate program, I now will be aware of the services available to me and will be sure to include in my search whether or not this support would be accessible before even applying to attend.

Libby

In truth, I did not come to "grips" with my disabilities until my freshman year of college. First and foremost, I was a "late label"; in other words, I was not labeled with a disability until the end of my sophomore year of high school. Why? Certainly, I was the "perfect" student; I did very well academically, socially, and athletically. Actually, I never presented a severe achievement gap; rather, my strong verbal, written, and organizational skills surpassed those of my classmates. As a result, any minor hint of a disability was overlooked. Finally, my freshman English teacher brought her well-founded concerns to the head of the "Student Assistance Team," who then approached my parents. I was tested and it was determined that I have a specific learning disability and attention deficit/hyperactivity disorder (ADHD).

Consequently, I did not deal with the issue of disclosure until my sophomore year of high school. Even then I compensated so well that I received very few services and only a handful of testing accommodations. I really came face-to-face with my disability in college. Ironically, I did not search long and hard for a school with disability awareness and accommodations, but instead the school found me. I applied early decision. I attended the "Early Orientation" for students with "special needs," which greatly facilitated my transition to my new school. Fortunately, the coordinator for Disability Services (DS) was outstanding. She was my best support and biggest advocate. Nevertheless, I, too, had to step up to the plate and advocate for myself. The DS coordinator sent out the letters to each professor, but the rest was up to me, and I was willing and ready to approach my professors, introduce myself, and address my needs. Amazingly, my professors were supportive, compassionate, and helpful. I received extra time, my own testing room, and the use of a computer for all exams. Over the course of 4 years, or 8 semesters, I encountered only one hint of discrimination, but when I addressed the issue, my professor realized that she was wrong. In any case, I made her confusion a teachable moment, and as a result she has become much more conscious and supportive of students with disabilities.

In truth, if I had not received the previously mentioned accommodations, I probably would not have graduated. In addition, if my professors had not been so supportive and understanding, I probably would have transferred. I certainly had an incredible college experience both academically and socially. Within the context of my undergraduate institution, I found a balance, which was key to my comprehensive success. In summary, I decided to disclose, come face-to-face with my disability, and, in turn, I had an exceptional academic and social college experience. In the end, I was "proud" of my disability and ready to surmount the "downside" but thrilled to embrace and make use of the "upside."

I am now near the end of my graduate program. I am pursuing my master of arts in special education with teacher certification. Upon completion of my undergraduate degree, I tutored for a year, and then decided to be a full-time student once again.

On the whole, at my graduate institution I have made the decision not to disclose. Interestingly, upon matriculation I sensed the general institutional environment as unsupportive of people with disabilities. Therefore, I have only disclosed to three professors. I had not met with the disability coordinator until a professor recommended that I meet with her "just in case." I am thrilled that I did because she has been a great support and a reliable source of information and helpful recommendations.

Even though I have not disclosed, I have sensed discrimination from one professor in particular. Even though I have not made even mention of a disability, I have a sense that she suspects that I have one. Sadly, she has picked up on the most conspicuous features of my multifaceted disability, and consequently, she makes me feel incompetent and insecure within the realm of her classroom. I wish I had sent a letter to this professor to let her know my background, and maybe she would have treated me differently. Nevertheless, I know I am strong, capable, and intelligent, and I will not let her "suspicion" obstruct my potential for well-deserved success. Fortunately, after nine classes and seven professors, she has been my only "problem."

At this juncture, I am getting ready to student teach, and I know I will soon encounter another institution and environment. I am not worried about student teaching; however, I am a bit concerned about moving into the working world. Even though I do not have a surface disability, I am fearful that an astute person will pick up on the surface characteristics of my hidden disability and treat me differently; but deep down I am hopeful that I will find a supportive school that will embrace me as whole and realize that I have a heart of gold and steel and I am an incredible teacher! I have the educational background, motivation, and desire to make a difference that will carry me onward.

Ways to Create a Campus That Is Safe for Disclosure

We have shared our own stories in order to illustrate typical concerns related to disclosure. One of us expresses it like this:

> I am left with an enduring question: to disclose or not to disclose? I have two hidden disabilities, but I am not required or expected (by societal norms and expectation) to disclose. Nonetheless, contingent on the respective situation, I have two options: (a) make known my disabilities and suffer through what is often frustrating and insensitive treatment, or (b) choose to withhold (not reveal) a monumental piece of my whole being. My ultimate dilemma: do I forsake my true identity to appease the environment (i.e., not disclose), or relinquish the entirety of my identity (disclose) and potentially suffer the consequences? (Libby)

In the following paragraphs we describe ways that students with hidden disabilities have suggested to make a campus safe in their eyes to disclose a hidden disability. They are arranged in the order that people with hidden disabilities have suggested to be most important to least important.

1. Seeing the person first: When we talk about people with disabilities, or think about them, too often we define them by their disability. For example, someone is a "learning disabled student," rather than being described as a "student with a learning disability." To describe a person in this manner has a dramatic impact, as we are only addressing one aspect of the student's identity, therefore overlooking the student's core characteristics and strengths separate from the disability. Instead, it is important to see the person first, because we then realize and emphasize that the disability is only a part of the whole. As a result, when we are supporting or interacting with a person with a disability, we view the individual as having similar needs and wants to those of all people, and not just as a person with a disability.

2. Using person-first language: When we begin to see the person first, we also need new language to describe a person with a disability, for example no longer the "mentally ill person," we refer to the "person with a mental illness." Utilization of person-first language emphasizes that the individual is of primary importance, and that the disability is merely one part of the person's identity. Until we begin not only to view but also to treat students with disabilities as people first, they will continue to be marginalized and hence their environment will serve as a barrier to their success.

3. Using and understanding appropriate and current disability terms: People on campus should be familiar with and understand the different terms used to describe disabilities and what each of these terms means. For example, they should be able to differentiate between Schizophrenia and Dissociative Identity Disorder (DID). A common misperception demonstrating the misuse and misunderstanding of terms is the frequent use of Schizophrenia to define a person with multiple identities, or DID, when Schizophrenia is an entirely different disorder. Further, when not current with disability terminology, it is easy to be hurtful through one's ignorance. An example of such an offense is to refer to someone with DID as having Multiple Personality Disorder (MPD). People with DID are now recognized as having multiple identities and to use the former label of MPD can invalidate a person with multiplicity, as the reference to personality will often signify that the individual's personality is flawed rather than recognizing the exceptionality of multiple identities.

Another point to consider when utilizing terms, or labels, to describe people is the

Figure 1. How to correctly apply person first language

Incorrect	Correct
Non-disabled people	People without disabilities
The mentally ill guy	The man with a mental illness
The CP girl	The girl with Cerebral Palsy
... which can be used by most disabled and non-disabled people.	... which can be used by most people with and without disabilities.
Granted, I am a hearing White person, so my knowledge on the subculture is limited. They felt like it was insulting the rest of the disabled community.	Granted, I am a person who is hearing and White, so my knowledge on the subject is limited. They felt like it was insulting the rest of the community of people who have a disability.
... while self-advocates rebel against professionals and the non-retarded world.	... while self-advocates rebel against professionals and the world of people who are not mentally retarded*.
He is handicapped**.	He has a disability.
... who are confined to a wheelchair***.	... who use a wheelchair.
The person is afflicted by mental illness.	The person is affected by his or her mental illness.
She is a victim.	She is a survivor.
He suffers from Schizophrenia.	He has Schizophrenia.

*"Mentally Retarded" is a term certain states use; many states have varying terms (e.g., in Connecticut, "Intellectual Disability"). **The term "Handicapped" is a derogatory term that should not be used. It is derived from a reference to a person begging with their "cap in hand." ***When referring to someone who is in a wheelchair, he/she should not be described as being confined to the wheelchair, as the wheelchair gives the person freedom to move and independence. Therefore, the wheelchair is a tool rather than an object of confinement.

fact that all individuals are unique and therefore many prefer to define their disability in their own terms or labels. A way to honor them is to use the terms or labels they use to define their disability. For example, over the past several decades different state officials have changed the label used to define people with mental retardation. Many people who have disabilities that are classified under any number of the mental retardation terms will usually adamantly prefer one term over another when describing themselves (Shapiro, 2007). It is also important to realize that because most labels suggest deficiency, allowing people to define their disability empowers them. Every individual is exceptional in certain ways. By using correct and appropriate terms when relating to students and individuals in general, people on campus will demonstrate that awareness and understanding of people with disabilities is fundamental to the campus environment.

4. Refraining from telling and objecting to disability jokes and the use of pejorative language: As we should not and do not accept racial or ethnic jokes under any circum-

stances, we should also renounce jokes about people with disabilities. Jokes about disabilities and about people who have them are offensive, and when these jokes are told, or tolerated (i.e., laughing at a joke despite finding it offensive), the effect is that people with disabilities are ridiculed and continue to be oppressed. For example, people saying that they are having a "Dyslexic moment" because they reversed two letters or numbers in writing something is insulting to a person with a learning disability (LD), as they are implying that having Dyslexia can simply be reduced to the reversing of digits or letters and therefore is not a significant disability. Any joke puts down the people who are at the brunt of the joke. Not telling disability jokes, or objecting when others tell disability jokes, shows respect and understanding for people with disabilities. Closely related to offensive humor is the use of pejorative terms like "spaz" or "retard" or "looney toons" whether referring to a person with or without a disability. In addition to reducing complex disabilities to a punch line, these terms are intended as "put downs" to be hurtful. Even when referring to ones own leg as "gimpy," the connotation is demeaning to anyone with a real physical impairment. Phrases like "the blind leading the blind" may not be intended by the user to imply that people with visual impairments are incapable of taking leadership roles, but can be interpreted that way. Similarly, the use of "blind copy" to indicate an undisclosed recepient and "double-blind peer review" to note that both the author and the reviewer are masked are inappropriate (Tregoning, in press).

5. Providing Disability Sensitivity Training: Increasing the understanding of an oppressed group for everyone working with any group that has been oppressed in this country has been shown to improve understanding of and equity for the oppressed group (Strandberg, 2007). Hence, Disability Sensitivity Training is essential. In Disability Sensitivity Training, participants begin to learn about the hidden biases and stereotypes that they have about people with disabilities. They also explore how society reinforces these stereotypes and generates an environment where it is difficult for a person with a disability to excel or even maintain one's place. Through the discoveries made and the knowledge gained during Disability Sensitivity Training, a better awareness of what life is like for people with disabilities will follow. As a result, one can contribute to the unraveling of some of the common biases and stereotypes people have, offering a greater understanding of and more genuine interactions with people who have a disability.

6. Having high expectations for all students with disabilities: The one matter that comes up again and again that hurts people who disclose their hidden disability is that once they disclose, people view them as incapable of achieving as much expected prior to disclosing. Many students report that professors often treat them as if they cannot pass their course upon hearing that they have a disability. Students also report that many professors think that the students will need so much support in order to pass the course that it will bring down the rigor of the course, when in actuality the only accommodation the students need is simple for the professor to facilitate. A student with disabilities should be viewed as any other student, one who is capable of doing well in the course. Faculty attitudes can play an important role because of self-fulfilling prophecies. If a teacher believes that a student will do well in a course, the student is more likely to succeed in the course than when a professor has low expectations for that student (Rosenthal & Jacobson, 1968). Therefore, when a professor views students with disabilities as students who are successful

and intelligent and as capable as any other student, the students with disabilities are more likely to succeed in that course and at their college or university.

7. Using Universal Instructional Design (UID): When UID is integral in course planning and implementation, students may not need to disclose, as accommodations are built into the course for students with disabilities and all others. Through the use of UID, faculty and staff exhibit an awareness of the multiple ways to learn and demonstrate knowledge. This awareness greatly benefits students with hidden disabilities as they will learn and demonstrate knowledge more easily and need to use fewer of their compensatory skills when learning and demonstrating knowledge in nontraditional ways. For example, a student who has a learning disability and has weak auditory processing skills will learn better in a course that does not rely only on a lecture format to present knowledge, but instead uses multiple formats including demonstration and hands-on-learning. Through the use of UID, faculty and staff no longer view students' disabilities as problems or hindrances to learning and therefore create a campus environment where even though students with hidden disabilities are not required to disclose, they feel safe and are safe to do so.

8. Enhancing faculty understanding of accommodations and encouraging them to provide accommodations easily and readily: Even when UID is used, there are still times when accommodations need to be made for students with disabilities. In postsecondary settings professors primarily rely on reading and lecture formats in order for their students to gain knowledge. There are, however, a multitude of other ways for students to gain knowledge (e.g., through visual demonstrations and simulations, by listening to radio segments, and by listening to others read aloud and then discussing what was read). It is also important to recognize that just as there are many ways for students to gain knowledge, there are also many ways in which they can demonstrate this knowledge. Aside from the traditional college formula of tests and papers, students can show what they have learned through means such as presentations, dictating (rather than writing) answers for an exam, demonstrations, case studies, and group exams. By being aware of and using these other ways for students to obtain (learn) and demonstrate knowledge, professors show that they can easily make accommodations for students with disabilities (Hill, 1996). Further, by knowing that these accommodations do not decrease the rigor of their courses or change in any way the essential knowledge of their courses, professors actually reinforce the fact that these accommodations are an integral part of the learning experience for all students.

9. Offering support for all forms of disabilities and the different degrees of disabilities: Many times campuses provide supports for students with learning disabilities and ADHD, as these are seen as directly connected to learning. However, supports need to be in place for all disabilities, because many others like mental illness and medical disabilities can also affect a student's learning and ability to attend classes (Weiner & Weiner, 1996). By providing supports for all disabilities, all students with disabilities can feel comfortable and safe at the college or university.

10. Offering disabilities support programs that are easily accessible: When support services are difficult to access, it serves as an indication to students with disabilities that they are not welcome. When students with disabilities are unable to access or are not provided with the proper supports, the resulting message is that their success at the college

or university is not of importance to the campus community. For example, if the location of the campus support services is not centrally located, the services are then physically inaccessible to many students. Making services accessible also includes detailed planning to be sure to include all students, including graduate students. For instance, if graduate students are primarily on campus during evenings, then the support system for students with disabilities should also be accessible during evening hours.

11. Ensuring that different support systems on campus work together: In addition to making support programs (e.g., counseling, academic supports, career services, academic advising, and health services) obvious and easily accessible, it is crucial to create programs that are collaborative and work well together in order to prevent students from being caught between systems (Scott, 1996). For example, when various programs are working together across campus, students who are receiving counseling services will be informed that they also may be eligible for support services through disability services or in academic support. In addition, when students with disabilities know that systems are working together, they feel secure that when they disclose to one service, it is safe to disclose to other services as well.

12. Ensuring that people in admissions know how to evaluate applications of students with disabilities: When students are applying to a college or university, why would they disclose a disability if they are unsure as to how they will be judged by doing so or not? Students are more likely to disclose a disability on their applications if they are informed that the review process includes an additional evaluation by someone who is educated about and aware of how varying disabilities present in order to determine whether the disability might affect the student's performance at the college or university. With such a process in place, applicants will disclose to their benefit instead of withholding pertinent information for fear of being discriminated against in the application process.

In addition, when a student is able to disclose a disability during the application process, support and accommodations for the student can be established before the student begins to study at the college or university. When students wait to disclose until they are in the midst of needing services, it is often too late for them to be successful in all of their courses. Hence, having these supports in place from the start will provide students with a better opportunity to succeed at the college or university.

13. Facilitating peer support: Peer support among people with disabilities is often overlooked, mostly because of confidentiality issues. However, when students are given the choice to disclose to peers with disabilities, generally they are not hesitant, because the uncertainty of how their disclosure will be received is no longer an issue. Through peers with disabilities coming together, they are able to support each other in classes that they take together, and by sharing information about which professors use UID or work with students to make accommodations and adaptations, and which do not. In addition, support is also given through the common experiences and knowledge they each have of what it is like to have a hidden disability. It is much more powerful and meaningful to be able to talk about successes, failures, and hardships with someone who has this understanding of what a hidden disability is than with someone who has not experienced this unique situation.

14. Providing orientation activities that introduce campus and academic services: By

having students with disabilities participate in special orientation activities, they immediately learn the support systems that are available to them, and become familiar with the people who run them. As a result, students with disabilities are able to take advantage of these supports early on in their academic career, instead of having to investigate where each of the services is while they become involved in their coursework. In addition, by being familiar with the people who provide these services, their fears of how their disclosure will be received are alleviated. These orientation activities are also beneficial for starting a peer support network for students with disabilities.

15. Ensuring that everyone on campus is on board with these steps to create a safe campus: As with any program developed to create a safe environment for an oppressed group, everyone on campus, or at least the majority, have to buy into not only the idea but actively support it in its implementation and beyond. All too often, students with hidden disabilities have been tangled up in situations where though people have verbally expressed their support towards students with disabilities, they then do not follow through in their practices. Accordingly, a professor indicating support for students with disabilities and actually supporting them are two very different things. One clear way to show students with disabilities that a campus is a safe place is through members of the administration, faculty, and staff demonstrating their understanding and support of students with hidden disabilities.

Conclusion

As evidence has widely demonstrated, students who disclose their hidden disability perform better in college. Despite this evidence, however, it continues to be difficult for students with hidden disabilities to disclose, as they worry about the risk involved and have experienced many negative consequences upon and after disclosure. As a result, many students delay disclosing their disabilities until they are in the position where they are forced to disclose in order to obtain the support they need. Even then, many students who reveal their disabilities for the purpose of receiving assistaaccomodations face numerous impediments toward their success due to others' misperceptions of their abilities. By creating a campus community that fully understands and supports students with hidden disabilities, students with hidden disabilities will feel safe and will be safe to disclose their disability early on in their academic career, and will in turn receive the support they need throughout their time in academia, allowing them to achieve to their fullest potential.

References

Barga, N. C. (1996). Students with learning disabilities in education: Managing a disability. *Journal of Learning Disabilities, 29,* 413-421.

Career Center–Cal Transitions. (n.d.). *Talking about disability: Disclosure.* Retrieved November 2, 2006, from http://career.berkeley.edu/Disab/Talk.stm

Career Services at the University of Delaware. (n.d.). *To tell or not to tell: Disclosure ... That is the question.* Retrieved November 2, 2006, from http://www.udel.edu/CSC/disclosure.html.

Career Services at Rutgers. (n.d.). *Disclosure of a disability.* Retrieved November 2, 2006, from http://careerservices.rutgers.edu/disDIS.html

Cooper, M.(1995). Epilepsy and employment: Employers' attitudes. *Seizure, 4*(3), 193-199.

Dalgin, R. S. (2005). *Disability disclosure in an employment interview: Impact on employers' hiring decisions and views of employment.* Unpublished doctoral dissertation, Syracuse University.

Disability Services, University of Wisconsin-Stout. (n.d.). *Time to disclose.* Retrieved November 2, 2006, from http://www.uwstout.edu/disability

Frieche, M., & Aune, B. (1996). Career services needs of college students with disabilities. *Career Development Quarterly, 44,* 289-300.

Glover-Graf, N., Janikowski, T. P., & Hadley, M. (2003). Rehabilitation counseling student disclosure of disability and use of educational accommodations. *Rehabilitative Education, 17,* 224-236.

Hill, J. L. (1996). Speaking out: Perceptions of students with disabilities regarding adequacy of services and willingness of faculty to make accommodations. *Journal on Postsecondary Education and Disability, 12*(1), 22-43

Huvelle, N. F., Budoff, M., & Arnholz, D. (1984). To tell or not to tell: Disability disclosure and the job interview. *Journal of Visual Impairment and Blindness, 78,* 214-244.

Kennemer, C. (1997). Blue space blues: Parking with a hidden disability. *Inside MS, 15*(1), 15.

KOKUA Program-University of Hawaii-Manoa. (n.d.). *Faculty.* Retrieved November 2, 2006, From http://www.hawaii.edu/kokua/faculty.html

Kravets, M. (1996). Hidden disabilities: Another diverse population. *Journal of College Admissions, 152-153,* 24-31.

Leahly, J. T. (1994). Don't ask, don't tell. *Business Week, 11*(6), 38.

Learning Plus, University of Hartford. (n.d.). *Information for current L+ students and faculty.* Retrieved November 2, 2006, from http://uhaWeb.hartford.edu/LDSupport/current-students.htm

Lynch, R. T., & Gussel, L. (1996). Disclosing and self-advocacy regarding disability-related needs: Strategies to maximize integration in postsecondary education. *Journal of Counseling and Development, 74,* 352-357.

National Center for Learning Disabilities. (n.d.). *How to disclose.* Retrieved November 2, 2006, from http://www.ncld.org/content/view/356/427/

National Collaborative on Workforce and Disability for Youth. (2005). *The 411 on disability disclosure.* Washington, DC: Institute for Educational Leadership.

Office of Disability Services, Appalachian State University. (n.d.). *Welcome.* Retrieved November 2, 2006, from http://www.gstudies.appstate.edu/dss/

Pearson, V., Ip, F., Hui, H., Yip, N., Ho, K. K., & Lo, E. (2003). To tell or not to tell: Disability disclosure and job application outcomes. *Journal of Rehabilitation, 69*(4), 35-38.

Roberts, L. L. & Macan, T. H. (2006). Disability disclosure effects on employment interview ratings of applicants with nonvisabile disabilities. *Rehabilitative Psychology, 51,* 239-246.

Rocco, T. S. (2001). *"My disability is a part of me": Disclosure and students with visible disabilities.* Paper presented at The Annual Meeting of Adult Education Research Conference, East Lansing, MI. (ERIC Documentation Reproductive Service No. ED 480965)

Rosenthal, R., & Jacobson, L. (1968). *Pygmalion in the classroom.* New York: Holt, Rinehart and Winston.

Scott, S. (1996). Using collaboration to enhance services for college students with learning disabilities. *Journal on Postsecondary Education and Disability, 12*(1), 10-21.

SFSU DPRC–The Students' Source. (n.d.). *Disclosure of a non-apparent disability.* Retrieved November 2, 2006, from http://www.sfsu.edu/~dprc/stusource/winter2k3/disclosure.html.

Shapiro, J. (2007). *Label falls short for those with mental retardation.* Retrieved March 21, 2007, from http://www.npr.org/templates/story/story.php?storyId=6943699

Strandberg, D. (2007). *Workshops teach awareness.* Retrieved March 22, 2007, from www.tricitynews.com

Training and Technical Assistance Providers. (2005). *Q & A on customized employment: Disclosure.* Boston:Virginia Commonwealth University and the Institute for Community Inclusion, University of Massachusetts.

Tregoning, M. E. (in press). Being an ally in language use. In J. L. Higbee & A. A. Mitchell (Eds.), *Making good on the promise: Student affairs professionals with disabilities.* Washington, DC: ACPA-College Student Educators International and University Press of America.

University of Vermont. (n.d.). *Admissions: Disclosure of a disability.* Retrieved November 2, 2006, from http://www.uvm.edu/access/?Page=disclosure.html&SM=submenu6.html

Weiner, E., & Weiner, J. (1996). Concerns and needs of university students with psychiatric disabilities. *Journal on Postsecondary Education and Disability, 12*(1), 2-9.

Witt, M. (1992). *Job strategies for people with disabilities.* Princeton, NJ: Peterson's Guides.

Your Florida-Department of Education. (n.d.). *Develop your disability disclosure policy.* Retrieved November 2, 2006, from http://www.myflorida.com/dbs/job_seeker/disclosure.shtml

CHAPTER 31

Empowering Students With Severe Disabilities: A Case Study

Jay T. Hatch, David L. Ghere, and Katrina N. Jirik
University of Minnesota

Abstract
This chapter is reprinted verbatim from Curriculum Transformation and Disability: Implementing Universal Design in Higher Education, *and was originally published in 2003. This chapter provides a case study of the empowerment of a student with multiple and severe disabilities. We outline accommodations provided in three college courses, describe classroom events that contributed to the student's success, and provide the student's own insights into her situation. We conclude that instructors must be thoughtful about what constitutes the essential elements of their courses and creative about how students can acquire and demonstrate knowledge in order to remove the instructional barriers that prevent students with disabilities from being successful in college coursework. Removing these barriers empowers students with disabilities to achieve their academic potential by building self-confidence and developing a realization that the responsibility for success is shared by the students, the instructors, and the institution.*

Empowering Students With Severe Disabilities: A Case Study

Data suggest seriously disproportionate barriers both to access and to success in higher education for persons with disabilities (U.S. Census Bureau, 2001). That the disproportionate success results in large part from inadequately designed curricula and skeptical or hostile attitudes of faculty is no longer a matter of conjecture (Foster, Long, & Snell, 1999; Kalivoda & Higbee, 1998; Seymour & Hunter, 1998; Hill, 1996; West, Kregel, Getzel, & Zhu, 1993). In this chapter we present a case study of Kate, a student who, because of her severe and multiple disabilities, easily could have been pushed to the edge of the classroom and the entire college experience. We show instead how Kate became fully integrated into three courses (one in world history taught by David Ghere and two in biological science taught by Jay Hatch), won the respect of her teachers and peers, and gained a strong sense of self-confidence and empowerment that resulted in her becoming an outstanding student. We also describe how she helped us to recognize the elements of Universal Instructional Design (UID) that are crucial to the academic advancement of students with severe disabilities (Higbee, 2001; Bowe, 2000; Silver, Bourke, & Strehorn, 1998). Some of these elements already existed in our courses, while others had to be invented to accommodate Kate and are now available to every student.

We begin by describing Kate's array of disabilities, followed by separate case accounts of the world history course and the biological science courses. In these case accounts, we describe what accommodations each of us made, how these accommodations and other course practices facilitated Kate's integration into each course, and how Kate responded to the integration. We conclude with a brief analysis of what we believe to be crucial elements of curricular modification that will empower students with severe disabilities to successfully achieve their academic potential.

This case study is unusual in that its subject, Kate, is also one of its authors. We strongly believe that the advancements made here and the knowledge gained resulted from intellectual contributions involving all three of us. Kate's participation as an author also brought a level of accuracy and authenticity to the writing that would not have existed otherwise. Finally, Kate thought it important to be identified both as subject and as author; hence, we do not employ a subject pseudonym.

Kate's Challenge

Kate was a challenge, a delightful challenge. In our combined 35 years of teaching, we have never encountered a more daunting prospect or a more successful conclusion. Both of us have had personal experiences with friends or acquaintances who have disabilities, and these experiences preconditioned us to view the potential of students with disabilities very positively. We each have had a number of successful experiences accommodating such students in our classes. Yet, confronted with the array of Kate's disabilities, each of us wondered if we could have any positive impact on her learning.

Kate has severe and multiple disabilities that affected motor control, sensory perception, communication, and learning. She is unable to walk or have complete control over her head and arm movements. Her motor disabilities cause her speech to be virtually unrecognizable. She speaks by typing words into an augmentative communication device with a synthetic voice output. Weak muscles make it necessary for an assistant to support her arm while she swings it slowly but deliberately to strike the keys. Typing is a very slow and arduous task; thus, real-time conversation is a very slow and sometimes frustrating process. Kate also is legally blind. She has limited short-range vision but a form of dyslexia affects even that capability by sometimes rearranging and distorting those things that she can see. The combination of untrustworthy vision and weak muscles means that Kate cannot control the movement of her wheelchair physically or electronically and has to rely on an assistant to move anywhere. Poor muscle control also results in uncontrollable drooling and a variety of guttural noises made during attempts to swallow excessive saliva. Often these noises exacerbate communication problems and initiate a level of irritability in classmates, some of whom interpret the noises as discourteous, juvenile giggling.

Finally, Kate has a "central processing difficulty" that interferes with word finding and retrieval, which makes it appear that she has memory problems and causes her to go about problem solving in an unusual way. Kate explains it this way.

> I'm beginning to realize that I think differently than a lot of people. I think in associative Webs. I do not memorize well. I have to have lots of information and a thorough understanding of the concept or theory in order to remember it. I need to know much more than other students just so I can remember the required informa-

> tion. The typical teaching method of simplifying things is a disaster for me. When I don't understand something, I need more information not less.

Despite our doubts concerning our abilities to adequately address Kate's needs, we both were determined to make our courses positive educational experiences for Kate. We each met with Kate to discuss what specific accommodations would be effective and set out to determine how we could implement those accommodations in our courses. We hoped Kate would learn from her experiences in our courses; we had little notion of how profound the experience would be for all three of us.

The World History Course

Kate enrolled in a ten-week freshman world history class covering the period from 1750 to the present. One simple accommodation was to have exams administered by the staff at the University's Office of Disability Services so that Kate could use their magnification equipment and have questions read out loud if necessary. I also provided Kate with copies of class notes and map transparencies so that she could review them prior to class and thus, be better prepared to understand class presentations and be more involved in class discussions. The world history class included four classroom simulations, active learning exercises that require students to assess the options available to historical figures, reach some decisions, and then explain or critique those decisions. I provided Kate with simulation materials in advance so that she could prepare and save voice messages on her communication device for possible use during the simulation. These materials are now posted on a course Website for the benefit of all students in the course.

Kate's presence prompted me to make greater use of techniques and methods that I already attempted to practice in the classroom. I routinely contrast opposing views or evidence by writing them on opposite ends of the blackboard, and I vary my tone of voice and speech patterns to emphasize different points. Also, I try to verbally provide detailed explanations of the important aspects of material being presented visually. The physical movement, the voice changes, and the detailed explanations helped all students to follow the logic of class lecture and discussion, but it was particularly beneficial for Kate due to her limited vision. Also, my questions in class are followed by long pauses before I select the person to answer the question. This allows all students to consider the question, facilitates involving more students in the discussion, and provides broader indications of student comprehension of the material. In this instance, it also provided Kate with the time necessary for her to answer questions.

Long before ever learning of the concept of UID, my teaching goals included promoting the widest and deepest acquisition of course material and providing students with the greatest opportunity to demonstrate their knowledge and understanding. Detailed review sheets were provided and essay topics were announced a week before each exam. This had the dual benefit of enabling students to focus their thoughts and energies while increasing the quality of work that could be expected by the instructor. In addition, when demonstrating their mastery of course content through written essays, students were given generous amounts of time, thus promoting and rewarding thoughtful analysis rather than writing speed. These practices enhance student learning while enabling instructors to evaluate each student's effort, knowledge, and understanding with more precision. While they were implemented to benefit all the students, these practices contributed to Kate's success in the course and limited the need for special accommodations.

A significant breakthrough was achieved during the first classroom simulation that occurred at the end of the second week of classes. In this simulation, Congress of Vienna, students were divided into groups of three and provided with outline maps of central Europe depicting the boundaries of France, Prussia, Austria, and Russia as well as smaller countries and principalities in central Europe. Each group had to decide how to reward the victorious countries with territory, reestablish the balance of power between the major powers, and reinstall autocratic governments following the Napoleonic Wars. The two students grouped with Kate were friendly, but seemed uncomfortable and uncertain about how to include Kate in the simulation. As they were discussing a possible territorial decision, Kate selected a prerecorded message and the mechanical voice from her communication device said, "Austria would not like that." Her two startled partners waited for Kate to type a further comment and were rewarded with a clear explanation of the dilemma posed by the simulation. Kate quickly emerged as the leader of the discussion group for the rest of the class period.

The simulations allowed Kate to demonstrate her capabilities in ways that would never have happened in a typical lecture-style classroom. Kate's high scores on exams and papers would have been largely unknown to her classmates, and her severe physical disabilities would have greatly limited her involvement in most classes. Yet, in the context of the simulation, the "tinny' voice of Kate's communication device caught students' attention throughout the classroom. They were aware of her active involvement in her group and her contributions were evident in the class discussion that followed the simulation. Kate was paired with a different set of students in each of the three subsequent simulations. Having observed Kate in that first simulation, these new partners immediately involved her in the discussions and waited eagerly for her contributions. In each case, Kate participated fully in the activities and her active involvement could be heard by others in the classroom. By the end of the quarter, everyone knew that the student with the most "medical" disabilities was also the most intellectually capable student in the class.

Kate is a unique student, possessing a truly gifted intellect and a determination to succeed. However, her success in the world history course was also dependent upon a body of class procedures, course assignments, and teaching methods that enabled her to demonstrate her ability. Throughout most of her previous educational experience, she had not had the opportunity to display her capabilities. Many teachers, staff, and administrators had assumed an intellectual deficit based upon Kate's physical disabilities and her inability to participate in typical class interaction. When Kate had done well on standard tests and papers, many had assumed that others must have written the papers and answered the test questions for Kate. In this world history class, Kate's acquisition of knowledge was promoted, her active involvement was fostered, and her mastery of the content was accurately evaluated. Kate achieved success because the instructional design barriers were removed that had previously prevented her from demonstrating her ability. All students regardless of their intellectual or physical abilities should be allowed to demonstrate that ability without having to overcome needless barriers created by instructional design.

The Biological Science Courses

Kate enrolled in two biological science courses one year apart. The first was a small-enrollment (i.e., 35 students) environmental science course and the second was a larger enrollment (i.e., 100 students) general principles course that included a laboratory component. For the environmental science course I made several of the same accommodations that Dave did in the world history course. All students received a detailed study guide at the beginning of the course. This guide included all of the exercises and study questions that were worked on and discussed in class, as well as examples of tests from previous quarters. I made the additional lecture information (tables, graphs and other illustrations) available to Kate at least one week in advance. This way Kate could formulate responses and her own questions ahead of time, program them into her computer, and participate in class much as other students did. I had already made in-class tests only 20% of the grade, with a variety of formal and informal writing assignments and a group project making up the remaining 80%. As an accommodation to Kate, I gave all students the option of taking in-class tests similar to those in the study guide (i.e., a mix of short-essay and objective questions) or completing overnight take-home essay exams. Both exam types tested exactly the same learning objectives. These were the accommodations that Kate said ahead of time were the most important. She needed to know in detail from the start what was expected of her so that she could set up her support system and lay out a work schedule that would allow her to stay up to date in the course. She needed to know that there was at least the possibility that she could meet each course requirement, one of which was class participation. In retrospect, this seems only fair and reasonable for any student.

There was one course requirement that Kate thought she might have trouble meeting: the group project. Because of her real-time communication difficulties, Kate was not accustomed to working in a group, especially during class time. To help facilitate the initial group work, I assigned Kate to a group with an older, experienced student who had done a great deal of group work inside and outside of academia. I also suggested to the group members that, as they discussed project issues, they might periodically pose "yes" or "no" questions to allow Kate to participate in a timely way. As the group work proceeded, fellow students realized that Kate possessed considerable intellect and that she brought an unusually focused clarity to what she wrote. Both my concerns and Kate's about her ability to successfully complete the project work faded quickly. Still, there was the vexing problem of the final class presentation of the project's outcome. No one, including me, expected Kate to present before the class. It was not a requirement for anyone. The requirement was that each member of the group had to contribute to the project in a meaningful way that was acceptable to everyone in the group. Nevertheless, when the day for presentations arrived, Kate was at the front of the room with the rest of her group. They presented a Jeopardy quiz show on the Siberian tiger. While other members of the group read the answers, Kate used the variety of voices available on her voice synthesizer, like Bubbly Betty and Freaky Frederick, to supply the question, "What is the Siberian tiger?" The entire presentation was superb and it received the only standing ovation in memory.

Not quite one year later, Kate asked me if I would help her with a course requirement issue. The University of Minnesota requires all students to complete a foundation course in biological science that has a significant laboratory component. Kate was eager to take the general principles course, but she thought the laboratory component might be inappropriate for her. After all, she reasoned, the purpose of a lab is to get students to manipulate things with their hands and make direct observations, and "I cannot do that." My immediate reaction was, "Not so, you've already proven that you can do science as well as anyone, better than most." However, as I thought about exactly what we required our students to do in the laboratory, I began to think that Kate might be right. In the past we had had students with sight impairments, students with hearing impairments, students with motor impairments, and students with a variety of learning disabilities truly engaged in our laboratory exercises. But we had never attempted to engage someone with Kate's array of impairments.

I thought the question of Kate's involvement was complicated enough that I arranged for a meeting with Kate, her mother, her personal assistant, her counselor at the University's Office of Disabilities Services, a representative from the state's Services for the Blind and Visually Impaired, and our college's laboratory coordinator. After brief introductions, the meeting began with a prepared statement from Kate delivered via her voice synthesizer. Kate had made it clear that she did not expect to "slide by" in any course; on the contrary, she wanted to have the same chance as any other student to learn about biology. Her concern, based on previous experiences in science labs, was that:

> I would be expected to do everything everyone else did in the same way they did it and it would not work. In the past, I always felt like I failed rather than the system failed. I need to have clear learning objectives and clear expectations of what I have to do, and those expectations should not change later on. Jay's environmental science class was one of the first times in science when I got to participate with what I could [emphasis added] do. Having had that class with Jay, I know we can work out the lecture part, but I am still worried about lab because I don't see well and I don't move well; and if the lab is based on those skills, I'm in trouble because I can't do them.

By the end of her statement, I realized how far askew my thinking had been. The real purpose of an introductory level laboratory experience is not to have students manipulate things with their hands or even to have them make direct observations. Its real purpose is to impart to each student a strong sense of how the process of science works; a student gains insight into how scientists discover knowledge. All at the meeting agreed that Kate could achieve such an insight and that she should participate fully in the laboratory exercises. The laboratory coordinator and I would work with Kate to determine exactly how she would engage in the process.

That day I gave Kate a copy of the laboratory manual and asked her erstwhile reader, her mother, to go through it with her and write out a list of accommodations that Kate thought would be necessary for each lab. The overall accommodations included (a) time outside of lab to write out answers to questions on the worksheets (we now offer this option to all students), (b) someone to do the physical manipulations of the experiments and someone to record data (the lab is collaborative and students work in pairs anyway), (c) large versions of some of the visual materials (most of the materials were available electronically and could be enlarged; all materials are now), (d) availability of some of the computer software we use in the lab for home use (we obtained permission to do so), and (e) a quiz format other than multiple choice (we worked out a way for Kate to do multiple choice by allowing her to answer a question with a short essay if she could not retrieve the information in the multiple choice format).

Kate also told us how she could participate in virtually every lab. Her strength was in understanding concepts, making connections, and making predictions. She could come to lab prepared to make contributions based on her knowledge. For example, in the mitosis (cell division) lab, she suggested she could come to lab prepared to explain to others how to obtain a representative sample of dividing cells and why it was important to have a representative (i.e., random) sample. As I read through the five pages of how she would participate, I realized that Kate was already deeply engaged in the lab experience. She was well on her way to meeting the central learning outcome of a laboratory experience: having insight into the process of doing science.

I was confident that Kate could be an integral part of the lab and that her experiences there would be true learning experiences. I also concluded that, even though Kate would be working with a lab partner, she would need a personal laboratory assistant. This assistant would verbalize to Kate exactly what her lab partner was doing and would record measurements and observations into the computer when it was Kate's turn to do so. Kate made it clear that she also needed to have agreed-upon alternatives for demonstrating accomplishment of certain objectives in the event that she could not meet them in the same way as other students. The laboratory coordinator and I wrote out these alternatives and provided them for Kate one to two weeks in advance of each lab exercise. For example, instead of viewing a life stage and identifying it in the life cycles lab, the task became "be able to ask the 'appropriate question' about a life cycle that would permit a sighted person to discover what stage was being viewed." Sometimes Kate used these alternatives, sometimes not, but having them available put her at ease in the laboratory so that she could concentrate on doing what she knew she could do. Lastly, I provided additional background information about various concepts being learned or applied in the laboratory. This last accommodation helped meet Kate's associative learning needs.

Of course, not everything went smoothly in the laboratory. It took time for Kate's personal laboratory assistant to work out a reasonable system for communication and to get over "trying to help too much." The time taken for communication tended to put Kate out of synchrony with the other students, thus segregating her from the rest of the class. Ultimately, we discovered it was best to keep up with the other students and let the communication lag. Kate was processing far more than she could let us know while lab was in session. The proof came in her written responses on the take-home worksheets and in her oral (voice-synthesized) presentation about life cycles.

Kate's analysis of her laboratory experience was very informative and encouraging. She acknowledged having learned a variety of things about biology and about how science works, but more importantly she learned a great deal about herself. She wrote:

> Most of what I learned was that it [my lab work] was a partnership with everybody working toward the same goal, my successful completion of the lab. I learned that if we tried something and it didn't work, that everybody, not just me, was responsible and it was a system failure not a personal failure. I learned I could use my strengths and do the same activities but in a somewhat different manner, like in identifying the life cycles. And if I have the data, I'm good at analyzing it. I also learned some things about socializing with other people. I even learned to feel safe enough to share my sense of humor.
>
> Here are some things I think are important. I never tried to use my disabilities to get out of hard work. I expected to work hard. I expected to try things that would stretch my capabilities. As long as I was trying, I didn't expect to be blamed when things didn't work. That gave me a lot of freedom to try new things that I didn't know beforehand if they would work out. Sharing responsibility for a failure was very new to me and a very remarkable concept. I didn't expect everything to be perfect and it wasn't, but it wasn't solely my responsibility to make things work.

Constructing a learning environment with shared responsibilities for success was the most important accommodation we made, and it was not until I read Kate's evaluation of her experience that I even realized we had made it.

The Take-Home Messages

We do not know how many students with multiple severe disabilities have had the kinds of discouraging and disenfranchising experiences that Kate did in her high school and early college tenure, but we suspect it is a high percentage. Such experiences erect their own barriers to seeking further education. For the few who press onward (32.6%), very few find the will and the opportunity to complete a college degree (9.4%) (U.S. Census Bureau, 2001). Our case study of Kate shows that such an outcome need not prevail. True, Kate is highly intelligent and a very hard worker, but even in sum these attributes were insufficient to overcome the barriers erected by curricula that were designed by and for those with few or no medically recognized disabilities. Thus, it is reasonable and prudent to conclude that college curricula must be modified in ways that will be inclusive of and invitational to students with severe disabilities. We also conclude that the modifications must go beyond simple accommodations, like alternative testing modes or conditions, multiple modes of access to course materials, adequate time for all to complete assignments, and so on.

As we have since discovered, the principles of Universal Instructional Design can guide us in making the kinds of modifications that will be truly inclusive of students with severe disabilities (Bowe, 2000). As Higbee (2001) points out, the first step in developing a universally accessible curriculum is to determine its "essential elements." We need to ask ourselves:

1. What is it that our students must be able to do by the conclusion of this course and what is it that they *must* know?

2. Why must they be able to do it or know it? Here we have to be very critical of our answer.

3. In what ways can a student demonstrate that she or he knows the information or can do the task? Here is where we have to rely on our creativity and the creativity of others. For most learning objectives, there is more than one valid means of demonstrating what one knows or can do. Often, as illustrated by Kate, the student can be the best resource for determining these alternative ways.

This is exactly what we did in part as we attempted to discover what Kate should be expected to do in our courses. For example, the study of history generally includes memorization of many dates, important personages, and events. But what is the real importance of knowing these things? What is the essential element here? The history teacher hopes that the student ultimately will be able to understand how and why events unfolded the way they did. In the world history course, students moved on to this level when they worked through the simulations. They demonstrated what they knew factually and, at the same time, learned to refine their ability to critically analyze history. In Kate's case, the opportunity to demonstrate her knowledge and analytical abilities in this way was crucial. It not only provided the instructor with an additional way of evaluating her achievement, it provided a means by which Kate became an integral part of the class. The same thing happened with the group project in the environmental science course and with the collaborative laboratory experience in the general biology principles course.

Kate had the opportunity to capitalize on her strengths and so was not faced with having to do things that she could not do (an important tactic, see Preston-Sabin, 1997). This approach allowed her to take part in all of the essential elements of the courses. Thus, Kate felt fully included and fulfilled intellectually because she accomplished the same learning outcomes that other students did (and in Kate's case better than most). It was very important to Kate, and it is very important to the integrity of college curricula, that the level of academic rigor in a course not be compromised in an effort to accommodate a student with disabilities. If we are thoughtful about what constitutes the essential elements of our courses and creative about how students can acquire and demonstrate knowledge, there need be no sacrifice of rigor in designing universally accessible courses.

Thoughtfully following the principles of Universal Instructional Design also places teachers in the position of already having "accommodated" virtually any student who enrolls in their courses. The stress and the inconvenience of last-minute accommodations, which burdens both teachers and students, are eliminated. Because Universal Instructional

Design principles incorporate well-established principles for good teaching, UID courses become better courses all around. Our courses are much improved, and we have discovered that virtually all students appreciate having alternative ways to acquire and demonstrate knowledge.

Another very important discovery of this case was the sense of empowerment that accrued to Kate as she engaged in these courses. In all three courses, Kate's self-confidence in her ability to achieve her potential rose markedly. As she became an integral part of group achievement, she learned that she could participate in and significantly contribute to group work, something she previously had believed she could not do. In the biology lab in particular, she learned that the onus for success was not hers alone but was shared by her and those who designed and delivered the curriculum. This realization, coupled with the availability of alternative ways of demonstrating her knowledge, gave her the confidence to explore new ways of learning. As her self-confidence and array of learning tools increased, she finally felt empowered to design her own unique and very challenging major: "public policy and the ethics of inclusion of minorities." Kate currently is completing her senior year with a cumulative grade point average of 3.9. She plans to attend graduate school in the areas of history of science and public policy. Kate's future is hers to determine and that is as it should be.

References

Bowe, F. G. (2000). *Universal design in education: Teaching nontraditional students.* Westport, CT: Bergin & Garvey.

Foster, S., Long, G., & Snell, K. (1999). Inclusive instruction and learning for deaf students in postsecondary education. *Journal of Deaf Studies and Deaf Education, 4,* 225-235.

Higbee, J. L. (2001). Implications of Universal Instructional Design for developmental education. *Research and Teaching in Developmental Education, 17,* 67-70.

Hill, J. L. (1996). Speaking out: Perceptions of students with disabilities regarding the adequacy of services and willingness of faculty to make accommodations. *Journal of Postsecondary Education and Disability, 12,* 22-43.

Kalivoda, K. S., & Higbee, J. L. (1998). Influencing faculty attitudes toward accommodating students with disabilities: A theoretical approach. *The Learning Assistance Review, 3*(2), 12-25.

Preston-Sabin, J. (1997). Angela: Capitalizing on individual strengths. In B. M. Hodge & J. Preston-Sabin (Eds.), *Accommodations—Or just good teaching?* (pp. 82-83). Westport, CT: Praeger.

Seymour, E., & Hunter, A. (1998). *Talking about disability: The education and work experiences of graduates and undergraduates with disabilities in science, mathematics, and engineering majors.* Boulder, CO: The University of Colorado.

Silver, P., Bourke, A., & Strehorn, K. C. (1998). Universal Instructional Design in higher education: An approach for inclusion. *Equity and Excellence in Education, 31*(2), 47-51.

West, M., Kregel, J., Getzel, E., & Zhu, M. (1993). Beyond section 504: Satisfaction and experiences of students with disabilities in higher education. *Exceptional Children, 59*(5), 456-467.

U.S. Census Bureau. (2001, March). Americans with disabilities: 1997. Retrieved October 8, 2001, from U.S. Census Bureau Access: http://www.census.gov/hhes/www/disable/sipp/disab97/ds97t3.html

CHAPTER 32

Disability and Diversity: Results From the Multicultural Awareness Project for Institutional Transformation

Jeanne L. Higbee, Patrick L. Bruch, and Kwabena Siaka
University of Minnesota

Abstract

Disability is not always included in conversations about students' diverse social identities. This chapter reports on the results of a study conducted in the General College at the University of Minnesota, which did include disability in the "diversity mix." Implications for enhancing the academic experience for all students, including students with disabilities, are discussed.

Disability is not always included in conversations about diversity in higher education (McCune, 2001), which tend to focus more on racial and ethnic aspects of students' social identities. Yet more students with disabilities are attending college than in the past. In 1988 7% of full-time college freshmen self-reported having a disability (Henderson, 1988); by 1999 this figure had increased to 9.4% (Henderson, 1999). By 2003-2004, National Center for Education Statistics data indicated that 11.3% of all undergraduates reported having

> a "long-lasting" condition such as blindness, deafness, or a severe vision or hearing impairment, a condition that limits "one or more basic physical activities such as walking, climbing stairs, reaching, lifting, or carrying"; or who responded they had any other physical, mental, or emotional condition that lasted 6 or more months and who had difficulty doing one of the following activities: getting to school, getting around campus, learning, dressing, or working at a job. (Horn, Nevill, & Griffin, 2006, Table 6.1).

Of undergraduates in the U.S. reporting one or more disability, 25.4% had orthopedic disabilities, 21.9% had a mental illness or depression, 17.3% had health impairments, 11.0% had Attention Deficit Disorder, 7.5% had a specific learning disability, 5.0% had hearing impairments, 3.8% had visual disabilities, 0.4% had speech impairments, and 7.8% indicated "other" (Horn et al.). Thus, students attending college today have a wide range of disabilities, ranging in type from physical disabilities to cognitive and psychological disabilities that may not be apparent to the observer. Some postsecondary faculty and staff do not believe that academic accommodations are "fair" and others may even question the existence of disabilities that are "invisible" such as learning disabilities (Hill, 1996; Kalivoda, 2003; Kalivoda & Higbee, 1998; Williams & Ceci, 1999). For students with "hidden" disabilities like Attention Deficit Hyperactivity Disorder (ADHD) and psychiatric disabilities, as well as learning disabilities, negative responses from faculty and staff may lead to "faking it" (Lee & Jackson, 1992) or attempting to appear outwardly to be "just like anyone else" without the need for accommodations rather than disclosing the disability (*Uncertain welcome,* 2002). What may result then is students with both hidden and apparent disabilities being left out, not just in social situations, but in the classroom as well, unless faculty create environments where all students feel welcome and have an equal opportunity to learn (Hatch, Ghere, & Jirik, 2003; Hodge & Preston-Sabin, 1997; Lee & Jackson; Linton, 1998; Shapiro, 1994). Even faculty with positive attitudes toward both students with disabilities and providing appropriate academic accommodations can end up excluding students simply by doing what is asked of them, such as providing an alternative test format with extended time to be administered in a separate location (Higbee, Chung, & Hsu, 2004). In other words, even faculty with good intentions who are strongly committed to equity can unintentionally contribute to segregating students. Thus, faculty who are trying to abide by the letter of the law by providing reasonable academic accommodations can actually become part of the segregation problem. That is one of many reasons why it is imperative that disability be included in the "diversity mix."

Defining Diversity and Multiculturalism

Definitions of "diversity" as used when referring to students in higher education can vary significantly. For purposes of this chapter, diversity will be used to refer to the existence of students' myriad social identities, whether characterized by race, ethnicity, culture, religion, spirituality, age, gender, sexual orientation, disability, social class, language, citizenship, or any other aspect of identity or combination thereof. Today postsecondary educational institutions in the U.S. are serving more diverse student populations than ever before (Horn, Nevill, & Griffin, 2006; Horn, Peter, & Rooney, 2002).

Frequently the terms "diverse" and "multicultural" are used synonymously in higher education. For purposes of this chapter, "multiculturalism" will refer to a proactive response to diverse social identities: "If diversity is an empirical condition—the existence of multiple group identities in a society—multiculturalism names a particular posture towards this reality" (Miksch, Bruch, Higbee, Jehangir, & Lundell, 2003, p. 6). Thus, while diversity is a fact, multiculturalism portrays a set of attitudes and behaviors.

Theoretical Framework

The Multicultural Awareness Project for Institutional Transformation (MAP IT; Miksch, Higbee, et al., 2003) is based on the theoretical work of James Banks (1981, 1994, 1997), who introduced five dimensions of multicultural education: content integration, knowledge construction, prejudice reduction, equity pedagogy, and creation of empowering school cultures. Although Banks' work has been in the area of elementary through secondary (K-12) education, his theoretical approach is equally applicable to higher education (Bruch, Higbee, & Lundell, 2003, 2004). Banks and his colleagues (2001) published Diversity Within Unity: *Essential Principles for Teaching and Learning in a Multicultural*

Society to assess and guide K-12 multicultural education. With Banks' permission, MAP IT adapted Diversity Within Unity for higher education and created the following set of "10 Guiding Principles for Institutions of Higher Education" (Higbee, Bruch, Jehangir, Lundell, & Miksch, 2003; Miksch, Higbee, et al., 2003) to create institutional structures that support multiculturalism and social justice in higher education, as follow:

> ***Institutional Governance, Organization, and Equity***
>
> 1. The educational institution should articulate a commitment to supporting access to higher education for a diverse group of students, thus providing the opportunity for all students to benefit from a multicultural learning environment.
>
> 2. The educational institution's organizational structure should ensure that decision making is shared appropriately and that members of the educational community learn to collaborate in creating a supportive environment for students, staff, and faculty.
>
> ***Faculty and Staff Development***
>
> 3. Professional development programs should be made available to help staff and faculty understand the ways in which social group identifications such as race, ethnicity, home language, religion, gender, sexual orientation, social class, age, and disability influence all individuals and institutions.
>
> ***Student Developmen***
>
> 4. Educational institutions should equally enable all students to learn and excel.
>
> 5. Educational institutions should help students understand how knowledge and personal experiences are shaped by contexts (social, political, economic, historical, etc.) in which we live and work, and how their voices and ways of knowing can shape the academy.
>
> 6. Educational institutions should help students acquire the social skills needed to interact effectively within a multicultural educational community.
>
> 7. Educational institutions should enable all students to participate in extracurricular and co-curricular activities to develop knowledge, skills, and attitudes that enhance academic participation and foster positive relationships within a multicultural educational community.
>
> 8. Educational institutions should provide support services that promote all students' intellectual and interpersonal development.
>
> ***Intergroup Relations***
>
> 9. Educational institutions should teach all members of the educational community about the ways that ideas like justice, equality, freedom, peace, compassion, and charity are valued by many cultures.
>
> ***Assessment***
>
> 10. Educational institutions should encourage educators to use multiple culturally sensitive techniques to assess student learning. (Miksch, Higbee, et al., p. 5)

The items on the MAP IT questionnaires (Miksch, Higbee, et al.), including the Student Questionnaire used for this study, are organized around these 10 guiding principles.

Method

This research project was conducted in the General College (GC) at the University of Minnesota, which at the time of this study provided access to students considered underprepared for admission to this large public research university.

Instrumentation

The questionnaire used for this research was designed to assess how students evaluate multicultural aspects of their collegiate experience (Miksch, Higbee, et al., 2003). When responding to the survey items, students were encouraged to think broadly and inclusively about such terms as "multicultural" and "diverse groups" and to consider diverse social identities from the perspectives of race, religion, gender, ethnicity, culture, home language, social class, sexual orientation, age, and disability. The Likert-type response scale provided options of 1 to 4 for which 1 was defined as "never or almost never," 2 indicated "occasionally," 3 signified "often," and 4 represented "almost always or always." In addition, students could select "not applicable" (NA) if they thought that the item did not apply to them, or "don't know" (DK) if they thought that they had inadequate information to respond. At the end of each set of items, students also had the opportunity to provide comments or clarify their answers. The survey also included four demographic items: (a) gender, (b) native speaker of English, (c) disability, and (d) racial or ethnic identity.

Population

The population for this research was made up of all students enrolled in GC 1422: "Writing Laboratory: Communicating in Society" during spring semester 2004. This course was selected because it was a requirement for all GC students; the majority of students who entered GC as first-year students in fall 2003 were enrolled in GC 1422 during spring 2004. Thus, the population for the study was made up of students who had completed a full semester in GC, but were unlikely to have been in college for more than one year.

Administration

During the first 3 weeks of the semester, the individual GC 1422 course instructors introduced the MAP IT project using a script and providing students with a handout supplied by the researchers and asked students to log on to a Web site and complete the questionnaire either during class time for sections taught in a computer classroom, or outside of class. The Web site provided additional information about MAP IT as well as notification of implied consent, meaning that when the student submitted the completed questionnaire online, he or she was consenting to participation in this research. No incentives were provided to encourage students to respond to the questionnaire. Although seemingly a disadvantage, this practice enabled students to complete the instrument anonymously; to receive an incentive, students would have to have been required to identify themselves.

Data Analyses

Initially, after deleting "not applicable" and "don't know" responses that had been assigned values of 5 or 6, the overall mean, median, mode, and standard deviation were determined for each item. Crosstabs and Chi square analyses were then conducted to determine whether significant differences occurred within and between demographic groups.

Results

Out of the 629 students registered for the course, 406 responded to the survey, for a response rate of 65%. Due to incomplete responses, only 403 of the questionnaires were used in the analysis of the results. Of the students who responded to the demographic items, 6% indicated that they have a disability. Complete results of the study are reported elsewhere (Bruch, Higbee, & Siaka, 2007; Higbee, Siaka, & Bruch, 2007a, 2007b). This chapter will focus on the results pertaining to students with disabilities.

Prior to the administration of the MAP IT Student Questionnaire, GC faculty and staff had received training in the implementation of Universal Design (UD; Bowe, 2000, Center for Universal Design, 1997; Higbee, 2003) and Universal Instructional Design (UID; Higbee, Chung, & Hsu, 2004; Silver, Bourke, & Strehorn, 1998). Thus, we perceived that the administration of the MAP IT Student Questionnaire in GC would provide a yardstick for measuring the extent to which the academic unit was meeting its UD and UID goals. There were far fewer instances of significant differences on the basis of disability than for gender or race and ethnicity, but there were significant differences between students self-identifying as having a disability and those who did not for 29 of the 69 items on the questionnaire. Two of the items for which students with disabilities provided significantly more positive responses than students without disabilities included, "Through your interactions with administrators, faculty, and staff in the General College, do you believe that they understand the ways in which factors (such as race, ethnicity, home language, religion, gender, sexual orientation, social class, age, and disability) influence all individuals and institutions?" ($p < .001$) and "Have you participated in university activities outside of class that promote multicultural understanding?" ($p < .005$).

Some of the items for which students with disabilities provided significantly less favorable responses were "Do your teachers know how to effectively teach students from diverse backgrounds?" ($p < .05$), "Does GC equally enable all students to learn and excel?" ($p < .005$), and "Do you have the same opportunity to achieve your academic goals as any other student here in GC?" ($p < .001$). Students with disabilities were also significantly less likely to be aware of scholarships available for participating in international programs ($p < .05$) or to think that support services were equally accessible to all students ($p < .05$). Students with disabilities were significantly less likely to believe that faculty and staff provide students with information to contradict misconceptions and stereotypes ($p < .05$) or teach students "that 'normal' is defined differently for different groups of people" ($p < .05$). In addition, 45% of the students with disabilities responded "often" or "almost always or always" when asked if they were concerned about their safety on campus, while only 24% of the students who do not have disabilities chose numerical ratings of 3 or 4 for this item ($p < .05$).

It is also important to report some of the items for which no significant differences were found on the basis of disability, including regarding the availability of appropriate role models on campus (for entire sample overall $M = 2.87$, SD = 0.944); the use of teaching strategies that accommodate diverse interests and learning styles (overall $M = 3.19$, $SD = 0.725$); opportunities to participate in extracurricular activities (overall $M = 2.88$, $SD = 0.986$) and to work with other students collaboratively outside of class (overall $M = 2.78$, $SD = 0.923$); and the accurate and respectful portrayal of their "cultural group" in classes (overall $M = 3.12$, $SD = 0.849$).

Implications

We are pleased that students with disabilities believed that faculty and staff in GC were sensitive to students' unique social identities and that they were as likely as students without disabilities to find appropriate role models. It is heartening to know that there were no perceived differences in opportunities for students with disabilities to work collaboratively with other students and to participate in extracurricular activities, and that in fact students with disabilities reported more frequent participation in activities that promote multicultural understanding than students without disabilities. On the other hand, the responses of students with disabilities to the item related to safety on campus provide a legitimate reason for concern. Further research, including qualitative approaches such as interviews and focus groups, should be used to follow up on this finding and determine what can be done to create a safer campus climate. This should be a priority on any campus.

Findings Related to Universal Instructional Design

Given that one of the foci of Universal Instructional Design is to provide students with multiple ways to acquire and demonstrate knowledge, we also believe that the finding of no difference between students with and without disabilities to the item that asked, "Do the teaching strategies used by faculty in GC accommodate diverse student interests and learning styles?" is an important one. However, with an overall mean of 3.19 ($SD = 0.725$), there is still room for further improvement in this area. Similarly, the overall mean in response to the item that asked, "In the courses you have taken, have a variety of types (e.g., multiple choice, essay) of tests and quizzes been offered?" was 3.20 ($SD = 0.817$). Again, there were no significant differences between students with and without disabilities, but this is an area that should receive further attention. If different types of quizzes and tests are not available, we would hope that students also have other means to demonstrate knowledge, such as papers, projects, presentations, journals, and so on. Meanwhile, the mean for students with disabilities in response to the question, "Do you have the same opportunity to achieve your academic goals as any other student here in GC?" was 3.29, while the mean for students without disabilities was 3.67. Thus, although most students with disabilities responded "often" or "almost always or always" to this item, there was still a significant difference between their perceptions of their opportunities for success and those of students without disabilities.

Definitions of Normal and Historical Approaches to Disability

One item on the MAP IT Student Questionnaire might have different meaning for students with disabilities than for other students because of how disability has been portrayed throughout history. The question asked, "Have your courses in GC included learning that 'normal' is defined differently for different groups of people?" Students from some historically marginalized groups, including students who are gay, lesbian, bisexual, or transgender (Connelly, 2000; Lopez & Chism, 1993), are more likely to have been considered "abnormal" than others. Spiritual and medical models of disability assumed that people with disabilities were abnormal as well (Griffin & McClintock, 1997; Marks, 1999). As noted by Evans and Herriott (in press),

> During the medieval period in Europe (i.e., 1200s-1700s), people with mental or physical impairments were thought to be out of favor with God or possessed by the devil. Considered witches, they were often tortured or burned at the stake. In England, the Elizabethan Poor Laws (1598-1601) forced people with disabilities to leave hospitals and shelters for the poor. To survive, they were given a cap in which to collect alms from begging. This form of humiliation is the origin of the term "handicap," which ... is offensive to many people with disabilities because of its connotation.

Griffin and McClintock (1997), Linton (1998), Michalko (2002), Pfeiffer (1993), and others have documented the many ways in which disability has been characterized as not merely different, but deficient or defective. People with disabilities have been ridiculed, ostracized, disenfranchised, institutionalized, prevented from marrying, sterilized, and euthanized because of the belief that they were not "normal." For many years the prevailing approach to disability reflected the medical model (Fine & Asch, 2000; Hughes, 2002). Evans and Herriott (in press) wrote,

> In a higher education setting, adherents of the medical model would most likely question the appropriateness of higher education for individuals who have impairments. Within the medical model, the ultimate goal would be to "cure" individuals and return them to "health." Under this model, a person with a disability would be seen as sick and therefore not appropriate to participate in "normal" activity. This model also places the onus on the individual, albeit with the support of appropriate medical professionals, to adapt, change, and work to meet behavior expectations of the environment. This approach relies heavily upon medical interventions, such as medication, to ameliorate symptoms of, or problems associated with, a disability. For individuals who have a visible or apparent disability, where a medical intervention to "cure" them is not available, there is a clear message that society has no inherent responsibility to create access for persons with disabilities as they occupy an outsider role as they await a cure. This pattern is clearly supported by the larger society whereby individuals deemed to be sick are excused from societal expectations such as work, school, or family; persons with disabilities are sick and therefore have no place in everyday social interaction.

Despite more recent models of disability, including the social construction approach and the social justice perspective (Evans & Herriott, in press; also see Chapters 2 by Evans and 3 by Hackman), terms that apply a deficit model to disability are still used in everyday conversation, and the medical model—with its underlying assumption that to have a disability is synonymous to being "sick"—still provides the foundation for many attitudinal barriers that students with disabilities must face on a daily basis. Thus, by failing to address how the term normal can be used as a mechanism for exclusion, we are failing to teach our students about a pervasive form of institutionalized discrimination against people with diverse social identities, including people with disabilities.

From Awareness to Implementation

In addition to issues specific to definitions of normal, institutionalized discrimination can be a factor related to research results for several of the other questions to which students with disabilities responded less favorably than those without disabilities. As previously reported, as a group, students with disabilities provided significantly less favorable responses to questions focused on equally accessible support services, teachers' demonstrated abilities to "effectively teach students from diverse backgrounds," and feeling that their learning contexts "equally enable all students to learn and excel." At the same time, these students were significantly more favorable than their peers regarding faculty understanding of "the ways in which factors (such as race, ethnicity, home language, religion, gender, sexual orientation, social class, age, and disability) influence all individuals and institutions," and equally positive when compared to other groups of students regarding faculty use of multiple teaching styles. For us, these findings suggest that students recognize faculty *awareness* and *understanding*, but, at the same time, still experience inadequacies in faculty *practices*. To put this insight in terms of a Universal Design image, it is as though students with disabilities are, as a group, saying, "Yes, we see that you understand that the traditional style of doorknob did not work, but the new one you designed does not work very well either."

Recommendations

Based on these findings, we offer the following recommendations:

1. Educators must include disability in their conversations about diversity and multiculturalism in order to challenge attitudes that create barriers for success for students with disabilities and ensure that *all* students have the invitation and opportunity to achieve their goals.

2. Faculty and staff should talk openly with students about social justice issues. These topics are relevant to *any* course or academic discipline. Students cannot learn if we back away from topics that are uncomfortable or spark dissent.

3. Faculty and student services staff members should implement Universal Design (Bowe, 2000; The Center for Universal Design, 1997) and Universal Instructional Design (Silver, Bourke, & Strehorn, 1998) in order to enhance access and create environments that are welcoming physically, academically, and socially for all students. We believe that UID provides a starting point for developing a model for multicultural education (Higbee & Barajas, 2007).

4. Faculty should continue to design and implement assessment tools that measure the learning outcomes of their teaching practices and innovations. As part of this, it is important to provide students the opportunity to report about both (a) their sense of whether faculty are trying to teach effectively given the diversity of their audiences and (b) in

what ways faculty efforts are succeeding or failing.

5. Faculty need to engage in ongoing reflection and development of teaching based on the goal of universal inclusion. Both individual and collective reflection and deliberation are important here. The approach of UID provides one promising framework for such reflection.

6. Faculty should engage in culturally responsive teaching (Gay, 2000; Howard-Hamilton, 2000; Lisi, 1997; also see Chapter 3 by Hackman) to ensure that all students feel included and that they have an equal opportunity to learn. Culturally responsive teaching involves exposing and challenging assumptions and recognizing and valuing the backgrounds, experiences, and ways of knowing of all students in the classroom. It requires using a wide array of pedagogical approaches and instructional tools to promote the learning of all students, and providing multiple forms of assessment to enable students to demonstrate their knowledge in a variety of ways. This inclusive approach to teaching benefits *all* students.

Conclusion

In the General College we considered multiculturalism central to our mission (Higbee, Lundell, & Arendale, 2005). After engaging in previous research to assess our colleagues' commitment to this mission (Bruch & Higbee, 2002; Higbee, Miksch, Jehangir, Lundell. Bruch, & Jiang, 2004), we determined that to get an accurate perspective it was imperative to assess students' perceptions as well. Overall, we found that students' attitudes toward our efforts were favorable. However, we did find some disturbing statistically significant differences based on students' social identities. This chapter has addressed just one dimension of these findings—those related to the experiences of students with disabilities—a group frequently ignored in research of this nature. We hope that this chapter will encourage others to conduct future research that does not look solely at disability, but instead includes disability when considering how students with diverse social identities experience higher education. Only then can we explore similarities as well as differences in the student experience and work to transform higher education institutions to ensure equal access and success for all.

References

Banks, J. A. (1981). *Education in the 80s: Multiethnic education.* Washington, DC: National Education Association.

Banks, J. A. (1994). *Multiethnic education: Theory and practice* (3rd ed.). Boston: Allyn and Bacon.

Banks, J. A. (1997). Transformative knowledge, curriculum reform, and action. In J. A. Banks (Ed.), *Multicultural education, transformative knowledge, and action: Historical and contemporary perspectives* (pp. 335-346). New York: Teachers College Press.

Banks, J. A., Cookson, P., Gay, G., Hawley, W. D., Jordan Irvine, J., Nieto, S., Ward Schofield, J., & Stephan, W. G. (2001). *Diversity within unity: Essential principles for teaching and learning in a multicultural society.* Seattle: University of Washington, School of Education, Center for Multicultural Education. Retrieved March 27, 2007, from http://depts.washington.edu/centerme/home.htm

Bowe, F. G. (2000). *Universal Design in education—Teaching nontraditional students.* Westport, CT: Bergin & Garvey.

Bruch, P. L., & Higbee, J. L. (2002). Reflections on multiculturalism in developmental education. *Journal of College Reading and Learning, 33*(1), 77-90.

Bruch, P. L., Higbee, J. L., & Lundell, D. B. (2003). Multicultural legacies for the 21st century: A conversation with Dr. James A. Banks. In J. L. Higbee, D. B. Lundell, & I. M. Duranczyk (Eds.), *Multiculturalism in developmental education* (pp. 35-42). Minneapolis: University of Minnesota, Center for Research on Developmental Education and Urban Literacy. Retrieved October 11, 2007, from http://www.cehd.umn.edu/crdeul

Bruch, P. L., Higbee, J. L., & Lundell, D. B. (2004). Multicultural education and developmental education: A conversation about principles and connections with Dr. James A. Banks. *Research & Teaching in Developmental Education, 20*(2), 77-90.

Bruch, P. L., Higbee, J. L., & Siaka, K. (2007). Multiculturalism, Incorporated: Student perspectives. *Innovative Higher Education, 32,* 139-152.

The Center for Universal Design. (1997). *The principles of Universal Design* (Version 2.0). Raleigh: North Carolina State University. Retrieved March 27, 2007, from http://www.design.ncsu.edu/cud/about_ud/udprinciples.htm

Connelly, M. (2000). Issues for lesbian, gay, and bisexual students in traditional classrooms. In V. A. Wall & N. J. Evans (Eds.), *Toward acceptance: Sexual orientation issues on campus* (pp. 108-130). Lanham, MD: University Press of America and the American College Personnel Association.

Evans, N. J., & Herriott, T. K. (in press). Philosophical and theoretical approaches to disability. In J. L. Higbee & A. A. Mitchell (Eds.), *Making good on the promise: Student affairs professionals with disabilities.* Washington, DC: ACPA-College Student Educators International and University Press of America.

Fine, M., & Asch, A. (2000). Disability beyond stigma: Social interaction, discrimination, and activism. In M. Adams, W. J. Blumenfeld, R. Castañeda, H. W. Hackman, M. L. Peters, & X. Zúñiga (Eds.), *Readings for diversity and social justice* (pp. 330-339). New York: Routledge.

Gay, G. (2000). *Culturally responsive teaching: Theory, research, and practice.* New York: Teachers College Press.

Griffin, P., & McClintock, M. (1997). History of ableism in Europe and the United States—A selected timeline. In M. Adams, L. A. Bell, & P. Griffin (Eds.), *Teaching for diversity and social justice* (pp. 219-225). New York: Routledge.

Hatch, J. T., Ghere, D. L., & Jirik, K. N. (2003). Empowering students with severe disabilities: A case study. In J. L. Higbee (Ed.), *Curriculum transformation and disability: Implementing Universal Design in higher education* (pp. 171-183). Minneapolis: University of Minnesota, General College, Center for Research on Developmental Education and Urban Literacy. Retrieved October 11, 2007, from http://www.cehd.umn.edu/crdeul

Henderson, C. (1988). *College freshmen with disabilities.* Washington, DC: American Council on Education.

Henderson, C. (1999). *College freshmen with disabilities.* Washington, DC: American Council on Education.

Higbee, J. L. (Ed.). (2003). *Curriculum transformation and disability: Implementing Universal*

Design in higher education. Minneapolis: University of Minnesota, General College, Center for Research on Developmental Education and Urban Literacy. Retrieved October 11, 2007, from http://www.cehd.umn.edu/crdeul

Higbee, J. L., & Barajas, H. L. (2007). Building effective places for multicultural learning. *About Campus, 12*(3), 16-22.

Higbee, J. L., Bruch, P. L., Jehangir, R. R., Lundell, D. B., & Miksch, K. L. (2003). The multicultural mission of developmental education: A starting point. *Research & Teaching in Developmental Education, 19*(2), 47-51.

Higbee, J. L., Chung, C. L., & Hsu, L. (2004). Enhancing the inclusiveness of first-year courses through Universal Design. In I. M. Duranczyk, J. L. Higbee, & D. B. Lundell (Eds.), *Best practices for access and retention in higher education* (pp. 13-26). Minneapolis: University of Minnesota, Center for Research on Developmental Education and Urban Literacy. Retrieved October 11, 2007, from http://www.cehd.umn.edu/crdeul

Higbee, J. L., Lundell, D. B., & Arendale, D. R. (Eds.). (2005). *The General College vision: Integrating intellectual growth, multicultural perspectives, and student development*. Minneapolis: University of Minnesota, General College, Center for Research on Developmental Education and Urban Literacy. Retrieved October 11, 2007, from http://www.cehd.umn.edu/crdeul

Higbee, J. H., Miksch, K. L., Jehangir, R. R., Lundell. D.B., Bruch, P. L., & Jiang, F. (2004). Assessing our commitment to providing a multicultural learning experience. *Journal of College Reading and Learning, 34*(2), 61-74.

Higbee, J. L., Siaka, K., & Bruch, P. L. (2007a). Assessing our commitment to multiculturalism: Student perspectives. *Journal of College Reading and Learning, 37*(2), 7-25..

Higbee, J. L., Siaka, K. , & Bruch, P. L. (2007b). Student perceptions of their multicultural learning environment: A closer look. In J. L. Higbee, D. B. Lundell, & I. M. Duranczyk (Eds.), *Diversity and the postsecondary experience* (pp. 3-23). Minneapolis: University of Minnesota, Center for Research on Developmental Education and Urban Literacy. Retrieved October 11, 2007, from http://www.cehd.umn.edu/crdeul

Hill, J. L. (1996). Speaking out: Perceptions of students with disabilities regarding the adequacy of services and willingness of faculty to make accommodations. *Journal of Postsecondary Education and Disability, 12*(1), 22-43.

Hodge, B. M., & Preston-Sabin, J. (1997). *Accommodations—Or just good teaching? Strategies for teaching college students with disabilities.* Westport, CT: Praeger.

Horn, L., Nevill, S., & Griffin, J. (2006). *Profile of undergraduates in U.S. postsecondary education institutions: 2003-04 with a special analysis of community college students.* Washington, DC: U.S. Department of Education, National Center for Education Statistics, Institute of Education Sciences. Retrieved September 14, 2007, from http://nces.ed.gov/pubs2006/2006184.pdf

Horn, L., Peter, K., and Rooney, K. (2002). *Profile of undergraduates in U.S. postsecondary institutions: 1999-2000. Statistical analysis report.* Washington, DC: U.S. Department of Education, Office of Educational Research and Improvement, National Center for Education Statistics. Retrieved March 26, 2007, from http://nces.ed.gov/pubsearch/pubsinfo.asp?pubid=2002168

Howard-Hamilton, M. F. (2000). Creating a culturally responsive learning environment for African American students. *New Directions for Teaching and Learning, 8*(2), 45-53.

Hughes, B. (2002) Disability and the body. In C. Barnes, M. Oliver, & L. Barton (Eds.), *Disability studies today* (pp. 58-76). Cambridge, UK: Polity Press.

Kalivoda, K. S. (2003). Creating access through Universal Instructional Design. In J. L. Higbee, D. B. Lundell, & I. M. Duranczyk (Eds.), *Multiculturalism in developmental education* (pp. 25-34). Minneapolis: University of Minnesota, General College, Center for Research on Developmental Education and Urban Literacy. Retrieved October 11, 2007, from http://www.cehd.umn.edu/crdeul

Kalivoda, K. S., & Higbee, J. L. (1998). Influencing faculty attitudes toward accommodating students with disabilities: A theoretical approach. *The Learning Assistance Review, 3*(2), 12-25.

Lee, C. M., & Jackson, R. F. (1992). *Faking it: A look into the mind of a creative learner.* Portsmouth, NH: Boynton/Cook.

Linton, S. (1998). *Claiming disability: Knowledge and identity.* New York: New York University Press.

Lisi, P. L. (1997). Developing culturally responsive and responsible curriculum in college classrooms: Excerpts from an annotated resource guide for university faculty. *MultiCultural Review, 6*(4), 36 39.

Lopez, G., & Chism, N. (1993). Classroom concerns of gay and lesbian students: The invisible minority. *College Teaching, 41,* 97-103.

Marks, D. (1999). *Disability: Controversial debates and psychosocial perspectives.* London: Routledge.

McCune, P. (2001). What do disabilities have to do with diversity? *About Campus, 6*(2), 5-12.

Michalko, R. (2002). *The difference that disability makes.* Philadelphia: Temple University Press.

Miksch, K. L., Bruch, P. L., Higbee, J. L., Jehangir, R. R., & Lundell, D. B. (2003). The centrality of multiculturalism in developmental education: Piloting the Multicultural Awareness Project for Institutional Transformation (MAP IT). In J. L. Higbee, D. B. Lundell, & I. M. Duranczyk (Eds.), *Multiculturalism in developmental education* (pp. 5-13). Minneapolis: University of Minnesota, General College, Center for Research on Developmental Education and Urban Literacy. Retrieved March 26, 2007, from http://www.education.umn.edu/crdeul

Miksch, K. L., Higbee, J. L., Jehangir, R. R., Lundell, D. B., Bruch, P. L., Siaka, K., & Dotson, M.V. (2003). *Multicultural Awareness Project for Institutional Transformation: MAP IT.* Minneapolis: University of Minnesota, General College, Multicultural Concerns Committee and Center for Research on Developmental Education and Urban Literacy. Retrieved October 11, 2007, from http://www.cehd.umn.edu/crdeul

Pfeiffer, D. (1993). Overview of the disability movement: History, legislative record, and political implications. *Policy Studies Journal, 21,* 724-734.

Shapiro, J. P. (1994). *No pity: People with disabilities forging a new civil rights movement.* New York: Times Books.

Silver, P., Bourke, A., & Strehorn, K. C. (1998). Universal Instructional Design in higher education: An approach for inclusion. *Equity and Excellence in Education, 31*(2), 47-51.

Uncertain welcome [video]. (2002). Minneapolis: University of Minnesota, General College and Disability Services. Retrieved March 26, 2007, from http://www.gen.umn.edu/research/ctad

Williams, W. M., & Ceci, S. J. (1999, August 6). Accommodating learning disabilities can bestow unfair advantages. *The Chronicle of Higher Education,* B4-B5.

CHAPTER 33

Using Universal Design for Administrative Leadership, Planning, and Evaluation

David Arendale and Robert Poch
University of Minnesota

Abstract
Universal Design (UD), Universal Design for Instruction (UDI), and Universal Instructional Design (UID) provide practical models to guide more inclusive learning practices within student affairs and also to serve as a useful evaluation measure for student outcomes. This chapter extends the utility of these approaches for a variety of settings within student affair units, addresses dynamics of change, identifies institutional and community assets that can support sustained change, presents a planning and assessment tool, offers several real-world scenarios for within student affairs, and concludes with several case studies of change at the institutional and state level.

Universal Design (UD) and have often been adopted to reduce barriers within the classroom to increase learning for all students, especially those with visible and invisible disabilities. UD also is a powerful approach to increasing learning for students outside the formal classroom within other units such as student affairs (Burgstahler, 2007b; Higbee, 2003). This chapter is devoted to exploring this new opportunity within postsecondary education.

Together we served as small-group facilitators for a group of student affairs administrators and higher education faculty members during summer 2006. This was part of the larger group convened through the Pedagogy and Student Services for Institutional Transformation (PASS IT) grant project described elsewhere in this book and through the project Web site (PASS IT, 2007). This chapter describes some of the conversations among these administrators and higher education faculty members concerning the application of UD and UID to their work as leaders and the creation of an assessment tool to guide and evaluate UD practices. In addition to the coauthors of this chapter, this team included Deborah Casey (then at Florida Atlantic University, Boca Raton), Robert Fox (Fresno City College), Sue Kroeger (University of Arizona), Karen Myers (Saint Louis University), and Erin Sember (Cornell University). Additional conversations continued during summer 2007 with several members of this group along with Alfred Souma, a counselor at Seattle Central Community College. Dr. Casey was appointed Assistant Dean of Students Affairs at Green River Community College during the past year.

This chapter extends the utility of UD for a wide variety of settings within student affairs units, addresses dynamics of personal and instructional change, identifies institutional and community assets that can support sustained change, presents a planning and assessment tool for use regarding UD, offers several real-world scenarios for UD use within student affairs, and concludes with several case studies of change implementing UD at the institutional and state levels. The next section explores the history and theoretical basis for UD and its application to units within student affairs.

Review of the Professional Literature

UD focuses on a transformative process of making systemic changes within the learning environment to reduce potential barriers for all students. An enriched learning environment meets the needs of not only students with disabilities, but all students within the class (Higbee, 2003; Pliner & Johnson, 2004; Silver, Bourke, & Strehorn, 1998). Elsewhere in this book a more detailed overview of the background and theoretical models of UD is presented. This chapter focuses on use of UD within student affairs.

A number of chapters that explored Universal Design within the classroom and also student affairs are reprinted in this volume. Kalivoda and Totty (2003a) proposed that the institution's disability services office can be more than an advocate for students with disabilities; it can also be a resource for the entire institutional community to improve access for all students. Higbee and Kalivoda (2003) explored the use of UD in services for prospective and new students, including traditional student affairs units such as admissions, orientation, registration, and first-year experience courses. Wisbey and Kalivoda (2003) detailed opportunities to apply UD within residential living and learning environments. Higbee and Eaton (2003) described how implementing UD helps to achieve the mission and objectives of a learning center. In an article published elsewhere and reprinted in this volume, Opitz and Block (2006) identified principles for the use of UD for learning support defined much more broadly than a learning center. Uzes and Connelly (2003) highlighted the use of UD within counseling center service areas. Previously, Kalivoda and Totty (2003b) examined the issues of accessibility to technology, both computer hardware and online materials. That information has been updated for the appendix of this volume. Shapiro (2003) also examined the issue of accessibility of online materials and provided numerous recommendations. This is an important issue for student affairs units due to their heavy reliance upon the institution's Web pages for delivery of information to students.

Burgstahler (2007j) identified six major areas where UD could be implemented within units in student affairs,

1. Planning, policies, and evaluation. Consider diversity issues as you plan and evaluate services. 2. Facility and environment. Assure physical access, comfort, and safety. 3. Staff. Make sure all staff are prepared to serve all students. 4. Information resources. Assure that publications and Websites welcome a diverse group and that information is accessible to everyone. 5. Computers, software, and assistive technology. If used, make technology accessible to all visitors. 6. Events. Assure that everyone feels welcome and can participate in events sponsored by the organization. (p. 5)

In addition, Burgstahler has applied these principles to a wide variety of areas in student services including: (a) advising (2007a), (b) career services (2007b), (c) computer labs (2007c), (d) financial aid (2007d), (e) housing and residential life (2007e), (f) registration (2007f), student organizations (2007g), and (g) tutoring and learning centers (2007i).

While this section of the chapter has sought to identify the underpinnings of UD and UID, the next identifies a historic model for effectively engendering change within a system. Success with implementing UD will require a systematic and sustained effort. Attention must be carefully paid to organizational dynamics and incentives for sustained innovation.

Employing an Effective Change Model

College administrators have a wide variety of responsibilities that are very demanding, including budget manager, strategic planner, student learning leader, personnel manager, and catalyst for positive change. In regard to UD implementation at the institution, change is often difficult not because of lack of interest by others, but rather because of the energy and resources needed for change itself. Every day new management books are published with a subset focused on higher education management. A key issue for a successful leader is not only leading others to a desired outcome, but also understanding the complicated stages of change that must occur before arriving at that destination. In this chapter we are relying on a classic model of change theory to guide implementation of UD within student affairs units.

Kurt Lewin was one of the early leaders in social psychology and focused his research heavily on organizational dynamics. Lewin's (1947, 1951) Force Field Analysis provides a model for understanding the forces that either foster or hinder change. He described a multistage process. The first stage requires the early leaders of the innovation to help engender dissatisfaction with the present system. Lewin argued that people would not even consider change unless the status quo was demonstrated to be seriously lacking. Applying this principle to higher education, this activity might include reports about the number of students with disabilities enrolled at the institution, drop-out rates for students, student satisfaction survey data, and so on.

The second stage occurs when people "unfreeze" from customary behaviors and implement new ones. Activities at this stage might include a few people at the institution experimenting with several practices as a pilot test. Data are collected from this pilot test, such as student survey data, changes in grade performance, and increase in utilization by students. The next stage builds upon the pilot stage by the change agents, in this case senior student affairs administrators, presenting a comprehensive model for implementing UD. This stage requires not only advocacy from the administrators for change, but sustained attention and resources such as training.

The final stage, according to Lewin, is the most important and also the most challenging. "Refreezing" occurs when people have deeply adopted the new behavior and feel as comfortable with it as they were with the previous behaviors before the change model began. It requires continued support and rewards for people to sustain the new behaviors. Lewin argued that this stage is the one where well intentioned pilot programs sometimes are not continued. Applying this principle to postsecondary education, practices could include supplemental pay for additional work outside of the normal job scope or work week, recognition for performing the new UD practices through the annual performance review system, and so on. The UD practices must not only be advocated, but valued in a practical way from the perspective of the front-line implementers of the practice.

This comprehensive model of change is reflected in the following sections of this chapter. It is not enough to advocate for adoption of new practices and policies. The entire cycle of change, especially the final stage of supporting ongoing implementation, is essential for systemic and sustained change. The next section of the chapter explores the assets that may be commonly available at the institution that could help support and sustain the change process.

Assets for Implementation, Extension, and Sustainability

The investments for implementation of change within an institution are often more heavily dependant upon human resources than financial resources. As the previous chapter section identifies, the change process requires a comprehensive approach. Additional partners are needed for the effective implementation of practices and policies within the institution. Evans, Assadi, and Herriott (2005) described an approach to gaining more advocates for support of students with disabilities. Evans et al.'s article provides a foundation for the rest of this section for identifying potential assets for supporting change. We encourage readers to conduct an inventory of potential resources within their institution and community. The availability of these preexisting resources may guide which UD practices can be most practically and successfully implemented initially. Additional funding and external grants could be explored for more challenging areas. These resources are essential for dealing with Lewin's (1947, 1951) stages of change as described in the previous section.

Gatherings of Faculty and Staff

Change often begins with awareness of an issue of concern or importance. Where could UD be first introduced? What are venues for training workshops? Rather than creating additional meetings, one might consider the following venues: (a) new employee orientation; (b) employee retreats, meetings, and workshops at the beginning of academic year; (c) periodic employee meetings during the academic term; (d) teaching and learning professional development seminars; and (e) online professional development venues provided by the institution for its employees.

Institutional Offices

UD requires a comprehensive approach for its effectiveness. Not only does an institutional priority for reducing barriers for learning require change by many, it also requires the expertise of faculty and staff at the institution. Where are these experts located? Larger institutions will have entire offices dedicated to these functional areas. Smaller institutions may have delegated these responsibilities to a single individual as just one part of the person's job scope. Offices that often have people with expertise include the following: (a) office for students with disabilities; (b) center for teaching and learning, which often hosts professional development resources and seminars for faculty members; (c) center for technology, which has staff responsible for Web page redesign, podcasting, and adaptive computer hardware; (d) learning center, which is primarily focused on providing learning assistance for students; and (e) department or school of education. Implementing a UD initiative through a preexisting department is a more natural venue than creating another place for faculty and staff to learn about it. Also, hosting the UD pilot program within a willing unit that receives additional resources increases the likelihood of continued support after the initial promotion and pilot phase.

Offices Outside the Institution

Additional resources are external to the institution within the local community. A formal or informal partnership with the local school district office for students with disabilities could provide needed expertise. A wide variety of Internet-based resources are available. The PASS IT project has a Web site (2007) with rich content and practical recommendations. DO-IT (2007b), another program funded through the U.S. Department of Education's (2006) Demonstration Projects to Ensure Students With Disabilities Receive a Quality Higher Education program, also has free resources. A free weekly Internet radio podcast series features interviews and practical recommendations for reducing barriers at the institution (Case, 2007). A Google search of the Internet as well as a search of online ERIC documents will identify many more.

Institutional Leaders and Influencers

Systemic change within the institution requires not only involvement, but also active promotion by others. "Buy in" by many is essential for long-term success. Who are the champions for instructional and service improvement? These are individuals who often are the first to attend optional talks and training seminars. They are often the early adopters of practices, whether those activities are within the classroom or elsewhere at the institution. Seek out these individuals to solicit their interest and support with a pilot test of the new UD practice. These individuals are often the unofficial leaders of institutional change.

It is also helpful to solicit involvement from administrators, staff, and faculty who are highly visible at the institution, and have formal leadership roles. Some of the following groups are ones that have what appears to be a more clear interest in UD: (a) the institution's retention taskforce members, (b) student affairs officers, (c) academic affairs officers, (d) academic department chairs, (e) enrollment management team members, (f) multicultural affairs office staff, and (g) disability services staff. Another group of leaders are formal representatives of students or employees: (a) student senate, (b) faculty senate, (c) staff bargaining unit, and (d) faculty bargaining unit. Too often the perception of these groups is that their interests circulate around student fees, job scope responsibilities, and annual salary increases. Although those responsibilities are high priority, the leaders from these groups can also be powerful partners for institutional change. Increased student graduation rates and higher tuition revenues as a result are helpful outcomes for everyone at the institution. Involving these individuals early in the UD change process can not only gain valuable allies but also help avert the inevitable call for maintaining the status quo.

Building and Classroom Assessment

Understanding the environment at the institution is essential for implementing some UID approaches. The most common inventory is a careful analysis of the physical environment regarding physical barriers and challenges for those with a disability. An outside evaluation may be necessary, because it is often difficult to detect small barriers that most people would not notice. This is more than just compliance with the Americans with Disabilities Act (1990). For example, those responsible for admissions and orientation need to ascertain any difficulty for students with mobility impairments, including those using wheelchairs, with navigating a tour of the institution. Administrators must determine the utilization of scarce resources such as computer classrooms and those with adaptive equipment and software. Can the existing resources be maximized further to serve more students than presently? Due to institutional procedures, sometimes such resources are restricted because they have been placed under departmental or unit access and not made available to the larger community at the institution.

Institutional Policies

Senior administrators can make several strategic decisions that can have a systemic impact on the learning environment. Textbook adoption guidelines can require that alternative formats are available by the publisher before purchases are permitted. Boilerplate language included in course syllabi can describe services for students with a disability and to whom appeals can be made. Course curriculum guidelines or requirements could require instructors to provide diverse modalities for both instruction and assessment. Student affairs units could be required to provide various means for completing tasks or accessing services.

Professional Development and Reward System

In addition to awareness presentations, short workshops, and distribution of training materials, the following activities may be essential for sustained adoption of UD practices: (a) travel to professional conferences related to UD, (b) purchase of materials such as books and journals related to UD, (c) summer stipends for those not employed at that time of year to attend workshops and work with one another on UD, (d) overload pay for faculty and staff to work on UD during their contract period, and (e) meaningful impact on annual evaluation and merit raise criteria.

Linking Change Theory With Needed Resources

As Lewin (1947, 1951) indicated, providing support for adoption of the new behaviors requires changes in the current system. Most faculty and staff already have extensive responsibilities. They need support during the process until they internalize the change and feel as comfortable with the new practice as they did with the previous one. This section of the chapter has focused on a wide array of possible resources for successful and sustained UD implementation. Obviously not every resource is needed for every UD pilot. However, careful identification of resources may not only provide greater support, but also more recommendations from stakeholders regarding other UD changes. The next section of this chapter provides an assessment and planning tool that could be used within student affairs or other parts of the institution.

Assessment and Planning Within Student Affairs

The Student Affairs Administrative Working Group during the PASS IT 2006 summer institute engaged in a variety of activities to contextualize UD for programs and services outside the classroom and within their areas of responsibility. Using UD within student affairs is certainly not a new concept (Burgstahler, 2007h; Higbee, 2003). The Working Group determined that assessment was a critical issue, both for identifying opportunities for integration of UD and also for assessing its effectiveness. The group decided that an assessment and planning tool was needed that could bring together the elements necessary for thoughtful management decisions. The following tool was created by the Working Group, with the assessment criteria based on the model for Universal Design of Instruction (UDI) proposed by Scott, McGuire, and Shaw (2003).

For purposes of this chapter, the tool appears as a one-page form to save space within this book. For actual use, it is suggested to recreate the form as a table through a word processing software program, permitting expansion of the size of the boxes to allow more or less space as needed to type or write responses. It would also enable sharing of the document with others as an e-mail attachment. To help illustrate use of the instrument, the following scenario will be used:

> One part of the new student orientation program is learning the locations and functions of buildings at the institution. Because students are not required to disclose a disability during the admission process, orientation leaders may not have any advance knowledge regarding participating students with disabilities, and in the case of invisible disabilities, may not at any point be aware of students' disabilities. How could the tour of the institution be designed to be inclusive for all students?

Top Section of the Tool

The top section of the tool provides a place to record the current situation regarding the activity under review. First, the program or service is succinctly described (e.g., tour of the institution for prospective students). The next item asks for a description of the goals of this program or service. This is a critical piece, because clearly identifying goals may permit the administrator to explore alternative ways to achieve the same goals through diverse means that present fewer barriers to students. The third item identifies who is currently being served. This item could include both demographic information and the number of students served. Continuing with the example of the tour, this could be the number of students who participate annually. The final item in this set identifies which resources are used currently. This item might include the types and numbers of students

Figure 1. Planning and assessment tool for higher education programs and services

Program/Service Description:			
Program/Service Goal(s):			
Who Involved and Served Currently:			
Existing Resources, Staff, and Policies Used Currently to Implement Program/Service:			
Program/Service Analysis by Assessment Criteria:			
Assessment Criteria	Rating (1 to 7)	Success Indicators	Barriers/Challenges
1. Equitable use			
2. Flexible use			
3. Simple and intuitive use			
3. Simple and intuitive use			
4. Perceptible information			
5. Tolerance for error and provision for contingency			
6. Low physical effort			
7. Size and space for approach and use			
8. Supportive community of learners (students, faculty, staff)			
9. Positive learning climate			
Current Overall Evaluation Rating of the Program/Service Circle one: 1 (lowest) 2 3 4 5 6 7 (highest)			
Recommendations for Change:			
Existing Resources, Staff, and Policies Needed to Implement Program/Service:			
New Resources, Staff, and Policies Needed to Implement Program/Service:			
Benefits of Implementing Program/Service:			

or staff who conduct the tours, the means and route for the tour, and what materials are used during the tour (e.g., handouts, audio and visual aids).

Middle Section of the Tool

The middle section of the assessment tool can serve two purposes for the administrator or evaluator of the program or service. On one hand the assessment criteria can be used to analyze a policy or practice to decide if it is a candidate for change. The second purpose is to apply the same criteria again after the change has occurred to analyze the outcomes to discern if significant improvement has occurred.

Each of the nine assessment criteria are drawn from the professional literature describing UDI (Scott, McGuire, & Shaw, 2003). As noted elsewhere in this book, UDI is a model that evolved during the same time frame as UID and Universal Design for Learning (UDL). Comparable assessment forms could also be developed using UID principles or the guiding principles proposed by Opiz and Block in Chapter 16 for learning support, or by Higbee in Chapter 15 for student development programs and services. Each of the criteria presents an opportunity to assess the effectiveness of the policy or practice. Column one allows for rating of each criterion. The next column asks the respondent to identify success indicators and milestones. The final column identifies the barriers and challenges with the practice before the introduction of UD, UDI or UDI. Continuing our example of the tour, some of the items in this section might be the following: One success indicator for "equitable use" would be that 95% of students become acquainted with the institution's environment. "Perceptible information" success indicator would be achieved through making all information regarding this activity available in a variety of forms (e.g., print, audio, computer text readable). A "barrier or challenge" under the "low physical effort" criterion might be that the tour cannot be easily conducted during inclement weather or is difficult for some students with a physical disability or is not inclusive of family members who do not speak English. Finally, the person completing the assessment is asked to make an overall evaluation rating of the program or service.

Final Section of the Tool

The final section of the assessment and planning tool focuses attention on effective implementation of the UDI activity. With the example used thus far, under "recommendations for change" one or more of the following might arise: (a) providing golf-cart type vehicles for campus tours, (b) using a bus with wheelchair accessibility to transport all students around the institution, (c) creating a narrated tour that could be played in the listener's choice of language via audio player while moving along the route or listened to alone, and (d) developing a narrated three-dimensional virtual tour using the institution's Web site or a Web site such as Second Life (Linden Research, 2007). Each of these potential responses should be keyed to fulfilling one or more of the nine assessment criteria of the middle section of the planning tool. The second item identifies existing resources that are being used to support delivery of the program or service. The next item in this section identifies "new resources and policies needed to implement" the revised program or service. In the previous section in this chapter we identified a wide range of UD assets that could be accessed to implement the desired practice or policy decision. Achievement of the desired student outcomes may require a combination of old and new resources. The final item in this section asks for identification of the benefits for implementing this program or service. Clearly identifying the tangible benefits to the students, staff, and institution of the UD or UDI practice or policy helps to ensure its continued support and implementation.

Reuse of the Tool as Assessment for Progress

After the program or service has been modified through the use of UD or UDI best practices, it is recommended that the form be used again. This time the primary purpose of the tool is assessing the modified practice. This step in the process provides feedback essential for further improvement and refinement. As with any other practice within academic or student affairs, the cycle of assessment, revision, and improvement is continuous. The members of the Student Affairs Working Group have taken the planning tool home to their institutions. Several case studies for transformation at the institutional or state level are presented at the end of this chapter.

Scenarios Involving Student Affairs

During the 2006 PASS IT summer institute, the Student Affairs Working Group explored the use of UD in general and the Assessment and Planning Tool in particular with a number of possible scenarios that related to student affairs, some of which are now provided here. Each presents a real-world scenario that is followed by several probing questions and finally several recommendations to consider that are consistent with UD principles. The recommendations are not intended to serve as comprehensive responses, but rather as catalysts for deeper consideration by the reader. In conjunction with most of the scenarios, we provide references to publications that explore that particular topic in more depth and provide additional practical recommendations.

Scenario #1: Expanding Access and Service to More Students

Professor Johnson's class is known for being extremely challenging for most students, especially regarding note taking, because the professor speaks so quickly and presents so much new content not covered by the text in each lecture. A student with a diagnosed learning disability received an accommodation for a note taker. Other students in the class learn about this and request copies of the notes, because their student fees help fund disability services. The issue is on the agenda for the next student senate meeting for discussion about a resolution demanding more assistance for students enrolled in classes with high failure rates.

This scenario prompts the following questions: How can the needs of the one student with a learning disability be met through an action or service that is also available for all students within the classroom? How can the institution leverage the limited budget to serve more students? Possible responses for this situation include the following: (a) copies of the note taker's lecture notes posted on the Web; (b) placement of the professor's PowerPoint slides on the Web; and (c) audio recording of the class lecture using

Podcasting technology, to be posted to the Web.

Scenario #2: Leveraging the Intellectual Assets of Those With Special Expertise

The institution has invested heavily in establishing an Office for Student Disability Services. The dedicated staff work one-on-one with students with diagnosed disabilities. The staff has considerable expertise in learning pedagogies that would be helpful for other faculty and staff members, but little interaction occurs due to the heavy caseload and priorities of the disability services staff members. They often argue that they cannot do more if more full-time qualified staff members are not hired.

The following questions can naturally arise from this scenario: How can the institution encourage knowledge transfer between the disability services staff members and the rest of the institution's community? How should work load priorities and expectations be changed through collaborative discussion? What would a new mission statement look like for the disability services office if dissemination was a high priority? Some possible solutions include the following: (a) staff with responsibilities for students with disabilities become regular presenters for in-service professional development workshops, and (b) these same staff spend 20% of their work time out of their office providing individual consultations and making presentations to faculty and staff (e.g., at departmental meetings) with a reallocation of their job responsibilities as a result. See Kalivoda and Totty (Chapter 22) for more ideas on this topic.

Scenario #3: Fostering Change and Innovation Among Faculty and Staff

The Office for Student Disability Services eagerly seeks to share information about mainstreaming accommodations within the classroom. However, some faculty and staff are reluctant to embrace change, because they perceive themselves as overworked and underpaid, and are therefore uninterested. Institutional budgets have been slashed and workloads increased in the past couple of years. Labor negotiations are contentious and morale is shaken. Questions that naturally emerge include: How do leaders encourage others to become dissatisfied enough by the current environment that they are open to change? How are others motivated to change? What are the motivators for individuals? What are the barriers that have to be overcome?

A clear understanding of how to encourage successful change is essential. The previous section of this chapter describing Lewin's (1947, 1951) approach provides the theory. Possible solutions were explored in the previous section on UD assets. Depending upon the individual, some of the incentives and support could include: (a) release time from some job responsibilities to work on the UD activity, (b) additional conference travel funds for professional development related to UD, and (c) supplemental summer pay for independent or group work on a UD practice. See Ouellett (2004) for more ideas on this topic.

Scenario #4: Sustaining Innovation

Early last semester Assistant Dean Mathers invested in new computer hardware and software, furniture, and space reconfiguration for the Student Information Center in the student affairs unit she leads. She now senses in staff meetings that her primary unit manager and staff believe that all necessary changes and innovations have been accomplished and that relief, comfort, and a commitment to the status-quo are becoming part of the professional office culture. Dr. Mathers is anxious to inspire an ongoing commitment to innovation in service to all students, but is uncertain how to do so while encountering staff resistance. Several questions are prompted by this scenario: How can a sense of need for ongoing innovation and change be inspired among staff who may tire or grow resentful of such change? What can Assistant Dean Mathers do? Is she facing complacency or possibly something else?

Some possible solutions include the following: (a) fully involve staff in the discussion and conceptualization of changes to inspire ownership of the need for change and innovation; (b) explore with staff how innovations in the past have assisted in developing learning and growth for all students and thus have produced meaningful change; (c) examine fully the rate at which such change and innovation have occurred and whether staffing patterns and the distribution of responsibilities have been adequate within the unit to sustain such changes as well as future needs; and (d) examine methods of creating a sense of dissatisfaction with the status quo through student survey data, persistence rates, and other measures. See Burgstahler (2007c), Kalivoda and Totty (2003b), and Shapiro (2003) for more ideas.

Scenario #5: Communicating Between Student Affairs and Academic Affairs

The director of a student services unit discovers that several faculty members who are teaching first-year courses in his college require students to explore careers relative to the subject matter that they are covering in the respective courses. The students are now coming to the career services office in the student services unit in sizeable numbers with the intent of meeting these course expectations. Although pleased to have the student interest, the director does not have all of the resources or physical space to enable all of the students to meet the class expectations. There are 95 students in these courses and only space to accommodate 7 students at a time in the career center with work stations separated by only one narrow passageway. Further, the computers are 5 years old and the software has not been upgraded in 3 years due to budget reductions. Career assessments and exploratory software available do not match up with the course requirements established by the faculty. This scenario prompts the following questions. How can this director respond? Is there anything that he can do to implement better communication patterns and resource attainment? What UD issues are present in this scenario? How might they be addressed?

There are a variety of possible solutions to the overwhelming response to accessing services from this student affairs unit. Communication is the first step in this process. The director needs to meet regularly with faculty and academic leadership. Based on current resources available, expectations need to be mutually established. Secondly, this situation presents an opportunity for the director to gain key sponsors for change in the career center by linking with faculty and student interests and demonstrating the value that can emerge from connecting academic and student services to UD. At many institutions, more resources are available from academic affairs than student affairs. Acquiring more access to classroom space, computers, and career software that is accessible for students with disabilities will be easier if the director within student affairs can gain key supporters and advocates within academic affairs. See Burgstahler (2007a, 2007b) for advising and career services, Uzes and Connelly (Chapter 18) for counseling centers, and Higbee and Kalivoda (Chapter 20) for first-year experience programs.

Scenario #6: Supporting Student Choice in Education and Work Venues

A graduate student in a college student personnel program who uses a wheelchair refuses an internship in Disability Services and requests placement in Student Activities or Residence Life instead. How might the administrator in charge of internship placements respond? How might the Directors of Student Activities or Residence Life respond? Key questions are: What are the requirements or essential components for internships in different areas? What systemic changes would be needed to enable wider participation in internships? UD best practices could include one or more about the following: (a) ensure that job descriptions include reasonable physical requirements to complete essential work tasks, (b) be vigilant about eliminating stereotypes of work assignments, and (c) distinguish between essential and secondary work tasks for positions and reallocate secondary tasks to others as needed and reengineer the essential tasks so that there are few or no barriers.

With each of these scenarios, the student affairs administrator is presented with an opportunity to draw upon preexisting resources within the institution and community to provide a creative solution. While the prompt for the administrative review was to meet the needs of an individual or a small group, the opportunity is presented to make systemic changes in the learning, working, and living environments that benefit all students and staff and faculty as well. This cumulative result of many small changes contributes to a transformative impact for the institution and the students who are served.

UD Use at Several Institutions

The following section focuses on two case studies of how UD has been implemented by several PASS IT grant participants at their home institutions and has even influenced an entire postsecondary system within a state. Both individuals serve at different institutions in the state of Washington.

Green River Community College

Dr. Deborah Casey is Dean for Student Affairs at Green River Community College (Auburn, WA). Nearly 9,500 students are enrolled at this public, 2-year institution in both academic transfer and vocational programs. The college employs nearly 700 faculty and staff members.

Dr. Casey is working with colleagues at different levels within the institution to engender interest and implementation of UD in various academic and student affairs units. She intentionally uses UD-related language and concepts when communicating with faculty, staff, and fellow administrators. After hearing about the PASS IT grant and reading relevant professional literature, senior academic and student affairs administrators have become champions for the initiative as well. Working with senior academic leaders, Dr. Casey has sponsored several UD awareness workshops with both faculty and staff members. The past year has been spent cultivating interest in change among these individuals. This approach is consistent with the first phase of Lewin's (1947, 1951) multi-stage model for engendering change. To aid in sustainability for the UID initiative, Dr. Casey has placed day-to-day responsibility for UD training with the Center for Teaching Excellence established in 2007. This effectively moves UD from a special project in the Dean's Office to an ongoing activity within a department that is supported by academic and student affairs. Plans are to provide more detailed follow-up UD professional development workshops as more resources are generated through the PASS IT grant. Dr. Casey returned with an institutional team for the 2007 PASS IT summer institute. Changes will naturally emerge as individuals and departments experience Lewin's change cycle and continue improving their practices and, as a result, student outcomes with the incorporation of UD principles.

Seattle Central Community College

Alfred Souma is a counselor at Seattle (WA) Central Community College. Approximately 10,000 students are enrolled at this public, 2-year institution. Students enroll in both academic transfer and vocational programs. Souma advocates for adoption of UD practices within academic and student affairs at his institution. This case study focuses on his work that influences postsecondary institutions across the state.

Due to his interest, past role as a coordinator for the institution's student disability services, and current vocation, Souma has served on the Washington State Disability Services Council. Partially influenced by the PASS IT grant and also by life-long interest, he has been advocating for UD as another way to reduce barriers for students with disabilities. Under his leadership, the Council recommended to the Washington Community College System of 33 institutions an important policy requirement that could make a significant impact. The policy would require all bid procedures for the 33 institutions to also require consideration of UD principles before purchasing instructional materials. This action potentially can require alternative and accessible formats being readily available from the publisher for all books, curriculum materials, and computer software programs. These are requirements above and beyond those of the Americans with Disabilities Act (1990). The potential impact for this policy decision may influence other institutions in Washington and throughout the U.S. As vendors incorporate best practices into their materials for sale to the State of Washington, those same materials may also be purchased elsewhere. Just as when textbooks are changed to meet the particular requirements of a state such as Texas (McInerney, 1991), the same materials are purchased elsewhere.

Different Institutions, Common Goals

Both Casey and Souma share similar goals for their institutions regarding the widespread implementation of UD: (a) increase awareness of UD knowledge among faculty, staff, and administrators; (b) create accountability of UD to respective outcome models, ensuring access to opportunity, engagement, and higher student outcomes; (c) implement effective UD practices within both classrooms and student services activities; (d) increase student retention; (e) build partnerships throughout the institution to aid in sustainability and support for UD; (f) tie UD to the institutional mission to ensure more resources for sustainability and wider impact on student outcomes; and (g) reduce cognitive and physical barriers at their respective institutions. These two case studies illustrate the multilevel approach that is needed to transform the learning environment for students. Casey has included in her implementation plan a "bottom-up" approach that is building desire for change and encouraging innovation at the individual and departmental levels. Souma has adopted among his strategies a "top-down" approach that influences state-level policy that can have a systemic impact on postsecondary institutions throughout the state. True and lasting change will require innovation and policy changes throughout the educational system.

Summary

U.S. postsecondary education continues its transformation with increasing access to education options and diversity of the student body. During the 1960s the Civil Rights Movement contributed to opening more widely the doors of higher education institutions to more students from families that had not attended college before. The 1990s saw the college doors open more widely to students with disabilities who had been accustomed to accommodations in elementary and secondary education through federal legislation. The 21st century has expanded this concept of reducing barriers for those with a disability by establishing principles of UD that create a more inclusive environment for all students within the classroom. This chapter and others in this book and other publications extend this work again by applying UD to student services and throughout the institution. This takes us all one step further in creating a supportive and productive learning community for all our students.

References

Americans with Disabilities Act of 1990. (1990). Public Law No. 101-336, § 2, 104 Stat. 328 (1991)

Burgstahler, S. (2007a). Equal access: *Universal Design of advising.* Seattle: University of Washington, DO-IT (Disabilities, Opportunities, Internetworking & Technology). Retrieved September 6, 2007, from http://www.washington.edu/doit/Brochures/PDF/equal_access_adv.pdf

Burgstahler, S. (2007b). *Equal access: Universal Design of career services.* Seattle: University of Washington, DO-IT (Disabilities, Opportunities, Internetworking & Technology). Retrieved September 6, 2007, from http://www.washington.edu/doit/Brochures/PDF/equal_access_cs.pdf

Burgstahler, S. (2007c). *Equal access: Universal Design of computer labs.* Seattle: University of Washington, DO-IT (Disabilities, Opportunities, Internetworking & Technology). Retrieved September 6, 2007, from http://www.washington.edu/doit/Brochures/PDF/comp.access.pdf

Burgstahler, S. (2007d). *Equal access: Universal Design of financial aid.* Seattle: University of Washington, DO-IT (Disabilities, Opportunities, Internetworking & Technology). Retrieved September 6, 2007, from http://www.washington.edu/doit/Brochures/PDF/equal_access_fa.pdf

Burgstahler, S. (2007e). *Equal access: Universal Design of housing and residential life.* Seattle: University of Washington, DO-IT (Disabilities, Opportunities, Internetworking & Technology). Retrieved September 6, 2007, from http://www.washington.edu/doit/Brochures/PDF/equal_access_hrl.pdf

Burgstahler, S. (2007f). *Equal access: Universal Design of registration.* Seattle: University of Washington, DO-IT (Disabilities, Opportunities, Internetworking & Technology). Retrieved September 6, 2007, from http://www.washington.edu/doit/Brochures/PDF/equal_access_reg.pdf

Burgstahler, S. (2007g). *Equal access: Universal Design of student organizations.* Seattle: University of Washington, DO-IT (Disabilities, Opportunities, Internetworking & Technology). Retrieved September 6, 2007, from http://www.washington.edu/doit/Brochures/PDF/equal_access_so.pdf

Burgstahler, S. (2007h). *Equal access: Universal Design of student services.* Seattle: University of Washington, DO-IT (Disabilities, Opportunities, Internetworking & Technology). Retrieved September 6, 2007, from http://www.washington.edu/doit/Brochures/PDF/equal_access_ss.pdf

Burgstahler, S. (2007i). *Equal access: Universal Design of tutoring and learning centers.* Seattle: University of Washington, DO-IT (Disabilities, Opportunities, Internetworking & Technology). Retrieved September 6, 2007, from http://www.washington.edu/doit/Brochures/PDF/equal_access_tlc.pdf

Burgstahler, S. (2007j). *Universal Design in education: Principles and applications.* Seattle: University of Washington, DO-IT (Disabilities, Opportunities, Internetworking & Technology). Retrieved September 6, 2007, from http://www.washington.edu/doit/Brochures/PDF/ud_cdu.pdf

Case, B. (Host). (2007). *Disability411 podcast.* [online]. Retrieved September 7, 2007, from http://disability411.jinkle.com/

DO-IT. (2007a). *Equal access: Universal Design of recruitment and undergraduate admissions.* Seattle: University of Washington, DO-IT (Disabilities, Opportunities, Internetworking & Technology). Retrieved September 6, 2007, from http://www.washington.edu/doit/Brochures/PDF/equal_access_rua.pdf

DO-IT. (2007b). *Web homepage.* Seattle: University of Washington, Do-IT (Disabilities, Opportunities, Internetworking & Technology). Retrieved September 6, 2007, from http://www.washington.edu/doit/

Evans, N. J., Assadi, J. L., & Herriott, T. D. (2005). Encouraging the development of disability allies. In R. D. Reason, E. M. Broido, T. L. Davis, & N. J. Evans (Eds.), *Developing social justice allies.* (New Directions for Student Services, No. 110, pp. 67-79). San Francisco: Jossey-Bass.

Higbee, J. L. (Ed.). (2003). *Curriculum transformation and disability: Implementing Universal Design in higher education.* Minneapolis: University of Minnesota, General College, Center for Research on Developmental Education and Urban Literacy. Retrieved

September 6, 2007, from http://www.cehd.umn.edu/crdeul/books-ctad.html

Higbee, J. L., & Eaton, S. B. (2003). Implementing Universal Design in learning centers. In J. L. Higbee (Ed.), *Curriculum transformation and disability: Implementing Universal Design in higher education* (pp. 231-239). Minneapolis: University of Minnesota, General College, Center for Research on Developmental Education and Urban Literacy. Retrieved September 6, 2007, from http://www.cehd.umn.edu/crdeul/books-ctad.html

Higbee, J. L., & Kalivoda, K. S. (2003). The first-year experience. In J. L. Higbee (Ed.), *Curriculum transformation and disability: Implementing Universal Design in higher education* (pp. 203-213). Minneapolis: University of Minnesota, General College, Center for Research on Developmental Education and Urban Literacy. Retrieved September 6, 2007, from http://www.cehd.umn.edu/crdeul/books-ctad.html

Kalivoda, K. S., & Totty, M. C. (2003a). Disability services as a resource: Advancing Universal Design. In J. L. Higbee (Ed.), *Curriculum transformation and disability: Implementing Universal Design in higher education* (pp. 187-201). Minneapolis: University of Minnesota, General College, Center for Research on Developmental Education and Urban Literacy. Retrieved September 6, 2007, from http://www.cehd.umn.edu/crdeul/books-ctad.html

Kalivoda, K. S., & Totty, M. C. (2003b). Universal Design and technology. In J. L. Higbee (Ed.), *Curriculum transformation and disability: Implementing Universal Design in higher education* (pp. 251-263). Minneapolis: University of Minnesota, General College, Center for Research on Developmental Education and Urban Literacy. Retrieved September 6, 2007, from http://www.cehd.umn.edu/crdeul/books-ctad.html

Lewin, K. (1947). Group decision and social change. In T. M. Newcomb & E. L. Hartley (Eds.), *Readings in social psychology* (pp. 459-473). New York: Holt.

Lewin, K. (1951). *Field theory in social science.* New York: Harper & Row.

Linden Research. (2007). *Second Life Web page.* Retrieved September 11, 2007 from http://secondlife.com/

McInerney, J. D. (1991). A biologist in wonderland: The Texas biology textbook adoption hearings. *American Biology Teacher, 53*(1), 4-5.

Opitz, D. L., & Block, L. S. (2006). Universal learning support design: Maximizing learning beyond the classroom. *The Learning Assistance Review, 11*(2), 33-45.

Ouellett, M. L. (2004). Faculty development and Universal Instructional Design. *Equity & Excellence in Education, 37*(2), 135-144.

PASS IT. (2007). *Web homepage.* Minneapolis: University of Minnesota, College of Education and Human Development, Center for Research on Developmental Education and Urban Literacy, PASS IT (Pedagogy and Student Services for Institutional Transformation). Retrieved September 6, 2007, from http://www.cehd.umn.edu/passit/

Pliner, S. M., & Johnson, J. R. (2004). Historical, theoretical, and foundational principles of Universal Instructional Design in higher education. *Equity & Excellence in Education, 37*(2), 105-113.

Scott, S. S., McGuire, J. M., & Shaw, S. F. (2003). Universal Design for Instruction: A new paradigm for adult instruction in postsecondary education. *Remedial and Special Education, 24,* 369-379.

Shapiro, B. (2003). Technology transformation and disability: Universally accessible Web tables. In J. L. Higbee (Ed.), *Curriculum transformation and disability: Implementing Universal*

Design in higher education (pp. 265-284). Minneapolis: University of Minnesota, General College, Center for Research on Developmental Education and Urban Literacy. Retrieved September 6, 2007, from http://www.cehd.umn.edu/crdeul/books-ctad.html

Silver, D., Bourke, A., & Strehorn, K. C. (1998). Universal Instructional Design in higher education: An approach for inclusion. *Equity and Excellence in Education, 31*(2), 47-51.

U.S. Department of Education. (2006). *Demonstration projects to ensure students with disabilities receive a quality higher education.* Retrieved August 27, 2006, from http://www.ed.gov/programs/disabilities

Uzes, K. B., & Connelly, D. O. (2003). Universal Design in counseling center service areas. In J. L. Higbee (Ed.), *Curriculum transformation and disability: Implementing Universal Design in higher education* (pp. 241-247). Minneapolis: University of Minnesota, General College, Center for Research on Developmental Education and Urban Literacy. Retrieved September 6, 2007, from http://www.cehd.umn.edu/crdeul/books-ctad.html

Wisbey, M. E., & Kalivoda, K. S. (2003. Residential living for all: Fully accessible and "livable" on campus housing. In J. L. Higbee (Ed.), *Curriculum transformation and disability: Implementing Universal Design in higher education* (pp. 215-229). Minneapolis: University of Minnesota, General College, Center for Research on Developmental Education and Urban Literacy. Retrieved September 6, 2007, from http://www.cehd.umn.edu/crdeul/books-ctad.html

CHAPTER 34

Computing Technologies, the Digital Divide, and "Universal" Instructional Methods

Jillian M. Duquaine-Watson
Texas Woman's University

Abstract
The Universal Instructional Design (UID) literature reflects a tendency to advance computing technologies as a means of achieving improved access to education for all students. In this chapter, I raise important critical questions about the "universal" benefits of UID methods that rely on computing technologies by situating the experiences of college students who are single mothers within relevant literature on the digital divide. In raising these issues, I hope to prompt additional research concerning the ability of UID to meet diverse student needs and, in doing so, encourage the continued development of teaching methods that effectively promote the principles of UID as well as efforts to improve access to computing technologies for all student populations.

With strong ties to the disability rights movement, Universal Instructional Design (UID) and other models such as Universal Design for Learning (UDL) challenge the construction of disability as an "illness" and, through a combination of "elements of the minority group model and social constructionist perspective" (Evans, Assadi, & Herriott, 2005), promote more inclusive educational environments for students with disabilities. Described by Johnson and Fox (2003) as a type of "curb cut" in the classroom, UID centers the needs and interests of students with disabilities. However, arguments concerning the benefits of UID frequently refer to the "universal accessibility" of UID-designed courses. Indeed, proponents regularly claim that courses designed using principles of UID will result in universal access and better meet the needs of all students.

In this chapter, I address what seems to me to be a gap between the theoretical promises of UID and the demonstrated achievements of the field. While I endorse the vision of UID and the ways in which it can help democratize access to education, I am concerned that the fervor surrounding UID overshadows the relatively small body of research that validates claims concerning UID's ability to facilitate universal access, particularly in regard to technology-intensive pedagogical models. While technologies can aid learning, the success of such models hinges on an ideal scenario in which all students not only have access to computing technologies, but also have adequate knowledge of both hardware and software and have sufficient time to access and utilize such technologies. This ideal, sadly, is not the reality for many students.

Drawing on my own research on college students who are single mothers and situating that research within relevant discussions of the digital divide, I raise critical questions concerning reliance on instructional technologies as a way to achieve universal access. I argue that while the use of instructional technologies may seem to reflect principles of UID, teaching models that are technology intensive do not necessarily meet the needs of all students, specifically those who find themselves on the far side of the digital divide. By attending to the social and material realities of single mothers attending college, I hope to contribute to discussions of diverse student learning needs. It is my belief that continued exchanges regarding these and related issues can help to further the aims of UID and are fundamental to the on-going development of teaching models and methods that enable practitioners to come closer to realizing the ideal of universal access to education upon which UID is predicated.

Principles of UID

UID reflects a holistic approach to education and has been influenced by a number of fields including architectural design, learning theories, and social justice education. Adopting the architectural concept of barrier-free design, UID promotes learning by creating a "design of [learning] products and environments usable by all people, to the greatest extent possible, without the need for adaptation or specialized design" (The Center for Universal Design 1997, p. 1). Brain research has also had a significant influence on UID, prompting increased attention to the different ways in which people learn (Gardner 2000; Rose & Meyer, 2002). Finally, UID reflects central tenets of social justice education, particularly in relation to "social responsibility, student empowerment, and the equitable distribution of resources" (Hackman & Rauscher, 2004). Consequently, UID both recognizes and celebrates the diverse experiences and identities of student populations and, thus, is ideally positioned to transform education through the promotion of multiculturalism (Barajas & Higbee, 2003). Though a relatively young model, UID has been successfully adapted to a broad range of academic disciplines, including both introductory and advanced-level courses (Brothen & Wambach, 2003; Bruch, 2003; Ghere, 2003; Higbee, Chung, & Hsu, 2004; Kinney & Kinney, 2003; Lightfoot & Gibson, 2005; McAlexander, 2003; Miksch, 2003).

The recognition of student diversity and diverse learning needs is central to the UID model and has enabled educators to challenge traditional pedagogical methods. As Burgstahler (2005) described it, UID means "rather than design your instruction for the average student, you design for potential students with a broad range of abilities, disabilities, age[s], reading levels, learning styles, native languages, and other characteristics" (p. 1). It is this conscious move away from an imagined generic, neutral, or "average" student that has led to a broad range of UID classroom strategies and modes of instruction intended to meet student needs more effectively and produce a more inclusive educational environment. Examples include modification of accommodation statements, the creation of learning communities and learning laboratories, inclusion of student-generated discussion, tactile activities, and enabling students to demonstrate knowledge in multiple ways (Bruch 2003; Higbee, Chung, & Hsu, 2004; Jehangir, 2003; Pedelty, 2003).

Another central theme reflected in the literature is the belief that UID enables instructors to make education more accessible to all students, including those with disabilities and those without. Rose and Meyer (2002) argued that Universal Design of Instruction (UDI) offers a "flexibility in methods and materials [that] maximizes learning opportunities not only for students with identified disabilities, but for all students" (p. 3). Similarly, Estes (2004) contended that instructors can "maximize learning for all students through the implementation of . . . principles of universal design for learning" (p. 87). Pliner and Johnson (2004) offered a similar assessment, indicating that "the concept of UID as it relates to instruction is an approach that benefits all students at the same time that it serves students with disabilities" (p. 105). And the Council for Exceptional Children (2005), while acknowledging that Universal Design for Learning (UDL) grew out of concerns specifically related to the needs of students with disabilities, maintained that all students benefit from the application of UDL principles and methods:

> The ultimate goal of UDL is to appropriately challenge and effectively engage the full range of students: those with disabilities and those without, those who are average, as well as those who are below and above average. This does not imply that UDL is a "one-size-fits-all" or a "do-it-yourself" solution to learning problems; it is not a panacea but is an achievable process that promotes success for all students working in the general education curriculum and classroom. (p. xii)

UID and Technologies

Recent research suggests that computers, media, and assistive technologies can affect learning in positive ways (Alavi, 1994; Chapelle, 2001; Piccoli, Ahmad, & Ives, 2001; Strijbos, Kirchner, & Martens, 2004). Thus, it is not particularly surprising that many UID practitioners advocate for the use of these types of technologies as a way to enhance teaching, learning, and assessment. For example, Knox, Higbee, Kalivoda, and Totty (2000) pointed out that "technology will allow those with disabilities to achieve fuller participation in the academic venture" (p. 153). Indeed, screen readers, voice input devices, assistive listening devices, specialized software, alternative keyboards, real-time captioning, and other types of assistive technologies continue to improve access to education for individuals with disabilities (Johnson & Fox, 2003). Yet support for computers and technology among UID advocates extends well beyond concerns related specifically to students with disabilities. Rose and Meyer (2002) argued that in the "digital age," communication technologies are increasingly available and can enable educators to "maximize learning opportunities not only for students with identified disabilities, but for all students" (p. 3). Similarly, Bowe's (2000) discussion of the ways in which the seven principles of UID can help serve the needs of nontraditional students relies almost exclusively on computer and technology-related examples including personal computers, listservs, and Web sites. Others offer similar praise for computers and technologies, suggesting that instructors can increase educational access by posting lecture notes on the Internet, promoting Internet research, adopting CD-ROMs rather than traditional print texts, using computer simulations or computer-based testing, or offering courses partially or entirely online (Boyd & Moulton, 2004; Brothen & Wambach, 2003; Campbell, 2004; Center for Applied Special Technology, 2003; Ketterlin-Geller, 2005; Kinney & Kinney, 2003; Lightfoot & Gibson, 2005; McAlexander, 2003).

The "Digital Divide"

The demonstrated ways in which technologies have enabled instructors to incorporate UID into their classrooms are certainly impressive as is the clear desire among many UID advocates to formulate teaching methods that more effectively enable educators to meet students' needs. Yet I am concerned both by what seems to be an over-reliance on computing technologies as well as related claims about the universal benefits of models such as UID, UDI, and, UDL. In this section, I discuss the "digital divide" as it exists for a particular college student population: students who are single mothers. Drawing on ethnographic research I conducted at three postsecondary institutions in the Midwest, and situating that research within relevant literature on the digital divide, I illustrate how the challenges these women face result in limited access to computing technologies. In doing so, I hope to demonstrate that teaching models that rely on computer technologies as a seemingly effective way to promote "universal" access can, in fact, exacerbate the digital divide and further marginalize members of this particular student population.

The tendency toward computers and computing technologies within UID literature is, in many respects, quite understandable. Computers have become smaller and more affordable in recent decades. Additionally, the Internet continues to expand and influence patterns of work, commerce, travel, social interaction, and other aspects of society. Higher education has also gone "high tech," something that is evident in the fact that student computing labs, classroom computers and Internet connections, and computing-related workshops have become regular features of the campus landscape. In fact, U.S. higher education has reached a point where it seems that students simply must have access to computing technologies in order to participate *fully*. They need computers to send and receive email, to complete research papers, to conduct research, to explore library databases, to participate in courses via WebCt or Blackboard, and to complete other course-related activities.

Despite the increasing centrality of computing technologies in higher education, it is imperative that educators consider the ways in which incorporation of these technologies into the classroom and course-related activities may place some students at a disadvantage. Put quite simply, the expansion of technologies has contributed to a digital divide, a situation which the National Telecommunications and Information Administration (2000) has recognized and defined as "the disparity between the 'have' and 'have nots' in the technology revolution." Yet the digital divide is, as Pippa Norris (2001) has explained, much more complicated:

> [T]he digital divide is a multidimensional phenomenon encompassing three distinct aspects. The *global divide* refers to the divergence of Internet access between industrial and developing nations. The *social divide* concerns the information gap between the rich and poor in each nation. And … the *democratic divide* concerns those who do, and do not, use the panoply of digital resources to engage, mobilize, and participate in public life. (p. 4)

Thus, when I use the phrase digital divide, I am referencing not only the disparities in access to and knowledge of how to use technologies, but also the ways in which such disparities are connected to economic, social, and political systems, both reflecting and replicating them. Research confirms that social inequalities including those related to gender, age, race, ethnicity, class, and ability are particularly relevant to this discussion as they shape both access to information technologies and patterns of cyber-participation (Kennedy, Wellman, & Klement, 2003; Merrifield, 1997; Mossberger, Tolbert, & Stansbury, 2003). Accordingly, women, low-income populations, and members of historically-oppressed racial and ethnic groups are among those most likely to find themselves on the far side of the digital divide. Furthermore, individuals facing multiple or "interlocking oppressions" (Young, 1990), especially poor women and women of color, may find their access to computing technologies especially limited (Gilbert & Masucci, 2005).

Challenges Facing Single Mothers in Higher Education

College students who are single mothers are certainly among those individuals facing a digital divide. For the past 5 years, my research has focused on the experiences of women who are attempting to balance their dual roles as sole, custodial mothers and college students. Relying on a combination of surveys, participant observation, and one-on-one interviews, I have sought to understand the reasons single mothers pursue a college degree, the specific challenges they face, and the ways in which they respond to such challenges. To date, over 100 individuals have participated in this research, including college students who are single mothers as well as faculty and staff members at three different institutions in the U.S. The first institution is the University of Iowa (UI), a major research institution located in Iowa City, Iowa. The largest postsecondary institution in the state of Iowa, UI offers undergraduate, graduate, and professional degrees. The second is Kirkwood Community College (KCC). In addition to a main campus located in Cedar Rapids, Iowa, KCC operates 12 satellite campuses and learning sites throughout a seven-county area in central Iowa and offers high school completion, GED, 2-year associate degrees, and job training programs. Texas Woman's University (TWU), the final institution included in the research, operates four campuses, offers undergraduate, graduate, and professional degrees, and enrolls approximately 12,000 students annually, approximately 90% of whom are female.

Although these three institutions differ in size, academic programs offered, and degrees available, the single mothers who participated in this research have a number of things in common. They are predominantly poor and struggle to make ends meet. They tend to describe the pursuit of a postsecondary degree as an avenue to achieving financial independence and self-sufficiency and take their student responsibilities very seriously. Most have only one or two children and prioritize their parental responsibilities over other things in their lives. And perhaps not surprisingly, they face some significant challenges as they attempt to reconcile their multiple and often competing roles as students, parents, and, in many cases, employees.

Paramount among these challenges is economics. Passage of the Personal Responsibility and Work Opportunities Reconciliation Act of 1996 (U.S. Congress, 1996), more commonly known as PRWORA, dramatically reduced the availability of state assistance available to poor populations pursuing postsecondary degrees. As a result, many poor single mothers have found themselves "shut out" (Polakow, Butler, Deprez, & Kahn, 2004) of colleges and universities across the U.S., with enrollment among welfare recipients dropping by nearly 80% at some institutions (Applied Research Center, 2001; Kates, 1998). Consequently, almost all of the women who participated in this project were deemed ineligible for cash welfare grants and were forced to rely on other sources of income. These sources included wages, child support, cash gifts from friends or family members, and even cash earned from selling personal belongings. Most often, however, they turned to student financial aid. While scholarships and need-based educational grants do comprise a portion of their total student aid, student loans constituted the primary source of income for the majority of participants. Indeed, it was common for them to take out the maximum amount available to them each year in student loans in an attempt to meet basic living expenses and pay for child care, tuition, and books. Yet even with "maxing out" student loans, many regularly fell behind on their bills and simply could not make ends meet.

A second major challenge facing college students who are single mothers is time constraints. As they attempt to juggle the multiple, often competing demands of single motherhood and higher education, participants frequently find there is simply not enough time in the day to get everything done. Those who have secured either part- or full-time employment in order to earn much-needed income must contend with even more complicated scheduling issues. Although they do attempt to manage their time in various ways, most often they sacrifice sleep, something that leaves them exhausted and, in turn, can affect their academic performance as well as the quality of the time they are able to spend with their children.

Child care is the third challenge. Finding child care that is high-quality and conveniently located can be a difficult task, particularly in university communities where the demand for such services is high. And although some colleges and universities facilitate on-campus or campus-affiliated child care centers, the waiting lists can be extensive or services may be limited to days and times when classes are in sessions and, thus, are not appropriate for mothers who both work and go to school. For those who are able to locate child care, affordability is another issue entirely. To put it quite plainly, child care is expensive and can cost $500, $600, and even up to $900 per month for one child, depending upon the type of care and the child's age. Some students who are single mothers attempt to reduce their child care expenses by only registering for classes that meet either 2 or 3 days per week. In doing so, they are able to reduce their reliance on child care, even part-time child care can be very costly and is often not much less expensive than full-time care. Other students recruit family members or friends to help with child care, an arrangement which may help save money but frequently proves unreliable. And regardless of how secure child care arrangements may be, a child's bout with the flu, an ear infection, or other illness can necessitate that a single mother forego her student responsibilities as she stays home and tends to her child.

Lastly, college students who are single mothers must contend with the "chilly" climate of higher education. While research suggests that the climate of postsecondary institutions marginalizes women in general (American Association of University Women, 2004; Sandler & Hall, 1982, 1986), students who are single mothers experience a particularly harsh climate (Duquaine-Watson, 2007). They encounter disparaging comments from faculty, staff, and other students both in and out of the classroom that reflect the type of conservative "family values" rhetoric that drove welfare reform in the first place. In addition, institutional policies seem to ignore their particular needs. For example, campuses may lack family housing. Where such housing exists, it may be geographically separated from the rest of the campus, the quality may be poor, and availability limited. In addition, these women are likely to find that institutional programming does not take their particular needs into account. For example, while institutions typically offer student groups, workshops, lectures, social organizations, or events designed to appeal to and meet the needs of a broad range of student populations, those aimed specifically at students who are single mothers are rare.

Intersecting Challenges: Single Mothers and the Digital Divide in Higher Education

How do the challenges facing members of this particular student population relate to UID? Do the barriers they face in relation to higher education more generally also affect their ability to enjoy full and equal access in courses that rely predominantly on computing technologies as a means of reflecting UID principles? Each of the challenges previously discussed is, of course, important in and of itself. However, these challenges also intersect with one another in ways that contribute to a digital divide for students who are single mothers and make it difficult for them to access the types of computing technologies they need in order to complete assignments and other school-related activities (Duquaine-Watson, 2006). Given the strong inclination among many UID advocates to turn to computing technologies in an effort to make their courses more accessible, it is worth examining how the digital divide may render such efforts ineffective in meeting the needs of this particular student population.

First, and most obviously, the cost of a personal computer is simply beyond the budget of many students who are single mothers. Those who own computers often indicated that the machines were old and either not functioning or only capable of running outdated software. And even among those participants who did own a functioning computer, Internet access was a luxury they typically could not afford. As a result, most participants relied on campus computing resources to complete assignments and conduct research.

Second, while campus computing centers are open to all students attending a particular institution, challenges relating to child care, time constraints, and institutional climate tend to limit the ability of students who are single mothers to utilize these resources. Limited access to child care can leave these women with little "free time" on campus, time they might use to access campus computing centers. While some participants will bring their children with them to campus computer labs while they check e-mail, write papers, and engage in similar activities, this arrangement can be frustrating for both child and parent. Campus computing centers are not particularly "child friendly." They are spaces designed with the needs of college students in mind, not those of infants, toddlers, or school-aged children. Participants reported that their children quickly get bored in these situations and may respond by becoming loud or behaving in inappropriate ways. And such responses, of course, can be stressful for the mother and make it difficult for her to focus on computing activities. Yet even when the children are well-behaved, other students make it clear that they do not approve of children being brought into that space. Participants reported that the climate of campus computing labs is especially "chilly" as they encounter disapproving looks and negative comments concerning the "inappropriateness" of bringing children into the computer labs. Some were even approached by computer lab staff and asked to leave, including one single mother who was told that the presence of her sleeping infant in the computer lab was making it difficult for other students to concentrate. In fact, some campus computer centers prohibit the presence of children or other non-students.

Computing technologies seem to fall nicely into line with the principles of UID. Indeed, Bowe (2000) indicated that through the use of computing technologies, educators can make their courses more accessible, accommodate a range of student abilities, increase effective communication, and minimize physical effort, thus making education more *universal* including to nontraditional students. Computing technologies may help educators better meet the needs of some student populations. However, it is simply inaccurate to suggest that turning to computing technologies and putting course materials online facilitates universal access and better meets the needs of *all* students. As indicated in the above discussion, the challenges facing college students who are single mothers are significant and contribute to a digital divide that can make it difficult for these women to access computing technologies. Thus, teachers who believe they are adhering to the principles of UID by posting lecture notes, assignments, and other course materials online, using CD-ROMs rather than textbooks, or offering their courses either partially or completely online may, in fact, be making it more difficult for these students to succeed.

Yet single mothers are not the only students who may find themselves on the far side of the digital divide. As noted earlier, the digital divide mirrors broader social inequalities of gender, age, race, ethnicity, class, and ability. Thus, other student populations also have limited access in regard to computing technologies. Students who are female, poor, members of historically-oppressed racial and ethnic groups, or those with disabilities as well as students attending school part-time or who work part- or full-time are especially vulnerable (Kennedy, Wellman, & Klement, 2003; Merrifield, 1997; Mossberger, Tolbert, & Stansbury, 2003).

Computing technologies can promote increased access to education for some students, perhaps even the majority of students. However, it is important to recognize that increased access *overall* does not mean equal access *for all*. Any method of teaching may undoubtedly serve the interests of some while simultaneously failing to address the particular needs of others. Consequently, we must remember that claims regarding the universal benefits possible through UID may not only be inaccurate but also overshadow attention to the diverse needs of our students and, consequently, contribute to the types of educational disparities and inequalities that UID proposes to eliminate in the first place.

Conclusion

In raising these issues, I do not mean to take away from all that UID has to offer. On the contrary, I fully support the aims and principles of UID. Yet I also recognize that the goal of universal access in education is quite complicated, most certainly beyond what can be addressed by simply relying on computing technologies to enhance traditional modes of instruction. On an individual level, it is imperative that educators continue to engage in critical self-reflection and examine the potential as well as the limitations of all teaching methods, including those they have adopted in an effort to foster universal access for their students. UID would also benefit greatly from quantitative and qualitative research designed to assess the relationship between particular teaching methods and the realization of UID principles. This type of data would provide a foundation to substantiate claims regarding improved access to education and, when such improvement does not occur, demonstrate the limits of particular teaching methods. Of equal importance, such data would provide a foundation for the continued development of a wide variety of teaching methods designed to meet the needs of single mothers and other students with similarly complicated lives and correspondingly diverse learning needs.

Finally, educators must become more aware of and sensitive to issues of computer access and use that knowledge to help address the digital divide and increase student access to computing technologies. Several models currently exist. For example, the Student Parent HELP Center, established in the 1960s at the University of Minnesota (UMN), offers a variety of "programs and services that are designed to promote access, retention, and academic success for … undergraduate students who have children" *(About the Student Parent HELP Center, 2006).* This includes providing a space on campus with four Internet-linked computers specifically for use by UMN student parents. The Women's Resource and Action Center (WRAC) at the University of Iowa provides another model. Recognizing that student parents face challenges that may limit their access to campus computing centers, the WRAC collaborated with the Office of the Provost, campus technology centers, and the Office of Family Services to create CAPRA: Computer Access Promoting Retention and Achievement. Instituted during the 2005-2006 academic year, CAPRA provides desktop and laptop computers for checkout from semester to semester for low-income student parents, thereby enabling them to take the computers home and use them at times that best fit their class, employment, and child care schedules (Duquaine-Watson, 2006). While both of the above programs may help increase access for student parents, other institutions have adopted more wide-reaching models that improve access for all students. The comprehensive technology program at Wake Forest University (n.d.) is one such program. Facilitated by the campus Information Systems office, the program provides a new notebook computer and color printer to all incoming and transfer students. Students "trade in" the computers every 2 years and, upon graduation, are permitted to keep both the computer and printer. By learning more about these and similar models, UID educators can work toward developing similar programs on their own campuses and, in doing so, promote universal access for *all* of their students, thus ensuring that computer-intensive models of teaching reflect both the spirit and aims of UID.

References

About the Student Parent HELP Center. (2006) Retrieved July 19, 2007. http://www.osa.umn.edu/help_center/.

Alavi, M. (1994). Computer-mediated collaborative learning: An empirical evaluation. *MIS Quarterly, 18*(2), 159-174.

American Association of University Women. (2004). *Tenure denied: Cases of sex discrimination in academia.* Washington, DC: Author.

Applied Research Center. (2001). *Welfare reform as we know it.* Oakland, CA: Author.

Barajas, H. L., and Higbee, J. L. (2003). Where do we go from here? Universal Design as a model for multicultural education. In J. L. Higbee (Ed.), *Curriculum transformation and disability: Implementing Universal Design in higher education* (pp. 285-290). Minneapolis, MN: Center for Research on Developmental Education and Urban Literacy, University of Minnesota.

Bowe, F. G. (2000). *Universal Design in education: Teaching nontraditional students.* Westport, CT: Bergin & Harvey.

Boyd, R., & Moulton, B. (2004). Universal Design for online education: Access for all. In D. Monolescu, C. Schifter, & L. Greenwood (Eds.), *The distance education evolution: Issues and case studies* (pp. 67-115). Hershey, PA: Information Science Publications.

Brothen, T., & Wambach, C. (2003). Universal Instructional Design in a computer-based psychology course. In J. L. Higbee (Ed.), *Curriculum transformation and disability: Implementing Universal Design in higher education* (pp. 127-147). Minneapolis: University of Minnesota, General College, Center for Research on Developmental Education and Urban Literacy.

Bruch, P. L. (2003). Interpreting and implementing Universal Instructional Design in basic writing. In J. L. Higbee (Ed.), *Curriculum transformation and disability: Implementing Universal Design in higher education* (pp. 93-103). University of Minnesota, General College, Center for Research on Developmental Education and Urban Literacy.

Burgstahler, S. (2005). *Equal access: Universal Design of Instruction.* [Brochure]. Seattle: University of Washington, DO-IT.

Campbell, D. M. (2004). Assistive technology and Universal Instructional Design: A postsecondary perspective. *Equity & Excellence in Education, 37*(2), 167-173.

Center for Applied Special Technology. (2003). *Tools for schools.* Albany, NY: State University of New York.

Center for Universal Design. (1997). *The principles of Universal Design.* (Version 2.0). [Brochure]. Raleigh, NC: North Carolina State University.

Chapelle, C. A. (2001). *Computer applications for second language acquisition.* New York: Cambridge University Press.

Council for Exceptional Children. (2005). *Universal Design for Learning: A guide for teachers and education professionals.* Arlington, VA: author.

Cox, K. L., & Spriggs, W. (2002). *Negative effects of TANF on college enrollment.* Washington, D.C.: National Urban League Institute for Opportunity and Equality.

Duquaine-Watson, J. M. (2006) Understanding and combating the digital divide for single mother college students: A case study. *Equal Opportunities International, 25*(7), 570-584.

Duquaine-Watson, J. M. (in press) "Pretty darned cold": Single mother students and the community college climate in post-welfare reform America. *Equity & Excellence in Education.*

Estes, M. (2004). Universal Design: Implications for instruction. In M. Orey, M. A. Fitzgerald, & R. M. Branch (Eds.), *Educational media and technology yearbook,* Volume 29 (pp. 86-92). Westport, CT: Libraries Unlimited.

Evans, N. J., Assadi, J. L., & Herriott, T. K. (2005). *Encouraging the development of disability allies.* (New Directions for Student Services, no. 110, pp. 67-79). San Francisco: Jossy Bass.

Gardner, H. (2000). *Intelligence reframed: Multiple intelligences for the 21st century.* New York: Basic Books.

Ghere, D. L. (2003). Best practices and students with disabilities: Experiences in a college history course. In J. L. Higbee (Ed.), *Curriculum transformation and disability: Implementing Universal Design in higher education* (pp. 149-161). Minneapolis: University of Minnesota, General College, Center for Research on Developmental Education and Urban Literacy.

Gilbert, M. R., & Masucci, M. (2005). Moving beyond "Gender and GIS" to a feminist perspective on information technologies: The impact of welfare reform on women's IT needs. In L. Nelson & J. Seager (Eds.), *A companion to feminist geography* (pp. 305-321). Malden, MA: Blackwell Publishing.

Hackman, H. W., & Rauscher, L. (2004). A pathway to access for all: Exploring the connections between Universal Instructional Design and social justice education. *Equity & Excellence in Education, 37*(2), 114-123.

Higbee, J. L., Chung, C. J., & Hsu, L. (2004). Enhancing the inclusiveness of first-year courses through Universal Instructional Design. In I. M. Duranczyk, J. L. Higbee, & D. B. Lundell (Eds.), *Best practices for access and retention in higher education* (pp. 12-26). Minneapolis: University of Minnesota, General College, Center for Research on Developmental Education and Urban Literacy.

Jehangir, R. R. (2003). Charting new courses: Learning communities and Universal Design. In J. L. Higbee (Ed.), *Curriculum transformation and disability: Implementing Universal Design in higher education* (pp. 79-91). Minneapolis: University of Minnesota, General College, Center for Research on Developmental Education and Urban Literacy.

Johnson, D. M., & Fox, J. A. (2003). Creating curb cuts in the classroom: Adapting Universal Design principles to education. In J. L. Higbee (Ed.), *Curriculum transformation and disability: Implementing Universal Design in higher education* (pp. 7-21). Minneapolis: University of Minnesota, General College, Center for Research on Developmental Education and Urban Literacy.

Kates, E. (1998). *Closing doors: Declining opportunities in education for low-income women.* Waltham, MA: Welfare Education Training Access Coalition, Heller School, Brandeis University.

Kennedy, T., Wellman, B., & Klement, K. (2003). Gendering the digital divide. *IT & Society,*

1(5): 72-96.

Ketterlin-Geller, J. R. (2005). Knowing what all students know: Procedures for developing Universal Design for assessment. *The Journal of Technology, Learning, and Assessment, 4*(2), 3-22.

Kinney, D. P., & Kinney, L. S. (2003). Computer-mediated learning in mathematics and Universal Instructional Design. In J. L. Higbee (Ed.), *Curriculum transformation and disability: Implementing Universal Design in higher education* (pp. 115-125). Minneapolis, MN: Center for Research on Developmental Education and Urban Literacy, University of Minnesota.

Knox, D. K., Higbee, J. L., Kalivoda, K. S., & Totty, M. C. (2000). Serving the diverse needs of students with disabilities through technology. *Journal of College Reading and Learning,* (30): 144-157.

Lightfoot, E., & Gibson, P. (2005). Universal Instructional Design: A new framework for accommodating students in social work courses. *Journal of Social Work Education, 41*(2), 269-277.

McAlexander, P. J. (2003). Using principles of Universal Design in college composition courses. In J. L. Higbee (Ed.), *Curriculum transformation and disability: Implementing Universal Design in higher education* (pp. 105-114). Minneapolis, MN: Center for Research on Developmental Education and Urban Literacy, University of Minnesota.

Merrifield, J. (Ed.). (1997). *Life at the margins: Literacy, language and technology in everyday life.* New York: Teachers College Press.

Miksch, K. L. (2003). Universal Instructional Design in a legal studies classroom. In J. L. Higbee (Ed.), *Curriculum transformation and disability: Implementing Universal Design in higher education* (pp. 163-169). Minneapolis, MN: Center for Research on Developmental Education and Urban Literacy, University of Minnesota.

Mossberger, K., Tolbert, C. J., & Stansbury, M. (2003). *Virtual inequality: Beyond the digital divide.* Washington, DC: Georgetown University Press.

Pedelty, M. (2003). Making a statement. In J. L. Higbee (Ed.), *Curriculum transformation and disability: Implementing Universal Design in higher education* (pp. 71-78). Minneapolis, MN: Center for Research on Developmental Education and Urban Literacy, University of Minnesota.

Piccoli, G., Ahmad, R., & Ives, B. (2001) Web-based virtual learning environments: A research framework and a preliminary assessment of effectiveness in basic IT skills training. *MIS Quarterly, 25*(4), 401-426.

Pliner, S. M., & Johnson, J. R. (2004). Historical, theoretical, and foundational principles of Universal Instructional Design in higher education. *Equity & Excellence in Education, 37*(2), 105-113.

Polakow, V., Butler, S. S., Deprez, L. S., & Kahn, P. (Eds.). (2004). *Shut out: Low income mothers and higher education in post-welfare America.* Albany, NY: State University of New York Press.

Rose, D.H., & Meyer, A. (2002). *Teaching every student in the digital age: Universal Design for Learning.* Alexandria, VA: Association for Supervision and Curriculum Development.

Sandler, B. R., & Hall, R. M. (1982). *The classroom climate: A chilly one for women?* Washington, DC: Association of American Colleges Project on the Status of Women

Sandler, B. R., & Hall, R. M. (1986). *The campus climate revisited: Chilly for women faculty, administrators, and graduate students.* Washington, DC: Association of American Colleges and Universities.

Strijbos, J, Kirschner, P.A., & Martens, R. L. (2004). *What we know about CSCL: And implementing it in higher education.* Norwell, MA: Kluwer.

U.S. Congress. (1996). *Personal Responsibility and Work Opportunities Reconciliation Act of 1996.* Public Law 104-193, H.R. 3734.

Wake Forest University. (n.d.). *Academic life: technology.* Retrieved July 22, 2007. http://www.wfu.edu/admissions/technology.html.

Young, I. M. (1990). The five faces of oppression. In I. Marion (Ed.). *Throwing like a girl and other essays in feminist philosophy and social theory* (pp. 141-159). Bloomington: Indiana University Press.

CHAPTER 35

Transforming the Community College by Eliminating Division Between Educational and Student Services

Melanie K. Wagner
Lake-Sumter Community College

Abstract
Community colleges are struggling to educate the increased number of underprepared students entering the system. Now more than ever educators see the need to tear down the silos between student services (e.g., staff involved in orientation, advising, counseling, and admissions) and educational services (i.e., those who are teaching and developing programs and curriculum). Instead of each division of the college focusing only on specific prescription-type solutions for the multitude of student differences, educators see value in taking an intentionally universal approach. This chapter offers research-based strategies for breaking down the silos between student and educational services in order to serve all students.

Faced with challenges of "No Child Left Behind" (2001), community colleges are struggling to find academic solutions to educate the increased number of underprepared students who are entering the system. Some classroom teachers, frustrated parents, and recent graduates will confirm that from August until February the typical school day in Florida is spent preparing for the Florida Comprehensive Assessment Test (FCAT). In fact, in 2006 during a regular session, several representatives in the Florida House introduced a bill that would "mandate that district school boards may not adopt a school year start date earlier than 7 days prior to Labor Day" (House of Representatives, 2006). Under current law, start dates were left up to the individual school districts. Statistics gathered by the Florida Department of Education and attached to HB 177 (2006) supported that school districts were clamoring for higher grades and increased funding and thus starting classes earlier each year. In 1998-1999, only 6 districts started school the first week of August; by 2005-2006, the number of districts doing so rose to 26. In fact, some districts had considered a July start date, hoping to get a jump start on FCAT curricula.

Even in this "teach to the test" environment, most college administrations still look exclusively to student services for identifying problems with student success and arranging accommodations for identified students. No doubt various programs and strategies have been a valuable resource for students who have documented disabilities. However, the majority of the students considered "underprepared" do not have documentation to support a disability. Perhaps more importantly, even if they do not have a documented disability, these students could benefit from a Universal Instructional Design (UID) approach to their education.

To date, educational services have remained primarily on the fringes, or at least in a separate camp. Graff (2003) argued that academic discourse alone alienates students, keeping them "clueless in academe"; community colleges need to do a better job of opening the open door. As proposed in *Learning Reconsidered* (National Association of Student Personnel Administration & American College Personnel Association, 2004), academic learning and student development must become integrated if learning is to become a "comprehensive, holistic, and transformative activity" (p. 2). Administrators, staff, faculty, and students need to be communicating; academic speak is not transparent to outsiders. To be truly successful, community colleges need to invite others, including colleagues and students, into the conversation. This chapter offers research-based strategies for breaking down the silos between student development and educational services in an effort to serve all students entering the open door of the community college system.

Since the Rehabilitation Act of 1973 and the Americans with Disabilities Act of 1990, the student services area of the community college has made great strides in providing better access to educational opportunities of students with all abilities. Over the years, colleges have established offices for students with disabilities; staff members not only work with the students, but also educate the faculty concerning the needs of these students. Yet often those in the classroom or other areas of educational services have remained on the fringe of the discussion, only participating long enough to approve extra testing time, scribes, or other such prescribed accommodations for individual students on a case-by-case basis.

Certainly, the open door policy of the community college presents another challenge. Students with disabilities are welcomed without discrimination regardless of test scores, just as are students who represent the first generation in their family to attend college, work full-time jobs, are displaced workers and homemakers, or are returning from military service with a scholarship "to spend." Among this wonderful kaleidoscope of students, community colleges are also seeing an increase in enrollment for the traditional college-age student. Higher tuition rates and closing access at the university level have made the community college even more attractive to high-achieving high school graduates. However, as community colleges in the state of Florida look toward the future and require student outcomes, faculty and administrators alike have become concerned about how core competencies will be met if the college's door continues to swing open to everyone who applies, especially as state and federal funding is shrinking.

Added to this mix is the idea of measuring college's success in a similar manner as the No Child Left Behind law outlines assessment of elementary through secondary schools. In a recent *USA Today* article, Marklein (2006) quoted Education Secretary Margaret Spellings as stating,

> If you want to buy a new car, you go online and compare a full range of models, makes and pricing options. The same transparency and ease should be the case when students and families shop for colleges, especially when one year of college can cost more than a car" (par. 3). Spellings wanted to make sure that parents and students are getting the best: "If we believe we must educate more Americans, particularly those of

> color and reduced economic means, how are we going to be able to do that without any information about how well we're serving that customer? (Marklein, par. 16)

Vickie Schray, deputy director of Spellings' commission, told Daniel Golden (2006) of *The Wall Street Journal* that "it is a misconception to think that the administration wants to have one standardized test for all institutions or to extend the testing requirements of the No Child Left Behind law for K-12 schools to higher education" (par. 18). Yet Golden reported that several colleges and universities are beginning to administer the Collegiate Learning Assessment (Council for Aid to Education, 2000), which measures critical thinking through performance tasks and writing prompts. Adjusting for SAT and ACT scores, this assessment allows "more meaningful comparisons of the value added by colleges" (par. 19). Increasingly it seems that emphasis is being placed on the "ends" rather than the "means." Where is the consideration for the students who do not persist to graduation?

Because of this educational climate, now more than ever educators see the need to tear down the silos between student services (e.g., staff involved in orientation, advising, counseling, and admissions) and educational services (i.e., those who are teaching and developing programs and curricula) in an effort to meet the needs of our ever-changing student populations. Instead of each division of the college focusing only on specific prescription-type solutions for the multitude of student differences, educators see value in taking an intentionally universal approach. Progressing with curriculum revisions that bring advisors, counselors, admission and records personnel, vice presidents, deans, department chairs, and faculty to the table will have a profound effect on student success. In addition, as a by-product, Secretary Spellings, as well as state legislatures, will have the improved success statistics that they "need" to measure student success.

I realize that this proposed curriculum revision is much more than taking an isolated look at each course in every program within the college catalog. After curricular changes are made, then what? Gregory (2001) reminded readers that "exposing students to a well thought-out curriculum is not the same thing as educating them, if educating them means ... helping them learn how to integrate the contents of the curriculum into their minds, hearts, and everyday lives" (p. 69). It is time for educators to ask what steps faculty, staff, and administrators need to take to "educate" all students, not on a case-by-case basis, but rather with a college-wide, universal approach.

Curriculum Revision

During Convocation at Lake-Sumter Community College (LSCU) at the beginning of the 2006-2007 academic year, the college president announced that the Board of Trustees, along with his cabinet, had made student success the strategic goal for the academic year. All energy would be funneled to making students at this community college more successful. Listening sessions were organized to give faculty, staff, administrators, and students an opportunity to define student success. During each of the sessions, individuals were first asked to define student success and discuss what role they played in achieving success for all students. When the feedback from the listening sessions was compiled, staff, faculty, and administrators were somewhat surprised to learn that their past goals and hard work were not as transparent to other divisions as these goals had been to them. As a result, many wished that they would have been able to participate in some of the other sessions. Now, the challenge was to find a way to bring all of the divisions out of their respective corners into a common dialogue.

Arising from that feedback, committees were formed and priorities were set. Members eagerly accepted the challenge of working on the curriculum committee, whose job it would be to examine the college curriculum as a whole, but only after taking a new look at the college's mission statement and values. Student services and technology committees were also formed; a distance learning committee followed quickly. Everyone soon realized, however, that achieving college unity on even such an important issue was not going to be as easy to implement as it was to envision. It was difficult to decide where to begin when so much needed to be accomplished.

Soon, however, committees began brainstorming about improving student success through a more integrated curriculum, more accessible student services, increased technology, and a new professional development center. As a result of the synergy from all of the divisions working together—as most committees had representatives from all divisions, including facilities and work force—a possibility emerged from the margins of discussion. Required math courses often serve as a tremendous roadblock for student success on our campus. If students persist through developmental math, they often leave our college before completion of Intermediate Algebra. Two plans that will require the teamwork of faculty, student services, and administrators are currently being designed and will be piloted in fall 2007 and spring 2008.

The first pilot is not unique, but nonetheless, Thom Kieft (personal communication, July 14, 2007), chair of the math department, believes it will have positive and powerful effects on student success. MAT 0024, Elementary Algebra, the second developmental math course, requires students to pass a state exit exam (Florida Department of Education, 1997). Because of the high-stakes pressure of a course that has an exit exam as a criterion for passing, as well as the desire to assist students with future success in math, this class will be linked with a Student Life Skills (SLS) course. Linking these courses will require coordination between academic departments because both professors will be present during every class session in an effort to integrate student life skills with the content matter.

A November 2006 Data Trend publication from the Florida Department of Education set forth statistical information that supported the benefits of "taking and successfully completing a Student Life Skills course" for all "students regardless of their preparation for college" (p. 7). If we pair these findings with data that indicate that the more remedial or developmental coursework that students are required to take, the less likely they are to persist (p. 4), then we quickly realize the importance of helping our students learn to be successful. "Learning to be successful" is key; many of our students come to our classes believing that they are as they are, and not much change can be made. They lack the "growth mindset" that Carol Dweck referred to in her February 7, 2007 interview with Lisa Trei (2007).

Fascinated that some people believe they can expand their intelligence, while others believe that intelligence is a fixed quotient, Dweck (Trei, 2007) has spent many years searching for possible connections between student success and how a student views intelligence. Dweck's research found that students who had a growth mindset were "energized by the idea that they could have an impact on their mind" (par. 10). Dweck, along with other psychologists, implemented a study skills intervention program. Along with the typical study skills strategies, students were taught that the brain was like a muscle; if it engaged in exercise, it would become stronger. A control group received the same SLS material, but did not receive the growth mindset theory information. After 2 months, students who had received the "expandable theory of intelligence" training together with the study skills strategies showed measurable improvement in both study habits and grades when compared to the control group (Trei).

Typically, students enroll in MAT 0024 during their first semester of college. If these students can have the benefit of working with two professors throughout each of the linked class meeting times, it is LSCC's hypothesis that these students will become more successful not only in MAT 0024, but also in their other college classes. As study and success strategies are covered throughout the semester, specific relevance to math will be at the forefront. For instance, during the unit on test-taking skills, the class discussion will specifically focus on math tests. The benefit of linking the courses is that faculty do not have to present the unit on test-taking strategies in a vacuum. Faculty also do not have to present the unit once and then move on to the next chapter. As faculty develop the course, we anticipate that faculty will integrate test-taking strategies with math content material as each test date draws near.

During the career unit that is an important unit in most SLS courses, careers that rely heavily on math education will be explored. However, the relevance of math in and to everyday life will be at the center of all discussions, not just during the sessions focused specifically on careers. LCSS wants its students to believe that their minds are not fixed, even when it comes to math. They can and will have the opportunity to learn, to expand their intelligence. Research supports what has been suspected. Learning cannot be defined as a process whereby students "simply take notes or regurgitate information on exams" (De Jong & Eckard, 2005, p. 10). Learning can be defined as the reflective activity that takes place when those same students make relevant connections with course material.

Universal Instructional Design is the perfect pedagogical method for accomplishing this goal. During the planning stages for the linked course, essential components have been established. Professors did not simply transfer a set of objectives and learning outcomes from an old syllabus to the new syllabus. Conscientious planning has resulted in a course that will appeal to all student learning preferences. LSCC recognizes that not all students learn through a professor talking about the math problem, working an example on the board, and assigning homework sections. The course curriculum embraces learning differences, rather than labeling those differences. "The universal in Universal Instructional Design does not imply that 'one size fits all.' Instead, it refers to universal access to curricula" (Higbee, Chung, & Hsu, 2004).

Drawing support from the previously-mentioned research, Kieft (personal communication, July 14, 2007), chair of the math department, proposed another plan to further the success of math students LSCC. In addition to offering MAT 0024 and SLS 1501 as linked classes, Intermediate Algebra will be offered in modules. In the past, when linked classes or stepped classes were mentioned, the ideas were often shut down with comments such as "The Registrar's office will never go for this idea—too tough to work out parts of term with student records"; or "Student services won't like it, not one bit!" One of the benefits of turning the focus from divisional territories toward a common goal of student success is that suddenly divisions are beginning to move past selfish motivations. Student success is the central focus of every decision; the focus is on what is best for not just one student through an individually-designed accommodation, but beneficial to all students through a universally-designed curriculum.

I wish that I could report that this shift in philosophy has gone without problems; however, such is not the case. Realistically, even though representatives from student services, educational services, and administrative (i.e., technology) services have participated in all phases of the planning, when the final pilot for this particular project was placed on the fall schedule, some student services administrators responded with surprise. Because LSCC is a small college, personnel often have many responsibilities, making it easy to get so entrenched in a department's projects and day-to-day activities that sight of the overall college vision is lost. Certainly, some infrastructure of those once sturdy silos built between educational and student services remains.

In addition, even though many professors are on board with new pedagogical strategies suggested by UID, others are still shaking their heads with doubt. Some department chairs are finding it difficult to slow the pace of rapid development of video streaming, Blackboard enhancement, a student response system (D. Guiler, personal communication, July 19, 2007), and Class Climate (2007) usage. Support personnel and funding for distance learning and technology are having a difficult time keeping up with the demand. Yet other chairs are finding that the innovative strategies are falling on deaf and unwilling ears. Comments such as "Oh, we tried something like that 15 years ago and it didn't work," or "It won't make any difference; students just don't want to do the work" are the replies of those who resist the challenge of redesigning a course, making a change. LSCC's goal is to offer the research and anecdotal evidence that indicates that making the courses more relevant and more accessible will result in a more enriched learning environment for both professor and student.

Therefore, I am happy to report that Dr. Mojock, our president, supports these efforts. He has recommitted himself, his cabinet, and the college to student success. The 2007-2008 Annual Plan (LSCC, 2007) has specific success goals outlined; each of those goals has planned strategies for implementation as well as a cabinet-level administrator to monitor progress and success. The course is on the fall schedule; the president, his cabinet, math faculty, and members of the developmental facilitators group are excited to see this innovative curriculum change make it from the drawing board to the classroom.

Although the Intermediate Algebra in modules sounds a little scary and perhaps not at all revolutionary, as previously noted, this proposal represents a huge philosophical shift for faculty and an increased opportunity for success for students. Three sections of MAT 1033 will be taught during the same time slot during the pilot semester. All three professors will begin with module one. After the first module of work is complete and the test results are in, students who scored below 70 will be given the option of repeating the first module.

Although over the years professors had suspicions that students who struggled with concepts presented at the beginning were unable to successfully complete the course, data they collected from the 2006 academic year clearly indicated that 90% of the students who made a 70 or below on the first exam did not earn a C or higher in the course (T. Kieft, personal communication, July 14, 2007). Further, the department's collected data indicated that 30% of enrolled students scored 70 or below on the first MAT 1033 exam. Kieft believed that just handing professors a book such as Paul Nolting's (2008) *Math Study Skills Workbook* was not the answer; nor was the answer attributing the lack of success to student apathy. Therefore, interventions such as workshops and conferences that focused on pedagogy for math, using manipulatives, computer-assisted labs, and student tutors, were added. The underlying belief is that if students can be given not only a little extra time to learn foundational concepts presented in the first module, but also a variety of modes of learning the skills, then they will be better prepared to move on to higher applications.

As a result of close planning with student services staff and administrators, students enrolled in MAT 1033 will not have the stress of withdrawing and waiting out a semester. Two professors will move on with module two, while the other professor will provide guided practice and review of key concepts introduced in module one. After the second test, students who have earned below a 70 will be given the option to repeat module two before moving on to complete the course, and so on throughout all three modules of the course. This approach will negate the need for most of the traditional accommodations that students require. Just as SLS classes benefit students of all abilities, this pedagogical approach to MAT 1033 will likewise prove beneficial.

The excitement being generated as our college shifts from a teaching-centered to a learning-centered college is contagious. As Barr and Tagg (1995) observed, the shift in paradigm that began over a decade ago continues to evolve. Certainly, some people will argue that a complete shift has occurred, yet we would argue that at least at LSCC, not all of our colleagues have been receptive to such a shift. Rather than embracing new pedagogical strategies, many professors see change equal to weakening standards. They believe that students who really want to learn should come prepared to learn and be ready to soak up the information being disseminated through lecture. The one-size-fits-all pedagogical strategy that was good enough for them should be good enough for today's students.

It comes as no surprise that this particular philosophy has resulted in a great deal of professorial frustration when professors realize that today's students are not receptive to having course content information delivered only in lecture format or "banked" (Friere, 2002). With the explosion of technology came the deluge of knowledge (Frechette, 2002). Students are entering into a new dialogue, an opportunity to engage in the conflict of ideas (Graff, 2003). LSCC wants to bring about philosophical and pedagogical changes that embrace these ideas and "asserts not only that all students can learn, but also that it is in the institution's responsibility to help all learners connect with knowledge to construct meaning" (McKusick & McPhail, 2003, p. 16). There truly is a difference between knowing *that* and knowing *how* (Carter, 2007, p. 387).

Therefore, as previously mentioned, a committee consisting of deans, professors, distance learning experts, and student development personnel has been organized for the purpose of developing core values that will guide the college's renewed commitment to student success. From these core values, each academic department will develop essential components for one or two pilot courses. Eventually, the entire curriculum will be evaluated, working closely with faculty as well as program deans and department chairs. Just as the divisions of the college are coming together, sometimes with hesitation or resistance, we hope to see the students realize that academic content is not compartmentalized, but rather joined together in a dialogue for success.

During this journey, some departments have designated lead instructors who serve as the liaison for a particular course to other areas of the college and colleagues. For instance, with a large percentage of LSCC's classes being taught by part-time instructors, strengthening the communication between the departments and the adjuncts will directly impact student success. Jacoby (2006) summarized statistical research in a recent article, noting that student success is directly and negatively impacted when part-time instructors teach the class. In fact, the higher the number of classes that students take with part-time faculty, the less likely they are to persist. Jacoby cited the students' lack of engagement into the structure of the college along with less challenging pedagogy and lack of curricular cohesion as the major areas for concern. If financial standings restrict the ability to hire new full-time faculty, perhaps a more cohesive and universally-designed approach to teaching and offering services to students would alleviate some of the negative outcomes of using part-time faculty.

LSCC committed grant dollars and then college dollars to the Scenarios program offered by Valencia Community College (2007). This program simulates a semester of teaching for a new instructor, adjunct, or seasoned instructor. Pedagogical strategies are modeled as participants work their way through the semester. A research library is offered as well. Perhaps the most valuable aspect of the program is the professional learning community that evolves from the first face-to-face meeting through the weekly online exercises until the final celebration of completion. Interestingly enough, to date participants have included staff, faculty, and administrators; interest has been high. From this program came the first questioning of the college's syllabus template. Interest in pedagogy and a permanent Professional Development Center no doubt arose from this small beginning as well. The Scenarios program was a beginning step that has infiltrated all parts of student success at LSCC.

For instance, a recent technology upgrade has given faculty members the opportunity to maintain Web pages similar to ones that were modeled in the Scenarios program and, of course, supported in UID. We are looking forward to potential benefits that faculty Web pages hold for making course materials accessible to all learners, including new professors and part-time instructors. As LSCC works through curriculum redesign as a college and course reevaluation as departments, we will keep Universal Design (UD) principles before us. The goal is to design courses and ultimately instruction for "students with a broad range of abilities, disabilities, age, reading levels, learning styles, native languages, and other characteristics" (Burgstahler, 2005, par. 1). Spreading the word that not only instructors, but also other college personnel should consider "the potential variation in skills, learning styles and preferences, gender, culture, abilities, and disabilities" (Burgstahler, par. 10) will be an easier task with the formation of the Professional Development Center.

Professional Development Center

Designing and implementing the Professional Development Center (PDC) as the mechanism for bringing all parties into the dialogue of creating a curriculum that is universally designed and instructed is a huge task, but a crucial one. Faculty, staff, and educational and student services administrators will take part in training sessions that will familiarize them with the goals of Universal Design for all areas of student development including instruction, advising, campus life, and physical structures. For instance, specialized workshops focusing on pedagogical strategies that embrace UD will be on-going, as will workshops educating all college employees about their respective roles for a UD campus. For a number of years, the professional library has been a library of neglect. With the advent of the PDC, however, current articles, books, and journals are being collected, but more importantly, integrated into daily practice.

Of course, having a professional library or even scheduled workshops is not always enough. Therefore, the PDC is developing a coaching system. Individuals who are interested in various topics can be connected with coaches who are experts in the field. Certainly some of the coaches on call will be available for technical support, such as providing information about how one actually gets his or her class notes to "appear" on the Web page. Other coaches will be ready to give hands-on assistance to help professors design lab activities for universal instruction. Having such an on-demand service for faculty, staff, and administrators will keep the dialogue moving forward. Loss of momentum is often a problem when ideas have to run up and down the bureaucratic pipeline; the PDC is in place to keep ideas and energy flowing.

The PDC will be the hub for continued education and exploration into the role of distance learning. The college has recently hired a Director of Distance Learning, whose degree is in curriculum design. The wealth of information that she brings to the college will be a valuable contribution toward student success. Syllabi, class notes, chapter outlines, reviews, and supplemental sources are suddenly popping up on the newly established faculty Web pages. Evolving capability of this resource now allows students uninterrupted access to class notes should they be absent or lose their notes. In addition, the librarians have worked with professors and the distance learning director to make direct links to resources possible. Video streaming augments the printed notes, schedules, and research resources. Certain learning center resources are on the way to becoming accessible to students 24 hours a day, 7 days a week. Because of the dedication of our Distance Learning Director, as well as the emphasis on professional development, those professors who may not be as savvy with technology now have a resource for learning through the PDC.

One of the biggest benefits of the PDC is that through the initial setup of the center all areas of the college have had to come to the same table to discuss what their areas needed in the way of professional development. Members from all divisions listened intently as desires and concerns were expressed. This collaboration will continue as advisory teams comprised of representatives from all constituent areas, like work force, student services, administrative council, career support, and educational services, come together to inform and guide the progress and evolution of the PDC. Because of the core design of the PDC as well as its ability to evolve, we see the success and growth of the PDC as a direct link to improved success for all students.

Learning Center

Another key factor to student success that has been all but ignored until recently at LSCC is the importance of offering a space on campus that can become a dedicated place for students who are in academic distress as well as those who desire to enhance their academic progress. Over the years the learning center's reputation has evolved. Initially, the learning center assisted students who were having academic difficulties in any subject area; tutors were either on demand for subjects like math and English or available by appointment or scheduled for open labs as posted. As directors came and went, the vision of the learning center became blurred. The once faculty- and student-friendly space became a punitive space. In keeping with the president's goal for student success, significant changes are underway. Today the learning center is being transformed into a space that offers tutoring for students in their current academic pursuits, as well as seminars, activities, and outreach programs. The old pencil-and-paper grammar tests have been replaced with interactive activities using Blackboard. Students at all levels interact in a common space: the student who wants to polish his or her punctuation skills before taking the Graduate Record Examination (GRE) may be working next to or with a student who is in developmental

English. In addition, students are being offered opportunities to explore topics of interest. For instance, debates on pop culture topics, updates on library services, and information about career activities are being sponsored by the learning center through a brown bag lunch series.

Until recently, the LSCC learning center existed with little more than part-time tutors who sat behind a tall counter and played solitaire on the computer because no one approached them for help. Higbee, Lundell, Barajas, Cordano, and Copeland (2006) reminded us that a "barrier-free and welcoming environment" is a key principle for UD. Their research supports our personal belief that the physical barrier of the tall counter as well as the psychological barrier that the environment presents are roadblocks to student success. Of course, exceptions do exist; according to records maintained informally in the learning center, as well as student anecdotes, many math students regularly sought tutoring from full-time and student tutors in the math lab. It is interesting to note, however, that this portion of the lab had tables and chairs for group interaction, as well as computer stations for interactive lab work. A whiteboard was also available for tutors and students to use. Students helping students was a common and welcomed sight. As part of LSCC's focus on student success, the institution wants to make the entire environment better; a welcoming learning center must be the rule, rather than the exception.

Fortunately, when the college hired an Interim Dean of Teaching and Learning in January, 2007, he immediately saw the need for redesigning the learning center. Through his support, the new director who began work July 1, 2007, has generated excitement for the coming academic year. Ideas that were bounced around, as she began bringing together a support team for the learning center, have generated amazing synergy. This team will continue to function much like the advisory teams for the PDC. Possibilities that have been suggested and are currently being considered include some of the "peer cooperative learning programs" that Arendale (2004) discussed in his article, "Pathways of Persistence." Other strategies such as a brown bag outreach series, tutoring both scheduled through appointment and on demand, increased faculty involvement, and a structured tutor training program will be piloted. With all of the unknowns and possibilities, one fact is certain: the newly designed learning center will be designed for and be accessible to all students, whether they come individually, in small groups, or in classes. Student success, which is fostered through student engagement, will be the "center" of this learning center.

Even in an extremely tight budget year, the president's commitment to student success is evident in his move to locate the PDC and learning center together in a building marked for renovation beginning fall 2007. The creation of this learning environment will send a strong message to the college community, from student to trustee, that LSCC is serious about the movement to break down the barriers. A clear sign of the change in philosophy that is occurring on our campus is that the aspect of this joint learning commons that generated the most excitement was not the issue of saving space and money. Rather, the excitement grew from the realization that this arrangement would bring faculty, staff, and administrators together with students in a common learning environment. LSCC could have found no better way to demonstrate to students the importance and relevance of life-long learning, and no better way to model for students that educators also need to approach learning from a variety of methods.

The space that may provide small group tutoring rooms for biology tutoring can just as easily be transformed into PDC coaching corners. A large computer classroom that a literature class has used to have interactive access with a publisher's material can become a training room for administrators; the list of possibilities continues. Willing participants are breaking down the silos that have previously segregated departments and divisions. The move is on to familiarize members of the college community members with UID in an effort to extend the barrier-dozing to the barriers that keep students from learning. The college has set student success as its number one goal, and divisions are coming together to make this 2-year college a college of destination, not a college of default.

Conclusion

The problem with measuring student success is that often those who are making assessments are determining results based on a single set of criteria. For instance, they may be looking at retention rates alone and making sweeping generalizations without exploring what factors went into the student being retained or leaving the college. Others may be quick to point a finger at the advisors or orientation programs, while yet others may jump to the conclusion that it is just that students are not as prepared as they used to be. I would propose that a better way to improve student success is to bring all of the variables to the table for discussion. If administrators and staff from student services are talking with the administrators, staff, and faculty of educational services, then possible disconnects that occur between initial advising and the classroom may become clearer.

I am are also thrilled by the interest and willingness of administrative services staff members to join the discussion. Their interest in designing classroom spaces and buildings for accessibility to all students is a key factor in UD instruction and overall student success. Recently, LSCC faculty and staff have witnessed purse strings being loosened to integrate technology into every classroom. Departments are joining together and allocating labor and dollars to accomplish the overriding goal of student success. The college's objective is not to point fingers, assign blame, or dismiss effort; the goal is to improve student success.

We are certain that by applying Universal Design to all areas of LSCC, with renewed emphasis on student learning, the advising process, instructional strategies, and academic support, students will be getting an education, not just exposure to "well thought out" curriculum. By working on curriculum only, LSCC is not addressing the entire issue. By tearing down the silos and building communication, our college is well on the way to constructing an exciting place of learning.

References

American with Disabilities Act of 1990, 42 U.S.C. S12101 *et seq.*

Arendale, D. (2004). Pathways of persistence: A review of postsecondary peer cooperative learning programs. In I. M. Duranczyk, J. L. Higbee, & D. B. Lundell (Eds.), *Best practices in access and retention in higher education* (pp. 27-40). Minneapolis: University of Minnesota, General College, Center for Research on Developmental Education and Urban Literacy.

Barr, R., & Tagg, J. (1995). From teaching to learning: A new paradigm for undergraduate education. *Change, 27*(6), 13-25.

Burgstahler, S. (2005). *Equal access: Universal Design of Instruction.* DO-IT. [Brochure]. Seattle: University of Washington.

Carter, M. (2007). Ways of knowing, doing, and writing in the disciplines. *College Composition and Communication, 58,* 385-418.

Class Climate. *Faculty evaluation feedback system.* Retrieved August 3, 2007, from www.scantron.com

Council for Aid to Education (CAE). (2000). *Collegiate Learning Assessment (CLA) project.* Retrieved July 21, 2007, from http://www.cae.org/cla

De Jong, M., & Eckard, S. (2005). Faculty and librarian cooperation in designing course projects for at-risk freshmen. *NADE Digest, 1*(2), 8-13.

Florida Department of Education. (1997). *Florida College Basic Skills Exit Test.* Retrieved July 26, 2007, from http://www.fldoe.org/asp/exitTest

Florida Department of Education. (2006). *Taking student life skills course increases academic success: Data trend #31.* Retrieved November 17, 2006, from http://www.fldoe.org/CC/OSAS/DataTrendsResearch/Data_Trend.asp

Frechette, J. (2002). *Developing media in cyberspace: Pedagogy and critical learning for the twenty-first century classroom.* Westport, CT: Praeger.

Freire, P. (2002). *Pedagogy of the oppressed.* New York: Continuum.

Golden, D. (2006). Colleges, accreditors seek better ways to measure learning. *The Wall Street Journal,* p. B1. Retrieved November 15, 2006, from http://wsj.com

Graff, G. (2003). *Clueless in academe.* New Haven, CT: Yale University Press.

Gregory, M. (2001). Curriculum, pedagogy, and teacherly ethos. *Pedagogy: Critical Approaches to Teaching Literature, Language, Composition, and Culture, 1*(1) 69-89.

Higbee, J. L, Chung, C. J., & Hsu, L. (2004). Enhancing the inclusiveness of first-year courses through Universal Instructional Design. In I. M. Duranczyk, J. L. Higbee, & D. B. Lundell (Eds.), *Best practices in access and retention in higher education* (pp. 13-25). Minneapolis: University of Minnesota, General College, Center for Research on Developmental Education and Urban Literacy.

Higbee, J. L., Lundell, D. B., Barajas, H. L., Cordano, R., J. Copeland, R. (2006, March). *Implementing Universal Instructional Design: Resources for faculty.* Presentation made at the 22nd Annual Pacific Rim Conference on Disabilities, Honolulu, HI.

House of Representatives Staff Analysis. HB 177. (2006) Retrieved July 25, 2007, from http://www.flhouse.gov

Jacoby, D. (2006). Effects of part-time faculty employment on community college graduation rates. *The Journal of Higher Education, 77,* 1082-1103.

Lake-Sumter Community College (2007). *Annual plan 2007-2008.* Retrieved July 25, 2007, from www.lscc.edu

Marklein, M. (2006). Should government take a yardstick to colleges? [Electronic version]. *USA Today.* Retrieved November 14, 2006 from http://www.usatoday.com/news/education/2006-11-13-spellngs-cover¬¬_x.htm

McKusick, D., & McPhail, I. (2003). Walking the talk: Using learning-centered strategies to close performance gaps. In J. L. Higbee, D. B. Lundell, & I. M. Duranczyk (Eds.), *Multiculturalism in developmental education.* (pp. 15-24). Minneapolis: University of Minnesota, General College, Center for Research on Developmental Education and Urban Literacy.

National Association of Student Personnel Administrators & American College Personnel Association. (2004). *Learning reconsidered: A campus-wide focus on the student experience.* Washington, DC:Authors

No Child Left Behind Act of 2001. Retrieved July 24, 2007, from www.ed.gove/nclb

Nolting, P. (2008). *Math study skills workbook.* New York: Houghton Mifflin.

Rehabilitation Act of 1973, Public Law 93-112, 87 Stat. 355.

Trei, L. (2007) New student yields instructive results on how mindset affects learning. *Stanford News Release.* Retrieved February 7, 2007, from http://news-service.stanford.edu/news/2007/February7/dweck-020707.html

Valencia Community College. *Learning scenarios.* Retrieved July 23, 2007, from www.learningscenariosonline.com

CHAPTER 36

Community Colleges and Universal Design

Judy Schuck
University of Minnesota

Jane Larson
Minneapolis Community and Technical College

Abstract
This chapter is reprinted verbatim from Curriculum Transformation and Disability: Implementing Universal Design in Higher Education, *and was originally published in 2003. Community colleges are committed to serving all segments of society through open access admissions, allowing equal and fair access to all students. The diversity of community colleges makes Universal Design's "one size does not fit all" approach very compelling. At the same time, community colleges face significant challenges in fulfilling the promise of Universal Design (UD) and Universal Instructional Design (UID) because of this diversity and the limited resources available to both students and institutions. This chapter presents a description of community college students, their diversity and challenges in accessing higher education, as well as the opportunities and challenges colleges encounter in the implementation of UD and UID.*

When we consider the history and mission of community colleges, it seems particularly fitting to include this chapter in a book on Universal Design (UD). In fact, we could view the community college model itself as a metaphor for this inclusive approach to delivering education. If we change the question an architect first asks in universally designing a building, "Who are the people who will need to access this building?" to "Who are the people who will need to access this education?" we get some idea of what the founders of community colleges had in mind.

Community colleges were formed in the early 20th century with the goal of providing a gateway to opportunity for many young people who otherwise would have been denied access to higher education (Phillippe & Patton, 2000). Although the earliest junior colleges may differ from today's comprehensive community colleges, this goal of access still remains central to the community college mission. This mission is characterized by a commitment to serving all segments of society through an open-access admissions policy (i.e., open enrollment) that offers equal and fair treatment to all students (Vaughan, 1999). Whether young or old, affluent or economically disadvantaged, new to college or returning after time out, planning to enhance basic skills or transfer to ultimately earn a graduate degree, students who attend community colleges are seeking an environment that has been designed to accommodate them. Such an environment calls for a flexible and inclusive model of delivering education and makes UD's "one size does not fit all" approach particularly compelling.

In this chapter, we will first present a description of community college students, addressing both their diversity and the characteristics that make it more difficult for them to access higher education. We will then consider the features of community colleges that facilitate the implementation of Universal Design and Universal Instructional Design (UID) as well as the special challenges community colleges face in its implementation.

Characteristics of Community College Students

For the students who enroll in them, community colleges are often the first student experience in accessing higher education, a first experience in education in this country, or a return to school after several years of absence. Community colleges serve students of all ages and ethnic and cultural heritages, students with life and time conflicts, and students possessing a great range of skill levels. Community colleges also serve as the entry point to higher education for many students with disabilities. More adult students than traditional-age students are likely to access education in the community in which they live. Students who are still in high school, or who have left school before the age of 18, also access community colleges through concurrent enrollment during high school. Only 32% of community college students are between the ages of 18 and 22, often considered the "traditional" college age. Forty-six percent of students are 25 years or older; 32% are age 30 years or older. On the other hand, 4% of students are under the age of 18. Across the nation the average age of students attending community colleges is 29 years (National Center for Education Statistics, as cited in Phillipe & Patton, 2000).

Ethnic and cultural diversity varies with the community being served. Nationally, over 30% of community college enrollment is comprised of students representing minority groups. This number is growing; minority student enrollment increased from 25% in 1992 to over 30% in 1997. Meanwhile, at four-year colleges, minority enrollment increased from 21% to 24% during the same period. In 1997 students of Hispanic origin represented 11.8%; Black students, 11.1%; and Asian students, 5.8% Today, more Native American and Hispanic students attend community colleges than all other postsecondary institutions combined (National Center for Education Statistics, as cited in Phillipe & Patton, 2000).

Nearly two-thirds of community college students attend college less than full time, compared to only 22% at four-year colleges. More than 80% of students work either full or part time, and 50% work full time. Many students under the age of 18 enroll part time as concurrent college students while still attending high school. Many students have additional responsibilities for raising children and caring for relatives (National Center for Education Statistics, as cited in Phillipe & Patton, 2000).

Open enrollment means that students enter community college with a large range of skill levels and preparedness, from students at remedial levels to those already having degrees. Thirteen percent of college students report that English is not the primary language spoken at home. More than half of all students report that neither of their parents had attended a postsecondary institution (National Center for Education Statistics, as cited in Phillipe & Patton, 2000).

The community college system is also the entry point for a majority of students with disabilities. Community colleges serve a higher percentage of students with disabilities than any other sector of higher education (Henderson, 1998). Over 50% of these students report a disability that affects learning (Henderson), and many bring additional complexities to the educational environment. Because community colleges serve as an initial higher education opportunity for students new to this country or a second chance for those who have previously failed, many of these students may have newly-acquired disabilities or disabilities that have gone previously undiagnosed. They may also have multiple disabilities or additional challenges associated with the other facets of college diversity already mentioned.

Because of the diversity described above, it is not possible to describe a typical community college student, but the following examples are representative of students who attend community colleges:

1. Fatima is 25 years old. She has lived in the United States for less than a year and, other than taking introductory classes in English as a Second Language (ESL), she has not attended school in this country. Her first contact with college is through the admissions, assessment, and orientation process. Her assessments indicate that she needs to complete ESL classes before she is ready for college level work. She also appears to have an undiagnosed hearing impairment.

2. Craig is 41 years old. For the past 20 years he has been employed in farming but is no longer able to work because of a back injury. He is married, has three children, and is very motivated to be employed again. He is undecided about a new career. He reports that he liked farming: it was hands-on work; there was variety in what he did all day; and he admits that he was not "much of a student" when he was younger. He attended one year of college after high school, but was not successful and dropped out.

3. Shawna is 19 and has not yet graduated from high school. She has an Individualized Educational Plan (IEP) because of a learning disability and is taking two classes at the community college as part of her transition program. As a high school student, she has had parents who have been very involved in her education and have advocated for her. This is the first time she has been independent in school.

These examples reflect the multiple challenges faced by students at a community college. The student with a disability often faces other challenges such as learning English, supporting a family, and learning to navigate a system that is new and unfamiliar.

Characteristics That Enhance UD Implementation

By their very design, community colleges have many characteristics that make them a setting in which Universal Instructional Design can flourish. An emphasis on teaching, small classes, hands-on and experiential learning, flexibility in designing and changing curricula, and meeting students where they are--all these features facilitate the implementation of UID.

At the heart of UID is the emphasis on flexible instruction and reflective teaching. Many of the strategies employed under the UID rubric could be considered "just good teaching"

(Hodge & Preston-Sabin, 1997); in fact, UID has been described as "a complement to the more flexible and innovative approaches to higher education that are currently proffered" (Silver, Bourke, & Strehorn, 1998). Because a commitment to teaching is an integral part of their mission, community colleges are a particularly good fit with UID. Unlike professors in most universities, who are often not trained to teach and who are experts in their own disciplines rather than in pedagogy, community college faculty members are hired for their pedagogical skills. They are also recognized and rewarded for good teaching and are not faced with the research and publication demands that generally are placed upon faculty in other institutions of higher education. Community colleges also have the advantage of small class size. Although applying UID principles certainly enhances instruction in all classes, it may require more creativity to utilize such recommended approaches as cooperative learning, multiple means for students to demonstrate knowledge, and experiential learning in large classes than in small classes. In fact, experiential and hands-on learning is central to much of the technical and vocational instruction in comprehensive community colleges. It is hardly necessary to encourage or train faculty in programs such as cabinet making, information technology, or practical nursing to offer labs, field trips, practica, or other forms of experiential learning when these experiences form the core of the curriculum.

A related advantage that technical and vocational curricula offer in the implementation of UID is that in most courses the identification of essential components and technical standards has already been accomplished in order to meet certification and licensure requirements. This identification, which is so critical in the execution of Universal Instructional Design, is especially important in open enrollment institutions if they are to fulfill their commitment to serving students of varying ability levels without compromising standards.

Flexibility is another characteristic of the community college academic environment that enhances the implementation of UID. Flexibility in design and delivery of instruction is a central tenet of UID (ERIC/OSEP, 1998) and a core principle of community colleges (Phillippe & Patton, 2000), which are designed to be responsive to the needs of students and the communities from which they come. Consequently, the processes for making necessary changes to the curriculum are generally less cumbersome and can be completed in a shorter period of time than those found in four-year colleges and universities.

Finally, one of the most important attributes that aids in the realization of UID in community colleges is their goal to meet students where they are, not where the institution might wish them to be. Universal Instructional Design is based on the premise that as long as standards are not compromised, the academic environment can be changed to meet the needs of diverse students (Center for Applied Special Technology, 2001), rather than requiring these students to change in order to fit into a static mode of instructional delivery. Community colleges often address this goal of meeting students where they are through their ESL and developmental or remedial education programs. Most community colleges test incoming students and require completion of prerequisites before students can take advanced classes (Phillippe & Patton, 2000). A recent study of remedial education in community colleges revealed that a majority of the institutions surveyed require assessment for all students and 75% of those institutions also require placement into remedial courses (Shults, 2000). The aim of these policies is not to keep unqualified students out, but to give them the tools in remedial classes that they need to succeed in their ultimate goals, which may include degree programs and highly technical vocational training (Phillippe & Patton, 2000).

Special Challenges

Although community colleges have many characteristics that facilitate the implementation of UID, they also face unique challenges that can make its implementation especially difficult. These challenges derive from both the diversity of their student population and from a lack of resources.

The student diversity that is one of the greatest strengths of community colleges also poses one of their greatest challenges. In spite of the best efforts of skillful teachers and advisors, it is often difficult and sometimes impossible to provide access, without compromising standards, to all of the students who may enroll in a particular course in an open enrollment institution. They may simply lack the prerequisite skills or have too many external conflicts in their lives to be successful in their academic pursuits. This diversity does not affect just the academic program in community colleges; it poses challenges in the delivery of student services as well. For student services to be universally designed, they must be accessible to the same wide range of students that instruction must reach, including students who may be very unsophisticated about higher education. This is particularly true in delivering disability services. When beginning college, many students with disabilities may have trouble determining how to access assistance even when the college has published and posted information on disability services. What may seem intuitive to others may not be to the student who comes from a high school with a different form of service delivery, who has never taken on the role of self-advocate, who speaks English as a second language, or who did not have a diagnosed disability at the time of last attendance in school.

Also related to the overall challenge posed by a diverse student body is the challenge posed by the large numbers of economically disadvantaged and older students who access community colleges without even a basic level of computer literacy. Findings of a recent survey of more than 100,000 students at 245 community colleges revealed that the cost of computers for education is a major problem for 20% of these students. A significant percentage of survey respondents--1% of credit students and 30% of noncredit students--also reported that they had never used the Internet (Phillippe & Valiga, 2000). Given that many recommended UID strategies, such as providing materials in multiple media and creating digital, networked learning environments (Center for Applied Special Technology, 2001), assume a basic level of computer competence, this lack of exposure and access to computers presents a formidable obstacle to be addressed.

In addition to the challenges inherent in an extremely diverse student body, the other major challenge that faces community colleges in the implementation of UID is a widespread lack of both staff and financial resources. Professional development is a key component in any institution that wishes to adopt Universal Design and Universal Instructional Design. Even in colleges where teaching has been the top priority, many of the principles on which UID is based will be new to a significant number of faculty members, and all faculty will benefit from an interdisciplinary exchange of strategies that promote access. In some disciplines where essential components have not yet been identified, training and time will be needed for departmental review of their entire curriculum.

The resources needed to accomplish this professional development effort are often not available in community colleges. In an ideal situation, members of the disability services staff can provide the training. Yet, in many of the smaller colleges, there is no disability services office. Services are coordinated by a single person who already fulfills many roles, and the additional role of "trainer" may not easily be assumed. The alternative to providing in-house training, hiring external consultants with expertise in UID, requires financial resources that are either lacking or already committed to other training that is mandatory, not merely desirable (e.g., compliance with the Americans with Disabilities Act [ADA]). Although this competition for scarce funding is a widespread problem throughout higher education, it is particularly acute in community colleges, which traditionally receive lower per-student funding than four-year colleges and universities (S. Nemitz, personal communication, May 2001).

A further challenge in providing community college faculty with training in UID is devising ways to reach the large number of adjunct faculty. In the academic year 1996-1997, 66% of the faculty in public community colleges was employed on a part-time basis (Phillippe & Valiga, 2000). As with the funding needed for UID training, there are many competing demands for the time needed when the training must reach so many part time instructors.

Still another challenge in finding staffing resources for UID implementation is inherent in the very structure of community colleges--the lack of an upper division. Many strategies that help make class content more accessible, such as Supplemental Instruction or tutoring, can be effectively implemented by juniors and seniors or graduate teaching assistants in four-year institutions, but are more difficult to accomplish in two-year community colleges.

Finally, the lack of financial resources mentioned above not only impedes the provision of staff training in UID, but it also severely inhibits community colleges from utilizing technology to its fullest degree. Just as many of their students have not been able to afford access to computers prior to enrolling in school, the community colleges themselves have had great difficulty finding sufficient funding to acquire the state-of-the art technology needed to realize the full potential of UID.

Conclusion

By their very nature, community colleges are educational institutions that provide a good fit with Universal Design and Universal Instructional Design. Their mission of access and their core values of diversity and flexibility create an environment in which UD and UID can flourish. At the same time, community colleges that seek to UD and UID will be faced with many challenges. In spite of these challenges, this model holds great promise as an approach that community colleges can adopt to enhance their commitment to providing access while maintaining excellence.

References

Center for Applied Special Technology. (2001). *Universal design for learning.* Retrieved January 25, 2002, from http://www.cast.org/udl/

ERIC/OSEP. (1998). *A curriculum every student can use: Design principles for student access.* (Topical Brief). Retrieved January 25, 2002, from http://www.cec.sped.org/osep/udesign.html

Henderson, C. (Ed.). (1998). *College freshmen with disabilities: A statistical profile.* Washington, DC: American Council on Education.

Hodge, B., & Preston-Sabin, J. (1997). *Accommodations--Or just good teaching?* Westport, CT: Praeger.

Phillippe, K. & Patton, M. (2000). *National profile of community colleges: Trends and statistics* (3rd ed.). Washington, DC: Community College Press.

Phillippe, K., & Valiga, M. J. (2000, April). *Summary findings. In Faces of the future: A portrait of America's community college students.* Retrieved January 25, 2002, from http://www.aacc.nche.edu/faces/

Shults, C. (2001, June). *Remedial education: Practices and policies in community colleges.* (Research Brief). Retrieved January 25, 2002, from http://www.aacc.nche.edu/Content/ContentGroups/Research_Briefs2/Remedial.pdf

Silver, P., Bourke, A., & Strehorn K.C. (1998). Universal Instructional Design in higher education: An approach for inclusion. *Equity and Excellence in Education, 31*(2), 47-51.

Vaughn, G. (1999). *The community college story.* Washington, D.C.: Community College Press.

CHAPTER 37

Assistive Technology

Margaret C. Totty and Karen S. Kalivoda
The University of Georgia

Abstract
The purpose of this chapter is to acquaint postsecondary educators with technologies available to ensure access for postsecondary students with disabilities and promote equal access. This chapter addresses the Web, computer hardware and software, and other technologies.

The purpose of this book is to promote the implementation of Universal Design, and thus reduce or eliminate the need for individual academic accommodations to the extent possible, and particularly those accommodations that identify or segregate students with disabilities. However, as noted in the introduction to this book, structural accommodations such as appropriate seating, ramps, and assistive technologies like screen readers and voice synthesizers will still be needed to provide access for students with some types of disabilities. The purpose of this chapter is to acquaint postsecondary educators with technologies available to ensure access for postsecondary students with disabilities and promote equal access. This chapter addresses the Web, computer hardware and software, and other technologies. This information will be updated periodically on the PASS IT Web site (www.cehd.umn.edu/passit) for the duration of the grant.

The World Wide Web

The World Wide Web (WWW) has played an important role in making information accessible to people with and without disabilities. The Web can open doors to people with disabilities, but can also close them if Web sites are not designed to be accessible. Educators can receive feedback on Web accessibility through WebXACT, a free online service previously named Bobby. This service will test local files or an entire Web site to help make Web pages accessible to those with disabilities. The link for the site is http://webxact.watchfire.com/. Another site that provides comprehensive guidelines for accessible Web development is the World Wide Web Consortium III or WC3 (http://www.w3.org/Consortium/new-to-w3c).

Hardware and Software Adaptive Technology

Recent developments in adaptive technology have assisted in overcoming many information access issues for people with disabilities. Hardware and software resources are provided here.

Kurzweil Educational Systems

The Kurzweil 1000 for Windows (http://www.kurzweiledu.com/) is software used in an integrated unit composed of a scanner with text recognition and voice synthesis hardware and software. To use the device with printed material, a person places a book or document face down on the scanner bed and presses a scan button. Once the printed material is scanned, Kurzweil 1000 recognizes the text, and speaks the contents of the page. A control keypad allows the user to maneuver within the document, to go backward or forward by line, paragraph, or page. This software is particularly useful for people who are blind or have low vision.

The Kurzweil 3000 for Windows is a similar system but provides unique tools for people who have acquired brain injuries (ABIs), attention deficit hyperactivity disorder (ADHD), learning disabilities (LDs), and other cognitive disabilities. In addition to text recognition and voice synthesis software for reading, it also provides writing assistance (Kurzweil Educational Systems).

Screen Reader Software

The primary means of computer access for people who are blind is screen reader software. Screen readers, such as JAWS or Job Access with Speech for Windows (Freedom Scientific, http://www.freedomscientific.com/fs_products/software_jaws.asp) translate the computer screen's contents into voice output. With the proliferation of graphic user interfaces, screen reading has become more complex for low vision users. Users must now maneuver through menu bars, icons, and folders. Fortunately, screen reader software offers a multitude of navigational tools for the virtual desktop. Screen readers not only give navigational information, but can also read the contents of windows, such as a word processing document. Key commands allow the user to go backward and forward in the document and speech output allows the use of menus. However, tables, graphs, and other visual images can still pose significant barriers when using a screen reader.

Additional screen reader software is uniquely designed to address the needs of people who have an ABI, ADHD, or LD. Read&Write by Texthelp (http://www.texthelp.com/page.asp) is a screen reader with spell checking and word prediction useful for professionals. Openbook, from Freedom Scientific, converts printed documents or graphic-based text into an electronic text format using optical character recognition and speech. The low vision tools in Openbook allow users to customize how documents appear on the computer screen, while other features provide portability (http://www.freedomscientific.com/fs_products/software_open.asp). Another common screen reading program is ReadPlease produced by ReadPlease Corporation (http://www.readplease.com/).

Scanning and Reading Devices

Freedom Scientific's SARA is a solution for those who are blind or have low vision (http://www.freedomscientific.com/fs_products/scanners_SARA.asp). It is used to read a wide variety of printed material including books, mail, newspapers, magazines, and more. This scanning and reading appliance uses optical character recognition (OCR) technology to scan text and then read it aloud in a variety of voices and languages.

To use SARA, the student places a book or document on the scanning area and presses the scan button. SARA automatically scans and recognizes the text and reads. During the reading, the student can adjust the voice rate and volume, as well as fast forward and rewind, or pause and take time to examine a document in detail. The student can even spell out words to get a better understanding of what is being spoken.

Braille Computer Output Devices

Books in a digitized format on a disk that can be read by a screen reader provide a different avenue of access to materials for people with vision impairments. Braille computer output devices such as BrailleNoteMPower and BrailleNote PK, made by the Humanware Group (http://www.humanware.com/en-usa/products/braille_and_speech/braillenotes), translate what is on the screen onto a tactile Braille pad. The effectiveness of such devices is dependent on the user's proficiency in Braille.

PAC mate is a Pocket PC solution that makes all the benefits of a mainstream PDA accessible to blind and low vision students, including Pocket Word, Internet Explorer, Windows Media Player and more. Additional features may include a Braille display, Global Positioning System (GPS) software, Digital Access Information SYstem (DAISY) players, a barcode reader, and many other applications compatible with a mainstream Pocket PC (http://www.freedomscientific.com/fs_products/PACmate2.asp).

Screen Enlargement Options

Computer accommodations can be provided for people with low vision by hardware or software screen enlargement devices. The software packages, such as ZoomText by AiSquared for Windows (http://www.aisquared.com/index.cfm), enlarge the contents of the screen from 2 to 36 times. Another low cost software option by the same manufacturer is BigShot.

Hardware screen enhancement devices include magnifiers such as the Aladdin Ultra made by Telesensory (http://www.telesensory.com/products2-1-12.html). Closed circuit televisions (CCTVs) enlarge and enhance printed material using video cameras. These are used primarily for reading, but also for writing, drawing, or magnifying hand-held calculators (http://www.visionaware.org/what_is_a_cctv_and_is_it_really_helpful).

With either software or hardware screen enlargement, it is advisable to have a larger monitor, a minimum of 20 inches. Options are available for portable screen enlargement hardware such as the OPTI Verso (http://www.ashtech.ie/tp_product_image.asp?pid=70).

Dictation and Voice Recognition Software Programs

People with manual dexterity impairments, whether they have limited or no hand use, will find dictation software programs useful. A common dictation software program today is Dragon Naturally Speaking, developed by Nuance (http://www.nuance.com/naturallyspeaking). The basic notion behind dictation software is that anything entered by keyboard or mouse can be accomplished via voice input. Navigational aspects of computer use can be achieved by voice command: opening, saving, and closing files; surfing the Web; moving within documents and applications; and operating control panels.

Alternative Keyboards

There are a variety of alternative keyboards to assist people with limited manual dexterity. Infogrip provides keyboards that are one handed, contoured, on screen, large print, and wireless (http://www.infogrip.com/). An example of a one-handed keyboard is the BAT personal keyboard (Infogrip). The BAT, either left- or right-handed, has seven keys and specific chords for the keyboard characters. Required hand movement is limited and users can input at a high rate.

Hands-Free Computer Control

People who do not have use of hands can have access to computers by means of devices such as CameraMouse, HeadMaster Plus, IntegraMouse, and Tracker Pro, also made by Infogrip (http://www.infogrip.com/). These devices are commonly worn on the head and consist of a sending unit and a receiving unit hooked up to the computer. For instance, the TrackerPro uses a sensor to track the movements of the head so the user can move around and operate the icons on the computer screen. It interfaces with a virtual keyboard that allows users to type with head movements.

Other Technologies

Numerous additional forms of technology are available to improve accessibility for people with disabilities.

Assistive Listening Devices

People who are deaf and hard of hearing, have cognitive processing deficits, or have ADHD will often use an assistive listening device (ALD). ALDs amplify and transmit voices of speakers to anyplace in a room, so it seems like listeners are situated in close proximity. Interference from environmental noises that are typical in large class or meeting rooms is reduced. The most common types are frequency modulated (FM) systems (http://www.comtek.com/), which operate on radio frequencies, and infrared systems, which operate on infrared light waves. The FM system uses a pocket-size transmitter and receiver, and is convenient and easily transportable. The speaker wears a lapel microphone attached to an amplifier and the user wears a receiving unit. Because amplification occurs solely for the speaker, comments from others should be repeated by the person with the microphone. Another alternative for group meetings is a conference table microphone adapter. New developments in ALDs incorporate digital technology to provide an improved system.

Telecommunication Devices

People who are deaf and hard of hearing or have other communication disorders may need to converse with people over the telephone. The Telecommunication Device for the Deaf (TDD), also referred to as TeleTYpewriter (http://www.deafzone.com/), has a keyboard and visual display to assist in communication. Both parties need these devices unless using Telecommunication Relay Services (TRS). TRS (http://www.fcc.gov/cgb/dro/trs.html) has trained relay agents to assist TDD users to communicate with others who only have access to a standard voice telephone. TDDs are becoming more obsolete with the advent of e-mail and text messaging. There are also new hand-held devices that allow users to e-mail, text message, and browse the Web. Examples of these devices are the SideKick by T-Mobile (www.sidekick.com), the Blackberry by Research in Motion (www.blackberry.com), and the iPhone by Apple (www.iphone.com).

Real Time Captioning

Lectures, speeches, and discussions in meetings can be made accessible to people who are deaf and hard of hearing. Especially useful for people who are deaf but never learned sign language, real time captioning can be connected directly from laptop to laptop or through a remote site. A transcriptionist accompanies the person who is deaf and types the lecture or discussion into a laptop and the text then appears on a monitor in front of the user. There are remote connections and hardwire connections. Most people seem to prefer the wireless connections because they are less cumbersome. They are, however, less reliable than hardwire connections. In remote captioning, the spoken information is transmitted to a remote site, where the captionist types the dialogue, which is then displayed on the user's computer.

Real Time Notetaking

More popular in many instances, real time notetaking uses different software. C-print by the National Technical Institute for the Deaf (http://www.ntid.rit.edu/cprint/) is based on the typist paraphrasing communications using phonetically-based condensing and paraphrasing. TypeWell (http://www.typewell.com/) manufactures another system used in real time notetaking where the typist uses abbreviations to paraphrase communications.

Closed Captioning

Closed captioning (http://ftp.fcc.gov/cgb/consumerfacts/closedcaption.html) provides access to television and movies to people who are deaf and hard of hearing by displaying the audio portion of a TV show or movie as text on the screen. Digital captioning (http://www.nad.org/site/pp.asp?c=foINKQMBF&b=180360) is the latest movement in response to the advent of digital television. This is a technique used to caption digitally as opposed to using analog format for television and movies.

Descriptive Video Service

Just as various mechanisms for captioning provide access for students with hearing impairments, the Descriptive Video Service (DVS) enhances inclusion for students with severe vision impairments by providing access to videos via oral descriptions of what is occurring in the "picture." The Descriptive Video Service Catalogue is available online (http://main.wgbh.org/wgbh/pages/mag/resources/dvs-home-video-catalogue.html).

Alternative Text

The Americans with Disabilities Act (ADA) requires that written materials be converted into alternative formats (http://www.usdoj.gov/crt/ada/adahom1.htm). Often a person who is blind or has low vision needs written material converted into audiotape, Braille, or digital text. Some people with cognitive disabilities might also benefit from using audio text to enhance their processing, visual memory, or attention to detail.

Recording for the Blind and Dyslexic (RFB&D) provides recordings on compact disks (CDs) from a comprehensive library of prerecorded books and takes orders for books not already recorded (http://www.rfbd.org/). RFB&D sells Victor Reading Vibes and Victor Reading Waves, portable digital players that are lightweight and easy to handle. These devices use a standard in alternative media called DAISY for digital talking books (http://www.daisy.org/about_us/dtbooks.shtml).

Books or materials may be scanned into a text file on a computer and used with different software and hardware applications. For instance, people who are partially sighted might use the font size adjustment that exists in most software applications. Screen magnification software is another avenue for readers. Electronic text (e-text) can be output to speech synthesizers and displayed in Braille. In some instances, text files can be converted into digital audio files such as MP3s, listened to through popular digital audio players. Posting text files on a computer to a WebCT site allows users to access the file using a screen-reader software program. Large educational textbook publishers have helped to make alternate media more accessible by providing their print material in different formats, including e-text, to educational institutions.

Cognitive Aids

Other resources available for professionals with an ABI, ADHD, LD, or other learning disorder include devices such as the WordFinder (http://www.wordfinder.com/), which provides speller-thesaurus-dictionary functions. Word prediction and completion programs, graphical word processors, and outlining and brainstorming programs such as Inspiration (http://www.inspiration.com/productinfo/inspiration/index.cfm) and Co:Writer by Don Johnston, Inc. (www.donjohnston.com), are also used. These programs assist the writer in organization, word prediction and suggestion, and sentence completion. There are also grammar and proofing tools available through Microsoft Word (http://www.microsoft.com/) and Corel WordPerfect (http://www.corel.com). Simple tools such as calculators can assist people who have dyscalculia and other disabilities that involve difficulties in mathematical problem solving.

Concluding Thoughts

CHAPTER 38

Institutional Transformation: Some Concluding Thoughts

Jeanne L. Higbee
University of Minnesota

Abstract
This conclusion to Pedagogy and Student Services for Institutional Transformation: Implementing Universal Design in Higher Education *picks up where the conclusion to* Curriculum Transformation and Disability: Implementing Universal Design in Higher Education *left off and provides specific guidelines for building upon the promise of Universal Instructional Design (UID) as the foundation for a model of multicultural postsecondary education.*

In the conclusion of *Curriculum Transformation and Disability: Implementing Universal Design in Higher Education* (Higbee, 2003), Heidi Barajas and I asked, "Where do we go from here?" (Barajas & Higbee, 2003). More than 2 years later a team of faculty and student services staff members from the former General College (GC; Higbee, Lundell, & Arendale, 2005) at the University of Minnesota, in collaboration with senior staff from the University's Disability Services, engaged in an unusual process of grant writing by large-group consensus. The Pedagogy and Student Services for Institutional Transformation (PASS IT) team decided that there were three primary goals we wanted to accomplish, to (a) explore implementation of Universal Design (UD) in student affairs as well as academic affairs and work toward breaking down the silos constructed around the two (see Chapter 35); (b) involve staff and faculty in creating discipline- and work-scope-specific professional development resources in their own areas of expertise; and (c) consider the full potential of UD as a model for multicultural education rather than merely as an alternative to some individual accommodations for students with disabilities. We continued to be concerned that beyond the membership of professional organizations like the Association on Higher Education and Disability (AHEAD), few postsecondary administrators, faculty, and staff are even marginally acquainted with Universal Design or Universal Instructional Design (UID; Silver, Bourke, & Strehorn, 1998) or other applications of UD in classroom settings, such as Universal Design for Instruction (UDI; Scott, McGuire, & Shaw, 2003) and Universal Design for Learning (UDL; Rose, 2001; Rose & Meyer, 2000).

We have wondered why UD and UID are not gaining prominence and support from a broader range of advocates, especially given increasing attention to disability allies (Casey & Souma, in press; Evans, Assadi, & Herriott, 2005; Higbee & Mitchell, in press; Neal, in press; Tregoning, in press a, in press b). We have hypothesized that one reason might be the use of the term "universal," which is intended to refer to universal access, *not* "one size fits all" (Higbee & Barajas, 2007). We certainly do not propose an assimilation model. In the world of architecture—from whence UD came—the term universal would not be open to the same misinterpretation as might occur in education.

It is important to us that all aspects of social identity be included in the "diversity mix." We understand the concerns of those who fear that if we think more broadly about UD and UID as models for multicultural postsecondary education, disability will once again be relegated to the margins of the conversation (McCune, 2001). We also agree with Heather Hackman, who indicates in Chapter 3 of this book that UD and UID may not go far enough in terms of the deeper levels of institutional transformation needed to create true access and equity in the academy. As noted in Chapter 32, we know through our own work on the Multicultural Awareness Project for Institutional Transformation (MAP IT; Miksch et al., 2003) that we still have much to accomplish in working toward achieving this goal.

So once again I, personally, find myself asking not only "Where do we go from here?" but also "Where do I go from here?" I know that on my own journey in search of social justice and exploring the role I can play in making a difference, I still have a long way to go before reaching my desired destination, and I look upon my experiences along the way as part of the process, hopefully contributing to positive outcomes, but not necessarily with an endpoint. To steer my progress I have benefited from numerous collaborations, including Curriculum Transformation and Disability (CTAD), MAP IT, and PASS IT. From these exceptional opportunities to learn from others, I have "borrowed" the following series of guidelines for Integrated Multicultural Instructional Design (IMID):

1. Value difference.
2. Articulate a commitment to diversity and multiculturalism.
3. Establish a learning environment that fosters trust and mutual respect in order to create classrooms in which all students feel welcome and supported.
4. Promote understanding of how knowledge and personal experiences are shaped by contexts (e.g., social, political, economic, historical) in which we live and work.
5. Determine essential course components.
6. Integrate skill (e.g., critical thinking, problem solving, written and oral communication) development with the acquisition of content knowledge.
7. Communicate clear expectations.
8. Provide timely constructive feedback.
9. Integrate multicultural perspectives into all aspects of the learning process.
10. Teach about the ways that ideas like justice, equality, freedom, peace, compassion, and charity are valued by many cultures.
11. Explore the use of natural supports for learning, including technology, to enhance access.
12. Use teaching methods that consider diverse learning styles, abilities, ways of knowing, and previous experience and background knowledge.
13. Create multiple ways for students to demonstrate their knowledge.
14. Use culturally-sensitive techniques to assess student learning.
15. Promote interaction among and between faculty and students.

Yes, these guiding principles might be considered simply "good teaching." But too often when striving to get papers graded and meet publication deadlines, I know that my own good intentions can get lost in the shuffle. And, to me, that is what distinguishes UD and UID and IMID from just good teaching. When UD or UID or IMID guides our work, we are intentional about every step we take along the way; as we plan we take into consideration myriad social identities and how what we say and do might impact different people in different ways. So to me, the answer to the question, "Where do I go from here?" involves the kind of careful reflection and intentionality that can do everything possible to ensure inclusion, knowing that my implementation will not be perfect, but that it is not good enough merely for my "heart to be in the right place."

When my children were little, the holiday program at their public elementary school always ended with the students on stage and the friends and family in the audience joining together to sing a song that began, "Let there be peace on Earth, and let it begin with me." I had two conflicting reactions. On the one hand, I responded to the mention of God within the song, knowing that among my friends and acquaintances in the audience there were many different religious and spiritual values and beliefs. And as a woman and mother of a young daughter who questioned everything, I was also aware of my feelings about being "brothers" in the endeavour of working toward peace and harmony. And yet, on the other hand, that very diverse group of children and their friends and relatives singing this song always brought tears to my eyes and a wish that we would remember these sentiments throughout the year, not just at holiday time. Just as peace requires the efforts of every individual every day, so does equality. Institutional transformation begins with me, with each one of us, and our efforts must be intentional and ongoing. And it is with that thought that we conclude this book.

References

Barajas, H. L., & Higbee, J. L. (2003). Where do we go from here? Universal Design as a model for multicultural education. In J. L. Higbee (Ed.), *Curriculum transformation and disability: Implementing Universal Design in higher education* (pp. 285-290). Minneapolis: University of Minnesota, General College, Center for Research on Developmental Education and Urban Literacy. Retrieved September 15, 2007, from http://www.cehd.umn.edu/crdeul

Casey, D., & Souma, A. (in press). Allies in our midst. In J. L. Higbee & A. A. Mitchell (Eds.), *Making good on the promise: Student affairs professionals with disabilities.* Washington, DC: ACPA-College Student Educators International and University Press of America

Evans, N. J., Assadi, J. L., & Herriott, T. K. (2005). Encouraging the development of disability allies. In R. D. Reason, E. M. Broido, T. L. Davis, & N. J. Evans (Eds.), *Developing social justice allies* (New Directions for Student Services No. 110, pp. 67-79). San Francisco: Jossy Bass.

Higbee, J. L. (Ed.). (2003). *Curriculum transformation and disability: Implementing Universal Design in higher education.* Minneapolis: University of Minnesota, General College, Center for Research on Developmental Education and Urban Literacy. Retrieved September 15, 2007, from http://www.cehd.umn.edu/crdeul

Higbee, J. L., & Barajas, H. L. (2007). Building effective places for multicultural learning. *About Campus, 12*(3), 16-22.

Higbee, J. L., Lundell, D. B., & Arendale, D. R. (Eds.). (2005). *The General College vision: Integrating intellectual growth, multicultural perspectives, and student development.* Minneapolis: University of Minnesota, General College, Center for Research on Developmental Education and Urban Literacy. Retrieved September 15, 2007, from http://www.cehd.umn.edu/crdeul

Higbee, J. L., & Mitchell, A. A. (in press). *Making good on the promise: Student affairs professionals with disabilities.* Washington, DC: ACPA-College Student Educators International and University Press of America.

McCune, P. (2001). What do disabilities have to do with diversity? *About Campus, 6*(2), 5-12.

Miksch, K. L., Higbee, J. L., Jehangir, R. R., Lundell, D. B., Bruch, P. L., Siaka, K., & Dotson, M. V. (2003). *Multicultural Awareness Project for Institutional Transformation: MAP IT.* Minneapolis: University of Minnesota, General College, Multicultural Concerns Committee and Center for Research on Developmental Education and Urban Literacy. Retrieved September 15, 2007, from http://www.cehd.umn.edu/crdeul

Neal, S. (in press). The role of student affairs allies: Creating welcoming spaces for students and staff. In J. L. Higbee & A. A. Mitchell (Eds.), *Making good on the promise: Student affairs professionals with disabilities.* Washington, DC: ACPA-College Student Educators International and University Press of America.

Rose, D. H. (2001). Universal Design for Learning: Deriving guiding principles from networks that learn. *Journal of Special Education Technology, 16*(2), 66-67.

Rose, D. H., & Meyer, A. (2000). Universal Design for Learning. *Journal of Special Education Technology, 15*(1), 67-70.

Scott, S. S., McGuire, J. M., & Shaw, S. F. (2003). Universal Design for Instruction: A new paradigm for adult instruction in postsecondary education. *Remedial and Special Education, 24,* 369-379.

Silver, P., Bourke, A., & Strehorn, K. C. (1998). Universal Instructional Design in higher education: An approach for inclusion. *Equity and Excellence in Education, 31*(2), 47-51.

Tregoning, M. E. (in press a). Being an ally in language use. In J. L. Higbee & A. A. Mitchell (Eds.), *Making good on the promise: Student affairs professionals with disabilities.* Washington, DC: ACPA-College Student Educators International and University Press of America.

Tregoning, M. E. (in press b). "Getting it" as an ally: Interpersonal relationships between colleagues with and without disabilities. In J. L. Higbee & A. A. Mitchell (Eds.), *Making good on the promise: Student affairs professionals with disabilities.* Washington, DC: ACPA-College Student Educators International and University Press of America.